The History
and
Haunting
of
Lizzie Borden

Rebecca F. Pittman

ISBN number: 978-0998369204

Published by Wonderland Productions, LLC
Colorado

First Edition

Printed in the United States of America
Cover Art by Rebecca F. Pittman
Lizzie Borden image courtesy of the Fall River Historical Society

www.rebeccafpittmanbooks.com

Dedication

For Lee-Ann Wilber, Donald Woods,
Kristee Bates, Michael Martins &
Dennis A. Binette: The Keepers of the Keys

Ronald Bueker: Photographer & Sage
&
LeRoy Peterson: Editor & Constant Friend

Table of Contents:

Table of Contents (Continued):

Acknowledgments

When one is writing a book that blends history and current accounts, it is never done without the enormous help and inspiration of those who came before, and those who are the guardians of the present. It is with a heartfelt "Thank You!" that I acknowledge the following people:

Lee-Ann Wilber & Donald Woods with the Lizzie Borden Bed & Breakfast Museum in Fall River, Ma.; Kristee Bates, owner of *Maplecroft* in Fall River; Michael Martins & Dennis A. Binette with the Fall River Historical Society; Stefani Koorey with LizzieAndrewBorden.com; Shelley Dziedzic with lizziebordenwarpsandwefts.com; Faye Musselman with phayemuss@wordpress.com/TatteredFabric.com; Leonard Rebello, author *of Lizzie Borden: Past & Present*; Ronald Bueker—photographer, researcher and general "idea-bouncer-off-of"; Danielle Cabral, Colleen Johnson, & Sue Vickery—docents extraordinaire; LeRoy Peterson—my Editor and eternal friend; Maggiemayfashions.com; CarsonDunlop.com; Frank Grace with Trig Photography; Maria, Raymond, Diana and Rayna Brigham, along with Jack Nolan of the Touisset Country Club, Swansea, MA.; Carl Becker with the Swansea Museum; the Swansea Library; Richard George with the Bristol County Superior Court House, New Bedford; and Lizzie Borden researchers, who gave so much of their time in publications, and interviews.

A big thank you to Leonard Rebello, author of *Lizzie Borden: Past and Present*, and to Shelley Dziedzic, for driving this Author and her husband, Ron, all over Fall River and Swansea, pointing out the pertinent landmarks of the Lizzie Borden murder mystery. These two partners in crime also sent maps, photos, and other relevant information for the book, as well as returning to locations to follow up on a few mysteries. You went beyond, and I thank you so much! You also know how to choose a great hot dog place!

And a big hug to Kristee Bates for the rare gift of allowing the Author and her husband to spend two evenings at Maplecroft, and for spoiling us rotten. Your generosity and hospitality is so appreciated.

Prologue

There may never be a final resolution of the Borden hatchet murders of August 4, 1892, in Fall River, Massachusetts. The tantalizing trail of clues and documentation is all 21st-century armchair sleuths are left to forage through. Yet the people who say there is nothing new to bring to light are incorrect. Actually, there is much. It is hiding between the lines of trial testimony, in dusty newspapers, and within the invaluable modern use of technology.

The mind of a sociopath is fascinating, albeit, a frightening mass of grey matter. They go through life with a sense of entitlement; seeing people as obstacles to their goals who must be manipulated...or...removed. Guilt and remorse are non-existent. It is a chilling thing to watch. I grew up next door to someone who had just that blend of personality traits, and I watched the trail of destruction left in her wake. That perspective of a borderline personality disorder gave me a unique insight into the writing of this book. These people do exist.

Lizzie was human, flawed in many ways, as we all are. I believe losing her mother at such a young age began a fear of abandonment, which Emma, her older sister, tried desperately to eradicate. Andrew, her father, followed suit until Lizzie saw herself as entitled to a life without obstacles. Was she spoiled? Yes. Was she fearful of loss? Yes. Did a hand in her face set off feelings of panic and depression? Yes. Would anything stop her from getting what she felt was her due? No.

This book is written from the facts born out from police interviews; Inquest, Preliminary Hearing, and Superior Court trial testimonies; newspaper reports; and research. None of the relevant dialogue has been tampered with. I have, as a means of providing atmosphere, added some background and trivial dialogue, based on the above-mentioned reports. Some of the people introduced here for the first time took a great deal of hunting down, but I think you will admit, it was worth it. Some of what I'm about to show you is a reasonable deduction if you look at the trail of breadcrumbs and connect the dots.

The book contains new evidence showing how the famous handleless hatchet was broken—and in just a few seconds. The burned roll of paper, found in the kitchen stove the morning of the murders, will also be confirmed through photographs.

The trials, in this case, are just as fascinating as the murders. The artful questioning put forth by the trial attorneys is sometimes masterful, other times patently transparent, but always revealing. That many witnesses were rehearsed, polished, and asked to lie is without a doubt. You learn as much from the missing words as you do from what made it onto the stenographer's pages. All grammatical and spelling errors found in the testimonies and dialogue of the involved parties has been retained for accuracy.

As a paranormal historian, I have researched and written about the most-haunted historic places in America. Paranormal events happen every day. The final section of this book is dedicated to the haunting associated with the Lizzie Borden Bed and Breakfast Museum at 230 Second Street in Fall River, Massachusetts. Listed in the top ten most-haunted places in America, it would seem the walls that witnessed the bloody tragedy of that sultry summer day do, at times, play back their memories. Read what the staff and guests report as ongoing paranormal events in this 124-year-old home.

Here then, is a tale stranger than fiction, that spread beyond the gate at 92 Second Street (the house number in 1892), and up onto "the Hill," where the Borden sisters locked their doors against the ubiquitous whispers and gossip. The strange occurrences that surrounded Lizzie's life on French Street show an unsettled mind that became increasingly unhinged.

This is a telling of one of America's biggest unsolved murder mysteries. It is the unauthorized diary of –

"Lizzie Borden: A woman with her face pressed up against the window of a world she could not enter."

Rebecca F. Pittman
November 2016

The History

Maplecroft

Chapter One

ALL HALLOW'S EVE

Maplecroft. Fall River, MA.
Oct 31, 1893

"Come away from the window, Lizzie."

The voice was tired; a melancholy resolution turning it at once into a flatline of emotion.

Emma Borden looked, and felt, much older than her 43 years. A gaunt woman with sad eyes, she had endured much in the past year and three months. She had returned home from a short-lived vacation with friends to find her father and stepmother butchered—their autopsied bodies packed in ice and laid out on the family dining room table. Her coveted privacy was sacrificed to the glaring spotlight of thousands of strangers gathered outside the house, and a score of policemen and newspapermen *inside* the house. Blood was splattered across the wallpaper and woodwork. There had been no time to grieve, as she immediately took over the care of a prostrated sister who could not face the milieu.

Within moments of entering her home at 92 Second Street, Emma was immediately interviewed by the police, her private things searched through, and the mantle of responsibility etched firmly upon her furrowed brow. The tears flowed only when she was finally cosseted alone in her room at night, and the morning she wiped her father's blood from the parlor door.

"Lizzie! Come away from the window," Emma urged more emphatically. She glanced past her younger sister's hand holding aside the lace curtain of the south-facing sitting room window on the second floor of their new home on French Street. Outside, the gaslight street lamps punched ragged holes in the darkness, their soft halos of light illuminating the small shapes darting about the neighborhood trees. Candlelight flickered through the carved eyes and mouths of macabre pumpkins and gourds peering through the window glass of the mansions lining the street. It was All Hallow's Eve in Fall River, Massachusetts, and the moneyed gentry of "the Hill" was enjoying the merriment.

A view of the Brayton house today from Lizzie's Sitting Room/Library window at *Maplecroft*. Photo © by the Author, courtesy of Twilight Enterprises, LLC.

Lizzie Borden ignored her sister's admonition. She stood, transfixed, at the window, eyes focused on the three-storied house caddy corner from hers. Carriages were arriving in front of the Brayton's home, their lanterns adding to the party atmosphere, as revelers in fancy dress spilled from their open doors. Their laughter carried on the night air, tightening the knot in the voyeur's stomach, until the familiar feeling of panic pulsed in Lizzie's head. Several of the party-goers turned to stare over at the house across the street, its turret, topped with a conical witch's hat roof, seeming ironically suitable to its inmate. "That's Lizzie Borden's house," they said in excited whispers, and then, seeing the silhouette at the upper window turned and hurried up the sidewalk to the party.

Emma pulled her from the window, a familiar feeling of dread sweeping over her. They had only been living at 7 French Street for a little under two months. She had hoped the new furnishings and prestigious address would give her sister the peace that had eluded her at their father's home on Second Street. Yet Lizzie had continued to complain as she watched neighbor after neighbor pass their front door without stopping to welcome the sisters to their private enclave. There were no calling cards left on the silver tray waiting expectantly by the front door, no flowers, pastries, or invitations. Though the neighbors peered at the gabled structure from beneath parasols and whispered to each other from behind gloved hands, they passed them by.

The arrival of bands of curious onlookers began occurring from the moment the ubiquitous newspapers announced the Borden sisters' purchase of the home on "the Hill," Fall River's most elite setting, and the addresses of the "Who's Who" of that New England hamlet. It sat looking down, both geographically and figuratively, on a city built upon the backs of cotton mill workers. People walked by, drove by, even stood, unabashedly pointing at the Borden sisters' new house, with varied looks of awe, bewilderment, and fear.

Only a few days earlier two families had moved into the newly-remodeled Andrew J. Borden home at 92 Second Street where the double murders had taken place. Lizzie and Emma had seen to the alterations. The fireplace in Lizzie's bedroom was, at some point, walled over. Perhaps, Lizzie had seen to it.

Louis Hall, the owner of the livery stable across the street from the Borden house; and William B. Peckham (a grocer), his wife and three daughters, unpacked their boxes, moved into the two newly-created living spaces, and became Lizzie and Emma's first tenants. For both men, it was a pragmatic move, placing them within walking distance of their businesses. Whether they grew accustomed to the ongoing spectators gawking at the infamous murder house, is unknown. Both men had witnessed the harrowing events played out there on August 4, 1892. Did they walk with trepidation through the hallways, and double check all those locks?

Did innocent shadows, caught from the corner of their eyes, cause their nerves to twitch?

To add to the circus-like atmosphere that had ridden into "the Hill," along with the Borden sisters' moving carts, came hacks carrying "drummers" from out of town. For a few coins extra, the traveling salesmen could pay a rented carriage driver to carry them by the house on French Street and hear a Penny Dreadful retelling of the murders of Andrew and Abby Borden.

"Yes Sir, Gents! There she sits…Lizzie Borden. She was acquitted of the crimes, but there are tongues still wagging—somewhat knows—that says maybe someone got away with murder." The eyes would then dutifully follow the outline of windows, hoping for a glimpse of the infamous woman about whom they had read so much. After a few minutes of hedonism, the driver would continue, "Next up, over on High Street, we'll see the home of Alfred D. Butterworth. Mr. Butterworth hung himself from a tree in a field only four months before the Borden murders, leaving behind a wife and family. Maybe money don't buy happiness, gents."

The newspaper headlines and dubious celebrity of their newest neighbor brought the Borden sisters few fans from the addresses surrounding them. The increased traffic, both by foot and buggy, was an unwelcome invasion among the manicured lawns and pristine Victorian homes.

The sound of thuds against the siding of the house suddenly sounded from below. Emma and Lizzie hastened to windows; one overlooking the east side of the house, the other looking to the front. Lizzie saw the small figures of several children darting across the street from her side yard. They were dressed in makeshift costumes—most appearing to be oversized castoffs from their parents' closets. Long, flapping coat sleeves and trailing dresses flitted about in the October night.

Annie E. Smith, the Borden sisters' 29-year-old maid, appeared at the entrance to the upstairs sitting room.

"Miss Borden," she said, directing her statement to Emma, "there is boys and girls outside pelting the house with eggs. Do you want me to tell Joseph to run 'em off?"

Joseph H. Terault was the sisters' coachman who lived on the property. He was 37-years-old, four years Lizzie's senior, and hailed from Rhode Island.

Just then, the stinging sound of thrown sand skittered across the glass window panes. Something hit the roof and rolled down. Shrieks could be heard coming from the small shadows racing to the safety of towering elms and maple trees skirting the Borden's property. The maid looked at Lizzie with panicked eyes; the infamy of her mistress perhaps becoming clearer with each assault.

The shrill sound of the doorbell split a short-lived respite of silence. It twilled on without cessation.

"They've put a pin in the bell, Miss," Annie said, wringing her hands. Her breathing was coming in short pants. "It's a mischief thing they do. They hope you will open the door, and then they throws flour in your face. It's just a children's prank," she said, more to convince herself of the harmlessness of the onslaught than to offer solace to the sisters who were both showing strain.

Emma left the room, her shoulders bowed beneath the weight of the past two years. Lizzie heard her steps on the stairs leading down to the front hall. Moments later the incessant shrill stopped, leaving their ears ringing. Annie and Lizzie waited in the stillness and listened. Moonlight shone through the lace curtains, throwing fluttering ghost-like images across the polished wood floor.

Seconds later, she heard it, rising in the still air from the stand of bushes beneath the windows:

> "Lizzie Borden took an axe,
> Gave her Mother forty whacks,
> When she saw what she had done,
> She gave her Father forty-one!"

Her throat constricting, Lizzie turned to the window nearest where she heard the voices. Three small girls and a young boy streaked up French Street and careened around the corner of Belmont, disappearing into the darkness. She stood there, the sounds of music and laughter spilling from the open windows of the Brayton house where the All Hallow's Eve party was in full swing. Her head filled with a thrumming noise; like the sound of water rushing in through her ears. The panic started in her

16

stomach and reached up to her heart in a vise-like grip, as her breathing became labored. She gripped the lace curtain, nearly pulling it from the wrought-iron rod.

"Miss Borden?" Annie asked in a frightened voice, as she watched the metamorphosis before her. Her mistress's cheeks were effused with a red tinge, and her lips had gone white.

All Lizzie heard were the words ringing in her ears:

"Lizzie Borden took an axe..."

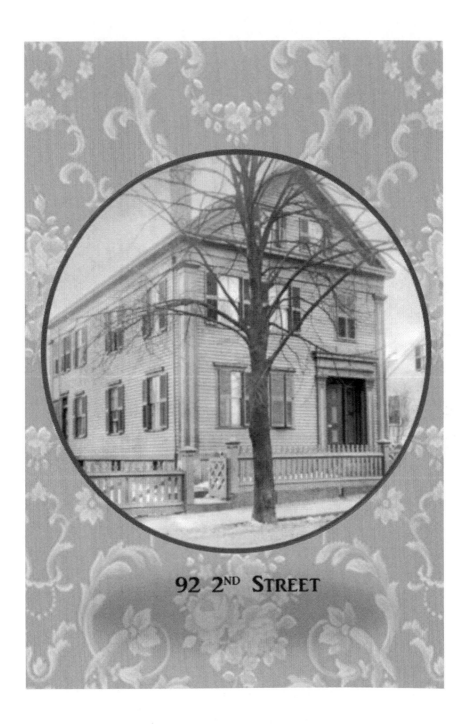

Chapter Two

"I don't know who she is."

For Lizzie Andrew Borden, the world was an uncertain place; one fraught with rules and boundaries over which she had no control. This realization that life would always have a hand before her face, blocking her way to things to which she felt entitled, began at the vulnerable age of two.

Sarah Anthony Morse Borden. Courtesy of Fall River Historical Society.

12 Ferry Street was a crowded home in 1853. Generations of families would often reside under one roof. Andrew J. Borden carried his new bride Sarah A. Morse over this threshold after their 1845, Christmas Eve wedding at the Central Congregational Church. For Sarah, a life that began beneath the ethereal glow of

Christmas bells must have seemed magical. Her young husband was establishing himself in the cabinet making business, and she did work as a seamstress.

Andrew J. Borden as a young man. Courtesy of Fall River Historical Society.

As Andrew's fortunes grew, along with his real estate holdings, his family followed suit. On March 1, 1851, his first daughter, Emma Lenora Borden, was born. Andrew's small family now resided elbow-to-elbow with Andrew's father Abraham, his wife Phebe, their youngest daughter Phebe Ann, and their older daughter Lurana, along with her husband Hiram Harrington.

Emma, at the impressionable age of four, witnessed her first, but certainly not her last, family funeral. Andrew's sister, Phebe Ann, died within the walls of 12 Ferry Street at the age of twenty-seven in August 1855. Andrew's sister Lurana and her husband Hiram moved across the street to 13 Ferry Street about this same time. For young Emma, it must have felt like a frightening change in the household to lose two Aunts at once, albeit one was only a few yards away.

The sadness of Phebe's passing was quickly replaced by the joy of a new addition to Andrew and Sarah's family. On May 3, 1856, daughter Alice Esther was born. Five-year-old Emma looked into the bassinet with mixed emotions at this new arrival who wrapped her small hand around her older sister's finger. Emma had been an only child for five years; a position some adolescents find hard to forego. She may have been filled with joy, however, at the prospect of having this new little playmate.

Whatever Emma felt, it was short-lived. At just under two years of age, young Alice died of *hydrocephalus acutus*— "dropsy on the brain." For the second time in only three years, the funeral wreath was hung at the door, the mirrors draped in black, and the sound of sobbing echoed throughout the small house.

On July 19, 1860, Andrew's third, and last, daughter was born. He gave the baby his name, perhaps realizing a boy was not in the making. Thus, Lizzie Andrew Boden made her triumphant entry into the world and changed the course of history.

For the next three years, life in the congested little house on Ferry Street saw several changes. Phebe Davenport Currier moved in; a relative of Andrew's through his mother's Davenport side. Perhaps a crying baby was not Phebe's thing, as she departed soon after Lizzie's birth.

There were also rumors at this time that Sarah Borden, Andrew's wife, was suffering from severe headaches and bouts of behavior causing acquaintances to label her as "peculiar." In photographs of Sarah, we see an intense woman, with an almost wild-eyed fierceness. Her brother John Vinnicum Morse has the same penetrating stare in photographs taken of him. Whatever plagued Sarah is uncertain. Tragically, in March 1863, she died at thirty-nine after succumbing to "uterine congestion" and "disease of the spine." Lizzie was only two, Emma twelve, and Andrew a widower at forty.

Sarah A. Borden with young Emma while posing for a daguerreotype by photographer Edward S. Dunshee.

In early images of Andrew, you see a man with a grim-set mouth, his visage showing a determination to overcome his father's fall from the Borden fortune. With unrelenting guile and business acumen, he set about to create his fortune, beginning with joining William M. Almy in an enterprise that would set the men up for the rest of their lives. Together they purchased the property at South Main and Anawan Streets and opened a furniture business, which later included undertaking services and coffin building. Borden & Almy opened in March 1845. The bond between the two men was ironclad. William gave his daughter Rachel, Andrew's name. Rachel Borden Almy and Lizzie Andrew Borden were classmates and friends. The Almy/Borden bond followed the two men to their graves. Their family plots at Oak Grove Cemetery are side by side.

Borden & Almy Furniture Store on South Main & Anawan.
Photo courtesy Fall River Historical Society

Emma would say in later years that she had stood by her mother's deathbed and acquiesced to one promise her mother asked of her...to "always watch over baby Lizzie." This was a promise Emma Borden fulfilled, beyond all human endurance, until the day she was lowered into her grave.

Emma

By the time adolescence merged into teenage years, Emma Lenore Borden had seen much sadness. A weight of responsibility has been placed with unrelenting heaviness upon her young shoulders. She may have taken over much of the care of baby Lizzie well before her mother's death, as any spinal disease probably made lifting a baby impossible. While the 1860 Federal Census shows a servant by the name of Caroline T. Gray residing at the Ferry house, it would seem she had her hands full caring for such a large household. It is doubtful the care and rearing of children were included in her "maid-of-all-work" description.

Emma's education was unremarkable. There are no records touting her grades or extracurricular interests. As she was a shy and retiring adult, it may be assumed she was of the same makeup at an early age, choosing the back row in school as opposed to the front; dutiful in her studies, but praying not to be called to the chalkboard in front of the eyes of watchful peers.

Lizzie was nine years Emma's junior. She may have followed closely in her big sister's shadow within the close walls of Ferry Street, but their personalities could not have been more different. Yet, Lizzie stated during her Inquest testimony, that Emma had been more like a mother to her as she grew. "I always went to her, because she was older and had the care of me after our mother died."

Emma during her elementary school days. This may have been taken on her 12th birthday on March 1, 1863, only 3 weeks before her mother's death.
Photo courtesy of the Fall River Historical Society.

Another mother was to shortly enter Emma and Lizzie's life. Andrew married again when Lizzie was five and Emma fourteen. Abby Durfee Gray was thirty-seven when she became the second Mrs. Borden. For Abby, a spinster by the era's reckoning, she may have given up hope of finding love. For Andrew (a widower with two young daughters and an empire to build), a wife to oversee things and be a female influence for a daughter entering her teenage years was pragmatic. There may have been romantic feelings between the couple, although a child from the union was never forthcoming.

Abby Durfee Gray Borden in her younger years.
Photo courtesy of the Fall River Historical Society.

Emma, age 16. She resembles Andrew, while Lizzie's full face was
closer to Sarah's. Photo courtesy of the Fall River Historical Society.

It was soon after, in April 1867, that Emma, at the age of 16, was sent away to Norton, Massachusetts, to the Wheaton Female Seminary for a year-and-a-half. The four terms, for which she stayed, came at the cost of $382.25. The rumors that Andrew Borden was miserly with his daughters is not born out, as here, he spends what was not a nominal amount in that era, to ensure his oldest daughter's education.

For the two sisters, this period of Emma's only absence from Lizzie's life since her birth must have had a traumatic effect on both of them. Emma's role as the little mother and housekeeper was suddenly usurped by a strange woman who lacked her mother's fire and intensity. "Fiery as a Borden" was a phrase used often in Fall River, and it was usually well-founded. Now, Emma was away from home for the first time, with only a few Fall River-ites, including a friend, Mattie Brigham, as familiar faces. Did she feel kicked out once Abby arrived? Was this the beginning of her hatred of her new stepmother?

Lizzie

Lizzie was also beginning a new education, as at the age of five she began elementary school. She was still living at home, doubtless lonely for Emma, and trying to adapt to this new female presence in their house who suddenly was calling the shots, albeit in an ineffectual, mild way. Lizzie called her "Mother," perhaps at her father's urging. It was all so different. Life held no consistency for her…no safety net. She could be batted about like a badminton at everyone's will but her own. The uncertainty of who would be in her life, and who would disappear just as suddenly, was frightening. Losing her mother at such a young age had brought about a fear of abandonment. In later years, this fear would resurface when people ignored her, or she felt control over her life slipping away. At times, it became an all-encompassing panic; at other times, it exploded into rage.

Lizzie in her high school days.
Photo courtesy of the Fall River Historical Society.

Lizzie began her freshman year at the Fall River High School in September 1875. The school was located on "the Hill" and was perhaps Lizzie's introduction to the address that would become her obsession throughout the rest of her life. The city's wealthy sons and daughters graced the halls of this former mansion. It was her first real taste of class segregation, and the burning need to "fit in."

According to the *Boston Herald* on August 7, 1892, Lizzie "as a scholar was not remarkable for brilliancy, but she was conscientious in her studies and with application always held a good rank in her class." Later in life, Lizzie was often described as a brilliant conversationalist, mostly due to her voracious reading. According to acquaintances, Lizzie was quite sensitive, and reticent when it came to making new acquaintances. Her reserve, her nemesis during the 1892-1893 double murder trials of her father and stepmother, seems to have been in place at an early age. Friends later remarked it had always been her manner. Other girls giggled, and flirted, Lizzie tended to hang back and watch through distrustful eyes.

A pattern began in young Lizzie's life that would follow her into her adult years. Her desire to be seen as "worthy" and "perfect" are evident in her routine of quitting things in which she did not excel. She did not finish high school, perhaps feeling the pain of falling short of excellent grades, or from watching from the sidelines as other girls were invited to dances, picnics, and house parties, from which she was excluded. Invitation after invitation to parties on "the Hill" would find their way into her classmates' mailboxes, but not to hers. Her testimony at her Inquest concerning her father's final minutes with her is prophetic. She stated she found him in the sitting room after his return from the Post Office. When she asked, "Is there any mail?" she claims he answered, "None for you."

Lizzie also quit other things in life if they became too difficult, or if she felt she had "fallen short." It was rumored she once, while teaching Sunday School to some Chinese children, became distraught when they would not mind her, and walked out, never to return to teaching. She would hold organization posts for only a short time, once again quitting if she felt she was underappreciated, or it did not fulfill her need for social advancement.

Lizzie was not without friends. Some of the acquaintances she made in High School stayed with her for many years. Two bequests in Lizzie's will went to Adelaide B. Whipp (Addie), and to Lucy S. Macomber (Lou), showing her lasting friendship with these young classmates.

Other friends came from church associations, daughters of her father's business acquaintances, and relatives. Adeline Maria Allen (Addie), was a classmate friend of Lizzie's and later became her neighbor on "the Hill." Addie, on June 2, 1881, married in what was called a "Brilliant Wedding", and quickly acclimated to the status of a Fall River clubwoman, and member of numerous social welfare organizations. She moved into a newly constructed Queen Anne-style home on Rock Street in 1892, the year of the murders.

Later in life, Lizzie became friends with Addie's daughter, Edith, who was quoted as saying there "were rumors that Lizzie stole some things from local stores when she really didn't need to. I don't know whether Lizzie was guilty or not. She had a very good and influential lawyer who was able to keep information out." The rumors of Lizzie's stealing would follow her from Second Street up onto "the Hill" in later life.

Louisa Holmes Stillwell (Lulie) maintained her friendship with Lizzie for many years. Her Uncle was Charles Jarvis Holmes, a friend of Andrew Borden's, and one who would stand by Lizzie's side throughout her long legal battles. His wife, Mary, would spend considerable time at the Borden house after the murders, supporting Lizzie and Emma, and even overseeing the police searches of the home. Their daughters, Mary Louisa and Anna Covell Holmes, were Lulie's cousins, and part of the group of girls who were to vacation with Lizzie in Marion during the time of the murders.

Lulie kept a prolific diary during her high school years, where boys, dating, and other teenage raptures are reported. As she describes who is flirting with whom, Lizzie's name never appears. She is conspicuously absent from the names mentioned attending parties, weddings, and outings.

Lizzie was to witness another grand wedding when this same Lulie married John Hiram Condict Nevius of New York in another of the elaborate receptions that made Fall River newspapers' social column headlines. Lizzie presented her with a set of delft-like sweat meat dishes, which are on display today at the Fall River Historical Society in the Lizzie Borden Museum section.

Lizzie attempted to learn how to play the piano during her high school days. With her usual doggedness and focus, she attacked the keys, determined to become an aficionado of the ivories. This did not last long. She quit when it became apparent she would not achieve the perfection for which she aspired. It may have also required more dedication to practice than she was ready to sacrifice.

Her friends' diaries during this time were filled with entries of parties, "splendid sleighing," tennis matches, seaside adventures, and travel. Lizzie escaped into a world of words. It was said she bought books not by the volume, but by the armful. Friends visited Lizzie at her home at 92 Second Street, but the feeling is not one associated with frivolity and fun. Lulie's diary, reporting on her few trips to see Lizzie during their high school days, stated that Lizzie was "rather tired," "rather blue," and "real miserable." These statements were made during different visits, and within one month of Lizzie's 16th birthday, a time when most girls are planning a party, and looking at boys with new interest.

Three of Lizzie's closest friends had been neighbors during her young days on Ferry Street: Elizabeth Murray Johnston, who was to receive a cryptic letter from Lizzie on the day of the murders; and sisters Mary Ella and Anne (Annie) Eliza Sheen, who would marry well, and become Fall River socialites, as, respectively, Mrs. George S. Brigham and Mrs. William Lindsey, Jr. Annie remained Lizzie's friend for the rest of her life, her correspondence with Lizzie giving much insight into a troubled mind. Annie rose high in her social circles, the pinnacle of which was her presentation to the Queen of England.

That Lizzie watched her friends marry, decorate lavish mansions and summer homes, travel in elite circles, and become mothers, must have colored her view of the world as she saw it from the lace curtains of her bedroom amidst the businesses and noise of Second Street. These girls had lived in the same working-class neighborhood as she, yet they were living her dream. Her father's money and name carried with it a clout that should have unlocked doors for her, but they remained as barred as the triple locks on the

Borden's front door. Her location in Second Street's business district was a deterrent to the young beaus of social breeding who may have sought her. She may have been oblivious that her "black spells," "sullenness," and frequent outbursts of anger were also walls to her popularity.

Lizzie entered her adult life with one unrelenting aspiration: to belong to the elite set of young women who belonged on "the Hill." She was, after all, a Borden. Her ancestors had played a part in the town's prosperity. Her father was one of the wealthiest men in Fall River, with a giant building named after him that took up half of a city block. Her Borden cousins lived on "the Hill." She was doing volunteer work through the Central Congregational Church, rubbing elbows with the city's wealthiest matrons, joining each committee, such as the Fruit and Flower Mission, the Christian Young Women's Temperance Movement, and others, all in an effort to be noticed and welcomed into that coveted inner circle.

The Central Congregational Church on Rock Street in Fall River, Ma.

Lizzie's church work finally bore "fruit" on June 21, 1890, when she was included, along with two other Borden ladies, to join some of the other church volunteers for a Grand Tour of Europe. That the other Borden girls lived on "the Hill," along with other moneyed passengers, would have caused Lizzie a dizzying feeling of finally having "arrived." Her traveling companions, Anna H. and Carrie L. Borden, were granddaughters of Colonel Richard Borden, and hence part of the elite branch of the Borden family tree.

The Cunard Line Steamer *Scythia* (the same steamship line that owned the *Titanic*) sailed for Liverpool, England, in June 1890, one month before Lizzie's 30th birthday. For the next eighteen weeks, Lizzie toured the elegant cities of Europe and witnessed first-hand how the "other half" live. The more prominent Misses Borden's took to the streets of Paris and Rome as young ladies "to the manor born." Lizzie watched as trunks and hat boxes were filled with the latest designs by Worth, and other maestros of fashion. She navigated through the confusing array of silverware surrounding the fine china plates at the fashionable restaurants they frequented, by watching the other ladies surreptitiously. This is where she belonged. This was her birthright!

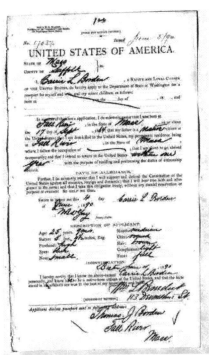

Lizzie's Grand Tour passport. Courtesy of Ancestry.com.

From the Blarney Castle in Ireland to Loch Lomond in Scotland; from Shakespeare's Stratford-upon-Avon, to Canterbury Castle in Kent; Amsterdam to Heidelberg; the Alps to Florence; Milan to Venice; Paris to the Tower of London, Lizzie collected postcards of her favorite sites, and purchased a few fashions of the *belle epoque* that she could afford. Each city unfolded its culture before her thirsty eyes. The museums and galleries were no longer just on the pages of her books at home, but here, where her eager fingers could touch them. At times, it must have seemed surreal to walk the crowded European streets where the fashions and languages wrapped around her mind like gossamer.

The return voyage in October of 1890, shows a Lizzie coming down from a high. The tour is over, and perhaps she felt during the trip that the other girls, though polite, were not as ingratiating toward her as she had hoped. Perhaps it was her imagination. The sinking feeling at the thought of the bleak house waiting for her was not imagined; it was all too real.

Anna Borden shared a cabin with Lizzie during the sea voyage. During Anna's testimony at the murder trial, she was asked, "You are I believe, not a relative of the prisoner?" "No sir," Anna replied, the indelible stamp of hierarchy firmly planted. Lizzie and Anna shared a great-great-grandfather, making them third cousins. Anna went on to say she had known Lizzie about "five years," a time that coincided with Lizzie's confirmation into the Central Congregational Church. It was indeed through Lizzie's Christian endeavors she had wrangled a Grand Tour ticket, and a stab at entering the circled wagons on "the Hill."

Anna was asked to testify to a conversation she and Lizzie had in their cabin on the voyage home. She related that Lizzie said, "she regretted the necessity of returning home after she had such a happy summer because the home that she was about to return to was such an unhappy home."

To belong to the Fall River "inner circle" upon her return was perhaps the wish Lizzie made at the famed Trevi Fountain in Rome, as she stood with her back to the 85-foot-high sculpture, held her breath, and tossed a coin over her shoulder into the water. That wish would never be realized.

On November 18, 1890, members of the Central Congregational Church threw a large "Welcome Home" party for the Fall River girls, who had just returned from the Grand Tour. Seventy guests were waited on by the young men of the church, and the returning travelers were spoiled beyond their dreams. Anna Borden stood and regaled the crowd with a few stories of their travels and thanked the committee warmly for the wonderful party. As the orchestra played, the guests departed. President Booth asked permission (and receiving it), escorted the two Misses Borden's home, while a young man named Fred Pearce, escorted Lizzie to her address because it was "the polite thing" to do.

If Lizzie had hoped to be part of the social in-crowd that traveled that summer to Europe would ensure her place within the carefully sewn folds of the Fall River nobility, she was to be let down and let down with a crash. Upon returning home to the austere house in the midst of businesses, stables, and a few scattered houses, she waited for party invitations from the girls on the cruise, but none appeared. Though she had been the secretary for the Fruit and Flower Mission before the trip, she did not return to that post upon her return.

Lizzie A. Borden in her 20s.
Photo courtesy of the Fall River Historical Society.

A letter was written by Mrs. William C. Davol, Jr. on April 25, 1890, to her daughter (two months before the trip), listing the girls who were included in the Grand Tour party, summed up Lizzie's place in society. This woman who knew "everyone who was anyone" in Fall River, wrote:

Nellie [Ellen] Shove, Elizabeth [Lizzie] A. Borden (I do not know who she is), Anna [H.] Borden and Carrie [Caroline L.] Borden, are going to Europe with Miss [Hannah D.] Mowry this summer."

"I do not know who she is."

Chapter Three

"This is where the trouble began; this is the starting point."

George Petty

The hatred towards Abby Borden had been growing since Lizzie's return from the Grand Tour. Emma saw the difference in her younger sister within a few short days after Lizzie unpacked her trunks and came down from the exhilaration of telling her travel stories and showing off her postcards and souvenirs. She spent hours pasting each picture postcard of the many wonders she'd seen into an album, carefully writing beneath each card her memories of that location.

After seeing her steamer trunk resting in the hallway, Andrew, it was said, bounded up the steps to greet his daughter the morning following her return. That he loved his daughters was evident to many, if not to them. It was said, one friend looked at Andrew's smiling face, as he went about his daily routine, and commented, "I can guess by that huge smile that someone is back."

But, the afterglow from the dizzying whirlwind of travel to so many cultural places soon faded. Lizzie was unhappier than ever. She complained constantly about her cramped little room, and the "ugly house" she had come home to. There wasn't even room to display the many wonderful treasures she had carefully selected from each European city.

Emma did what she always did. She took a back seat to "baby Lizzie's" wishes, and in an effort to head off a maelstrom, offered to change bedrooms with her, as Emma's was twice as large. While the new sleeping arrangement may have mollified Lizzie for a time, it quickly wore off.

It is unknown at what point Lizzie learned of the plan to turn the Upper Farm at Swansea into a major business operation. Andrew owned two farms in Swansea, Massachusetts—the Upper and

Lower Farms. He had accumulated the property through acquisitions over the years and stubbornly held onto the water rights of that area. The Upper Farm was a huge acreage for cattle, other livestock, and crops. The Lower Farm was where the family "summered," and where Lizzie had learned to fish. Both farms were only minutes from Warren, Rhode Island, and the home of Uncle Charles M. Morse.

The Lower Farm at 1205 Gardner's Neck Road in Swansea, today, where the Borden's "summered." Photo courtesy of the Author.

It is possible Andrew went to visit his brother-in-law John Morse in Hastings, Iowa, while Lizzie was away for eighteen weeks on the Grand Tour, in 1890. Plans for a new business concerning the Upper Farm may have begun at that time. John did testify in 1893, that Andrew came to see him "some years earlier."

John Vinnicum Morse was the brother of Andrew's first wife, Sarah, who died when Lizzie was only two. He was a bachelor who had been born and raised in Fall River but had headed west to the frontier to try his hand at farming and horses. Using his Yankee thrift, and good business head, he soon amassed a sizeable bankroll. John visited the Borden's often, staying a year-and-a-half in 1879. He tended to bounce around from relative-to-relative when traveling. Andrew found in him a friend and shrewd business confidant. Both men were loners, seldom letting others close until their motives and loyalty had been proven. They pinched pennies, distanced themselves from frivolous adornment, and saw real estate holdings and expansive businesses as the Golden Goose.

John Vinnicum Morse. Courtesy Fall River Historical Society.

John rented his Iowa farm and moved to Warren, Rhode Island (a mere 8 miles from Swansea), in 1890, the same year Lizzie was traveling. He stayed with his Uncle Charles Morse, his wife Mary, and their two spinster daughters, Elizabeth (52) and Henrietta (47). Both Charles and Mary were getting on in years. In 1890, Charles was 80, and Mary was 78.

A year later, John rented his Iowa farm for an additional year and moved to South Dartmouth, Massachusetts, to join his friend William A. Davis, who was operating a horse trading and butcher business. The 1880 Federal Census shows William A. Davis (28), his wife Sophia S. Wilcox Davis (26), Issac C. Davis (2), and Alice P. Davis (5). Sophia's father is also living with them by 1892. William is listed as a "meat Pedder [Peddler]".

John told friends around this time that he had brought 80 mustang horses with him from Iowa. For a time, they were pastured at Westport, Massachusetts, where some itinerant horse traders had set up camp. The local authorities began investigating the set-up two days before the Borden murders. John suddenly moved the horses to Fairhaven, Massachusetts, possibly to his relatives' farm there. In Fairhaven lived another Charles Morse—Charles L. Morse, who was married to Marinda (Mary) C. Morse, a second cousin. They had 3 young children: Betsy (12), Charles M. Morse (4), and Emma L. Morse (2). Yet *another* Mary Morse (Mary L. Morse), who was widowed after her husband Joseph died, was cited as living in Fall River in the 1900 Federal Census, at the age of 76. This is the Aunt Morse Emma mentions during the trial. The tradition of naming generations the same name has caused more than one genealogist to reach for the aspirin bottle.

The storm within the walls of 92 Second Street had truly begun in 1887 when Andrew stepped in to help Abby's relative. Sarah Gray Whitehead was Abby Durfee Gray Borden's half-sister, and a good 32 years younger. When Sarah and Abby's father, Oliver Gray died, the Fourth Street house, where Sarah was living, was divided four ways: one-fourth to Mrs. Gray, the widow; one-fourth to Mrs. Priscilla Fish, Gray's daughter; one-fourth to Sarah Gray Whitehead; and one-fourth to Abby. Abby gave her one-fourth to her sister, Sarah. At Abby's urging, in 1887, five years before the murders, Andrew bought the Widow Grey's share and gave it to Sarah. Sarah was struggling, and her husband wasn't doing right by her, according to Abby. This generous gift would give her beloved half-sister security and a home of her own.

For the penurious Andrew J. Borden, this strange largesse made his two daughters sit up and take notice. Lizzie, never one to sit quietly by, confronted him. Her Inquest testimony summed it up when Attorney Hosea Knowlton asked her about her response to the gift.

"We thought what he did for her [Abby], he should do for his own," Lizzie said haughtily.

And indeed, the sisters were given their grandfather's house on Ferry Street where they had been born. It was worth a good deal more money than the Fourth Street house. They owned it outright, but soon found that the rent payments they received from tenants there were minimal, and the house was in constant need of repairs.

On July 18, 1892, only two weeks before the murders, they suddenly sold the deed for the house back to their father for $5,000; $2,000 more than what it was valued when he gave it to them. That the sisters opted out for cash so soon before his death gives one pause. Did one, or both, fear that should their father die, they would be stuck with a house that was proving to be a money pit, and prefer ready cash instead? Would extra money in their banks prove there was no motive on their behalf to kill their wealthy father?

A Burglary in Broad Daylight

One of the many people allowed to view the dead bodies of Andrew and Abby Borden on the day of their murders was George Petty of Number 98 Second Street. He had lived at 92 before the Borden's moved in, twenty years prior to their death. He was interviewed by Officer Phillip Harrington concerning what he saw the day of the murders.

"Went upstairs, got down on my knees to examine Mrs. Borden's head. At once I saw she had been dead some time, and told the Doctor [Bowen] she must have been dead an hour. I further said, this is where the trouble began; this is the starting point."

No truer words were spoken concerning the mysterious circumstances of that day. Abby was indeed where "the trouble began."

On June 24, 1891, two important events happened. John Morse was moving to South Dartmouth to join the William A. Davis family's meat business, and the Borden's house was robbed.

It was a unique burglary; happening in broad daylight on one of the busiest business streets in the city. It happened while Andrew and Abby were summering at the Swansea farm. Captain Dennis Desmond, Jr., of the Fall River Police Department, responded to a summons made by Andrew Borden. Upon Desmond's arrival, he said, "in a small room on the north side of the house, I found Mr. Borden's desk. It had been broken open." Andrew told Desmond "$80.00 in money and 25-to-30 dollars in gold, and a large number of horse car tickets had been taken. The tickets bore the name of Frank W. Brightman." They were a gift to Andrew from a business associate. Due to the name written on them, the tickets were seen as a way to apprehend the burglar if, and when, they were used. An idea Lizzie Borden later ridiculed.

Abby was interviewed and stated that her "gold watch and chain, ladies chain, with slide and tassel attached, some other small trinkets of jewelry, and a red Russian leather pocket-book containing a lock of hair had been taken." She said, "I prize that watch very much, and I wish and hope that you can get it; but I have a feeling that you never will." Her husband Andrew echoed her sentiments when he told Captain Desmond "three times within two weeks after the robbery," "I'm afraid the police will not be able to find the real thief."

Perhaps it was obvious to Andrew and Abby that the burglary could have only been committed by someone within the heavily-locked house, and who knew just where to go to find the room where the Borden's valuables were kept. An intruder from the outside would need to know when the coast was clear, as Emma, Lizzie, and Bridget were all home that day. He would have to find the rare time when the rear door wasn't hooked, the front door's three locks unlatched, enter, traverse that confusing layout of rooms, get past more locked doors, break open a desk without alerting anyone to his presence, grab the "good stuff" and exit, again without passing any of the inmates.

Lizzie was ready with an answer to at least one of the obstacles. She dramatically showed the police officers an open door in the cellar, and pointed out an old "6 or 8 penny nail" which she "found in the keyhole of a door leading to "a bedroom on the east side of the house." The description of the door "leading to a bedroom on the east side of the house," matches the location of the door to Andrew and Abby's bedroom. It would appear that door was in the habit of being locked *before* the burglary of 1891, and a burglar used the unlikely nail as a tool of entrance.

As you will see, Lizzie anchors her lies with objects. As though leaving a trail of bread crumbs for others to detect her cleverness, no material object goes without a hint to her deception:

Attorney Knowlton (during the Inquest questioning of Lizzie):

"All the reason you supposed there were sinkers there [in the barn] was your father had told you there was lead in the barn?"

Lizzie: "Yes, lead; and one day I wanted some **old nails**; he said there was some in the barn." [Bold print by Author]

"This is where the trouble began…"

1890s streetcar ticket with the name at the bottom.

The streetcars were watched for several weeks after the burglary. Finally, a breakthrough occurred when the "tickets were traced to some person." Oddly, Andrew told the police to "drop the case." Not so oddly, it was later stated that Officer Desmond reported he had told Andrew that the stolen tickets had been traced to his youngest daughter after people using the horse car said the tickets had been given to them by "Lizzie Borden."

1903 Gold Lady Elgin watch.

The stolen watch, so highly prized by Abby, was quite probably the one Andrew bought for her on August 5, 1871. It was a Gold Htg Lady Elgin, in a hunting case, and priced at $75. In 2015, $75 is the equivalent of $1,470, a prodigious amount for someone with

Andrew's reticence for spending on things that weren't absolutely essential. That the gift did not fall on a birthday, anniversary, or another special occasion, gives it even more importance. It was a gift from the heart, not from an obligatory observation of an event. Abby's watch, along with the other items, was never recovered.

That Andrew suspected Lizzie, was possibly the reason that from the day of the burglary forward, he lay the key to his bedroom in plain sight on the left-hand corner of the sitting room mantle. Without uttering a word, the key notified the thief that Andrew "trusted the housemaid, and if stealing from your father is that important to you, then here...here's the key. No rusty nail necessary." That key sat there, day in and day out, taunting Lizzie with her father's distrust, until the day he was found murdered only a few feet from the mantle where it sat.

A skeleton key, like the one Andrew left, on the sitting room mantle of the Lizzie Borden B&B and Museum. Kitchen door (l). Photo by the Author.

"This is where the trouble began..."

The fireplace in the Borden sitting room. The key is on the left-end of the mantle. The couch where Andrew was found murdered can be seen on the left.
Photo by Ron Bueker

The burglary of Abby's watch is significant. During trial testimony, Emma reported that Andrew wore on his little finger "the only article" of jewelry with which he adorned himself. He carried a pocket watch but wore no other rings. The ring was a small gold band Lizzie had given to him "10-15 years" before the murders, according to Emma. That would make Lizzie around 17-22-years-old at the time she gave it to him. We know she did not graduate from High School, and the presentation of school rings was not yet popular.

Was the small gold ring something that had belonged to her late mother Sarah? Was it Lizzie's way of reminding her father where his loyalties should lie? Or, more ominously, was it her way of tying him to her, due to her jealousy and hatred of Abby? Perhaps Abby's watch was the first outward sign of affection that the usually non-demonstrative and remote man showed to his wife. For Lizzie, it was a sign of betrayal and abandonment, no matter how erroneous her feelings were. The watch goes missing, but Lizzie's gift still glitters from her father's little finger.

During Lizzie's Inquest testimony, Attorney Knowlton asked her:

Knowlton: "Were your father and mother happily united?"

(Witness pauses a little before answering)

Lizzie: Why I don't know but that they were."

Knowlton: Why do you hesitate?"

Lizzie: "Because I don't know but that they were, and I am telling the truth as nearly as I know it."

Lizzie's hesitation may have been caused by a flashback of Andrew's gift of the watch to Abby. It was obvious Lizzie had not really thought of her father and step-mother as a loving husband and wife, other than that unexpected romantic gesture on her father's part.

That two things of obvious sentimental value to Abby were taken says quite a bit as to the perpetrator's mission. A small leather pocket-book with a lock of hair would hardly seem tempting. The hair was doubtless from someone Abby loved dearly.

Andrew's gift of a deed to the house on Fourth Street in 1887, further cemented Lizzie's growing fear that this woman had not only taken over her mother's role but may be close to replacing his love for his daughters as well. It was at the time of the Fourth Street transfer that Lizzie stopped calling Abby "Mother." When Attorney Knowlton asked her during her Inquest testimony, "You did not regard her as your mother?

Lizzie: "Not exactly, no; although she came there when I was very young."

Knowlton: "Were your relations toward her that of mother and daughter?"

Lizzie: "In some ways it was, and in some, it was not."

"This is where the trouble began..."

Knowlton: "In what ways was it?"

Lizzie: "I decline to answer."

The Borden house burglary in June of 1891, was the beginning of a plethora of strange happenings at 92 Second Street. That winter, Lizzie began reporting seeing a strange man running around the house in the shadows.

Chapter Four

"Something Wicked This Way Comes"

The spring and summer months of 1892, leading up to the murders of Andrew and Abby Borden, were fraught with strange occurrences and disclosures. The threatening clouds hanging over the house at 92 Second Street were as prevalent as the industrial smoke from the mills skirting Fall River. The pressure was building, and it was apparent to those in the Borden's inner circle something was about to blow.

In March of that year, Mrs. Hannah Gifford measured Lizzie for an outer garment. She had been creating capes, cloaks, and "sacks" for the Borden ladies for "seven or eight years." During the trial in June of 1893, Mrs. Gifford was asked to state a conversation between herself and Lizzie Borden that occurred in March 1892, while she was working on a "sack" for Lizzie. [A sack is a short, loose-fitting coat for women and children.]

> Knowlton: "Now Mrs. Gifford, will you state the talk, what you said and what she said?"
> Gifford: "I was speaking to her of a garment I made for Mrs. Borden, and instead of saying "Mrs. Borden," I said "Mother" and she says, "Don't say that to me, for she is a mean, good for nothing thing." I said, "Oh Lizzie, you don't mean that?" And she said, "Yes, I don't have much to do with her; I stay in my room most of the time." And I said, "You come down to your meals, don't you?" And she said, "Yes, but we don't eat with them if we can help it." And that was all that was said."

Barn door with hasp lock. During the day, a pin was placed through the hasp.

In April 1892, only four months before the murders, someone broke into the barn at the Borden residence. Bridget, the housekeeper, testified it was "at night." That something was taken was addressed during her Preliminary Hearing testimony a few weeks after the murder.

> Mr. Adams (for the Defense): "Within a few months [of the murders], the barn was broken into, and something was taken or tried to be taken out of that, so far as you know?"
> Bridget: "Yes, Sir."
> Adams: "Has the barn been broken into more than once? It has been twice, has it not?"
> Bridget: "I do not remember."
> Adams: "You only remember once?"
> Bridget: "Yes, Sir."

Lizzie told Miss Alice Russell about the barn break-ins, on the night before the murders. Alice said it was "just teenage boys up to mischief trying to steal the pigeons." What is telling about the above testimony with Bridget is the cagey way the question to her from Mr. Adams is presented.

Mr. Adams: "…something was taken, or tried to be taken out of that, so far as you know?"

Nine pages of Bridget's Preliminary Hearing testimony are missing from the time the prosecutor, Mr. Knowlton, is questioning her. Her entire Inquest testimony has been missing since the Superior Court trial in June of 1893. The testimony she gives Mr. Adams during cross-examination, concerning the barn break-in, corresponds to the questions from the missing nine pages of the Preliminary Hearing that were under Direct examination.

If you look at the way the question to her by Mr. Adams is phrased, you can infer that when the question was first asked of her in the missing pages, under Direct examination by Knowlton, it was probably objected to. If the "something" taken from the barn had been pigeons, then why not say pigeons? Why the cloak and dagger? But, if the "something" had a more ominous meaning, such as a hatchet, that *is* something that would be objected to. The break-in was in April, and the Defense would have objected to any object which could be construed as relating to the murders, by saying "it was too removed in time from the murders;" an excuse they had used before to defuse ticking bombs.

Bridget's answer of "Yes, Sir" when asked if something was taken, shows she had knowledge that a burglary had occurred. Let's see just what might have happened.

Andrew was a shrewd businessman who never missed an opportunity to make a buck. He sold vinegar and other sundries from his cellar, and was known to peddle eggs from his farm on the downtown street; something which caused Lizzie no end of embarrassment. His father and Abby's father had both been peddlers, and he saw no shame in it.

The breeding and raising of pigeons as a business was a popular one in the 1800s. Young pigeons were called squab. They were considered a delicacy and were in demand both at restaurants and at meat markets. Andrew, after ridding himself of his only horse the year before, took the barn loft and turned the east-end of it, above a window, into a pigeon coop.

An article from *Mother Earth News* says the following:

"A point to remember is that it is just about as easy to raise twice the number of squab you will want for your family, as it is to raise barely enough. You can then easily sell the surplus to cover all your costs (first class hotels and restaurants are always in the market for squabs), or you can swap the surplus with neighbors for things they raise, and you don't."

The timing of when young pigeons were considered squabs is important to note. The USDA's definition for squab is "a young pigeon that is marketed just before it is ready to leave the nest, usually from 25-to-28 days of age, when it weighs from 12-to-24 ounces." Most people raising squab made sure there were several males and females in one coop to keep the eggs coming at different intervals, thus supplying the breeder with meat every "25-to-28 days," or...every month.

In April, a break-in at the barn occurred. That is also the month Andrew Borden found it necessary to buy a new hatchet; a large one with a 5" blade and claw head at the back. He took it over to his farm in Swansea and handed it to Mr. Frank Eddy, the foreman there for sixteen years, to have it sharpened.

Mr. Eddy, on August 11, 1982, during the police investigation in the early days after the murder, reported to Detective George F. Seaver, "I have seen axes and hatchets at Mr. Borden's. The large hatchet was comparatively new. When it was bought, it was brought over here, and ground sharp. After being ground, Mr. Borden was here, and it was carried out and put on the wall by the gate for him to carry home. When he went away, he said, "I won't take the hatchet. You'll be coming over in a day or two, and you can bring it over; which I did."

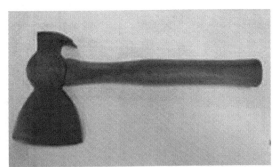

An 1892 clawhead hatchet like the one Andrew bought.

The fact that Andrew told the farmer to bring it when he came, may intimate that this way Lizzie couldn't steal it again. He left it with Mr. Eddy.

Bridget testified that she hadn't seen Lizzie go to the barn since the horse was taken away the year before. That Lizzie did visit the barn when the horse was in residence is another testimony to her love of animals that followed her throughout her lifetime. She may have seen the removal of the horse as a thoughtless gesture from a father she was beginning to see as the enemy. When the pigeon coop was installed, Andrew, a man nearing 70, may have given her the job of climbing the steep barn steps to the loft to feed and care for the birds. It may have been a way to mollify her after getting rid of the horse. [Horse cars ran near Second Street during this time, and electric streetcars had just begun to make an appearance in Fall River. Andrew probably felt the expense of harboring a horse unnecessary. It is possible the horse was removed to the Swansea farm.]

If Lizzie had begun tenderly caring for the birds, she may have been horrified to find them beheaded by a hatchet sometime in Spring. When Andrew explained the birds were a business, not pets, she would have realized the beheading would be happening every time the helpless things were of age…about once a month. Lizzie may have stolen the hatchet Andrew was using in the barn, and for good measure, hidden the others that were in the cellar.

Alfred Johnson, the young Swede who was in charge of the Lower Farm at Swansea, told Detective Seaver, August 11, 1892, that he "has worked for Mr. Borden for nine years. Have done his work at the house, cutting wood and cleaning up the yard, when not busy at the farm. Think the two last times I cut wood was early in the Spring, and again just before planting. Mr. Borden had two axes, a single hatchet, and a shop or bench hatchet. The bench hatchet has never been used much since it was sharpened. I ground it over here to the farm in early Spring. The hatchets and axes were always kept in one place, in a box in the wood room at the left of the furnace. Never found them in any other place and always put them back after using them, as Mr. Borden was particular about having one place for all tools. When I have been working for Mr. Borden, I have stayed there."

It is unclear when Andrew first realized the hatchet was missing. He kept the barn locked at night, and had the key with him on his extensive key ring. While obviously knowing the barn had been broken into in April, he may not have realized the hatchet was missing until it came time again to "dispatch" of the birds, which would have been sometime in May.

If Alfred arrived to do some work at the house, "just before planting," which was probably May in Massachusetts, he may have gone to the cellar for a hatchet to chop wood and found the box where they were kept, empty. He would have asked Bridget if she knew where they were, and after looking, she, perhaps, mentioned it to "Miss Emma." In Emma's Inquest testimony, a few days after the murder, she was asked by Attorney Knowlton concerning the cellar:

Knowlton: A short-handled hatchet...was found there [later, after the murders] ...do you know anything about that?"
Emma: "No, Sir."
Knowlton: "Do you know whether your father kept such an instrument?"
Emma: "I know the farmer used to come over and cut up wood. I suppose he had something to do with it."
Knowlton: "Whether any such instrument had been previously kept there, you don't know?"
Emma: "No, Sir. I never saw one, but there must have been one."
Knowlton: "Assume there were three found— "
Emma: "Yes, Sir, I think I have seen a hatchet down there in the wood room. I am quite sure I have— "
Knowlton: "When do you think you saw, whatever you did see, there?
Emma: "I should say it might have been several months [before the August murders] that I have been in the wood room for anything."
Knowlton: "You don't know of anything being done with an ax or a hatchet that would cause blood to come on it, do you?"
Emma: "Not unless father killed pigeons with them; I don't know whether he did or not."
Knowlton: "You did not see him kill the pigeons?"
Emma: "No, Sir."

Emma tries to dodge the subject of hatchets, only to finally admit she had been to the wood room in the cellar "several months" before August. That tallies nicely with Alfred being there in May to chop wood. It is hard to believe Emma would need anything in that dark and dirty wood room. She may, indeed, have been looking for the missing hatchets for Alfred Johnson's use.

Andrew Borden could be an obtuse man when it came to relationships. While he had a mind for business, dealing with women's emotions and drama was so outside his wheelhouse, he may as well have come from Pluto. Yet here he was, living in an all-female home, where hormones and "spells" swirled like the Falls for which the city was named.

Rather than confront Lizzie about the missing barn hatchet, he handled it in the same way he had left a silent message with the key on the sitting room mantle. He fought back, not with words, but with actions.

Knowlton: "Did you have any occasion to use the axe or hatchet?"

Lizzie: (During Inquest testimony August 10, 1892): "No, Sir."

Knowlton: Did you know where they were?"

Lizzie: "I knew there was an old axe down cellar, that is all I know…the last time I saw it, it was stuck in an old chopping block."

Knowlton: "When was the last you knew of it?"

Lizzie: "When our farmer came to chop wood."

Knowlton: "When was that?"

Lizzie: "I think a year ago last winter; I think there was so much wood on hand he did not come last winter."

Knowlton: "Do you know of anything that would occasion the use of an axe or hatchet?"

Lizzie: "No, Sir."

Knowlton: "Assume they had blood on them, can you give any occasion for there being blood on them?"

Lizzie: "No, Sir."

Knowlton: "Can you tell of any killing of an animal? Or any other operation that would lead to … blood on them?"

Lizzie: "No, Sir. He killed some pigeons in the barn last May or June."

Knowlton: "What with?"

Lizzie: "I don't know, but I thought he wrung their necks."

Knowlton: "What made you think so?"

Lizzie: "I think he said so."

Knowlton: "Did anything else make you think so?"

Lizzie: "All but three or four had their heads on, that is what made me think so."

Knowlton: "Did all of them come into the house?"

Lizzie: "I think so."

Knowlton: "Those that came into the house were headless?"

Lizzie: "Two or three had them on."

Knowlton: "Were any of their heads off?"

Lizzie: "Yes, Sir."

Knowlton: "Cut off, or twisted off?"

Lizzie: "I don't know which."

Knowlton: "How did they look?"

Lizzie: "I don't know, their heads were gone, is all."

Knowlton: "Did you tell anybody they looked as though they were twisted off?"

Lizzie: "I don't remember whether I did or not. The skin I think was very tender, I said why are these heads off? I think I remember of telling somebody that he said they twisted off."

Knowlton: "Did it look as if they were cut off?"

Lizzie: "I don't know; I did not look at that particularly."

Pigeon with young squab

In the same dysfunctional way Andrew left a small key on a mantle do his talking, his twisting off the heads of the birds when his hatchet was taken, shows the "fiery Borden" trait and iron will. He knows Lizzie was responsible for the theft of Abby's things the year before. It may have been at that time he installed a sliding bolt between the shared door to his bedroom and Lizzie's. Her erratic behavior had taken a toll. He would not be victimized by his daughter. He would fight back. That Lizzie was made of the same unyielding will was Andrew's undoing.

 ## Lizzie's Testimony:

In **Lizzie's testimony,** we find the following clues:

1) She lies about the last time Alfred "the farmer" came to chop wood. She said it was "a year ago, last winter." Alfred says he chopped wood in early Spring and "right before planting," only a few months earlier. It is suggestive that she needs to distance herself from him being there in need of a hatchet.

2) She admits to knowing Andrew "killed some pigeons in the barn last May or June." This is in response to finding blood on a hatchet, which shows us Andrew did use one to kill the birds previously. Emma also mentions him using one to kill pigeons.

3) Andrew, in his strange symbolic way, brings the beheaded birds into the kitchen and lays them out before the horrified Lizzie on the kitchen table. Startled, as she knows she has hidden the hatchets, she blurts out, "Why are these heads off?" Based on her next response, it appears Andrew, angry and determined, tells her, he twisted them off. His habit was to use a hatchet with them—why not now? Because the hatchet has been stolen.

4) Knowlton says "Those that came into the house…" Lizzie didn't say they came into the house before he asks this question. Did Bridget tell him about the birds in her missing Inquest testimony, or in private?

A Blue Bedford Cord & a Pink Wrapper

In May, three months before the murders, a dressmaker made her appearance on the scene; one whose testimony concerning an important dress she made for Lizzie would be of great interest.

Mr. Jennings [Lizzie's attorney during the Superior Court trial in June of 1893, one year after the murders]: "What is your name?"

Raymond: "Mary A. Raymond."

Jennings: "What is your business?"

Raymond: "Dressmaker."

Jennings: "Where do you live?"

Raymond: "31 Franklin Avenue."

Jennings: "Fall River?"

Raymond: "Yes, sir."

Jennings: "Have you done dressmaking for Miss Lizzie Borden for a number of years?"

Raymond: "Yes, sir."

Jennings: How many?"

Raymond: "Ten at the house…ten at my home."

Jennings: "What portion of that time, if any, have you also done dressmaking for Mrs. Borden and Miss Emma."

Raymond: "I worked for Mrs. Borden, not for Miss Emma—for Mrs. Borden during that time."

Jennings: "Where did you do the work for Mrs. Borden?"

Raymond: "In the same room I did Miss Lizzie's."

Jennings: "Did you make any dresses for Miss Lizzie last Spring [1892]?"

Raymond: "I did."

Jennings: "Do you remember at that time making a Bedford cord dress?"

Raymond: "Yes, sir."

Jennings: "Before I pass to that, I will ask you what time you went there?"

Raymond: "In May."

Jennings: "What time in May?"

Raymond: "The first week in May. I was there three weeks."

Jennings: "And do you remember in what order the dresses were made, as to when this Bedford cord dress was made?"

Raymond: "I made that the first one."

Jennings: "Why?"

Raymond: "Well, she needed it, needed it to wear, and had it made first."

Jennings: "How long did it take to make?"

Raymond: "I couldn't tell the exact time, but I should think three days." [Emma, who helped with the sewing, said it took two days.]

Jennings: Can you describe the dress?"

Raymond: "It was light blue with a dark figure."

Jennings: "How light a blue?"

Raymond: "Well, quite a light blue…"

Jennings: "What they call a baby blue?"

Raymond: "No, I think not, not as light as baby blue."

Jennings: "Do you remember what the figure was upon it?"

Raymond: "I can't remember the shape of the figure. It was a dark figure."

Jennings: "In what manner was it made?"

Raymond: "It was made a blouse waist, and a full skirt, straight widths."

Jennings: "How was it to the sleeves?"

Raymond: "The sleeves were full sleeves, large sleeves."

Jennings: "How was it as to the length?"

Raymond: "Longer than she usually had them."

Jennings: "How did the length compare with those of her other dresses made for her *at that time*?" [Italics are the Author's]

Raymond: "Well, I should certainly say it was half a finger longer, two inches longer."

Jennings: "Did you make a pink wrapper for her at this time?"

Raymond: "I made a pink-striped wrapper."

Jennings: "Was this dress longer or shorter than that?"

Raymond: "I should think longer."

Jennings: "Now what was the material of which the Bedford cord was made?"

Raymond: "Why it was a Bedford cord. That was the name of the material…It was cotton, a cheap cotton dress…trimmed with a ruffle around the bottom."

Jennings: "A ruffle of what?"

Raymond: "Of the same."

[Keep in mind the order the dresses were made. It may have been for another reason than simply needing something new to wear.]

1890s shirtwaist. It hooks down the front (l). 1890s Day Dress with Train (r). Photo courtesy maggiemayfashions.com.

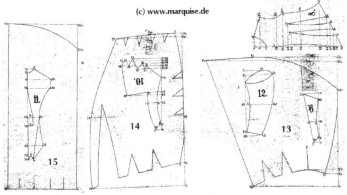

1890s dress pattern. Courtesy of www.marquise.de

During the Superior Court trial in June 1893, Officer Phil Harrington was asked to describe the dress Lizzie had on when he interviewed her in her room the afternoon of the murders.

Harrington: "It was a house wrap, a striped house wrap, with a pink and light stripe alternating; the pink the most prominent color. On the light ground stripe was a diamond figure formed by narrow stripes, some of which ran diagonally or bias to the stripe and others parallel with it…the sides were tailor fitting or fitted to the form. The front from the waist to the neck was loose and in folds.

The collar was standing, plaited on the sides, and closely shirred in front. On either side, directly over the hips, was caught a narrow bright red ribbon, perhaps three-fourths of an inch or an inch in width. This was brought around front, tied in a bow, and allowed to drop, with the ends hanging a little below the bow. It was cut in semi-train or bell skirt, which the ladies were wearing that season."

Officer Harrington's description brought some twitters from the female spectators in the courtroom, and some sarcasm from the prosecution team, as to his overt knowledge of lady's fashions.

The *Boston Record* had this summation of Harrington's testimony: "If Officer Phil Harrington of the Fall River police ever loses his job he ought to have no difficulty in getting a situation in a millinery store or as a reporter on a society journal. His description of the dress that Lizzie Borden wore the day of the murder was so elaborate in detail as to arouse the suspicion that it was carefully prepared beforehand. It is a pity, in the interests of justice, that he and his brother officers of the Fall River police were not so observant of other details on that fatal morning as he was of Lizzie Borden's apparel. His knowledge of the details of a woman's costume is painfully accurate even for a policeman."

A 1890s wrapper. These were a looser fit and faster to take off and put on.

The description of the dress Lizzie wore the morning of the murders before she changed into the pink wrapper at noon that day, did not fare as well in the detail department. Witnesses' accounts of what she wore were vague, and in some cases, non-existent.

During Lizzie's Inquest testimony on August 9, 1892, only five days after the murders, she was asked by Attorney Hosea Knowlton, the District Attorney, "What did you wear the day of the murders?"
Lizzie: "I had on a navy blue, sort of Bengaline silk skirt with a navy-blue blouse. In the afternoon, they thought I had better change. I put on a pink wrapper."

Two-piece blouse waist (shirt) with a skirt. The blouse hooked down the front. Narrow ruffle at the bottom and leg-o-mutton sleeves. This the design of the Bedford cord dress.

Note that the name of the person who told her to change is not mentioned. It is an ambiguous "they." Alice Russell testified that she did not tell Lizzie to change, and did not hear anyone else instruct her to do so. Doctor Seabury Bowen testified he suggested Lizzie go upstairs after the crowd out front was becoming overwhelming. Their shouts and conversation were, no doubt, coming in through the dining room windows. Even if Bridget had left them closed after washing them a little over an hour earlier, the chaos would have been heard from within the house.

It is interesting to note only two people, during the trial testimony, agreed with Lizzie on the color of the dress she wore that morning.

What Dress Did Lizzie Have On?

Dr. Bowen stated Lizzie's dress that morning was sort of drab, not much color to attract my attention, a sort of morning calico...a common dress that I did not notice specifically. I should call it dark blue."

Mrs. Phebe Bowen (his wife): "...dark blue, with a blouse waist, a white spray design on it, a round figure or flower."

The other witnesses describe the color differently:

Bridget Sullivan (the maid): "It was a blue dress with a sprig on it...light blue, it [the sprig] was a darker blue, I think, than the under part was." In previous testimonies, Bridget said she did not notice what dress Lizzie wore that morning, yet she recalled what she was wearing the day before the murders (Wednesday) vividly. "...light blue wrapper on her; shirt [misspelled, probably skirt], and basque." [Basque was a blouse waist.]

Officer Patrick Doherty: "I thought she had a light blue dress with bosom in the waist or something like a bosom. I thought there was a small figure on the dress, a little spot like."

Mrs. Churchill recalled a "light blue and white ground, with a darker figure, the shape of a diamond...box pleat and loose in the front."

Alice Russell, in her usual flustered dialogue, could recall nothing about the dress, even though Lizzie laid with her head on Alice's shoulder during the morning of the murders, was fanned and administered to throughout the early hours, her hands rubbed, forehead bathed, and helped to sit down. Alice did remember the bottom of Lizzie's blouse waist was open, and she tried to unhook it further to allow Lizzie to breathe. Lizzie stopped her, saying "I am not faint."

Only the Bowen's collaborate Lizzie's description of a "dark" blue dress. Lizzie described it as "navy" blue. She also said it was a Bengaline silk, which is a ribbed cotton fabric threaded with silk to give it a sheen. It differs from a calico, or cheap cotton, that has no ribbing. Bengaline fabric is a thick-grained taffeta. It is a durable plain weave fabric characterized by widthwise cords formed by using fine warp yarns and course weft yarns. Bengaline was first made of silk in Bengal, India. Calico is an unbleached cotton, often showing small husks. It was a cheap material and popular in the 1800s due to its ease in receiving dyes and patterns.

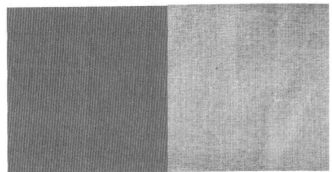

Bengaline fabric is on the left, calico on the right. Note the ribbing in the Bengaline that does not appear in cotton or calico.

That Bowen aided Lizzie and cared about her, was obvious. He and his wife had known her, and the family, for twenty years, both as neighbors, and as the family physician. He even accompanied Lizzie to the Catholic Central Congregation Church when her parents were summering in Swansea, although he was himself Baptist. It resulted in the Fall River "hens" having a "cluck fest."

Perhaps Dr. Bowen was merely mimicking what his wife had told him of Lizzie's dress, within the seclusion of their own walls. It would not be the first time he took credit for something she witnessed.

The fact that Bridget described her own dress that fateful morning as "a dark, indigo blue calico skirt and blouse with a white clover leaf background" is interesting. Perhaps Phoebe Bowen confused Bridget's dress as Lizzie's during the excitement. Later that day Bridget changed to a light blue gingham dress with two white borders running around the bottom portion of the skirt.

The reason Lizzie was in a hurry to change out of the dress she was wearing that morning will become clear later. The innocent view is a wrapper was much less restricting; something the Victorian female looked for in everyday house dresses and tea gowns. The ubiquitous corset they were forced to wear was difficult enough without being pinned in by more hooks and unyielding fabrics.

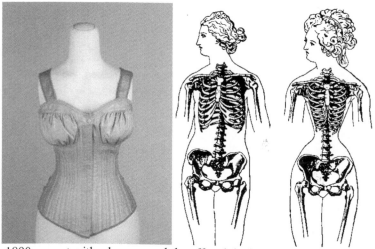

1890s corset with a bosom, and the effect it had on the female ribcage.
Photos courtesy of maggiemayfashions.com

A Paint-Stained Bedford Cord Dress

Lizzie's father had announced he would be having the house painted in May. Whether Lizzie offered to choose the color (in an uncharacteristic move on her behalf), or Andrew asked for her assistance in an effort to lessen the tension that had accumulated inside the house between Lizzie, Abby and himself, we don't know. As a transparent olive branch, in an obvious effort to placate her, Lizzie would still have seen the offer as perfect timing.

THE ARSENIC WALTZ.

The new Dance of Death. (Dedicated to the Green Wreath and Dress-Mongers.)

A cartoon in the 1800s depicting the deaths associated
with wearing the popular green-dyed fabrics.

Lizzie was a voracious reader. One of her excursions between the pages had trumpeted the deaths caused by a dye called Emerald Green. This popular color of the 1800's was derived from mixing Verdigris in vinegar and warm water. Arsenic was then added to achieve the green color. When reacting with the copper particles, it achieved a brilliance, unlike previous greens, replacing the popular Scheele's, and Paris green pigment. At the peak of its popularity, people began dying. It was found the flocked emerald green wallpaper was releasing the arsenic into the air; women, wearing silk ball gowns created by the green dye, were absorbing the poison into their skin; even fake flowers dyed with Paris green were infecting households. It made headlines—and Lizzie took notice.

Lizzie accepted the offer to choose the color (or volunteered to do so) and moved forward to oversee the painting of a house she detested.

On May 9, 1892, only three months before the murders, John Grouard arrived at the Borden home to begin preparing the paint color Lizzie had chosen: Drab. Drab was the name of a green paint of medium-hue found on a palette of Victorian color choices.

Victorian color palette showing **Drab Tint** (3rd from the top on the right).
It was a medium-green hue.

John Grouard testified during the Superior Court trial concerning his interaction with Lizzie Borden during the time he was hired to paint the Borden residence at 92 Second Street.

Jennings: "Can you tell when you took the paint up there, Mr. Grouard."
Grouard: "The ninth of May."
Jennings: "Did you see Miss Lizzie Borden there on or about that time?"
Grouard: "Not that day...the next morning early...in the back yard, near the barn."
Jennings: "Where was your paint?"
Grouard: "In the barn."
Jennings: "What was it in?"
Grouard: "Tubs, pots, etc."
Jennings: "Now won't you tell what was done by you and she at that time in regard to paint?"
Grouard: "The color was not satisfactory that we had mixed in the tub, and so I made the color to suit--to suit her."
Jennings: "...was she about the premises?"
Grouard: "Oh, yes, she was, and I mixed the colors to get a satisfactory color. Of course, I mixed the color in the large tub."

Jennings: "Will you state what part of the barn the tubs of paint were in?"

Grouard: "Well, near the door...the south door."

Jennings: "And was she during any portion of that time in the immediate vicinity of those tubs or not?"

Grouard: "I think she was."

Jennings: "Did you paint the house?"

Grouard: "We did...the next morning, of the 10th," Outside"..."dark drab" ... the trim was a "darker drab" ..."

Jennings: "Do you remember whether or not any tests were made from time to time by you and her in regard to the appearance of the paint when you were mixing it?"

Grouard: "Well, the paint was carried there on the afternoon of the 9th and her father said that she was to select the color, and I better not go on with it until the color was determined, and she not being present, it was delayed until the next morning. That evening, she came to my house and said the color was not just what she wanted."

Jennings: "She came to your house. In consequence of what she said to you an appointment was made for the next morning?"

Grouard: "The next morning early before the men came to go to work, that was about six o'clock in the morning...I mixed the colors then satisfactorily."

Jennings: "She was there at the time?"

Grouard: "Yes, sir."

Jennings: "You painted the steps and everything connected with the house, I presume?"

Grouard: "Yes, sir."

Knowlton [**during cross-examination**]: "Where were the paints in the barn, near the door or in the stall?"

Grouard: "Well, probably partially—there was two tubs, one dark and one light color."

Knowlton: "Well, don't you remember whether they were in the stall or not?"

Grouard: "Well, one color may have been, but one color was near the door."

Knowlton: "You did all the mixing?"

Grouard: "Yes, sir."

Knowlton: "Who else besides you did it?"

Grouard: "Well, I directed the mixing of it."

Knowlton: "Well, either you or some of your men did all of the mixing?"

Grouard: "Yes, sir."

Knowlton: "Well, she looked on and saw it done?"

Grouard: "Yes, sir."

Jennings [**on re-direct**]: "After it was mixed, did you take it out and try it at the house?"

Grouard: "Yes, sir, on the corner of the house near the back steps."

Jennings: "In consultation with her?"

Grouard: "Yes, sir."

Jennings: "So as to show how it looked on the house?"

Grouard: "Yes, sir."

1890s bottle of arsenic (l). Paris Green paint, 1890s, stamped with POISON label. (r)   Photo courtesy shutterstock.com.

 The Green Paint

Several things are apparent in Grouard's testimony:

1) A color had already been mixed and it "was carried there on the afternoon of the 9th and her father said that she was to select the color, and I better not go on with it until the color was determined, and she not being present, it was delayed until the next morning. That evening, she came to my house and said the color was not just what she wanted."

The color had been mixed at Grouard's home and "carried over." Lizzie had not been present to watch the making of it. Paint in that era required pigment, vinegar, linseed oil, and, in the case of green paint, copper mixed with arsenic. She asked him to come back "early" the next morning.

2) Lizzie was not an early riser. She typically made her appearance around 9 in the morning. The painter may have requested an early appointment so his men could get started, or she may have. 6 a.m. was before Bridget even came downstairs to begin breakfast.

3) Both attorneys were interested in the location of the paint tubs. Knowlton's curiosity may have leaned toward more nefarious reasons. It is interesting that he pushes whether the tub was by the door, or in the stall, which is farther back from the entrance. It may be the question was to see if Lizzie had more room to navigate around the tubs (without brushing up against them and getting paint on her dress) than she would have if the tub was sitting right next to the door. Or, it may have been to see where the paint ingredients were kept: near the door where it would have been more difficult to take something without being seen, or, if they were in the back of the barn, in the shadows.

4) Neither attorney comes right out and asks "Did she get paint on her dress?" You would think Jennings would have asked that question in order to nail down Lizzie's later actions concerning the Bedford cord dress. But he didn't. Why? He probably already knew the answer. Every attorney preps his witness before trial. Obviously, Grouard said he didn't know if she got paint on the dress. Jennings decides not to open that door and give the jury any reasonable doubt. Knowlton lets it slide, possibly knowing it will avail him nothing, and only put the paint stains back in the jury's mind, as a reason for later burning the dress.

5) Most importantly, during the painting, the barn was "broken into," again. Is it possible some of the arsenic used in the paint recipe was taken?

Shortly after Mary Raymond completed the sewing of Lizzie's Bedford cord dress, Lizzie may have accidentally brushed against the back steps' railing on her way to the backyard one afternoon while the paint was still wet. The painters had gone for the day, without warning the household of the hazard waiting outside the back-entry door. Or perhaps, they had. It had ruined the lower part of her skirt and beneath the ruffle, as she descended the steps, her skirt caught up in her right hand. Good enough for mornings around the house, for now. The cheap cotton was, at least, a cooler option than her fancier dresses. Later, it would be suitable for some saved scraps and burning.

During the Superior Court trial of June 1893, Lizzie's attorney, Andrew Jennings questioned Mary Raymond, the dressmaker who was at the Borden resident for two weeks in May 1892.

> Mr. Jennings: "Do you remember at that time you were there they were painting the house or did paint the house?"
> Raymond: "They did paint the house at that time, yes, sir."
> Jennings: "Do you know anything about whether at that time there was any paint got upon the dress?"
> Raymond: "There was."
> Jennings: "How soon after it was made did Miss Lizzie begin to wear it?"
> Raymond: "Just as soon as it was finished."
> Jennings: "And how soon after that, as you recollect, that she got paint upon it?"
> Raymond: "I can't tell you that, I don't remember."
> Jennings: "Was it while you were there?"
> Raymond: "Oh, yes, sir." [Mrs. Raymond was there the first week of May and stayed three weeks. The painters began work on May 10 and were there three weeks, a little longer than the dressmaker.]
> Jennings: "Where was the paint, if you recollect?"
> Raymond: "It was on the front of the dress and around the bottom of the dress, around the ruffle, on the underneath part of the hem."

Chapter Five
"All Around the Town"

The months of April and May of 1892, had been busy ones in the Borden murders' countdown. In April, pigeons are beheaded, the barn is broken into (and "something was taken from it"), and Andrew finds the need to buy a new hatchet and put it in the safekeeping of his farm foreman.

May ramps up with several occurrences: a blue Bedford cord dress is made, only to become stained with paint immediately after; and the Borden barn is broken into, again, during the time paints are being mixed there. Pigeons are once *again* beheaded and cruelly showcased on the family kitchen table. And, Uncle John Vinnicum Morse returns for another visit—this time to ride with Andrew Borden over to the Swansea farm and talk about future plans.

Attorney Knowlton [during the Preliminary Trial August 25-September 1, 1892]: "Did he say anything about his farm, about giving that away?"

John Morse: "We were going over—that was sometime in May of this year...we were riding over by his place, we got to speaking about the Old Ladies' Home, you know. He says "I would give them some land here, if I thought they would accept of it, something to that effect."

Knowlton: Nothing about a will then?"

Morse: "No, sir."

Knowlton: "About giving it to them?"

Morse: "Yes, sir, that is all."

John Morse's testimony came after much probing by Attorney Knowlton. It was obvious, John did not want to talk about the farm or the plans for it.

> Knowlton: "Did he [Andrew Borden] ever tell you about any bequests he had a notion of making?"
> Morse: "I think he said something about making…he did not say how or anything like that."
> Knowlton: "Whether he ever did say anything to you about any purpose?"
> Morse: "I think sometime he made a remark about a bequest."
> Knowlton: "When was that?"
> Morse: "I think somewhere within a year."
> Knowlton: "Where were you at the time?"
> Morse: "I think on South Main Street."
> Knowlton: "What doing, walking together?"
> Morse: "Just walking along."
> Knowlton: "What was it he said?"
> Morse: "That is all he said."
> Knowlton: "What?"
> Morse: "Something about some bequests that he would make; he did not say what they were, or anything about it; something about giving something away, bequests to somebody, he did not say who; something about these bequests that he—he did not say anything more about it."
> Knowlton: "What did he say?"
> Morse: "He did not know but he might make some public bequests; words to that effect."
> Knowlton: "Won't you tell me what he said?"
> Morse: "He talked like he was going to make some public bequests; just in that way."
> Knowlton: "That was sometime within a year."
> Morse: "Yes, Sir."
> Knowlton: "Can you fix the time any better than that?"
> Morse: "I could not."

In the testimony, above, as John is pushed to state what the bequests were, he suddenly switches to the words *public bequests*, in an effort to distance the topic from a closer recipient.

John's tap dance concerning Andrew's will and its contents was witnessed earlier during the Coroner's Inquest, five days after the murders. He is still vague as to when certain conversations took place.

Knowlton: [Attorney Hosea Knowlton, DA]: "Did he ever talk with you about a will?"

Morse: "Yes, sir, he has."

Knowlton: "When was the last time?"

Morse: "Somewhere within a year."

Knowlton: "Were you in the house?"

Morse: "No, sir, I think we were outside at the time."

Knowlton: "What was the talk?"

Morse: "He said he thought he should make some bequests outside to charitable purposes. He did not say any more either one way or the other."

Knowlton: "Did he talk as though he was intending to make a will?"

Morse: "I judged from that that he was intending to, I drew my conclusions that he had not, but was thinking of it."

Knowlton: "Did he mention the bequests outside he thought he should make?"

Morse: "He did not."

Knowlton: "How came he to be speaking about it?"

Morse: "Common conversation, I suppose, same as about his land. Before he bought the Birch land, I was down there with him. He says let's go up Main Street. We went up. He says "here is a piece of property, don't say anything about it, I have a chance to buy. What is your opinion about it?" I asked what it could be bought for. I don't know he told me direct, but about. I says "I think it is good property in the heart of the city. The city will be coming towards it all the time. I believe it would be a good investment." Several months afterwards, one Sunday, he says "John, I did as you told me to." I says "what is that," I forgot all about it. "I bought the Birch land.""

Knowlton: I wish you would recall the conversation about the will as explicitly as you have this."

Morse: "That is all he said about a will, he thought of making some bequests out, you know, for charitable purposes. His farm over there, he was talking about the Old Ladies' Home, "I don't know but I would give them this, if they would take it."

Knowlton: "Was that the same talk?"

Morse: "I don't think it was the same time.

Knowlton: "Did he talk to you any other time about a will?"

Morse: "Years ago, out West at my place one time, he said he had a will; several years ago, he told me had destroyed it."

Knowlton: "How long ago did he tell you he had destroyed it?"

Morse: "15 years ago."

Knowlton: "Did he tell you anything about the contents of the will?"

Morse: "He did not."

The timing here is interesting. When Lizzie was asked about Andrew's property during her Inquest testimony, she mentions the Birch land, stating "a short time ago he bought some real estate…that belonged to a Mr. Birch." John says several months after the conversation about the Birch property with Andrew, Andrew tells him he did indeed purchase it. Andrew bought the Birch land May 22, 1892. The talk about "the Old Ladies' Home" happened in May when John and Andrew drove over to the Swansea farm. John can only manage to say the original Birch land conversation, and "other bequests," is "within a year." John says Andrew told him "several months after" he mentioned thinking of buying it, that he had bought it. Was it several months earlier it was mentioned originally or is it possible this elusive time was in April, a visit he has not alluded to.

We first hear about the pigeons in April, during the first barn break-in. Was John there around the 1st of April? Did his evasiveness concerning when his conversation occurred with Andrew about bequests and the Birch land have something to do with not wanting to mention April, in case he was asked if anything out of the ordinary happened while he was visiting Andrew? Would a barn break-in and a stolen hatchet be a subject to avoid?

Did Lizzie overhear any of the conversations concerning the Swansea farm and bequests? It is interesting that the two big discussions concerning Andrew's will and bequests happened on South Main Street, and at the farm, away from listening ears.

The Birch Street purchase was not a small one. Andrew bought the area for $23,000. That's $400,000 in today's dollars. His plan was to erect a substantial brick building at the corner of Spring and South Main, comparable to his large Andrew J. Borden building farther north on Main Street. He told a *Fall River Daily Globe* reporter, "I could secure tenants readily for two floors, but it wouldn't be just the thing in my mind to leave the third floor for hall or dancing purposes. Second street will eventually become an overflow business highway, but it won't be in my time. I don't like to move off the street in my lifetime and dances wouldn't be just the thing I'd want around me in my sleep." [Andrew says he has no intention of moving off Second Street in his lifetime, something Lizzie and Emma contradict in later interviews.]

When John Morse is questioned by Attorney Knowlton at the Inquest and in the Preliminary Hearing, he confesses to only three dates, leading up to the murders that he was with Andrew, prior to his visit the day before Abby and Andrew are killed. He says he is there May, the end of June, and the middle of July. The murders occurred on August 4th. John is suddenly with Andrew every month, talking over this strange "bequest to the Old Ladies Home."

The Swansea Upper Farm area was large—over 220 acres—and was a huge acreage with cattle, other livestock, crops, and various income-producing commodities. Mr. Eddy managed this farm. On a separate parcel was the Lower Farm, where the Borden's "summered" and Lizzie spent time fishing with her father in Cole's River, just down the slope. An 1895 map (next page) shows Andrew owned two "estates" on this parcel along Gardner's Neck Road, one of which is still standing—the summer home. Albert Johnson was the overseer here.

Whenever John Morse is interviewed about Swansea, he never says "the Lower Farm" or the "Upper Farm," he simply says "the farm." This is convenient if you look closely. John says, "his farm over there, he was talking about the Old Ladies' Home." The other "public bequests" conversation is cloaked in secrecy. Not just the contents, but the date the conversation occurred. What if…John wasn't talking about one farm or the other—the Upper Farm or Lower Farm—but both farms?

"The Old Ladies' Home" (according to the Author's belief), was the nickname he and Andrew came up with for the Lower Farm where the family spent their summers. This was not the income-producing farm, but a beautiful home near the river. This may have been slated to be set aside for Abby, her mother, half-sister, and other elderly women who were without support in the Borden family. Some of these in the Borden/Morse lineage were John's Aunt Catherine Boudray (Boodry), the elderly Mrs. Vinnicum (Abby's friend), Mrs. Mary Morse (the widow in Fall River), and possibly for the other Aunt Mary Morse, who lived in Warren, and whose husband was already 82. This couple had two spinster daughters, Elizabeth and Henrietta, in their 40s' and 50's. It would be a secure place for the women to live out their days in peace, when the time came, without worry about rent or companionship. Andrew was turning 70; his time was getting short by 1892 standards.

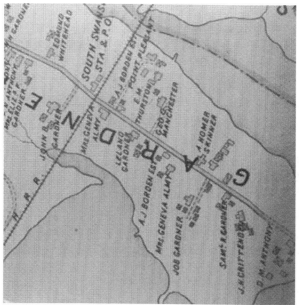

In this map of the Swansea farm areas, we see clearly there are two Andrew J. Borden estates, on Gardner's Neck Road. This is the Lower Farm area. The house near the middle of the map is where they "summered." Cole's River is on the left. Map courtesy of Leonard Rebello/*Lizzie Borden Past & Present.*

Lizzie and Emma had stopped joining Andrew and Abby at the annual summer vacations at the Lower Farm five years earlier when the cold war began between Andrew's daughters and his wife. Lizzie's own testimony admits she has not been to the farm "in five years." Why leave this home that Abby loved, and treasured her vacation time there, to two daughters who had turned their backs on it?

That brings us to the Upper Farm and the epicenter of the storm. This was set up for cattle, horses, and crops. That there were already cattle there is witnessed by John Morse coming over to the farm the night before the murders and Mr. Eddy asking him about the "two oxen" he was to take to Butcher Davis. Morse admits during his Inquest testimony that on the morning of the murders, following breakfast, that "we went out in the sitting room from the dining room...Mr. Borden and I talked about some cattle I had, and then I went away."

Why was John talking about cattle *he* had? His "sole reason" for coming to Fall River the day before the murders was to *pick up* two oxen for William Davis who ran a butcher and horse trading business in South Dartmouth. John lived with the Davis's and helped with the logistics of running it. Thursday morning, the day of the murders, John wrote to William Vinnicum in Swansea, whom he had just visited for supper the day before, "about some cattle." Vinnicum was related to John through his maternal grandmother's side. John also just brought 80 mustang horses in from Iowa. There were other players in this dangerous chess game, as we will soon find out, who also had an interest in the Upper Farm...a business deal so far-reaching, that it may as well have been called "All in the Family."

Andrew may have been contemplating deeding not one, but both of the farms under Abby's name: one for the "Old Ladies' Home," (Lower Farm) and one for the Upper Farm, with John Morse actually running a huge cattle and horse-trading operation. And it was all about to explode.

Other Players Enter the Plot

By the summer months of 1892, there was much activity concerning the Upper Farm at Swansea. John Morse was spinning more plates than an accomplished circus act. But at some point, there's usually the sound of crashing glass.

On John Morse's visit to Fall River, at the end of June, he brought with him William Davis's daughter, Alice. Alice was 17-years-old and had known John most of her life. He lived with her family many years before, and was now back, living with them in South Dartmouth, and helping with her father, and grandfather's meat business. The butcher trade was also one involving horse trading and cattle—an area in which John V. Morse was well acquainted.

According to John Morse's Inquest testimony about his June visit, he said he "came over in the morning and went back at night. I can tell about that time if you want me to. There was a lady came over Mr. Davis's daughter, with me. We drove over in the afternoon. I hired a horse, and Mr. Borden's daughter went to ride, we went down to the steamboat. I took her home after dark."

In one paragraph, John Morse contradicts himself. He first said he "came over in the morning," only to say two sentences later, "we drove over in the afternoon." I believe both are correct. John was an early riser, as most farmers are. When at the Borden's, he was up by 6:00. It is possible he drove Alice Davis over to the Swansea farm first, to show it to her. As we will see, John was showing the farm to another young woman. Was he shopping for a future housekeeper for the Lower Farm homestead; one to help with the "Old Ladies' Farm," or, was there another farmhouse, up Gardner's Neck Road (shown on the map at the top, pg. 74) that is no longer standing?

"About the 10th of July," John was back. "I did not stay but a short time," John testified to Attorney Knowlton during the Inquest. "I was here overnight, but I went down to an Aunt's on the Stafford Road at that time…Catherine Boudray (Boodry)." Catherine Boodry is John's mother, Rhody's, sister. He testified he did not see Lizzie during either visit.

During this July return to Fall River, John took a detour to Warren, Rhode Island, where he picked up his niece, Annie Morse. Annie was questioned by a *Fall River Herald* reporter the day of the murders concerning her Uncle John Morse. At the time of the interview, Annie and her brother William were staying with the Daniel Emery family on Weybosset Street, a mile from the

Borden's house. She was vacationing there from her home in Minnesota. Her father, William Morse, is John's brother.

The Fall River Herald, August 4, 1892: "Morse's niece was asked if she had ever seen her uncle [John] before, and replied that she had. She had met him when she was five years old, and three weeks ago, he had taken her from the cars at Warren to the Borden farm, Swansey [ms]."

When Morse is asked about his niece during his Inquest testimony, his answer is quite different.

> Attorney Knowlton: "Did you see the relatives you went there to see?" [Referring to John's visit to Daniel Emery's home the morning of the murders.]
> Morse: "I saw one; the young man was out; I did not see him."
> Knowlton: "What was the young woman's name?"
> Morse: "Annie Morse, she was indisposed while I was there, she was on the lounge part of the time. She is my brother's daughter."
> Knowlton: "Did she come from the same part of the West you lived?"
> Morse: "She belonged up in Minnesota. I went there first." [When he moved out West years earlier]
> Knowlton: "The first you heard of her being there was from Mr. Borden?" [Morse testified Andrew Borden told him the night before the murders to go over to the Emery's to see his relatives who "were stopping there."]
> Morse: "No, I was at her Grandmother's, they told me she was there, and had gone to Providence with one of her cousins. When I got off the cars, they got on. I just barely saw her."

John's need to lie about something as innocent as giving his young niece (Annie was 19 at the time) a ride to see the Borden farm, is strange, to say the least. It smacks of secrecy. Was Annie being shown the farmhouse as a possible housekeeper for a future business concern, as well?

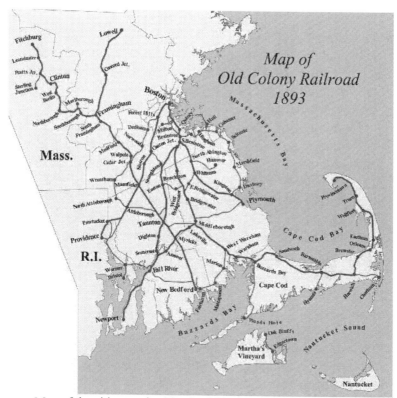

Map of the cities serviced by the Old Colony Railroad. Swansea (Somerset/Warren) is only a ten-minute train ride from Fall River. Dartmouth, where John lived with the Davis family, has access to Fall River via a 30-minute train ride from New Bedford.

He was wearing what looked like "baseball shoes."

During John's July visit, he and Andrew drove over to the Swansea farm. He was asked about it by Attorney Knowlton during his Inquest testimony.

Morse: "Mr. Borden, when I was over here sometime in July, that I speak of, wanted to know if I knew of a man he could get on his farm to take charge of it, I told him I did not know, I would see. When I got back [to South Dartmouth] I wrote him I knew of a man I thought would suit him, I would send him over. He wrote back to me he had rather I would wait until I saw him. I have his letter in my pocket, if you want to see it." (Witness produces the letter dated July 25, 1892.)

As we will see, John did send a man to see Andrew when they thought Lizzie was safely away on her vacation to Marion. They had not expected her to return home unexpectedly Monday morning, August 1st. It was too late to warn John, and the young man he had found to take charge of the Swansea farm.

The New York Times. Fall River, Ma., August 6, 1892.

"Some interesting clues were worked out by the police today relative to two mysterious visitors at the Borden homestead prior to the assassination of old Mr. and Mrs. Borden. No positive light was thrown on the mystery of the murders, however.

"Last Monday morning, about 9 o'clock, a horse and buggy turned into Second Street out of Spring and stopped in front of the Borden residence. A man who is employed nearby sat in his buggy almost opposite and facing south. He had ample opportunity and time to take a careful look at the vehicle, and the circumstances of the two strange men calling at the Borden house made an impression on his mind which he remembers distinctly. One of the men got out of the buggy and rang the doorbell. As he stood there the observer saw him plainly and remembers that his description was that of a man about twenty-five-years-of-age, with a sallow complexion, soft hat, dark trousers, with a wide strip of dark material running down the leg, and russet, or [ms] baseball shoes. He was about 5 feet 9 inches high. The shoes, in particular, attracted his attention, as they were of a peculiar make and color and were laced. Mr. Borden opened the door and the man spoke a few words and was admitted. The man who remained in the buggy was as not as closely scrutinized, and his description not so well remembered. The man who entered remained about ten minutes and then came out with his hat in his hand. The team was driven off in the direction of Pleasant Street.

"The circumstance is considered of importance when the fact is known that the police have in their possession knowledge of the only person who tells of having seen a strange man at the Borden house at the time of the murders."

The mysterious caller was never identified by the police. He came and went, shrouded in a cloak of mystery…leaving only one clue…he was wearing russet baseball shoes.

The stranger appearing on Andrew Borden's doorstep the Monday before the murders was carefully chosen. He had to be someone Lizzie would not have recognized, and more importantly, he had to be a relative who would benefit from his connection with the Swansea farm. Andrew had asked John to find him a man to take charge of the farm, and John sent one to him. His name was James "Jim" Chatterton. And he was a professional baseball player for the Kansas City Cowboys, and the Salem Fairies.

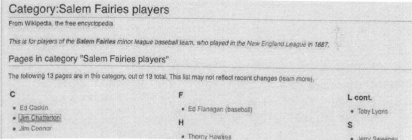

Jim Chatterton's listing in the New England League's short-lived Salem Fairies, in 1887. Jim is also listed in the Baseball Encyclopedia.

Kansas City Cowboys. Pitcher seen in long "trousers"
Russet Brown Uniforms. with a dark stripe down the leg.

| Jim Chatterton | | | | | | | | | Select Team | | | | |
| James M. Chatterton | | | | | | | | | | | | | |

		Best Season		Career Totals	
Born: 10/14/1864 (Brooklyn, NY)		BA	-- --	BA	0.133
Died: 12/15/1944 (Tewksbury, MA)		HR	-- --	HR	--
Height: -	Weight: -	RBI	-- --	RBI	--
Debut: 06/07/1884		R	4 1884	R	4
Final Game: 06/15/1884		SB	-- --	SB	--
Position(s): 1B(2);OF(2),P(1)		OPS	-- --	OPS	0.435

Cards		Statistics			
Batting - Reg. Season		Pitching - Reg. Season		Fielding - Reg. Season	

Regular Season Pitching Stats

Year	Team	G	GS	W	L	SV	IP	H	ER	R	HR	BB	SO	SO/9	WHIP	ERA
1884	KC (UA)	1	1	0	1	0	5.0	11	2	7	0	2	2	3.60	2.60	3.60

Jim Chatterton's baseball stats as a pitcher for the Kansas City Cowboys in 1884. He played only one week.

For the first time ever, we find out who the mysterious man was ringing Andrew's doorbell, three days before the murders. James "Jim" Chatterton was born in 1864 in Williamsburg, New York. He was 28 in 1892. ("He was about 25-years-of-age," the witness said of the man he saw on Andrew's step that Monday.) He married Mary "May" Dwight, Jan. 10, 1891, in Raymond, New Hampshire. In 1884 and 1887, he played for the Kansas City Cowboys and the Salem Fairies, respectively. In 1884, he was living in Lynn, Massachusetts, two hours from Fall River. He was the sole supporter of his widowed mother and his disabled older brother. He had another brother, Joseph, who was also living in Lynn and was 31. Their brother William H. Chatterton likewise was living in Lynn and was 20-years-old in 1892. Together, they worked with Joseph's wife's parents in a shoemaking business; each one with a different skill set, such as "stitcher," "stretcher," "tanner," etc.

James and Joseph's father was James Martin Chatterton. He was the brother of Elvira Chatterton, who married Charles E. Morse of Hoboken, New Jersey. Charles was a salesman in the jewelry business. James Martin Chatterton (Jim, Joseph and William's father) was John Vinnicum Morse's uncle, making the three boys John's cousins.

Lizzie may not have been very familiar with this side of the family, who were living in New York. Jim traveled a lot in the baseball circuit and bounced around from one address to another. His baseball career had pretty much fizzled out. He was now a newlywed and living two hours from Fall River. John Morse may have felt it safe to send him to see Andrew to interview as a foreman for the Swansea farm, hoping Lizzie wouldn't recognize him if she did see him. At the time, Jim was sent to the Borden house, it was thought Lizzie was safely away in Marion, and Emma in Fairhaven. She had materialized out of thin air before they could call off Jim's visit to see Andrew.

Was it a coincidence the Chatterton's were in a family-run shoe business requiring an ongoing supply of leather? Would that make a nice fit for a farm about to expand its cattle connections? And, Jim's mother was a widow, who would later die in 1921, at the age of 84. Was she to be part of the "Old Ladies' Home," even though she was only 55 in 1892? If Jim and his new wife moved into one of the two Swansea Lower Farmhouses, his mother may have needed a place as well, as he had been supporting her. Perhaps an "Old Ladies' Home."

Jim was not the only one of his family to play a part in the mystery. It's just possible his brother, Joseph, had a role to carry out on the morning of the murders.

Carousel Horses

John Morse's plates were still spinning, faster and faster, as July continued on in the unrelenting New England heat. The trips from South Dartmouth to Westport, Westport to Fairhaven, Fairhaven to New Bedford, New Bedford to Fall River, and Fall River to Swansea and Warren, must have been dizzying. Lizzie wasn't the only one following his every move. The police were showing an active interest in his pursuits, even before the day of the murders.

New Bedford Daily Mercury, Tuesday, August 9, 1892:
State Officer, George F. Seaver, Fall River, Ma.
"Westport promises something, and again comes to the front in the flat contradiction of John V. Morse's statement that he had no knowledge whatever of the horse traders at Westport," State detective Seaver said, "before I knew anything about this case whatsoever, I heard that a large consignment of wild

horses to John V. Morse had arrived at Westport, and I went down to see them. I wanted to see the Mustangs, and see them lasso them. There were 80 horses, I should think together. I went down there with a gentleman from Westport factory and saw the horses in a field. They were consigned to John V. Morse of South Dartmouth. There are farmers there and it is the best place to make a trade. There had been an auction, and about 12 horses had been sold by the auctioneer, that was a week ago today, exactly, and Morse was the man to whom they were consigned. The murders happened about 2 days later, and I knew nothing of the case until Thursday night."

According to the *New Bedford Daily Mercury*, Tuesday, August 2, 1892:

"Two carloads of horses direct from Iowa, have been pastured on the land of Stephen P. Kirby during the past week. They have attracted many visitors, and several of them have been sold."

When confronted during his Inquest testimony by Knowlton about the horse business making headlines before the murders, the attorney asked John Morse:

Knowlton: "Have you any connection with the horse business?"
Morse: "Not recently. I bought some horses here when I came her two years and a half ago."
Knowlton: "All sold out now?"
Morse: "Yes, sir."
Knowlton: Have you had any dealings in horses since then?"
Morse: "A little along occasionally, not to amount to anything."

John's business partner, Mr. William Davis, was also heavy into horse trading. Mr. Davis was involved with the band of traders at Westport. When police interviewed him, concerning his involvement with the itinerant horse dealings, he denied any connection, and backed up John Morse later when a reporter cornered he and Mr. George Howe, when they visited Morse a few days after the murders."

Wild Mustangs.

Stephen P. Kirby owned the land where the horses were pastured. He was a farmer, born and raised in Westport, Massachusetts. He was married twice. His first wife was Harriet N. Brownell of Westport. She died and was buried in Fairhaven, Massachusetts. It is probably not a stretch to consider her a relative of the Brownell's, with whom Emma Borden was vacationing in Fairhaven during the time of the murders. Helen Brownell and her mother, Rebecca, were more than just good friends of Emma's, they were related to the Borden's through their great-great-grandmother, Penelope Read. If Harriet Brownell was indeed related to Helen Brownell, then Stephen P. Kirby was related to the Borden's (and hence John Morse) through a convoluted chain of familial events. A Charles T. Kirby owned the livery at 13 Rock Street in Fall River; the same livery from which John Morse rented a horse and buggy the day before the Borden murders.

If that isn't enough to give Kevin Bacon's "Six-Degrees" a run for its money, George E. Howe is also cousins with John and involved in the horse deal. This is the same George Howe that John visited the morning after the murders. George owned a drug store in Fall River across the street from the Post Office. John came into the store, Friday, one day after the murders, to "purchase a stamp" for a letter he would send "in haste" to William Davis.

He then dashed across the street to the Post Office; a Post Office, obviously without stamps.

So, the horses are on Kirby's farm two days before the murders. On the day of the murders, the *Fall River Herald* said, regarding John Morse, "Nothing definite about his affairs is known other than that he had told friends that he had brought a train load of horses with him from Iowa to sell, and they were now at Fairhaven."

Fairhaven. Emma is vacationing in Fairhaven, and Kirby's ex-in-laws may be living in Fairhaven. It would appear the horses were hurriedly moved to Fairhaven, as the police interest in Westport ramped up. To where?

Helen Brownell's father, Allen Brownell, was a Sea Captain. He married Rebecca Delano in 1837, and they had several children, one of which was Emma's friend, Helen. Sadly, two of Helen's brothers died young. When Allen Brownell retired from the sea, he took up his dream of being a "gentleman farmer." The 1870 census states his occupation as "farmer." The 1880 census lists him simply as "agriculture." He is also listed that year as a retired "Sea Captain" and 80-years-of-age.

Helen and her elderly mother, Rebecca, are living in Rebecca's brother's house, Moses Delano, at 19 Green Street during Emma's vacation with them during the murders. Helen's father Allen passed away in 1884, and the women were probably unable to keep the farm up. Did the farm Helen's father owned still exist, run by someone else in the family? Would it be a good temporary stop for a herd of wild mustangs? There are also Morse relatives living in Fairhaven, as mentioned earlier: Charles and Mary Morse. Did they own some property suitable to pasture a herd of horses, just passing through on their way to their new home in Swansea?

During the days leading up to the murders, the players in this dangerous game tried desperately to move each piece into place. The horses resembled a whirling carousel by this time, as they were moved from Iowa to Westport, to Fairhaven. The next stop would be to move them over to the Swansea farm within a few days and begin a new venture.

But Lizzie had other ideas.

Chapter Six

A Train Ride to New Bedford

On July 15, 1892, only two weeks before Andrew and Abby Borden are found hacked to death in their home on Second Street, the two sisters decided to sell their deed to the Ferry Street house back to their father.

Charles C. Cook was questioned by Officer Medley shortly after the murders. Mr. Cook stated, "I am business manager for Mr. Andrew J. Borden, for the Borden Block. I did not see Mr. Borden Thursday [the day of the murders]. I have had the charge of the Block almost since it was built. He used to come in once and awhile, but not every day, nearly always alone. The only other person who ever came with him was his wife, excepting once when Lizzie came with him to sign a deed conveying some property she owned to her father. This property was owned jointly by the two sisters and was situated on Ferry Street. Lizzie has been in three or four times, once [she] came to ask me about the value of the property she was going to convey to her father. I told her and she went away."

> Officer Medley: "Mr. Cook, do you know of anything that would lead you to imagine that Lizzie and her father did not get along well together?"
>
> Cook: "I do not like to answer that question on account of my position as custodian of property, as I do not know what my relations may be with the family, when this thing [the murder case] is settled."

Several things are of interest here: one, that Lizzie has been in several times to see a man who is the "custodian of property" for her father's real estate holdings. At that time, Lizzie's and Emma's only owned property was their grandfather's house on Ferry Street, which their father gave to them to placate the sisters after their blow-up concerning his gift of the house on Fourth Street to Abby's sister. What other business did Lizzie have with Charles Cook? Was she fishing to find out if transfers of deeds were in the making? Asking to see the Swansea files?

The second thing of interest is Lizzie's apparent lack of trust in her father. She wanted to know the value of the Ferry Street house before she sold it back to her father; a question Andrew could have answered. Yet, she asked his manager. As it happened, Andrew paid Emma and Lizzie $5,000 for the deed--$2,000 more than its value.

And thirdly, when asked if Lizzie and her father got along, Mr. Cook declines to answer, as it is possible he will continue to act as property manager for the sisters, as they will inherit their father's properties; which he did. If the relationship between Lizzie and Andrew was amicable, you would think he would answer to that point. The fact that he declines to answer is suggestive. Had Andrew asked Cook to specifically keep details from Lizzie pertaining to his affairs, should she ask? Did it become apparent to the manager that all was not well in the Borden household?

Three days after the sisters deeded back the house on Ferry Street to their father, they headed off for their summer vacation. As mentioned earlier, that they chose this time to sell Andrew back the property is interesting.

New Bedford and Fairhaven

On July 21, 1892, Emma and Lizzie Borden boarded the train for New Bedford from the Fall River Bowenville depot. For Emma, the trip was long overdue. According to Rebecca Brownell, the mother of the friend with whom Emma was traveling to stay, she told a reporter for the *New Bedford Standard* on August 25, 1892, "Emma had intended to remain in Fairhaven all summer." Yet, she had waited two months into her treasured vacation away from that house of hate. Why? Was it to make sure Lizzie boarded the train with her?

Lizzie was expected in Marion, a seaside resort about 25-miles from Fall River. It was home to some very elite families who had summer "cottages" there. Dr. Handy was one such denizen. He offered his cottage to his daughter, Louisa, and her friends to enjoy for their summer vacation. Many of the girls had gone over earlier to begin their fun near the water. Lizzie had waited.

Whether Emma watched her younger sister's face nervously as the train passed through heavily-wooded scenery is not known. The dramatic events escalating at the Borden home in the preceding months were certainly not lost on her. Break-ins, fights, beheaded pigeons, and rumors of theft. Was there relief that she was finally getting Lizzie away, and would be free of her sister's theatrics and rages for a full, glorious, peaceful six week, with friends she held dear? The Brownell's cozy home was only steps from the popular Fort Phoenix Beach, with all its recreation and soothing sea breezes.

Fort Phoenix Bathing Beach, Fairhaven, Mass.

Fort Phoenix Beach, Fairhaven, Ma.

The Brownell's House, 13 Green Street, in Fairhaven, Massachusetts, before restoration. Photo courtesy of Stefani Koorey/lizzieandrewborden.com.

The Brownell's House today, 39 Green Street, in Fairhaven, Massachusetts, after restoration. Photo courtesy Stefani Koorey/lizzieandrewborden.com.

As the conductor shouted out the New Bedford stop ahead, Emma may have reassured Lizzie, "It will all be alright. Go and enjoy yourself in Marion."

Interior of Pullman car on New Bedford train, circa 1900.

Emma and Lizzie alighted from the train. Emma would continue the short distance to Fairhaven by electric car, and, she believed, Lizzie would continue on to Marion, a short ride away. The sisters hugged and parted ways. Emma's trolley car turned a bend and vanished from sight. Lizzie did not continue on to Marion. She headed into downtown New Bedford, to begin a secretly planned 5-day visit.

The Plot Thickens

According to Office Medley's statement made the day following the murders, on August 5th, "In accordance with instructions, I visited New Bedford. I find that Lizzie Borden arrived in that city on Thursday, July 21st, and went to Mrs. Poole's, the mother of a friend, a former schoolmate, living near South Water Street. While there she never went out alone, always going in the company of the family, with one exception, that being Saturday morning, July 23rd, when she went on the street to buy a piece of dress goods of some cheap material, being gone about one [hour] and 30 minutes. She went alone and returned alone. No one called to see her while there. She never made mention of her family affairs. On Tuesday, Mrs. Poole, and Mrs. Poole's daughter went to ride to Westport to see Mrs. Poole's daughter who was a schoolmate of Lizzie's, and who is now married to Cyrus W. Tripp. They spent the day there, leaving time enough for Lizzie to connect with the train at New Bedford for Fall River. That was the last time the Poole's saw her. While at Westport, Lizzie saw no one outside of the family."

The report states Lizzie went out alone on Saturday, July 23rd, two days after her arrival in New Bedford. She returned with "a piece of dress goods of some cheap material." Lizzie never testified about buying "cheap material" while in New Bedford; in fact, her Inquest testimony quickly changes to a purchase of a "dress pattern," instead. The report does not mention two other excursions Lizzie made during her trip to New Bedford; one of which occurred during that one hour and 30 minutes she stepped out alone onto the New Bedford Streets.

New Bedford, 1890s. Purchase Street.

Attorney Knowlton questioned Emma Borden during the Superior Court trial in June of 1893:
Knowlton: "Had you seen Lizzie during the two weeks?" [Emma was vacationing with the Brownell's in Fairhaven]
Emma: "Yes, sir."
Knowlton: "When?"

Emma: "Well, I can't tell you what day it was; some few days after; she had been in Fairhaven."

Knowlton: "Was it Saturday?"

Emma: "No, sir."

Knowlton: "Was it on her way over to or back from Marion?'

Emma: "Oh, I do know. She went to New Bedford when I went to Fairhaven, and I think it was the Saturday following our going Thursday."

Knowlton: "That is, she went to New Bedford the same day you went to Fairhaven?"

Emma: "Yes, sir."

Knowlton: "How long did she remain in New Bedford?"

Emma: "Until the following Tuesday."

Knowlton: "This is, from Thursday until Tuesday. During that time, do you know, did she go to Marion?"

Emma: "No, sir, she did not."

Lizzie's secret trip to Fairhaven on that Saturday morning, when she returned with "a piece of dress goods of cheap material" gives one pause. Obviously, Mrs. Poole didn't know her visitor had hopped an electric car that made a straight run from New Bedford to Fairhaven. And why was it hidden from the police reports early in the investigation?

New Bedford/Fairhaven Trolley car across the bridge, 1890s.

Officer Medley, concerning Fairhaven, made out police reports on another matter. On August 13, 1892, Medley states "Went to New Bedford today to investigate about a man acting strangely in a druggist's store on North Second Street, kept by Wm. H. Drummond. A man stopped into the store, said he was hungry, bought a glass of soda and a few sticks of candy, lounged around the store a little while, looking once or twice up and down the street. He said he lived on Chestnut Street, Fairhaven; and went away. Description of the man: 5 feet 6; age 45 or 50; complexion dark; wore blue clothes."

Did Lizzie make a quick run to Fairhaven to talk to a farm hand she may have known earlier—either from working on her father's farm, or the Brownell farm in Fairhaven? At 45 or 50, the man may be out of work and looking for money. The description of "dark complexion" and "blue clothes" sounds like it could possibly be describing a Portuguese or farm hand. Men in that era did not wear blue suits.

Lizzie was also friends with the Brownell's and doubtless spent time with them over the years. Mrs. Brownell was interviewed by the *New Bedford Standard* on August 25, 1892. "In speaking of the tragedy, Mrs. Brownell did not hesitate to speak strongly in support of Lizzie's innocence. She said, that both of the girls always spoke in endearing terms of their father."

Fairhaven, Ma., today.

That Lizzie found the need to buy a piece of cheap dress material to show the Poole's as her reason for being away that Saturday morning is suggestive. The material is never seen again.

Did Emma lie for Lizzie on the stand when she said Lizzie's reason for being in Fairhaven was to visit her? Or, was Lizzie there to see someone else? Perhaps to run by the Morse relatives living in Fairhaven, and see if they just happened to have 80 mustangs running around? To meet with a "dark complexioned" farm worker? Or, a more chilling thought is, did Emma know about Lizzie's intent to kill Abby (a woman Emma detested even more than Lizzie, according to Emma's testimony)? Was Andrew's murder a tragic follow-up, based on the turn of a clock's hands?

Would this give a more ominous meaning to Lizzie's warning to Doctor Bowen the day of the murders, when she asked him to telegraph Emma in Fairhaven, "but don't tell the facts, for the lady whom she is staying with, is old and feeble, and the shock may be too much for her." When Bowen left to send the telegram, Abby's body had not yet been found. Was Lizzie afraid the shock would be to Emma (not "the lady" who is "old and feeble") that their father was dead when the plan had been only to kill Abby? The telegram is stamped 11:32 am. Emma does not arrive home until 5:00 pm.

Yachting in Marion

The yacht *Mabel F. Swift*, full sail, 1899.
Photo courtesy of the Fall River Historical Society.

Fall River Evening News, July 27, 1892, "Sloop yacht *Mabel F. Swift* was at Marion, Monday, where the following ladies from Fall River are stopping at Blake's Point: Mrs. James F. Jackson, Misses Edith Jackson, Jennie Stowell, Anna C. Holmes, Mary L. Holmes, Mabel H. Remington, Louise O. Remington, Alice Buck, Isabelle Fraser, Louise H. Handy, Elizabeth Johnston, Annie C. Bush, and Lizzie A. Borden."

The owner of the yacht, "Charles W. Anthony, is cruising with a party of friends, including Hon. Simeon Borden, Hon. James F. Jackson and Messrs. Holder W. Durfee, William Winslow, and R.W. Bassett."

Mrs. Poole's testimony to Officer Medley was that Lizzie was only out of their sight once, which was the clandestine outing Saturday morning, July 23rd, resulting in her trip to Fairhaven. Yet, she is spotted, and reported on, during an outing to Marion, only minutes from New Bedford, on Monday, July 25, with the ladies with whom she was to vacation. On July 26th, she and the Poole's visit Augusta Tripp in nearby Westport. Westport was also where John V. Morse's horses were being pastured. Suddenly, the trip to New Bedford to visit old friends shows a different agenda; one that went beyond horses.

Lizzie plans a 5-day trip to New Bedford when she is supposed to begin her holiday in Marion. Why? The sudden visit to stay at a boarding house run by Mrs. Poole, her friend Augusta Tripp's mother, seems an unlikely choice. When Lizzie disappears that Saturday for an hour and a half, she returns with some "dress goods of cheap material." What if the material was not just to establish an alibi? What if the real reason for a side trip to New Bedford was to buy some cheap material and have a dress made, one with special features, and one she wouldn't mind disposing of later?

"Don't send a man. Wait until I see you."

Is it a coincidence Andrew Borden mails a letter on July 25th, 1892, to John Morse, telling him not to send the man John has found to take charge of "the farm," and to "wait until I see you?"

Had word reached Andrew that Lizzie had not traveled on to Marion, but had made a detour to New Bedford? For whatever reason, Andrew told John to wait.

Andrew's premonition that Lizzie was up to something became apparent when she suddenly arrived home Tuesday evening, July 26th. Indeed, she had not gone on to Marion and begun her month-long vacation after all. The panic Andrew and Abby must have felt at this sudden turn of events when the wheels were turning on the deed transfer of the Swansea farm, and the horses were in-route, must have bordered on epic. From that Tuesday night's arrival, until Lizzie suddenly leaves again for Marion on Saturday, July 30th, we know nothing of the excuse she gave as to her seemingly random movements.

She did go to Marion and spend the day with the girls at the Handy cottage, Saturday—five days before the murders. But her thoughts were elsewhere. While seated around the table in the Handy kitchen, one of the girls asked her, "Lizzie, why don't you talk?" Lizzie admitted to Alice Russell a few nights later, that at that moment, "something came over her that she could not shake off." Lizzie left, and headed back to Fall River, to put into action the events that would culminate in two deaths, and the destruction of multiple livelihoods.

That Mysterious Sunday

From the time Lizzie boards the train from New Bedford to Fall River, we have no reports of her for five days. There is nothing in the testimony or witness reports that show where she was during that time, up until she shows up at home unexpectedly early Monday morning, August 1. It could be she didn't return home at all. Yet, we do know one thing: Alfred Johnson, the overseer at the Swansea Lower Farm, and Frank Eddy, manager of the Upper Farm, were both taken sick within the days leading to the murders. Andrew Borden sent John Morse to check on Mr. Eddy Wednesday afternoon, August 3rd, as he had been ill for a while. Alfred Johnson was still "indisposed" on Thursday, the day of the murders, August 4th, when Marshall Hilliard, the Fall River Police Chief, drove over to the farm to interview the men.

Before Lizzie arrived home Monday morning, August 1st, she believed Andrew and Abby were headed to the farm that Monday to begin their summer vacation at the Lower Farm. People around town voiced surprise that Andrew was not over there, and Andrew had told John to "write to him at the farm so I won't have to bother with it" when John was ready to get the two cows for William Davis. Abby told John the afternoon before the murders that they were expecting to go, but had changed plans at the last minute when Mrs. Vinnicum couldn't accompany Abby to the farm. It was assumed they were going there. If Lizzie had a murder plot in mind, it would be the farm where it would need to be carried out.

The South Swansea Depot for the Old Colony Railroad, that ran from New Bedford and Fall River to Swansea, was only a short five-minute walk from the Borden's Lower Farmhouse, where the family "summered." Carl Becker, with the Swansea Museum, told the Author-it was nothing for women to walk in those days; often a mile or more. Leonard Rebello, author of *Lizzie Borden: Past and Present*, walked it while helping with the research of this book. Five minutes. Farm wagons and hacks were always at the depot, and happy to give someone a lift if they were heading that way. Lizzie hadn't been around the farm for at least five years, as she testified. It's possible no one in the vicinity of the depot recognized her.

Lizzie walked down Gardner's Neck Road. It was after five in the afternoon, and Alfred Johnson would be home at Andrew Borden's other house up the road, across from the station, or over at the Eddy's for supper. She knew the routine. Abby and Andrew were expected the next morning to begin their August vacation.

Looking about her, Lizzie walked up the short dirt walkway to the farm house's kitchen door and inserted her key. She stepped into the room with its wood-burning stove, hand pump sink, and small table and chairs. It smelled of stale air, after being shut up for so long. Alfred Johnson, who lived up the road, checked on it, kept the trees trimmed and the well primed, but for the most part, it remained empty when the Borden family was not in residence. The ghosts of summers past when the family sat around the old kitchen table, eating the fish Lizzie and Andrew caught that day, rose from the worn flooring and shimmered across the faded curtains. Ignoring the sudden fluttering in her stomach, she left the room.

The Borden's Lower Farmhouse where the family "summered."
Photo courtesy of Shelley Dziedzic.

Lizzie walked down the hall to the back bedroom she used when she and Emma vacationed with their father and stepmother. Five years had barely changed it. She felt a tug on her heart when she saw the old apron hanging on a hook in the closet that she would wear when she fished Cole's River with her father, just down the slope outside. Her mood sank, bordering on depression, and she slumped into a chair near the window. She sat there until the shadows deepened, the room's furnishings blurring in the ensuing darkness.

At 4:00 the next morning, Alfred would leave a can of fresh milk on the porch step outside the kitchen, in preparation for the Borden's arrival. The milking was done at the barn on the Upper Farm, only a buggy ride, or train depot, away.

A new dress had been made in New Bedford for her, one with a loose "pigeon" blouse and full skirt. The new hatchet was obtained, in a way that could not be traced back to her, and the arsenic was in her purse. She had written to her Aunt Mary Morse, who lived only eight minutes away in Warren, that she would love to visit her and "the girls" tomorrow before she headed down to Marion to begin her August vacation.

Today, a large barn at the Upper Farm location is the pro shop for the Touisset Country Club. It sits directly on Pearse Road, only 10 minutes from the old Cole's Depot. The golf course claims the barn is "original to the property." It may, or may not, be the same barn where the Borden cows were milked. It could have belonged to a different family leasing some of Andrew's farmland. It may, however, be sitting in the correct location, if the Borden barn *was* demolished, as the foundation and drive were already in place. The original cow stalls can still be seen, and the barn is said to be "very old." This was to be the location of a huge cattle endeavor for Andrew Borden and John Morse.

As the final rays of light filtered into the small bedroom on Gardener's Neck Road, Lizzie reached into her satchel for the pouch of arsenic. She felt the soft weight of it in her hand, and thought back to the night she broke into the Second Street barn to steal it from the painter's supplies. Would it be enough? She knew nothing of poisons, only what she had read. Would it mix with milk, and kill them?

By 5:00 the next morning, Lizzie was locking the kitchen door to the farmhouse, as she prepared to head home. As she walked down the dirt path, that leads from the small barn past the farmhouse to Gardner's Neck Road, she glanced back to see the milk can, waiting on the kitchen steps, glinting in the early morning sunlight.

Chapter Seven

Monday, August 1, 1892
Three Days Before the Murders

92 Second Street, Fall River

It had not worked.

The clouds above 92 Second Street hung low and dark; pregnant with rain. Although the temperatures had dropped from the debilitating heat wave that had suffocated the city the week before—claiming 90 lives in its oven-like maw—the humidity at 8:45 that Monday morning clung to her bedroom drapes and wrapped around her face like a hot washcloth. Her corset shut off what breath had mustered its way up from her lungs, and perspiration puddled beneath the fabrics of her chemise, petticoat, waist blouse, and skirt.

The two windows of her bedroom were opened wide in hopes of a vagrant breeze. It served only to allow the relentless sound of horses' hooves, metal buggy trappings, people shouting, and the constant banging of metal against stone coming from Crowe's mason yard, only 50 feet east of her window. The pounding found its way into her temples—a staccato rhythm mirroring the thoughts that would not abate.

It had not worked.

All her planning: the secret trips to New Bedford, Fairhaven, and Swansea...all for naught. *They hadn't gone to the farm after all.* She heard her father's voice coming through the wall that separated her bedroom from his. She had planned only to stop at the house, pick up a few things, and head to Warren to see her Aunt Mary, and then on to Marion. But they were still here. They usually left by 8:00 when they vacationed at the farm. Their plan to rob her of her inheritance would go through now. *Perhaps they were still going over later this morning. The milk would still be sitting on the kitchen steps at the farm.* She had to hope for that.

A loud bang from the Fall River Ice Company, only two lots away, made her jump. Her nerves were on edge. The constant sound of ice sliding down metal chutes played like background music to the repetitive beat of the stone cutter, and the rhythmic sawing from the laborer just on the other side of the fence, creating a jarring symphony with the clatter of carts out front.

It was never quiet here. 92 Second Street was surrounded by commercial concerns as varied as any main street. From laundries to liveries, grocery stores to restaurants, the Borden house sat in the center of it all. While up on "the Hill," homes were encased in flower gardens, and the sounds that floated in through the glass lace curtains were those of birds and small children playing.

Lizzie Borden sat upon her bedroom lounge that rested between the two windows facing south. A petite woman of 32 years of age, she stood 5' 4" tall. Her eye color depended on the descriptor: many described them as a light blue; others, brown; and her passport from 1890 listed them as "grey." Large, catlike in shape, and slightly protruding, they looked out upon the world with an unwavering calm, though at times, they flashed with anger, and a "look," described as "peculiar" by those on the receiving end.

Those same eyes darted about the room now, as her thoughts raced. Her mind was in overdrive. If they didn't leave for the farm this morning, all her plans would have to change—and quickly. They thought she was so stupid; that she hadn't always been one step ahead of them.

The arsenic she'd stolen from the barn when the house painter was there in May was now inside the milk can at Swansea. She had placed the white powder into the fresh milk, stirred it around with a nearby stick, and held her breath. It finally blended with the white foam, and she screwed the metal lid back into place. It had taken only moments.

Yet, there had been a risk: going there on the Old Colony Railroad that ran right by the farm in South Swansea, hoping no one would recognize her, and praying the farmhand had finished the afternoon chores and was gone—it was risky—but she was desperate. And no one had noticed her. It was perfect! Abby and her father would drink the tainted milk and die. On her way to see her Aunt Mary, only a few minutes by train from the summer home, she would stop and use the hatchet on their bodies, making it look like a maniac came in and killed them. By the time they were found, she would be safely away at Marion for her long-planned vacation, and everything would be wonderful. It didn't matter now. They hadn't gone to the farm as planned. They were still here.

An unbidden thought flitted through Lizzie's mind—what if someone else at the farm drank the poisoned milk—Alfred Johnson, the overseer, or Mr. Eddy? It caused her only a moment's hesitation, and she swatted away the image like an annoying fly.

The lace curtains lifted beneath a momentary breath of air. The fetid odor of the Quequechan River wafted into the room. From only three blocks over, the biting, acrid smell of smoke billowing from the Fall River Iron Works' chimney stung her nostrils. The smokestack rose an impossible 350-feet in the air, its soot covering the town in a perpetual dusting that maids washed from their employer's windows each Thursday. Her stomach tightened. She felt dizzy and nauseous. What would she do now?

Lizzie Andrew Borden. Photo courtesy of
The Fall River Historical Society.

View from the sitting room window today. You can see the Kelly house to the south. Just to the left of the house is Crowe's mason yard & barn.
Photo courtesy of the Author.

Lizzie bent forward, lowering her head in an effort to quell the spinning sensation in her head. A sound like that of a rushing freight train filled her ears. Her father, obviously having gone downstairs, was saying something to Bridget below. Her eyes fell upon the dark paint stains along the lower portion of her blue Bedford cord skirt she was wearing. The paint. Another plan—so perfect in its conception and execution—gone. She was sick of the old, faded dress, one she had not planned on wearing today, or ever again. She was sick of the house, sick of the noise, sick of her life.

Just then the bell on the other side of her wall sounded in her father's bedroom. It was the extension of the front doorbell. She glanced at her small clock. 9:00. Who would be calling? Most everyone knew her father was supposed to be spending August at the farm.

View from top of stairs looking down to the front door.
Photo by Ron Bueker.

Lizzie crept out of her room onto the second-floor landing and tried to see the front door. She took two tentative steps down the staircase and watched as her father crossed the front entry.

Andrew Borden opened the door and said something in hushed tones to the person on the outside step. The noise from the street rushed in over his shoulder, along with a blast of humid air. Finally, he stepped back and allowed a young man in strange clothing to enter the front hall. The stranger wore dark pants, with a darker stripe of material running the length of his leg. His shoes were most peculiar. Lizzie had never seen anything like them. They were a russet brown flat shoe that laced up, with odd rubber-looking heels. He was carrying his soft felt hat in his hands as Andrew led him into the sitting room.

Sitting room looking west to the front entry (middle door), parlor (right door), closet (far left), and dining room door (far right, closed). Ron Bueker.

Lizzie turned and climbed quickly to the landing, crossing into the guest room that sat next to her own bedroom. She hurried across the Brussel carpeting to the west-facing window and looked down to the busy street below. A hooded carriage was parked in front of the house. She could see only the knees and hands of the driver who was waiting inside.

Tiptoeing to her room, she shut her door. Quietly, she closed her two windows to shut out the noise from outside. She knelt down before the unused fireplace in her room. Reaching into it, she pulled loose the brick on the south side that shared a flue with the sitting room below. Picking up a 4'-length of plumber's pipe she had gotten from the box in the barn, she placed one end into the brick opening, and after seating herself on her bed placed the other end to her ear. Seeing an ear trumpet used by an elderly person had given her the idea.

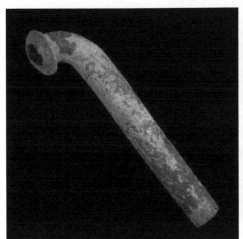

1890s plumber's pipe like the kind found in the Borden's barn (l), and a 1890s ear trumpet, used to amplify sound.

She had opened the flue in the sitting room fireplace over a year ago, to overhear the conversations from that room, knowing no one would check it. That the fireplace in her room sat directly above the one in the sitting room below had allowed her a private means of eavesdropping; one she discovered by accident one evening when muffled voices drifted from the open flue into her room. She'd found by removing a brick from the south wall of her fireplace, that shared the flue with the room below, she could hear plainly what was being said. That her father and step-mother sat there exclusively to hold their discussions had been perfect. It was also where they sat with John Morse, and conducted other business.

At first, Lizzie had tried listening from her open window facing south, which sat directly above the sitting room windows, but the noise of the street and Crowe's stonecutters made that impossible. Sitting on the stairs leading down to that room had garnered her only snippets of words, and murmuring.

The Author's sincere thanks to the Pointer Family, owners of the historic Lemp Mansion in St. Louis, for conducting a double fireplace experiment for me. Lemp Mansion was built in 1868 and features the same design of two fireplaces, one floor above the other, sharing a flue. They said they could hear voices coming through the flue, although it was muffled. Removing a brick, and amplifying the sound through a pipe, would allow the listener to make out the words.

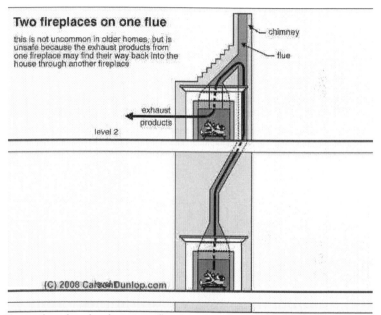

Illustration showing how two fireplaces stacked above each other share a common flue, which would have been made of brick in the 1800s. Courtesy of Carson Dunlop, © 2016. www.CarsonDunlop.com

Once the radiators had been installed, the fireplaces were strictly ornamental. A large bed was pressed before the fireplace in the guest room. One can still see the mantel behind it. Only the opening in the dining room had been walled over with a fake front of brick to offer room for more furniture, and to keep out drafts. Its old wooden fireplace front rested against the north wall of the barn loft outside the day of the murders. (Only one fireplace front is found during the investigations, and only one is mentioned as being walled up; the dining room. That the other fireplaces were still there is evident by the case drawings of the time and the position of Lizzie's bed.

Old fireplace front at a local antique store. It was amazingly light, which helped in getting something like it to the Borden barn loft. Photo by the Author.

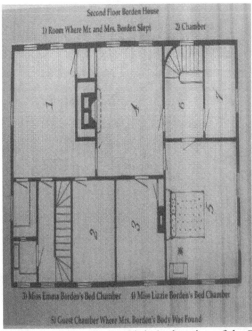

Edwin Porter with the Fall River Daily Globe's drawing of the Borden's second floor. Lizzie's bedroom (4) shows a fireplace is still in residence. Her bed layout is seen on the map on page 118.

Andrew and Abby's bedroom had been used as a kitchen when the house was originally built to accommodate two tenants—one upstairs, and one down. A stovepipe opening, identical to the one in the kitchen below their room, was closed off, a separate chimney opening allowing the release of wood and coal smoke from the cook stove below to the outside. It is still visible today.

Old Stove pipe opening behind Andrew's bed.
Photo by Ron Bueker.

As Lizzie crouched in her bedroom, her breathing becoming more labored, muffled voices came through the fireplace opening, and she pressed the pipe closer to catch their words.

It was obvious her father was keeping the conversation with the stranger low. She heard only snippets of words: "Out of town" … "Partner" … "You are mistaken." The young man's voice was stronger, and she realized from his words the plot to take away the Swansea farm from her went deeper than she thought. The deed would be signed over to Abby on Wednesday—only two days from now. Her lips pressed into a white chalk line. The game was on.

The conversation ended, and Lizzie tiptoed out of her room and back into the guest room next door, her cheeks aflame. As she was crossing the landing, she heard her father say, a little too loudly, in what appeared to be a fake farewell to a person pretending to be interested in renting his store—and for her benefit— "Come again when you are back in town, and I will let you know."

She looked down from the guest room window and watched as the young man walked down the short walk, opened and closed the front gate, and climbed into the waiting buggy, gesturing to the driver. He had only been with her father ten minutes. She noticed a man in a buggy seated near Hall's livery across the street to the north watching the two men as well. The reins snapped and the buggy carrying the young visitor merged into the Second Street traffic.

Hooded Horse and Buggy from the 1890s.

Lizzie strained to see the driver's profile through the opening at the back of the buggy. He appeared to be a young man as well, and she did not recognize him. She was running out of time. Her mind spun as she tried to come up with an alternate plan to stop Wednesday from coming—at least for two members of her home.

A crack of thunder sounded from outside. The day was dark and the air sodden with moisture. Lizzie hid the plumber's pipe beneath her bed and left her room. She crossed along the short landing to the door facing her room. Inserting a skeleton key into the lock, she entered a large room that functioned as the Borden sisters' dress closet. The room measured about 5 feet by 8 feet, and was called a "clothes press." The sole window was padded with an oil cloth, and a long white sheet covered the dresses, to alleviate dust, and the sunlight from fading the brilliant colors of the silks. She selected a blue walking dress. As she left the room and turned to lock the door, her eyes fell on Abby's only garment hanging in that closet, on a hook toward the back corner. Lizzie's heart raced. There would be an empty peg in the crowded closet very soon now.

The lingering odor of breakfast was fast being replaced by the fresh smell of soap flakes dissolving in hot water in the cellar. The pungent smell of starch wafted up through the open cellar door, as Bridget Sullivan, the Borden's "maid-of-all-work" sloshed the family's clothes in the washtub below. Thunder shook the house as Lizzie entered the kitchen, dressed to go out. Andrew had gone downtown on his routine rounds of business transactions.

Open cellar door leading off kitchen area/back entry & wash tub.

Lizzie poured herself a cup of coffee, watching the darkening day unfold from the window above the sink. Abby entered the kitchen from the dining room. She jumped slightly at seeing Lizzie there. She and Andrew were still showing ragged nerves. Lizzie's unexpected return from her trip to Marion to begin her vacation had unsettled them a great deal. This was the second time she had started off, only to pop up like a Jack-in-the-Box, days later.

"Good morning, Lizzie," Abby mustered, as she stood there in the doorway. "Did things not go well in Marion? You're not ill, I hope."

Lizzie eyed her from over the cup's rim as she sipped slowly at the hot coffee.

"I was worried about father," she said, in low, measured tones. "With you away at Swansea, I did not want him eating his noon meals alone here during the week. He works so hard, and he is no longer a young man."

Abby paused, and then said, in a voice that sounded meek and vulnerable, "We have had to postpone the trip for now." She noticing a sudden flush on Lizzie's face. "Mrs. Vinnicum was going to accompany me to the farm, so I wouldn't be alone when Andrew is taking care of his business concerns. She is waiting to hear if her sister from out West is coming to visit or not. There is no need for you to forego your plans with your friends. You go on ahead. We can always go another time."

Lizzie's thoughts were racing as she studied the short, stout woman before her. Abby was fidgeting with her skirt and smoothing a stray strand of hair, her nervous actions giving her away.

"I cannot go right now," Lizzie finally managed. "I am expected to attend the Christian Endeavor Society meeting Sunday, as I was asked to substitute as secretary for the recording of attendance and the minutes. It's the first Sunday of each month, and I can't break my word. I shall go to Marion on Monday. As I won't be needed at home, perhaps I shall write to Aunt Mary in Warren and see if I might visit with her a day or two, perhaps Thursday and Friday. I have not seen Elizabeth and Henrietta for a while now." Abby was not aware the letter had already been sent, or the dates requested for Lizzie's visit were much sooner. If they didn't leave for the farm today, Lizzie would have to change her plans.

Abby's face, never one to mask its feelings, became a kaleidoscope of emotions. They went from surprise, to fear. She struggled to find another excuse to get Lizzie away from the house before Wednesday afternoon, but she could find nothing.

Lizzie set down her cup and walked past the woman she detested, only giving way to her feelings as she mounted the stairs to her room. She sat down on her lounge and tried to drown out the noise thrumming against the outside glass of her windows. She was tired of the panic constantly gripping her heart.

An antique writing desk in Lizzie's bedroom today (l), standing before the locked door into the Guest Room, as it would have been the day of the murders in 1892. According to John Morse's testimony that Lizzie had "some desk" in front of the door, and the mention of a bookcase by a snooping journalist, it is possible Lizzie's desk resembled the large antique secretary at the right. Alice Russel held vigil with Lizzie from a similar chair (pictured at left) in the bedroom on the day of the murders. Photo by the Author.

She sat there, wheels turning in a fevered mind. *They weren't going to the farm today…or anytime this week. She had to change gears. The plan formed slowly in her mind. She played with it, moved this piece here, rearranged that segment there until it was solidified. This could work. Saying she would stay with the Morse's a day or two bought her time; Abby couldn't force her to leave for Marion. And, if Abby and her father did suddenly leave for the farm, she would be only 8 miles away at Warren; easy access to Swansea, the farm, the milk can...and them. Whether she killed them here or killed them in Swansea, she would need more poison. She used all she had stolen from the painter's supplies.*

Rain began to fall, plopping on the hard-packed road, and striking the metal roof of Crow's barn to the east of her. She checked her hair in the dressing mirror, picked up her satchel, and descended the stairs.

Abby was moving about the kitchen, absent-mindedly checking the pantry, her thoughts somewhere else. She jumped when Lizzie entered the room, wearing a "waterproof" and carrying an umbrella from the hall coat stand.

Abby stepped from the pantry into the open kitchen area, as though to speak to the girl. She watched, her heart thudding, as Lizzie passed her, managing a small smile, and walked down the back entry to the side screen door. As she opened it, she glanced back at her stepmother, still rooted in place, the dark clouds outside casting the kitchen into shadows.

The rain picked up in intensity, falling in pelting droplets that hit Lizzie's opened umbrella in a rhythmic tattooing. The roads would be muddy soon, but at least the constant dust raised from horse's hooves would be lessened. As she headed "downstreet," people passing her on the sidewalk nodded her way, some offering a "Good morning, Miss Borden," or a more familiar, "Miss Lizzie."

Lizzie hastened to a nearby drug store on Pleasant Street. Philias Martel, the owner, was not in, but his clerk, young Hypolyte Martel, greeted her. After slowly perusing the aisles of merchandise, giving the impression of an innocent shopping trip, Lizzie approached the counter and asked the clerk for some arsenic. When Hypolyte paused, she said, "Price is not a problem." Finally, finding his voice, he informed her that "as the druggist is not present, I cannot possibly comply with your wishes."

Lizzie left, clearly showing her disappointment.

Undeterred, she headed north to E.S. Brown's general merchandise store on North Main Street. She approached the pharmacy counter at the back of the store and informed the clerk there, by the name of Gifford, that she wished to buy "some poison." He refused her.

1890s drug store interior. Photo courtesy unknown.

Lizzie had always believed arsenic would be a simple thing to obtain. It was readily sold at drug stores, and had been used by so many people in the Victorian era to dispose of wealthy relatives, that it had been given the nickname "the Inheritance Poison." Possibly due to its widespread overuse for nefarious reasons, it now required a doctor's prescription to obtain it.

Remembering another book she had read concerning poisons, she seized upon a new plan. Perhaps it was only arsenic being regulated. She would ask for another poison, although she was not as familiar with its application.

Marching back into the Philias Martel drug store on Pleasant Street, she approached the apprehensive face of Hypolyte Martel and said simply "How about Prussic Acid?" The clerk again said his hands were tied, and it would be best if she "returned when the druggist was back from dinner." Hypolyte later described her to the police as being about twenty-six years old and weighing around 150 pounds. As many newspapers would later report, Lizzie looked a good "ten years younger than her age."

As Lizzie Borden dashed about Fall River's downtown district, she may have just missed her father as he came and went from various banks and businesses he either owned or sat on the board of directors. He was taking inventory of his businesses, and directing a deed to be drawn up; one that would cause his funeral procession through the streets of Fall River only five days later.

As the rain increased, beating down on his stovepipe hat, Andrew Borden's mind was in turmoil. What was he to do with his youngest daughter, Lizzie? Hadn't he given her everything within his power to make her happy? Even a 5-month Grand Tour of Europe had only intensified her fiery temper and mood swings when she returned home.

Andrew's thoughts turned to his eldest daughter Emma, and how she had given up her larger bedroom to Lizzie in an effort to ease her younger sister's transition back to the little house after seeing the world. Emma moved into the small, closet-like room that abutted Lizzie's new domain, and hoped the exchange would make her sister happy.

Emma's small room. The bed was against the other wall in 1892.
Photo by Ron Bueker.

The exchange of rooms lifted her spirits, for a time, as Lizzie turned it into a bedroom/parlor, complete with red hanging portieres, a private wash area, lounge, writing desk, bookcase, and dressing table. Picture postcards of the many places she visited in

Europe were proudly displayed, along with a few precious souvenirs. Her bed was placed diagonally near the corner door leading into Abby and Andrew's bedroom. The fireplace mantel and hearth prevented the bed from going corner to corner, leaving a space where one could walk around the bed's headstand to the door that was bolted on her parent's side and hooked on her own. One door, separating daughter from father, double-locked…against what? Against whom?

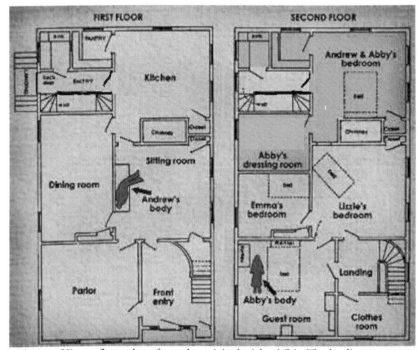

Thomas Kieran floor plans from the original trial exhibit. The bodies were not included in the original drawings.

Chapter Eight

Tuesday, August 2, 1892
Two Days Before the Murders

Tuesday morning dawned with oppressive heat and the mugginess that hangs on after a rainstorm. The sun was shining, and the noise of business trade on Second Street could be heard through Lizzie Borden's open bedroom windows. Rather than waiting until breakfast was over, as was her custom, this day she made it a point to join her family at the table. She was dressed to go out, a letter she had penned to her sister resting in an oversized satchel.

The tension at the breakfast table was palpable. As Bridget brought in fresh coffee, the maid glanced apprehensively at the strained faces of the three people seated in the dining room. Abby looked pale, her eyes darting between her plate and her husband's face. Lizzie merely sipped at her coffee, a slight flush to her cheeks.

Once the maid left the room, closing the dining room door behind her, Abby took a deep breath and began, Andrew, twisting nervously in his seat:

"Lizzie, are you sure you won't go on with your plans? As you can see, I will be here to take care of your father and you need not postpone your trip to Marion. You can always come back on Sunday to take care of your church meeting."

Abby's small smile, meant to look reassuring, merely came off as nervous and faltering. Tension hung over the table as heavy as the August humidity outside.

Abby Borden. Photo courtesy of The Fall River Historical Society.

Abby Borden was a short woman, only slightly smaller than Lizzie, at 5' 3". Her face was round with a somewhat vacuous look about it, created by a mouth that turned down at the corners, and eyes that looked trusting, yet tired. Her dark brown hair was threaded with grey and caught up atop her head, a fake braid twisted and pinned to add style and convenience. She was 64-years-old. Her weight was remarked upon often, as she tipped the scales at 220 pounds. Her simple joys in life were her husband, her family on Fourth Street, and her immaculate home. She sat and waited for Lizzie's reply, sweat puddling along the folds of her neck.

Lizzie let her steady gaze wander from Abby's face over to her father's, who would not meet her eyes. A wave of mixed emotions flashed through her as she studied the balding head fringed with white hair, now bowed, as he picked at the last of his food. She had loved him so much. Images of them fishing, and Andrew taking her with him as a child, as he worked in his early carpentry business, rippled through her mind, causing a momentary stirring of pain. He would be 70 next month, and he looked it. His face once chiseled and determined, looked beaten and strained. She noticed the habitual twisting of his lips, his short beard moving with them.

Andrew Jackson Borden. Photo courtesy of The Fall River Historical Society.

After several uncomfortable moments, Lizzie set down her cup and said, in quiet, even tones, "I am quite sure. I have already written to Aunt Mary, and expect a reply from her today."

The reaction she received from her father was more than she could have hoped for. His slender frame actually flinched, and his dark eyes shot across the table at her in unveiled anger. He had not known the letter to Aunt Mary was, at this moment, being delivered in Warren.

Lizzie rose and left the room. As Andrew and Abby sat there in stunned silence, they heard the opening and closing of the front door.

Lizzie walked determinedly along the downward slanting sidewalk toward town. There was a lot to do before the noon meal. That the Swansea deed would be signed over tomorrow at one of her father's banks was a certainty. She had pieced together that much from overheard conversations and glimpses of her father's letters from Uncle John Vinnicum Morse, found in his Prince Albert coat pocket. Her trips over the past few weeks bore out her suspicions that a horse deal was being put together that involved the Upper Farm at Swansea; a farm that had been in the Borden family for years. That she and Emma were being kept in the dark meant only one thing—some business transaction was going on that would take the farm away from their inheritance. Just like the house on Fourth Street Andrew had put in Abby's name five years earlier. Like players in a chess game, each of the involved parties moved to outmaneuver the other. Yet Lizzie was always circling; like an omnipresent vulture hovering overhead.

Andrew Borden's routine never varied, and in the days and hours leading up to his murder, it was his undoing. He wore the same dark suit and Prince Albert coat, morning, noon and night; Spring through Winter. Each morning he left the house around 9 a.m. unless he was attending to business matters at home. Not only did he deal with tenants from his many commercial holdings, but he also sold some merchandise from his cellar. Large barrels of vinegar were stored in the earthen first cellar room, along with other sundries as they became available. If he could store it, make it or get a good deal on it, he hoarded goods for sale. Vinegar was always needed for pickling, and his neighbors, including Charles Sawyer, had bought from him.

Keep cellar with preserves and vegetables. Barrel of vinegar.

Prince Albert double-breasted coat.

His daily rounds included a stop at the Post Office, where he mailed letters and picked up the morning post. Mail was delivered twice daily. Lizzie and Emma often handed him letters to post for them as he left the house each morning. When he returned for the noon and evening meals, he was usually greeted by his daughters asking if there were any letters for them.

The Fall River Post Office and Customs House was a large stone building on Bedford Street, a block over from City Hall and the Police Station. From the Borden House, it was a mere 5-8-minute walk. Market Square, sitting a half block away, would become the scene of mass frenzy when the Inquest and Preliminary Hearing into the Borden murders took place.

Fall River Post Office and Customs House, March 1912

Andrew also picked up a copy of the *Providence Journal* newspaper, for which he had a subscription. For one cent, you could buy plain white wrappers, which you would address, and leave at the Post Office for your reserved copy.

Newspaper wrapper with 1 cent stamp.

A newspaper with a wrapper that Lizzie hoped could pass as a "small white package."

After the Post Office, Andrew typically stopped at Pierre Leduc's for a shave. It was the only extravagance for which he indulged. Barbershops in the 1800s were a mainstay for businessmen and were relatively inexpensive. You could get a haircut for $0.25, and a shave for $0.10.

Typical barbershop in 1892.

From there, he would make the rounds of his three banks, stop by the various stores he owned, and often stop to see his property manager, Charles Cook, who had an office in the Andrew J. Borden building, on the third floor.

Charles C. Cook's primary business was insurance. He had charge of the Andrew J. Borden Building at the corner of Anawan and South Main Street in Fall River. Andrew entrusted him with collecting rents and acting as a general property manager. It was his custom to visit Charles at least 3-4 times a week. After Andrew's murder, Charles became the Borden sisters' property manager, as they inherited their father's many business concerns. According to Mr. Cook, Lizzie had visited his office several times. She was no stranger to deeds and their overall appearance.

Andrew Borden was as close to the Dicken's image of Ebenezer Scrooge as Fall River could hope to find. Gaunt, white-whiskered, and dressed habitually in a long black coat and top hat, he walked the blocks near his home with his small notebook and tiny pencil in hand, jotting down figures, and overseeing tenants. Although he loved his family, his world was one of cyphers and cold, hard cash.

Fall River looking north on North Main Street. Late 1880s.

At 11:00 in the morning, Andrew typically arrived home. He hung his Prince Albert coat in the dining room closet, or laid it over the arm of the lounge there, and donned a smoking jacket he kept hanging on a nail by the kitchen door that leads into the sitting room. If there was business to be conducted, he took care of that from 11-12. If there were no transactions to be handled, he would often sit in the sitting room and read his mail and the *Providence Journal.* If there was time for a nap, he put on his slippers kept in the closet of that room and lay down on the sofa. The key to his locked bedroom door was kept on the mantel shelf near the doorway leading into the kitchen.

This was the nature of the Borden residence. Mind-numbing routine. It rarely varied, and in that house with inter-connecting rooms, and without hallways, there was no privacy. Each of the denizens knew each other's patterns. Bridget's was especially regimented. In 1890s New England, the chores were done on a daily routine, relegated to each day of the week.

A Sun Bonnet Babies plate, popular in the late 1800s, depicting each day of the week, and its chores. Note Thursday is washing the windows. Lizzie was fond of giving Sun Bonnet Babies dishes as gifts in later years.

Close-up of Thursday "Scrubbing Day".

Monday was wash day and for hanging out clothes. Tuesday was ironing. Wednesday was mending. Thursday was for scrubbing, and the maids on Second Street could all be seen on that day washing windows. Friday was sweeping (which for Bridget, only happened every other Friday in the front hallway). Saturday was baking, and the Sabbath afternoon was usually a maid's day off. This predictable time-table gave a person with black motives a distinct advantage.

That Lizzie had access to the Prince Albert coat at times when her father was asleep on the sofa, or upstairs for a moment, was a certainty. Whether he stuffed a letter or two from Uncle John, after reading them at the Post Office, into its pocket, is unknown. A letter *was* found in his pocket the day of the murders. Emma recalled her father would burn correspondence, but not business letters. He may have kept them in his desk in his small safe room adjoining his bedroom. When the safe was opened, under the direction of the District Attorney and Marshal Hilliard during the Inquest, it contained no letters. They found deeds, business papers, and bank statements, but not the hoped-for will, or...letters. Perhaps, not dreaming one of his daughters would rifle through his coat pockets, he may have put off the trip, on occasion, to the hot upper floor after returning home for lunch to put important letters away. He would be going out again after dinner (lunch), and there would be a second post to collect in the afternoon.

As Andrew Borden made his rounds about town that Tuesday morning; Bridget was hanging the family's clothes in the backyard (a day late due to Monday's rain); Abby was alerting her sister that she could babysit little Abbie on Thursday after all, as they were canceling their plans for the farm; and Uncle John was scurrying around Westport and Fairhaven, trying to come up with Plan B, now that Lizzie was back home and watching like a hawk from its aerie. Sometime that day, word reached Andrew that over at the two Swansea farms, Mr. Eddy and Alfred Johnson (the Swede), had been taken suddenly ill.

Lizzie meanwhile, had taken a train to New Bedford, a mere 30-minute ride. The morning sun baked down on the shoppers as Lizzie hurried to meet the man who would help her with her plan. If she kept asking for poisons, people were bound to become suspicious. Yet, she had so little time. The plan she had hatched for poisoning the milk at the Swansea farm had been sound. She could use it again, now at home, as poison found in the milk can would point to someone outside the house—an enemy. Each morning the milk from the farm was left in a can on the side porch around 4:30. Bridget brought it in and poured it into manageable milk bottles that were kept in the ice box. She then rinsed out the pail and left it on the porch to be replaced the next day with a different can of fresh milk.

But the hatchet...that had to change. She had planned to use the old one in the barn at the Swansea house, making it look like a weapon of convenience the murderer picked up. She couldn't do that now. And she couldn't use one from the Borden cellar. It had to be from outside the house. She would have to get a new one.

1890s milk cans in 5- and 10-gallon containers.

Rough on Rats

Arsenic could be found in several over-the-counter products. Rough on Rats was something she had read about. The white powder resembled flour. Perhaps a dusting on the bread, like the bakers did. It also came in crystals, like the painter used. That could be placed in milk. But arsenic poisoning wasn't a fast-acting method.

Lizzie stepped into the drug store of E.E. Wright in New Bedford and boldly asked for Prussic Acid. She was prepared for the usual speech, and she received it. It was denied her. She left the store in a mood that mirrored the summer heat, as the city, and her thoughts spun around her.

She would have to settle for arsenic, even if she had to steal it. It had to look like an intruder. A maniac. No one would think to look for poison after seeing them hacked to death. But rather than risk being caught, she brought in her new accomplice from Fairhaven.

A few minutes later, a Portuguese entered Hillman and Vincent's Hardware Store in New Bedford. He spent some time with the axes and hatchets at one of the counters. Finally, he selected a small shingling hatchet with a 3 ½" blade and carried it to the counter. The shiny new hatchet with the gold gilt emblem stamped upon it glinted in the store light. Mr. Vincent studied the man. He was obviously a laborer from somewhere. He casually asked where the man worked, and he said "The Davis farm in Dartmouth," in broken English. The store owner rang up the sale, along with a box of rat poison, which was a typical purchase by farmers and their employees. The man paid him in cash. The proprietor wrapped the hatchet carefully in several layers of white paper and tied the package with twine. The foreigner picked up his purchases and exited the store, disappearing from view into the crush of shoppers.

Minutes before entering the hardware store, the Portuguese stopped in a drug store. He bought a soda and some candy, then loitered near the front door. The store owner was watching him. He was at the front of the store, sipping his soda, and looking out the window for the lady he was to meet. He glanced up and down the crowded sidewalk, then feeling the store owner's eyes on him, opened the door and walked out.

His errand accomplished, he handed over to the lady the packages from Hillman's. He stepped into an alley, reached into his pocket, and counted his cash. He may not be able to read, but he knew money. It had been the easiest work he had ever done. She had asked him only one question about his purchase in the hardware store: "Did you mention the Davis farm in South Dartmouth?" He had forgotten to say "South," but he nodded in the affirmative anyway. There would be more money if he kept his "errands" for the lady quiet. It all sounded fine to him.

Lizzie cradled her satchel in her lap as the train headed back to Fall River; a white package, tied in twine, peeking from its depths. A small box rested next to it. She would kill them tonight. She would drop a quick note to her Aunt when she reached Fall River.

The town hall clock struck 11:00 am. Andrew Borden hastened to finish his rounds and go home. His head was down, the sidewalk a blur of cracks and debris. His thoughts tumbled like maniac acrobats in his tired mind. A pair of shoes appeared suddenly and he stopped. One of his associates stood before him, smiling.

"I thought you were spending summer at the farm," the man said. He noticed his friend was uncharacteristically agitated, his face creased with tension.

"No," Andrew blurted out, contrary to his private nature, "I have had so much difficulty in my family, I have not felt like going away."

Suddenly embarrassed at his lack of propriety, he merely tipped his hat and hurried up the street, the man staring after him.

Andrew entered his home through the side door. Bridget unlatched it for him and returned to her cooking. The cloying smell of fried swordfish hung in the air. A loaf of baker's bread, a soft dusting of flour coating the golden surface, rested on the kitchen table.

After changing from his Prince Albert to his smoking jacket, Andrew sat in the sitting room near an open window in his large, armed chair, slid the mailing wrapper from the *Providence Journal,* and snapped the pages open. But his mind would not focus on the black ink before him. Abby entered and sat near him in the rocking chair. Their conversation was in hushed whispers.

Lizzie surprised her father and step-mother by once again joining them at the table for dinner. Lizzie placed her napkin in her lap and poured herself a cup of tea. She glanced at the pitcher of cold milk sitting at the center of the table, droplets of condensation running down its glass.

Abby and Andrew filled their plates with fried swordfish, and large slices of toasted baker's bread. Andrew reached for the milk pitcher and poured the liquid all over his toast. Bridget had just entered the room to set the cakes and cookies on the table, and departed, not noticing if Abby also drenched the bread and cake in milk, as was the New England custom. She returned, placing a plate of some bread she had made herself on the table, in case they ran out.

Lizzie nibbled at her fish, watching the actions of her parents surreptitiously. They gobbled their food, and made light conversation, obviously nervous to suddenly have so much of Lizzie's unexpected company. Andrew mentioned that there was sickness over at the farm. Lizzie cast a quick glance at him. Comments on the weather, some store sales, and other innocuous conversation filled the noonday meal time.

Abby rang the bell, signifying to Bridget that they were finished. The three rose; Lizzie going upstairs to her room, and Andrew and Abby retiring to the sitting room. Once they heard Lizzie's footsteps overhead in her bedroom, they began talking. A small puff of brick dust fell silently inside the sitting room fireplace.

Tuesday night's supper was to be a repeat of dinner: warmed over swordfish, with baker's bread, cakes, cookies, and tea. Bridget, noticing the bread was nearly gone, donned the shawl that hung on the peg in the back entry, her soft felt hat, and headed over to the bakery on Borden street, a block away. The smell of baking bread and cake filled her nostrils as she opened the door of the shop; a small bell tinkling overhead.

She asked for dinner rolls but was told they were out. She settled for another loaf of flour bread, paid them the 5¢, and headed back with her bundle.

1890s Ice Box. Note the large block of ice and the milk bottles.

The maid hurried along Borden Street with her purchase. The cicadas were so loud, they nearly drowned out the carts and horses that passed her along the way. Lizzie heard their evening song as well through the screen door, as she hurriedly opened the ice box nestled in a closet nearby in the old sink room. She filled the remaining bottles containing Tuesday's milk with a white powder and swirled it around. She had barely finished and was leaving the sink room when Abby entered the kitchen from the dining room. Lizzie barely glanced at her, as she headed for her room.

Bridget entered the side yard and closed the gate behind her. Abby met her at the screen door as she climbed the side steps and reached for the handle.

"Did you get dinner rolls?" Abby asked.

"No, Marm," Bridget said in her thick Irish brogue. "They was out of 'em. I got a loaf of baker's bread."

Abby handed her 5¢ to replace the change Bridget had spent for the bread from her own money. The young servant went back to preparing the evening meal, this time setting three plates at the table, as it appeared Lizzie had taken a sudden fancy to eating with the old folks; something she and Emma rarely did. *Maybe now there would be some peace around here*, Bridget thought. *Maybe she is going to try to get along. Maybe she just misses Miss Emma.*

Bridget Sullivan was a 26-year-old Irish immigrant who had worked for the Borden's for two years and nine months. She was a pretty woman with thick dark hair, a full figure, and at times, a temper, which flared up occasionally during the later murder trials' inquisitions. An Irish Catholic, she was steeped in her religion's traditions and believed flagrant lying could send you to hell. Lying by omission, however, might let her squeak by.

Bridget Sullivan. Photo courtesy unknown.

Her duties at the Borden's were light compared to the usual chores required of a maid. When Attorney Knowlton questioned her during the Preliminary Hearing, after the murders of Andrew and Abby Borden, he asked her the following:

Knowlton: "What were your duties?"

A. "Well, I done the washing, ironing, and cooking."

Q. "Anything else besides that?"

A. "A little sweeping and scrubbing."

Q. "Which part of the house did you have the sweeping of?"
A. "I had the front hall to do, the front entry."
Q. "What days did you sweep the front hall?"
A. "Every other week, Friday."
Q. "Did you have any care of the beds?
A. "No sir."
Q. "None of them at all?"
A. "No Sir."
Q. "Did you have any duties in any of the bedrooms upstairs?"
A. "No sir."

Bridget brought in the dishes of swordfish, bread, cakes, and cookies and set them in front of the three silent members comprising the Borden's household. Emma Borden, Lizzie's older sister, was still away on vacation in Fairhaven.

Lizzie watched as Andrew's afternoon ritual of soaking his toast in milk was repeated. The baker's bread, and Bridget's homemade loaf were liberally doused until there remained very little milk in the pitcher. Abby had only eaten the cakes and bread, foregoing the fish. Lizzie watched their faces closely, looking for any change in their behavior or countenance.

Abby rang the bell for Bridget, and she and Andrew, once again, removed to the sitting room for their evening conversation. Bridget sat down in Andrew's chair and had her dinner. Lizzie angrily climbed the front stairs.

She entered her room and sat on the edge of the bed. She could hear the soft murmuring of their voices coming through her fireplace, but it did not matter now what they were saying. If it all went well, they would be dead by morning. Surely, the arsenic would show some effect soon! She glanced at her small, packed valise she would take to Warren in the morning early for her visit to Aunt Mary Morse. Word would get her to in Warren that her parents had been tragically murdered. There would be no trip to Marion.

Emma Borden sat in the cozy parlor of her dear friend Helen Brownell. The briny smell of ocean water wafted in through the open windows and fluttered the lace curtains in a rhythmic dance of moonlight. She had not felt so peaceful in a long time. Here, she was away from the constant drama her younger sister insisted upon creating. She was finally away from the tension and pretense. She shared no affection for her stepmother Abby, and the strain of maintaining a civil façade was draining.

At 42-years-old, Emma had given up any hope of marriage and creating a family of her own. She had an angular face with a prominent nose, warm eyes, and wavy dark hair pulled back severely into a bun. Where Lizzie was big-boned and wide-shouldered, Emma was ram-rod straight, slender and unremarkable. She wished only to live her life in peace, enjoying close friends, and life's simple pleasures.

Emma Borden. Photo courtesy of The Fall River Historical Society.

Ironically, as she sat there revering her escape from her unhappy home, she was handed a letter by Helen's mother. She recognized her sister's familiar scrawl. The glow faded. Now what? She was already aware Lizzie had canceled her trip to Marion to vacation at the seaside cottage of their friend, Dr. Handy. She stayed in New Bedford for five days…doing Lord knew what.

With trepidation, Emma read the lines written on the expensive stationary, and a feeling of dread overtook her. Helen, noticing her friend's sudden change of pallor, asked what was wrong. Emma handed her Lizzie's note and watched for her friend's reaction to the words. Helen looked up in confusion. What did it mean? A strange man running around the Borden property at night, trying the side door, darting into the back yard? Their father having angry words with visitors to the house? Enemies? Predictions of doom? Emma felt a sudden wave of panic. Something was wrong. Something was very, very wrong.

Fall River City Hall with its four-sided clock.

The City Hall clock in downtown Fall River struck nine bells. From its perch, only a couple of blocks away from the Borden residence, the sound of the hourly alert was deep and sonorous. Lizzie lay on her bed in the ensuing shadows and listened for sounds coming from the sitting room below, where her parents were talking. She could hear the low tones of Andrew's deep voice, followed by the soft replies of Abby. Lizzie's heart was racing. Why weren't they showing signs of the poisoning? Had she not put in enough? Minutes later, she heard them enter their bedroom next to hers. The sound of creaking bedsprings came to her as they climbed onto the old mattress. Minutes passed.

Suddenly, the sound of retching came to her through their closed bedroom door, directly behind her headboard. Her pulse raced, and she held her breath. Would they die? The reality of it hit her hard in the face. It was one thing to plan a murder, it was another to hear your victims in their death throes.

Abby and Andrew were both vomiting now, exclamations of pain filling the brief reprieves. Lizzie's heart was pounding. The noises from the street irritated her as she strained to hear what was happening in the room beside hers. She suddenly thought of Bridget, whose room was in the attic. If she heard them vomiting, she would come to check on them and wonder why Lizzie wasn't.

Pulling on a robe, she pulled aside the red portiere hanging at the back of her bed and tapped on the door separating their bedrooms. She called out, asking if they were alright. A bolt sliding back sounded and Andrew opened the door. The smell of sickness assaulted her nostrils, and she felt her stomach lurch in response.

"What's wrong?" Lizzie asked them. Abby was cradling a slop pail, several towels lying next to her on the floor. "Can I do anything for you?"

Her father said simply, "No." Lizzie heard a renewed binge of vomiting from Abby's direction. Swallowing the bile rising in her throat, Lizzie managed to say she was sick as well and would be lying down on her bed if they needed her. She lay there in the darkness, the sounds of their pain coming through the thin wall separating the two rooms.

It dragged on for hours. Nervous excitement turned to anger, as the sounds of sickness were still going on as the town hall clock struck midnight. It was at this time that Lizzie mimicked their sounds of retching, realizing, she would need to look like a victim as well.

Sometime during the wee morning hours of Wednesday, August 3rd, the house became quiet.

Chapter Nine

Wednesday, August 3rd, 1892

The pale sunlight of early morning streaked across the floral carpeting and the white counterpane bedspread. Lizzie was seated at her writing desk, penning a note to her Aunt Mary. She wouldn't be coming after all, as they were all taken ill. She angrily stuffed the letter into her purse. With the Swansea deal going through, she had to stay here and figure out a way to stop them from going forward with it.

If the poison had worked, the plan was to kill them with the new hatchet early Wednesday morning before Bridget arose. Lizzie would take the key from the sitting room mantle, enter their room, find them dead from the poisoning, and attack them with the blade, making it look like a madman had come in the morning when the house was quiet and killed them. She planned to be on her way to her Aunt Mary before Bridget was up, leaving the front door's spring lock not quite latched. No one would suspect her—a Borden, and a Christian woman—of committing such a heinous act. But, as she discovered, when the first rays of sunlight pierced the lace curtains of her bedroom, they were still alive. She heard them coughing.

Murmurings came from the bedroom next to hers. They were awake. She glanced at her sister's empty bedroom that connected to her own and felt a sudden pang. She missed Emma. She needed her to lean on right now. But Emma would not have approved of the mission Lizzie was on…not all of it, anyway.

Andrew and Abby Borden's bedroom. Photo by Ron Bueker.

Lizzie opened her bedroom door leading out to the second-floor landing. She paused and listened. The faint sound of the stove fire door being opened and closed came to her. She could hear Bridget setting out her pans and feeding wood into the heavy black oven. She could picture her, setting out her supplies, pushing her bangs from her forehead as she moved about her kitchen.

Kitchen utensils from the 1890s at the Lizzie Borden B&B and Museum.

The kitchen at the Lizzie Borden B&B and Museum,
set as it was the day of the murders. Photo by Ron Bueker.

Bridget looked up in surprise as Lizzie walked through the room. The girl was usually not down before 9:00. The maid glanced at the kitchen clock; it wasn't even 7:00. Mr. and Mrs. Borden had come down earlier and were in the sitting room. Bridget noticed they did not look well. Mrs. Borden said they had all been sick throughout the night.

Attorney Knowlton questioned Bridget during her Preliminary Hearing for the Borden murder case about that morning:

Knowlton: These people had been sick, had they not?"

Bridget: "Yes, sir."

Knowlton: "Mr. and Mrs. Borden had been sick, and Miss Lizzie had been taking care of them, and had been sick herself?"

Bridget: "That is what they said."

Knowlton: "She looked sick, did she?"

Bridget: "I did not notice. She told me she was sick that morning.

Knowlton: "Wednesday morning?"

Bridget: "Yes, sir."

Knowlton: "It was the night before Mr. and Mrs. Borden were ill...did you hear them up around?"

Bridget: "No, sir."

Knowlton: "Miss Lizzie's was right next to theirs...her room opened into their room?"

Bridget: "Yes, sir."

Knowlton: "They were vomiting?"

Bridget: "Yes, sir, that is what they said."

Knowlton: "Mrs. Borden said she was sick, or had been taken sick that night, and was sick nearly all night?"

Bridget: "Yes, sir."

Knowlton: "Did they all come down to breakfast?"

Bridget: "Yes, sir."

Knowlton: "What did they have for breakfast?"

Bridget: "Pork steak, and Johnny cakes, and coffee."

Lizzie glanced at the pork steak sizzling in the skillet. The grease sputtered and popped; it could have been any Wednesday morning in the Borden home. Except, Andrew Borden was lying prostrate on the sitting room lounge, his stomach roiling from the smells coming from the kitchen on the other side of the door. His arm was bent and flung across his pale face, his upper lip pebbled with perspiration. Abby was half-way laying in the big overstuffed chair across from him; wringing her hands and talking some nonsense about being poisoned. Andrew was in no mood for it today. He had more serious matters to deal with. As soon as he could muster, he had to get downtown.

Bridget asked Lizzie if she was also "real sick" the night before. She did not look anything like Abby, who was pale. She admitted she was, and that she had tried to help her father and step-mother. Lizzie would later report she too was vomiting around midnight.

As Bridget busied herself in the kitchen, Lizzie crept to the back stairs leading to the attic. She caught sight of the empty milk can sitting on the floor of the sink room as she passed by. Bridget had already rinsed it out after emptying Wednesday's milk into the bottles. Another plan that had not worked. But Lizzie had not given up. The bank deal was today. She doubted they would still go; they were both still very ill. But just in case, she had to hurry.

The attic was already warm. For the first time, Lizzie felt sorry for Bridget. Her room was just ahead of her at the top of the attic stairs. The maid withered up here in the summer months and froze during the winter when the door atop the attic stairs was usually closed to keep the heat trapped below. Bridget had always seemed like a fixture to Lizzie, one whose purpose was to serve, no more important than the last maid, "Maggie," yet, for one moment, Lizzie felt empathy for her.

Attic door at the top of the stairs. It was designed to be lowered in the winter months to keep the heat below stairs. Photo was taken by the Author at the Lizzie Borden B&B & Museum.

The door to Bridget's room is at the top of the attic stairs, straight ahead.
Photo by the Author.

Lizzie stepped out into the large attic area and hurried to the locked door of one of the storage rooms. Unlocking it, she entered the side room with the chimney. The room was filled with trunks, crates and seasonal clothing. She headed for a row of hanging bags. Taking one down, she removed a seal skin cape. Draping it over her arm, she left the room, relocking the door.

Chimney room in the attic that served as a storage room in 1892. Today it is the Hosea Knowlton guest room at the Lizzie Borden B&B & Museum. Photo by Ron Bueker.

1890s Seal Skin Cape

Bridget's bedroom at the top of the attic stairs.
Photo courtesy of Ron Bueker.

Her timing was perfect. As she descended the back stairs, Bridget was in the dining room, setting out the pork steak, Johnny cakes, and coffee. Her father and Abby were settling in, uncertainly, to the breakfast before them. Lizzie walked quietly through the sitting room, and past the open dining room door. Keeping the cape hidden from their view, she hurried into the front entry and up to her room. She left the cape and returned to the breakfast table. The unhappy threesome nibbled dubiously at the breakfast, thoughts of poison running through Abby's mind. Gratefully, she saw no baker's bread, or sugar cakes, present at the table. When Bridget entered the dining room to have her own meal, she found plenty of left-over food

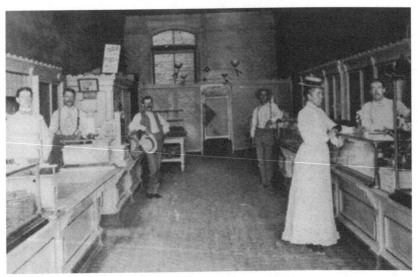

1890s Bakery.

Abby and Andrew headed back to the sitting room, where Andrew once again lay down on the sofa. Abby made him as comfortable as she could, and then headed down the entry to the front door.

"Where are you going?" Andrew asked feebly.

"I'm going for Bowen," Abby said determinedly. Perhaps their family physician, Doctor Seabury Bowen, would believe they were being poisoned, even if Andrew would not.

"My money shan't pay for it!" he hollered angrily, as his wife's stout form disappeared out the front door.

Abby waddled across Second Street, her face covered in perspiration from the heat, the sudden exertion, and the illness. She stepped to the second door of the Southard Miller home, that Dr. Bowen and his wife, Phebe, shared. Southard Miller was Phebe's father, and she and her husband had set up a home and a doctor's practice in the second half of the large house, just catty-corner from the Borden's.

Attorney Hosea Knowlton questioning Dr. Bowen on the stand during the Coroner's Inquest:

Knowlton: "You had not been called that week to the family?"
Bowen: "No, sir. I had not been called over to see them. The day before [the murders], Wednesday morning, about eight o'clock, or before eight, Mrs. Borden came to the door and said she was frightened, said that she was afraid she was poisoned. I told her to come in. She sat down, and she said the night before about nine o'clock, she and her husband commenced to vomit, and vomited for two or three hours until twelve, I understood...I asked her what she had eaten for supper, and she told me. She said she had eaten some baker's white bread, and she had heard of baker's cream cakes being poisonous, and was afraid there was something poisonous in the bread that made her vomit. She said she only ate cake and baker's white bread. At that time, she had a sort of an eructation of vomiting, slightly. I was afraid she was going to vomit there; I rather got ready for her. I told her to go home, and told her what to take, and she took it."
Knowlton: "Do you recollect what it was you prescribed for her?"
Bowen: "I told her to take some castor oil, and take it with a little port wine, to take the taste off, and probably that would be all she would want. I think immediately after breakfast, I thought they were neighbors, I would just go over. Before that, she said Lizzie came down, she heard them vomiting, I think she was in the next room, and she was up, too, and she commenced to vomit at that time, about twelve. I thought if they did not call me I would go over and make a friendly call. I went over after breakfast. I think Bridget let me in, I am sure it was the front door. I says "Mr. Borden, what is the matter?" He looked at me and wanted to know

if anybody had sent for me. I told him no, Mrs. Borden was over, I thought I would just come over and see. He seemed well enough then. He said he felt a little heavy, and did not feel just right, but said he did not think he needed any medicine. I did not urge him at all, of course, and I went home. I did not think much about it. I saw Mr. Borden out two or three hours afterwards. When I went in, I saw Lizzie run up the stairs. Mrs. Borden, I did not see, because I had seen her before."

Knowlton: "Where did you afterwards see Mr. Borden?"

Bowen: "I saw him Wednesday, walking along between the side door and the gate. Lizzie, I saw walking up the street, and I concluded they were all right."

[It was later determined that it was actually Dr. Bowen's wife, Phebe, who had seen Lizzie and Andrew Borden leaving their home that day. Phebe Bowen said she saw Lizzie leave a little after 6 o'clock in the evening, heading "downstreet." She was sure of the time, as it was just after the Bowen family was finishing supper. Why Doctor Bowen took credit for the sightings is not known, unless he wanted to keep his excitable wife out of the murder case spotlight, or Lizzie had left the house twice that day. Mrs. Bowen was called to testify anyway.]

Southard Miller/Bowen house, #91 and #93 Second Street. Dr. Bowen's door is on the right, #91. Photo courtesy Fall River Historical Society.

Andrew Borden rallied enough to get dressed in the same black suit, and Prince Albert coat, and head "downstreet," about 11 o'clock. He stopped into the building named for him and collected the rent checks from Charles Cook. It is probable he left his deathbed to do more than to pick up a check he could have easily gotten the next morning, just before he deposited it in the bank. It may be he was telling Mr. Cook that the deed transfer would have to go forward tomorrow, as they were all sick. He may have also tried to reach John Morse.

Abby was lying down, Bridget was in her room (washing some windows to get a head start on the next day's work schedule), and Andrew was downtown. Lizzie seized the opportunity to grab the cape and slip from the house. She walked quickly up the street to a drug store she did not frequent, as it was in the "wrong part of town" for someone with her name and aspirations. She made a beeline for D.R. Smith's Drug Store at the corner of Spring and Columbia streets, only a few blocks from her home.

[It is interesting here to note that in Doctor Bowen's testimony, he said he saw Lizzie walking "up" the street Wednesday, while his wife reported seeing her at 6 o'clock walking "downstreet." Is it possible they both saw Lizzie at different times? Second Street sloped down toward the city hub. The term "downstreet" was always used when someone was headed that way. When Phebe saw Lizzie at 6 o'clock, she was supposedly heading for Alice Russel's, whose home was down one street, and over, on Borden. A certain drug store, however, was "up" the street from the Borden house. The Prosecution later brought it up to Dr. Bowen, during the Superior Court trial.]

"Ten Cents Worth of Prussic Acid"

The shop bell tinkled as Lizzie Borden entered D.R. Smith's Drug Store. The atmosphere was a laid back, lazy afternoon of August temperatures. Outside, the clouds hung grey and threatening. A fan buzzed softly, as store clerk, Frederick B. Harte looked out through the colored bottles that filled the storefront window, and idly watched the traffic go by. He glanced at the woman in dark clothing, who was making her way to the counters at the back of the store, without taking special notice of her. She had something draped over her arm that looked like a cape, or "sack."

It was not until the young woman asked for something unusual that the employees at D.R. Smith's took notice. "I would like to buy ten cents worth of Prussic Acid," she said, in a rather tremulous voice. "I need it to clean a seal skin cape."

The still air in the store seemed to vibrate from her words. The employee behind the counter, Frank H. Kilroy, seemed relieved when Eli Bence, the head clerk, stepped over to offer her his assistance. She repeated the request. There was something in her manner, strange eyes, and guttural tone that stuck with him.

Cyanide Poison, a form of which is Prussic Acid.

"We do not sell Prussic Acid without a doctor's prescription," he said.

"I need it to put on the edge of a seal skin cape," she said emphatically, as a way to sidestep its medicinal requirement.

"I cannot sell it to you without a doctor's prescription," he reiterated. "It is very dangerous, and we do not sell it."

"I have purchased it before," she said undaunted.

When the clerk stood firm, she turned haughtily and exited the store.

"That's Miss Borden," Frank Kilroy said, as they watched the woman disappear down the street.

D.R. Smith's Drug Store, looking north on Rodman and South Main, is the first one on the left. Photo courtesy of the Fall River Historic Society.

Prussic Acid bottle sitting next to the newspaper headline that announced Lizzie Borden had been spotted the day before the murders attempting to buy poison. This photo is of the display case in Lizzie's room at the Lizzie Borden B&B & Museum. Photo by Ron Bueker.

Wednesday, August 3rd, 1892

Uncle John Comes for A Visit

Bridget came down from her room about half-past eleven and was surprised to see Lizzie standing in the kitchen. Not only was the girl eating meals "regular" with Mr. and Mrs. Borden for a change, she was actually early for the noon meal. Bridget took down her pots and set them on the stove. She checked the fire and found it low. With a sigh, she headed "down cellar" for a hod of coal.

 Lizzie's Dress Wednesday

During Bridget's Superior Court testimony, she said the following, concerning what Lizzie had on that Wednesday when they were all sick:

Bridget: "I saw her around the house before dinner [lunch]. I saw her down in the kitchen at breakfast time and before dinner was served on the table."

Robinson (Defense): "That is the day you said she had on the light blue wrapper?"

Bridget: "Yes, sir."

Robinson: "Did she have it on when she came down in the morning?"

Bridget: "Yes, sir."

Robinson: "And kept it on during the forenoon and had it at the dinner table?"

Bridget: "Yes, sir."

Robinson: "And the dinner was at 12 o'clock?"

Bridget: "Yes, sir."

Robinson: "Do you remember seeing her about that same day again, later in the day, Wednesday?" Bridget: "No, sir. I did not see her."

Robinson: "I used the word "wrapper."

Bridget: "It was a basque [blouse] and skirt."

Re-direct by Mr. Moody (Prosecution):
"Is this dress that you are speaking of that she had on Wednesday, the one you referred to as having been made in the Spring?"
Bridget: "Yes, sir." [The Bedford cord dress]

This means Lizzie would have had on the Bedford cord Wednesday morning at breakfast, changed to the dark-colored street dress Eli Bence and his clerks testified to seeing her in before 11:30 that forenoon, and then come back and changed into the Bedford cord again before dinner when Bridget saw her "early" for the noon meal. The effect was to show she had been home all day "sick."

We don't know where Abby was during the time both Lizzie and Andrew are out. She may have been lying down in her room, as she would have heard Lizzie coming and going out the front door if Abby was in the sitting room. Abby told John a few hours later that Lizzie had been in her room all day, "sick," proving she did not know Lizzie had gone out earlier.

Just then, Andrew arrived at the side door. Bridget left Lizzie, sitting in the large overstuffed chair by the small kitchen table, and hurried to unhook the screen door. He entered, with a curt greeting, his face pale and sickly, and walked into the dining room, where he laid his Prince Albert over the lounge arm. He settled in the sitting room.

Bridget's lunch of mutton soup, broiled mutton, cakes, cookies, and tea, was placed on the dining room table. Once again, Lizzie and her parents ate in tense silence. Andrew's stomach felt as though it would betray him with each bite. Abby appeared to be faring a little better, although she nibbled cautiously at the fare. She asked Bridget to serve Mr. Borden the Garfield tea she had prepared for him, and Andrew drank it, his face pinched in revulsion at the taste. The castor oil had been bad enough.

Lizzie left the table, barely touching her food, and climbed the curved staircase to her room. Locking her door, she collapsed onto the lounge. *What would she do now?* She managed to doze off, last night's vigil catching up to her. It wasn't until she heard voices in the sitting room below that she realized John Morse was in the house. Her pulse quickened. He had come to help facilitate the Swansea deed transfer! She listened through the pipe set into the fireplace opening until their "voices annoyed" her. Finally, she replaced the brick, and with panic filling her chest, formed a plan.

Attorney Knowlton, during the Inquest testimony of John Morse:

Knowlton: "Who did you see when you got there that noon?"

[John actually arrived at the Borden house at 1:30 p.m., after taking the 12:35 train from New Bedford.]

Morse: "The servant girl [Bridget let him in the back door]. I asked if Mr. Borden was at home, or Andrew, I don't know which. She said he was on the lounge. I went in. He got up. He asked if I had been to dinner [lunch]. I said I had not, but was not hungry at all. Mrs. Borden said, "We have just had dinner, a little while ago, it is all warm, I will put it on." She did in the dining room. I sat down and ate, and we went back into the sitting room and chatted until about 3 or 4. I was going to Swansea. I came over to Kirby's stable, hired a horse and buggy and went over to Swansea."

[Kirby's stable was located at 13 Rock Street and was owned by Charles T. Kirby, probably related to Stephen P. Kirby, John's close friend (and a possible relative) in the horse business. There were two livery stables within steps of the Borden house on Second Street, yet John chose to walk several blocks to Rock Street to hire a horse and buggy.]

Knowlton: "With Mr. Borden?"

Morse: No, sir. I asked him to go. He said he did not feel able to; they were indisposed, all them that day."

Knowlton: And the daughter [Lizzie]?"

Morse: "Yes, Mrs. Borden said they had been sick."

Knowlton: "Who did you see at the farm?"

Morse: "An American, Frank Eddy…I saw what I supposed to be his wife; I never was acquainted with her."

Knowlton: "Any other farm hands?"

Morse: No, sir."

Knowlton: "Stay to supper over there?"

Morse: "No, sir. I ate supper at William Vinnicum's; a little beyond there."

Knowlton: "In Warren?'

Morse: No, in Swansea."

Knowlton: "Got back home [Borden's house] about what time?"

Morse: "I got back to the house probably quarter to nine, not far from that, after dark."

Knowlton, during Preliminary Hearing, August 23, 1892:

Knowlton: "Did you see Mr. Eddy when you were over at the farm the night before [the murders]?"

Morse: I did."

Knowlton: "Did you give him any message from Mr. Borden?"

Morse: "No, sir."

Knowlton: "Or tell him Mr. Borden sent you over?"

Morse: "No, sir. There was one thing I forgot. I got some eggs from there for Mr. Borden; that is all."

Knowlton: "For him?"

Morse: "Yes, sir."

Mr. Frank Eddy's interview with Detective George F. Seaver on Thursday, August 11, 1892 [before the start of the final day of the Inquest testimony]:

> Detective Seaver: "Early Thursday morning, August 11, went to Luther's Corner, Swansea, with Marshall Hilliard to the farm of the late Andrew J. Borden, and had an interview with Frederick [Frank] Eddy and Alfred C. Johnson, who have been employed on that place, Mr. Eddy sixteen years, and Johnson for nine. [*The Fall River Herald*, on the day of the murders, stated: "...the only Portuguese employed on the upper farm is Mr. Johnson, and he is confined to his bed by illness...an attempt was made to try and reach Swansea by telephone, but no answer was received."] [Alfred Johnson was a "Swede." The term 'Portuguese" was a catch-all term for many

immigrant ethnicities. Also, notice, a phone at the farm is mentioned.]

A house stands today where Frank Eddy's was located, at the Upper Farm in Swansea, Ma. This is where John Morse picked up the eggs the day before the murders. Photo courtesy of Leonard Rebello, author of *Lizzie Borden: Past and Present.*

Seaver continues: "Frederick Eddy made the following statement. "John V. Morse came over to his house Wednesday evening, August 3rd, between 7 and 8 o'clock. He drove a horse and top buggy; said it was a stable team. He came into the house and brought a rattan basket, took out three pears and laid them on the table, said he brought them over from the Borden house. He said Mr. Borden sent him over to see how I was, and get the eggs. Said Mr. Borden was coming with him, but he, his wife and Lizzie were all taken sick last night, and he couldn't come. He said he stopped to supper to Mr. Vinnicum's, who lives a short distance from here. I said to him, after he got his eggs, 'how about the oxen Mr. Davis of South Dartmouth was to have to use?' 'I am going back and see Mr. Borden, and think we will make arrangements to get them back over Saturday morning,' was the reply. Mr. Morse stayed here 10 or 15 minutes. Since hearing of the murder, it has seemed to me a singular coincidence that he should have come over that night for the eggs, for, had he not, I should have taken the train and gone to Mr. Borden's Thursday morning [the day of the murders], arriving at the house about quarter to eleven or eleven."

The William Vinnicum house in Swansea, just down the road from Mr. Eddy's house at the Upper Farm, on Old Warren Road. This is where John Morse had supper on August 3rd, the day before the murders. Photo by the Author.

John's Visit to Swansea:

1) John's late arrival for dinner [lunch] Wednesday, August 3rd, is meant to make his visit look unplanned—for Lizzie's sake. He arrives without luggage. Andrew got word to him that things had gone wrong; the deed wasn't signed, and they were too sick to make alternate plans. John hops a train.

2) He, Andrew & Abby spend up to 2 hours talking in the sitting room. John leaves, hiring a horse & buggy several blocks away; travels to the Vinnicum's, and to the Swansea farm to see Mr. Eddy. The result of the meeting with Mr. Eddy is that the egg delivery the next day, planned for 11 o'clock, is now unnecessary. John even brings pears, to mask the rattan basket's true purpose...to carry back the eggs. The trip to the Vinnicum's for supper is to talk to their two visitors from Lynn, Massachusetts: the Chatterton boys.

3) Knowlton asks Morse during the Inquest if he saw any "of the other farm hands" during his visit to see Mr. Eddy. He says "No." We later learn from a newspaper report that Alfred Johnson was sick on Thursday, the day after John's visit, and quite possibly was ill at the time of the visit, along with Mr. Eddy. *Two people at the Swansea farms are ill.* When Knowlton asks Morse if Mr. Borden sent any message for Mr. Eddy, or that Mr. Borden sent John over, Morse replies, "No." Yet, Mr. Eddy states John said Andrew sent him over to see how Mr. Eddy was feeling.

Why did John deny such a simple request as to see how Mr. Eddy was? Why ask Morse if he saw "any other farm hands?" We know arsenic has been ruled inadmissible in the trials. Knowlton's hands are tied

He's hoping Morse will open the door by mentioning Eddy and Johnson are sick. But Morse sidesteps the trap. He denies any knowledge the two men are ill. By this time, is the wind up that it's possible Mr. Eddy and Alfred Johnson were poisoned, along with Andrew and Abby? Does John, as the first suspect in the murders, need to distance himself from anything to do with possible poisonings?

4) John testified, and it was reported in the *Fall River Herald*, that he came to Fall River Wednesday, August 3rd, with only one purpose, and that was to pick up the two oxen for Mr. Davis. He did everything but.

5) The plan, hurriedly hatched in that sitting room Wednesday, after dinner, was Plan B. Plan A had been for the Swansea deed transfer to happen Wednesday, with Lizzie safely away in Marion. Two things went wrong: Lizzie came back, and Andrew and Abby are violently ill.

Plan B is to send a messenger Thursday morning with a note for Abby to go help a "sick friend." At 10:00 a.m., a man will arrive to drive her to the "friend's" house. She will be driven, instead, to the signing of the deed transfer. The messenger and driver will need to be two people Lizzie won't recognize, in case she sees them. William Morse, John's 16-year-old nephew, visiting from Minnesota and staying at Daniel Emery's, will be the messenger. Joseph Chatterton, the 31-year-old brother of James "baseball shoes" Chatterton, will be the driver to pick Abby up. The deal is now on for Thursday, August 4th.

Many have wondered why Abby didn't just pretend she was going over to her half-sister's on Fourth Street. Because it was known "Bertie" was going early to the Rocky Pointe clam bake. In fact, Abby was supposed to babysit little Abbie for her that day, but called Bertie and canceled, saying she was sick. That Abby had few friends, and few places to go, was a sad reality. Even Bridget guessed the note from a "sick friend" must have come from Bertie Whitehead, as she was the only person Abby frequently visited.

Wednesday, August 3rd, 1892

In Alice Russell's Parlor

Alice Manley Russell was a woman who had seen her share of disappointment. She was considered a spinster at the age of 42. Though closer to Emma's age, she was friends with both of the Borden sisters, having known them for eleven years in 1892.

Alice's father, Frederick W. Russell, died in 1878, leaving Alice and her mother, Judith Manley Russell, on their own. Her mother was a respected nurse and was able to move herself and Alice into the home next to the Borden's at 96 Second Street, one they shared with John B. Chase, a quintessential entrepreneur with talents such as florist, paper hanger, and music teacher. Alice and her mother lived there until October 1890, only 8 months before the daylight burglary at the Borden's next door.

The house at 96 Second Street had made headlines in 1848, when a tragedy, that would give the Borden murders a run for its money, occurred there.

Fall River Weekly News, May 4, 1848. "The second wife of Lodowick Borden, the former Eliza Darling, and Aunt to Andrew J. Borden, who resided in the house on Second Street, later occupied by Dr. Kelly [and Alice Russell before him], "took her two youngest children [six-month-old Holder and three-year-old Eliza], went down cellar, and drowned them in the cistern; then, stepping behind the chimney, cut her own throat with a razor, and died almost instantly." A contemporary diarist noted that Eliza had been "considered a little out of her head for a few days past." She was left alone in the house with the children, her maid having "stepped out to draw a pail of water," and at that time Eliza "committed the lamentable deed in a paroxysm of insanity." The only one to be spared from being a victim of her mother's demented act was the couple's eldest child, Maria. Once the tragedy was discovered, it was said that a "great excitement prevailed in town." [Courtesy of the Fall River Historical Society]

It is interesting to note that in both the Borden's murders (one at 92 Second Street, and the other next door at 96) a maid was outside "to draw a pail of water." While Abby Borden was being murdered in her upstairs' guest chamber, her maid, Bridget, was filling a pail to wash the exterior windows.

During the trials after the murders of Andrew and Abby Borden, an insanity defense was considered for Lizzie. The connection between her and Eliza Borden was looked at to see if a strain of madness ran in the Borden family. As Eliza was a Darling, and only married a Borden, the bloodline theory fizzled out.

On the evening of Wednesday, August 3rd, 1892, only fourteen and one-half hours before the brutal murder of Abby Borden, Lizzie arrived on the doorstep of Alice Russell. The evening was cooler, a mild 66 degrees, overcast, with a slight wind coming off the water. The smell of baked goods from the bakery next door wafted on the night breeze.

Alice admitted her guest, and they sat down in the small parlor. Alice had moved to the boarding house at 33 Borden Street only a little over a year earlier. She testified at trial that her new home was only "300 yards" from the Borden house. Her mother had moved to Maple Street and continued working as a nurse. Alice was employed as a bookkeeper for the Leander D. Wilbur & Company Clothing Store at the corner of South Main and Pleasant Streets, a short walk from her home.

Newspaper drawing of Alice Russell during the Borden murder trial.

Alice noticed the strange frenetic movements of her guest, as she poured tea and make polite conversation. Lizzie looked tired, strained, and keyed up.

According to Alice's Superior Court trial testimony, a year later, "when she [Lizzie] came in, she said 'I have taken your advice, and I have written to Marion that I will come." I don't know what came in between, I don't know as this followed that, but I said, "I am glad you are going," as I had urged her to go before." [Lizzie obviously at some time told Alice about her misgivings for going on the trip.]

"...I said something about her having a good time, and she said, "Well, I don't know; I feel depressed. I feel as if something was hanging over me that I cannot throw off, and it comes over me at times, no matter where I am." And she says, "When I was at the table the other day, when I was at Marion, the girls were laughing and talking and having a good time, and this feeling came over me, and one of them spoke and said, "Lizzie, why don't you talk?" I don't know what was said after that. I don't remember any more conversation about Marion. Whether there was or not, I don't remember."

Much has been said about this conversation, and Lizzie's cryptic statements. Some Borden scholars see her words to Alice as a cry for help. Depression, moods that come over her, and even lapses in memory to where entire conversations are forgotten are presented. It very well could have been the desperate attempt of a woman with murder in mind, hoping her close friend would see her struggle and help her before she did something irrevocable.

Or, was it more? A possible precursor to an insanity plea? People suffering from depression, as those who struggle with bi-polar disorder, will sometimes act out in rage and claim they have no memory of the event or only a hazy, segmented reality of it. Time in a mental facility, should she be found guilty, was preferable to hanging. As her conversation with Alice continues, she switches gears, perhaps realizing Alice is not picking up the need to rescue her and moves into the "father has an enemy" mode.

Miss Russell continued her retelling of Wednesday night's conversation with Lizzie: "I suppose it was followed right on after that. When she spoke, she says, "I don't know; father has so much trouble." Oh, I am a little ahead of the story. She said, "Mr. and Mrs. Borden were awfully sick last night." And I said, "Why, what is the matter; something they have eaten?" She said, "We were all sick...all but Maggie." And I said, "Something you think you have eaten?" She said, "We don't know. We had some baker's bread, and all ate of it but Maggie and Maggie wasn't sick." And I said, "Well, it couldn't have been the bread; if it had been the baker's bread I should suppose other people would be sick, and I haven't heard of anybody." And she says, "That is so." And she says, "Sometimes I think our milk might be poisoned." And I said, "Well, how do you get your milk; how could it be poisoned?" And she said, "We have the milk come in a can and set on the step, and we have an empty can. They put out the empty can overnight, and the next morning when they bring the milk they take the empty can." And I said, "Well if they put anything in the can the farmer would see it." And then I said—I asked her what time the milk came if she knew. She said, "I think about four o'clock." And I said, "Well, it is light at four. I shouldn't think anybody would dare to come then and tamper with the cans for fear somebody would see them." And she said, "I shouldn't think so." And she said, "They were awfully sick; and I wasn't sick, I didn't vomit; but I heard them vomiting and stepped to their door and asked if I could do anything, and they said No." [Attorney Knowlton asks her to repeat Lizzie's words about not vomiting; Alice repeats it, adding Lizzie's words "I wasn't sick enough to vomit, but they were." Knowlton is aware Lizzy testified she vomited also.]

"I think she told me they were better in the morning, and that Mrs. Borden thought that they had been poisoned, and she went over to Dr. Bowen's—said she was going over to Dr. Bowen's."

Knowlton: "Anything about trouble with tenants, or anything of that sort?"

Alice: "She says, "I feel afraid sometimes that father has got an enemy. For, she said, "he has so much trouble with his men that come to see him." And she told me of a man that came to see him, and she heard him say—she didn't see him, but heard her father say, "I don't care to let my property for such business." And she said the man answered sneeringly, "I shouldn't think you would care what you let your property for." And she said, "Father was mad, and ordered him out of the house." She told me of seeing a man run around the house one night when she went home. I have forgotten where she had been. She said, "And you know the barn has been broken into twice." And I said, "Oh well, you know well that was somebody after pigeons; there is nothing in there for them to go after but the pigeons." "Well, she says, "they have broken into the house in broad daylight, with Emma and Maggie and me there." And I said, "I never heard of that before." And she said, "Father forbade our telling it." So, I asked her about it, and she said it was Mrs. Borden's room, what she called her dressing room. She said her things were ransacked, and they took a watch and chain and money and car tickets, and something else I can't remember. And there was a nail left in the keyhole; she didn't know why that was left; whether they got in or out with it or what. I asked her if her father did anything about it, and she said he gave it to the police, but they didn't find out anything, and she said father expected that they would catch the thief by the tickets. She remarked, "Just as if anybody would use those tickets."

"She said, "I feel as if I wanted to sleep with my eyes half open—with one eye open half the time—for fear they will burn the house down over us."

She said, "I think sometimes—I am afraid sometimes that somebody will do something to harm him; he is so discourteous to people...Dr. Bowen came over. Mrs. Borden went over, and father didn't like it because she was going; and she told him she was going, and he says, "Well, my money shan't pay for it." She went over to Dr. Bowen's, and Dr. Bowen told her—she told him she was afraid they were poisoned—and Dr. Bowen laughed, and said, 'No, there wasn't any poison. And she came back, and Dr. Bowen came over. I was so ashamed, the way father treated Dr. Bowen. I was so mortified." And she said after he had gone Mrs. Borden said she thought it was too bad for him to treat Dr.

Bowen so, and he said he didn't want him coming over there that way."

Lizzie left Alice's house sometime around 9 o'clock and walked the 300 yards to her home along shadowed sidewalks, stepping stones of light from the street lamps leading her way. Her mood was black. So much had gone wrong, and Alice had not been sympathetic to her tales of doom. At least she had planted the seed of imminent danger lurking in the form of an enemy, who wished her father harm.

As Lizzie approached the Borden home, she felt like a prisoner ascending the gallows. She was trapped now. The sitting room windows were dark; in fact, all the windows watched her through blackened squares. It was not until she unlocked the front door with her key that she saw the glow from the kerosene lamp sitting on the entry hall table; Abby's thoughtful touch to make sure she could see her way when she arrived. Lizzie knew another one would be burning in the kitchen for Bridget.

Lantern burning in the entry of the Lizzie Borden B&B and Museum. The door to the sitting room is at the right. Photo by Ron Bueker.

Lizzie's Conversation Warning Signs:

1) Statements concerning depression, and moods that come over her no matter where she is.

2) Poisoning of baker's bread and milk; both come from sources *outside* the house. Alice's mention that the farmer would have seen something added to the milk can must have given Lizzie pause, based on her trip to the Swansea farm Sunday.

3) String of harrowing events, *all happening during the time Emma is away*: two barn break-ins, a strange man running from her side door at night, and Andrew's trouble with tenants. The daylight burglary occurred while Emma was home. Emma admitted on the stand she had never heard of her father having trouble. Lizzie is setting the stage, and has sent letters to Elizabeth Johnston and Emma with the same reports of danger.

The murmurings Lizzie heard briefly, coming from the room ahead of her, suddenly stopped at her entrance. The sitting room was dark, its three occupants conspiring in the soft glow of the kerosene lamp on the hall table. *They are in there, talking and plotting*, she thought, spots of color coming to her cheeks. She shut the door and triple-locked it, as she always did when she was the last one in at night. Without a word to the three people sitting in the shadows of the sitting room, she climbed the stairs, entered her room, and locked the door. Tossing her purse onto her bed, she crouched in the darkness by the fireplace and listened.

Lizzie heard Abby enter their bedroom, around quarter to ten that night. Fifteen minutes later, John Morse climbed the stairs and entered the guest room. Lizzie boiled with anger. They had put him in the guest room, instead of the attic where he usually stayed. Why? To keep an eye on her? She listened for the sound of a closing door coming from that room but heard none. Several minutes later, she heard him climbing into bed. He was leaving the bedroom door open!

Lizzie's bedroom. Photo by Frank C. Grace (Trig Photography)
In 1892, her bed was angled diagonally in front of the door leading to Andrew and Abby's bedroom, & a lounge was between the windows where the bureau is in the photo. (left of photo).

At the same time, John Morse was preparing for bed—opening the shutters and windows in the guest room, in the hopes of catching a breeze—Bridget Sullivan was unlocking the back door. It was 10:05. She saw the lamp Abby left for her burning brightly on the kitchen table. She hung her hat and shawl on the pegs lining the entry wall. The pears Mr. Borden had brought in earlier that morning were still lying on the small table beneath the south kitchen window. The clothes she had ironed earlier that day from 1:30-4:30, hung from a clothes horse near the stove. She would fold them during breakfast tomorrow and leave them on the kitchen table for the family to take to their rooms. With Miss Emma gone, she had less to do. It had given her time that afternoon to go upstairs to the attic for an hour, from 4:30-5:30, and get a head start on tomorrow's window washing.

The house creaked around her as Bridget stood for a moment in the kitchen, looking over things, and going over in her mind the things needed for breakfast the next morning. Moonlight spilled in through the south-facing window curtains; its ghostly dance with the lace flitting across the worn floor.

Bridget's Window Washing

Edwin Porter was the police reporter for *The Fall River Globe*. It was admitted by the police that some leaks from the closed Coroner's Inquest, that ran August 9th-11th, found their way into the papers. Bridget's Inquest testimony, which went missing during the Superior Court hearing, was reported in segments in the *Globe*. When asked about her actions Thursday (the day of the murders), she said in part, "I washed the breakfast dishes. I saw Miss Lizzie pass through the kitchen, and she may have passed through again. I finished my work downstairs and resumed window washing on the third floor, *which I'd begun the preceding day* [Wednesday]." The *Globe* went on to say, "While she was washing windows on the third floor [Thursday], she talked down to a friend on the sidewalk. She said she might have made considerable noise as she raised and lowered the windows." *This is leaked Inquest testimony.*

The New York Herald reported that "Bridget Sullivan was up in the third story cleaning windows in the front room," around 11 o'clock when Andrew Borden was being murdered." Great pains were taken to remove that testimony concerning the attic window washing. From then on, the story changed...Bridget went upstairs at 11 to lie down and rest, not to wash windows.]

Bridget's Glass of Milk

Police Witness Statement: Bridget Sullivan, to Officer Harrington: "No, I never, at any time, saw Lizzie put anything in, nor did I ever throw any milk away. Whatever milk was left, and there wasn't much of it, I drank it, for I don't like tea." Although Bridget took a glass of milk with her upstairs Wednesday night, it seems odd, if there was arsenic in it, that it didn't hit her until the next morning, after her breakfast. Andrew and Abby were sick within an hour and a half of finishing supper around 7:30 Tuesday night; they began throwing up at 9.

As the family was sick Wednesday, and there is no mention of milk served that day (rather, they are devouring tea), Bridget probably had a surplus of milk in the ice box when Thursday's milk was delivered. Did she, needing more bottles for the excess of milk from Wednesday, and now Thursday, find a half bottle at the back of the ice box with the remains of Tuesday's milk, and drink it to free up some empty bottles? This would be about the perfect timeline for the arsenic to kick in later that morning:

Bridget brings in the milk from the back steps when she comes downstairs Thursday morning at 6:15. She drinks the remains of Tuesday's milk ("Whatever milk was left, and there wasn't much of it, I drank it, for I don't like tea.") By 6:30, just as Abby comes down, Bridget has drunk the last of Tuesday's milk, and filled more bottles with the fresh milk delivered that morning.

There are now bottles of Wednesday's and Thursday's milk in the ice box. As Lizzie comes down to the kitchen, a few minutes before 9, Bridget is doing the breakfast dishes. She suddenly runs into the back yard to vomit---only a few hours after drinking the milk. The dull headache she rose with that morning, was dismissed by her, as she "was always having headaches."

The fact that Bridget drank the last of Tuesday's milk is bolstered by one glaring point:

Dr. Dolan, under Bridget's guidance, was shown which bottles of milk in the ice box belonged to what days. He emptied some from Wednesday's bottles, and some from Thursday's bottles, into jars and labeled them "Wednesday's Milk" and

"Thursday's milk." The jars were sealed with wax and sent off to Professor Wood in Boston to test for signs of poison. The salient point here is that Andrew and Abby were poisoned *Tuesday night!* Wednesday and Thursday's milk were a moot point, as they were delivered after the sickness began. Bridget "drank the last" of Tuesday's, leaving none to be sent off for testing. They sent off the wrong milk. Results from the lab showing no poison was found in the milk would be worthless!

Superior Court testimony: I went and took the lamp off of the table, and went to the ice chest, and took a glass of milk…That was all I did; I went upstairs…I *guess* it was the milk we had that day…Wednesday's milk." [Italics are the Author's.]

During Bridget's testimonies, she tried valiantly not to admit to being out back vomiting Thursday morning, as Knowlton pressed her as to why she didn't know when Mr. Borden left. Not wanting to admit she was sick a *second time* that morning, may be why she and John Morse's testimony of when Abby asked her wash the windows differed. Abby probably asked her during breakfast, as John testified, but Bridget moved it to later, after John left, that Abby asked her to do the windows, in an effort to conceal a missing 20-30 minutes she may have been out throwing up again. Instead, she said she spent the time "straightening my kitchen."

Crossing to the kitchen table, Bridget picked up the lamp and carried it to the sink room. Opening the ice box, she poured herself a glass of milk and made her way to her room in the sweltering attic.

Chapter Ten
Thursday Morning, August 4, 1892
The Day of the Murders

Thursday morning dawned with a layer of humidity already sending droplets down the windows of the Borden house at 92 Second Street. Bridget Sullivan turned in her bed, her pillowcase damp beneath her neck, and looked at her small bedside clock. 6 o'clock. She sighed and pressed her fingertips to her temples. She had "a dull headache," and sensed the heat that would mount throughout the day. At least she had the afternoon off. This brightened her spirits and she swung her legs over the bed to rise.

Bridget headed down the two flights of stairs to the kitchen. She swirled water into the empty milk glass from her room, watching as the film that coated its edges melted away. Her head throbbed. *Not now*, she thought. She was meeting her friends downtown this afternoon for a bit of fun. As she began arranging things for breakfast, she glanced at the closed sitting room door. Everything was quiet.

She unlocked the wooden door in the back-kitchen entry and left it open. She then unhooked the screen door and brought in the milk can waiting for her from the Swansea farm. She poured the milk from the can into clean, manageable bottles, and rinsed it out, leaving it to sit on the sink room floor until later.

Bridget made two trips to the cellar; first to carry up the wood for the stove, and then returning down the stairs to get a hod of coal. Perspiration was pebbling her forehead, and she wished she could sit down for a bit. She paused in the cool cellar, bending slightly from the hip, as she tried to manage her aching head. Crossing to the washroom, she splashed cold water on her face from the sink. The brick floor of the room lay bare before her. She glanced at the dry sink inside the chimney notch. The washing was done until next Monday. Today would be window washing. She took a deep breath and steadied herself for the day ahead. Picking up the coal, she mounted the steps to the kitchen.

Minutes later, at 6:30, Abby Borden entered the kitchen. She told Bridget Mr. Morse was in the house.

"Did he sleep in the attic?" Bridget asked, somewhat surprised.

"No. He slept in the guest chamber. What have you for breakfast?" Mrs. Borden asked, kindly. Bridget noticed some of her employer's color was back in her face, and she appeared to be feeling better.

"Soup and cold mutton," Bridget replied.

"Warm it over, but save enough for dinner." Abby turned and opened the sitting room door. John Morse's voice greeted her. He had been the first one up at 6:00 o'clock and was reading the paper.

At 6:45, there was a knock on the screen door. Bridget opened it for the ice man. He hauled a chunk of ice into the sink room and deposited it into the ice box for her. Normally, Bridget would have paused for a chat, but this morning she was not feeling up to it.

Ten minutes later, Andrew Borden came down the back stairs from his bedroom. He set down his slop pail and crossed to the sitting room door. A short dressing coat hung there on a nail. He put it on and opened the sitting room door. Bridget saw him place the key to his room on the mantle there and greet John. He returned to the kitchen, picked up his pail and went out to the back yard.

Bridget was at the window beneath the window overlooking the yard. She watched as he threw the contents of the slop pail onto the ground beneath the large pear tree. He then unlocked the barn, entered it, filled the pail with water from the faucet beneath the barn stairs, and returned to the house. He gathered up some rotten pears from the small kitchen table, took them out and flung them under the barn. Finally, he returned with several that had fallen from the tree overnight and placed them on the table.

Crossing to the sink, Andrew washed his hands in preparation for breakfast and entered the dining room. Bridget finished her cooking and opened the dining room door. John Morse, Abby, and Andrew were at the table. The maid placed some cold mutton, mutton soup with potatoes, Johnny cakes, sugar cakes, molasses cookies, and coffee on the table. She returned to the kitchen and closed the dining room door. [The two doors leading from the kitchen to the sitting room and dining room were habitually kept closed. In the Victorian era, the smoke from the stove wood and coal would dirty the wallpaper and furnishings. The closed-door also helped to trap the heat in the kitchen during the summer months.]

Kitchen doors looking toward sitting room (on left) and dining room (on right). Andrew would hang his dressing coat on a nail behind the open door on the left. Photo by Ron Bueker.

Bridget began tidying the kitchen and folding the clothes that hung on the clothes horse from the day before. She separated the clean clothes into two piles—one for Abby and Andrew, and one for Lizzie. The heat in the kitchen felt suffocating, as the temperature outside climbed to 66 degrees, with high humidity as a chaser.

Dining Room at Lizzie Borden House. The kitchen door is at the top, the open door to the right leads to the sitting room. Andrew's dining chair is top right. In 1892, a lounge chair was where the sideboard is now in the photo.
Photo by Frank Grace (Trig Photography)

Abby rang the bell and asked for more coffee. As Bridget poured their cups, Abby asked her, "Do you have anything, in particular, to do today, Bridget?"

Bridget swallowed, knowing what was coming next. "No, marm," she said.

"Well, I would like you to wash the windows, please."

"How?" Bridget asked, hoping Mrs. Borden would want only the inside windows, as it was already hot and humid. Her hopes were dashed, when her employer said, "Inside and out."

Bridget walked to the kitchen and placed the coffee pot on the stove. Abby rang the bell in the dining room at 7:30, signaling Bridget they had finished eating. The three adjourned to the sitting room. Bridget carried in her own plate of white ware, and sat in Andrew's chair, as it was closest to the kitchen door. She pushed his plate aside and placed some Johnny cakes and cold mutton onto her own. She could hear the three of them talking in the sitting room next door, although their tones were low.

Bridget finished her meal and took the dishes into the kitchen. She poured hot water from the kettle into the zinc-lined recess, added soap flakes, and placed the dishes into the sudsy water. She went about cleaning the kitchen, delaying the trip outside to wash the windows.

The front entry with coat tree. The sitting room can be seen at the back. The dress is a period piece. Photo by Frank Grace (Trig Photography)

Meanwhile, in the sitting room, Andrew and John talked, while Abby popped in and out, dusting and straightening. John had asked her first thing how she was feeling, and she answered him, "a good deal better." Andrew was still moving rather tenderly, his face wane and drawn. At 8:30, Abby headed into the front entry, feather duster in hand. John and Andrew spoke for another fifteen minutes. At 8:45, John retrieved his hat from the hall tree, just on the other side of the sitting room door, inside the front entry. Andrew walked him to the back-kitchen door.

John testified that he saw Bridget in the kitchen as he and Andrew walked to the back screen door. They stepped outside and talked for a moment. Bridget did not hear what they said. Suddenly, Andrew called out, "Come back to dinner, John!" Andrew then entered the house and went into the sitting room to get the key to his room. He then "cleaned his teeth in the sink." Filling a large basin with water, he carried it up the back stairs to his bedroom.

Bridget continued to wash dishes. It was only moments after John left that Lizzie suddenly entered the kitchen from the sitting room.

"What will you have for breakfast, Miss Lizzie?" Bridget asked, her wrists buried in the hot water.

"I'm not very hungry," Lizzie replied. "Maybe just some coffee and a cookie." Lizzie took a cup and was pouring herself some coffee at the head of the kitchen table that stood in the center of the room.

Bridget's breakfast suddenly rebelled. The nausea she had been fighting for the past hour, took over. She made a dash for the screen door and raced to the back fence, where she placed a hand on the rough boards, bent over and threw up.

Andrew came downstairs, adjusting his thin lariat tie. Lizzie was seated in the big overstuffed chair near the south kitchen window. She asked if he would mail a letter for her. He took it from her, but said he "may not make it to the Post Office this morning." The simple statement underscored Lizzie's feelings of betrayal—the signing of the deed was taking up his time that morning. He could not do the small favor of mailing her letter.

Back kitchen entry. The side door is straight ahead. Immediately to its left is the railing for the stairs leading up to Andrew's room and the attic. Bridget's hat, shawl, and apron hung on the pegs. The door to the cellar can be seen at the far left in the foreground. The door to the sink room would have been immediately to the right of the back door. It is no longer there. Photo by Ron Bueker.

Lizzie watched him enter the sitting room and heard the soft *clink* as he returned his bedroom key to the mantle. The daylight burglary of Abby's things had been over a year ago, yet he insisted on placing the key to their locked room where she could see it. She felt the anger rise in her, along with the panic—her companion for most of the past two weeks.

Andrew sat for a moment in the sitting room, glancing at the *Providence Journal*, until the clock chimed 9:00. Just then, the front doorbell shrilled near Lizzie's head in the kitchen. She jumped.

Lizzie stepped to the open sitting room entrance and watched her father's back as he walked to the front door. Every nerve fiber in her was tingling. They are going through with it! She had hoped against hope her father would change his mind. That he would remember how much he loved her, and their wonderful times together at the farm. Surely, he would not give away her inheritance! But when Andrew opened the door, and she saw a young man standing there holding out a note, her faith came crashing to the ground.

"I have a note for Mrs. Borden," the youth said, in a rather nervous voice. "It's from a sick friend of hers."

Andrew thanked him, pressed a coin into the lad's hand, and shut the door. Abby came down, hearing the bell from upstairs. Andrew handed her the note. He came into the kitchen and hung his dressing coat on the nail behind the door, and put on his Prince Albert from the dining room. Lizzie was not in the kitchen chair. He thought he heard her in the cellar, as he walked down the kitchen entry to the back screen door, and stepped out.

As he was about to descend the steps to the side yard and make his way to the north gate fronting Second Street, he heard a noise from the back yard. He stepped down the four stairs and looked around the jog by the barn. Bridget was throwing up near the pear tree. He hesitated for a moment, feeling too awkward to assist her, and turned back toward the side steps. A thought stopped him. *Now Bridget's sick.* Was there really someone trying to poison them? With unsteady steps, he walked toward the gate.

[Mrs. Churchill testified that she saw Andrew Borden standing by the side steps of his home, near the barn, a little after 9:00 on the morning of the murders. She said, "He stood at the east side of the back steps [closest to the barn] …he was standing at the steps…as if he was coming around the steps…I finally saw him heading toward the street."]

Abby stood in the front entry holding a feather duster in her hand. The note shook slightly in her hands. She was alone here with this deception now. Andrew was gone. Bridget would be outside soon, out of earshot if Lizzie should go into one of her black moods. She had been nervous from the beginning about the whole thing. Look what happened over the small house on Fourth Street Andrew had helped her with. The girls had been furious…alienating themselves from her. Lizzie even stopped calling her "Mother," after all those years. Her relatives would not even visit her at the house, as the tension was so severe, and the girls snubbed any of her guests. *What was she doing?*

Side yard steps to back kitchen entry door today at the Lizzie Borden B&B. Bridget would have been roughly where the car is pictured, at the back fence near a pear tree "being sick." Photo by Ron Bueker.

Lizzie emptied her slop pail in the cellar, just as Andrew stepped onto the sidewalk to head downtown. She heard her step-mother's heavy footsteps as she walked through the dining room. Abby entered the kitchen, with the feather duster in her hand. She laid the duster on the kitchen work table. She then scooped up the pile of clean clothes Bridget had folded for her and Andrew and headed up to their room. A few minutes later, she came down with fresh towels and pillow shams for the guest room. Picking up the feather duster, she entered the dining room. Laying the shams and towels on the sofa, she began dusting the bric-a-brac and furnishings of the room.

Lizzie came up from the cellar and set her slop pail down in the kitchen. She stepped into the dining room where Abby was dusting, closing the kitchen door behind her. Abby seemed nervous to see her.

Bridget entered the back entry. She had been out back sick to her stomach for almost fifteen minutes. While the emptying of her breakfast had helped, her head had a pounding feeling, and her throat hurt. She stepped over to the sink and finished the last few breakfast dishes. The murmur of two voices came from the dining room. She recognized Abby's, the rising inflection sounding as if she was asking Lizzie questions. Lizzie answered in a civil tone, although Bridget could not make out the words.

"Are you feeling better?" Abby asked Lizzie, as they stood awkwardly, face-to-face in the dining room.

"It's better, thank you," Lizzie said.

Abby's nerves were showing as she suddenly blurted out that she had received a note from a sick friend this morning, and would be going out soon. "I just need to put the pillow shams on the guest bed. The room is all done, so you needn't worry about it," she said, hoping to win Lizzie's good will, on this morning, most of all. It was usually Emma and Lizzie's chore to clean the guest room unless the guest was Abby's, which was not often. With Emma gone, Abby was sure Lizzie would resent cleaning the room. She did not want to provoke her this morning.

Lizzie studied her, enjoying the effect she was having on the nervous woman. Abby was not a good liar, and it showed. Her face was effused with color, and she twisted the feather duster's handle in her hands. Lizzie played with the idea of tormenting the woman by prolonging her agony with questions such as "Who is sick?" "Who is picking you up?" Instead, she merely walked into the sitting room and sat down, waiting for Abby's next move…and Bridget's.

Just as Lizzie sat down, she heard the dining room door open from the kitchen, Bridget entered, with a flurry of clashing dishes. The maid began laying out the clean whiteware on the table, in readiness for dinner. Abby may have spoken to her again about the windows, not realizing the girl had been out back throwing up. Bridget finished laying the table and crossed to the kitchen door. She looked back to see Abby dusting the door frame between the sitting room and dining room. Bridget would never see her alive again.

Lizzie's Conversation with Abby

According to Lizzie's Inquest testimony, Abby said the following during their brief conversation in the dining room:

Lizzie: "She asked me how I felt. I told her. She asked me what I wanted for dinner. I told her not anything, what kind of meat I wanted for dinner. I told her not any. She said she had been up and made the spare room, and was going to take up some linen pillow cases for the small pillows at the foot, and the room was done. She says: "I have had a note from somebody that is sick and I am going out, and I will get dinner at the same time." I think she said something about the weather, I don't know. She also asked me if I would direct some paper wrappers for her, which I did."

Problems with this story:

1) Abby has already told Bridget that morning to warm over the mutton soup for dinner, and serve the cold mutton, as well. She would not have asked Lizzie what she wanted for dinner [lunch].

2) Directing [addressing] the paper wrappers was Lizzie's way of introducing the idea of the *Providence Journal* "white" wrapper, hoping the police would believe that's what Andrew had in his hand that afternoon when he returned home, and it was the newspaper that was burned in the stove (not a farm deed), should someone see the burned remains.

Twenty-to-thirty minutes later, with a heavy heart, Bridget walked down the cellar steps to get the pail. She would have to wash the windows. Lizzie now made her move. She grabbed the key from the sitting room mantle, eased open the door to the kitchen, and hurried to the back stairs.

Abby had finished her dusting, and entered the kitchen from the dining room, just as Lizzie's skirts disappeared around the corner of the back stairway. Abby returned the feather duster to the closet near the kitchen stove where the cleaning things were kept. She took a large, blue, silk handkerchief from the rag box; it had been Andrew's. She walked into the sitting room. Picking up the clean pillow shams, and guest towels, she started for the front stairs and the room John Morse had vacated.

Bridget came up from the cellar with the pail. She crossed to the closet Abby had just closed, and took down a brush for the windows.

1890s kitchen sink with running "city water." Typically, the sinks were zinc. Note the large basin, such as the one Andrew filled and took to his room the morning of the murders. Photo courtesy unknown.

Where Was the Sink?

During trial testimony, Officer Doherty, who was the second policeman to arrive, said he "saw Bridget standing by the *sink* in the southeast corner of the kitchen." That would put her at the opposite end from the "sink room" by the back door. The new "City Water" plumbing in the kitchen was directly above the sink in the wash room below in the cellar. The old sink room by the back door probably still had an old pump handle and was no longer used, as the well had been filled in when the new plumbing was put in. The sink room housed the ice box, and it drained into the old sink. Bridget called this room "a closet." Due to the room being labeled "sink room" on the trial drawing, many have assumed it was still used as such.

Attorney Knowlton during the Preliminary Hearing: "This back entry way that comes in at the north door, and goes into the kitchen, was a pretty large entry way? Where did you keep the ice chest?"

Bridget: "A closet that goes from the entry, in, and the ice chest sets in there."

Knowlton: "It was in a closet that opens off the entry? You do not have to bring the ice into the kitchen?"

Bridget: "No sir."

Knowlton: "Was there anything else that opened off that entry way but that closet or room where the ice chest was?"

Bridget: "No sir."

Knowlton: "Where is the sink, right opposite the screen door?"

Bridget: "It is the left of the kitchen, next to the back yard."

Knowlton: "That is where the back entry comes out?"

Bridget: "It is way in the back of the kitchen."

Knowlton was describing the sink room as one comes in the back-entry door. But, Bridget says "way in the back of the kitchen." She is telling him it is pretty far away from the back door, in the kitchen area. Not once in her testimony does she call the closet where the ice box goes "the sink room." It is no longer used as a sink, other than to drain the water from the ice box. She says Mr. Borden "washed up at the kitchen sink," and "brushed his teeth in the kitchen sink." We will see Emma standing at this sink the Sunday after the murders.

Lizzie unlocked Andrew and Abby's door with the mantle key. She hurried to the door that separated her room from theirs and slid back the bolt, leaving it touching just enough so someone glancing that way would not notice it was open. Hurriedly, she left the room, relocking their bedroom door to the second-floor landing. She reached the bottom of the stairs just as Bridget stepped out onto the side steps, carrying her pail and brush. The servant had just gone through the sitting room and dining room, closing the windows. Lizzie had not been there. Yet, she appears within seconds at the back door.

"Are you going to wash the windows?" Lizzie asked, unnecessarily. Thursday was window washing day, and Bridget was standing there with a pail and brush.

"Yes," Bridget said. "You've no need to lock the screen door. I will be around here. You may lock it if you want to. I will get clean water in the barn."

Bridget may have hoped Lizzie would take pity on her. Although the temperature was around 74 degrees, the humidity was suffocating. Her head was pounding, and with each step she took, her stomach sloshed like a ship listing to the leeward side. *Lizzie had to have seen me out back throwing up,* Bridget thought, *the girl was right there in the kitchen when I ran out of the door.* But if she hoped for a reprieve, there was none forthcoming. As Bridget headed to the barn for the pole that attached to the brush, she looked back at the screen door. Lizzie was gone.

Chapter Eleven
Thursday, August 4, 1892
The Stage Is Set

As the August sun beat down on the "Spindle City," none of its inhabitants could have known, that by the time the City Hall bell struck 11 o'clock, an act, so brazen and heinous that it would make national headlines, would occur inside a modest home in the heart of the city. Nor, did they realize the name Fall River would forever become irrevocably connected to the name of Lizzie Borden, and the murders at 92 Second Street.

Andrew Borden spent his last two hours on the planet, going about his typical routine. *The Fall River Herald* said he stopped into Pierre LeDuc's for a morning shave around 9:30 a.m. The police never interviewed the barber or verified this. We do have at least thirty minutes of missing time concerning Andrew's whereabouts after Mrs. Churchill saw him "standing near the steps" by his back door at 9:05, and his arrival at his first place of business around 9:35. Had he met up with someone concerning the clandestine transaction about to occur? As we will see, his missing time, and one other's collide.

Andrew Borden walked into the Union Savings Bank at No.3 Market Square "about half-past nine" Thursday morning, according to Officer Medley. Mr. Borden spoke to Mr. Abram G. Hart, Treasurer, and explained to him the reason he had missed the Wednesday meeting of the Board of Directors was because he had been ill. Mr. Hart said he remained "but a few minutes—not more than five," and went north from the bank. He was alone when he came and went away from the Bank. "He did not look strong," Mr. Hart said during his Preliminary Hearing testimony. "He was in after that [his first visit of 9:30], but I was out. I know he was in, by the word that came to me."

John T. Burrell, a cashier at the National Union Bank, testified that Mr. Borden came into the bank "between quarter past nine and quarter to ten, but I would not swear to that." He stayed "from five to ten minutes. I saw him talking to two gentlemen, and Mr. Hart in front of my end of the room." Attorney Knowlton asked him if he was in the same building as Mr. Hart. Mr. Burrell answered, "Yes, sir." Mr. Burrell, when originally interviewed by Officer Medley before the Hearing, stated, "Andrew J. Borden came into the Bank, as near as we can place the time, **about ten o'clock**. He went to the rear of the Bank, and looked in the rooms, probably for Mr. Hart; and finding no one, went out, remarking something about calling again. He did not call again. He was alone."

Everett Cook was the cashier for the First National Bank. Andrew Borden was a director for the Trust Company affiliated with that bank. Mr. Cook testified that Mr. Borden "entered the bank at quarter of ten, and went away at five minutes of ten." He told Officer Medley that Mr. Borden "deposited a check which was made payable to him by Troy Mills. While making the deposit, Mr. William Carr came in. They talked together a few minutes, and Mr. Borden left the bank. He was here not more than ten minutes. While he was here, I noticed that he looked tired and sick; knowing him so well, I could not help noticing he looked real sick. I did not speak to him about it because I thought he might consider it none of my business. He was alone when he came and went away from the bank."

First National Bank today, in Fall River, Ma.
Photo courtesy of Shelley Dziedzic.

Andrew's Thursday Morning Timeline:

1) He leaves home at 9:05.
2) He may have been shaved at LeDuc's *around* 9:30, a barber whose shop is within steps of the banks.
3) He enters Union Savings Bank *around* 9:30 and stays "not more than five minutes."
4) He enters National Union Bank "between 9:15 and 9:45." It is probable he was there closer to 9:40.
5) He enters First National Bank at" 9:45 and leaves at 9:55."

6)We are missing time between 9:05 – 9:20+.

7) Edith Francis, clerk for Charles C. Cook (Andrew's property manager) sees Andrew "in Mr. Borden's Block on South Main Street going south on the east side of the street, shortly after **10 o'clock**. He was alone."

8) Jonathan Clegg, Gent's Furnisher at No. 6 North Main, states Andrew was in his store to discuss his lease of the new store on South Main at **10:20**. He left at 10:29 to go to that store.

9) Joseph Shortsleeves and James Mather, carpenters, saw Andrew at his store at 92 South Main. He went upstairs for a few minutes, came down, picked up an old Yale lock laying on "a window stool," and left between "**10:30 and 10:45**," heading south toward Spring Street. The lock was in his hand.

10) Mary Gallagher, at McManus, saw Mr. Borden at the corner of Main and Spring streets, just turning up Spring, with "a small package in his hand."

11) Lizzie Gray, at the corner of Spring and Second, says she saw Andrew Borden, carrying "a small white package" and coming toward her along Spring Street. He turned north on Second Street. It was "between **10 and 11 o'clock**."

Andrew's Thursday Morning Timeline (continued):

12) Caroline Kelly left her house for a dentist appointment at **10:35** and saw Andrew coming around from the north side of his house, carrying "a small white package, about 5" long and 1" high." He climbed the steps to his front door and was putting his key into the lock when Mrs. Kelly went past him. [Between the time Andrew leaves the South Main store with the lock in his hand, and turns onto Spring within 2 minutes, he has a "small white package." He may have wrapped the rusty lock in a used newspaper wrapper from his pocket.]

13) Bridget Sullivan heard someone trying to get in the front door at 10:35-10:45. She unlocked three locks and admitted Andrew J. Borden into his home.

14) **We have missing time from 10:00-10:20.**

Andrew entered Union Savings, which shares a lobby with National Union, at 9:30. He spoke to Mr. Hart and two gentlemen, which was witnessed by Mr. Burrell of National Union. He stayed "5-10 minutes."

He enters First National at 9:45 and leaves at 9:50.

Andrew *returns* to Union Savings & National Union Banks at 10:00. He looks in the back rooms for someone, and finding no one, leaves and says *he may return.*

We will see that 10:00 was the designated time for a driver to deliver Abby Borden to the National Union Bank. She did not appear. Andrew checks the rooms for her and finally leaves. He is seen at 10:00 heading south toward Spring Street, which would carry him home. He is not seen again until 10:20 by Johnathan Clegg. Did Andrew stop somewhere and call John Morse at the Emery house, where John was "stopping" that morning, to ask him why Abby has not been delivered? John may have said he would find out.

Andrew continues on to his store at 92 South Main, the same number as his house on Second Street and only one street over. He climbs the stairs at the store to the second story. There is a lot across the street from his house, that is nothing but trees. Could he see his house out the east window from the second floor of his store?

Andrew's Thursday Morning Timeline (continued):

Was he looking to see if a buggy is still parked there? Did he call John again from a phone in an upstairs office?

The missing time from **9:05 – 9:20**, or so, that morning, may be a clandestine meeting with John Morse at Charles Cook's office to look over the Upper Swansea Farm with James Chatterton as overseer, and John running it. Now, all that's left is to bring Abby to National Union Bank at 10:00, to put the Lower Farm (Old Ladie's Home) and Upper Farm (cattle business) into her name. Notice John's testimony about his whereabouts that morning, next.

John Mathers testified that Andrew picked up an old, broken Yale shop lock. The above photo is a 1890s Yale shop lock. It measures 5" wide and is 1" tall, the same description Mrs. Kelly gave of the "small white package" Andrew had in his hand as he was coming around the corner of his house at 10:35, Thursday morning. If it was "old and broken" it was probably rusty.

John Morse's Timeline

John Morse left the Borden house at 8:45 on the morning of August 4, 1892. He spoke with Andrew for a few moments in the side yard, and then started away, Andrew calling after him, "Come back to dinner, John!"

According to John's words to Officer Fleet on the afternoon of the murders, this was where he went when he left the house:

"Leaving Mr. Borden at the door, went to the Post Office, wrote a letter from there, went as far as Third Street on Bedford, from Third to Pleasant Street, through Pleasant Street to No. 4 Weybosset Street, arriving there about 9:30 a.m. Saw relatives from the West. Remained at the house from 9:30 to 11:20 a.m., or thereabouts. Left, taking a horse car, and stopped at the corner of Pleasant and Second Streets, and to Mr. Borden's house at, or near twelve o'clock. Saw a number of persons around the house, and was told Mr. and Mrs. Borden was killed. That was the first I knew of their deaths." [Officer Medley stated that John Morse told Reporter [Edwin] Porter of the *Daily Globe* that the first he knew of it [the murders] was when he was telephoned for [at the Emery's]. Morse also told the *New York Herald*, August 7, 1892, that he went to the Post Office, and "*several other places* about town, and finally to Daniel Emery's." [Italics are the Author's.]

During John Morse's Preliminary Hearing testimony, two weeks after the murders, his story is improved upon:

Morse (during his time with Andrew in the sitting room that morning before he left for the Emery's): "We talked about some cattle I had. He [Andrew] was telling me the night before, up at Emery's I had a nephew and niece from the West, and he told me where they lived, and wanted me to go and see them. Then I went away. I came to the Post Office and got a car. I wrote a postal, and went up Bedford Street to Third Street, and went from there to Pleasant Street, and up to Weybosset Street, No. 4, Dan Emery's."

Attorney Knowlton: "Did you see relatives you went there to see?"

Morse: "I saw one; the young man was out. I did not see him."

Knowlton: "What was the young lady's name?"

Morse: "Annie Morse; she was indisposed while I was there, she was on the lounge part of the time. She is my brother's daughter."

Knowlton: "Did they ask you to stay to dinner?"

Morse: "Yes sir. I told them I had another engagement."

Knowlton: "That engagement was to dine with your brother [Andrew]?"

Morse: "Yes, sir."

Knowlton: "Did you walk up?"

Morse: "No, sir. Came on the street car...got off at Second and walked up."

Knowlton: "When was the first you heard that Mr. Borden was killed?"

Morse: "When I went into the door. I went around, before I went into the house, to a pear tree to get a couple of pears. When I came back, the servant girl met me at the door, and asked if I had heard the news. I said no. She said Mr. and Mrs. Borden were both murdered. A man named Sawyer stood there at the time."

Knowlton: Were there people out in the street?"

Morse: "I did not see them when I went in."

Knowlton: "You did not see any excitement in the yard or the street?" [By noon, it was reported 400-500 people were in front of the house; many running around the yard and going into the barn.]

Morse: "Nothing to attract my attention at all."

Officer Medley, "to prove the truth or falsity" of Mr. Morse's statements, went to the home of Mr. Emery at No. 4 Weybosset Street, about a mile from the Borden's home. He spoke with Mrs. Emery. "She said Mr. Morse did come there at 9:40, and left there at 11:20, or thereabouts; that he *did meet his nephew* and niece. She also said Mr. Morse had not been to her house before in several years. She asked him to remain to dinner, but he declined, saying something about going to New Bedford, to which place they understood he was going after leaving the house. He left by the front door, but she does not know whether or not he took a streetcar."

In 1892, Fall River offered both horse cars (left) and electric streetcars (right).

Daniel Emery's home at #4 Weybosset Street today. This is where John claims to have spent the morning of the murders. Photo by Ron Bueker.

The *Fall River Herald* reported Officer Medley's interview with Mrs. Emery as well. A few other details are relayed. Mrs. Emery: "I had several callers that day, one of whom was Mr. Morse." When asked how she fixed the time as 11:20 when Morse left her house, "after some little hesitation, Mrs. Emery said that one of her family was sick and that Dr. Bowen was her physician. 'Dr. Bowen came in just as Mr. Morse left." "Did they meet?" queried the officers. "No, they did not," said Mrs. Emery. The niece entered the room at this time and collaborated the information that Morse left at 11:20, although they originally said 11:30."

John's Thursday Morning Timeline:

1) In John's first report the day of the murders to Officer Fleet, he left the Borden's at 8:45, went to the Post Office (a 5-minute walk), mailed a letter, and walked to the Emery's, arriving at 9:30. That means it took him at least 40 minutes (after walking to P.O., writing a letter and mailing it) to walk one mile; a distance that would typically take about 15-20 minutes.

2) In Morse's Preliminary Hearing testimony, he says he did not see his nephew (William Morse) at the Emery's. Mrs. Emery tells Officer Medley, Morse did see both the nephew and niece.

3) Morse testifies the first he heard of the murders was when he arrived at the house and Bridget told him Abby and Andrew were dead. He told Edwin Porter of the *Fall River Daily Globe*, he first heard of it when he was telephoned for. Dr. Bowen, who had just come from covering Andrew's bloody body with a sheet at 11:30, passed John as he was leaving the Emery's.

We have unverified time from 8:45-9:30.

4) John first tells Assistant Marshall Fleet, the day of the murders, he saw "a number of persons around the house when he arrived "at, or around 12 o'clock," a time when the crowds swelled to 500 people, and the police were pushing them back from the yard. He changes his story during subsequent questioning, saying he arrived earlier, closer to 11:45 or so, in order to get there before the crowds did. It would be tough for him to explain why a man seeing hundreds of people, talking about murder, in front of the Borden house, would nonchalantly go to the back yard, lean against the barn and eat three pears. Morse already knew about the murders. Why? Because Dr. Bowen called him at the Emery's to tell him Andrew was dead.

There was a brief, 4-or-5 minutes, after the discovery of Andrew's body, that Dr. Bowen and Lizzie were alone. It was when Mrs. Churchill and Bridget went up to Abby's dressing room to get a sheet to cover Mr. Borden's body. Lizzie could have asked her friend, Dr. Bowen, to get hold of John Morse quickly, and tell him her father is dead. She tells Bowen where John is…the Emery's on Weybosset…something she could only have known if she was eavesdropping on their sitting room conversations. [Morse testified Andrew told him the relatives from Minnesota were staying at the Emery's at #4 Weybosset, as they sat in the sitting room the night before the murders.] When Bridget and Mrs. Churchill return with the sheet, Lizzie simply asks Dr. Bowen to please telegraph her sister Emma, without relaying the bloody details. Bowen leaves, going first to his house where he says he was checking train schedules for Emma, when he was actually calling John at the Emery's. He then runs to telegraph Emma (stamped 11:32) and races in his buggy a short mile to the Emery's, to talk with John.

5) John has the same missing time slot as Andrew: roughly from 9:00 to 9:30, when John admits he also ran "several errands around town." Did they meet up to finalize the plan for the Upper Farm deed?

6) John's nephew William Morse is 16-years-old, from Minnesota, and staying at the Emery's with his sister for a visit. This is the messenger that arrives at Andrew's door at 9:00 that morning, with a note from a "sick friend" for Abby.

Lizzie mentions "a boy brought the note," as she saw him when Andrew opened the door. This is a relative she is unfamiliar with. Annie Morse, the niece said she hadn't seen

Uncle John for over five years, before he picked her up in Warren three weeks prior to the murders. The messenger is why John distances himself from the nephew, saying the boy wasn't home at the Emery's, and he only saw the niece, while Mrs. Emery says he saw them both.

7) Mrs. Emery says something strange when asked if John Morse was there that morning. She says, "I had several callers, one of whom was Mr. Morse." Why volunteer she had several callers? In an effort to give herself an alibi that she was too busy to keep tabs on John, in case her timeline she gave of him is found in error, or he was out, and seen, during the time he was supposed to be visiting her? The Author believes she had "several callers." Two of whom were Jim and Joseph Chatterton, waiting for John to give Joseph the signal to go and pick up Abby at 10:00 for the deed transfer. Joseph is someone Lizzie will not recognize as he is from the New York City branch of the family. Jim "baseball shoes" Chatterton will be the new overseer at the Swansea farm.

8) John tells Mrs. Emery he is headed back to New Bedford when he leaves her, which was probably the plan. He mentions in his interview with Fleet that he went to the P.O., and got "a car." His plans were to travel to New Bedford after leaving the Emery's. But when the murders occurred, he had no choice but to return to Andrew's. This was Lizzie's plan when she asked Bowen to hurry and contact John. She needed to catch him before he could leave town and establish an alibi. This was her bargaining chip.

9) The Author believes Morse left the Borden house at 8:45, and walked to the Kirby stable on Rock Street, procuring a horse and buggy. The Chatterton's, meanwhile are arriving at the Emery's on Weybosset. At 9:00, William Morse, John's young nephew, arrives at the Borden's to deliver the note for Abby. He returns to the Emery's. It is shortly after 9. Andrew leaves his house and heads downtown. John takes the buggy and meets Andrew at Charles Cook's office in the AJ Borden building to go over the deeds. He then mails a letter at the P.O. to William Vinnicum, "about some cattle." It is now 9:20. He rides the buggy to Weyboseet. It's 9:30. The lie about walking to the Emery's is to cover the time he is actually downtown with Andrew.

John may also be talking to Howes and Kirby at this time, as the transfer of the horses to the Swansea farm is probably Friday or Saturday. There may have been a business transaction or auction set up for the horses, but it's apparent the deed transfer had to be done then, or they simply would have waited for Lizzie to go to Marion on Monday, and forego the cloak and dagger arrangements they were undertaking. John also told Frank Eddy he "would pick up the two oxen on Saturday. It appears there are some dealings set up for that day, and the transfer of titles is part of it.

John makes sure to notice each street he drives past, so he can foster his alibi that he walked to the Emery's. As he later drove the team back to Kirby's, he made note of the streetcar numbers, passengers, and anything else that would establish his alibi of taking a streetcar to Andrew's. If he *had* taken a car from Weybosset at 11:20, as was stated, why did he arrive at Andrew's "close to 12:00?" This is a 10-minute car ride, and a 4-minute walk up Second Street. It is, however, enough time to return a buggy to Rock Street, talk over business, and walk to Andrew's.

Chapter Twelve
Thursday, August 4, 1892
"She Was Struck 18 Times"

Abby Borden found it difficult to concentrate on what she was doing. Straightening the guest chamber at least gave her nervous energy an outlet. The bed linens, and the shams—that went over the little pillows at the foot of the bed—had been changed. John had lain atop the spread and put his feet, with his dirty socks, on the small pillows at the end of the bed. She replaced three dirty hand towels from the rack near the wash basin, John had used that morning, with fresh ones. She poured his dirty wash water into the slop pail and filled the basin with clean water from the pitcher. She would take the slop pail, along with the soiled towels, to the cellar when she finished here. Then, she would have to hurry and change to her street dress. The driver was picking her up at 10:00. She glanced at the small bedside clock—it was 9:15.

Andrew's large blue handkerchief was put to use polishing the bric-a-brac on the dressing bureau and the large rectangular mirror. The cloth was almost in tatters, but the silk material made the glass shine.

Guest room w/sewing machine & wash basin.
Photography by Frank Grace (Trig Photography)

She next moved to the windows. Bridget's window washing did not include the private chambers; the girls were responsible for their own, and Abby took care of her and Andrew's room. Emma usually kept the guest room clean, as it was used primarily as the sister's sitting room for their friends. It also doubled as the sewing room. A sewing machine sat against the west wall, while a basket of notions rested on the cane chair by the north window. A yardstick was propped up by the machine.

The Guest Room, looking north toward Mrs. Churchill's.
Photography by Frank Grace.

Abby pushed aside the shutters that faced Second Street. Taking one of John's used hand towels, she dipped it in the clean wash water and scrubbed the glass. She repeated this on the other window facing west and then moved to the window overlooking the side yard and Mrs. Churchill's house. When she finished, she added the wet towel to the other two laying on the washstand. Taking Andrew's silk handkerchief, she began to polish the windows facing the street. Her breath was ragged. All the extra work, and the heat of the second floor was taking a toll on her. She felt her extra pounds all the more on these humid summer days. The cheap calico dress clung to her like wet tissue paper.

Lizzie picked up her pile of freshly folded clothes from the kitchen table and started for the stairs. She stopped in the dining room and removed her low tie shoes. She could hear Abby moving about the guest chamber in great thudding steps. As she passed the front door, she checked the three locks. Everything was secure.

Cradling the clothes in both arms, Lizzie climbed the steps in stocking feet. As she reached the curve in the stairs, she looked toward the open door of the guest room. Abby was swiping at the window glass straight ahead of her, near the dressing bureau. *Why was she taking so long?* Lizzie thought angrily. *She was supposed to be in her room, changing to go out.*

Abby didn't hear Lizzie enter her bedroom and lay the clothes on the bed. Voices wafted into Lizzie's room from the open window facing the Kelly house to the south. She walked over to it and pulled back the lace curtain. Bridget was standing at the fence, laughing with Mary Doolan, the Kelly maid. She hasn't even begun to wash the windows, Lizzie thought in a panic. *Her timeline was falling apart!*

It will have to be now, she thought, her heart pounding. She couldn't swallow and her head felt dizzy. She would have to kill her in the guest room, while Bridget was on the opposite side of the house. She couldn't wait anymore. She glanced at her clock. It was 9:30.

She pulled the shiny hatchet from the mattress and placed it between the layers of clean clothes. A linen handkerchief rested on top. Taking several deep gulps of air, she again tried to swallow, panic pushing bile up into her throat until she thought she would vomit. With a final deep breath, she walked out onto the landing and into the guest room.

1890s Shingling Hatchet

A flash of blue swept across the dressing bureau mirror as Lizzie walked quickly across the room in her Bedford cord dress. Abby didn't turn until Lizzie was standing directly behind her.

"I think I have one of your handkerchiefs," Lizzie said, her voice trembling.

Abby was caught off guard. Lizzie was holding out the pile of laundry toward her, careful not to spill the pile of clothes that rested in both hands. Abby hesitated, not recognizing the handkerchief that rested on top of the pile. Lizzie suddenly pulled the hatchet from the clothes, tossing them aside. They fluttered to the ground in a heap near the sewing machine. Before the startled woman could cry out, Lizzie swung the hatchet and caught her stepmother on the left side of her face, near the back, by her ear. The wound hung open like a flap.

Abby's look of shock, as her eyes locked with her attacker's, gave way to mind-numbing pain. She doubled over in an instinctual move to cover herself. A flash of motion came from the second-floor bedroom window of Adelaide Churchill's house, directly across from the Borden's, and a stone's throw from where Lizzie stood. She quickly threw the small half shutters together, in an effort to block the outside view into the room. It was suddenly much darker.

She saw Abby place a hand on the wound, dazed. Lizzie swung the hatchet into the air, her teeth set with hatred. The next two blows hit her stepmother atop her head, leaving small incisions in her scalp. Abby, now in full panic, whirled in a mindless attempt to flee; the only path not blocked by Lizzie was toward the bed. Again, the hatchet fell, this time finding its mark. The blade sliced through the calico and buried into the skin near the nape of Abby's neck, going in a full two inches between her shoulders, leaving a gash 4-inches wide; the entire width of the steel. The flesh spurted, drops hitting the pillow shams on the left side of the bed. Cast-off from the raised hatchet flew through the air, a small drop landing atop Lizzie's white petticoat lying on the floor a few feet away.

Abby hit the floor with a resounding thud. The boards shook beneath Lizzie's feet, as she watched her victim fall face first on the floral Brussel's carpeting. The blue handkerchief flew from Abby's hand, landing near her head. Lizzie paused only a moment, her chest heaving.

The rage she had held inside for five years exploded. It came rushing out in a flurry of attacks. The hatchet swung through the air, sending droplets of blood onto the top of the swollen bureau drawers, the marble base, the mop board and bed frame. Only a few drops shot forward onto the wall before Abby's head. Straddling her enemy, Lizzie bent forward, her stocking feet hidden beneath her ruffled hem, and struck again, and again, at the exposed right side of her stepmother's head, until the blade was hitting brain and bone. She gripped the hatchet in both hands, using shorter strokes, and lost count of the strikes.

Finally, her anger spent, and her forearms tired from wielding the hatchet, Lizzie straightened, trying desperately to catch her breath. A dark blur caught her eye off to her right. There was something long and brown lying on the pure white counterpane. During one of the blows, Abby's fake braid of hair had caught on the blade, and landed on the bedspread.

Abby's braid found on the bedspread of the guest room. This is the original photograph by Charles Carroll. Fall River Historical Society.

She stood, panting. In the soft shadows of the room, she stared down at the motionless form. The copper smell of blood filled the air. Her breathing began to slow. The room came into focus as her head cleared. A strange calm overcame her. She had done it. It was over.

The original plan had been to kill Abby in her bedroom as she changed to go downtown. It was the only certainty Lizzie had awoken with: sometime this morning, before 10 o'clock, Abby would go to her bedroom to change her shabby calico for a street dress. The bolt on the door separating their bedrooms had been pulled back. Everything was ready. But she had taken too long in the guest room—stopping to go down for the note, reminding Bridget about the windows…

Perhaps, this was better, Lizzie thought. There was no locked bedroom door from the landing a madman would have to negotiate, like the one to Abby's room. This looked easier. An open door at the top of the front stair landing; a helpless old lady making a bed, her back turned...

Abby Borden crime scene photo. This is after the police disturbed the bedspread, and moved the bed back into place. What appears to be a man, seated, can be seen at the top, right. James Walsh photograph.

Lizzie crossed to the wash basin and plunged the bloody hatchet into the fresh water. A red stain spread through the bowl. She rubbed it first with her hands, gliding them gently over the sharp blade, and up and down the smooth hickory handle. She picked up one of the wet towels and scrubbed it, careful not to cut herself. The water was now a deep crimson. There was a stubborn puddling of blood at the base of the helm. She would take it to the cellar and use the sink there. She dropped the bloody towel into the slop pail and grabbed another of John's soiled towels.

The smell of death filled the room. It was an odd mixture of bodily fluids and the unmistakable odor of blood. It was nothing like the poor pigeons she had seen beheaded. An odd thought pressed up through the images of violence: Her father was a widower again. She paused to contemplate it. Bridget's laugh from outside rose incongruously through Lizzie's open bedroom window across the hall, bringing her back to reality.

For the first time, Lizzie looked into the oval mirror at a face speckled with blood...Abby's blood. She was surprised to see only a few large drops. She scrubbed at her cheeks, nose, and forehead, and dabbed at the several droplets resting in her brown wavy hair. The back of her hands was covered with blood. She eased them into the crimson basin water and rubbed them. She could not see them beneath the bright red surface. Finally, she took the wet towel to them until they were clean. Her nails were kept short, and the blood beneath their edges came away when she scraped them.

In her reflection, she saw that her bodice was covered with small, tear-drop-sized blood drops. Two or three larger blotches covered the small, dark figure adorning the front. Grabbing the last wet towel, she dipped it into the fresh water in the pitcher, avoiding the bloody wash basin. She rubbed at the crimson spots, at first gently, then with more vigor. Some had soaked into the ribbed weave of the dress, and would not come out. Lizzie held up her skirt and studied it. The old, dull paint stains still rimmed the lower left side of the skirt, but she saw only a few drops of cast-off blood from the hatchet. All-in-all, it was far less blood than she expected. Bending low over the body, and keeping the blows short, had served to keep the blood spatter to a minimum.

She dropped the other two towels into the slop pail and poured the bloody basin water in with them, and then refilled the bowl with clean water from the pitcher.

Small blood-stained towels. Several police officers testified to seeing "small bloody towels," soaking in water in a pail in the cellar. Officer Mullaly pulled them from the pail at one point and laid them on the cellar floor. He was later asked by Dr. Dolan to take them away as evidence.

The morning heat reached in through the half-closed shutters, amplifying the smell coming from the area between the bed and the bureau. Lizzie stepped to the window facing the street, and looked down, looking for Bridget. She drew the still air into her lungs. Her pulse quickened. A cart of pond lilies was standing in front of her house. Mrs. Manley, Alice Russell's sister-in-law, and another woman were looking at the flowers and speaking to the peddler, who Lizzie recognized as Mrs. Manley's nephew. The noise from the street filled the room. A strange thought flashed through her mind. *Life is going on as usual. There goes a drummer, heading for the Daily News office; the Miller's maid is outside cleaning windows, just like every other Thursday; and someone is yelling over at Hall's stables. Nothing has changed, except Mrs. Borden is dead.* She looked down at the street, pregnant with people. *How soon before they all know?*

And then she saw him. There...standing boldly in the gateway of her side yard, was a young man, his arm resting upon the post, waiting. Was he waiting for Abby? He was early. Lizzie ran to her room.

She looked at her clock. It was 9:55. She heard the sound of scraping outside her window and peered out. Bridget was standing in the tall grass, pushing the long pole with the brush attached, along the upper sitting room windows. She had obviously been talking with the Kelly maid for some minutes.

Her thoughts suddenly changed to her father. *He would be home at 11 o'clock to handle business or rest in the sitting room before the noon meal.* She knew her Uncle John was not expected back for it; she had overheard the entire plan last night and this morning. Still, she had made sure the triple locks were bolted on the front door.

She paused for a moment, taking stock. Abby was dead. The farm deed was to be put in her name. Did she really need to kill her father, too? The Swansea deal would not go through now. She and Emma's inheritance were safe. Her father would be 70 next month and the grave would claim him soon enough. She pictured bringing the hatchet blade down onto his head, and she froze. She couldn't do it. Poisoning was different. It gave one distance from the act of murder. But killing someone up close—their eyes looking at you in shocked disbelief as the blows fell—that was terrifying. She had just done it! Now that she knew what it felt like to sink a steel blade into someone's brain, she could not reach a place in her mind where she could do that to a man she had loved so much...until *she* came along and manipulated him into taking money away from his own daughters.

A thought suddenly struck her. *When Abby doesn't show up at the bank this morning, her father will come looking for her!* She didn't have as much time as she hoped.

Now, the thoughts came flooding into her mind, as once again, she had to change directions. If she wasn't going to kill her father, what would she do with the blood-stained dress? She could try and burn it in the stove, but Bridget could enter and smell it. A burned dress with a body upstairs might look suspicious. Her thoughts raced. She would stick to her plan. She would slip the new dress over it, convince Bridget to go on some errands with her, and by the time her father came home, they would both have an alibi of being downtown when a maniac entered and killed Abby. She would remove the Bedford cord dress somewhere while they were out, and dispose of it. *That would work!*

Lizzie ran to the dress closet at the end of the hall, unlocked it, and selected the new, light blue, calico pigeon blouse waist and skirt she had made in New Bedford the week before. It was her longest dress, with a loose bodice, and inexpensive; one she wouldn't care about damp blood getting on it from inside. Hurrying back to her room, she tried shoving her arms into the sleeves of the calico blouse waist. The large mutton sleeves of the Bedford cord bunched into the tight fabric and refused to budge.

Lizzie tugged on the sleeves, trying to force the outer blouse to cover the other. As she pulled on the tight forearms, a button loop snapped. Angrily, she pulled off the blue calico and struggled with an answer. The sleeves of the Bedford cord would have to go.

Without a thought, as to the woman lying on the floor in a pool of blood, Lizzie dashed into the guest room and picked up the sewing box from the cane chair, a mere three feet from Abby's shoes. She hurried back to her room and removed the Bedford cord blouse. Taking scissors from the sewing box, she cut away the voluminous sleeves of the old dress. Sitting on the lounge, she hurriedly basted the small button loop on the calico back into place.

[During Lizzie's only testimony, at the Coroner's Inquest, she stated: "I had only been upstairs just long enough to take the clothes up and baste the little loop on the sleeve."]

She put the Bedford cord blouse back on—sleeveless this time—and hooked the front. Standing, she pulled the light blue dress with the dark figure over the old blouse and hooked it as well. It was a tight fit. The area around the waist bulged slightly; she unhooked the bottom of the top blouse to give it some space.

Lizzie stepped into the calico skirt and pulled it up over the stained one. While hooking it in the back, she looked down in dismay. The narrow ruffle of the Bedford cord showed. She sat on the lounge, and taking the scissors, cut away the ruffle at the seam; half-cutting, and half-tearing it, as she hurried to finish.

[Mrs. Raymond, the dressmaker stated in her testimony that the Bedford cord "was two inches longer than her [Lizzie's] other dresses." She also said its large sleeves would not fit beneath another dress.]

She looked about her for a place to hide the sleeves and ruffle scraps. Emma's room! *If she needed to, she could lock that door and say Emma locked it when she left! Perfect!* [Officers Doherty and Mullaly found Emma's door open on their first pass through the house. It was found locked later that day.]

Lizzie entered her sister's room and opened her small closet door. There were some spare pillows and a blanket on the shelf. Taking down a small pillow, Lizzie stuffed the fabric scraps into the sham and replaced it on the shelf. She closed Emma's bedroom door.

Emma's room, looking northwest toward the guest room wall.
Photo by the Author.

She would need to get rid of the hatchet. It must look like the murderer lost it during his escape. The hatchet could not be traced back to her. It was new and had been purchased from a man with no ties to her. Knowing Alfred, the Swede from the farm would detect a hatchet missing from the cellar, buying a new one had been her only choice.

Lizzie had selected the perfect place to put the hatchet; one in plain view, and yet where it might be picked up and carried away. She looked out her window toward the southeast. She could see the foreign-looking man sawing wood just on the other side of her fence in Crowe's yard. She could also see the woodpile where a hatchet would not look out of place. Whether the police found it and connected it to an escaping murderer, or the woodman happened upon it and happily took a brand-new hatchet home with him, her purpose would have been served. It was away from her.

Lizzie's bedroom. Her two windows faced south toward the Kelly house next door. Photo by Ron Bueker.

She glanced down at the side of the yard. Bridget had moved to the other side of the house.

The view from Lizzie's bedroom window looking south at the Kelly house. Crowe's barn was to the left. Photo by the Author.

Chapter Thirteen

Thursday, August 4, 1892
Timing

At 9:45 Thursday morning, while Lizzie was cleaning Abby's blood from her body and dress, Joseph Chatterton arrived at the Borden house to pick up Andrew Borden's wife and deliver her to the National Union Bank on North Main Street. He was early, in case she was waiting out front. He parked his buggy down a way, between the Borden and Kelly houses. The day was hot and muggy. He eyed the shade of one of the two large oak trees standing like sentinels before the Borden house. After several minutes, he got out of the buggy and planted himself beneath the north tree, nearer to Mrs. Churchill's home. The sidewalk was busy, so he stepped up onto the stoop of the north gate of the Borden property, and leaned his arm against the fence post.

Mrs. Delia S. Manley and her friend, Mrs. Hart, were walking along Second Street at 9:45 a.m. They stopped to look at a cart with pond lilies for sale, standing between Mrs. Churchill's house and the Borden's. As Mrs. Manley stepped back up onto the sidewalk, she came face-to-face with a young man standing on the stoop of the north gate of the Borden house. She described him during trial testimony as "young...about thirty...wearing light gray clothes. He was "standing in the north gateway, leaning his arm on the gatepost...that gatepost is higher than this [pointing to a photograph of the Borden house], and that is the one he was resting his arm on...He seemed to be looking at us, taking in what we were talking about, I should judge."

Borden house, facing east. The gate post closest to the tree is taller than the other three. It is directly beneath the guest room windows on the second floor (windows are middle and at far left, second floor. There is also a window on the north side. The window next to that is Emma's room. Photo by Charles Carrol.

If Mrs. Manley had looked up at the house, she might have seen Lizzie Borden looking down at them, only moments after washing Abby's blood from her hands. [During the Preliminary Hearing, Officer Mullaly was asked by Lizzie's Attorney, Mr. Adams: "When Miss Lizzie said something about seeing a man around there [that morning], did not she say she saw a man under the tree, or something like that, by the front fence?" Mullaly: "I do not remember just what she did say." Adams: "You would not say; she did not say in substance something like that?" Mullaly: "No, sir, I could not." Officer Mullaly's Witness Statement, a statement that was required and turned in by every officer involved in the Borden murder case, is mysteriously missing from the reports. We hear of Lizzie seeing a man under a tree by the front fence only in the Preliminary Hearing.]

Dr. Handy's "Wild-Eyed Man"

Lizzie stepped into the guest room and took one last look at Abby's prone body. She had not moved. She would not move again. The metallic smell of blood was dissipating, as the pool beneath her head soaked into the carpet. Crossing to the washstand, Lizzie checked that all was in order. She picked up the hatchet and the pail of bloody towels. Glancing back at the room, she walked out, leaving the door open. She looked into her room. It too was in order. She suddenly thought of the 4-foot-long pipe, lying beneath her bed. She would no longer need to eavesdrop on her stepmother and father's conversations through her secret hole in the fireplace. A metal plumber's pipe could be misconstrued into a weapon with which to beat someone over the head. She grabbed it.

The sun beat down on Bridget Sullivan as she continued washing the windows. It was 10:00 and her dress stuck to her, perspiration matting her thick hair to the back of her neck. Mary Doolan, the Kelly's maid was also going about, washing the windows. It was Thursday. Maids all throughout Fall River were on ladders or struggling with long poles, brushes, and pails.

Lizzie knew Bridget's window washing schedule by heart. She always started with the sitting room windows on the south side, moving around to the west to the parlor windows near the front door, and finally the one parlor window and two dining room windows on the north, across from Mrs. Churchill's. She would wash them first with the brush, and then go around again, in the same order, throwing water up on them with a dipper.

[George Petty said he saw Bridget washing windows at 10:00. Mrs. Churchill stated she saw Bridget "throwing water on the parlor window with a dipper that morning...the parlor window closest to my house [north side] between 10 and 10:30."]

Bridget stood on the ground, reaching up with the long pole, washing the parlor window next to the front door. The front of her dress was wet, from wash water and sweat. She did not notice the young man who had, only moments before, been leaning on the Borden gate post, become nervous of her presence, and walk across the street.

Joseph Chatterton watched the front door of the Borden's expectantly. The City Hall clock had struck 10 o'clock only moments before. His shirt was damp in the heat and humidity. He watched the maid across from him pick up her pail, a long pole pressed beneath her armpit, and circle around to the north side of the house.

Lizzie Borden watched Bridget's movements as well from the cellar. She could see the maid's feet through the small cellar windows as she moved from window to window, and went to the barn for fresh water. She was almost finished with the first part of the work. It would take her only fifteen-to-twenty minutes to finish up the rinsing with the dipper.

Cellar windows running around the stone foundation of the Lizzie Borden House. Windows on the first floor are (left to right) shuttered window by front staircase, two sitting rooms windows, two kitchen windows. Second floor (left to right) stair window, two windows in Lizzie's room, and two in Andrew and Abby's room. Photo by Ron Bueker.

Lizzie filled the cellar sink with cold water. She grabbed Bridget's bar of lye soap and scrubbed the new hatchet along its edge. The gold gilt emblem from the manufacturer remained intact at the hatchet's center. The place beneath the blade, where it met the handle, was the hardest part. Some of the blood had seeped up under the opening. The handle had cleaned up nicely, as it was new hickory wood, and deep crevices had not yet formed. She took one of Bridget's small scrubbing tools and worked on the stubborn stain. It would not need to be perfect. An escaping murderer would not be expected to have a pristine weapon.

Outside the Borden house, as Bridget came back around to the Kelly house side of the building, to begin rinsing the windows, Dr. Benjamin Handy was passing up Second Street, taking particular notice of the Borden house. His daughter, Louise, may have told him of a strange letter Elizabeth Johnston had received from Lizzie in the morning mail. Elizabeth Johnson was at the Handy cottage at Marion, with the other girls vacationing there. They were expecting Lizzie on Monday morning. But the letter Elizabeth received from her friend was so frightening, she showed it to the other girls. Strange tales of poisonings, enemies, and a man running about the Borden house in the shadows. Louise may have asked her father to drive by the Borden's to see if he saw anything out of the ordinary...any "strange men running about the house." The letter also mentioned a hatchet.

Dr. Handy was questioned extensively by Attorney Knowlton about what he saw on Second Street that morning:

Knowlton: "Were you in the vicinity of the house during the forenoon at any time?"

Handy: "I passed it twice...once in the morning about nine, and returning about somewhere between 20 minutes past ten and twenty minutes of eleven...I was in a carriage."

Knowlton: "Did you see any person in the vicinity of the Borden house at this time?"

Handy: "I did. He was opposite the space between Dr. Kelly's house and Mr. Wade's Store...He was a stranger. I noticed he was very pale, exceedingly pale individual, and he was passing very slowly up the street, south. He was just beyond Dr. Kelly's house, south, opposite the space between that and the store. He was a young man of medium height, dressed in a light suit of clothes...sort of grayish. There was something about him that attracted my attention, so I turned and looked at him the second time, as I went by him."

Knowlton: "Did you ever see the man before?"

Handy: "My opinion is that I had seen him before...within a few days on Second Street. I have the impression that he had a mustache. He was a small man, five feet four; five feet three or four."

Knowlton: "Short, was he?"

Handy: "Yes, sir. He had a very full, and very white forehead, full face. I spoke to my wife, and to the officers that are stationed at the patrol station nearly opposite my house."

Knowlton: "What time in the morning did you say it was?"

Handy: "Somewhere between 20 minutes past 10, and 20 minutes of eleven; in that twenty minutes."

Knowlton: "Which way was he going?"

Handy: "He was facing south. He did not always face the south. He turned partially around several times while I was going by, that is moving...He had on an ordinary sack coat. He was alone...looked agitated."

Knowlton: "You understand quite active efforts have been made by the police to find such a man? And they have followed down every rumor?"

Handy: "Yes, sir."

Re-Direct by Mr. Jennings (Lizzie's attorney):

Jennings: "What did he appear to be doing when he turned around?"

Handy: "He did not turn clear around. He seemed to be moving or vacillating or oscillating on the sidewalk...looking down on the sidewalk."

[Both of the Chatterton brothers—James and Joseph—are described as pale complexioned. The witness who saw James in his baseball shoes on Monday described him as having a "sallow" complexion; a synonym for pale. James is described as 5'9", and Joseph as a "small man" of 5'3 or 5'4" tall. Dr. Handy says he feels he has seen the young man before a few days earlier. Perhaps Handy saw him as Joseph waited in the buggy at the Borden's for James on Monday. Mrs. Manley describes the young man waiting out in front of the Borden house, "leaning on the gate post," as about "30." Joseph Chatterton was 31-years-old. Both brothers worked inside, making shoes. That may contribute to pale complexions, or it may be a family trait, such as redheads inherit.]

Lizzie walked carefully up the cellar steps to the kitchen. She wasn't sure if Bridget might come into the house again. She had heard her several minutes ago, getting the dipper from the sink; the screen door slamming behind her as she went back out. Watching the open door, Lizzie grabbed Bridget's soft felt hat from the pegs lining the back entry. She picked up the hatchet and placed it sideways inside the hat. Carefully she rubbed the felt along the handle and blade. She had read that a new kind of forensic technology was now being used by the police. It was called "fingerprinting." She wasn't sure if Fall River had it yet, but she heard Boston might be using it.

Lizzie peeked through the screen door. No Bridget. She should be at the front of the house, Lizzie thought. She hurriedly picked up the plumber's pipe, hat, and hatchet, and ran out the side door to the back yard. She dropped the pipe in the tall grass and hurried for the lumber pile at the back of the property. Her heart pounding, the noises of the neighborhood caused her nerves to fray with each sound.

Borden yard facing east to Crowe's barn. Photo by Charles Carroll.

Looking about her constantly, she climbed up onto a few boards and reached up for a pear—just an innocent outing in the morning hours should anyone be watching her. The felt hat, still gripping the hatchet, was in her left hand, away from the house. The pear branches poked her as she adjusted herself on the boards, the wood making a "scraping sound" against the rough timbers of the fence. Lizzie took one last look toward the street, and back again at the side jog by the barn, and then flung the hatchet from the hat over the fence. Her sleeve just missed becoming snagged on the barbed wire with which her father had lined the top of it. A loud bang sounded. She had missed her mark. Underestimating how far a top-heavy hatchet would fly, she heard it land on the metal roof of Crowe's barn, farther back from the woodpile she had hoped for. The loud clang of mason's metal hitting stone had covered the noise. She thought she heard the hatchet slide down the metal roof, but she wasn't sure.

Illustration from *The Boston Daily Globe*, June 15, 1893.
#1 is the Borden house; #2 is Crowe's barn. The Author has added #'s 12 and 13. #12 shows where Lizzie probably stood to throw the hatchet over the fence. #13 is the location of the hatchet mentioned in the newspaper article stating a hatchet had been found on Crowe's barn roof June 15, 1893, while the Superior Court trial was in session. Note the fence line of the Crowe's barn property goes farther back toward the Kelly house (#8) making it an easy pitch for the hatchet to land where it did.

The sound of sawing continued uninterrupted. The foreign-looking man on the other side of the fence had noticed nothing. Lizzie climbed down from the woodpile. Once again, she scouted the yard and street and peered up at the curtained windows of her neighbors' houses. It didn't appear as if she had been seen. She dropped the pear into the grass.

A young Russian immigrant, Hymon Lubinsky, was driving his ice cream cart north on Second Street, coming from Charley Gardner's stable on Second Street and Rodman. He saw the pretty Irish maid up ahead, closing the tall shutters to the window near the front door. She looked as though she was in a hurry. He had sold ice cream to her in the past couple of weeks. Perhaps he would come back after he picked up his merchandise.

Lubinsky was asked about what he saw that day. His original report to the police was that he passed the Borden house at 10:30 that morning. His timeline had changed by the Superior Court trial, one year later. The rest of his story had not:

Mr. Jennings (Lizzie's attorney): "When you got to the Borden house, did you see anybody on the premises?"

Lubinsky: "Yes, sir. I saw a lady come out the way from the barn right to the stairs back of the house—the north side stairs, from the back of the house. She walked slow."

Jennings: "Can you tell how she was dressed?"

Lubinsky: "She had on a dark colored dress."

Jennings: "Did she have anything on her head?"

Lubinsky: "No, sir."

Jennings: "She was going towards the steps. Did you see her go in the house?"

Lubinsky: "I don't know; I couldn't tell this."

Jennings: Had you ever seen the servant who worked in that house?"

Lubinsky: "Yes, sir."

Jennings: "Had you ever delivered ice cream to her?"

Lubinsky: "Yes, sir…two or three weeks before the murder."

Jennings: Was the woman you saw the servant?"

Lubinsky: "I saw the servant and the woman too."

Jennings: "Was the woman you saw the day of the murder the same woman as the servant?"

Lubinsky: "No, sir."

Jennings: Are you sure about that?"
Lubinsky: "I am sure about that."

Hymon Lubinsky dropped a bomb shell during his testimony. He stated he saw "the woman" *and* the servant **at the same time**. That can only mean he saw Lizzie coming around the side of the house from the back yard at the same time Bridget is finishing the windows. Bridget testified she finished the windows about 10:30...she had only one thing left to do. Close the parlor shutters; something Lizzie testified she had asked Bridget to do to keep the heat out from the west-facing windows.

Lubinsky originally told Officer Mullaly he saw "the woman coming from the barn area" at 10:30 that morning. Now, his story has changed to see her at 11:05. During the cross-examination by Attorney Knowlton, Lubinsky was pressured into saying he had been in Mr. Jennings office before the trial to talk with Mr. Phillips, a detective working on the case for the Defense. His point was that Mr. Lubinsky has suddenly changed the time he saw "the woman" coming around the side of the house from 10:30 to a little after 11; a time that collaborates Lizzie's timeline of being out in the barn when her father is killed. Basically, Hymon Lubinsky saw Lizzie's venture into the back yard, not as an alibi for Andrew's murder, but as her returning from disposing of the murder hatchet used on Abby, at 10:30. He witnessed the wrong murder!

Quickly, fearing Bridget would head to the barn at any moment, Lizzie grabbed the pipe from the grass and ran to the open barn door. She lobbed the plumbing pipe at the box near the door, where other metal pieces were kept. Her aim was off. The pipe hit the side of the box and rolled out onto the barn floor. She had no time to retrieve it. *What did it matter anyway if it was seen there?* she thought. Lizzie walked slowly to the side of the house where the back stairs were, and stepped around the corner, looking for Bridget. She did not see her. What she did see was a young foreigner in a cart looking right at her.

[Officer Medley reported seeing "a piece of lead pipe about 4 or 5 feet long laying on the ground floor of the barn; distance from the door about five feet. This lead was in full view and could readily be seen by anyone. I saw it on the afternoon of August 4th."]

Bridget Sullivan closed the tall dark Drab parlor blinds, and headed around the corner of the house toward the barn, just missing the screen door as it closed silently behind Lizzie. The servant emptied the dirty water in the yard, and returned the long pole to the horse stall in the barn, stepping over a piece of pipe on the floor. Her head was throbbing, and her stomach still felt queasy. She entered the side door to the kitchen and latched it behind her. The sudden darkness of the back entry felt like an oasis after being in the unrelenting sunshine. Her flesh pebbled at the change of temperature as she trudged down to the cellar to return the pail, dropping it at the base of the stairs.

The Borden house showing the two closed parlor blinds (behind the tree) by the front door. The barn & back yard is at the rear of the house.
Photo by Charles Carroll, 1893.

Bridget walked back up the cellar stairs and placed the brush back in the closet by the stove. She took out two small wash rags, hand basin, and a small step ladder. Crossing to the sink, she filled the basin with water and walked to the sitting room. She removed the screen of the window closest to the front door, climbed her small ladder, and began to wipe the dirty glass.

Lizzie sat on the lounge in her room, her head spinning. Had she covered her tracks? The hatchet was away from the house. She had almost forgotten to return Bridget's hat to its peg after she laid it on the kitchen table and headed for her room. Only after she was halfway to the front stairs did she remember she had left it there. She placed it back on the peg, making sure its shape was the same as when she borrowed it.

Danielle Cabral, tour guide at the Lizzie Borden B&B and Museum, on the lounge in Lizzie's room. Photo by the Author.

Wearing two dresses was taking a toll on her, but she could hear Bridget raising and lowering the window in the sitting room. She would be finished in about 15 minutes. She had only the two sitting room windows to do, and two in the dining room. She was not in charge of the parlor, and only rarely cleaned the kitchen windows, as they did not show for company. She could handle wearing the double layer of clothing for a little while longer. She only hoped the girl hurried with her work before her father returned.

Looking at her reflection in the dressing table mirror, Lizzie smoothed her hair. She backed up and twirled slowly around. You could not see the hemline of the Bedford cord she wore beneath the calico. She leaned close to the mirror, checking for any blood she may have missed. Her large, catlike eyes looked suddenly foreign to her. There was a dullness to them as if the light had gone out. They looked puffy from lack of sleep.

Straightening, she double-checked that the hooks on the front of her blouse waist were holding firm against the extra bulk. Her hands looked clean. She breathed a little easier. Remembering the hatchet, she stepped to the window closest to the back yard and peered out. While she could see the top of the wood pile and the man sawing wood, the pear trees blocked her view of the roof of Crowe's barn. She wanted desperately to see where the hatchet had landed, but she didn't dare go and look.

Picking up her purse, Lizzie stepped into the guest room, unable to stop herself from taking one more look at her handiwork. Standing at the bottom of the bed, she looked down at the rotund woman she had grown to hate. It was all so surreal. She had to keep reminding herself that Abby Borden was dead. In a few more minutes, she and Bridget would be headed downtown, checking sales and running errands; something the two had never done before. In only a few more minutes, she would be in the clear.

Just then, someone began rattling the front door knob. Bridget, not expecting Mr. Borden yet, walked into the parlor and peeked through the crack in the parlor blind at the front door stoop to the left. It was Mr. Borden...home early. He was fumbling with the lock. Bridget hurried to the front door to let him in. Lizzie heard the commotion and stepped onto the landing to listen. There was a rattling at the front door as if someone was trying to get in. Her breath caught. She stepped quietly down two steps, into the curve of the staircase where she had a clear view of the front door. She saw Bridget's back, turning the spring lock. The maid turned to head back to the sitting room, only to hear the door rattle again.

She returned, sighing deeply and struggled to slide back the top bolt. Finally, she unlocked the last latch and swore.

The profanity Bridget used, so strange, and so indicative of the moment, took Lizzie by surprise. Her nerves screaming, and her plan of escape shattered, she looked at Andrew Borden striding into the front entry and turned to see Abby Borden's body beneath the bed, through the stairwell spindles. She was trapped. She was, in essence, the word Bridget just used. Lizzie laughed.

The view beneath the guest room bed as seen from the third step of the front staircase. Photo by the Author.

Chapter Fourteen

Thursday, August 4, 1892
The Hands of Fate

John Morse sat in the sitting room of the Emery's at Number 4 Weybosset Street. A very pale, and agitated Joseph Chatterton was sitting across from him, hunched over in the chair, and practically ruining his soft hat as he twisted it in his hands. His brother James was seated in an armchair next to him, looking none too pleased. Mrs. Emery was in and out of the room, catching snippets of the conversation. Her niece was in the kitchen, working on a cup of chamomile tea, after being ill most of the morning. The mantle clock in the sitting room chimed 10:45.

John Morse was clearly upset. He pressed Joseph to tell him again what happened. The young man sputtered out that he was there early to the Borden house to pick up Mrs. Borden. He swore he was out front in the buggy at 9:45. He got hot, and went and stood under the tree by the gate, but could see the front door plainly. He waited in that spot until some ladies looking at a peddler's cart took notice of him, and a maid came around the corner of the Borden house to clean the window near the front door. He didn't want to look like he was just hanging around, as the plan was to be secretive about the whole thing, so he walked across the street, and kept an eye on the door for Mrs. Borden to come out.

It was hot...he had no shade there, and he heard the City Hall clock strike 10:00. He figured she would come now—that was the appointed time. But she didn't come out. He watched the maid move around to the side of the house where he had just been standing, lugging a wooden bucket. He watched her mop her forehead and push her bangs away. She didn't look like she felt really well.

The minutes ticked by. He heard the big clock chime the quarter hour—it was 10:15. He had been told not to knock...just wait for her to come out. He couldn't just stand there staring at the house. He began moving slowly south on the sidewalk, only to turn back, and look again at the door. Back and forth he paced. His suit felt like an oven of fabric. He worried people were going to notice his strange actions. There were men and women everywhere: loitering out in front of the store across from him, talking to each other on the sidewalk, going in and out of the laundry just steps away from him.

Time dragged on. The clock struck 10:30. He gave up. He would go back to the Emery's and see what to do. Something must have happened. He got into his buggy, took one last look toward the door with number 92 next to it, and flicked the reins. He headed down Second Street, glancing back to see the maid closing up the large shutters of one of the two windows by the front door. He caught a glimpse of a young foreigner directly behind him, driving an ice cream peddler's cart.

As Joseph told his story to his cousin John Morse, he could see how angry, and nervous, the older man was. Andrew Borden had already rung the Emery's twice, asking where Abby was. The deal had to be done today!

Emma Borden was staring out the window of the Brownell's parlor, not seeing anything in her worried state. Her stomach was clenched in panic. When Lizzie was in one her moods, it could be frightening. It was like a runaway train of emotion, and anyone in her path was in danger of being pressed into the rails. She could change so quickly: one minute that unnerving calm, looking at you as though you were a bug beneath a glass. The next, her face would color, those same eyes flash with a hate that withered, and she would act out...without thinking. There were no brakes. The family had learned to run for cover, or just give in to her demands. The letter from Lizzie, Emma was clutching in her hand, worried her. She feared something terrible was about to happen.

At 92 Second Street, Bridget finally managed to undo the three locks securing the front door and swung it open. A disgruntled Andrew Borden pressed in past her, without a word. She noticed he "was carrying a small white parcel." He swept his top hat from his head and planted it impatiently on the peg of the hall tree. Bridget shut the front door and returned to the sitting room to complete her window washing, leaving Andrew to re-bolt the door.

Seeing Bridget cleaning in the sitting room, Andrew walked into the dining room instead. No Abby. She didn't appear to be in any of the downstairs' rooms. She must have gone out. Somehow, they had missed each other. Perhaps John's cousin had gotten lost, or gone to the wrong house. When he talked to John by phone, only ten minutes earlier, he was told the young Chatterton cousin had not come back to the Emery's, so he must be with Abby downtown. She would realize they missed each other and return at any minute. There was still time.

Andrew's head throbbed. He dropped the lock, still wrapped in the sleeve of the *Providence Journal*, into his Prince Albert coat pocket. He would add it to the other locks in the box in the barn later. He reached into the inside pocket of the coat and removed the folded deed for the Swansea farm. It was several pages thick, resembling "a small book," and laid it on the dining room table. Removing the coat, he laid it across the arm of the lounge chair that sat along the south wall of the dining room. Abby or the girls would sometimes lay there when the summer heat was too much to be upstairs in the daytime. He preferred the sofa in the sitting room.

A 1890s, deed packet. To Bridget, it looked like "a small book, or papers."

Lizzie, who had seen many of her father's deeds, and signed one with him for the Ferry house, would know exactly what Andrew had in his hands.

He picked up the deed and carried it to the dining room window where the light was better. Looking out through the glass Bridget had just washed outside, he noticed someone moving about in the Churchill's kitchen. Paying no attention, he opened the deed and checked over a few of the conditions he had added there.

Bridget walked into the kitchen. She was surprised to see Lizzie coming down the *back* stairs. Bridget had just heard the girl laugh at the top of the *front* stairs not five or ten minutes ago. Knowing the door separating Lizzie's and her parent's room was always locked, Bridget was confused as to how she came down.

Lizzie Came Down the Back Stairs

The New York Sun, August 28, 1892, during the Preliminary Hearing ran the following story quoting Bridget's testimony as she is washing the inside windows:

Bridget: "I went into the sitting room and washed the windows there. It was then about 10:35 o'clock. I saw and heard nothing of Lizzie or Mrs. Borden. Suddenly, I heard a noise at the front door. I walked through the parlor into the hall. Lizzie was not in the parlor. I tried to unlock the front door. It was fast, I kept trying, and when it would not open, I said, "Oh, ---! That is, "Oh, pshaw!" As soon as I said it, I heard a laugh upstairs. It was Miss Lizzie. I looked up but I didn't see Miss Lizzie. Finally, I got the door open and let in Mr. Borden. He locked the door after him.

"I am sure Mrs. Borden was not downstairs then. I walked through the house back to the kitchen. Mr. Borden went into the dining room. Lizzie came down the back stairs as I reached the kitchen. She went into the dining room where her father was."

"If Lizzie Borden was within ten feet of that door at 10:30 o'clock, when she laughed at Bridget's swearing, why did she not see Mrs. Borden dead or alive in that room? The laugh showed that she was near that door. The fact that she came down the back stairs a few seconds later proves that she walked from the front hall upstairs, past the door, to the back stairs."

What the reporter missed, was that Lizzie coming down the back stairs also proves she had unlocked the door separating her bedroom and Abby's from *both* sides; something she could only have done if she had taken the key from the sitting room mantel, unlocked her parent's bedroom from the second-floor landing, and slid back the bolt on the door leading into her bedroom. She would have already unhooked her side of the door.

Bridget also said she went through the parlor. This is missing from her Direct Examination.

The most compelling aspect of this part of Bridget's testimony, is that it fell within the 9 missing pages of her Preliminary Hearing transcript! It mysteriously disappeared after the hearing. Andrew Jennings, Lizzie's attorney, even makes a pencil note of the missing page (number 34) in the margin of Bridget's cross-examination transcript. What may be the word "stairs," is scribbled next to it.

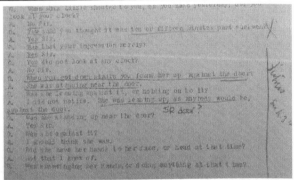

Section of Bridget's Preliminary Hearing transcript. Lizzie's attorney, Andrew Jennings' scribbled note is seen at the right. The word may say "stairs." Below it is the notation "see h [page] 34." Page 34 is the exact location where Bridget's testimony under Direct Examination is missing and has been, since 1893. Nine consecutive pages, beginning with page 34 are gone. The "X" at the top is Jennings'. The underlining and the "SR door?" markings are those of the Author.

Bridget's Term for "Front Entry"

During the Preliminary Hearing in August of 1892, and the Superior Court Trial in June of 1893, the attorneys for the Defense and Prosecution needed to prove where Lizzie was when her father came home early that fateful morning at 10:35-10:40. As Lizzie's Inquest testimony was an explosion of confusing statements regarding that crucial moment ("I was upstairs," "I was on the stairs coming down," "I was in the kitchen reading a magazine...") they relied on Bridget's testimony to get at Lizzie's movements. The following Superior Court testimony concerning what Bridget called the Front Entry is important:

Mr. Robinson (for the Defense): "Is there a room connected with the kitchen beside the closet?"

Bridget: "Why, there is the sitting-room, dining-room, closet and sink room."

Robinson: "Anything else?"

Bridget: "Front hall—front entry."

Robinson: "Small hall leading to the outside door? Is there a room there in the corner, the northeast corner?"

Bridget: "Downstairs?"

Robinson: "Yes."

Bridget: "There is a parlor there."

Robinson: "Leading out of the kitchen?"

Bridget: "There is a closet there."

Robinson: "Well, you call it a closet." [Big pantry]

Bridget: "Yes, sir."

Robinson: "Is that the only closet there in the kitchen?"

Bridget: "That is the closet, the kitchen closet. There is a little closet there, where the wood and coal was kept, and there is a sink room there where the refrigerator was."

Robinson: "Then there is a closet, and that is quite a large closet--a sort of pantry, wasn't it?"

Bridget: "Well, I always called it the kitchen closet. I don't know what anybody else called it."

In Bridget's Preliminary Hearing testimony, here is her location of the Front Hall:

Mr. Knowlton (for the Defense): "Which part of the house did you have the sweeping of?"

Bridget: "I had the front hall to do, the front entry."

Knowlton: "Did you have any other duties in the front part of the house, except sweeping the front hall?"

Bridget: "No, Sir."

If you look closely at Mr. Robinson's brilliant strategy in twisting Bridget's words in the Superior Court testimony, you will see he is trying to show when Bridget said "Front Entry" during her testimonies, she was referring to the back-entry area where the stairs come out from the back of the house. The Defense needs to get Lizzie away from the front stairs where Bridget claims she heard Lizzie laugh when Mr. Borden came home; an area adjacent to Abby's dead body. If the Front Entry is Bridget's name for the back stairs area, then they can back up Lizzie's testimony that she was in the kitchen area when Andrew came home, not at the top of the front stairs.

Watch how cleverly Mr. Robinson gets Bridget to call the back-door area the Front Entry:

Bridget: "Why, there is the sitting-room, dining-room, closet and sink room."

Robinson: "Anything else?"

Bridget: "Front hall—front entry."

Robinson: **"Small hall leading to the outside door? Is there a room there in the corner, the northeast corner?" [He asks two questions, sidestepping the first part of the query. He makes the jury think it's the small kitchen hall leading to the outside door, but Bridget answers the second part of the question.]**

Bridget: "Downstairs?"

Robinson: "Yes."

Bridget: **"There is a parlor there." [This shows Bridget thinks he is referring to the front of the house—the front entry.]**

Robinson: "Leading out of the kitchen?" [He reels her back in.]

Bridget: "There is a closet there."

When you look at Knowlton's question in the Preliminary Hearing concerning where Bridget swept, it is clear, Bridget called the area by the front door the "front entry," at the front of the house.

Mr. Robinson's strategy with Bridget shows the Defense's desperate need to put Lizzie near the kitchen, not the guest room.

The Defense still has the sticky wicket regarding Lizzie needing to unlock her parent's room door in order to come down the *back* stairs, after Bridget just heard her laugh at the top of the *front* stairs. They may have been hoping the jury forgot that little impediment to traveling from one part of the house to the other. That door was always kept bolted on Andrew and Abby's side of the door connecting to Lizzie's bedroom, and, you needed the sitting room mantle key to unlock their door to the second-floor landing where the stairs led down to the kitchen area.

As Lizzie came tiptoeing quickly down the back stairs, she looked a little startled to find the maid in the kitchen, having assumed Bridget was in the sitting room. She hesitated for a split second near the back door. Bridget paused only a moment, scenarios running through her mind of how Lizzie accomplished this feat of prestidigitation, but then continued on to the sitting room, anxious to be finished with her work. She climbed the small step ladder and ran the wet cloth over the top window pane. She thought she heard the sound of a small *clink* behind her, and turned to see Lizzie near the sitting room mantle. Keeping her face a mask, the girl walked through the room, ignoring Bridget, and turned right into the dining room.

Andrew was seated in his chair at the dining room table. He quickly put away the deed and stood up as Lizzie entered the room. Bridget heard Lizzie's voice, speaking low, and very slowly.

"Is there any mail for me?" Bridget heard Lizzie ask her father.

Mr. Borden answered, but his voice was too low for Bridget to hear his reply. She next heard Lizzie tell him that "Abby had a note from a sick friend and has gone out." There was no reply from Andrew.

Bridget climbed down from the step ladder and began washing the bottom half of the window, behind the rocking chair. She saw Andrew come from the dining room, into the kitchen, and from the kitchen into the sitting room, picking up the key from the mantel to his bedroom. This was the first chance Bridget got a good look at him. His complexion was pasty, and his usual erect stature had given way to unseen weight. He looked sickly, tired and stressed.

Andrew walked through the kitchen, heading for the back stairs. Bridget finished the window and adjusted the two screens, pulling the chairs back into place where she had moved them to accommodate her ladder. She took the basin into the dining room and set it on the table. Lizzie was nowhere to be seen. Just as Bridget picked up her ladder from the sitting room, and headed into the dining room, Andrew came back downstairs. He looked fidgety and distracted. As she placed her ladder before the window on the northwest corner of the room, she looked back through the open dining room door and saw Andrew open the window in the sitting room, nearest the front hall, and sit down in the armchair there. He once again had a "small book, or papers" in his hands, and was looking it over.

Bridget went for clean water in the kitchen. As she was coming back to the dining room, she passed the open cellar door. It sounded like someone was down there rummaging around. *It could only be Lizzie,* she thought, *as Mrs. Borden is out, and Mr. Borden is in the sitting room. What can that girl be doing?*

1892 hand basin

Sitting room. Andrew was seated in armchair in the foreground. The key was
kept on the fireplace mantel, next to the kitchen door. The sofa is at left.
Photography by Frank Grace (Trig Photography)

Bridget's view from the dining room of Andrew's reading chair.
Photos by the Author.

Andrew's view of Bridget washing the first dining room window.
The sofa where he would be found dead 25 minutes later is near the door.

Bridget moved her ladder to the last window in the dining room. She could no longer see Mr. Borden, due to the wall behind her. Lizzie suddenly came in from the sitting room, walked through the dining room, opened the door to the kitchen, went through, and shut it. There was no sound coming from the sitting room. She had heard no conversation pass between Lizzie and her father as the girl came through a few seconds before.

The kitchen door opened and Lizzie entered the dining room, carrying a small ironing board and some handkerchiefs. She went back into the kitchen and returned with a flat iron. Bridget hadn't heard her add fuel to the small coal fire in the stove. She glanced over and saw a roll of sprinkled handkerchiefs on the dining room table.

Lizzie began to iron. There was still no sound from the sitting room.

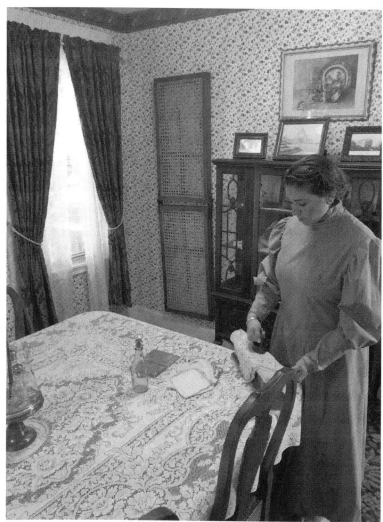

Danielle Cabral, a tour guide at the Lizzie Borden B&B and Museum, standing where Lizzie did that day, ironing. The window Bridget was washing is directly across from her. Photo by the Author.

"Are you going out today?" Lizzie asked, watching Bridget's back as the servant wiped the top half of the northeast window. She would have preferred not to have Lizzie watching her. She would have to slow down and do a polished job of it.

"I might and I might not," Bridget answered in her thick brogue. "I'm not feeling well."

"Well," Lizzie said, "be sure and lock the door if you do," ignoring Bridget's illness. "I may go out, and Mrs. Borden is out on a sick call."

"Oh, who is sick, Miss Lizzie?" Bridget asked.

"I don't know. A boy came to the door with a note. It must be in town."

Bridget finished her lower window and placed a hand on her back. Lizzie had been ironing for "8 or 9 minutes," three or four handkerchiefs were still rolled in a ball. The maid took her step ladder and basin and walked into the kitchen. She replaced the ladder into the closet near the stove and crossed to the sink, where she emptied the basin. She turned to the stove and hung a cloth behind the pipe to dry.

Lizzie followed her into the kitchen.

"There's a sale of dress goods at Sargent's today," Lizzie said casually. "Only eight cents a yard."

"Aye, and I'm going to have one," Bridget said tiredly. Without another word to Lizzie, she headed through the kitchen to the back stairs. She did not see the spasm of anger run along Lizzie's face, only the girl heading back into the dining room.

[Mr. Adams for the Defense asked Bridget at the Preliminary Hearing about this conversation between herself and Lizzie:

Bridget: "I got through with my work, and was in the kitchen. Then she told me there was a sale of dress goods at Sargent's, eight cents a yard. I said I would have one. That is all."

Adams: Did not she make the statement about the sale of dress goods at Frank Sargent's, that is the name, two or three days before that?" [A big ad for a sale on dress goods ran Monday.]

Bridget: "No sir."

Adams: "Did she ever tell about any sale at Sargent's before that?"

Bridget: "No sir. Emma had a good many times told me about bargains."

Adams: "Miss Lizzie had not before, so far as you recollect?"

Bridget: No sir...I went upstairs directly after that."]

Bridget's Window Washing Inside:

1) Bridget heard no conversation between Andrew and Lizzie in the sitting room while cleaning the dining room window. Lizzie testified she asked her father if she could help him get comfortable on the sofa, asked if he wanted an afghan over him (on a sweltering day), and helped him to take off his shoes, put on his slippers, and change from his Prince Albert to his smoking jacket (reefer). She said her last words to him were to ask if he wanted the shutters adjusted for the light. The crime scene photographs show Andrew with his Gator Congress shoes still on...no slippers in sight. His coat is now rolled up and bunched under his head, something he would not have done.

2) Bridget is asked if Lizzie's handkerchiefs were part of the Monday wash that Lizzie carried up to her room earlier. She said "No." When did Lizzie get the handkerchiefs and sprinkle them? It seemed obvious she was looking for something to do to be near Bridget, and to try during two conversations to get the maid to leave the house. Bridget didn't take the bait.

Gator Congress Shoes

Andrew's crime scene photo. His Congress shoes are still on. His coat is
bunched under his head on the arm of the sofa. Dr. Bowen said that the photo
showed Andrew lower than he was originally. His head had been higher on the
sofa arm. He had been moved as his pockets were checked, and Dr. Bowen had
lifted the coat to check its pockets, as well.

Bridget Sullivan climbed the two sets of stairs to the attic. The
temperature rose with each step. As she passed Mr. and Mrs.
Borden's room on the second landing, she wondered who the sick
friend was Abby was visiting. The only person that ever called on
Mrs. Borden was her half-sister, Mrs. Whitehead, who lived two
streets over. It was also the only place her employer visited. But if
Mrs. Whitehead was sick, would she have sent a messenger boy?
Wouldn't her mother, or another relative get hold of Mrs. Borden?
Besides, Lizzie said it "was probably someone in town."

The bed in Bridget's room looked inviting. Her head was still
swimming, but at least her stomach had settled somewhat. She
still had at least thirty minutes before she had to stoke the stove
fire to heat over the mutton soup for the noon meal. She would
just finish the front-facing window in the attic storage room that
she had started yesterday and wash the window in her room, and
she would be finished. The other attic windows were done. After
the noon meal, she had the rest of the day off. Her mind focused on
spending time with her friends downtown. Perhaps they would
grab a pint.

She crossed to the closet in her room and opened the door. An old wooden water tank sat on a shelf. She took a rag and dipped it into the clean water. With a sigh, she headed for the attic storage room.

Wooden water tank in Bridget's closet. Photo Ron Bueker.

Lizzie stood in the dining room. She heard the soft sputtering sounds coming through the open sitting room door, only steps away from her. Her mind was awash with panic. Bridget didn't take the hints to leave. She couldn't force the maid to go downtown; it would look suspicious later. Even asking Bridget to go on an innocent errand at that time, would come back to her. It had to be her idea to go shopping or run a personal errand, but she had chosen to climb the stairs to her attic room, instead. She had mentioned something about "fixing her room."

Andrew's sputters turned into a rattling snore. Lizzie felt nauseous. How could she kill him? She thought of Abby lying dead upstairs, her head sliced to a pulp. Could she do that to her father? It would have to look like the same maniac killed them both—that meant at least a dozen thrashes with the hatchet. *The hatchet.* She looked down at the weapon in her hand she had found in the cellar, while Bridget was busy with the dining room windows. It was older than the one she had used on Abby. She had thrown the new one away into Crowe's yard, not realizing her father would choose this day, of all days, to come home early. She should have gone out after she killed Abby and not waited for Bridget. But, if they found Abby, and Bridget was the only one home, the girl would hang. Lizzie couldn't do that to her.

Taking deep gulps of air, she laid the hatchet on the dining room table and bent over to untie her low-tie shoes. Slipping her feet from them, she carefully picked up her father's Prince Albert coat lying across the arm of the lounge. Andrew's snoring stopped. Lizzie stood frozen to the spot. Seconds passed, and his rattle resumed, catching at times as his fevered mind drifted in and out of sleep.

Quickly, she slipped into the coat, buttoning it to her chin. Pulling the lapels upward, the lower half of her face was covered to her nose. It hung on her to the floor—her father's 7" height difference providing the perfect cloak. Something felt heavy on her right side, but she ignored it for now. She had to hurry.

Lizzie picked up the hatchet, its weight so heavy now in her hands. The handle was rough and the head top-heavy, causing an ache to rise in her sore wrists. She swallowed, over and over. There was no saliva in her mouth. A gag reflex threatened to betray her. Breathing hard, she took two steps to the open sitting room door and peered around the corner.

His head was right there. It was so close to her. His white hair looked wispy against the embroidered pillow he rested against. Her father's knees were bent, his feet obviously resting on the floor, although she couldn't see them from this angle. His hands rested limply in his lap. The small gold ring she had given him so long ago glinted in the soft light.

Bridget lifted the attic storage room window, removed the screen and began to run the wet rag over the dirty glass. She doubted Mrs. Borden would check her cleaning up here, so she hurried along, giving the window a mere spit polish. The City Hall clock struck 11. Below her, life on Second Street drifted by. The smell of chimney smoke from the mills, the sweat of horses, and an occasional whiff of the Quequechan River rose and fell on the slight breeze. The sound of metal trappings and clopping horse hooves was as pervasive as ever. Inside the house, it was quiet.

Andrew Borden lay in his sitting room, his head turned to the right, as he slept fitfully on the black horsehair sofa. His lips made small movements in his sleep, like that of a baby.

View the murderer would have of Andrew's head from the dining room door. Photo by the Author.

Lizzie stepped into the room, her breathing short and erratic. She stood just inside the dining room door, her body at an angle so that the blood would not reach her. Tears rimmed her eyes, her head screamed, and with a final breath, she lifted the hatchet over her head, and paused. Trembling, she took a deep breath, raised it higher into the air, and let it fall against the left side of her father's face. The thin skin split, exposing his cheekbone. The blade sliced through his nose and cut through his lips. His hands flew up in a convulsive muscle reaction and then fell, the fingers clenched. Her breath coming in panicked bursts, she lifted it again and brought it down. It cut through his left eyebrow, shattering his eye socket. His eye fell forward onto his cheek, sliced in half.

In a frenzy of swinging motions, Lizzie hit him again, and again; shorter blows that lessened the amount of blood that was forming. One of the first blows hit his artery and an arc of arterial spray splashed across the wallpaper near his body. As she raised the hatchet on each subsequent blow, the cast-off blood hit the parlor door to her right and slightly behind her. One drop flew up to the ceiling, and several others splashed onto the framework of the kitchen door at the base of the couch. She kept striking, her mind a blur of emotion.

Bridget, unaware of what was happening two floors below her, picked up the screen to replace it into the front-facing attic window. Before she slid it into place, she looked down to see Mary Doolan from next door pass the side fence that separated the Kelly and Borden houses. The Kelly maid was hauling a pail and brush, finally finished with the outside windows. Bridget laughed and called down to her. "Are you coming with me later?" she yelled, her voice carrying down past the open sitting room windows.

Attic window facing Second Street. Today it is the Andrew Jenning's Room.
Photo by Ron Bueker.

Lizzie stopped—the hatchet raised, ready to strike the mutilated head again. The sound of Bridget's voice, calling down past the open sitting room window, startled her. She froze, hatchet still raised. Chest heaving, she blinked and looked down at the bloody mess that had been her father's face. As if coming out of a trance, Lizzie stepped back in horror. Her hands were shaking now. She had lost count of the blows. Swallowing the bile rising in her throat, she wiped the bloody hatchet head on her father's coat which she was wearing. She laid the hatchet on the couch arm and unbuttoned his coat with trembling fingers.

She once again felt the weight pulling the jacket down on the right side. Reaching into the pocket, she felt something large and smooth. She pulled out a small white package, hastily wrapped in a newspaper sleeve. Unwrapping it, she found a large rusted lock. Her heart skipped, and her eyes blurred. *So like him to keep something broken and useless,* she thought. She swallowed back the tears and laid the lock on the white sofa tidy, dropping the wrapper to the floor. [Police found an unexplained rust stain on the sitting room sofa tidy near Andrew's head.]

A loud bang sounded from the attic. Bridget was still raising and lowering windows. She wasn't taking her usual nap before fixing the dinner meal. Lizzie would have to hurry. The maid could come down unexpectedly for something. Her Uncle John might show up, changing his mind about dining with them. One of her father's tenants might drop by. Panic shot through her nerves until she thought she would come undone.

Lizzie rolled up the Prince Albert and shoved it down slightly behind her father's head, wincing as the blood trickled down into his shirt and dressing jacket. *If blood is found on the coat, the police will assume it came from his wounds,* she thought. She stepped to the deed he had left on the small table by the window and picked it up. Glancing only at the first page, she saw the words "Swansea Plat." Anger overtook the terror momentarily, and her resolve came flooding back.

Hurrying now, she picked up the hatchet, the lock, and the newspaper wrapper from the floor, and ran to the kitchen. She set the lock on the big table, and the hatchet on the floor. Taking the lid from the stove, she peered in. The coal was barely burning. She grabbed a "stick of wood" from the basket of kindling by the stove and thrust it into the fire door, poking it into the only red glow of heat she could find. Quickly, she rolled the deed into a tight tube and placed it on the metal grate closest to the fire. She crumpled the newspaper wrapper and dropped it down into the hot coals.

Grabbing the hatchet, Lizzie ran in stocking feet down the cellar steps. She turned on the faucet in the washroom and ran the cold water over the blade and handle. She had wiped most of the blood from the blade with her father's coat. The rest came off with a little scrubbing. The hatchet handle, however, was harder. It had small fissures running along the weathered grain. The blood had not been nearly as bad as with Abby's wounds, partly due to her father's long coat sleeves covering her hands to the fingertips.

Lizzie let the hatchet lay in the sink beneath the running water as she washed the small blood droplets from the back of her fingers. She checked her nails and pushed back her sleeves to make sure her wrists were clean. Turning off the water, she stared at the hatchet. She couldn't throw this one away. Alfred Johnson would spot it as missing, and it would lead back to her. A murderer isn't going to take the time to look around the house for a weapon...he would bring his own. So, what to do with it? She couldn't get all the blood out of the cracks in the handle.

Bridget made one last swipe at her bedroom window. She looked down at the Borden's back yard. Several pears had fallen, which meant Mr. Borden would be bringing more into her kitchen in the morning. She sighed. *How many pears did one family need?* She glanced at the barn door and froze. It was standing ajar. She must have forgotten to lock it after washing the windows. If Mr. Borden saw it, he would not be happy with her.

Bridget opened her door and crept quietly down the stairs, grateful the last flight to the kitchen was carpeted. As she reached the entryway floor, she paused and listened. Nothing. Quickly she hurried out the screen door, making sure to close it gently, and ran to the barn. She quickly peeked inside, saw no one, and shut the door, pinning the hasp. With a sigh of relief, she hurried back to the screen door. She entered, and just as she was about to head back up the stairs, she heard noise coming from the cellar. She paused and then gave it no more thought, as she tiptoed up the back stairs to her room.

Bridget walked around her bed to the window and looked down, just to make sure. The barn door was locked. She sat down on the edge of her bed with a grateful sigh. Only dinner to prepare and the rest of the day was hers. At least the mutton broth was almost gone. She would be grateful for a nice joint of beef from the farm, a chicken—anything but more lamb. She swung her legs up onto the bedspread and laid down, her head grateful for a moment of stillness. No sound floated up the stairs from below. Only the rhythm of the street sounds ran through her tired head.

Bridget's room, and her window overlooking the back yard. You can see the barn through the window sheer. Photo by Ron Bueker.

View of the barn from Bridget's attic window today. It would have been closer to the house in 1892. The barn door is right of the bench.
[This is not the original barn.] Photo by Ron Bueker.

The cellar smelled of earth and brick. Outside, the sound of pounding stone was barely muffled. Lizzie hardly noticed. She had come up with a plan. The old starch box where she had found the shingling hatchet she just used, was filled with dusty tools. If she covered the hatchet in the dust, it would look like no one had used it for a while. She took it to the back room where the coal was kept. Ashes from the stove and furnace were everywhere. She rolled the hatchet in the ash and looked at it. Most of the ashes fell away as she moved it through the air. Carrying it back to the washroom, she ran water over it, returned to the coal room, and rolled it again, being careful to only touch the small piece of wood at the top of the blade, and the bottom of the handle, with a finger from each hand. The coarse, white ash stuck to the blade and wood.

She studied it and realized it wasn't enough. Someone might still look closely at it, and see the blood on the handle. It would need to be broken. No one would suspect a broken hatchet as being a murder weapon. But it had to look like a break…not cut, or sawn.

Lizzie had often watched as her father made things from wood. As a child, she had followed him about like a shadow. His carpenter's trade fascinated her; building beautiful things from plain wood. One of the tricks she had learned from him was how to break poles quickly. He would lay a chip of wood on a chopping block or table, lean the pole against it at an incline, and strike it. It always split cleanly, and fast.

She laid a wedge of wood onto the chopping block near the furnace and placed the hatchet at an incline, its head resting on the wedge. Lizzie stepped into the wood cellar back of the furnace and reached into the old starch box where the hatchets were kept. She removed a large one that was standing, head down; one with a 5" wide blade, and claw on one end. It felt huge compared to the smaller one she had used. Walking back to the chopping block, she looked down at the small shingling hatchet and considered. I can't use the sharp blade edge, she thought, it will look cut. She turned the hatchet over to the square, flat, block edge of the blade where the claw turned down. She would hit the little hatchet near where the handle was thinnest, about 4" down from the blade. [The hatchet breaking experiment is on page 821.]

Fearing the blade would flip up and cut her when she struck it, she placed her hands as far along the claw head handle as possible and stood back. Taking a deep breath, she raised it high above her head and swung it down hard on the shingling hatchet handle. A loud crack sounded, and the head flew into the air, missing her by mere inches. The small chip of wood, that had elevated the hatchet, fell onto the floor.

Lizzie picked up the head with two fingers and looked at it. It looked good. It looked like a break, not cut or sawn. She carefully picked up the handle, keeping her fingers at the top and bottom, and carried into the wood cellar to the starch box she had left sitting on the floor. Doing the same with the hatchet head, she placed them inside; she was pleased. While the ashes covering her hatchet looked somewhat different from the thin layer of dust coating the tops of the other tools, it might just pass.

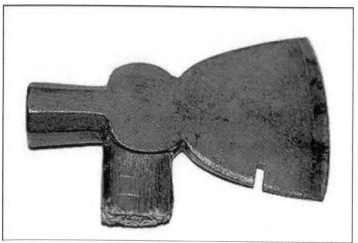

The 3 ½" blade shingling hatchet head believed to be the murder weapon of Andrew Borden. On display at the Fall River Historical Society.

She quickly washed the claw head hatchet to remove some ashes that had transferred to it, and for extra measure, swiped it down with a cloth, to remove any fingerprints. Holding it with her skirt, she put it into the starch box. As she took a hasty look at the washroom to make sure all was in order, her eyes fell on the small wedge of wood. "I picked up a chip from the floor," Lizzie said in her Inquest testimony, always one for small details. She tossed the fragment into the wood room and headed for the cellar stairs to the kitchen.

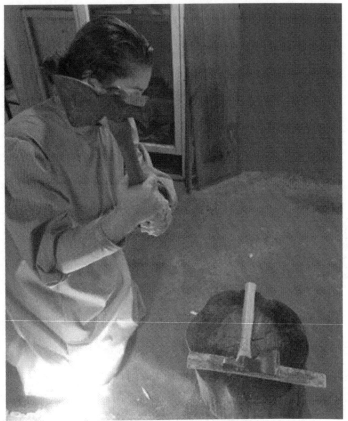

Danielle Cabral, a tour guide at the Lizzie Borden B&B in Fall River, Ma., in the Borden cellar, reenacting the way the hatchet was broken that day. She is holding an actual 1890s clawhead hatchet, and aiming it at a shingling hatchet, the same as was used that day in Andrew's murder. Photo by the Author.

Her heart racing, Lizzie rushed to the stove and lifted the lid. The roll of papers was "smoking and smoldering" just about to catch. *Hurry up!* she thought desperately. She tiptoed quickly through the dining room, her breath catching as she neared where her father lay. Without looking at him, she crossed through the sitting room and into the front entry where she checked her reflection in the mirror of the hall tree. She pushed aside the small curls flanking her forehead. She could see no blood. Her dress had been completely covered by the coat, but she carefully looked it over anyway. There was coal ash flecking the front of the skirt and the hem.

A chimney in the cellar of the Lizzie Borden cellar. Behind it, and to the left, was the chopping block, and coal dust. Photo by Ron Bueker.

Bridget felt the sweat trickle down along her neck. The attic was so close and stuffy. It was hard to sleep in the heat of the forenoon. Her mind went over her chores. The windows were done now for another week or two, depending on Abby's wishes. The attic wouldn't need it for another month. Tomorrow was just some light sweeping, and Saturday, some baking. The worst of the week was over, and she had tonight and half of Sunday off. She sighed with relief.

Just as she felt herself becoming hazy, a shout from the back stairs jarred her awake.

"Maggie! Maggie!" It was Miss Lizzie…hollering at the top of her lungs. Miss Lizzie rarely hollered. Something terrible must have happened.

Heart pounding, Bridget ran to the top of the attic stairs and called down, "What's wrong?"

"Come down quick!" Lizzie screamed. "Father's dead! Someone's come in and killed him!"

Lizzie Borden in her 30s. Photo courtesy of the Fall River Historical Society.

Chapter Fifteen

Thursday—August 4, 1892
"Where Was You, Miss Lizzie?"

Bridget Sullivan hurried down the back stairway, past her employer's shut bedroom door, and around the bend to where she found Lizzie standing at the back screen door. Lizzie looked dazed and was leaning against the door's wooden frame.

View down attic steps from outside Bridget's room.
Photo by Ron Bueker.

"Miss Lizzie, what is the matter?" Bridget asked, breathless. She had never seen Lizzie Borden look so shaken. The girl never showed any emotion, other than flashes of anger when things did not go her way.

"Go for Dr. Bowen as soon as you can, I think Father is hurt."

Bridget instinctually headed for the last place she had seen Mr. Borden—the sitting room. Lizzie stopped her. "Oh Maggie, don't go in. I must have a doctor. Go for Dr. Bowen."

Bridget was confused. Lizzie had just yelled up the stairs that her father was dead, and "someone had come in and killed him." It sounded more than he "was hurt." She passed Lizzie and hurried out the screen door, running for the doctor that lived only steps across the street to the north.

Lizzie watched as Bridget's back disappeared. She turned to face the kitchen and saw the old lock sitting where she left it on the kitchen table. Quickly, she picked it up and ran to the back door. Looking about at the street, and the windows of Mrs. Churchill's house, Lizzie hurried to the barn. She unlatched the hasp and stepped in only enough to toss the old Yale lock into a box of "old truck" a few feet from the door. It landed among a few other broken shop locks her father kept there, along with some sheets of iron and tin. Her gaze fell on the plumber's pipe, half-hidden in shadow. Someone closed a door nearby; she let it go and hurried out, pinning the door. Brushing the rust from her hand, she hurried back and entered the house. Leaning against the inside door to the back entry, she finally caught her breath. Her head spun, her nerves were shattered. Had she really just butchered her father?

Bridget pounded on the Bowen's door at 91 Second Street. Finally, Phoebe Bowen, the doctor's wife, opened the door and looked in surprise at the harried girl standing there. Bridget sputtered out that Dr. Bowen was needed at the house—Mr. Borden was dead. Mrs. Bowen, taken aback, told her the doctor was out on calls, but as soon as he got back, she would send him right over. The time was "shortly after" eleven.

The view from the Bowen's house (right foreground), looking diagonally across the street at the Borden's (behind the trees). Mrs. Churchill's house is at the left of the photo. Photo by Charles Carroll.

Bridget hurried back across the street, the dust from the road puffing up beneath her feet. She climbed the side steps to the screen door and found Lizzie where she had left her—leaning up against the wooden frame.

The maid told Lizzie Dr. Bowen was out, but that Mrs. Bowen said he would be back soon, and she'd send him over.

"Miss Lizzie, where was you?" Bridget finally asked. "Didn't I leave the screen door hooked?"

"I was out in the back yard and I heard a groan and came in, and the screen door was wide open," Lizzie said in a strained voice.

Lizzie asked Bridget if she knew where Alice Russell lived, and the maid said she did.

"Go and get her," Lizzie said. "I can't be alone in the house."

Bridget grabbed a hat and shawl from the pegs in the back entry and hurried out the screen door.

As soon as she left, Lizzie crossed to the stove and looked in. The roll of Swansea papers had finally caught and was burning. She worried about the smell of burning paper that escaped slightly through the stove vents. There was nothing she could do about it now.

At 11:10, Adelaide Churchill was returning up Second Street from M.T. Hudner's Market on South Main, only a quick walk from her house next door to the Borden's. Mrs. Churchill's house was still called the Buffington House, named for her late father who had at one time been the mayor of Fall River and lived in the house in the mid-1800s. A widow, Adelaide Churchill had her hands full, caring for a house filled with relatives, a son, and a handyman named Thomas Bowles. She had just purchased "three items" from Hudner's meat market for her noon meal and was walking home when she saw Bridget running frantically from Dr. Bowen's house toward the Borden's.

"She looked frightened, to me," Adelaide Churchill stated during her Preliminary Hearing testimony.

Mrs. Churchill entered her gate and carried the groceries into her kitchen at the south side of the house. She placed the parcels on a long bench beneath a window facing the Borden's dining room window. She then stepped to a window further east and looked out to see Lizzie Borden standing inside the back-screen door of her home.

"She looked as if she was distressed or frightened about something," Mrs. Churchill testified. "She was leaning against the side of the door. I do not know but she put her hand to her head; and looked as if she was distressed. I opened one of the windows and said, "Lizzie, what is the matter?" She said, "Oh, Mrs. Churchill, do come over; someone has killed father."

Bridget hurried to the house at the corner of Second Street and Borden, only a few houses down from the Borden's. It was the wrong house.

Mrs. Churchill ran through her house, yelling "Mr. Borden has been murdered," shocking Mrs. John Gomeley, who was in the dining room pushing "a sick baby to-and-fro." She ran through her gate and into the Borden's side yard. When she opened the screen door, she found Lizzie sitting on the second stair of the back staircase, directly right of the entry door.

"O, Lizzie," Mrs. Churchill said, placing her hand on Lizzie's arm, "Where is your father?"

"In the sitting room," Lizzie said in a strained voice.

"Where was you when it happened?" Adelaide asked breathlessly.

"I went to the barn to get a piece of iron, and came back, heard a distressed noise, and came in, and found the screen door open," Lizzie said.

"Where is your mother?"

"She had a note to go see someone that was sick. I don't know but that she was killed too. I wish someone would try to find Mrs. Borden, for I thought I heard her come in. Father must have an enemy, for we have all been sick, and they thought the milk had been poisoned. Dr. Bowen is not home," Lizzie continued on in a rush of words. "I must have a Doctor!"

"Shall I go and try to find someone to get a doctor?"

"Yes."

Danielle Cabral, a tour guide at the Lizzie Borden House, sitting on the second stair where Lizzie sat waiting for Bridget that morning. Photo by the Author.

Adelaide hurried diagonally across the street to L.L. Hall's Livery Stable where her handyman, Thomas Bowles, had just taken her carriage, after washing it. She asked Mr. Hall for Thomas. When she found him, she blurted out, "Thomas, will you go and try to find a doctor. Somebody has killed Mr. Borden. Any doctor!"

Just a few houses over from them, and across the street, Bridget had hurried to the home at the corner of Second Street and Borden in search of Miss Russell.

Thomas hurried off and ran into Bridget, who had just found she had the wrong house. She asked him if he knew where Miss Russell lived, and he gave her directions. Meanwhile, Lizzie was alone in the house.

Lizzie's Mind Set:

1) Lizzie stops Bridget from going toward the sitting room to see Andrew. It may have been to spare the maid, or to insure she kept her wits about her so she could run for help. It may also have been to keep her away from the stove where the Swansea deed was "smoldering and smoking," about to catch fire.

2) She tells Bridget she was out in the back yard and hears a "groan." The sitting room is on the other side of the house, away from the back yard, behind a door that is always closed to the kitchen. This sound changes to a "distressed" noise, by the time she gives her version to Mrs. Churchill. She tells Mrs. Churchill she was out in the barn looking for a piece of iron. She has now moved farther away from the murder than just the back yard. When she tossed the lock into the box of scraps minutes earlier, did the iron she saw there set her mind to working? "There is iron in the barn. What can I do with iron to form an alibi?" She will later use it for fixing a screen, and in another version, for fishing "sinkers."

3) Lizzie says she heard Mrs. Borden come back from her sick note call. How is that possible? It was only moments before Bridget went up to her room before dinner that Lizzie said Abby had a note and was gone out. Andrew is home. The front door is once again, triple locked, and the back-screen door is hooked; both barring Abby from getting in without help.

4) In Lizzie's one and only testimony during the Coroner's Inquest, she says she was in the kitchen waiting for her irons to get hot and looking through a Harper's Magazine when her father got home.

Abby could not have come through the back door without Lizzie seeing her. When Bridget goes upstairs a few minutes before 11, Andrew has already made a quick trip to his bedroom, and found no Abby upstairs. She is nowhere on the first floor, and Lizzie has told Bridget and her father Abby is out of the house. The only time Lizzie could have "heard her come in" is when she is "out in the barn" during her father's murder. When she hollers up the back stairs shortly after 11 to inform Bridget her father is dead, there is no sign of Abby, yet Lizzie's scream would have gone right past Abby's bedroom door. And when Abby is found, it is in the guest room where she started that morning, still in her plain house dress.

Lizzie's urgency for someone to begin looking for Abby is two-fold: it is too nerve-wracking to wait for someone to stumble upon the body, and, the murders need to look like they happened at the same time. Abby can't lay there undetected much longer, as her wounds are already congealing. And, two, the sooner the bodies are both found, the police will go in search of the murderer, and leave her alone. She is wearing two dresses on a hot August day.

5) Lizzie tells Bridget to go and get Miss Russell for "I can't be alone in the house." Yet, she sends away two people who were there with her: Bridget and Mrs. Churchill. Her father has been butchered within the last few minutes. The murderer could still be in the house. Yet, she stays in the house, only a few feet away from an open cellar door, and a back staircase, instead of running outside where all the people are on that busy street. That she sends Bridget for Miss Russell is an interesting choice. Alice just heard all of Lizzie's tales of poisoning and enemies the night before. She will back up Lizzie's fears of doom. And notice, she draws attention to poisoned milk, already directing the attention to the possibility of someone *outside* the house putting something in the can of milk. Now, if poison *is* found in the milk, or inside the bodies, it bolsters her story of an enemy.

The Chaos Begins

As Bridget hurried up Borden Street toward Alice Russell's house, the rumor of Andrew Borden's murder was spreading beyond the door of Hall's stable. John J. Cunningham, a freelance writer in the newspaper business, had just walked up to Hall's, where he saw Mrs. Churchill speaking excitedly to some men. He asked "what was the matter," and a boy by the name of Albert Pierce told him that someone had "stabbed" A.J. Borden at his house.

Mr. Cunningham darted into Mr. Gorman's paint store, a few steps away at the corner of Second and Borden streets, and telephoned what he had heard, first to John Manning of the *Fall River Daily Globe,* Mr. Stevens of the *Fall River News,* and finally, to Marshall Hilliard at the Central Police Station. Edwin Porter, a police reporter for the *Fall River Globe,* covered the news for the police, in the guise of an investigative reporter. He would later write the first book on the Borden murders, called *The Fall River Tragedy: A History of the Borden Murders*; one that caused Lizzie Borden great angst. It was 11:15 in the morning when the phone shrilled in Marshall Hilliard's office.

Alice Russell was "doing my work" near her window overlooking her front walk when she saw a breathless Bridget Sullivan come racing up to her door. With Lizzie's tales of poison from the night before still ringing in her ears, Alice feared the family had taken a turn for the worse. She left her accounting books to hurry to the door before Bridget could knock.

"What is it, Bridget? Are they worse?' Alice asked.

Bridget, out of breath and panting, said, "Yes, he is worse. I don't know but Mr. Borden is dead," she said ominously. Alice stared, hoping the maid was exaggerating. She assured Bridget she would be right over as soon as she changed her dress. Bridget took off on the run again, as Alice dashed into her small bedroom upstairs to change into her street clothes.

Dr. Seabury Bowen arrived home in his horse and buggy, to find his wife hurrying down the steps to catch him before he alighted. His driver, James Leonard, told the police Mrs. Bowen said "something terrible has happened" at the Borden's, and to "go right over." Dr. Bowen, like Alice, assumed it was something to do with the food poisoning from the day before, yet there was something in his wife's urgency that concerned him. Surely, no one had died from the malady! It was now 11:25.

For the past ten minutes, Lizzie Borden had been alone in the house. She had plenty of time to make sure all the loose ends were tied up. She walked through the dining room, and peered with a tight stomach into the sitting room, avoiding looking at the prone body on the sofa. Nothing seemed out of place. The blood spattering the closed parlor door turned her stomach. It was too real, too graphic, and final. As she returned to the kitchen through the dining room, she absentmindedly picked up the small ironing board and carried it to the kitchen table. The smell of burning paper scented the air, as she lifted the stove lid to peer inside, all the while keeping an eye on the screen door.

The Swansea deed was still burning through the tightly rolled layers of papers, most of it blackened and leaving only a ring of white paper at its center.

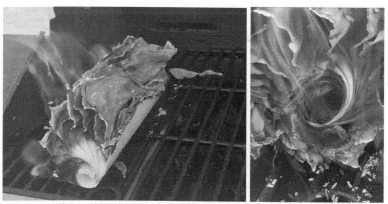

Actual experiment burning a tube of rolled paper over a low fire. It took ten minutes to burn, from the time of its beginning to smoke to the fire burning out after the paper was consumed. It left a recognizable cylindrical shape (right). Test performed by the Author.

Lizzie heard voices shouting outside. The news was out. Replacing the stove lid, she hurried back to the rear door and sat on the second stair next to it, where Mrs. Churchill had left her.

Adelaide Churchill. Photo courtesy of the Fall River Historical Society.

Adelaide Churchill hurried back to the Borden's, entering through the screen door. She told Lizzie people were looking for a doctor. She was unaware Dr. Bowen had just pulled up in his buggy across the street.

Seabury Bowen stepped down from the carriage and hurried across Second. He was a man of medium-height, bewhiskered in the style of the day with mutton chops, and sported a high collar. His face was warm—the kind patients find comforting. He had known Lizzie and her family for twenty years. He was not prepared for what he was about to find.

Bridget hurried up Second Street without waiting for Miss Russell. She hadn't run this much in a long time. Her head was swimming from the heat, exertion, and the remains of the stomach flu she had been fighting all day. Up ahead, she saw Dr. Bowen step down from his buggy and hasten across the street. *Thank goodness*, Bridget thought. *He will know what to do.*

"He is murdered! He is murdered!"

Doctor Seabury Bowen

Dr. Bowen opened the screen door and entered without waiting for an invitation. Mrs. Churchill and Lizzie were still in the back entry. A few minutes later, Bridget came in the back door.

"What is the matter, Lizzie?" Dr. Bowen asked breathlessly.

"I am afraid father has been stabbed or hurt," she said.

After recovering from the shock of hearing of a stabbing, instead of a man suffering from poisoning, the doctor asked: "Where is he?" "The sitting room," Lizzie said, beckoning for Dr. Bowen to follow her through the dining room, instead of opening the sitting room door leading from the kitchen. It may have been to spare Mrs. Churchill and Bridget, or, that she couldn't bear to see her father like that again.

The three women followed Dr. Bowen into the dining room and waited as he continued through into the sitting room. Lizzie held her breath. It would be the first reaction to what she had done.

Seabury Bowen bent over the ruined head of the man he had spoken to on this very sofa only the morning before. He did not recognize Andrew Borden. The gashes were so severe, that only a fraction of the man's upturned face remained. Only a glimpse of the right side of his features, pressed into the decorative pillow, resembled the austere businessmen he had known for so long. The doctor felt for a pulse; an unnecessary but instinctual routine. He found none. He realized he was visibly shaken. Murder victims, and ones as brutally mutilated as this were not his daily experience. His was the world of pill bottles and remedies, stitches and delivering babies. He walked nervously back into the dining room, where three expectant faces turned toward him.

"He is murdered. He is murdered," Dr. Bowen said. "That is just awful." He turned to Lizzie and asked, "Has there been anybody here?"

"Not as I know of," Lizzie said. "I overheard father several times talking loud recently, and I was afraid some of the tenants had some trouble with him. [Attorney Knowlton hit the point hard during the trial that Lizzie offered the information to Mrs. Churchill and Dr. Bowen within minutes of their seeing her that "father has an enemy."]

Dr. Bowen looked at Mrs. Churchill and said, "Addie, come and see Mr. Borden."

Adelaide Churchill recoiled. "Oh, no Doctor. I don't want to see him. I looked at him out in the yard this morning, he looked nice to me, I don't want to see him."

"Perhaps it's just as well," Doctor Bowen said. Mrs. Churchill's remark brought him back to the delicate situation at hand with so many women in the house. He asked for a sheet to cover Mr. Borden.

Bridget said the sheets were kept in the bedclothes drawers in Mrs. Borden's dressing room, and they would need a key to get into the locked room. Dr. Bowen went into the sitting room and reached up into the Prince Albert coat rolled beneath the dead man's head. As he did so, Andrew's body slid down somewhat lower onto the couch. Finding no keys, he gently felt into Andrew Borden's pants' pockets. Finding the ring of keys, Dr. Bowen returned and handed them to Bridget. She told him that was not what they needed. It was a single key, she told him, sitting on the mantel in the room where Andrew lay. He brought out the key and handed it to her.

Bridget was nervous about going upstairs alone. Mrs. Churchill offered to go with her. The two mounted the back stairs slowly, nervously listening for sounds in the attic, or any movements that might betray a murderer secluded in the shadowy recesses of the stairwell area. They unlocked the Borden's bedroom door on the second landing and went in. There was no Abby. They went to the bureau in the small room and opened the drawer with the clean linens.

As the two women went about their task, Lizzie quickly asked a favor of her neighbor, Doctor Bowen, as they waited in the dining room. Would he please contact her uncle, John Morse, to let him know Mr. Borden is dead? "He is in town and visiting at the Emery's on Weybosset," she explained quickly. She kept her voice low.

"Do you think two sheets will do?" Bridget asked Mrs. Churchill in Abby's dressing room, wanting to hurry and return to the safety of the kitchen.

"I would think one would cover a body," Mrs. Churchill said, the word "body" feeling foreign on her tongue. She shuddered.

Bridget took two anyway, perhaps in a moment of clairvoyance, as there would soon be two bodies to deal with. They left the rooms and relocked the door to the landing.

Drawing of Bridget Sullivan for the Borden Murder Trial.

Mrs. Churchill and Bridget handed Dr. Bowen the sheets. He took one and went into the sitting room. Mrs. Churchill left the other on the dining room table. Lizzie called Bridget into the kitchen. A few minutes later, Bridget called to Mrs. Churchill, who had remained waiting in the dining room.

Almost before Mrs. Churchill stepped into the kitchen, Bridget, obviously nervous, said, "Mrs. Borden had a note to go and see someone that was sick. She was dusting in the sitting room, and she hurried off. She did not tell me where she was going. She usually does."

If Adelaide Churchill thought this sudden revelation strange, it was probably one of many strange occurrences happening on this macabre day.

Lizzie suddenly blurted out, "I shall have to go to the cemetery myself."

"Oh, No," Mrs. Churchill assured her quickly. "Lizzie, the undertaker will attend to all such things as that for you; they generally do."

Alice Russell, her prim hat and visiting dress arrayed as nicely as she could manage with shaking hands, hurried along the upward slanting street to the Borden's house. Her mind was in a daze. Was Lizzie's story of an enemy and poisoning true?

Charles Sawyer, a beefy decorative painter who lived nearby on Second Street, had heard the news. He was at the machine shop of Augustus C. Rich at 81 Second Street, above Hall's stables when he saw Alice Russell hurrying up the street. Knowing she was a friend of the Borden's, he hurried across Second in an attempt to learn what was going on.

Miss Russell was in no mood to talk. She answered his queries with vague and breathless bursts. As she reached the Borden's house, entering in through the north gate, Sawyer gave up and turned away. Just then, Officer Allen from the police station hurried up Second and told Sawyer to come along with him to the Borden's.

Alice opened the screen door and stepped into the back entry, not knowing what to expect. She saw Lizzie leaning against the kitchen door frame at the end of the entry hall.

"Lizzie," Alice said, "sit right down here in the kitchen." "She sat down in the rocker and I sat down next to her in a chair," Alice testified days later at the Coroner's Inquest. Lizzie laid her head on Alice's shoulder. Mrs. Churchill took a towel and wet one end of it. She bathed Lizzie's forehead and cheeks. The kitchen was stifling hot, partially due to Lizzie's attempt to restart a fire in the stove. The smell of burning paper had dissipated. The two women fanned her with a newspaper until Lizzie asked Bridget to get a fan from the dining room closet.

"Rub her hands," Alice instructed Mrs. Churchill, as she feared Lizzie was faint. As Addie reached for Lizzie's hands to do so, Lizzie shook her head, no.

Doctor Bowen took one of the sheets and covered Andrew, watching as the fresh blood quickly soaked through the linen weave at his head. Just then, a man in plain clothes appeared at the back door, along with Charles Sawyer. Doctor Bowen said they couldn't come in, and that he needed a policeman. Sawyer informed the doctor the other man was a policeman. Doctor Bowen let him in.

Newspaper drawing of Officer George Allen, 1892.

Officer Allen was lead into the sitting room by the doctor, while Charles Sawyer, waited outside. The physician pulled back the sheet and showed the astonished officer the bloody remains of Andrew Borden's face. The portly man gulped. He was merely a clerk at the police station—one who checked prisoners in and out. This was a sight he was not used to seeing.

"Now you go back and tell Marshall Hilliard all about it," Bowen said.

Officer Allen walked shakily through the house where he barely registered seeing Lizzie "sitting at the kitchen table." He checked the closet by the front door, the one in the dining room, and other places where someone might be hiding on the first floor. Finding no one, he hurried to the back entry. He passed out through the screen door and told Charles Sawyer to guard it.

"Don't let in anyone but the police," he told the surprised young man. With rubbery knees, Allen half-walked, half-ran, back to make his traumatic report to Marshall Hilliard.

Charles Sawyer stepped inside the door and peered down the back entry into the kitchen.

"Miss Borden sat in a chair in the kitchen," Sawyer testified at the Coroner's Inquest, five days after the murders. "She seemed to be considerable excited I thought, as though she was apparently grief-stricken, or something, although I might not be a judge in that respect. She seemed to be considerably excited and very uneasy, and the ladies seemed to be ministering to her, that is bathing her face. I can't say that she was crying. I could not tell exactly. I did not go way into the kitchen at all [until] after that some little time. I stood near that door. You know that is quite a little entryway."

"The servant girl appeared to be well," Mr. Sawyer continued, "somewhat frightened, I thought she acted as though she was considerably excited, although she talked intelligently, anything that was said to her, and she seemed very willing to give any information that she knew anything about. I heard her say something about Mrs. Borden saying she had received a note, but I can't seem to recollect just how she put it, whether she said Mrs. Borden told her, or somebody else told her. I also heard Mrs. Churchill mention that fact."

When Charles Sawyer was, in essence, deputized to guard the back door, he knew very little of what had happened within the walls of the Borden home. His nerves were on edge. All he knew was a man had been "stabbed" within the last half an hour. What if the knife-wielding man was still in the house? He eyed the open cellar door only steps away. When no one was looking, he hurriedly pulled the basement door closed and bolted it.

Doctor Bowen replaced the sheet across the still form of Andrew Borden and walked into the kitchen. Lizzie suddenly asked if he would please go and telegraph her sister Emma, who was staying at the Brownell's in Fairhaven. "Don't tell her the worse, as there is a feeble old lady there and it would shock her," Lizzie said. No mention was made again in the presence of Mrs. Churchill and Bridget, of contacting her Uncle John.

"I will do anything for you," Dr. Bowen, said sincerely, and hurried out to carry out his two directives; Officer Allen not far ahead of him.

Bridget thought suddenly of Mrs. Borden.

"Miss Lizzie, if I knew where Mrs. Whitehead [Abby's half-sister] was I would go and see if Mrs. Borden was there and tell her that Mr. Borden was very sick."

Lizzie paused and said, "Maggie, I am almost positive I heard her coming in. Won't you go upstairs to see?"

"I'm not going up there alone," Bridget cried. She and Mrs. Churchill had already been in Abby's bedroom up the back stairs. That left only the rooms at the top of the front steps.

"Come, Bridget," Mrs. Churchill said. "I'll go with you."

The two women buoyed themselves up for the passage through the sitting room. Keeping their eyes focused on the open door to the front hall entry, they hurried through and walked to the base of the front stairs. Looking up the winding stairway, they hesitated. Both were praying Abby Borden was still out on a sick call.

[It is interesting to note that Bridget's first thought of where Abby Borden had gone on that "sick call" was to her half-sister, "Bertie" Whitehead's, on Fourth Street. Knowing Mrs. Borden had few friends, other than Mrs. Miller across the street, and a few nodding relationships with other neighbors, Bridget thought it was the only logical place her employer could be. People did not send for someone to come and help them unless they were very close. Lizzie hurries and changes the direction of the conversation...sending the women off to look for Abby within the house.]

Front entry stairs to the second landing where the guest room is. As it curves, you can look to the left through the spindles and see beneath the bed in the guest room. Lizzie's room is at the top of the stairs to the right. The door to the sitting room is at the left bottom.

Photo by Ron Bueker.

Chapter Sixteen

Thursday—August 4, 1892
"Is There Another?!"

As Bridget and Mrs. Churchill climbed the front stairway, Alice Russell waited with Lizzie in the kitchen. She fanned her continually as the thick heat of the room threatened to rob them of breath. Charles Sawyer stole a glance at them from time-to-time, wondering what had happened inside the modest house. He managed to ask Mrs. Churchill as she went about the kitchen, "Is he dead?" "Oh yes, he is dead," she answered. Later that morning, Dr. Bowen asked him to come in and see the murdered man. Sawyer saw "a sheet with some blood on it," and was shown the butchered head of Andrew Borden.

Charles Sawyer watched the side yard from inside the door. Small boys, one he recognized as Augustus Rich's son, were running through the yard, and several men had walked through as well. He hoped some reinforcements were on their way, as people were continually coming up to him and asking to be let in. One man, stating his name was John Manning, and that he was a reporter with the *Fall River Daily Herald*, was told he could not enter. The dogged journalist planted himself on the side steps.

John Cunningham, the man who had first phoned the Marshall after hearing Mrs. Churchill's claim that Mr. Borden was dead, had himself, meandered over to the house. He walked into the back yard and spying the door to the cellar, reached over and tried the handle. It was locked tight. Other would-be detectives were trying hard to peer into the windows through half-closed shutters and lace curtains. It was only the beginning of the crowds that were to come running at the shout of "murder!"

Bridget and Adelaide Churchill climbed the front stairs slowly, peering up through the spindles, watching for any sign of movement. Bridget was a few steps ahead of the older woman when Mrs. Churchill happened to look to her left through the stairwell railing and into the open door of the guest room. The light was not as strong inside the room, but she could see beneath the guest bed. She suddenly stopped and gasped. There was no mistaking a prostrate form lying on the floor on the other side of the large bed. She went no farther.

Bridget turned to see the whitened face of the lady behind her. Following Mrs. Churchill's gaze to the bed, the maid suddenly bolstered her courage and darted into the room. She stepped to the end of the bed frame and looked down on the still form splayed across the carpet; something round and black spilling out from her head.

Adelaide, finding her feet, hurried down the front stairs. In her haste to get back to the kitchen, she forgot to avert her eyes as she bolted into the sitting room. Two legs, bent at an angle, their feet resting on the floor, were before her. The rest of the body was beneath a white sheet, its head area covered in blood. Her heart gave way and she stumbled into the kitchen where she finally doubled over, letting out a small shriek.

"What is it?" Alice asked in alarm. "Is there another?"

Mrs. Churchill nodded, her hand to her stomach. "She's upstairs," she finally managed, holding onto the door frame.

Lizzie was pale. Alice Russell looked at her and her instincts took over her own quaking nerves.

"Let's go into the dining room, Lizzie. It will be cooler there." Lizzie allowed the woman to lead her into the dining room. She threw herself down on the lounge.

"Go and get Mrs. Bowen," Lizzie told Bridget in a strained voice, as the maid returned to the room. Bridget may have supposed Lizzie meant for Mrs. Bowen to inform her husband that Abby had been found and needed attention. Without waiting for further instructions, the maid ran out the screen door, past the confused Charles Sawyer standing there. Mrs. Churchill stepped forward and told him "Mrs. Borden is dying! I think from the shock!"

[Lizzie has Alice Russell and Adelaide Churchill with her. Why does she ask Bridget to "go and get Mrs. Bowen?" Could it be due to Abby's visit to the Bowen house the day before, claiming the family was being poisoned? Did Lizzie want yet another witness in the house when the police came, testifying the family had an enemy?]

According to the Witness Statements supplied by the Fall River police, "Bridget came out of the house on a run, and went over to Southard H. Miller's house, and went in. Soon after, Mr. Miller came to the door and called Alexander B. Coggeshall, a stable-keeper on Second Street, who had stopped to talk to Mrs. Buffington in front of Mrs. Churchill's house. 'Here Alex, I want you to listen to what this girl says.'" Bridget then told them that Mr. Borden and his wife had both been murdered. Mr. Coggeshall then went to dinner at Mrs. Tripp's [restaurant next door to the Churchill's] at 80 Second Street, and he told her of the murder. It was then 11:20 by the clock in the restaurant."

Southard Miller had known the Borden's the longest. He had employed Andrew Borden as a young carpenter years before the ambitious man made his fortune. Miller had built the house in which the two bodies now lay. He listened in astonishment to Bridget's breathless tale.

Phoebe Bowen, overhearing the fuss, walked quickly over to the Borden home. She had known the family well, and had just the day before, admitted a sick and frightened Abby Borden into her parlor to see her husband.

Doctor Bowen was still out on Lizzie's errand to telegraph her sister Emma in Fairhaven, and to contact her Uncle John Morse at the Emery's on Weybosset Street. According to Dr. Bowen's testimonies, he sent the telegram to Emma, time-stamped 11:32 at the *Western Union Telegraph Company* in the Richard Borden Block and walked across the street to Baker's Drug Store. There he spoke to his friend, Mr. Samuel Flint, before returning to the Borden house. According to Mrs. Daniel Emery, the good doctor had also slipped in a visit to her house during his errands, to see to her ailing visitor. That John Morse was also there, was a fortunate "coincidence." She said the two "did not meet," although they came and went through the same door seconds apart.

Doctor Seabury Bowen returned up Second Street shortly before 11:40. He had reached John Morse by telephone at the Emery's, and possibly spoken to him privately outside the house after he took a look at Annie Morse, who was lying ill on the sitting room sofa. According to police, and Edwin Porter, the police reporter for the *Globe*, who interviewed Morse that day, Uncle John knew of Andrew's murder by 11:30. Morse told Porter he had been telephoned for, and that was when he first learned of the murder. When he arrived at the Borden house around 15-to-25 minutes later, he had not yet been told Abby was dead as well.

Doctor Bowen climbed wearily from the buggy, leaving James Leonard, the driver, in charge of the team. He entered through the Borden's screen door to find Charles Sawyer still at his post. He had barely made it into the entryway when Mrs. Churchill came running up to him.

"They have found Mrs. Borden," she told him.

"Where?" Dr. Bowen asked in shock.

"Upstairs in the front room. You better go up!"

When Bowen entered the guest room at the top of the stairs, he first noticed how dim the light was. The north shutters, facing Mrs. Churchill's were almost closed, casting the room in subdued shadows. At first, he saw nothing to alarm him.

Doctor Seabury Bowen's Preliminary Hearing testimony:

"I went up the front stairs. As I got at the top of the stairs, as soon as I got up on the second story, I could look right over the bed, and I saw her lying there flat, prone. My thought was, that she had run up there and fainted. I went right around the foot of the bed and satisfied myself in an instant that she was not living. I don't know whether I got hold of her pulse, but I satisfied myself some way, I don't know how, that she was not living. I went right down stairs again and told them Mrs. Borden was dead, killed the same instant, I think I said that. When I came down, my wife was there, and I told her to go right home."

[Dr. Bowen changed his story, during the Superior Court trial a year later, in an effort to appear as if he had handled it better. He said he placed his hand on her head and felt the cuts there. He testified he felt of her right wrist for a pulse and found none. He also changed his story that he said they were "killed the same instant;" he now stated they were "killed with the same instrument," as by then, it was accepted knowledge Abby died at least an hour and a half ahead of her husband.]

Phoebe Bowen had only been in the house a few minutes. She was standing behind Lizzie who was lying on the dining room lounge, where Alice and Mrs. Churchill were still trying to make her as comfortable as possible. The tension in the room was heavy as the women waited for Doctor Bowen to return from upstairs. When Phoebe Bowen's husband finally came down and made the announcement that Mrs. Borden was dead also, Mrs. Bowen let out a gasp and became upset. Lizzie asked who that was that just made the sound behind her. Miss Russell explained it was Phoebe Bowen. Doctor Bowen sent his wife home, perhaps to man the office phone line, or, possibly, because his wife was not helping the situation by becoming emotional. Phoebe Bowen testified later that "they sent me home. They said I was not fit to stay."

Policemen and Questions

At 11:35 that morning, twenty minutes after the call came into Marshall Hilliard's office, the police began to arrive at the Borden house in rapid succession. With a large portion of the officers away at the annual Rocky Point clambake, at the amusement park on Narragansett Bay in Warwick, Rhode Island, the day patrol was about to be thrown into a mystery that defied logic, ruined careers, and changed the lives of those sucked into its vortex, forever.

Doctor Bowen had just delivered the news to the women waiting in the dining room that Abby Borden appeared to be deceased as well when two officers appeared at the screen door. Bowen hurried forward to greet Officer Patrick Doherty and Deputy Sheriff Frank Wixon.

"I'm glad to see you," Bowen said, with a great deal of relief. He admitted the men into the house, a happy John Manning with the *Fall River Daily Herald* following in behind them.

The *Fall River Herald* is still going strong today, in Fall River, Massachusetts.

Officer Patrick Doherty, 1892. Captain Patrick Doherty, 1893.
Officer Doherty was promoted to Captain following the Borden murders.

"What is the trouble?" Officer Doherty asked. He noticed Bridget standing in the far southeast corner of the kitchen, near the sink.

"Mr. Borden is dead," Bowen said and led the officers and the reporter into the sitting room. When the doctor pulled back the sheet, the men were surprised to see the extent of the elderly man's wounds.

"I noticed there was one wound down here, across the eye, that was very deep," Officer Doherty testified at the Preliminary Hearing. "It looked to me on the left side of the face, the right side was on the sofa, and the eye seemed to be knocked out, hanging by some thread or something. There was another wound came down by the nose, or down the cheek bone, the cheek bone was wide open, by the cheek bone clear down to the neck was laid right open."

In low tones, Doctor Bowen told Officer Doherty and Deputy Sheriff Wixon, that he was satisfied something was wrong, for they were all sick the day before. "To make matters worse," Bowen continued, "Mrs. Borden is lying dead upstairs. I suppose she saw the killing of her husband, and run upstairs, and died with fright from the shock."

[Dr. Bowen, clearly embarrassed, denied during later testimony that he said any such thing. He now stated that he said she died from shock from her wounds.]

Newspaper drawing of Officer Frank Wixon

Officer Doherty requested to see Mrs. Borden's body. He found her lying face down between the bed and dressing case. "Several spots of blood were on the bed, and also a large tuft of hair," he later testified. "On examining the body, I found she was lying in a pool of blood. I informed the Doctor of the fact, and he expressed much surprise. I wanted to examine the woman, but there was no room between the bed and dressing case to walk. I walked back to the foot of the bed, up around the north side of the bed, and I pulled it out about three feet, away from her. I stooped down and I saw she was lying in a pool of thick black blood, and her head was all cut. I put one finger here [under one of Abby's arms that lay above her head] and raised this a little bit so I could see under the hair around the ear better. I asked the Doctor, Mr. Wixon, and the reporter to remain by the bodies until I notified the Marshall."

Officer Doherty hurried downstairs and out of the house. He ran the short distance to Gorman's Undertaking business at the corner of Spring and Second, where he knew he could find a phone. He called Marshall Hilliard with his findings at the Borden home, and then hurried back across the street. He passed the ever-vigilant Charles Sawyer at the door and stopped into the kitchen to question Bridget, who was still standing there.

"Mr. Borden came in the front door at 10:50," Bridget said, in answer to Officer Doherty's question. "I was upstairs [when the murder occurred] and heard no noise until Miss Lizzie called me."

Moments later, at 11:37, Officer Mullaly, Mr. George Allen, and Mr. Devine arrived at the house. This was Allen's second trip, after originally giving the alarm when he returned to the police station, after seeing Mr. Borden's wounds. Officer William H. Medley arrived within a few minutes of the others, around "twenty, or nineteen minutes of twelve."

Officer Doherty turned his attention to Lizzie, who was sitting next to Alice Russell in the dining room. Mrs. Churchill was fanning her.

"Miss Borden," Officer Doherty began, "where were you when your father was killed?

"I was in the barn," she answered quietly.

"Is there any Portuguese working on the farm over the River for your father?" [Bridget may have mentioned a Portuguese working at the Swansea farm, possibly referring to Alfred Johnson, who was actually of Swedish decent.]

"No, sir."

"Who works for your father?"

"Mr. Eddy, and Mr. Johnson; and Mr. Eddy has been sick."

"Have either Mr. Eddy or Mr. Johnson been in town this morning, or up here to the house this morning?" Doherty asked.

"No, sir," Lizzie said emphatically. "Neither Mr. Eddy nor Mr. Johnson would hurt my father."

"Miss Borden, did you hear any screams or outcries?"

"No, sir. I heard some kind of peculiar noise."

"Can you describe the noise?" Doherty asked.

"No, not very well; something like "scraping"."

Officer Michael Mullaly entered the dining room as Officer Doherty went into the sitting room. He approached Lizzie.

Officer Michael Mullaly

She looked up wearily from the lounge, and to his questions, repeated again her actions of the morning. She told the officer that she had been out of doors, and when she came in, she found her father dead on the sofa.

"Do you know what kind of property your father had on him?" Officer Mullaly asked, his mind focusing on a possible burglary as the motive for the murder.

"He has a silver watch and chain, a pocket book with money in it, and a gold ring on his little finger," she said.

Officer Mullaly testified at the Preliminary Hearing that the following happened:

"By that time, Officer Doherty had appeared in the doorway, and I told him to look and see if Mr. Borden has the property on him. He went to look and came back. He reported to me that his watch and chain was on him. He did not say anything about a pocket book. I then inquired of Miss Borden whether she knew if there was a hatchet or axe on the premises, and she said yes. She told me Bridget Sullivan would show it to me in the cellar. I then came out, and I went upstairs where Mrs. Borden laid on the floor in a pool of blood." [Sheriff Wixon removed Andrew's watch from the body. It was attached by a black braid to his lapel.]

Alice closed the door from the dining room to the kitchen, shutting out the heat from the stove, and the noise of the constantly-arriving police, reporters, and doctors. She sat by Lizzie on the lounge and noticed the last hook of her waist blouse was undone and the fabric "pulled out." Alice reached to unhook the next one, to allow Lizzie to breathe easier. Lizzie quickly stopped her, saying, "I am not faint. My clothes are loose." Alice stopped and fanned her instead. They would not have respite for long.

Charles Sawyer watched from the screen door as people continued to arrive. The front fence was lined with curious citizens, staring at the three-story house in excitement. Children were standing on the stringer of the fence and the gate. Others, without trepidation, entered the yard and walked about the house and grounds. John Cunningham and reporter Walter P. Stevens of the *Fall River News*, walked along the lawn between the Kelly house and the Borden's, peering into the long grass for footprints or clues. They tried the cellar door and found it locked. The wood pile at the rear fence was glanced at, as well as Doctor Chagnon's orchard at the rear of the property. It was a free-for-all for the public. Crime scene contamination was yet to become a buzz word in forensic terms. To say the least, the Borden scene was hopelessly trampled over.

[John Cunningham would later report they saw no footprints in the tall grass between the Kelly and Borden homes; a curious fact as Bridget had just been all over that area washing windows and making runs to the barn for water.]

Dr. Bowen stepped into the dining room where Lizzie was lying on the lounge.

"Lizzie?" he asked quietly. "Do you know what became of the note your stepmother received? I have looked in the waste baskets and not found it."

Lizzie said she did not know anything about it.

"Did you look in her pocket?" Dr. Bowen asked, meaning Abby's purse. Lizzie shook her head.

"Well, then," Alice spoke up. "She must have burned it."

"Yes," Lizzie agreed. "She must have burned it."

Chapter Seventeen

Thursday, August 4, 1892
Searches and Discoveries

The First Search

Officers Patrick Doherty and Michael Mullaly began a quick search of the house. They decided to begin with the attic. They found Bridget seated on the back stairs near the rear door and told her they needed to search the third floor. She went up with them and unlocked her bedroom door.

Bridget's attic room. Her only closet can be seen to the right.
Photo by Ron Bueker

The police officers peered into her small closet, where they noticed a wooden water tank. They asked to see inside her trunk and were shown a few articles of clothing, and some mementos, wrapped carefully in tissue paper. The servant seemed to have only a few dresses. They peered under her bed, and satisfied, went into the room next to hers. There they found spar furnishings with a bed that appeared not to have been used for some time. When asked, who stayed in that room, Bridget replied Mr. Morse sometimes used it when he visited, or an occasional farmhand. The other two attic rooms got a quick cursory look. Officer Mullaly testified later they were looking for a man, or a weapon, anything that would figure into the murders.

The two men left the attic and began their descent down the stairs. Stopping at the room on the second landing, they were informed that was Mr. and Mrs. Borden's bedroom. Bridget unlocked the door with the key she had been given to retrieve the sheets earlier. The men entered and looked beneath the bed and around the room. They peered into the room where the safe sat, along with a desk and bureau. At some point, they approached the door leading to Lizzie Borden's room and slid back the bolt. It would not open.

Abby and Andrew's bedroom looking south from the attic steps on the second-floor landing. The stairs to the kitchen are right of their door. Photo Ron Bueker.

At some point, Alice Russell entered the Borden's room to watch the proceedings. Alice testified during the Preliminary Hearing:

"I remember being up in Mr. and Mrs. Borden's rooms with some officer, I remember their asking me about the rooms that went out of it. The door into Miss Lizzie's room was hooked. They pulled the screw out, I judged. I remember, I asked them to let me look in first; I did not know what the condition of the room was. I pulled the portiere [curtain] aside, and looked in, and said it is all right, and they went in. I do not recollect if I went with them or not...That was before Miss Lizzie went up to her room."

Lizzie Borden's bedroom door that connected to Andrew's and Abby's room. You can still see the holes today from where the police pulled the screw out to open her door from the other side. Photo by the Author.

[In the upcoming paragraphs, it will become apparent, that at the time Doherty and Mulally made their initial search of Lizzie's room area, Emma's door is open and they merely "peeked in" to her room. The dress closet, at the end of the short hallway, outside Lizzie's bedroom door, is unlocked. After Lizzie comes upstairs to her room, and changes into the pink wrapper, both Emma's bedroom door and the dress closet (clothes press) are locked and required a key to open them. Why? What circumstance required the need to keep people out?]

Borden's bedroom. Lizzie's door is straight ahead. Right of it is the door to Abby's dressing room where the safe & linens were kept. The door at right foreground leads to second-floor landing. Photo by Ron Bueker.

Officers Doherty and Mullaly testified they went into all the rooms on the second floor "they could get into." Officer Doherty admitted they did not go into Miss Emma's room. He said they did go into the clothes press [dress closet at the end of the hall] and looked there. Attorney Knowlton seemed surprised they had looked in that room, asking them three times if they did go in that closet at the time. It was doubtless due to the fact that the "clothes press" door was found locked later when Officer Fleet tried to open it. Lizzie had to unlock it for him—after protesting there was nothing to be found in there.

Bridget then led the officers to the cellar, and what started as a routine search, exploded during the Superior Court testimonies of Officer Mullaly and Assistant Marshall Fleet, into one of the biggest mysteries of the case.

Axes in the Cellar

During the Preliminary Hearing, August 25-September 1, 1892, Officer Patrick Doherty was asked about the initial search of the Borden cellar the day of the murders on August 4th. He gave the following testimony:

> Attorney Knowlton: "Who were with you when you went into the cellar?"

Doherty: "Mr. Mullaly and the servant girl directly behind us, went down."

Knowlton: "The cellar is a very light cellar?"

Doherty: It is…the washroom is very light."

Knowlton: "As you go down the cellar stairs from the back entry, you come into a room that is used for what?"

Doherty: "The water closet, I believe…when you get to the bottom of the stairs there is a kind of hallway or space."

Knowlton: "Did you see Mr. Mullaly find the axes and hatchets?"

Doherty: "Not when he found them."

Knowlton: "You saw him reaching up for them?"

Doherty: "Yes. I turned to the left and went over to the sink and I looked at this pail that was spoken of the other day [during testimony]. Of course, I called Mr. Mullaly's attention to it. I was at the time probably 12 or 14 feet from Mr. Mullaly [who was in the next room]. He was looking at something in his hand. I walked over, and he had a hatchet. I guess I took and glanced at it, and said "that looks all right, Mike," something like that, and left him. The girl was standing with her hand about as high as her head…they were both reaching up."

Knowlton: "When you say "the girl," you mean Miss Sullivan?"

Doherty: "Yes, sir."

Knowlton: "I want the location of the place where you found the axes and hatchets."

Doherty: "Near the furnace there."

Knowlton: "On a shelf?"

Doherty: "Yes. It was about five or six feet high, ran east to west."

Knowlton: "So he had to reach up a little above the line of his shoulder to get them?"

Doherty: "Yes, sir."

Knowlton: "Were they in anything?"

Doherty: "I could not say; I thought they were on a shelf; I could not say as there was anything else there."

Knowlton: "Do you know what he did with them?"

Doherty: "He laid one down beside his feet, and came over and looked at the pail where I was."

Knowlton: "That would be in the part of the cellar near the foot of the stairs where he laid it down?"

Doherty: "Yes, sir."

Knowlton: "What became of the other three axes?"

Doherty: "I do not know; I was interrupted just at that time."

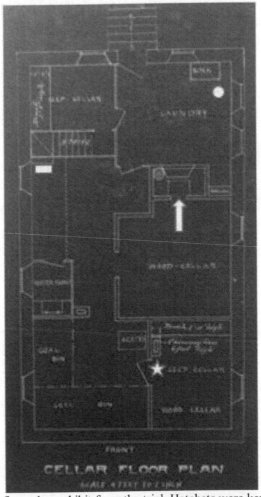

Borden cellar floor plan exhibit from the trial. Hatchets were kept in the wood cellar at the middle of the drawing (arrow). Axes, right of the furnace (heater), on the chimney base ledge, 6' up (star). Base of stairs (rectangle). Pail of bloody towels (circle). Drawing by Thomas Kieran, Engineer, 1893. [White symbols by the Author].

Officer Michael Mullaly gave the following testimony concerning his actions in the cellar at the same time as Doherty's:

Mullaly: "Went down cellar. Bridget led the way to the left. We went in, and in a small box, I would not say whether it was a partition across there, or not, but reached up, and took two hatchets out of this box, and passed them to me. We came out of there and went into an apartment south of the furnace, I believe, or hot water heater, I believe it was. In there we found two axes. I took them down."

Knowlton: "Where were they?"

Mullaly: They were on the south side of the cellar up against the wall. I would not say whether they were on a shelf, or whether there was something put there to hold them up. I know I reached up and took them down."

Knowlton: "Was this a covered box, these two hatchets were in?"

Mullaly: "No, the top was open."

Knowlton: "What did you notice about them?"

Mullaly: "On the large one, there was a small rust spot. On the axes, both handles were covered with ashes."

Knowlton: "Anything else?"

Mullaly: "Then, while I was in the washroom, I believe it was Mr. Doherty called my attention to some cloths in a pail. We took them out, and looked at them, and put them back again. No, I won't say I put them back again."

[At this point in Mullaly's testimony, and in Doherty's with respect to the pail of bloody cloths, Attorney Knowlton and Mr. Adams (for the Defense) back away from them, "making no claim" to them as a possible connection to the murders, as they have been told they were Lizzie's menstrual towels. Attorney Knowlton did say "I do not bind myself to any accidental future discoveries." He was leaving the door open, concerning the towels, to future evidence that might see them in a different light.]

Mullaly's testimony was brought back to the hatchet discoveries:

Knowlton: "As you go down, you have kind of a walk there, and a passageway that leads right to the water closet, if I remember?"

Mullaly: Yes, sir."

Knowlton: "Go by the water closet?"

Mullaly: "No, sir, just before you get to the water closet, on the south side of the house, we found those hatchets. The cellar steps are on the north side of the house. Just before you get to the water closet, we went into this department in the cellar where there was a lot of wood piled up. We carried out the hatchets, and put them on the cellar floor."

Knowlton: "Did you later see them in Dolan's hands?"

Mullaly: "Yes, sir. They were the same ones I carried out."

Mr. Adams on cross-examination:

Adams: "The axes you say were in the room where the furnace was, or one [for] sure?"

Mullaly: "No. That is further towards the street, coming towards the Second Street."

Adams: "They were up so you had to take them down?"

Mullaly: "They were up so I had to reach up and take them down...lying down lengthwise on a cross piece, I should say. They were covered with ashes, they were. When I brought them in, I laid them on the floor in the washroom."

Adams: "That is a brick floor?"

Mullaly: "Yes, Sir."

Adams: "How did you know this was a rust spot; could you tell by rubbing it?"

Mullaly: "By looking at it; I did not touch it. The larger hatchet was quite sharp. The smaller hatchet was not as sharp. I did not see any blood on any of them, axes or hatchets, that I could call blood. I did not see any hair on them either."

Adams: "Do you know how Dr. Dolan came into possession of those axes and hatchets?"

Mullaly: "He came down in the cellar, and I gave him this large hatchet, and he looked at it."

Adams: "What did he do with it then?"

Mullaly: "I don't know what he did do with it. The other axes laid there; I do not know whether he examined them or not."

Bridget Sullivan collaborated the Officers stories, with one, major, exception. She vehemently denied reaching up or touching, the hatchets. Officer Mullaly said she "passed them" to him. She did not remember how many hatchets and axes there were. She did say the hatchets were "standing with their heads down in the box [old starch box], and their handles sticking up." When asked about the wood she used for the stove, she denied needing to go into the wood cellar where the axes were kept: "I had no business in that part of the cellar at all." [There were two wood cellars. The wood cellar Bridget used was the first one where the hatchets were found. The second wood cellar contained the two axes.]

The cellar at the Lizzie Borden B&B and Museum. The first opening at the left leads to the wood cellar where the hatchets were found. In the back center of the photo (towards the street) is a white column that is the west chimney. This chimney comes up between the parlor and dining room on the first floor and the guest room on the second floor. To the left of the chimney is the second wood cellar where the two axes were found. To the right of the chimney, and behind was the coal cellar. The water closet was to the right of the photo. It is no longer there. The washroom is at the left front of the photo (not in view), just past the small white stool, and to the left. Photo by Ron Bueker

Chapter Eighteen

Thursday, August 4, 1892
John Morse and Changing Tales

If the strange case of Abby and Andrew Borden's murders was beginning to look like a fall down the rabbit hole, the arrival of Lizzie's secretive Uncle Morse would only add to the confusing testimony of the day.

John Morse Arrives at the Murder Scene

Newspaper drawing of John Morse for the Borden murder trial.

John Morse walked up Second Street from Pleasant Avenue. His stomach was in a knot. Andrew Borden, dead. Murdered! His mind was whirling with the fallout that was about to happen. He knew of only one person who would have done this...yet the implication staggered the mind.

He had barely begun the uphill climb toward the Borden house when he saw the activity ahead of him. People were running toward the house with excited exclamations. The words "stabbing," "murder," and "police" hung in the stagnant air. By the time he reached the white fence that fronted number 92, he could barely see the side door for the wave of bodies. He needed to think.

John opened the north gate and walked to the back yard of the property. There were people trying to peer into the kitchen windows, and they were looking around the grape arbor and trees. Someone said, "Mrs. Borden's dead upstairs," and he stopped dead in his tracks. Both! Both dead! His heart pounding, he tried to think. How could this happen? He just saw Andrew a few hours ago. Without noticing, he picked up a pear and bit into it. That the Swansea deal was over was without a doubt, a thought that made his stomach clench. So many people would be affected by that alone. It was not until he saw a policeman eyeing him that he realized his troubles could go much deeper.

Mrs. Churchill was in the back entry when she saw John Morse come from the direction of the back yard, eating a pear. Some spectators reported later they had seen Morse, leaning nonchalantly against the barn, as the crowd swelled. One police officer said he watched him eat three pears while standing there. Mr. Morse admitted to only "one." Strangely, Charles Sawyer testified he saw John Morse come toward the side steps from the direction of the front gate in the side yard. He did not know who the man was. The following is from Charles Sawyer's Inquest testimony concerning John Morse's arrival at the house:

"He came towards me from the gate. I stood on the steps at the time, standing outside of the door and holding the door outside. He came along to the steps, and he says "for God's sake, what has happened here?" I looked at him, I had not seen him, he was a stranger to me, I told him Mr. and Mrs. Borden have been murdered, been killed, something to that effect. "My God," he says, "and I left Mr. Borden right at this door, and he told me to come back to dinner." He was coming from the gate, along the walk; whether he had come through the gate or not, I don't know. At that time, there was quite a little crowd there. They had been driven out of the yard by an officer there in attendance. There were people in the street. My view was limited, not more than the width of the yard, but the fences appeared to be pretty well filled up, and previous to that, there had been quite a crowd in the yard."

Attorney Knowlton: "Did you notice whether Mr. Morse was eating a pear or not, eating anything?"

Sawyer: "No sir, he was not when he spoke to me, at that time."

Knowlton: "What did he do when you told him?"

Sawyer: "What kind of a God have we got that will permit a deed like this to be done?" He stood there a few moments, and then went inside.

Back yard at the Borden's. The cellar door is straight ahead, leading to a bulk head, and then into the cellar. You can see two rugs hanging from the wash line to the left. The pear tree, center, is where John Morse and Lizzie claim to have gotten fruit. The barn door used by Bridget, Andrew Borden, and allegedly Lizzie that day, is at the right. The jog to the side door steps is at the end of the barn (center).

View of the side yard facing Second Street. Kelly house is at left.
John Cunningham said he saw no footprints here in the tall grass.

6-foot-tall John Morse talking to police officer in front of the Borden house.
Unknown source for newspaper illustration.

John Morse's Arrival at the Borden's:

Mrs. Adelaide Churchill's testimony about John Morse's arrival is a little different from Charles Sawyer's. She said, "Both Mr. and Mrs. Borden had been found when he came. I think I was the first one to let him in. I says "Mr. Morse, something terrible has happened, somebody has killed both Mr. and Mrs. Borden." He says "What?" and hollered "Lizzie!" as loud as he could holler, and rushed into the dining room. Alice Russell heard him, and I think let him in, and he went into the sitting room and the door was closed between the sitting room and the kitchen." Mrs. Churchill testified she saw Mr. Morse come from "the back part of the yard. He stepped up on to the steps. I think he came from the east, the steps that come from the yard, but I am not sure. He was eating a pear."

The testimony here concerning John Morse's arrival is confusing. Charles Sawyer saw him coming from the gate area, Mrs. Churchill says he came from the back yard eating a pear; that he came from the "east." The front gate is to the west. It may be that Mrs. Churchill saw Mr. Morse coming from the side yard with the pear as the police were driving the crowds back from the yard to the street. Charles Sawyer may have stepped away at that moment to go upstairs and see Abby's body; something he says he did for a few minutes. When Sawyer returned to his post at the door, he may have seen John coming forward from the gate after being driven back, possibly telling the police he was a relative of the family. Sawyer said John waited a few moments before entering the house. Mr. Sawyer was on the outside of the rear door, and Mrs. Churchill met Mr. Morse in the entry as he entered to tell him the news. That John acted surprised to hear the news by yelling "What?" after Sawyer has just told him they are both dead, is not out of character with the great performance Morse is undertaking as he tries to sidestep the mess Lizzie has landed them all into. That he screamed "Lizzie!" is telling in and of itself.

You will notice that the first thing John says to Charles Sawyer is "and I left Mr. Borden right at this door, and he told me to come back to dinner." He is already establishing an alibi: that he was here and went away, and that he had a reason for returning...a dinner invitation. It is an odd thing to say.

John Morse testified that when he arrived at the Borden house, "shortly before noon," there was no crowd...nothing to draw my attention." Attorney Knowlton is incredulous, and hammers home the point that there were people in the yard, in front of the house, and in the barn. Morse holds firm that nothing "attracted my attention," not even the burly Charles Sawyer manning the door. It only made Morse look more suspicious, along with his absurdly detailed description of the street car he supposedly rode on his way to the Borden home.

Alice heard John bellowing Lizzie's name and opened the dining room door. She stepped back in surprise as John Morse burst into the dining room, leaving a rattled Mrs. Churchill in the kitchen. He barely glanced at Lizzie, laying on the lounge near the dining room table, as he flung open the sitting room door. He was not prepared for the number of people gathered there. The entire thing was too surreal. As Doctor Bowen once again peeled back the sheet for John to see, he reeled. This could not be happening. He couldn't bear to take more than a sideways glance at his brother-in-law's mutilated features. Swallowing hard, he asked where Abby was. He was told upstairs.

Gripping the stairway railing, John climbed up toward the room he had just slumbered in the night before. It was a nightmare...a walking nightmare. He barely registered the many doctors crouched around the form, lying near the dressing bureau whose mirror he had peered into that morning as he adjusted his collar. Holding onto the rear bedpost for support, he looked down.

The image registered in his mind in snippets: he saw the tired morning dress she had worn as she dusted, while he and Andrew put the finishing touches on their brilliant plan that morning in the sitting room; the moved bed; and something lying on the white bedspread that looked like hair. Her small feet, encased in worn house shoes, could be seen beside some man's knees, as the doctors probed and measured. As one of them moved aside, John saw the bloody pulp that had been Abby Borden's head.

His stomach roiling, he turned and fled the room. His knees threatened to betray him as he made his way down the front stairs. By the time he surged into the dining room, the fear, nausea, and tension had reached the boiling point. Lizzie looked up from the lounge at the reddened face of the six-foot man towering above her, and she waited heart pounding. If anyone would guess who had murdered her father and step-mother, it would be her Uncle John. Nerves screaming, he exploded, "What in God's name happened here?" As he hollered the words, he glanced up at the ceiling, in the direction of the guest room upstairs, where Abby Borden lay.

It was that simple movement—that upward glance—that was the first revelation to Alice Russell that these two people were not dead from poisoning...they had been murdered.

[Alice Russell, during her Inquest testimony, stated: "Something he [John Morse] said about their being murdered and looked up to her, then it dawned on my mind that it was cold-blooded murder. That is the first idea that I had that it was murder."]

Mrs. Churchill stood by in horrified silence. The tension in the room was palpable. She looked at the man's clenched fists, Lizzie's flushed face, and Alice Russell's quaking form, and decided she could stand no more. The noise of the crowd was coming through the dining room windows. It must be near dinner time and she had seven mouths to feed waiting for her next door. Just as she was about to speak, John Morse whirled and left the room, slamming the dining room door that led to the kitchen after him.

"Lizzie," Mrs. Churchill said, her voice quaking. "I must go home now. If there is anything I can do for you, I am willing to do it."

Lizzie Borden heard the voice, as if it were coming up from the depths of a well. The freight train noise was back, rushing through her head, causing the room to spin. She finally turned toward the speaker and comprehended what had just been said to her.

"I'm sure there will be, by and by," she said mechanically.

Mrs. Churchill left the dining room, closing the door behind her. She saw Bridget in the kitchen and stopped to talk to her. After more police arrived, including Assistant Marshall Fleet, she finally headed home to begin the noon meal. It was close to twelve. As Adelaide Churchill left the Borden house and paused next to Charles Sawyer (who still stood on the outside step), she was shocked to see the number of people crowding the street, sidewalk, and pressing up against her fence. As she exited the house, a buzz spread through the crowd. She heard her name whispered among several women. The enormity of what she had just been a part of hit her full in the face.

Stepping gingerly down the stone side steps, Addie happened to glance back and saw John Morse making his way to the back yard. The police held back the crowd as she walked through the north gate of the Borden property. The press of strangers was everywhere. It wasn't until she stepped through her door into the familiar furnishings of her home, that she allowed herself to collapse. [A rumor spread that Adelaide Churchill told a friend she had seen something that day at Lizzie Borden's that she would never speak of, "not even if they threaten to tear out my tongue." Mrs. Churchill did not return to the Borden house—not that day, or the ones following.]

The headlines, one of many, beginning the day of the murders.

VIEW OF THE VICINITY OF THE MURDERS.

I. Borden house.
II. Borden barn.
III. The well.
IV. Fence with barbed wire on top.
V. Side entrance.
VI. Churchill residence.

VII. Dr. Bowen's house.
VIII. Dr. Chagnon's house.
IX. Kelley house.
X. Yard from which officers watched the Borden house.
XI. Kelley's barn.
XII. Pear orchard.

The layout of Second Street, drawn for the trial. The Borden house is marked I; their barn II; their well III; the fence along the east of their back yard, IV; the Borden house side entrance, V; Churchill residence, VI; Dr. Bowen's/Southard Miller's house, VII; Dr. Chagnon's house, VIII; the Kelly house, IX; yard from which the officers watched the Borden property, X; Crowe's Barn, XI; and the Chagnon's pear orchard, XII. To the south of the Kelly house, the partially drawn building is Wade's store. North points "downstreet" toward town, and Borden Street where Miss Alice Russell lives. The police station, City Hall, the Post Office, and train station, are all north (left) of the Borden house.

Doctor William H. Dolan

Doctor William H. Dolan had stumbled across the Borden murders quite by accident. He had been traveling down Second Street when he saw the commotion going on in front of the house next to Mrs. Churchill's. It was 11:40-11:45.

Second Street looking south. Mrs. Churchill's house is at far left. Borden house is next, and the Kelly's after. The Miller/Bowen house is on the right foreground.

Medical Examiner, Doctor William H. Dolan

During a rather confrontational inquisition by Lizzie's attorney, Mr. Adams, during the Preliminary Hearing in late August, Doctor Dolan was asked a series of questions pertaining to his movements, at the Borden house that day:

Adams: "I understand you had been a Medical Examiner a year?"

Dolan: "Yes, sir, about. Surgery is not my specialty, but I do considerable in that line. I'm a general physician. I have overseen one homicide since becoming a Medical Examiner."

Adams: "You spoke of repairing to this house [Borden's] the 4th of August at a certain hour?"

Dolan: "Yes, sir."

Adams: "Was it a pleasant day?"

Dolan: "It surely was not a rainy day."

Adams: "Was it a very hot day?"

Dolan: "It was, sir."

Adams: "Whenever you went there the sun was about meridian?" [noon]

Dolan: Yes, sir."

Adams: [Referring to where Dr. Dolan went when he entered the side door of the Borden house] "Who was in the kitchen when you went in there?"

Dolan: "Bridget Sullivan and Dr. Bowen. Dr. Bowen met me just as I went in. He was coming from the sitting room."

Adams: "You went into the sitting room out of the kitchen?"

Dolan: Yes, sir."

Adams: "That brought Mr. Borden so that he faced you? Who were in the sitting room at that time?"

Dolan: "Officers, Mullaly and Doherty." [Lizzie was in the dining room at this time with Miss Russell and Mrs. Churchill]

Adams: "What did you do then and there?"

Dolan: "I took down the corner of the sheet and saw the face of Mr. Borden. I asked where Mrs. Borden was; I was informed she was upstairs. I went up and saw her."

Adams: "When you went upstairs, you went up the front way?"

Dolan: "Yes Sir."

Adams: "Are those winding stairs?"

Dolan: "They are to a certain extent."

Adams: "I did not ask you that, did I?"

Dolan: "You asked if they were winding stairs; they are to a certain extent," the doctor replied, nonplussed.

Adams: "What was the carpet, if any on the floor?"

Dolan: "I should say Brussels."

Adams: "What was its color, as to being dark or light?"

Dolan: "I do not think it was either very light or dark, I considered it medium. I think it was figured, I am not positive."

Adams: "Do you remember whether the wall was papered in the hall?"

Dolan: "I think they were."

Adams: "If they were, what were they papered with?"

Dolan: "Paper."

[The courtroom erupts in laughter.]

Adams: "What sort of paper? When I asked you what they were papered with, did you understand me, or did you desire to create a laugh?" the attorney asked hotly.

Dolan: "I do not know what you mean," Dolan answered with mock innocence. "You were so explicit with your terms, I thought I would be with mine."

The confrontation continued as Mr. Adams finally elicited from Doctor Dolan what occurred in the guest room pertaining to Abby Borden's "viewing." [A viewing is merely a name given to a doctor's brief viewing of the body. It is not an autopsy.]

Dr. Dolan admitted to Attorney Adams to having Dr. Bowen, Dr. Tourtellotte, and Dr. Handy with him in the room, examining Abby's wounds. Dolan said he could see Abby's feet while standing at the guest room door, projecting from the bed. "Her hands were extended over her head, not over it, but around the head…not resting on the arms; the head in a circle. Her head was three to four feet from the east wall."

Dr. Dolan, when asked whether anyone moved her body, admitted he and Dr. Bowen raised her up to get a better look at her wounds. The area between the bed and bureau was in partial shadow. When the body was returned to the floor, they tried to approximate the original position in which she was found, but, as shown in the photographer's photo taken later that afternoon, her hands are now beneath her, rather than arched out above her head.

Reenactment of Abby Borden's position before she was moved.
Courtesy of LizzieBordenwarpsandwefts.com. Shelly Dziedzic, actress.

Abby Borden's body as it was photographed on August 4th, at 3 p.m. Her dress was obviously arranged for modesty reasons, as it looks perfectly straight and pulled taught. Photo by James Walsh.

The testimony of Dr. Dolan continued during the Preliminary Hearing, with Attorney Adams for the Defense in his usual sparring form:

Adams: "Mrs. Borden was a well-nourished woman?"

Dolan: Yes, sir."

Adams: "She was five feet three or four inches in height?"

Dolan: Three."

Adams: "She weighed over two hundred pounds?"

Dolan: "Yes, sir."

Adams: "That made her more than stout? A fat woman?"

Dolan: "Yes, she was fat." [Dolan testified earlier that Abby was from two hundred and ten, to two hundred and twenty-five pounds.]

Adams: "Did you, either [Bowen] or both of you put your fingers or hands in these wounds, or any of them?"

Dolan: "I put my hands in; I do not know whether he did or not."

Adams: "Did yours get bloody?"

Dolan: "Yes, sir."

Adams: "Do you know whether any blood dropped from your hands?"

Dolan: "I am quite confident it did not. I beg your pardon; I did get two or three spots on my pantaloons; I think that was downstairs though."

Attorney Knowlton for the Prosecution asked Dr. Dolan to describe how Abby was dressed:

Dolan: "She was dressed, as you would expect to find a housewife at that hour in the morning, in some calico dress."

Knowlton: Anything on her head?"

Dolan: "No, sir. There was a silk handkerchief; whether it had been around her head or not, I cannot say. It was not around the head when I saw it, but near the head. It was a silk one. A pocket handkerchief I should say, same as they tie around their heads sometimes when dusting. It was very near her head, practically touching the head, but not on it. It was not knotted. It was so old. It was torn very freely. I should not think it was cut. There was blood on it from the surrounding blood."

Doctor Dolan admitted that the first time he saw Abby Borden's body that day, he only looked at it, and then returned downstairs to focus on Andrew Borden's body. He felt of his wounds, looked at the blood spatter covering the wallpaper at the rear of the sofa, the parlor door, and a long string of blood inside the dining room door frame. He then returned upstairs for his second viewing of Abby's body, and it was then he felt of her wounds, and along with Dr. Bowen, lifted her to a sitting position.

The doctor would later testify that there was a blood spot near the north window facing Mrs. Churchill's, that could have only gotten there during the first wound inflicted upon Mrs. Borden. In the doctor's opinion, Abby was standing at that window and turned to face her attacker when the first blow fell. Blood was also found on the mop board on the east wall before her head, along the bed frame where the counterpane had been originally tucked in during the attack. [It shows hanging out in the crime scene photograph, as the police had searched the bedding before the photographer arrived late in the afternoon. It was hastily put back together, and the bed moved back into place after Officer Doherty moved it in his initial viewing of the body.] More blood spatter was found along the top of the swollen drawers of the dressing bureau, the marble base, and the pillow sham on the bed nearest Abby's body. As mentioned, her fake switch of hair was lying on the white bedspread.

Dolan testified that Abby's clothing was soaked with blood halfway down her back, and her entire bodice, wetting her underclothes. The pool of blood beneath, and around her head, had soaked through the Brussel's carpeting to the floor below.

Doctor Dolan, in the role of Medical Examiner, was allowed to question witnesses to get at the facts of the homicides. He questioned Lizzie, but he was not the first to corner her in her bedroom.

Adams: "Did you ever have any talk with the defendant, Lizzie Borden, at any time?"

Dolan: "Yes, sir. I had a few words with her."

Adams: "Did you have any talk with her then?"

Dolan: I do not recollect if I had any words with her when I went in or not."

Adams: "Where was she?"

Dolan: "In the dining room, sort of reclining on the lounge, Mrs. Churchill was with her and Miss Russell. I saw her then pass out the door, and go upstairs."

Adams: "When was it you had any talk with her, if you can remember?"

Dolan: "When she was sitting in her room upstairs, that same day...it must have been quarter to one or half-past one."

Adams: "What was it?"

Dolan: "I asked her if her mother had received a note; she said she had. I asked her if she had seen the note, and she said no. I asked her if she knew who brought it; she said she did not know and thought it was a boy. I asked her what her mother did with the note; she said she did not know; in all probability, she burned it in the kitchen stove. That is all I can remember [about his conversation with Lizzie]."

"When it is necessary for an undertaker, I want Winward."

Alice Russell did her best to keep Lizzie calm. "There were always people coming and talking to her," Alice would testify. With the interconnecting rooms of the house's layout, there was no privacy to be had, as men came through the dining room on the way to the kitchen, or new policemen, doctors, and reporters came in through the screen door and entered into the dining room in search of the sitting room.

The crowd outside the open windows had now spread throughout Second Street. Charles Sawyer admitted that there were over 500 people filling the street outside. The Fall River newspapers said mill workers had walked off the job as the gossip trickled down through the factories. It didn't help that most of the rumors of murder found their mark at the noon meal hour. Food was forgotten as citizens left their homes and jobs to stand gawking at the Drab green house with the two gates. The police had their hands full keeping the crowd from entering the yard. Many found a way to penetrate the barricade.

Lizzie sat on the lounge in the dining room, a flood of activity around her. The Bedford cord dress she wore beneath the calico was taking a toll on her. As the temperature outside climbed, she felt her resolve faltering. She could barely breathe, and parts of the Bedford were sticking to her.

Alice glanced nervously at Lizzie as the shouts of the crowds, only a few feet from the open dining room windows, reached their ears. Lizzie looked pale. Her head was lolling and her breathing was becoming labored. At that moment, Dr. Bowen walked in, and came toward Lizzie, whose chin was resting on her chest.

"Maybe you should take her up to her room," Dr. Bowen testified to saying. He could hear the raised voices outside, shouting such words as "murder," and "Old Man Borden." [Alice would later testify during the Inquest that she did not remember hearing anyone telling Lizzie to go to her room.]

Alice was relieved to stand, and help Lizzie from her seat. Several of the officers turned to look at them as they entered the sitting room and stepped through to the front entry doorway. As they came to the staircase, they waited for several more men to come down past them. Alice was shocked the little house could hold this many people. She stepped into the parlor for a few moments to see several officers searching there. Lizzie was unaware that Miss Russell had actually helped them in their search of the bedrooms on the second floor earlier, as Mrs. Churchill kept vigilance in the dining room. Lizzie's hook to her bedroom door was now pulled from its frame.

Parlor looking toward front door entry and staircase. Photo Ron Bueker.

Finally, they climbed the front stairs, both women holding onto the railing for support. This was Alice's first glimpse of the second floor that day, and she feared she would see Abby's body there. No one had told her just where Mrs. Borden was lying. The sound of men's voices was everywhere; several coming from the guest room. She couldn't help herself as she and Lizzie came to the curve in the stairs—she glanced to the left through the open door.

From this angle, all she could see was an ocean of men's trouser legs. The bed had been moved and was close to blocking the door. The old fireplace, that had always been covered by the massive headboard, was now in full view, making the room she had sat in so often, look alien and foreboding. Alice could see nothing of Mrs. Borden's form.

Lizzie stepped onto the landing, and taking a ring of keys from her dress pocket, unlocked her bedroom door and gratefully stepped inside. Alice scurried in after her, shutting the door behind them. The room was hot and close, but it was blissfully free of strangers. It was then Lizzie realized Alice was holding her handkerchiefs from the dining room table. "Those are the ones I was ironing," she said to Alice. Some were still damp.

"You can lay those in the top drawer over there," Lizzie said of the ironed linens. Alice took the others that were damp and hung them on Emma's towel bar in the next room. At this time, Emma's door is still unlocked.

Before Alice could say anything, Lizzie faced her and said, "When it is necessary for an undertaker, I want Winward."

Alice didn't need to ask what she meant. James E. Winward's Undertaking was considered the finest in Fall River. All the elite on "the Hill" used Winward. For Lizzie Borden, he was the only choice to handle the funeral arrangements for her father. James C. Renwick actually prepared the bodies for burial, but it was Winward's establishment that oversaw the details.

That Gorman's Undertaking was literally steps away at the corner of Spring and Second did not even register to Lizzie. This was the establishment to which Officer Doherty dashed to use the phone, due to its close proximity to the Borden house. It would be Winward, or nothing.

Winward's ad in the 1892 Fall River Directory.

Alice paused and then realized telling Dr. Bowen of Lizzie's preference in preparation of the bodies could be time-sensitive. She left the room and threaded her way down past the people on the stairs. She asked someone to give Dr. Bowen a message that she needed to speak with him, as she was not willing to go into the sitting room. She waited in the front hall for over ten minutes for him to come to her; occasionally peeking into the parlor at the search still going on.

As soon as Alice left her bedroom, Lizzie walked quickly to the dress closet at the end of the second story landing. The men in the guest room had their backs to the open door and took no notice of her. She heard someone ask to be handed the yardstick that sat near the sewing machine.

Opening the door to the clothes press, she quickly selected a dress that was loose, with a trailing hemline. She could no longer stay in a two-piece blouse waist and skirt. Lizzie took a pink and white striped wrapper from a peg and went into the hall. She left the closet, locked it, and walked back to her room.

Knowing Alice could return at any time, Lizzie stepped to the only place there was privacy—her sister Emma's small room. She closed the door and hurriedly began unhooking the blue calico dress. Perspiration stained the armpits. With both hands, she opened the front, to find that it was sticking in places to the Bedford cord beneath it. The blood spatter had done as she feared: while still moist, it had stuck and dried to the outer dress. She pulled the fabric free of the stains. Releasing her arms from the calico's sleeves, she felt a huge weight lifted from her. The air pimpled her damp arms.

Lizzie looked at the underside of the calico blouse waist. There were several areas with dried blood stains. She looked down at the torn Bedford cord blouse she was still wearing like a chemise, now sleeveless. Several spots of blood speckled its bodice. Running a hand over the Bedford's stains, she was relieved to see they were dry. The calico she had just removed would be a problem, however.

Someone rattled the doorknob to her bedroom that leads to the guest chamber on the other side. She froze. She knew it was locked and bolted, her heavy writing desk pressed against it. Still, it was unnerving to hear them trying to get in. She had to hurry.

Stepping from the calico skirt, she turned it inside out and looked. There were a few dried blood spots that had transferred from the Bedford cord. How she wished she could take off the corded dress as well, but for now, it was the only safe place she could keep it. No man in Victorian New England would dare look under her dress in search of another one.

Lizzie put on the pink and white wrapper with the soft sheen and shirred bodice. It gave her so much more room and freedom of movement. The half-train swept the floor, which was exactly what she needed. The Bedford cord was completely covered.

Lizzie picked up the two halves of the calico dress and hung them on the peg in Emma's closet. Only a few of her sister's items remained there, as Emma had planned to stay a month with the Brownell's, and packed nearly all her belongings. She glanced up at the small pillowcase hiding the torn sleeves and hem of the Bedford cord dress. She felt easier. Shortly it would be over. Lizzie doubted anyone would pay attention to their bedrooms. When things settled down, she would hide the dress somewhere else, until she could destroy it. Surely the police had all they needed to now go out and look for the murderer.

Just as she closed the small closet, she heard someone opening her bedroom door. She stepped from Emma's room, tying the red satin ribbon of her gown as Alice Russell entered from the landing. Surreptitiously, Lizzie locked Emma's door behind her.

Emma's closet, looking in from Lizzie's room. Photo Ron Bueker.

Alice breathlessly told her that she had spoken with Doctor Bowen and he would handle notifying Winward. If she was surprised Lizzie had changed dresses, she didn't show it. She later testified that Lizzie was merely doing what any woman would do. "Making herself more respectable to receive the people who kept coming to talk to her."

Lizzie's bedroom door could not be in a worse place. It sat to the right at the top of the stairs, inches from the top rung. Each person coming to see Abby's body was taking the opportunity to peer into the other rooms on the landing. The clothes press was opposite her door; leaving only her room and the guest room. Lizzie finally crossed to her door and locked it. Alice slid into the small chair next to Lizzie's writing desk.

Examples of wrappers. The one on the right resembles the one described in detail by Officer Harrington during the trial.

Lizzie sank down onto her lounge across from Alice. She carefully arranged the long folds of the wrapper about her shoes. Alice was relieved to see Lizzie's nerves seemed to have rallied. She appeared steadier and there was some color in her cheeks. As she watched her smooth her wavy hair into place, Alice finally asked the question she had waited all morning to ask her. She had heard so many people inquire of Lizzie where she was when the murder of her father transpired. "Out in the barn" seemed an odd place to be on such a hot August morning.

"Lizzie?" she began, quietly. Alice was still rattled. In fact, she had to clasp her hands in her lap to keep them from shaking. "What were you out in the barn for?"

Lizzie looked at her old friend with those clear, protruding eyes that held so many secrets. In the early afternoon light of the bedroom, they appeared green, the whites glistening as if they were underwater. She paused only for a moment and said, "I went to the barn to get a piece of tin or iron to fix my screen. I was ironing handkerchiefs, and my flat iron was not hot, and I thought I would go and get that while I was waiting. You know, there is everything up there, and I went to see if I could not get a piece of tin or iron to fix it."

Lizzie Andrew Borden. Photo by the Fall River Historical Society.

Alice tried to process this new information. It was a lot to take in. The town hall clock had barely struck the half past hour of noon. The murders were only discovered a little over an hour ago, yet it felt like the morning had dragged on forever. The voices of the men in the guest room were ever present; sometimes soft and conspiratorial, other times calling out for assistance. And every few minutes, someone rattled the doorknobs to Lizzie's room. The door to the guest room was right next to where Alice was seated— directly behind the writing desk. Each time someone grabbed hold of it from the other side and shook it, she would jump. Her nerves were frayed. She knew the dead body of her friend Abby Borden was just on the other side of that door. And just beneath her feet, in the sitting room below, lay Andrew Borden, beneath a bloody sheet.

Abby Borden's crime scene photo, taken at 3:00 that day, by James Walsh.

Crime scene photo was taken of Andrew at 3:00 the afternoon of the murders. A gentleman is seen right, resembling the man seen in Abby's crime scene photo from page 204. It is possibly Dr. Dolan, who ordered the photos and was there to oversee them taken. See his photo on page 298. Photo by James Walsh.

Lizzie moved restlessly about her bedroom. At one point, she pulled back her red portiere behind her bed and noticed her hook and eye had been pulled from her door. Gritting her teeth, she screwed the hook back into the door frame and latched it, as Alice looked on.

Chapter Nineteen

Thursday—August 4, 1892
Bloody Towels and Barn Dust

A Pail of Bloody Towels

Between 11:39-11:40 a.m., Officer William Medley arrived at the Borden house. After inquiring for Assistant Marshall Fleet, who had not yet arrived, he walked around to the cellar door at the back of the house and tried it. Finding it locked, he looked around generally and went into the house. Mr. Fleet had by then arrived. When Medley entered the house, he saw Fleet, Mr. Mullaly, Miss Russell, Mrs. Churchill, one or two doctors, and Lizzie Borden.

Minutes later, Officer Medley entered Lizzie Borden's bedroom to talk with her.

Medley: "Where was Bridget [when Andrew was murdered]?"
Lizzie: "She was upstairs in her room."
Medley: "Where were you?"
Lizzie: "I was upstairs in the barn."

Officer Medley's Witness Statement report concerning his conversation with Lizzie went as follows:

"She said she was upstairs in the barn, and upon coming into the house, found her father all cut and bleeding on the lounge. She then called Maggie, and then Mrs. Churchill. She did not have any idea who could have done it. I inquired about some cloths which looked to me like small towels, they were covered with blood, and in a pail half filled with water, and in the wash cellar. She said that was all right; she had told the Doctor all about that. I then asked her how long the pail and its contents had been there, and she said three or four days. I asked the Doctor about it, and he said it had been explained to him and was all right."

"I then had a talk with Bridget about the pail and its contents. She said she had not noticed the pail until that day, and it could not have been there two days before, or she would have seen it, and put the contents in the wash, as that was the day she had done the washing."

 A Pail of Bloody Towels

The Pittsburgh Dispatch, Aug. 8, 1892: "On Friday [the day after the murders] there was found in the cellar of the Borden house a bundle of rags. These rags were concealed under a bucket turned upside down. They were smeared with blood as though an axe had been wiped on them. Dr. Dolan took these rags and sent them to Professor Wood of Boston. He also sent a strip of carpet dyed with the blood of Mrs. Borden. "Professor Wood today said that the blood is human blood."

Because of Professor Wood's pronouncement, Bridget was summoned immediately to the police headquarters. She went willingly. [Bridget was first questioned in Marshall Hilliard's office, and then taken upstairs to the court room where a Coroner's Inquest officially began.] "Bridget was taken before Judge Blaisdell where she told and retold her story."

When the Inquest adjourned for the noon meal, Bridget was placed in charge of the jail matron, Mrs. Russell. Bridget told the matron her story, saying she "could not tell all before, as there were so many men about."

That Bridget mentions she could not tell all, due to men being present is suggestive. It was probably related to the men asking her about the bloody cloths in the cellar, that were supposedly Lizzie's menstrual cloths.

What couldn't she say in front of them regarding the pail of bloody towels that Bridget claimed were not there before the morning of the murders? That it was not Lizzie's time of the month, so she was lying about them? That these were not sanitary towels that the girls usually wore, but were ordinary bath towels? Or, could it be, that American women had been introduced to disposable "feminine towels" in 1890? They were available by catalogue, and at all department stores. Perhaps Bridget knew Lizzie used this convenient disposable option, and not the outdated cloth towels. Was that the indelicate matter she could not discuss in front of all those men?

Ads for disposable feminine towels from the 1890s.
They were lauded for their small, compact travel size. Made of rayon, they were supposedly more absorbent than cotton. Lizzie may have used them while traveling in Europe.

The bucket, or pail, of bloody rags in the Borden cellar had been looked over the day of the murders. It was originally standing, half-filled with water as Officer Medley testified. It was later found overturned on the wash room floor with the towels nestled beneath it. Was this the slop pail, filled with three bloody towels, from the guest room where Lizzie cleaned up after murdering Abby?

Typical wooden bucket used in the 1890s.

Barn Dust

Officer Medley, after hearing Lizzie's statement that she had been in the loft of the barn, left her bedroom. He came down stairs and "went through the room where Mr. Borden lay, and out of the house, into the barn and upstairs." He found the door to the barn "fast with a hasp over the staple and an iron pin in it." He saw "quite a number of people outside and in the yard, one or two officers, Mr. Sawyer [at the back-door step], and Mr. Wixon, and someone else." He couldn't recall them all.

Officer Medley testified at the superior court trial that "I went upstairs [in the barn] until I reached about three or four steps from the top, and while there, part of my body was above the floor, above the level of the floor, and I looked around the barn to see if there was any evidence of anything having been disturbed, and I didn't notice that anything had or seemed to be disturbed, and I stooped down low to see if I could discern any marks on the floor of the barn having been made there. I did that by stooping down and looking across the bottom of the barn floor. I didn't see any, and I reached out my hand to see if I could make an impression on the floor of the barn, and I did by putting my hand down...and found that I made an impression on the floor."

"There was hay dust and other dust on the floor. I could see the marks I made quite distinctly when I looked for them. Then I stepped up on the top and took four or five steps on the outer edge of the barn floor, the edge nearest the stairs, I came up to see if I could discern those, and I did. I could see the prints plainly. There were no other footsteps in the dust but mine. I came down the steps and searched around a pile of lumber and other stuff that was in the yard, looking for anything that we could find, and after a while, I met Mr. Fleet. The little door for hay, and the two windows in the barn loft were all closed. It was very hot up there."

When asked how soon after he arrived at the house Officer Medley went up into the barn loft, he answered "Perhaps eight or ten minutes."

This view of inside the Borden barn, taken during the demolition of the building in 1938, shows the stairs and loft floor. It is easy to see how Officer Medley could have looked right and seen the floor level with his head a few steps from the top. Courtesy of the PIC Album, Dec. 13, 1938.

Alfred Clarkson arrived at the Borden house around 11:40. He looked about the property, and said he finally entered the barn "around 11:48." He testified three or four men went up into the loft before him. When he did ascend the steps, someone had opened the small hay door on the south side of the loft, and he saw an indentation in the hay that looked as though a man may have laid there. His testimony was treated with derision during the superior court trial, as his measurements of a few inches in the indentation of the hay could hardly be the size of a man lying there.

If Mr. Clarkson did enter the barn, it is likely he just missed Officer Medley, who had just vacated it a minute or two before. His testimony as to the time he entered the barn may have been "suggested" by the Defense, to put him there earlier than he was.

Others came forward, claiming to have been in the barn loft before Officer Medley. One by one, their testimonies were tossed aside. Two young enterprising boys, Thomas E. Barlow and Everett Brown, who were dubbed "Brownie and Me" by the newspapers, claimed to have been the first ones in the barn loft at 11:23. They testified to seeing Officer Doherty dashing back across Second Street as they came up to the Borden house. Officer Doherty arrived at the house at *11:35*, and had been there at least ten minutes or more, before he ran to make a phone call to Marshall Hilliard, and came dashing back. That puts the time they saw Doherty closer to 11:50, or later. So much for "Brownie and Me," and their timeline.

When Thomas Barlow testified that the loft was "cool" that forenoon, Attorney Knowlton was incredulous. "It was cool up in the loft of that barn?" "Yes, sir," the young boy answered. The two boys were later found to be delinquents, with a history of missing work, and vandalism.

"She is not my mother!"

Assistant Marshall John Fleet arrived at the Borden home between ten and fifteen minutes to 12. Officer Gillian had been stationed at the front door to keep the onslaught of curious onlookers at bay. Fleet inched his way through the crowds, his civilian clothing doing nothing in the way of granting him the authority he needed to hurry his arrival. As he finally entered in through the north gate, he saw Officer Medley in the side yard. The two stopped to talk for a few minutes. It may have been at that time Medley informed the Assistant Marshall of his talk with Lizzie Borden, her statement that she had been up in the barn loft, and that he had just returned from looking at that area, and found no footprints in the layer of hay dust there.

ASSISTANT MARSHAL FLEET.

Assistant Marshall John Fleet

As John Fleet approached Charles Sawyer at the side steps, he saw Reporter John Manning, of *The Fall River Herald*, interviewing anyone who would talk to him. Edwin Porter with the *Fall River Globe* was at the front door, also gathering notes for his newspaper column. The two journalists had already been all throughout the house, along with others. The public was regaled with the gruesome details before the end of the day.

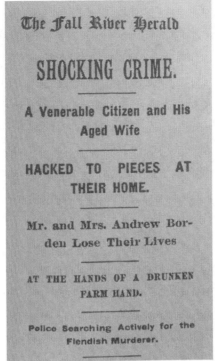

The Fall River Herald the day of the murders.

Drawing that accompanied *The Fall River Herald* that day.

Assistant Marshall John Fleet entered the Borden house. He found John Morse, Bridget Sullivan, and Mrs. Churchill in the kitchen. Adelaide Churchill left the house to go home moments later. Alice Russell was now upstairs with Lizzie in her bedroom. As Fleet passed through the sitting room, he saw Dr. Dolan leaning over the body of Andrew Borden. He stopped long enough to look at Mr. Borden's wounds and asked where the second body was. He was told upstairs in the "spare room."

Fleet found Abby Borden dead, between the bureau and the bed. He noticed her head was all "broken in." He came from the room and turned right, where he found a locked door. Dr. Bowen was standing there and Marshall Fleet asked if any of the family was around so that he could have the door unlocked. Dr. Bowen directed Fleet to the only other door on that landing; the one to the left of the guest chamber...Lizzie Borden's bedroom.

Marshall Fleet tapped on the partially-open door and found Lizzie seated on her lounge against the wall with the windows. Next to her sat Reverend Buck, her friend from the Central Congregational Church. From that day forward, Reverend Buck was to be seen constantly by Lizzie's side; a position the newspapers found to be cloying and attention-seeking. Alice Russell was seated near Lizzie's desk where she had been earlier.

During the Superior Court trial in June of 1893, Marshall Fleet gave the following testimony of his interview on his first visit with Lizzie Borden:

"I went in there and told her who I was---made known who I was (I was in citizen's clothes, as I am now), and I asked her if she knew anything about the murders. She said that she did not; all she knew was that Mr. Borden, her father, as she put it, came home about half-past ten or quarter to eleven, went into the sitting room, sat down in the large chair, took out some papers and looked at them. She was ironing in the dining room some handkerchiefs, as she stated. She saw her father was feeble, and she went to him and advised and assisted him to lay down on the sofa. She then went into the dining room to her ironing, but left, after her father was laid down, and went out in the yard and up in the barn. I asked her how long she remained in the barn; she said she remained up in the barn about half an hour. I then asked her what she meant by "up in the barn." She said, "I mean up in the barn, upstairs, sir."

[Notice Lizzie says her father took out "some papers and looked at them." If it had been a newspaper, she would have said "the paper." She let it slip that she noticed he was looking at something other than the *Providence Journal*, a slip-up no one caught."

Fleet continued: "She said after she had been up there [barn loft] about half an hour she came down again, went into the house, and found her father on the lounge, in the position in which she had left him, but killed, or dead. I then asked her what she did, finding him in that condition, and she said that she went to the back stairs and called Maggie. And I asked her who Maggie was; she said Maggie was the servant girl [Bridget]. She told Maggie to go for Dr. Bowen, he was not in his house, she then told her to go for Miss Russell, and Miss Russell came, and so did Dr. Bowen soon after, so she stated.

I asked her, "Who was in the house this morning or last night?" She said that "no one but her father, Mrs. Borden, and Bridget, and Mr. Morse, and herself." I asked her who is this Mr. Morse?" She said, "He is my Uncle, and he came here yesterday and slept in the room where Mrs. Borden was found dead." She said she didn't think Mr. Morse had anything to do with the killings, because Mr. Morse left the house this morning before nine o'clock, and did not return until after the murders. I asked her if she thought Bridget (Maggie) could have done this, and she said she didn't think that she could or did because Maggie went upstairs previous to her father's lying down on the lounge, and when she came from the barn, she called Maggie downstairs.

I then asked her if she had any idea who could have killed her father and mother. She said, "She is not my mother, sir; she is my stepmother—my mother died when I was a child."

How Alice Russell and Reverend Buck reacted to Lizzie's outburst concerning Abby, would be interesting. The woman lay on the other side of the guest chamber door, only a few feet away, butchered and lying in a pool of blood. Lizzie's denouncement of her, at such a time, was cold and unfeeling. While Alice later testified the feelings between the sisters and their stepmother was "not congenial," this showing of hatred for the dead woman may have surprised her greatly.

Marshall Fleet continued his testimony: "I then asked her if there had been anyone around this morning whom she would suspect of having done the killing of these people, and she said that she had not seen anyone, but at nine o'clock that morning a man came to the door and was talking with her father. [The person at the door was young William Morse, delivering Abby's fake 'sick call' note.] I asked her what they were talking about, and she said she thought they were talking about a store, and he spoke like an Englishman. [Johnathan Clegg, who had just rented Andrew Borden's store on South Main the day before the murders, had an English accent. He came to see Andrew Borden at home both on Tuesday and Wednesday, before the murders on Thursday. Lizzie is building a patchwork quilt of lies based on various visits to the Borden home that week. Another tenant dropped off keys to a store a few days before. It might be noticed here that Lizzie doesn't seem to miss much concerning people coming to the house, including the man in the baseball shoes on Monday.]

As Lizzie paused, Alice Russell suddenly spoke from her chair by the door.

"Tell him all; tell him what you was telling me," Alice coaxed, referring to Lizzie's tales of terror the night before in Alice's parlor.

Lizzie looked at Miss Russell [with that indefinable gaze that people around her committed upon]. Finally, she said, "About two weeks ago, a man came to the house, to the front door, and had some talk with father, and talked as though he was angry." And I asked her what he was talking about. She said, "He was talking about a store, and father said to him, "I cannot let you have the store for that purpose—the man seemed to be angry. I then came downstairs." [This was probably the conversation Lizzie eavesdropped on Tuesday and Wednesday when Johnathan Clegg came to talk to Andrew about "hiring the store." The polite exchange between her father and the businessman (who was only a day later already remodeling Andrew's store Clegg was moving into) has now become a bitter argument, between an Englishman demanding a store, and a reluctant Andrew Borden.]

Marshall Fleet made notes of the conversation. So far, Lizzie has made no mention of looking for sinkers in the barn loft; her alibi she gave at the Coroner's Inquest days later, for why she was up in the stifling hot loft, during the critical time her father was being hacked to death. She has only told Alice Russell that she was looking for iron or tin, to fix her window. Mrs. Churchill and Dr. Bowen were simply told she was "looking for iron," and Bridget was informed by Lizzie that she "was in the yard" when Andrew was murdered.

At 11:45 that morning, Lizzie's dear friend, Marianne Holmes, received the shocking news of the grizzly deaths of the Borden's. She made arrangements to hurry to Lizzie's side.

During Lizzie's inquisitions and the comings and goings of doctors, police officials, reporters, and friends, Andrew Borden's lifeless body was gone over. Not only his wounds and the condition of his blood were noted; Dr. Bowen and Officer Wixon went through his pockets and documented Andrew's personal property.

"A large ring of keys; a large shop key [possibly belonging to the broken Yale lock he brought home with him]; a can of fine chewing tobacco; a pocketbook with $81.65 in paper and coin; a letter; a silver watch and black braid, and a memorandum book."

The memorandum book was a small notebook, often carried by businessmen to make notations of transactions, receipts, etc. Dr. Dolan, who made an accounting of Andrew's effects, found something in the notebook he found interesting enough to give to Attorney Knowlton, the Prosecuting Attorney, on September 2, 1892, enclosed in a brief letter:

Hon. H.M. Knowlton
Dear Sir,
In looking over the old memorandum book of A. J. Borden, I found the enclosed slip. Please return it to me if you have no desire to retain it.

Respectfully
W.A. Dolan

Mr. Knowlton's return of the slip carried with it a cryptic reply: It said simply, "Keep it safe."
(Letters courtesy of the Fall River Historical Society)

Was the paper possibly a receipt? Had Andrew kept the sales receipt for the clawhead hatchet he was forced to purchase when Lizzie stole his others? Would this small slip of paper join his other non-verbal remonstrations, like the sitting room key to his locked bedroom, and the beheaded pigeons? Was he saving it for some future gesture, or, was it to be his proof that he had purchased such a hatchet for his home, in case, it too, went missing? Would the police be called in for any more of Lizzie's shenanigans?

Dr. Bowen made several trips up the stairs to check on Lizzie. It may have been during one of those trips that he carried to her a letter he found in Andrew's pocket. As there is no report that Andrew ever went to the Post Office that morning, and Lizzie admitted during her Inquest testimony that he told her he may not have time that forenoon, we have only her word that he did go. Bridget heard Lizzie ask her father upon his return that morning, "Any mail for me?" Bridget did not hear Andrew's reply. Only Lizzie claimed he replied, "None for you." It was important to her that it be believed Andrew *did* stop at the Post Office, mail her letter to Emma, and return with a *Providence Journal*, in a white wrapper, tucked under his arm. If a roll of burned papers was found in the stove, it would simply be the newspaper that she finished as she sat in the kitchen, waiting for her irons to get hot.

If Dr. Bowen found Lizzie's un-mailed letter to someone in Andrew's pocket, it would be natural to take it to her. The other letter found among his personal property was returned to Lizzie at the trial. The letter Lizzie gave her father to mail, was to Emma. It was never mailed. But when asked about it during her Inquest testimony, Lizzie is ready with an answer. Lizzie stated the letter was mailed and was later returned to the house, as Emma, after receiving Dr. Bowen's telegram, had hurried home and missed the post in Fairhaven. We do know Dr. Bowen is seen shortly after being in Lizzie's room, standing in the kitchen near the stove, with a torn letter in his hands.

By 12:25, not long after Marshall Fleet departed Lizzie's room, another policeman arrived at her bedroom door—Officer Phil Harrington. Other officers are arriving quickly: Officers Devine, Cogswell, and Riley.

Of all the officers questioned during the days and months of the murders, Phil Harrington's testimonies were the most articulate and detailed. It was not just his keen eye for women's fashion that stood out; there was not much that escaped this man's attention.

Officer Phillip Harrington: "I stepped into the hall [after coming from viewing Abby in the guest room], turned toward to go to the head of the stairs, and as I did so the door on the east end of the hall was ajar. In that room, I saw Miss Russell and Miss Borden. [Officer Harrington testified that when he arrived a few minutes earlier, he saw "several women in the kitchen." As Alice was upstairs with Lizzie, it may mean Mrs. Holmes has arrived and is there with Bridget. Mrs. Churchill has gone home, and Phoebe Bowen sent away earlier; any other females on the premises have not been mentioned.]

"I stepped into the room, and, taking the door in my right hand, I passed it back. Miss Russell stood on my left, and she received the door and closed it. Miss Russell stood in front of a chair which was on the north side of the door which I entered. Miss Lizzie Borden stood at the foot of the bed, which ran diagonally across the room. That is, the head of the bed was up in the north-east corner, forming a triangle with the north and east sides of the wall. She stood at the foot of the bed on the north side. I asked her to tell me all about this matter.

"She said, "I can tell you nothing about it." I asked her when she last saw her father, and she said, "When he returned from the Post Office, with a small package in his hand and some mail. I asked him if he had any for me, and he said, No. He then sat down to read the paper, and I went out in the barn. I remained there twenty minutes. I returned and found him dead."

"I then asked her, "When going to or coming from the barn, did you see anybody in or around the yard, or anybody going up or down the street?" She said, "No, sir." "While in the barn did you hear any noise in or about the yard as of anybody walking there?" She said, "No, sir." I said, "Not even the opening or closing of the door? Why not? You were but a short distance, and you would have heard the noise if any was made?" [The "scraping" sound is now missing.] She said, "I was up in the loft." I then asked her, "What motive?" And she said, "I don't know." "Was it robbery?" "I think not, for everything appears all right, even to the watch in his pocket and the ring on his finger." She said the rest of the house was all right, too.

I then asked her if she had any reason to suspect anybody. [After hesitating, Lizzie retells the story of the angry stranger coming to the house, not twice now, but three times in the past three weeks. So far, she has been careful to keep the harrowing events happening at her home within the two-week absence of her sister. This is the first time she adds a visit with angry words three weeks prior to the murders.]

"A few weeks ago," Lizzie stated, "father had angry words with a man about something...they were very angry at the time, and the stranger went away. They were in another room, but from the tone of their voices, I knew everything was not pleasant between them. About two weeks ago, he came again. They had a very animated conversation, during which they got angry again, and I heard father say, "No, sir; I will not let my store for any such business." But, before they separated, I heard father say, "When you are in town come again and I will let you know about it."

[The last words Lizzie quotes hearing the stranger say are quite possibly the only fabric of truth. Andrew may have told James Chatterton on Monday, to "come again when you are in town, and I will let you know about it." James was from out-of-town. He lived in Lynn, Massachusetts. Andrew would then talk to him later about running the Swansea farm. It is interesting to note Officer Harrington's note in the Witness Statements he submitted to Marshall Hilliard later. It reads, "Although Lizzie did not see the man who called about the store, still she did not explain how she knew it was he who called the second time." Lizzie also testified later at the Inquest that "it was dark" when the man called, and she did not see his features.]

What Lizzie did not realize, is that the Officers were constantly comparing notes that day. Her discrepancies in her stories to different policemen were being monitored on a play-by-play account. Thus, when another officer entered her room to question her, he had in mind what story she had already told. Officer Harrington, noting a few embellishments and omissions, said to her:

"Owing to the atrociousness of this crime, perhaps you are not in a mental condition to give as clear a statement of the facts as you will be on tomorrow. By that time, you may recollect more about the man who wished to hire the store. You may remember of having seen him, and thereby be enabled to give a description of him. You may recollect of having heard your father say something about him or his visit. So, by that time you may be in a better condition to relate what you know of the circumstances."

"To this, she made a stiff courtesy, shaking her head, and she says, "No, I can tell you all I know now just as well as at any other time." I asked her again about her time that she was in the barn. She said twenty minutes. I asked her wasn't it difficult to be so accurate about fixing the time. Said I, "May you not have been there a half an hour or perhaps only fifteen minutes?" She says, "No, sir; I was there twenty minutes." [She just told Assistant Marshall Fleet 30 minutes.]

"Miss Russell looked very pale," Officer Harrington noted in his Witness Statement report. "She was pale and much agitated, which she showed by short shallow breathing and wringing her hands. She spoke not a word. Lizzie stood at the foot of the bed, and talked in the most calm and collected manner; her whole bearing was most remarkable under the circumstances. There was not the least indication of agitation, no sign of sorrow or grief, no lamentation of the heart, no comment on the horror of the crime, and no expression of a wish that the criminal be caught. All this, and something that, to me, is indiscernible, gave birth to a thought that was most revolting. I thought, at least, she knew more than she wished to tell."

A Quick Trip to Swansea

According to *The Fall River Herald* that day, the following story ran under the sub-text, "Went to Swansey [ms]."

"At 12:45 o'clock, Marshal Hilliard and Officers Doherty and Connors procured a carriage and drove over to the farm, hoping that the suspected man would return there in order to prove an alibi. The officers will arrive at the place sometime before the man, as the distance is some ten miles, though it is hardly probable that he will return there. What makes it rather improbable that the man suspected is a Portuguese laborer is the statement of Charles

Gifford of Swansey [ms]. Mr. Gifford says that the only Portuguese employed on the Upper Farm is Mr. Johnson, and he is confined to his bed by illness. Another man might be employed by Mr. Borden on the lower farm for a few days, but he does not believe it. An attempt was made to reach Swansey [ms] by telephone, but no answer was received."

[Alfred Johnson was of Swedish descent. Portuguese, as mentioned earlier, was a catch-all phrase, at times, for foreigners. Bridget was asked about people in Andrew's circle, and especially those that had business at his home. She may have mentioned Alfred Johnson as a man from the farm who sometimes came to chop wood for them. It is possible that she mentioned he was coming that day to bring the eggs, not knowing John Morse had negated that visit the day before when he traveled to Swansea with a basket in which to bring them back.

Notice, Alfred is confined to bed by illness. He and Mr. Eddy are both ill. Was it from poisoned milk?]

Chapter Twenty

Thursday—August 4, 1892
Burning Paper and Hidden Hatchets

Officer Harrington left Lizzie Borden and Alice Russell a confused man. He had never seen a woman so cool and detached as Miss Borden appeared to be. Her father was lying brutally murdered in the room below hers, and her stepmother was also deceased only a few feet from where the lady stood coldly detailing her movements of the morning. He was still brooding over it when he came downstairs and entered the kitchen. There he saw Drs. Bowen and Dolan, Assistant Marshall Fleet, and Bridget.

"Just as I went to pass by Dr. Bowen," Officer Harrington testified in the Superior Court trial, "between him and the stove, I saw some scraps of notepaper in his hand. I asked him what they were. He was standing a little west of the door that led into the rear hall or entryway. I asked him what they were, and he said, "Oh, I guess it is nothing." So, he started to arrange them so as to determine what was on them, or to learn their contents. They were very small and it was rather difficult, but on one piece, on the upper left-hand corner, was the word "Emma." And that was written in lead pencil, as well as other pieces I saw.

"I asked him again what they contained, and he said, "Oh, I think it is nothing. It is something, I think, about my daughter going through somewhere." He then turned slightly to his left and took the lid from the stove and threw the papers in, or the pieces in. As he threw the papers in I noticed the fire box. The fire was very near extinguished. On the south end, there was a small fire which I judged was a coal fire. The embers were about dying. It was about as large as the palm of my hand. There had been some paper burned in there before, which was rolled up and still held a cylindrical form. It was twelve inches long, I should say, and two inches in diameter."

The Letter

The torn letter Dr. Bowen was holding was possibly the letter Lizzie had written to Emma and asked her father to mail for her that morning, but he did not go to the Post Office. Dr. Bowen found it in Andrew's pocket and gave it back to Lizzie. She may have torn it up, and as the police kept coming to search her room, asked him to burn it for her, making some excuse about its contents being misconstrued due to the tragic happenings of the day.

For instance, it may have said, "I am going through with my plans." If Emma knew Lizzie was going to kill Abby, this would be enough said. Lizzie may have told Dr. Bowen, "I am going through with it," was harmless---it merely meant she was going through with her plans to go to Marion on Monday for her vacation, but she feared the police would see it as something nefarious.

Dr. Bowen, when confronted by Officer Harrington looking over his shoulder, may have worried the policeman saw snippets of the writing. The good doctor quickly changes the meaning of the sentence he fears the officer has seen, to be about his own daughter...something "about my daughter *going through* somewhere." His daughter was expected that morning, but didn't come. Bowen's wife may have just used those very words with him earlier—that their daughter "went through" rather than stopping. It is fresh in his mind. He then quickly throws the scraps into the fire. Officer Harrington's first report of the incident stated the doctor dropped the pieces down past the side of the grate, making it impossible to fish them out.

Stove opening over the firebox section of a stove similar to the one where Officer Harrington saw the remains of the burned paper.

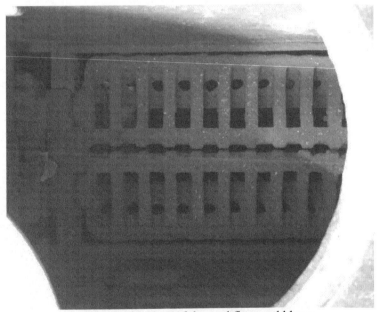

Close-up. The glow of the coal fire would have been seen through the grate, the burned paper resting on top. The stove pictured is on location, & courtesy of, MacDonald Book Shop in Estes Park, Colorado. Photos by Ron Bueker.

Remains of 12" long roll of paper. It still retains its cylindrical shape, as Officer Harrington testified. Could it have been the Swansea deed?

Comparison of a rolled deed and a rolled newspaper.

Lizzie made sure during her Inquest testimony that they knew she had a *Providence Journal* in the kitchen that morning, even though she admitted to not reading it. The fact that she was never asked about the burned paper in the stove was just one of many "lucky" breaks she was afforded that day.

Just about the time, Officer Harrington noticed the burned roll of paper in the kitchen stove, Dr. Dolan came in and called him over to the table. He had placed two cans of milk there, along with three hatchets, and told Harrington to watch over them. "Phil, I want you to take care of this milk, the family has been sick, and I don't want you to leave it until I relieve you."

Assistant Marshall Fleet then instructed Officer Harrington to go and check Bay Street. He also sent Officers Divine and Garvey at that time to cover Stafford Road in search of suspicious people who may have committed the murders. Officer Harrington told Fleet, Dr. Dolan had just told him to watch over the cans of milk. "Yes, I heard him when he spoke to you," Fleet said, "I will take care of the milk, and you go down to the lower road." Officer Harrington departed.

Hatchets in the Cellar

Shortly before Assistant Marshall Fleet arrived in the kitchen to instruct the officers to cover the major roads out of town, he had been "down cellar" to see what his officers had found there. Officer Mullaly showed him four weapons lying on the brick floor of the washroom, only a few feet from the cellar door that led outside.

Mullaly pointed out the spots on the larger hatchet—the one with the claw head at its back. There was a round spot on the blade that might be blood, or possibly rust. There was also a suspicious-looking spot on the handle. To Fleet, it appeared as if the hatchet had been recently washed and wiped. He testified the blade was a bluish tint, as if wet. He decided to separate the hatchet from the other tools lying on the floor. He stepped to his left into the keep cellar where barrels of vinegar, shingles and boxes sat. He placed the clawhead hatchet behind the barrels.

Assistant Marshall Fleet was asked in the Superior Court trial if he "discovered anything else there in the shape of an instrument— while you were down there at that time?" Fleet's answer was "Not at that time."

Fleet went upstairs where he met with Marshall Hilliard, who had just arrived in the yard. The two men discussed the situation. Officers were dispatched to areas around Fall River. Officer Medley was instructed to catch the 12:29 train to Providence, which was departing within a few minutes, and he hurried away.

"They Kept Coming to Talk to Her"

Bridget Sullivan remained in the kitchen throughout the day, watching as the parade of people passed through her domain. The noon meal had never been prepared, and her afternoon off was a mute point. She was questioned about the morning's events, her own movements, and asked to guide officers about the premises, unlocking the myriad keyholes as they went.

How much of Lizzie's conversation with the police and friends she overheard is unclear. Lizzie told Bridget she was in the backyard when the murders occurred. The maid must have overheard her, at least once that morning, mention she was in the barn when Mr. Borden was killed. The majority of the questions were asked of Lizzie in the privacy of her bedroom; a place from which Bridget was absent. But the police were comparing notes downstairs. Had Bridget overheard them? Was she already forming an impression of Lizzie's changing stories?

Mrs. Marianne Holmes arrived at the Borden home to find Lizzie in a state of nerves. She lay on her lounge, an arm flung across her forehead and let the calm façade she had shown to the police slip away. Her head was throbbing, and the ubiquitous sound of men's voices and footsteps outside her bedroom door were taking a toll on her.

Lizzie Borden was becoming frantic. Something was wrong. She imagined the police would come, see the bodies, look into the closets downstairs for a possible murderer, search the grounds and neighboring yards for clues—or an abandoned bloody weapon— have Winward remove the bodies, and leave her in peace. But that wasn't happening. They kept coming to her door, asking her more and more questions, trying to trip her up. The bodies were still here. She needed it all to go away. She needed Emma. She needed Dr. Bowen.

Mrs. Holmes hurried across the street to Dr. Bowen's home, who had been there only a few minutes, possibly to eat something and check on patient's calls. At Mrs. Holmes urging, he returned with a dose of Bromo Caffeine for Lizzie. It was a mild sedative, comparable to today's aspirin, and was to help with the headache and nervous condition.

Lizzie lay in the heat of her room, her friends and family physician comforting her. She wanted desperately for the day to end and to rid herself of wearing two dresses. The layers of fabric, along with a corset and petticoat, weighed her down like anchors. Perhaps it was almost over. Just then, a knock came at her door. It was shortly before 2 o'clock in the afternoon.

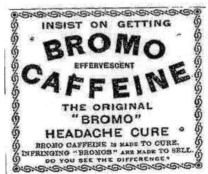

1890s ads for Bromo Caffeine, (l). Bromo Caffeine bottle from 1906. It was an effervescent added to water like Alka Seltzer.

"This is Making Me Tired"

Dr. Bowen walked to Lizzie's door and opened it "about six or eight inches" to peer out at three policemen standing there—Assistant Marshall Fleet, along with Officers Minnehan and Wilson.

"What do you want?" Dr. Bowen asked bluntly.

"We're here as officers to search the room, and the building," Fleet informed him.

"Just a moment," the doctor said and shut the door in the man's face. A few seconds passed, and he opened the door again.

"Miss Borden wants to know if it is absolutely necessary for you to search the room?" Dr. Bowen said.

"Yes," Fleet said flatly. "Murders have been committed. As Officers, we wouldn't be doing our duty if we didn't search, and we would like to come in."

"Just a moment." The doctor once again shuts the door in the face of the Assistant Marshall, who was becoming more and more agitated.

Finally, the door opened, and the doctor stood back to admit the three officers.

Lizzie lay on the lounge, visibly upset at the intrusion.

"I hope you will get through with this quickly," she said thickly. "All this is making me sick. I am very tired."

"We will finish as quickly as we possibly can," Officer Fleet said in a professional manner. "It's an unpleasant duty, considering your father and stepmother are dead." If he hoped the last statement would evoke any kind of emotion in the prostrate woman, he was disappointed. Lizzie bluntly announced, "There is no use in searching this room! Nobody can get in here, or throw anything in. I always lock my door when I leave my room, even if it is to only go downstairs."

Mr. Fleet nodded to the men, and they began to search the room as quietly as possible. They pulled aside the other red portiere in the bedroom that hid Lizzie's little wash area. They opened a few bureau drawers and did a general inspection of the bed.

Officer Fleet addressed Lizzie as the other two men continued their search of the room.

"You said this morning that you was up in the barn for half an hour," the Assistant Marshall said. He had heard from the other policemen who interviewed Lizzie about her timeline in the barn. "Do you say that now?"

Lizzie realized her error and said, "I don't say half an hour, I say twenty minutes to half an hour."

"Well, we will call it twenty minutes, then," Fleet said, making an entry into a notebook.

The color came into Lizzie's face. "I say from twenty minutes to half an hour, sir," she retorted hotly.

Fleet's jaw muscle jumped, but he continued on calmly.

"When and where was the last time you saw your stepmother?" he asked.

"I saw her about 9 o'clock as I was going downstairs. She was making the bed in the guest room," Lizzie replied. It was a concession she changed during her Inquest testimony, where she then stated she first saw Abby dusting in the dining room that morning.

Lizzie continued, hoping to get it all out and have the men leave her in peace. "Someone brought her a note this morning from a sick friend, and she went out. I did not know she had returned."

Fleet walked around Lizzie's bed and pulled aside the red curtain there. He tried to open it and Lizzie spoke up, "That door is locked and bolted from the other side. You can't go through there." Fleet noticed it was also hooked on Lizzie's side of the door.

The men finished their cursory search of her room. Mr. Fleet walked into the guest room next door and noticed the blood stains on the pillow cases and dressing case. He saw Abby Borden lying in a pool of blood. He tried the door to the right of the guest room bed and found it locked on Lizzie's side. This was the door he had seen her writing desk pressed against in her bedroom.

Fleet left the room and once again knocked on Lizzie's door. Before any protestation could be made concerning his intrusion, he asked her bluntly what was in the locked door at the end of the hallway, opposite her room. She answered it was just a clothes press [closet]. He informed her he wished to see inside it and that it was locked. Lizzie met him in the hallway with a ring of keys and unlocked the door. She watched as he and the other two officers looked over the dresses, up on the shelf, and around on the floor where there were some trunks and boxes. They exited and she locked the door.

"How do I get into Mr. Borden's room?" Fleet asked her as she turned to go back to her room.

"You must get the keys. Maggie will give you the keys." Lizzie turned away, entered her room and locked the door.

[Alice Russell, during her trial testimony, stated that she saw Lizzie go to the clothes press [closet] at the end of hall twice that day, both times unlocking the door to get into it. When asked if one of those times was with Officer Fleet, Alice replied, "No." When Officer Doherty first looked into the closet earlier that morning, he found it open. At some point, Lizzie may have taken the blue calico she had been wearing over the Bedford cord that morning and hidden it beneath a heavy winter silk dress in the closet at the end of the hall. The officers later admitted there were two dresses they never checked in that clothes press, as they were obviously winter dresses and would not have been worn in August. Lizzie's second trip to the locked closet may have been to check that the dress had not been discovered during subsequent searches.]

The Handleless Hatchet

Assistant Marshall Fleet, Officers Minnehan, and Wilson followed Bridget up the back stairs to Abby and Andrew Borden's room. She unlocked their bedroom door from the second-floor landing and stepped back to let them enter. They looked about the room and into the adjoining two rooms: one being Abby's dressing room where the safe sat, and the other a remodeled pantry from the days the room served as a kitchen for the upper floor tenants. This may have served as Andrew's clothes closet and the couple's toiletry area.

Mr. Fleet stepped over to the door connecting to Lizzie's bedroom and inspected the bolt; it was secure. If the enormity of locked doors in the house made a strange impression upon him, it did not make it into his notes.

The three men followed Bridget to the attic where they did a more thorough search of her room, closet, and trunk. They then searched the small bedroom next to hers where John Morse would find himself sleeping that night and following that, inspected the two attic rooms serving as storage closets. Finding nothing suspicious, they headed back down to the kitchen; the sound of Bridget relocking the doors echoing behind them.

Mr. Fleet went directly to the cellar, where he found Dr. Dolan and Officer Mullaly, still standing guard over the hatchet and axes that lay on the wash room floor. At this time, he asked Michael Mullaly where he had found the hatchets. The officer led him to the middle cellar room, explaining as they went how Bridget showed him the hatchets that morning.

Officer Mullaly would later testify that it was then he and Mr. Fleet took notice of a third hatchet. As the two men looked into the old starch box where Bridget had first found the hatchets, Mullaly took out a hatchet head without its handle. It looked suspicious to both men, as it appeared as if someone wanted it to appear unused, matching the other tools in the box that lay beneath a thin layer of fine dust. But the "dust" on the handleless hatchet head was of a coarser substance—what appeared to be white ash from the coal pile. Further, it was not just covered on one side, like the tools found in the box, but on both sides, as if it had been rolled in ashes.

The two men commented on the ragged end of the hatchet head, where the rest of the handle was missing. Both stated it looked as if it had recently been broken. The wood there looked "bright;" a fresh break.

Mr. Fleet later testified that he then put the hatchet head back into the box and left it there. This was a mistake that came back to haunt him.

After checking the cellar door, and finding the outer door leading to the yard bolted, he went back upstairs. He questioned Bridget in the kitchen.

According to Fleet's notes in his Witness Statements, Bridget gave the following statements at that time:

"Mr. Borden came in the house about 10:40 a.m. Saw him come in the dining room, go to the window and look at some papers which he had in his hands. He then went in the sitting room, sat down in the large chair near the window, and left Lizzie ironing some handkerchiefs in the dining room. I went upstairs at 10:55 to fix my room. After I had been in the room about ten minutes, Lizzie called me downstairs, saying that her father was dead, someone had killed him, and go and get Dr. Bowen. I went for the Doctor; he was not in, and I went for Miss Russell on Borden Street."

"Did you see anyone you think would have done the killing?" Fleet asked her.

"No, I did not. I was washing windows outside and did not see anyone but Mr. Morse that morning; and he went away before 9 o'clock. Am very sure that I was not upstairs more than ten to fifteen minutes. I did not hear the door opened while I was upstairs, nor did I see anyone from my window."

[Bridget's statement, "nor did I see anyone from my window" will take on new significance when her version of the morning's events are tampered with for her later testimonies.]

Mr. Fleet left the house and found John Morse hanging out in the backyard. The man did not look happy, as Fleet approached him, and began his questions as to his movements in the past 24 hours.

"Last night I stopped here," Morse began, his mind racing. "I slept in the room where Mrs. Borden was found dead. I arrived here yesterday afternoon from New Bedford. Called upon Mr. Borden. Afterward got a carriage from Kirby's stable, and went to Mr. Borden's farm, arriving at the house again about 8:30 p.m.

We sat up I think until about ten o'clock. Went to bed in the room, as before stated. Got up about six o'clock this morning, got breakfast about seven o'clock, stopped in the house till about 8:40 a.m. Leaving Mr. Borden at the door, went to the Post Office, wrote a letter from there, went as far as third Street on Bedford, from Third to Pleasant Street, through Pleasant Street to No. 4 Weybosset Street, arriving there about 9:30 a.m. Saw relatives from the West. Remained at the house from 9:30-11:20, or thereabouts. Left, taking horse car, and stopped at the corner of Pleasant and Second Streets, and got to Mr. Borden's house about, or near twelve o'clock. Saw a number of persons around the house, and was told Mr. and Mrs. Borden was killed. That was the first I knew of their deaths."

[Note that here John Morse admits to seeing "a number of persons around the house." That statement completely disappears, and is, in fact, hotly disputed by him during his court testimonies. He also says he left the Emery's at 11:20 and took a horse car to Pleasant and Second, walked up, arriving at Andrew's at, or near, noon. A horsecar trip would have taken 10 minutes, and walking another five. Where was he the remaining 20-25 minutes?]

"Have you any idea who did this?" Fleet asked him.

"I can't see who could do this; do not know that he has an enemy in the world."

"Have you seen, or have you heard Bridget or Lizzie say that they had seen anyone around who they suspected?"

"No, I have not."

John Morse then asked Mr. Fleet if he suspected that the murderer could have been concealed in the house last night. Fleet replied that he did not. He amended it to say that a murderer might have been in the house, but could not see how he could have been there without some of them seeing him. Morse said it is very strange that this should be done in the daytime, and right in the heart of the city. It put him in mind of the Nathan murder which was twenty or twenty-five years ago. "In that case, they never found the murderer," Morse stated ominously.

Chapter Twenty-One

Thursday, August 4, 1892
"It's Incredible!

Marshal Rufus B. Hilliard

At 2:00 in the afternoon, Marshall Rufus B. Hilliard arrived at the Borden property on Second Street. He could barely reach the house with his buggy due to the mass of humanity crowding the sidewalks and roadway. His men were valiantly trying to control the crowd. He had never seen anything like it in Fall River.

After hearing the reports from his officers, concerning their interviews with the inmates of the house, he turned his attention to the barn and yard.

Officer Phil Harrington arrived back at the Borden house and was put to work searching the barn. Marshall Hilliard rolled up his sleeves and joined Harrington, along with Officers Doherty, Conners, and Riley, as they overhauled the barn's main floor. It was at that time Harrington made known to his superior his suspicions concerning Lizzie Borden.

"I don't like that girl," Harrington blurted out, as they looked through the old carriages and sleigh.

"What's that?" Hilliard asked, out of breath in the heat.

"I don't like that girl. Under the circumstances she does not act in a manner to suit me; it is strange, to say the least," Harrington said.

The men continued their search of the barn's first floor. It contained a number of barrels, a large collection of old window frames—some with glass, some not— and a general assembly of odds and ends. Finding nothing, they ascended to the loft, the Marshall leading the way. "I want you men to give this place a complete going over; every nook and corner must be looked into, and this hay turned over."

The north side of the barn loft was almost completely filled with the hay that had been stored for the horse no longer residing there. Officer Harrington later testified there was "close to half a ton" of hay. An old fireplace front, a workbench with a basket filled with odd bits of scrap and iron, lumber, and an old pigeon coop took up most of the area. As the officers searched through it all, their uniforms drenched in sweat, Mr. Harrington once again spoke up:

"If any girl can show you or me, or anybody else what could interest her up here for twenty minutes, I would like to have her do it."

The Marshall shook his head, and said, "It's incredible!"

Marshall Hilliard then instructed Officer Harrington to go with him to the cellar of the house. Harrington stated he saw Assistant Marshal Fleet, Dr. Dolan, Michael Mullaly and Officer Riley there, searching the cellar. He changed his original statement in his Witness report, to something different weeks later in his Preliminary Hearing testimony. He now remembers seeing Fleet, Dr. Dutra, and Officer Devine.

"When we went into the wash room, laying on the floor were two axes and a hatchet. I had seen another hatchet that day which was not in the collection," Officer Harrington stated.

He went in search of the missing hatchet and found it laying on an old chopping block at the west end of the cellar near the entrance to the coal room; the opposite end of the cellar from where Fleet had hidden the hatchet earlier that morning. It was the large hatchet with the claw head on one end. Harrington showed its location to Mr. Fleet, who then took the hatchet and returned it to the hiding place behind the vinegar barrels in the keep cellar near the wash room. It was never ascertained who moved it to the chopping block. This was between 3 and 4 in the afternoon.

Headlines and Theories

The crowd outside 92 Second Street watched as police officers came and went through the two small gates affronting the murder house. Each arrival and departure sent off twitters of excitement. The armchair sleuths postulated their theories as the newspaper men documented the day in minute detail.

The New York Herald (by telegraph to the Herald):
Fall River, Mass., August 4, 1892:
Lizzie is Suspected
At this hour police suspicions rest upon persons who were in the family circle, particularly on John W. Morse, brother-in-law of Mr. Borden by his first marriage, also on the daughter, Lizzie...The police say the only motive for murder was gain, else one of the victims would have been spared.

The Fall River Herald, August 4, 1892.

Twenty minutes were all the time the murderer had to finish his terrible work; conceal the weapon with which he accomplished his crime, and conceal it in such a way as to leave no trace of blood on the carpet or through the house that would reveal how he escaped; to pass out of the house by the side door within 15 feet of the barn where the daughter was engaged, and a like distance from the Buffington house on the north; pass the length of the house and disappear up or down Second Street.

Historic Photographs

At 3 o'clock on that humid August afternoon, a buzz of excitement swept through the crowd. A local photographer, James E. Walsh, alighted from a carriage carrying a tripod and camera equipment. There were to be photographs of the salacious scenes! The gawkers could barely contain themselves.

Although the police and the attending doctors were ridiculed in the press repeatedly for their mishandling of the case that day, Dr. Dolan's request for a photographer was redemptive and groundbreaking. Crime scene photographs were not the norm. Jack the Ripper's victims were shown in photographs only after being removed from the scene of the crime. Documenting crucial evidence while the bodies still remained in the location of their slaying was a directive of historic proportions.

There was, however, one fall back in the Borden case. The bodies had been moved throughout the day, along with furniture and vital evidence. In Abby's case, the bed had been pulled away, stripped, remade, and shoved back in an effort to duplicate its original placement. Her body had already been turned over, lifted up, and replaced; her arm placement only guessed at. In an act of decency, her clothes were arranged primly along her body.

Andrew's body had met a similar fate, although not as drastic. As his clothes and the Prince Albert coat behind his head were searched, his body had slipped downwards along the horsehair arm of the sofa. The couch itself had been pulled away to look for blood stains and a possible hiding place for a weapon. His wounds had been studied, and his face tilted to look for marks on the opposite side.

But, as the afternoon sun shifted through the sitting room and guest room windows, James Walsh did his best to capture the gore of that fateful day.

Mr. Moody for the Prosecution (during the Superior Court trial): "What time in the day was this taken?" [Referrring to the crime scene photo of Abby.]

Walsh: "Probably half past three."

Moody: "Under whose direction were the body, the bed and bureau adjusted to the position seen in the view?"

Walsh: "They were that way when I went in the house. I didn't see anyone move them."

[The photographs of Abby's body, from behind, and with the bed moved away, are marked exhibits 15, 16, and 17]

Moody: "In whose presence were these views taken?"

Walsh: "There were several officers there and Dr. Dolan...I could not say he was present at all of them; he was at some of them...I could not say any officer was present at all—going in and out of the room."

[Exhibit 18 was entered as a view of Abby Borden's head, and Exhibit 19 was of Andrew Borden's head, taken later that day at half-past four during the partial autopsies at the house]

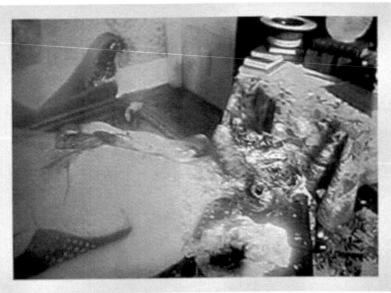

James Walsh's photograph taken of Andrew Borden at 4:30 during his partial autopsy in the sitting room where he died. Trial exhibit #19.

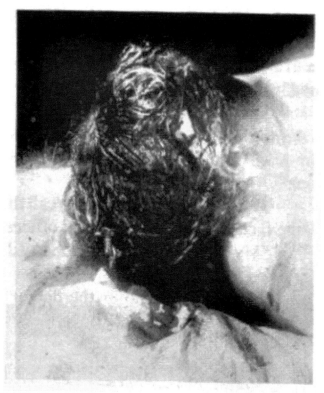

James Walsh's photo of the close-up of Abby's head. The would to her neck is seen. The braid of fake hair found on the bed next to her would have sat upon the crown where it appears flattened. Trial Exhibit #18.

Abby Borden was finally carried from the room where she had lain since her murder that morning. Several men labored beneath her weight, and the obstacles of the staircase, to transport her body to the dining room where she was laid out on an undertaker's board. At 3:30 p.m., she was undressed—her bloody clothing, stiff with dried blood, laid aside. Several doctors stood over the prostrate form, including Dr. Gunning and Dr. Learned, along with Doctor Dolan and Mayor Coughlin, who was also a physician. Abby's body was sponge bathed, and a partial autopsy began.

The notes made of Abby that day stated she was a 64-year-old woman, well-nourished, weighing approximately 210-220 pounds, with a full head of dark brown hair "getting to gray." The hair was cut by the hatchet blows, "as though done with a razor." Dr. Dolan reported that upon opening her stomach and taking her temperature inside, that it "was quite warm, due to the fat." Abby's stomach was removed and tied off at both ends to protect the contents. This was placed in a jar, sealed with wax, and labeled. It would be sent, along with Andrew's, and the two cans of milk from Wednesday and Thursday, to Professor Wood in Boston for analysis.

The dining room at Lizzie Borden B&B with undertaker's board on the back wall.
Photo by the Author.

Andrew Jackson Borden's body was lifted from the blood-soaked sofa and placed upon a second undertaker's board in the sitting room. He too was washed, and his stomach removed, tied off, and placed in a sterilized jar, sealed and labeled. It was noted his core temperature was cold, unlike his wife, even though she had died approximately an hour and a half before him.

James Walsh photographed both bodies at this time, before leaving the house. You can see his camera on the tripod reflected in the mirror of the guest room.

James Walsh's camera & tripod are reflected in the mirror.

Charles Carroll was sent to the Borden home the Saturday before the Superior Court trial in June of 1893, to take photographs of the house and surrounding property. At that time, Miss Emma was still living at the home. John Morse had gone back to Iowa but returned for the trial.

The Afternoon Wears On

Emma Borden stood at the train platform in New Bedford and held fast to her friend Helen Brownell's gloved hand. Although the telegram from Doctor Bowen had simply said her father was sick, and she was needed at home, she knew in her heart it was far worse. Letting go of Helen's hand, so warm and reassuring, and stepping into the train bound for home, would be the last normal moments of her life—she felt it as strongly as the humid air that pressed upon her. For the first time in her steady life, she faltered. She would have given her last cent to turn around and return to the safety and warmth of the Brownell's parlor on Green Street.

At 3:39 p.m., on August 4, 1892, the New Bedford train bound for Weir Junction in Taunton departed the Pearl Street Railway Station. The last leg of the trip would end at the Bowenville Station in Fall River. Emma lifted the red velvet curtain near her head and waved to her friend, who stood on the wooden platform. With a great blast of steam and squealing wheels, the train jerked away, taking her toward the small house on Second Street, and God knew what.

At 3:40 that afternoon, Officers Edson and Mahoney arrived at the Borden house. They found Abby and Andrew undergoing partial autopsies. The officers were told a distraught daughter was closeted in her upstairs bedroom, and that several weapons capable of inflicting the fatal wounds had been found in the cellar. The information was also imparted that the crime scene was suspect, no murderer had been found, and there was no trail of blood leading away from either victim. It didn't take long to realize the tide of suspicion was flowing toward the occupant of a locked room at the top of the front stairs.

Charles Sawyer remained on guard at the side screen door. His stomach rumbled, reminding him he had missed the noon meal, and the supper hour was arriving with the waning afternoon. The crowds surging around the house had not abated. The police ringing the parameter had their hands full keeping the morbid from trying to get into the yard to peer through the first-floor windows. The sitting room and dining room shutters were open wide to let in the natural light needed for the autopsies and photographs. The windows, with their screens in place, were raised to ventilate the rooms. Luckily, the windows were too high to peer into, especially the ones on the north where the drive dipped toward the barn. The shouting crowd outside was a constant background of noise as the police and doctors tried to unravel a mystery that would still capture the world's imagination over a hundred years in the future.

As the doctors worked over the disemboweled bodies of Abby and Andrew Borden, Charles Sawyer found himself in a suddenly quiet entryway. The kitchen was empty for the first time that day. He turned from the screen door and eyed the hatchets lying on the kitchen table. His curiosity got the better of him. He crossed quickly to the kitchen table standing center of the room and picked up the big hatchet with the strange claw head end.

"I think the police officers were downstairs searching, and some of them brought up I think two axes that I know of and this hatchet, and I do not know but what there was another one, but I am not certain...there was one or two," Charles Sawyer testified during the Preliminary Hearing.

Mr. Jennings (for the Defense): "Do you recollect whether one of the hatchets they brought up had a claw on it, or not?"

Sawyer: "The one I saw here yesterday in Court looked very much like it."

Jennings: "Do you know who brought it up?"

Sawyer: "I do not. The first I saw of it, His Honor the Mayor was looking at it...Mayor Coughlin. He stood in the back entry door leading into the kitchen. He stood there. I do not know whether he laid it on the kitchen table or not, but that is where I found it. It was about the time they were making the autopsy, as I supposed."

Jennings: "How long should you think the hatchet remained on the kitchen table?"

Sawyer: "I could not say that. I do not know how long it had been there when I picked it up. I saw it there with some cans of milk setting on the table. I looked it over pretty thoroughly, and I rubbed my finger on the side of it."

Jennings: "You was the man that did the scraping on that hatchet?"

Sawyer: "I do not know as I scraped it any, I rubbed it, and got a dried yellow rust off. I didn't see any blood or hair on it. I don't know when it was taken away."

Looking for a Murderer

Lizzie Borden remained on her red lounge in her bedroom as the afternoon sun made its way slowly toward the Taunton River. Her friends had come and gone throughout the day, always making sure someone sat with her. She asked each time they entered her room what was happening outside her door. No one had been in to question her for some time, and she hoped it meant the police were now out looking for the murderer. Tactfully, they answered her questions as best they could. They could tell by the questions put to them downstairs, that the police found Lizzie's statements and demeanor disturbing.

Her friends didn't need to shield her from the knowledge that Abby's body had been removed from the guest room next door. Lizzie had heard the voices of the men carrying Mrs. Borden past her door, as they tried to navigate the tight curve in the stairway, grunting beneath their burden. *She is gone now*, Lizzie thought with relief, as the voices descended the staircase. *She will be gone from this house...MY house...and Emma and I will be free.*

Minutes later, as her friends brought her tea and comfort, she noticed the strain about them. Something was happening downstairs that was upsetting—something they wanted frantically to keep from her. Although the voices from the sitting room had risen in muffled waves through her bedroom floor throughout the day, Lizzie had tried to distance herself from the image of her father laying there dead; separated from her only by carpet, wooden struts, ceiling plaster, and space. She did not realize they had lain him out on a perforated board and cut him open.

As Lizzie had hoped, however, a massive search had been ongoing throughout the day for the perpetrator of the Borden murders; spreading from her yard to the surrounding areas like a stain.

Officer Frances [Frank] Wixon began the search earlier that day, leading out of the Borden yard. Soon after, the City Hall bell struck 12. He was in the backyard searching through the tall grass. The movement of a man's hat on the other side of the fence to the southeast captured his attention. He climbed onto the pile of lumber at the Borden's backyard and stepped along the fence. He jumped down into Crowe's yard where a masonry business was run. The yard was filled with odds and ends, lumber, and weeds.

A barn sat near the fence, a pile of lumber west of it. Twenty to twenty-five feet from the fence separating Crowe's yard from the Kelly house—south of the Borden's yard—stood a man sawing lumber near the pile; his back was to the Borden property. Officer Wixon approached him and asked him a question. The man did not understand and replied in French. Two other men were there; one, John Denny, a stone cutter, stayed back, closer to Third Street, that Crowe's yard abutted. Wixon asked them if they had seen anyone that morning, or heard anything from the Borden house. They said they had not, and seemed surprised to hear about the murders.

Patrick McGowan worked for Crowe's masonry. He was in the stone yard that day working. At one point he walked over to the fence where the Borden and Chagnon properties met at the northwest corner of Crowe's yard. He stood on the pile of lumber on Crowe's side and reached up to a branch of pears hanging over from Chagnon's orchard on the other side of the fence. The Frenchman sawing wood, Joseph Derosier, told him in broken English the pears were not ripe yet, but the ones hanging over the fence to the west were. These were the Borden's pears. Patrick got up on the fence where he could reach them better and plucked off three pears.

Mrs. Mary A. Chase, who resided over Wade's store next to the Kelly house, saw McGowan up on the fence at 10:45, the morning of the murders, filling his pockets with pears. He saw her and jumped down near the barn on Crowe's side. She reported it when the police questioned the inhabitants of the neighboring houses. It was Patrick McGowan's luck to be caught pilfering pears from the yard of a house where two brutal murders were taking place not far from the time he was there. Due to this, he lied—stating he left Crowe's yard by 10 that morning.

Dr. Chagnon's pear orchard sat behind the Borden back fence, to the east. To the north of the orchard were the doctor's home and residence. On the morning of the murders, he and his wife were going to the Rocky Point clambake and amusement park. Officers Harrington and Doherty went to the house to question the people there. They spoke to Dr. Chagnon's assistant, John Normand, who told them he was at Bowenville during the forenoon, driving the Doctor and his family to the train station, to catch a train to Pawtucket, Rhode Island, at 10:45. The assistant had called Dr. Collet's and asked the doctor's son to go and care for Dr. Chagnon's house until he returned that day. Someone needed to be there to answer the phone in case patients called, or in the event, they dropped by.

The son was busy at the drug store, and could not go, so Dr. Collet's daughter, Lucy, was sent to Chagnon's to await callers. The 18-year-old girl found herself locked out at Dr. Chagnon's, so she sat down on the piazza in the yard from 10:50 a.m. to 11:45, when Mr. Normand returned. She could see the Borden's back fence and swore she saw and heard no one during that time. She later testified that she did talk to two patients who dropped by, which would have taken her focus away for a few moments. One gentleman came at 11:00 and waited for ten minutes until finally giving her a pill bottle to be filled and left. The other man did not stay after hearing the doctor was out.

Officers Harrington and Doherty went to the south of Crowe's yard to Mrs. Crapo's. She and her servant girl were home all day and heard no unusual noise, nor did they see anyone go through their yard.

The Fall River Ice Company was south of Mrs. Crapo. In the yard were several men constantly employed there. They reported to the officers that no one came their way. Mrs. Kelly's girl, Mary Doolan, who had been talking to Bridget that morning, before the two set about washing the exterior windows, was interviewed. She stated she and Bridget saw no one in or around the yard.

Dr. Bowen's wife, Phoebe, told the officers she had been sitting at her front window, which is directly opposite the Borden yard, and in full view of the front and side doors, waiting and watching for the coming of her daughter, Florence. She was at the window until 10:55 a.m.. The daughter was away and was expected on the forenoon train. At this point, Mrs. Bowen arose, and said, "well, she will not come now." [Mrs. Bowen did not mention seeing

Andrew Borden come home to the front door at 10:40-10:45 that morning.]

The officers knocked on every door and questioned each person loitering along Second Street. The stories were repeated: saw no one suspicious, and heard no noise out of the ordinary. Men were sent to check depots and roadways. They rounded up a few suspicious characters, one of which was a poor Portuguese who made the mistake of emptying his savings account that day of a measly $60 and change. He was brought to the jail for questioning, and let go.

The police interviewing potential witnesses were focused on a particular time: after 10:30, when Andrew was headed home. At 10:30, Joseph Chatterton was just giving up on waiting for Abby to come out the front door and was heading back to the Emery's on Weybosset Street.

If the officers had asked questions concerning an earlier segment of time that morning, they may have garnered more information about the clandestine meeting that resulted in the elderly couple's murders. Each witness's statement they jotted down had time stamps of 10:30 or later—moments after Lizzie Borden came around the side of the house from the backyard, after hurling a hatchet over the east fence. Some did report seeing Bridget washing windows between 10 and 10:30.

[If Lizzie had gone into the backyard only fifteen minutes later that morning, at 10:45, and stood on the woodpile at the southeast corner of the yard, she would have come face to face with Patrick McGowan reaching for the pear branch where she stood. Lucy Collet, sitting only 40-feet away on the piazza of Dr. Chagnon's house, would have seen an arm flinging a hatchet into Crowe's yard. Bridget would have finished the windows at that time as well, and witnessed Lizzie returning to the house. The planets had aligned for Lizzie Borden that day.]

In a scene reminiscent of Mayberry, the good people of Fall River had gone about their business that morning:

Fredrick A. Pickering, No. 8 Forest Street, was on Second Street and saw nothing.

Mark Chase was around the Express Company's stable, opposite the Borden house all forenoon. He wandered back and forth to Wade's Store, next to the Kelly house, several times between 10:30 and 11:15, and saw nothing suspicious.

Wade's store seemed to be the place to be for those in no particular hurry on that hot morning. Leander A. Wilson had been loitering there when Mary Wyatt, the woman living over Dr. Bowen's, told him and several others within earshot about the crime. Macy C. Macomber was standing in front of Wade's, before walking down to Louis L. Hall's stable, when Mrs. Churhill ran down.

Sarah Gray was in the store, at 103 Second Street, "not busy, saw nothing."

Harry Pearce of No. 25 Third Street, was standing around Hall's stable for some time before Mrs. Churchill hurried over.

Not one person noticed anything out of character, with the exception of Dr. Handy and Mrs. Manley, who reported a strange, pale man standing near the Borden house between 9:45 and 10:30 that morning.

Borden's old well near the barn. Mrs. Churchill's window is at left.
Photo by Charles Carroll, 1893.

The neighboring homes and businesses were not the only places receiving the officer's full attention. The Borden yard, privy, old well, grape arbor, barn and lumber pile had been gone over several times. The well had been covered over years before and was filled with debris. The vault beneath the privy was, admittedly, not probed to its dregs, but a cursory view of it seemed to satisfy the officials nothing had been dropped into the "goop." The lumber pile had been investigated at least a half dozen times that day by various officers, at one point the boards were removed a foot down from the top of the squared-off planks. Nothing.

Borden's privy in the barn. Photo by Charles Carroll.

Alfred Johnson, the farmhand from Swansea, had meticulously stacked the wood planks against the east fence in the Borden's yard into a square formation, placing the boards atop each other, leaving a "well" of space in the center. Other piles lined the fence as well.

Thursday—"It's Incredible!"

At the top and bottom of the east fence, flanking Chagnon's pear orchard, was barbed wire. Interestingly, no other neighbor in the area was reported to have gone to such lengths to fortify their property. Was it the barn break-ins that caused Andrew to add an additional obstacle to entry into his yard? Was it the nearness of the mill tenements only a few streets over, or the rash of fires in the area set by an arson's hand? Perhaps it was to keep people from pilfering his pears. His paranoia is obvious in his house of locks and the rules given to the latching of the three doors that provided entry from the outside; there was also that barbed wire fence.

Charles Carroll's photo of the Borden backyard in 1893. Note the lumber pile along the back of the fence with its crossed boards. The Chagnon pear orchard is at the rear, on the other side of the fence. The barbed wire ran along the top and bottom of that fence.

A view from Bridget's window looking east today. The wall is higher than the 6' height it was in 1892. The peaked roof on the other side of the fence, in front of the cars, was the location of Changnon's pear orchard. Third Street is in front of that. Dr. Chagnon's house would have been a little farther to the north than the white house at the left now shows. Crowe's yard would be where the large dark house at the right stands. The Kelly house still stands at the right of the wall (not shown). Photo by Ron Bueker.

Chapter Twenty-Two

Thursday, August 4, 1892
Evening

Emma Borden's bedroom.
Photography by Frank Grace (Trig Photography)

Emma Arrives Home

Emma Borden rode through the town of Fall River in the rear of a rented hack. The train had arrived at the Bowenville Station on time, and she was now headed home. Her small valices rested beside her on the seat. She worried a loose piece of yarn from the carpetbag pressed against her hip as the buggy passed the familiar buildings of South Main Street. Thoughts of Dr. Bowen's telegram ran through her mind, telling that her father was ill, and she was needed at home. Not Abby...her father. What did it mean?

As they approached Pleasant Street, she noticed clusters of people hurrying toward Borden Street. *It must be another fire,* her tired mind thought, as it seemed there was always one starting somewhere in the city. She tipped her head and cast her eyes upward through the buggy window. No smoke appeared above the treetops and rooflines.

The driver of the hack hesitated at Borden Street. He had intended to turn left onto the road, and then a right onto Second Street. But the street was completely choked off by people, who were standing like a human wall, refusing to budge. They poured out of shops and seemed to seep up from the pavement, making travel along South Main Street almost impossible. He snapped the reins, and the horse pressed forward up Main Street— foregoing a turn onto Borden—as people reluctantly gave way to the traffic.

By the time the hack turned left onto Spring Street, Emma's heart began to race. She could see that the wave of motion was towards Second Street. Shouts of "Murder!" came into the buggy as invasively as a hoard of wasps. She felt dizzy, and terribly, terribly frightened. Several hours earlier that day, her father had walked along this very street on his way home for the noon meal, and to find out what had happened to his wife, who not shown for a very important appointment. This rush of strangers had eradicated his last footprints.

The driver came to a stop at the corner of Spring and Second. Crowds blocked the way. Up ahead he could see policemen frantically trying to keep them to the sidewalks, but there was no room. There had to be close to a thousand people jockeying for a view of the greenhouse four houses down on the right.

Emma leaned from the buggy and stared, aghast. This could not be her street. Nothing looked familiar. It was distorted and foreign; these bodies of strangers that blocked her normal view of the neighborhood had turned it into something else. It would never appear the same. She shrunk into the carriage and pulled her bag onto her lap, her fingers gripping its handle until the flesh shown white.

A sudden surge of movement, the creaking of wheels, and the buggy pulled forward. She saw a sea of faces peering into the carriage at her, as the hack slowly progressed toward the house.

"It's Miss Emma!" she heard someone shout. It sounded ugly and invasive to her ears. It was to be only the beginning of the peeling back of her coveted privacy.

The crowd moved aside and allowed the buggy to pull up before the front gate of 92 Second Street. Climbing down from his seat, the driver opened Emma's door and took her two carpet bags. She clutched the smaller valise in her left hand, while accepting his with her right. A strange hush had settled over the people immediately around the house, while the steady thrum of voices could still be heard outside this sudden bubble of stillness.

She looked up to see a policeman standing at her front door. His face looked both stoic and sad, at the instant their eyes met. As she moved toward the gate, the hack driver was holding wide for her, she felt gentle pressures upon her back and sleeves. People were touching her as she passed. This was the only member of the family to which they had been given access. In some morbid fascination, they reached out to feel her; a souvenir of the morbidity going on inside those protected walls.

The hack driver delivered her bags to the front doorstep, and doffing his cap, turned back to the buggy. People were leaning into the window of the back seat where Miss Emma had sat, perhaps hoping for something she had left behind. The driver climbed up onto his seat, and flicked the reins. In deference to the carriage that had born Emma Borden home, they made way for him to pass the short distance to Borden Street. In his head, he was already rehearsing the story he would tell at his supper table that night. He had driven Emma Borden to the murder house...he had carried her bags.

The tolling of five bells rang out over the housetops, each tone seemingly more deep and sonorous than the one preceding it. Five bells. Five people, who had lived within the walls of that austere building. Two of those people were now dead; their bodies lying on the other side of the front door.

Emma stepped into the front hallway and stopped. Mrs. Holmes had been told she had arrived and was waiting for her at the bottom of the front stairs. The doors to the parlor and sitting room were closed, turning the entry into a small box, with the stairs the only way out. She took a step toward the sitting room door, but Mrs. Holmes hand on her arm stopped her. She was lead, instead, to the stairway, where her younger sister Lizzie waited above.

"The bodies were delivered to me at 5:30."

James Winwood stood inside the sitting room and watched as Doctor Dolan, and his team of associates, finished with the partial autopsy of Andrew Borden. Abby Borden's body lay in the dining room atop a coroner's board, where several other doctors were finishing their examination of her, and stitching up the Y-incision that had been made from her collarbone to her pubis. Both hers, and Andrew's stomachs, were in sealed jars sitting on the kitchen table. Melted wax had been used to form the protective seal, and each jar had been labeled. Whether Bridget had melted the wax for those seals, or stood by to see her employer's stomachs sitting in jars like macabre preserves, is unknown.

Attorney Knowlton questioned undertaker Winwood during the Preliminary Hearing as to his duties concerning the bodies of the two deceased Bordens:

Knowlton: "Did you have something to do with the bodies of Andrew J. Borden and Mrs. Borden?"

Winwood: "I had charge of them, yes."

Knowlton: "Were you the one who removed the effects from the body?"

Winwood: "I took the things from Andrew J. Borden's clothes."

[As it was already noted earlier, several people had taken Mr. Borden's effects from his clothes and looked at them, including Assistant Sheriff Wixon, Dr. Bowen and Dr. Dolan. Evidently, they were returned to their original place before the autopsies began.]

Knowlton: "Did you give whatever you took to Dr. Dolan?"

Winwood: "I did…There was $78 in bills in the pocketbook."

Knowlton: "What was the pocketbook in?"

Winwood: "In the inside pocket, inside the coat."

Knowlton: "Not inside the vest. What else in the shape of valuables?"

Winwood: "In that pocket there was some minor papers, which we did not examine into, just opened them, and saw there was no more money in there, or notes. That is all we examined for.

Knowlton: "There was a watch and chain?"

Winwood: "Yes Sir, in his vest."

Knowlton: "Anything else?"

Winwood: "In his pants pockets some loose change, two or three dollars in silver."

Knowlton: "What size bills were these?"

Winwood: "I think about $5...all in bills."

Knowlton: "Whatever you took, you turned it over to Dr. Dolan, the Medical Examiner?"

Winwood: "Yes, sir."

Knowlton: "Did you find anything valuable in her pockets?"

Winwood: "I did not have anything to do with her pockets at all."

[Some things are brought in wrapped in a handkerchief.]

Mr. Jennings during the **Cross-Examination** for the Defense:

Jennings: "Were these keys all upon the ring?" [Referring to two loose keys in the handkerchief.]

Winwood: "I do not remember; I should think they were; but I would not be positive about it."

Jennings: "Did you find either of the keys lose in his pocket?"

Winwood: "I could not say...I did not put any of them on the ring."

Jennings: "So all the keys that are on the ring now, so far as you know, were there when you took them from his pocket?"

Winwood: "They were."

Jennings: "Do you recall if you found any of these keys in his vest pocket?"

Winwood: "I should think not."

Jennings: "You think they were in his pants pocket?"

Winwood: "Yes."

Jennings: "Did you personally attend to preparing the bodies for burial?"

Winwood: "I did."

Undertaker James E. Winwood was called during the Superior Court trial almost a year later, in June of 1893, and asked about only one topic—Andrew J. Borden's small gold ring Lizzie had given him.

Mr. Jennings (for the Defense): "Did you have charge of the funeral of Andrew J. Borden and his wife?"

Winwood: "I did."

Jennings: "While you were preparing Mr. Borden's body for the grave, did you observe whether or not he had any ring upon his finger?"

Winwood: "I cannot remember positively now."

Jennings: "Did you see him have any ring upon his finger while you were having anything to do with him?"

Winwood: "I cannot remember so long ago."

Jennings: "That is all, sir."

Attorney Knowlton for the Prosecution: "Nothing." [No cross-examination of the witness.]

This was the totality of Winward's testimony during the Superior Court trial, other than to state his name and occupation. Why call him about the ring? Jennings is Lizzie's attorney. Was it to bolster Emma's testimony that the ring was the "only article" of jewelry Andrew ever wore (underscoring he and Lizzie's closeness), and that he was buried with it? Or was there another reason to ask if it went with him to his grave?

Emma Borden's testimony concerning the ring during the Superior Court trial:

Mr. Jennings (for the Defense): "Did your father wear a ring, Miss Emma, upon his finger?"

Emma: "Yes, sir."

Jennings: "Was or was that not the only article of jewelry which he wore?"

Emma: "The only article."

Jennings: "Do you know from whom he received it?"

Emma: "My sister Lizzie."

Jennings: "How long before his death?"

Emma: "I can't tell accurately. I should think ten or fifteen years."

Jennings: "Do you know whether previously to his wearing it she had worn it?"

Emma: "Yes, sir."

Jennings: "Did he constantly wear it after it was given to him?"
Emma: "Always."
Jennings: "Do you know whether or not it was upon his finger at the time he was buried?"
Emma: "It was."

[Was the ring on Andrew's finger when he was finally buried at Oak Grove Cemetery, a week after his murder? Did, perhaps, Alice Russell know something about it? A look at her testimony concerning what happened the night of the murders, when she accompanied Lizzie to the cellar, may provide a clue. We will look at this shortly.]

James Winwood "took charge" of Andrew and Abby Borden's bodies at 5:30 in the afternoon, the day of the murders. Emma was probably upstairs with Lizzie, along with Mrs. Holmes, and Alice Russell. Alice said she finally left the house at 6:00 to return home for supper, and to pack a few things, as she would stay the next four days with the sisters.

The bodies were laid out on the dining room table and washed. As they were not embalmed, it is possible that Winwood wrapped the bodies with herbs, such as myrrh and sandalwood, to offset the odor that would have been inevitable in the August heat. This was often done in that era, as bodies sometimes awaited burial for days, as relatives traveled great distances to attend the services. Typically, there was a rush to have the burial performed within two days of the death.

It was also a custom in the late 1800s to place the bodies within a cooling tent, on nickel-plated boards. This helped keep the remains, packed in ice, frozen for a time. With the legs folded, these tents would have enveloped most of the dining room table. As the family was known to have breakfast in the kitchen the following morning, it can be assumed the odor was kept to a minimum, which would imply some kind of freezing.

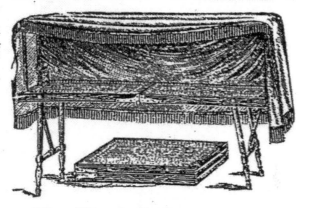

GREATLY IMPROVED
COOLING BOARD !

B. F. GLEASON,

A PRACTICAL UNDERTAKER of long experience, submits this **COOLING BOARD** to the profession as combining all the essential qualities to meet every requirement for the proper care of dead bodies. The simplicity of this Board recommends it over all others in the market, and its price places it within the reach of every Undertaker in the land. It is manufactured of the very finest materials, nickel plated, &c.

For prices, apply to the Manufacturer,

B. F. GLEASON,
Brockport, N. Y

Cooling board from the 1890s.

The shutters in the Borden's dining room were now closed to the curious onlookers outside. The bloody clothes had been removed, and were eventually taken to the cellar wash room, along with Abby's hair switch, and shards of her bone. The section of carpet where she lay had also been cut up, and placed along with the clothes on the brick floor of the room. They were later loaded into a wash tub and left in the southwest corner. Winward's final administration was to have the sofa where Andrew died removed from the house and stored in a room at his office. Though covered with blankets, as it was carried out the front door of the Borden home, the crowd was a twitter as the large bundle was loaded onto a cart and hauled away.

That Voice!

The news was spreading rapidly throughout Fall River about the double murder at the Borden house. Inside D.R. Smith's drugstore, Dr. Dutra was talking it over with his friend there, Eli Bence, the young 27-year-old clerk who had refused to sell Prussic Acid to Lizzie Borden the day before. The news was taken with surprise by those inside the store. Fredrick Hart, the assistant clerk, called it "a singular incidence" that the Borden murders should follow so closely on the heels of Miss Lizzie's Borden's request for poison.

Eli Bence reported to Doctor Dutra Miss Borden's actions on Wednesday, the day before. The doctor reported it to Officer Doherty, who, within an hour, went to the drug store that evening, along with Officer Harrington. Bence told them of Lizzie's attempt to buy Prussic Acid. They asked him if he was sure it was Lizzie Borden, Andrew Borden's daughter. He said he had seen her many times on the street, and that he believed he sold to her six years earlier when he worked at Riddell's Drug Store.

Between 8 and 9 that evening, the two officers took Mr. Bence to the Borden residence. They escorted him through the side screen door and asked him to wait inside the entryway, not far from the doorway leading into the kitchen. Officer Harrington asked for Lizzie, who appeared in the kitchen wearing a "loose wrapper." With Eli Bence within earshot, Harrington asked Lizzie some innocuous questions about whether or not she had seen anyone around the house. She answered him three times, stating "she had not seen anybody."

Eli Bence stood within her view and listened to her answers. She took no notice of him. If she recognized him from the drug store, she did not show it.

"The peculiarity was in the way she spoke it," Eli Bence testified during the Preliminary Hearing "it was kind of ---a little tremulous. I am sure it was the same woman I had seen down there."

[*The New York Herald* described Lizzie as "a masculine-looking woman, with a strong, resolute, unsympathetic face. She is robustly built, thirty-three years of age, and of average height. Her voice has a peculiar guttural harshness." Emma Borden was said to have a coarseness to her voice.]

Mr. Bence also testified that there was something about her eyes that he remembered as well. His testimony was excluded from the Superior Court trial. The findings were that the Borden's were killed by a hatchet, not poison. Although Knowlton battled hard to have the testimony allowed, showing it pointed to "the intent to kill," it was ruled inadmissible, and the jury never heard it.

Bridget Leaves

As the shadows lengthened outside the Borden house, Bridget's nerves gave way. She had seen the slain body of Mrs. Borden in the guest room, the bloody sheet covering Mr. Borden as he lay on the sofa in the sitting room, and watched as hatchets and axes were brought up from the cellar, and jars of body parts placed on the kitchen table. She had been questioned, her few personal possessions gone through, and been given the dubious honor of tour guide for myriad police officers throughout the day.

Bridget was invited to spend Thursday night across the street at the Southard Miller house. She could bunk with their maid in the attic. Although John had told her he would be spending the night in the attic next to her (or because of it), she chose to stay away from the house. There were two dead bodies in the dining room; she was confused about the things she had seen that day; and the murderer had not been found. Police outside the doors, be hanged! It was more than a young Irish maid could deal with. She packed up a few things, and was escorted across the street.

The door to the guest room was judiciously closed. The room sat in darkness; Abby's blood on the bed frame, dressing bureau, and wallpaper were the only reminders she had been there that day. A large rectangular piece of missing carpet where she had lain was a testament to her final resting place within the house.

John Morse would take the attic room near Bridget's. The heat in the upper story would not be the only thing that would keep him awake that night.

Lamplight in the Darkness

The crowd on Second Street had diminished somewhat. Three police officers had been placed around the Borden house to keep watch and stop intruders from entering the yard. Those tenacious onlookers who stood along the sidewalk, and tried to view the windows of the house from every angle, were relegated to only the occasional view of a moving lamplight through the closed shutters.

At 8:30 p.m., Alice Russell walked through the kitchen to the back screen door where Officer Hyde stood watch. She told him the family was now going to bed, and if he needed anything, he could knock, and she would come. She closed the wooden door and locked it. Somehow, it did not make her feel any safer. She felt as if she was locking her only security outside—away from her.

She passed the closed door to the dining room and shivered. Without success she tried to imagine it as she had always known it: a nice room with flowered paper, a table draped in linen, and small touches of warmth and hominess. Her nervous mind, instead, served up images of two bodies lying in the darkness, shrouded in white sheets.

Alice entered Lizzie's room from the front stairs landing, her lamplight playing across the closed door to the guest room. Inside, Emma was seated on Lizzie's bed, still wearing her street clothes. Their whispered conversation ceased as Alice's light preceded her into the room.

Lizzie rose from where she had been seated on the lounge. Both sisters looked worn, their faces aged in the lamplight. Emma appeared to be somewhat in shock. Her eyes had a vacant stare to them. It was only her tightly gripped hands and pressed lips that betrayed the emotions she was trying to control. She had only had a few hours to register that both her father and Abby had been butchered, and that they were still within the walls of the house. Lizzie watched her sister's face for some indication of what she was thinking.

Alice went through the now open door in Lizzie's room that led into Abby and Andrew's bedroom. She would sleep there, nearby in case Emma or Lizzie needed her. She looked at the bed where the slain couple had slept, and her nerve threatened to desert her. She could see their impressions in the pillows. The police had merely looked over and under the bed that day, leaving it basically the way Abby had made it that morning. Her simple toiletries lined the dressing case.

Alice stepped to the open door of the room that housed the safe and a few furnishings. Abby's dresses hung from pegs along one wall; most of them practical in their makeup, only one or two made of fancier fabric. A faint smell of lavender wafted over from them. She turned to see Lizzie watching her through the open connecting door. Quickly, Lizzie turned away from her and pulled aside the red curtain hiding her toilet area in her bedroom. She picked up the slop pail and poured her dirty wash water from the basin into it.

Emma went into her room and returned with her basin of water that she had used to freshen herself, upon her return that afternoon. She poured it into Lizzie's pail. As Alice added the water from the basin in her room, she said to Lizzie, "I'll take that down."

"No," Lizzie said, "I'll take it if you'll carry the lamp."

If Alice assumed they would take the back stairs leading out of Andrew and Abby's bedroom to the kitchen below, she may have been surprised, and chagrined, to see Lizzie head off toward the front stairs. This would take them through the sitting room to the kitchen. Her father's blood was still on the walls, doors and carpet. She could only follow Lizzie down the stairs, her heart pounding.

The sitting room door was closed. Lizzie opened it, and stepped through, Alice following her into the room. Hurriedly, Alice walked through the dark room, her hands shaking. To her left was the closed door to the dining room, where her friend's bodies were laid out. She and Lizzie reached the closed door to the kitchen, opened it, and stepped through.

Officer Joseph Hyde

Officer Joseph Hyde, who was in charge of the north side of the house, and keeping an eye on the backyard, saw something shimmer across the window glass of the kitchen on the east side. He stepped closer and watched as Lizzie Borden came through the open sitting room door into the kitchen, with Alice Russell directly behind her, carrying a kerosene lamp. The light lit their faces in an eerie halo as the two seemed to float through the darkened kitchen. They walked to the cellar door just inside the back entry and started down the stairs.

Once again, Alice must have been confused. There was a sink right there in the kitchen, with running City Water. Why go to the cellar? It was only dirty wash water that could be poured out into the sink. All she could do was hold the lamp and follow.

Officer Hyde made the following report of the two women's movements as they descended into the dark cellar:

"I was standing at the east side of the house. Miss Lizzie and Miss Russell came out of the sitting room. Miss Russell was carrying a small hand lamp. Miss Lizzie had a toilet pail. They came through the kitchen into the entryway, down the cellar stairs, into the cellar. Miss Russell, she stood at the foot of the stairs with the lamp. Miss Lizzie went along the north side of the cellar to the water closet, and emptied the slop pail. She came from the water closet into the wash cellar, to the sink, and I heard something that sounded like water when she got there. She returned from there to where Miss Russell stood and they came upstairs, went back through the sitting room—through the kitchen into the sitting room. It was fifteen minutes of nine.

"A few minutes after, perhaps ten or fifteen minutes, Miss Lizzie came out of the same door, of the sitting room door, into the kitchen, in the same way, down into the cellar. She came into the wash cellar, and she puts her lamp on to a table on the west end of the cellar. She comes over to the east end of the house, where the sink is, and stooped down opposite to the sink. What she did I don't know. She was all alone. It didn't take her above two minutes before she went upstairs again."

Mr. Moody (for the Prosecution during the Superior Court trial:

"At that time was there anything else in that wash cellar?"

Hyde: "Yes, sir. There was the clothes that had come off Mr. Borden and Mrs. Borden."

Mr. Robinson (for the Defense): "Now, were there any other officers in the yard that evening?"

Hyde: "Yes, sir. Mr. Ferguson and Officer Minnehan. I was on the east end of the house, by the cellar door. One was on the north side and one was on the southwest corner. John Minnehan was on the west end...the street end. Mr. Ferguson was standing around on the steps, on the north side of the steps, the front door. Neither of them were with me.

"I could see into the cellar through the window, the east window; I could see through the window on the southeast end of the corner. When Miss Lizzie came across from the water closet to the sink, Miss Russell was nervous then. She was hanging back over there by the stairs with the lamp, as though she would not go. She stood about three or four feet from the bottom of the stairs. She acted like she didn't want to go into the wash cellar, she seemed to be frightened, kind of shaking. She didn't say anything."

Robinson: "Where were those clothes you spoke of?"

Hyde: "They were on the south side of the wash cellar."

Robinson: "How far were they from the sink?"

Hyde: "Quite a ways; I should think five or six feet."

Robinson: "Which corner did the sink stand in?"

Hyde: "The sink stands in the southeast corner."

Robinson: "Do you know whether there is a door under it [sink] or not?"

Hyde: "I believe there is a door to the sink."

Robinson: "A door that opens and swings around?"

Hyde: "Yes, sir."

Robinson: "You didn't see her do anything except you say she stooped down?"

Hyde: "Yes, sir."

Robinson: "Had you seen that pail there with the cloths in it?"

Hyde: "Yes, sir."

Robinson: "And that pail was pretty near the sink, wasn't it?"

Hyde: "Yes, sir."

Robinson: "And then she took the light and went upstairs?"

Hyde: "Yes, sir."

   Mr. Moody for the prosecution then asks Officer Hyde: "But where you stood, you could see into the sitting room?"

Hyde: "I was looking through the kitchen window on the east end."

Moody: "Then you could only see when the door was open?"

 Hyde: "I could only see when the door was open."

Kitchen window at the Borden house today, where Officer Hyde looked in from the backyard. It faced the sitting room door. Photo by the Author.

What was Lizzie Doing?

The pail of bloody cloths had been turned upside down earlier in the day, and the three small towels hidden beneath it. They would be taken away by Officer Mullaly the following day, upon Doctor Dolan's request. When Lizzie came down to the cellar with Alice the first time that night, she poured out the bath water into the water closet toilet, then crossed to the wash cellar where there were three things of interest: her parent's bloody clothes, and carpeting, along with Abby's hair and parts of her skull; one hatchet and two axes laying on the wash room floor; and, a turned over bucket that had contained three bloody cloths.

As she rinsed out the pail, and refilled it with clean water, she had seen all three of those items. Taking a sideways glance at the axes and hatchets, as Alice trembled across from her, Lizzie may have wondered where the 5" clawhead hatchet was. Did they take it away, thinking it was the murder weapon? She didn't know Mr. Fleet had hidden it only a few feet away.

She may have only glanced at the bloody clothes in the corner; not wishing to see her father's things there. The overturned pail, however, was the true reason for her clandestine mission to the cellar without Alice. Lizzie stooped down, out of Officer Hyde's eye line, and peeked beneath that bucket to see if the cloths were still there. If they had taken them, it would have meant they suspected them of being something other than menstrual towels. They were still there.

She breathed a sigh of relief. Straightening, she picked up her lamp from the small table on the west side of the wash room and walked back toward the stairs, once again casting a sideways glance at the hatchet and axes.

An unwanted thought pushed its way through: The clawhead hatchet was not among the tools they had laid there—what of the hatchet she had broken? Had they found it? Was it still in the starch box in the next room, or had they taken it away as well? There was no way she could go and look, not with police watching. She walked up the cellar stairs.

When Alice was questioned about the two cellar visits that Thursday night, she said she was not aware Lizzie had gone down a second time without her. As Mr. Moody, for the prosecution, is questioning her during the Superior Court trial, something very odd occurs. Alice surprises him by becoming vague as to what happened after she and Lizzie came up from the cellar on the trip down with the slop pail:

Mr. Moody: "Did you go down cellar again that night?"

Alice: "No, sir."

Moody: "Either alone or with her?"

Alice: "No, sir."

Moody: "Did you know whether anybody else went down cellar later that night?"

Alice: "No, sir."

Moody: "When you went upstairs, where did you go?"

Alice: "I don't know. I think right up stairs; I think the second story, but I don't know."

Moody: "Right upstairs: what do you mean by upstairs? On the dining room floor?"

Alice: "No, the second floor. Still, I don't know—"

Moody: "Did anyone go up with you?"

Alice: "I don't know that."

[Emma testified she was hanging up her dress in the clothes press at 9:00 that night. It appears she was getting ready for bed as Alice and Lizzie made their nocturnal trip.]

Moody: "What room did you sleep in that night?"

Alice: "What was Mr. and Mrs. Borden's room."

Moody: "Do you remember when you parted after coming up from the cellar with Miss Lizzie Borden?"

Alice: "No, sir."

Moody: "Did you see her again that night?"

Alice: "Yes, sir."

Moody: "How soon after?"

Alice: "I don't know."

Moody: "Do you know where she had been in the meantime?"

Alice: "I think she had been in her room. Our doors were open."

Moody: "Were the doors opened all the time?"

Alice: "Yes, sir, all the time up to that time."

Moody: "Up to that time."

Alice: "Up to that time."

Moody: "Well, then, after that time were the doors open?"

Alice: "No, they were closed a short time."

Moody: "After the doors were closed did you see her again until morning?"

Alice: "Yes, sir."

Moody: "What time?"

Alice: "After I opened the door."

Moody: "How long was that after you closed the door?"

Alice: "I don't know for sure; I think fifteen or twenty minutes."

Moody: "How long after you came upstairs was it before you closed the door between the two rooms?"

Alice: "I don't know."

Moody: "Can't you give me any idea?"

Alice: "I cannot: I don't know whether we went right upstairs or not."

Moody: "You don't remember whether you did or not?"

Alice: "No, I did not: I can't tell anything about it."

Moody: "In any event, the doors were closed at the time you say?"

Alice: "Yes, sir. I was getting ready for bed. I read an account of this affair in the News."

Moody: "Anything else?"

Alice: "I don't think I did anything else."

Moody: "Any toilet operation of any sort?"

Alice: "Bathing."

Moody: "How long did you remain at the Borden house after the day of the murder---homicide?"

Alice: "I went there when I was called, and I came away the next Monday morning. I occupied what was Mr. and Mrs. Borden's room Thursday and Friday nights: Saturday and Sunday nights I occupied Miss Emma's room."

Moody: "Miss Emma's room?"

Alice: "Miss Emma's room."

[It is obvious Alice is a reluctant witness. The number of "I don't know" answers is remarkable.]

Abby & Andrew Borden's room. In 1892, the door to the left led into Abby's dressing room, where the safe was kept. It is today a guest room. The door on the right leads out to the second-floor landing. Photo by Ron Bueker.

What was Alice hiding?

It is apparent from Alice Russell's testimony that she and Lizzie did not go straight upstairs to their rooms, once they came up from the cellar and into the sitting room, closing the sitting room door behind them. Officer Hyde was pointedly asked if he could see into the sitting room from outside the kitchen window that night, and he said, "only when the sitting room door was open."

Alice almost acts as if she is hoping Mr. Moody will pursue her statements about not knowing if they went straight upstairs or not. She brings it up three times. Keep in mind, this is the Superior Court trial. Alice has already testified at the Grand Jury, and now the trial, about seeing Lizzie burn a dress—the biggest piece of damning evidence that caused the Grand Jury to indict Lizzie to start with. Did something happen that night as the two women made their way through the sitting room in the darkened house, that Alice wishes she could tell, but is withholding for some reason?

The only places between the closed sitting room door to the kitchen, and the front staircase, are the parlor and dining room. Did Lizzie pause outside that dining room door, and open it to peer in at the dead bodies of her parents? Was it too much for someone with Alice Russell's Victorian upbringing?

You can see Moody's suspicions that Alice went upstairs alone. He even asks if anyone went up with her; an odd question since she and Lizzie made the sojourn to the cellar, and back, together. And, there are the questions of how soon she saw Lizzie once Alice got back to her room.

Three times Alice says "I am not sure we went straight up..." Why would she volunteer that? It would have been easy just to say they went upstairs. Her abhorrence of lying is coming into play.

Did Lizzie go into the dining room? Did Alice go ahead rather than get a glimpse into that room, leaving the lamp on the entryway table where the light would reach Lizzie, as well as light her way up the staircase; just as it did Wednesday evening as Andrew, Abby, and John sat within its glow in the sitting room? Would mentioning Lizzie had done such a thing throw suspicion on her actions, as no woman of that era would be callous enough to look at the butchered bodies of her parents?

And now, the questions brought forward earlier to undertaker Winwood about whether or not Andrew was buried with his ring: Had Lizzie, whether on that trip with Alice to the cellar, or on the second one she took alone, gone into the dining room and removed the gold ring from Andrew's finger? Dr. Bowen may have told Lizzie that Andrew's effects had been tied up in a handkerchief and taken away as evidence. Did she go into the dining room to see if the gold ring had been taken as well? Did she remove it rather than have the police take it? It had been her gift to her father...no one had the right to it.

Had Emma covered for Lizzie when she said her father was buried with the ring intact on his finger? Alice said her door was closed Thursday night, and Lizzie was out of her sight for 15-20 minutes after returning from the cellar. Officer Hyde said Lizzie was in the cellar no more than two minutes. Did Lizzie make a side trip through the dining room before returning upstairs, as Alice read the news of the murders in Andrew's bedroom?

As an interesting side note: Lizzie gave a young male friend of hers a gold ring years later, from her home at *Maplecroft.*

The three policemen kept watch during the night: Officers Hyde and Minnehan, and Mr. Ferguson. Alice Russell testified she could hear them whispering beneath her window as she lay in the darkness of Andrew and Abby's room. She did not sleep all night.

Lizzie lay awake in her room as well, her windows open to the sounds of the night. The din of people talking had finally faded as the throng of strangers headed home to their dull lives; anxious to read what the local papers had served up in the way of details. Occasionally, there came the whisperings of the policemen beneath her window, as they discussed the case and compared notes. She could not make out their words; only a buzzing like flies. Her mind kept going down the stairs and into the dining room where two shrouded bodies lay. She was told the funeral would be Saturday. Her father would be with her only one more day. She heard Emma move on her bed in the room next to hers. Emma was here. Emma would fix everything.

Emma Borden, alone in the darkness of her small room, turned her back to the bedroom door, and sobbed quietly. It had all happened so quickly. Her prayers that it was a bad dream had gone unanswered, as she saw the blood sprayed across the sitting room wall. That room seemed so hollow and changed. It wasn't just the blood on the doors, but the sofa was gone. A section of carpet near the wall— where the sofa had been—was cut away.

Up in the sweltering attic, John Morse lay with an arm flung across his forehead. The sound of cicadas thrummed the still night air. His mind would not settle. All the planning—gone! All the lives the ruined Swansea deal would impact. The money he would lose on the horse and cattle deals that had been put in place. But, worse...so much worse...Andrew and Abby were dead...murdered. And, the newspapers were suspecting *him!* His heart raced as he watched the shadows from the pear trees play across the ceiling in the moonlight.

Across the street, Bridget lay in a fetal position, her back to Minnie Green, the maid with whom she was sharing a small bed. She couldn't sleep. So much had happened that day. Only now, in the silence of a strange room, with moonlight filtering in through the unfamiliar designs on the lace curtain across from her, did she begin to have nigglings of fear. Something was wrong with Lizzie's story. The things she told people. They just weren't true!

Chapter Twenty-Three

Friday, August 5, 1892

The Boston Daily Globe

DISCOVERY!

A Woman Inquired
for Poison.

Said That Drug Clerk
Identified Her.

Strange Story Told by
Lizzie Borden.

Members of the Family
Are Shadowed.

Stepmother the Cause
of Trouble.

Reward of $5000 Has
Been Offered.

The Boston Daily Globe
Friday, August 5, 1892

The morning sunlight, filtering through the factory smoke of
Fall River, Massachusetts, that Friday morning, shone down on a

city that would be forever changed—its name inextricably linked to the Borden murders. As storm clouds moved in, so did the crowds, arriving early at 92 Second Street to secure prime viewing of the day's events. Many clutched the morning papers in their hands, feverously reading over the latest developments, glancing up only if someone entered, or left, the Borden home.

The Boston Daily Globe

Fall River, Mass. Aug. 5.—In the closely shuttered dining room of the Borden residence on 2nd St. are the bodies of the victims of yesterday's tragedy, which will tomorrow, with brief burial services, be consigned to the grave.

At the front door is a police officer whose instructions are to pass no one into the house unless in authority, without the consent of the family. A second officer stands in a sheltered nook at the rear of the premises. Still a third sentinel is at the outer gate, his duty is to keep the sidewalk clear and open for travel.

A crowd of men, women, and children are braving a severe shower this forenoon for the privilege of lingering on the street and watching the scene of the tragedy. Among them are officers in citizen's clothing, who are instructed to shadow and follow closely any member of the household who may go out.

Very little of importance has transpired around the house this morning. The family was astir at 6:30 o'clock, and about an hour later breakfast was served. There were the Misses Borden, Mr. Morse, and a lady friend of the daughters present, and from the statements of the servant girl, Bridget Sulivan, they ate but little and talked less.

Miss Emma Borden, who was absent from home at the time of the tragedy, returned late yesterday afternoon. She appears very calm and self-possessed, and was seen this morning and interviewed by officers in the case. Miss Lizzie has not yet decided to speak for publication, and has denied all press visitors an interview. The city marshall will call on her today and take her statement, together with that of the servant.

The details of the funeral have not been arranged as yet, but will be before the day ends.

It is becoming well settled that there was not perfect harmony in the Borden household. It is said Lizzie and her stepmother never got along together peacefully, and that for a considerable time back, they have not spoken. When seen this morning, however, Mr. Morse denied the story, saying Lizzie and Mrs. Borden were always friendly.

Mr. Morse made his first appearance about 8 o'clock. He had a basket in his hand, and was evidently on his way to a store. He walked down 2nd St. with a policeman at his heels, and soon after returned and went indoors. He came out later on another errand, and again was trailed by the sleuth-hound of the law. Then he stayed indoors until noon.

The writer has the assurance of the chief of police that no move will be made by his department until after the funeral tomorrow. Then the procedure will depend upon a combination of circumstances that are now being investigated.

F.L. Edson, with the Fall River police, left the station house on Friday morning, August 5, at 5:55 a.m.., arriving at the Borden residence at 6 a.m. According to Mr. Edson's police report, he did the following:

"I entered the house by the side door on the north side of the house. Officer Harrington was on duty at the door. The door from the entry to the kitchen was open. J.V. Morse was in front of the stove; we did not speak. I went down cellar from the entry, went into the wash room in the southmost corner of the cellar. On the floor were two axes and a single hatchet. On a bench or table were a number of wet towels. There was blood on the towels. I went upstairs with the axes and hatchet, met Harrington at the door. Harrington said "there was one more hatchet in the cellar." I went down cellar again, Harrington with me. In the vegetable cellar, off the wash room, Harrington handed me a hatchet from a shelf or scaffold. We then went upstairs, and out of the house.

"On the steps I saw John V. Morse coming from the backyard. I said "good morning," he answered. I went from there directly to the Police Station; arriving there about 6:23 a.m. At the Police Station, I examined the axes. They were common ones, had been used rough; the single hatchet the same. The large hatchet was in good condition and very sharp. On the back of the blade, near the handle was a spot of rust or blood. From this spot to the handle was a light colored hair. There were dark spots on the handle; do not know whether they were dirt or blood. The blade appeared to have been in water. The extreme length of this hatchet was about 17 inches; the blade about 5" broad; the head, and claw on the end, about one inch wide, and about two and a half inches long.

"Officers Harrington, Doherty, Minnehan, Regan and McCarty saw me when I left the premises; and Officer Mahoney and Steward Cummings when I arrived at the Police Station. I carried the axes and hatchet openly in my hand."

Captain F.L. Edson

[The reason for Officer Edson's detailed, and vehement report, of how the axes and hatchets were conducted to the station-house, is that John Morse claimed to see Mr. Edson stuffing the four tools into a brown burlap bag at the steps of the rear door, as he came around the corner of the house from the backyard. Edson denies he did anything but carrying them "open handed" to the station; a sight that must have given the rain-drenched crowd their money's worth.

John Morse's insistence that he saw Edson placing them in a bag, may have been to insinuate that any hairs or spots found on the tightly packed weapons could have been caused by transference of hairs already in the bag. Spots of rust could have rubbed off onto each, as they were herded in a sack down the street. The argument was never rectified. It is hard to believe John would need to lie about something as innocuous as a bag; especially since the hair was proven to be bovine—not human at all. It is more likely the police were covering their hides in a case already riddled with mishandling of evidence.]

At 7:15 that morning, Officer Edson was back. "I went into the house with Officer Doherty. Bridget Sullivan and John Morse were in the kitchen. I also inquired of Morse about his relatives in New Bedford and vicinity. I also inquired about Mrs. Borden's relatives. Morse called Miss Emma, and she answered the questions. While I was talking to Miss Emma, Miss Lizzie came in. She said, "Bridget, are you sure the back cellar door was fastened?" Bridget said, "Yes, marm.""

It is apparent from the testimonies that Bridget had returned to the Borden house that morning between 6:30 and 7:15. As no one had gone to get her, it was probably arranged the night before that she would come back to the house in the morning and prepare breakfast for the family. She is spotted in the kitchen with John Morse at 7:15, and Lizzie and Emma arrive in the kitchen about the same time. The newspaper reported the small group sat down to eat around 7:30 that morning.

The atmosphere in the kitchen on that Friday morning must have been thick. Outside stands a bevy of policemen, rain is pouring down, perhaps dampening the excitement of the crowd, and bringing some semblance of peace. Plans may have been discussed for the funeral the next day, as flowers and caskets would have to be ordered. Undertaker Winward would handle the funeral procession and buggies, along with preparation of the bodies and graves. It would be a small service, with only a few close family members and friends.

If Lizzie hoped the removal of the hatchets would be the last of the police presence in their home, she was to have a rude awakening. As the subdued foursome ate their breakfast, Marshall Hilliard, and Detective Seaver of Taunton, were already in a closed room discussing their next move.

Sometime that morning, perhaps during breakfast, a plan was hatched between Emma, Lizzie, and possibly John Morse, to place an ad for a $5,000 reward, to run in the Friday evening papers:

$5,000 REWARD

The above reward will be paid to anyone who may secure the arrest and conviction of the person or persons who occasioned the death of Andrew J. Borden and his wife.

Emma L. Borden
Lizzie A. Borden

This reward may have been at the encouragement of Andrew Jennings, the family attorney, who Emma admitted she contacted in the early days of the murder investigation. Mr. Jennings had handled all of Andrew Borden's affairs, and was a trusted friend of the family's. It was a shrewd move. It showed the public a unified front by the family to find the murderer, and offer, what was in that day, a huge amount of money. If a member of the family was the guilty party, then they were out nothing, as no information would be forthcoming. As the papers were already pointing the finger at John and Lizzie, Morse may have been "all in" with this decision to divert attention away from the family.

The reward was never claimed.

John Morse Does Damage Control

At 8:30 that morning, Officer Harrington stated that John Morse left the house and pushed his way through the throng of people, as he crossed Second Street to rap on the door of Southard Miller's house. He "called" Bridget, who stayed there that night. Since Bridget was already at the Borden's during the breakfast hour, it is assumed she went back across to the Miller's afterward. Bridget did spend Friday night back at the Borden house. Had John convinced her to come back, telling her he would be right there in the attic to protect her? It appears he and Bridget were seen together on several occasions. Was he recruiting her as an ally? Or simply finding out all she knew about the movements and motives of that day?

After leaving the Miller house, John made his way down to the Post Office, an officer hot on his heels. He entered the Post Office, stayed a moment, and then came out and walked across the street to George E. Howe's, where he purchased a two-cent stamp. John then returned to the Post Office, and at 8:32 a.m., dropped a letter addressed to Wm. A. Davis of South Dartmouth. It bore the words "in haste." On his way home, he tried the *Daily News* door, but it was not open.

 John's Mission

Friday morning is John's first chance, after the murders, to start doing damage control for the botched Swansea deal. He enters the Post Office, only to come out, and go across the street to Howe's for a stamp! The Post Office had no stamps? It was stated earlier that George Howe is related to John Morse, and had a background in horse trading. John's quick trip into the store was probably to talk to Howe quickly about the situation, and to possibly ask him to alert a few key players. Morse then returns to the Post Office and sends a letter to his partner William A. Davis in South Darthmouth "in haste." By that afternoon, a Mr. Morse of New Bedford, is tapping on the Borden's door, and asking to see John.

Meanwhile, Detective George F. Seaver, with the Massachusetts District Police, has arrived at the Borden house "between 8:00 and 9:00 a.m.," and is searching the barn, and "down cellar." According to Mr. Seaver, and Marshall Hilliard, that was the only search of the Borden home, or premises made that day.

Marshall Hilliard and Detective Seaver arrived that afternoon and questioned Lizzie and Bridget. No record states what was gleaned from those two interviews. As a result of the conversation with Lizzie, however, Officer Medley was dispatched to New Bedford to follow-up on Lizzie's purported visit there.

Lizzie's Visit to New Bedford

This is Mr. Medley's report:

"In accordance with instructions, I visited New Bedford. I find that Miss Lizzie Borden arrived in that city on Thursday, July 21st, and went to Mrs. Poole's, the mother of a friend, a former schoolmate, living near South Water Street. While there she never went out alone, always going in the company of the family, with one exception, that being Saturday morning, July 23, when she went on the street to buy a piece of dress goods of some cheap material, being gone about one [hour] and 30 minutes. She went alone and returned alone. No one called to see her while here. She never made a mention of her family affairs. On Tuesday, Lizzie, Mrs. Poole, and Mrs. Poole's daughter went to ride to Westport to see Mrs. Poole's daughter who was a schoolmate of Lizzie's and is now married to Cyrus W. Tripp. They spent the day there, leaving time enough for Lizzie to connect with the train at New Bedford for Fall River. That was the last time the Poole's saw her. While at Westport, Lizzie saw no one outside the family."

Burying the Bloody Clothes

Sometime during Marshall Hilliard's interviews with Bridget and Lizzie, John Morse stepped forward to complain about the bloody clothing and artifacts of the murder, lying in the cellar. He asked them to be removed, out of decency for the family. Subsequently, Officer Albert E. Chase was sent in the afternoon to the house. Mr. Chase made the following report:

"The following articles and wearing apparel were this afternoon taken from a washtub in the cellar wash room of the Borden house by orders of the City Marshall and Medical Examiner, and were buried under my direction in the yard back of the barn.

"1 soft pillow and tidy, one large piece of Brussel's carpet, one roll of cotton batting, one sheet and several pieces of cotton cloth, three towels, one napkin, one chemise, one dress, one pair of drawers, one skirt, two aprons, one hair braid, and several pieces of hair from Mrs. Borden's head, from five to eight inches long, one necktie, one truss, one piece of black silk braid or watch guard.

"I also found mixed in with the hair of Mrs. Borden, a piece of bone, which from its nature I took to be a piece of Mrs. Borden's skull, it was cut so smooth, that I thought it might be of use in determining what kind of instrument was used, as the bone and hair both had the appearance of being cut with a very sharp instrument; I gave this piece of bone to Dr. Dolan.

"About the middle of the next week [during the Inquest] Dr. Dolan ordered all the articles dug up. After taking out pieces of clothing, and of the carpet, they were ordered buried again. This time they were put in a box."

[During the original burying of the clothes, John Morse, whose nerves had reached their breaking point, had an altercation with David P. Keefe, who hired a man to bury the clothes and artifacts for $5.00. John Morse pronounced the amount robbery. Keefe said, he wouldn't do the job for $100, but under the circumstances, said he might be persuaded to do it for free. Morse finally paid him $3.00.]

Relatives and Insights

By now, the pressure in the Borden household was at a boiling point. Lizzie spent the day sequestered in her room, leaving Emma to deal with the visitors, one of whom was reportedly Mr. George Fish, Abby Borden's brother-in-law from Hartford, Connecticut.

Hiram Harrington, the husband of Andrew Borden's sister, Lurana, claimed to have "had a long talk with Lizzie" on Thursday, the day of the murders. His statements to Officers Harrington and Doherty concerning Lizzie were less than kind.

"I am not at all satisfied with her statement or demeanor. She was too solicitous about his comfort, and showed a side of character I never knew or suspected her to possess. She helped him off with one coat and on with another, and assisted him in an easy incline on the sofa, and desired to place an afghan over him, and also to adjust the shutters so the light would not disturb his slumber. This is something she could not do, even if she felt; and no one who knows her, could be made to believe it. She is very strong-willed, and will fight for what she considers her rights. She went to the barn, where she stayed twenty minutes, or half an hour, looking for lead from which to make sinkers for fishing lines, as she was going to Marion next week. She said she was cutting the lead into sizeable sinkers." He did admit that Lizzie was an "enthusiastic angler." [Here, for the first time, we hear the "sinkers" alibi, one that was never mentioned during the police interviews of that day.]

Officer Doherty said Mr. Harrington told about the Ferry Street estate being given to the girls, and afterward being returned. Harrington also mentioned Mr. Borden giving "each girl ten shares in the Crystal Spring Bleachery Company, which he paid $100 a share for. They sold them very soon after for less than $40 a share. He also gave them bank stock at various times, allowing them, of course, the entire income from them. In addition, he gave them a weekly stipend amounting to $200 a year.

"In spite of all this," Mr. Harrington continued, "the dispute about their not being allowed enough went on with equal bitterness. Lizzie did most of the demonstrative contention, as Emma is very quiet and unassuming, and would feel very deeply any disparaging or angry words from her father. Lizzie, on the contrary, was haughty and domineering with the stubborn will of her father, and bound to contest for her rights. There were many animated interviews between father and daughter on this point. Lizzie is of a repellent disposition, and, after an unsuccessful passage with her father, would become sulky and refuse to speak to him for days at a time.

"Lizzie moved in the best society in Fall River, was a member of the Congregational Church, and is a brilliant conversationalist. She thought she ought to enter as others did, and felt that with her father's wealth, she was expected to hold her end up with others of her set. Her father's constant refusal to allow her to entertain lavishly angered her. I have heard many bitter things she has said of her father, and know she was deeply resentful of her father's maintained stand in this matter."

During Hiram Harrington's Inquest testimony, he mentioned his views of Lizzie, and of his severing ties with Andrew Borden:

Mr. Harrington [referring to Andrew]: "We never had no words, or anything of that kind. Some years ago I thought he was hard [referring to Andrew], and I cut his acquaintance; that is, he came to my house, and I would leave the room; and he very soon saw I cut his acquaintance; and he did mine."

Knowlton [referring to Lizzie's attitude toward Abby]: "Did Lizzie speak to you about it more than once?" [The dispute over the Ferry house being put in Abby's name.]

Harrington: "Sometimes it has been mentioned in a joking way, about the difficulties. I don't know as I could put enough together to say what really passed."

Knowlton: "How long ago was the last time she said anything about it?"

Harrington: "I think last Winter sometime. I have not seen her at the house for, I might say all Summer, and I have inquired of my wife how it was that Lizzie had not been down. Emma has always come. And the reply I would get from her was that Lizzie was into everything, that is, works in the church, and her time was occupied; that is all I would get from her."

Knowlton: "When she spoke about it last Winter, what did she say about it?"

Harrington: "I don't know as I could tell any more than to speak kind of sneeringly of Mrs. Borden. She always called her Mrs. Borden or Mrs. B. It was unfriendly. Abby never mentioned it to my wife."

Knowlton: "It was understood there was trouble in the family?"

Harrington: "O, yes, there has been I guess. For several years, I guess, of his early marriage with her, everything was very, very pleasant, uncommonly so for a step-mother."

Knowlton: "This trouble is of recent years?"

Harrington: "Quite a number of years, I should think."

Hirum Harrington was not the only Uncle to throw disparaging remarks Lizzie's way. Unce John Vinnicum Morse told a reporter "Lizzie is a peculiar girl, given to fits of sullenness."

After Marshall Hilliard's interviews, it became clear to the people residing inside 92 Second Street the police were not focusing their attention very far from the Borden's home. The newspapers were reporting in minute detail every move being made by the police, and the inmates of the house. Lizzie was coming undone. Although Alice, John, Bridget, and Emma were all keeping the papers and the news away from her, Lizzie knew things were not going as planned. Her panic grew with each passing hour. *They keep coming back, questioning where I was, who I saw in the days leading up to the murders, all of my movements yesterday morning...* The freight train roared again inside her head, the room spun, and she finally snapped. Dr. Bowen was hastily sent for.

Dr. Bowen arrived in Lizzie's room to find a woman whose nerves had completely unraveled. Knowing the bromo caffeine was no longer strong enough, he left her with a dose of sulphate of morphine— one-eighth of a gram. It was a low dosage, dissolved in water. It would calm her, and perhaps steady her nerves for the ordeal of the funeral the next morning.

John Morse was dealing with his heightened fear in another way. Sick of the invasiveness of the public, he acted out by locking two Boston reporters into the Borden's barn, who were helping themselves to some private snooping. Only after the men pounded on the locked barn door, and threatened lawsuits, did Morse let them out. They reminded him a $5,000 reward had been offered, and people were intensely interested in snooping out clues. He paced, and made every effort to relay news back and forth to his friends in South Dartmouth, Fairhaven, New Bedford and Westport; the going was rough, as his every movement was shadowed by a policeman.

By evening, the people in the street outside the Borden home had grown restless. The papers were rife with suspicions concerning Lizzie and John Morse, yet nothing seemed to be happening. The wait, the humidity, rain, and the constant jousting for a good position, had taken its toll on the crowd, numbering close to 600 people.

An Ill-Advised Trip to the Post Office

At 8:00 Friday evening, John Morse, once again left the house, desperate to get to the Post Office for any news from William Davis. He needed to be reassured that the entire horse and cattle transactions were under wraps. If word got out that he and Andrew were in the middle of a major deal, that involved the signing over of deeds to the Swansea farms, all hell would break loose. It could be imagined Andrew backed out at the last minute, and John murdered him because of it.

John Morse as he appeared in 1892.
Photo courtesy of Faye Musselman

John Morse, six-feet tall, with gray hair and beard, and wearing the same rumpled grey suit he always sported, was an easy target as he elbowed his way through the crowds. Bridget Sullivan was walking along with him down Second Street. People began to follow them, saying "That's John Morse!" By the time Mr. Morse had dropped a letter into the box at the Post Office, the crowd had swelled to 1,000 people.

"Murderer!" someone cried. The crowd turned from curious to a lynch mob within seconds. "Hang him!" they screamed. Office Devine, who had been tailing Morse, raised his club and ordered the crowd to stand back. He and another officer, who had been detailed to follow Bridget, escorted the rattled Mr. Morse and frightened servant, back to the Borden house, where John remained the rest of the night.

Fall River Post Office and Customs House

Andrew and Abby Are Prepared for Burial

That evening, James Winward arrived at the Borden house. It was time to prepare the bodies for burial the next day. Undertaker Winward had rarely faced something as daunting as making Andrew and Abby presentable for the family viewing the next morning. Emma undoubtedly provided the funeral director with Andrew's best suit, and Abby's relatives may have chosen her nicest dress, along with hairbrushes, and clips.

The bodies were touched up with mortician's makeup to hide bruising and discoloration. The three bruises on Abby's forehead and bridge of her nose, formed when she fell face first into the carpet, were carefully concealed beneath a pancake makeup. The caskets remained ready to receive Mr. and Mrs. Borden.

The bodies were lifted into the coffins. The undertaker carefully turned Andrew's head to the left on the satin pillow, obscuring the mutilated side of his head. Only the right side of his face was now visible. Abby's head was turned slightly to the right. Although her hair was carefully arranged to hide the multitude of blows to the right side of her head, there was still evidence of several of the attacks that had landed over her right ear.

The cooling boards were taken away, and Abby and Andrew Borden were left in the darkness of the sitting room, where their caskets had been carried, to await the morning.

Darkness settled over the Borden home. Bridget and John, were sequestered together in the muggy attic, their whisperings merging with the soft patter of rain on the roof overhead. Little by little, they pieced together what must have happened the day before. A trust formed between the two; one whose ties were not strong enough to keep them from contradicting the other's statements on the witness stand. With the public's suspicions printed each day, in bold black ink across the Fall River rags, it was every man for himself. It was not lost on the maid, or the relative, huddled in the shadows that evening, that if push came to shove, the church-going, Borden-bred, youngest daughter of one of the town's wealthiest citizens, would hold favor over an Irish immigrant, and a disheveled, horse-trading Uncle from the West. Another axe, born of fear and suspicion, could fall from the public pulpit at any time.

Chapter Twenty-Four
Saturday, August 6, 1892

Saturday morning's papers were full of theories and musings. Any clue worth mentioning, and some that weren't, were heralded in bold print. *The New York Times* ran several columns covering everything from the mysterious stranger who stood on the Borden's front doorstep the preceding Monday—dressed in baseball shoes—to the funeral services happening that day:

Fall River, Mass. Aug. 6—The bodies of the murdered couple were buried today. As early as 9 o'clock the house was surrounded by a great crowd of curiosity seekers. Reporters, artists, photographers, and policemen were active among them. Mr. Morse came from the house and talked freely with a group of reporters. He said it was a terrible thing to be suspected and shadowed as he has been, but he courts the fullest investigation and is anxious and willing to do all that he can to trace the perpetrators of the great crime. He said Miss Lizzie Borden's health was in about the same condition as it was last Thursday afternoon. She did not mingle with the family to any great extent. When Mr. Fish of Hartford, a nephew [should read brother-in-law] of her stepmother, appeared she gave him a very cool reception. About 11 o'clock preparations were commenced for the funerals. People numbering between 3,000 and 4,000 assembled in front of the house and about twenty policemen maintained a clear passageway.

[On the morning of the funerals, with the caskets laid out in the sitting room, John Morse's focus is on alerting the media of his innocence, doubtless due to the frightening mob scene the evening before. Rather than tout Andrew and Abby's virtues on this somber day, he chooses to hold a press conference outside the house declaring his innocence.]

The newspaper report continued: "The Rev. Dr. Adams of the First Congregational Church and City Missionary Buck soon arrived. The bodies were laid in two plain black, cloth-covered caskets in the sitting room where Mr. Borden was killed. An ivy wreath was placed on Mr. Borden's bier and a bouquet of white roses and fern leaves, tied with a white satin ribbon, was placed beside Mrs. Borden. There were about seventy-five persons present at the services in the house, which consisted of reading from the Scriptures and prayer. There was no singing, and no remarks. The mourners were Mrs. Oliver Gray, stepmother of the dead woman; G.H. Fish and wife of Hartford, the latter a sister of Mrs. Borden; Dr. Bowen and wife; Southard Miller, and a few of the neighbors.

[This included Adelaide Churchill and Mrs. Thomas Cheetham. Oddly, Alice Russell is not mentioned as being in attendance, although we know she and Mrs. Holmes remained behind after the funeral departed to keep an eye on the house. Hiram Harrington and his wife Lurana (Andrew's sister,) were also there, along with Mrs. Rescombe Case, Mrs. J.D. Burt, William Wilcox and John Durfee.] The burial was private, that is, only a few of the immediate friends were asked to accompany the remains to the cemetery.

"The pallbearers for Mr. Borden were Abram C. Hart, cashier of the Union Savings Bank; George W. Dean, a retired capitalist; Jerome C. Borden, a relative of the deceased; Richard B. Borden, Treasurer of the Troy Mills, in which Mr. Borden was a director; James M. Osborn, an associate of the deceased in several mills; and Andrew J. Borden, Treasurer of the Merchant's Mill, in which Mr. Borden was a large owner.

[It is interesting to note that of Andrew's pallbearers, only one was a relative. An insight into his lifestyle is evident: business dealings replaced social acquaintances, and even familiarity with the Borden relatives that blanketed Fall River. That John Morse was not one of the men who respectfully bore Andrew's casket to the hearse, is worthy of note.]

"The pallbearers for Mrs. Borden were James C. Eddy, Henry C. Buffington, Frank L. Almy, J. Henry Wells, Simeon B. Chase, and John H. Boone.

"As the procession wended its way along North Main Street many old associates of Mr. Borden were seen to raise their hats. Miss Lizzie Borden and Miss Emma Borden were, of course, the principal mourners. Miss Lizzie went out of the house first, leaning on the undertaker's arm. Her nerves were completely unstrung, as was shown by the trembling of her body and the manner in which she bore down on her supporter. When she reached her carriage, she fell back exhausted on the cushions.

Early Saturday morning, before the mourners arrived, Emma Borden and Mrs. Marianna Holmes scrubbed down as many of the blood spots on the parlor door and wallpaper as they could. Dr. Dolan testified that he gave precise orders that nothing was to be cleaned up in either of the murder rooms. John testified Emma did the cleaning of the parlor door Saturday morning. She probably could not bear her father's funeral service being held in a room spattered with his blood for all to see. Some of the spots did remain, but by the time Dr. Dolan arrived that Saturday afternoon to take a closer look at the room, they were greatly diminished.

Lizzie entered the sitting room early, and had a private moment with her father as he lay in his open casket. Mrs. Holmes led her to the coffin, and stood by as Lizzie wept. Placing her hands on the casket, she leaned in and kissed her father.

It was said that the casket of Andrew was closed during the services, while Abby's remained open. This is not substantiated. Whether Emma had a similar moment with her father, is also not documented. If Andrew's small gold ring was, indeed, missing, it was a simple thing to hide; by the placement of his hands, or, that the coffin lid may have hidden his body from the chest down. It is possible Emma chose not to see him, and only took Lizzie's word that he was buried with his ring.

The Boston Globe wrote that Andrew's casket "bore three heavy silver handles on each side, and on the lid the inscription: Andrew

Borden, Died August 4, 1892, Aged 70 Years. The inscription on the other casket was confined to the deceased name and age."

It is possible that Emma and Lizzie made the arrangements for their father's casket and floral arrangement, while Abby's may have been left to her stepmother and stepsister, Bertie. The flowers adorning Abby's of white roses, sweet pea, and fern were significant: sweet pea represented simple pleasures and is often found in bridal bouquets. White roses were for purity and innocence. These sentiments seem more likely to have come from Abby's family, than from Lizzie or Emma. Andrew's simple wreath of ferns stood for fidelity and sincerity.

Much was made of Lizzie's funeral dress that day. It was black with beaded trim and very form-fitting. One newspaper commented "it fitted her round and shapely body faultlessly." Funeral dresses of that era were typically black wool with plain crepe adornment. Lizzie had chosen to wear something more stylish. Her small black hat was adorned with tiny flowers. Neither she, nor Emma, wore veils—another thumbing of the nose to propriety—and it was commented on by those who saw the sisters exit the house that morning.

John Morse was the last to leave. He walked quickly to his carriage, and seated himself next to Reverend Buck and Reverend Dr. Adams. Mr. Morse looked straight ahead, his head steady, as the crowd of people stared.

At 11:00 o'clock, eleven hacks and two hearses began the funeral procession away from the Borden house. The going was slow, as throngs of people numbering in the thousands jockeyed for a view of the mourners. The procession traveled north on Second Street to Borden Street, on to South Main Street and past the Andrew J. Borden Building. Whether Lizzie, Emma, or John Morse felt a lump rising in their throat as they passed the stone façade that bore Andrew's name, is unknown. It then continued north to Cherry Street, to Rock Street, and east on Prospect Street and to the main gate at Oak Grove Cemetery.

The procession arrived at the cemetery at 12:20, where several hundred people stood about the grounds awaiting the burial. A dozen policeman, under the direction of Sergeant John Brocklehurst, held the crowd back. A few artists began busily sketching the scene. Representatives from every major New

England paper were there, awaiting the entourage. If they were hoping to capture cameo moments of the sisters at the gravesides, they were disappointed. Lizzie, Emma, and the other mourners remained in their carriages. Only John Morse emerged, along with the clergy, pallbearers and funeral director's assistants.

The two graves were near the northeast corner of the lot. The tops of the graves were lined with cloth, and the tops of the open cavities covered in fir branches. A brief service, lasting only a few minutes took place. Reverand E. A. Buck read from the New Testament, inciting "I am the resurrection and the life." Reverend Dr. Adams took the occasion to ask for "spiritual guidance of all and the inclination of all to submit to divine control...that the ends of justice might be delivered without mistake...and all might be delivered from the domination of evil."

Lizzie's ears may have heard more in those words than others. She remained in the carriage, as did the rest of the family, for five minutes following the service. There was no sound. Suddenly, an elderly woman in a simple dress, made her way quickly to the graves, and was about to kneel, when an officer moved her away. She went to the fence surrounding the grounds, and cried. Some whispered she had worked for the Bordens years earlier.

The carriages bearing the mourners pulled away, leaving the caskets still standing near their fir-covered graves. Unbeknownst to the family, Undertaker Winward had received word from Dr. Dolan that morning at 9:00 that the bodies were not to be buried, but rather placed in the cemetery receiving vault for further examination. The sisters would not learn of this until weeks later.

1890s funeral hearse.

Oak Grove Cemetery entrance in Fall River, Massachusetts. Photo Ron Bueker.

Oak Grove Cemetery Receiving Vault. Photo Ron Bueker.

Saturday's Searches

By the time the last hack in the funeral procession turned the corner of Second Street, heading for the cemetery, the police were at the back door of the Borden house. If Mrs. Holmes and Alice Russell were unhappy to see them, it would not be a surprise. It was their duty to make sure nothing was taken away. Left in charge of the house, they felt a huge responsibility to protect Lizzie's and Emma's privacy. That was not to happen.

Mrs. Charles Jarvis Holmes, (Marianna)
Photo courtesy of the Fall River Historical Society

At around half past 12, Detective Seaver, Marshall Hilliard, and Captain Desmond, entered the house and made a beeline for the second floor. This would be their first time having access to the sisters' bedrooms without the ladies being there. Oddly enough, they restricted their searches to the beds. They took off the bedding, shook out the mattresses and peeked at the back of Lizzie's lounge where it sat against the wall beneath the windows. According to Detective Seaver, they did not look into the bureau drawers. Marshall Hilliard watched as Detective Seaver took apart the bed in the guest room where Abby was killed.

Alice Russell, who remained at the house that morning, had a different version of what the police searched in Lizzie's room. Her Superior Court testimony included the following:

Alice Russell: "I think one of the officers took the keys that lay on the bureau after Miss Lizzie had left, and unlocked one or two drawers in her bureau, and didn't search any farther there. I think they opened what she called her toilet room, pulled the portiere one side, just looked there a little. I don't know how much they searched. I don't think very much; and they went into Miss Emma's room and looked around, and opened the cupboard door in her room, and I remember one of the officers pressing against a bundle after he shut it, I think so, some pillow or blanket, something of that kind, and the bed was taken to pieces. That is all I saw."

[If this "bundle" was the small pillow in which Lizzie may have hidden the sleeves and hem from the Bedford cord dress, it would be interesting to know if the men searched it. Had she removed the damning evidence earlier, realizing the men were going to continue returning to her room?]

Marshall Hilliard was questioned about the search during the Preliminary Hearing. He too denies any knowledge of the bureau drawers being searched. He does say something interesting concerning the search:

Hilliard: "That search was made from something that came to my knowledge, in fact, was handed to me; and I went there after the funeral procession left the house, and made a partial search of three rooms...Miss Lizzie's room, the room to the northward [Emma's room], and the front room [guest room], upstairs."

[It may have been Officer Medley's report from his trip to New Bedford the day before that was handed to Marshall Hilliard. That report listed Lizzie as going into town alone to buy some "cheap dress goods." The fact that the men limited themselves at the time of the morning search to just the bedding and "looked back of" a lounge in Lizzie's room, shows they were not looking for something bulky. Was it the dress goods they were searching for in an effort to validate her movements in New Bedford? Did they hope to find something hidden inside it?]

The police went away before the funeral party returned. Alice and Marianna Holmes may have hurriedly tried to make the three beds, so as not to upset the sisters, especially Lizzie, who was showing strain.

There is no mention of the hours between 12:50—when it is likely the family returned home—and 3:00 that afternoon. If the customary tradition of bringing food to the house was carried out, there was no mention of it. This was an unusual funeral, to say the least. The couple had been brutally murdered in the house; something much different than the usual death. The walls were still speckled with blood, and the dining room had been used as a mortician's laboratory. Perhaps the serving of food to guests would have been in poor taste.

The Mysterious Club

Alice Russell testified during the Coroner's Inquest that something on Saturday morning frightened her. She told Attorney Knowlton the following:

Alice: "The morning of the funeral I went out to do some errands, sometime between 9 and 10; and when I came back my hair was tumbled, and I took my dress waist off, and combed my hair. When I had gotten through, I put my waist on again, and had nearly finished it, and I turned and I saw something in under the bed that frightened me almost to pieces. It was a big stick, that I think it was something their father kept in the house. It was at the head of the bed, plainly visible, I saw the end of it. It was not out from under the bed at all. I could see it a little way under the bed. I told it to Detective Hanscom; and he asked Emma. I don't think the girl knew anything about that I found it. I was terribly alarmed, because I felt as if in some way it implicated me. I had not seen it there before, and I should think I would have."

Alice called Officer Hyde and pointed it out to him. It was subsequently handed over to Marshall Hilliard.

[Officers Doherty, Mullaly and Mr. Fleet looked under Abby and Andrew's bed the day of the murders, and saw nothing. Other officers looked over the room as well. When was the club placed there? Who would have done so?

One thought is this: the club is first seen on the day of the funeral. Lizzie's bed had not been searched up to that day. Had the stick been secreted beneath her mattress for some reason? Knowing as soon as she left for the funeral the police would probably search her room, had she tossed it beneath her father's bed? Was it her intention to scare Alice into leaving so that she could have some privacy and dispose of the Bedford cord she had been wearing for three days beneath her outer clothing? Or, was it, just to get rid of it, rather than be found with a club, large enough to bash someone's head in, hidden in her bed? Alice says she was gone from 9-10:00 that morning. Lizzie did not leave with the funeral procession until after 11:00.

At 3:00, the police were back. It appears quite callous on the surface; after all, the sisters had just buried their parents, or so they thought. Through the side door came Marshall Hilliard, Assistant Marshall Fleet, Andrew Jennings, Dr. Dolan, Captain Desmond, and State Detective Seaver. They headed directly for the attic.

Marshall Hilliard stated that "we commenced in the top of the house, what I should call the attic rooms. We searched the whole landing clear through." Every box, drawer, trunk, barrel, bed and bundle was searched. Mr. Fleet even went up on to the roof, along the ridgepole and searched around under the eaves. They searched every room, "clear down to the cellar." They once again searched Lizzie's room, along with the others.

Hilliard testified that as he was searching Lizzie's room again, Detective Seaver, Mr. Fleet and Captain Desmond were giving the clothes press [closet at the end of the hall] a thorough going over. He, himself, did not go into the dress closet at the time.

[That the search team heads straight to the attic on Saturday afternoon, maybe a continuation of the search for a certain item they began looking for during the funeral that morning. First on their list was to search the trunks and boxes in the attic. Were they still looking for the dress goods Lizzie claims she purchased on that one secretive outing in New Bedford, when her whereabouts are unknown?]

Captain Desmond

Marshall Hilliard elaborated on their search of the cellar:

Hilliard: "We looked around the cellar; it was not what I call a thorough search. There were barrels piled up in one of the cellars off of what I call the laundry or wash room. Then west of that room, of the laundry, was another cellar where there was a great quantity of wood. Then west of that again, there was another cellar or room and also a space where the furnace set, the boiler, or whatever it was, and also the foundation, or top of the foundation. We looked Saturday afternoon there to see if there was any place where a brick or stone could be removed, or had been removed, but there was nothing of the kind. We had a mason come in on Monday to see whether anything could have been thrown down the chimney...a weapon or anything."

[Had the police found Lizzie's loose brick in her fireplace and wondered if a weapon could have dropped down inside the flue? Obviously, nobody was going to climb up on the roof and pitch it down from the chimney openings. It could be tossed up a flue opening, but it would have to turn a right angle to go down. Marshall Hilliard notified Andrew Jennings on Saturday that they would be coming back on Monday to dismantle the chimney in the cellar. This report to Jennings is significant, and facilitated a drastic move on Lizzie's part the day before they were to return.]

Andrew Jennings (for the Defense): "Take the search of Saturday, as to whether you received any assistance or information that you requested from the girls in the house there, Miss Lizzie and Miss Emma I mean?"

Hilliard: "Yes, sir. Miss Emma came into the kitchen while we were there, in fact all that were there on the search, even to yourself [Jennings], stood on the kitchen floor, when Miss Emma, I can't say her exact words, but as near as I can, she told us that she wanted us to make as thorough an examination as possible of every part of the house, everything in the house; and if there was any place or box or anything else that we did not understand, could not open, why the keys would be given to us. I think she handed you, or someone of the party, the keys to the upper floor."

Jennings: "That was before we started?"

Hilliard: "Yes, sir."

Jennings: "Afterwards, when it was found there were one or two things which apparently could not be opened, they furnished whatever information or means were necessary?"

Hilliard: "There was one trunk in the room at the west and south side of the house that bothered all of us a little, about the top part of it. I noticed it was not a great while after we had been at work on it before I think Miss Emma and Miss Lizzie both came in."

Jennings: "Don't you remember the steamer trunk we could not get into, Miss Emma showed us where the key was hanging?"

Hilliard: "Yes, sir, that is the one I'm speaking of."

Jennings: "Was not that Lizzie that showed us where the key was tied on to that low trunk there?"

Hilliard: "That I could not say; it was one or the other; which I won't say."

Jennings: "They both came there to explain the thing to us, so we could get into it? So far as you know, in any and all of these searches, did there appear to be any attempt on their part to obstruct you, or hinder you in any way, in making a full examination of the house?"

Hilliard: "Not that I am aware of, sir."

Jennings: "On the day of the search, Saturday, what was delivered to you?"

Hilliard: "A dress."

Jennings: "What kind of a dress?"

Hilliard: "A dress skirt, with a blue figure in it. It was blue ground with a white figure...similar to a navy-blue color. The dress waist, perhaps part of it in the front, was loose. There was also a white underskirt, with a pin head size spot of blood."

Jennings: "Was there anything else given to you that day, Marshal?"

Hilliard: "Yes, sir, there was I think a lounge cover that was taken from the dining room."

[The lounge cover may have had blood on it from Abby's autopsy, and the sisters wanted it removed, or it may have been to wrap Lizzie's dress and petticoat in to keep them from the prying eyes of the public.]

(Cross-Examination by Attorney Knowlton during the Preliminary Hearing)

Knowlton: "Mr. Hilliard, did you look in the trunks in the attic?"

Hilliard: "Yes, sir."

Knowlton: "All of them?"

Hilliard: "Yes, sir."

Knowlton: "Did you examine their contents?"

Hilliard: "Yes, sir."

Knowlton: "Did you see anything up there of an unmade dress pattern in the attic?"

Hilliard: "Well, there was some of the trunks that I looked into, but I did not look into all of them. I did not, to my recollection, see any dress pattern in any of the trunks I saw."

Knowlton: "What other officer looked into the trunks in the attic besides you?"

Hilliard: "I think Mr. Seaver, I am not sure but what Mr. Fleet did. I think Mr. Desmond."

Knowlton: "Have you been to inquire for a dress pattern there since?"

Hilliard: "I have not, but under my orders other officers have."

Knowlton: "Who did go?"

Hilliard: "Mr. Fleet."

Knowlton: "Have you been able to get the dress pattern, or any dress pattern?"

Hilliard: "No, sir."

Knowlton: "When was it you sent for it?"

Hilliard: "I think the first officer that went there was Mr. Medley. After that, I think, I am pretty positive I sent Assistant Marshall Fleet. Week before last I think was the first time the officer went there. I think Mr. Fleet was there a week ago last Saturday night. I think he was there some day the first part of the week, of last week."

Knowlton: "And you have not got it?"

Hilliard: "No, sir."

Knowlton: "I now call for it, Brother Jennings, and ask you to bring it, not now, but this afternoon."

Detective Seaver was questioned shortly after Marshall Hilliard. Only the short testimony of Dr. Learned separated the two police officers. The dress pattern was once again addressed:

Knowlton: "Did you see anything of a dress pattern not made up, there?"

Seaver: "No, sir."

Knowlton: "Did you see the trunks Mr. Fleet looked into, did you look into the contents of them?"

Seaver: "I did not."

Knowlton: "You did not find any dress pattern at all up there in the garret?"

Seaver: "Not up there."

Knowlton: "How many trunks were up there?"
Seaver: "I could not tell you, three or four."

[The interesting thing here is that the policemen are looking for a *dress pattern*. Officer Medley's report from his trip to New Bedford (see page 390) to follow-up on Lizzie's time spent there, nine days before the murders, clearly states that Lizzie went into town alone to buy "a piece of dress goods of cheap material." That indicates it was *fabric* Lizzie bought, not a dress pattern. The definition of "dress goods" is lightweight fabric, usually cotton or calico. Did the officers, being men, assume Medley's report that Lizzie bought some dress goods, assume it was a dress pattern?

It is also significant that the first man who went in search of the pattern was Officer Medley. Knowlton repeatedly asks if the officers found any dress patterns not already "made up"—cut up and formerly used to make a dress. When he asks Lizzie about the dress pattern during her Inquest testimony, she shows surprise that he asks about a dress pattern, and not fabric, and she quickly takes advantage of it.]

A portion of Lizzie Borden's Inquest testimony (*Miss Borden recalled, Thursday, August 11, 1892*):
Attorney Knowlton: "Is there anything you would like to correct in your previous testimony?"
Lizzie: "No, sir."
Knowlton: "Did you buy a dress pattern in New Bedford?"
Lizzie: "A dress pattern?" [She is surprised at the question.]
Knowlton: "Yes."
Lizzie: "I think I did."
Knowlton: "Where is it?"
Lizzie: "It is at home."
Knowlton: "Where at home?" [The searches found no pattern.]
Lizzie: "Where at home?" [Buying time to think.]
Knowlton: "Please."
Lizzie: "It is in a trunk."
Knowlton: "In your room?"
Lizzie: "No, sir; in the attic."
Knowlton: "Not made up?"
Lizzie: "O, no, sir."
Knowlton: "Where did you buy it?"

Lizzie: "I don't know the name of the store."

Knowlton: "On the principal street there?"

Lizzie: "I think it was on the street that Hutchinson's book store is on. I am not positive."

Knowlton: "What kind of a one was it please?"

Lizzie: "It was a pink stripe and white stripe, and a blue stripe corded gingham."

[Lizzie, who anchors all her lies with physical objects, has just described the dresses made for her in the Spring by Mrs. Raymond. Attorney Knowlton may not yet be aware of that fact, as this is the initial Inquest, and Mrs. Raymond was not called until a year later for the Superior Court trial to appear on behalf of the Defense. Lizzie's mind must have been racing, knowing if they do find the dress pattern she just described, they will find it had already been "made up."

Lizzie pulls out the name of the store in which she undoubtedly spends a good deal of time in New Bedford—Hutchinson's books. Her love of books was well known. She may have simply grabbed some cheap fabric from a store she took no notice of on her way back to Mrs. Poole's, to show what she had been doing during her time away. This fabric would be turned into a loose-fitting dress.

Yet, the dress pattern is not found during the Saturday search preceding the Inquest. Did Mrs. Raymond, the dressmaker, keep patterns after she made the dresses for her customers, in case repairs were needed? It seems odd the men don't find a dress pattern of any kind in the home.

Detective Seaver's response to Knowlton's question, "You did not find any dress pattern at all up there in the garret?" is strange. Seaver answers, "Not up there." Does that mean they did find one elsewhere?

When Knowlton asks Hilliard the date an officer was sent to ask for the pattern, he says "a week ago, last Saturday." That would be August 20th, based on his date of testifying at the Preliminary Hearing. Lizzie is under arrest at that time, and sitting in the Taunton jail, which means the request was put to Emma.

Hilliard sends Fleet again early the next week to ask for the pattern. The Preliminary Hearing was scheduled to begin August 22nd, a Monday, which coincides with the date Fleet returned to the house.   He seems desperate to secure the dress pattern for the Hearing. As it turns out, the Preliminary Hearing is postponed by Knowlton, stating he is not in possession of all the evidence he needs. This incident will play out in the matron's rooms at the courthouse on the day before the hearing begins, in a showdown between Lizzie and Emma.]

After Detective Seaver leaves the stand during the Preliminary Hearing, two other witnesses are called: John Donnelly and Doctor Draper. Dr. Draper is questioned to some length. He is followed by Doctor Handy. An hour to two hours has now passed since Attorney Knowlton has asked for the dress pattern to be produced.

Half-way through his interrogation of Dr. Handy, during the Re-Direct, Attorney Knowlton interrupts the procedure. He has been handed the dress pattern. He says, "I made some public allusion to the dress pattern. I am satisfied that is the dress pattern; so that whatever may have been supposed to have been in the case, is out of it. I say that in justice to the defendant. I ought to say I never supposed there was anything about it; I simply wanted to see it, that is all."

As Alice would say, "Curioser, and curiouser!" It appears the dress pattern has miraculously appeared, after it could not be located at the house during a detailed search on several occasions. Did Jennings have it all along? Did Lizzie, or Emma, send someone out to buy the exact pattern to have on hand in case the prosecution wanted it? Or, to pick up the one they used from Mrs. Raymond and replace the used patterns inside with new ones from a different pattern—ones that were unmade? Surely no man would look farther than the cover of the envelope to see that the dress pictures matched the ones she described, and to peek inside to see the patterns had not yet been cut.

The mystery remains…what pattern was handed to Attorney Knowlton during Dr. Handy's testimony? If he looked inside, he must have seen a new pattern, "not made up," and was satisfied. Or, if he did find a used pattern, he may have realized it did him no good. He would not have another shot at Lizzie to ask her about it. She testified only once…at the Inquest.

It makes Knowlton's words somewhat cryptic: "I am satisfied that is the dress pattern…I never supposed there was anything about it; I simply wanted to see it, that is all." Once again, Lizzie has slipped away. If they *had* been looking for the cheap material she really bought, would they have found it?

One more item of interest in relation to the dress pattern, is that Lizzie's attorney, Andrew Jennings, never called Mrs. Raymond, the dressmaker, to the stand during the Preliminary Hearing. Did he fear, with the intense focus on the dress pattern, that Knowlton would question her and find out the pattern Lizzie described is the exact one the dressmaker made up for her in the Spring? Mr. Jennings did call Mrs. Raymond as a witness for the Defense during the Superior Court trial, almost a year later, to do damage control relating to the burning of the dress. As Alice has told no one about the dress burning at this point, other than Detective Hanscom (who told Mr. Jennings), there is no need to bring Mrs. Raymond in yet. She will do more harm than good at this point. It would be interesting to see Mr. Knowlton's face during the Superior Court trial when he recognizes the description of the two dresses made up for Lizzie three months before the murders, and realizes he has been duped.

The Clothes Press

On Saturday afternoon, as Marshall Hilliard once again went through Lizzie's room, Detective Seaver and Fleet tackled the large dress closet at the end of the short hallway outside Lizzie's bedroom door. The ladies had gone down to the second floor to give the police full sway over the upper rooms.

The clothes press, as it was called, contained the dresses of Lizzie and Emma Borden, along with some trunks and boxes. The dresses were hung on two rows of hooks, circling the room. The first row of hooks was screwed into the bottom of a shelf that rimmed the perimeter. The second row was screwed into the wall, thus allowing two layers of dresses packed up against each other.

Detective Seaver was questioned during the Preliminary Hearing regarding the search of the clothes press. He described the closet as 4' by 8' feet, with a large window facing the street.

Illustration of 1890s dress closet with one row of garments.
The Borden clothes press had two rows of hanging dresses. The capes and sacks
were kept upstairs in the attic. There would be hats, hat boxes, shoes, and
possibly gloves in the room as well.

Attorney Knowlton: "When you went in there, were there any clothes hung in front of the window?"

Seaver: "I think not, directly in front of the window. The window blind was closed very carefully by oil cloth, or something pinned in the sides and on the top as a guard so the light came in very little when we came in there. We took the clothes down, and opened one half of the shutter so we could see inside."

Knowlton: "Perfectly light was it in there? So you could see as well there as any room?"

Seaver: "Yes, sir."

Knowlton: "What did you do in there?"

Seaver: "We examined all the boxes, and I think there was one trunk there."

Knowlton: "Did you take everything out of those, and look at them?"

Seaver: "I cannot say that we took everything."

Knowlton: "Looked them over?"

Seaver: "It was satisfactory to us that we could not find anything we were looking for."

Knowlton: "Did you examine all the dresses in there?"

Seaver: "We examined about all the dresses. I think there was one or two silk dresses I did not particularly look at. I looked at the common dresses, the woolen dresses there. There were two dresses I did not examine; they were silk dresses. I did not think it was necessary to examine those."

Knowlton: "Every other dress you examined? Examined carefully with a view to determine whether there was blood on them or not?"

Seaver: "Yes, sir. That is what we were looking for."

Knowlton: "You found none?"

Seaver: "No, sir."

[The two overlooked silk dresses could have provided a hiding place for a dress to be placed inside of one, and both then suspended from a peg. Saturday, there is nothing to hide there, as Lizzie is once again, wearing the two dresses from the day of the murders.]

By 6:00, the searchers called it quits. Dr. Dolan admitted to Emma Borden they had done everything but rip the wallpaper from the wall and tear up the carpet. Marshall Hilliard went one better; he declared the searching completed. They would be back Monday to do some masonry work in the basement, but he gave Emma the impression, the searching of the rest of the house was finished.

The Mellon House

On Saturday morning, as the funeral of the Borden's was underway, a stranger rolled into Fall River. He checked into the Mellon House, the "Spindle City's" finest hotel, and in a central location of town. His name was Superintendent O. M. Hanscom of the Boston office of the Pinkerton Detective Agency. He was not there on behalf of the Mayor or the Marshall. Word quickly spread the prestigious detective had been hired by the Borden sisters. Mr. Hanscom arrived at the Borden home that Saturday afternoon, and along with Mr. Jennings, sat in consultation with Lizzie and Emma for about two hours. John Morse's whereabouts are unknown. Detective Hanscom remained in Fall River for two days, running down leads and questioning the sisters, along with Alice Russell. And then, just as suddenly as he arrived, he disappeared, leaving behind the rumor that there had been a falling out between the Marshall and the famous Pinkerton's.

Pinkerton's logo with the slogan "We Never Sleep."

The Mellon House would become home to more than just Detective Hanscom that day. Marshall Hilliard was up against the wall. The newspapers were impaling him and his force, for not making an arrest in the murders. Public opinion was that if Lizzie had been a poor girl, and not a rich Borden, she would already be in jail. He needed advice.

After all the searching and gathering of clues, Marshall Hilliard and his officers decided the case was important enough to call in the District Attorney, Hosea Knowlton, of New Bedford, Massachusetts. He arrived from his home in New Bedford, Saturday, and attended a short consultation at police headquarters. The gentlemen then agreed to meet in a private room at the Mellon House later that afternoon to go over what they had so far in the case.

The Mellon House, Fall River, Massachusetts. 1912.

According to Edwin Porter, the police reporter for the *Fall River Globe,* the following happened within the walls of the Mellon's House's private room, Parlor B:

"The Marshall took all the evidence which he had collected in the shape of notes, papers, etc., together with other documents bearing on the case, into the room with the five men closeted there: District Attorney Knowlton, State Officer Seaver, Mayor Coughlin, and Dr. Dolan. At the close of the conference, the District Attorney advised the officers to proceed with the utmost caution, and was extremely conservative in the conclusions he found. At that time he had not been made acquainted with all the details.

"At the Mellon House consultation, the same caution was observed. The quintet were working on one of the most remarkable criminal records in history, and were obliged to proceed slowly. Marshall Hilliard began at the beginning and continued to the end. He was assisted in the explanation by the Mayor and the Medical Examiner. Mr. Seaver listened. There were details almost without end, and all of them were picked to pieces and viewed in every conceivable light.

"Considerable new evidence was introduced, and then the testimony of officers not present was submitted, which showed Miss Lizzie Borden might have been mistaken in one important particular. The Marshall informed the District Attorney that the murder had occurred between ten minutes of 11 o'clock and thirteen minutes after 11 on Thursday morning. The time was as accurate as they could get it, and they had spared no pains to fix it.

"The Marshall, Medical Examiner, and Mayor then carefully rehearsed step-by-step, the summoning of Dr. Bowen, who was not at home when the murder was committed, and his ghastly discovery on the second floor. No theory other than Mrs. Borden was murdered first was entertained. Miss Lizzie Borden's demeanor during the many interviews which the police had with her was described at length, and the story of John V. Morse's whereabouts was retold.

"The missing note, the failure to find anyone who had sent it or brought it to the house, the lack of footprints in the barn loft, and the inconsistencies of Lizzie's stories were gone over in painstaking detail.

"After this extended conference of the highest authorities in the county, it was given out that the District Attorney was much pleased with the work of the police and that an inquest would be held immediately before Judge Josiah C. Blaisdell, of the Second District Court of Bristol, which is the Fall River Court."

"You Are Suspected."

As the long day drew to a close, the few people remaining within the walls of the Borden house sifted through their individual thoughts. Lizzie was once again wearing the blue calico dress she had worn the afternoon of the murders, and throughout the day before, on Friday. If it seemed strange to those around her that she remained so attired, it is unknown. The Bedford cord, devoid of sleeves and hemline, was still beneath the blue calico she was wearing. She had worn it out of the house, concealed under her black dress with the beaded trim, that day. She had kept her arms crossed before her as she left the house for the funeral, leaning heavily on the arm of the undertaker. At the cemetery, she remained seated in the carriage. The black dress was snug, and she feared her secret would be exposed at any minute. The weight of the Bedford cord, and the constant reminder from the blood stains that spotted the fabric, had taken their toll. She needed desperately to be rid of it. To do that, she needed some privacy.

By 7:30 Saturday evening, two of the three women in the house may have been feeling a sense of relief. The searches had been thorough and nerve-wracking, and the funeral an ordeal, but the Marshal said the searches were over all but the cellar chimneys. The family was still in shock at the number of people who had crammed the streets to the cemetery; you would have thought a United States President had died. For Lizzie, the searches of her room meant only one thing—they suspected her. Why else would they tear apart the beds in the upper rooms? No murderer would have been able to access her room, as it was always locked. She had told the police that. And the questions...so many, many questions. She felt as if a noose was tightening around her neck.

As if in some ironic manifestation of her feelings of doom, a knock came at the door. It was fifteen minutes to 8 o'clock; still light outside, but too late for normal callers. Emma opened the door and found Marshall Hilliard standing there, along with Mayor John Coughlin. Emma's heart skipped a beat. It looked terribly official. She stood back demurely, and asked the two men to enter. She caught sight of the crowd outside, pressing forward for a glimpse of her, and inside the Borden's front entryway. A flash of anger passed through her. *Why don't they all go home?* she thought. *We are not a sideshow.*

Mayor Coughlin did all the talking, as the Marshall stood nearby, his eyes alert to the surroundings. He asked that they all assemble in the parlor for a few minutes. John Morse, looking nervous, entered and reluctantly sat in a balloon-backed chair in the corner. Lizzie walked in, her mask of detachment firmly in place. Alice Russell perched like a bird about to take flight on the edge of a sofa.

Mayor John Coughlin

Mayor Coughlin began by asking Lizzie a few questions. She repeated the story of her trip to the barn and finding her father murdered. She recalled Mrs. Borden's movements, and that the last she saw of her was around nine that morning. The note to the sick friend was gone over, with Lizzie deducing it had probably been burned in the stove.

John Morse was asked a few follow-up questions. For a man with an iron-clad alibi, he came off as highly nervous, and suspicious. His penetrating stare was a tad unnerving.

Finally, Mayor Coughlin rose, and with a slight sigh, looked at each upturned face.

"I have a request to make of the family," he said, "and that is that you remain in the house for a few days, as I believe it would be better for all concerned."

"Why?" Lizzie blurted out. "Is there anybody in this house suspected?"

The Mayor may have looked surprised at this sudden outburst. After a brief pause, he said, "Well, perhaps Mr. Morse can answer that question better than I, as his experience last night, perhaps, would justify him in the inference that somebody in this house was suspected."

Lizzie's eyes flashed. She would not be mollified by such an obvious evasion.

"I want to know the truth," she demanded. Emma shot her a glance.

Mayor Coughlin looked to Marshall Hilliard, who, remembering the District Attorney's words to tread lightly, looked for an answer.

"I want to know the truth," Lizzie said again, more forcefully.

Before Marshall Hilliard could stop him, the Mayor made a huge mistake.

"Well, Miss Borden," Mayor Coughlin said, "I regret to answer, but I must answer yes, you are suspected."

Marshall Hilliard flinched, the room became deadly quiet, and all eyes were on Lizzie.

"We have tried to keep it from her as long as we could," Emma said, her voice tremulous. The color rising in Lizzie's cheeks was as indicative of a storm coming, as a sudden gust of wind.

"Well," Lizzie said, standing and facing the Mayor. "I am ready to go anytime."

The gauntlet was thrown down, not for the last time, in the days that would follow. The Marshall and Mayor were completely taken aback. This woman was incredible! They had never seen anything like her. Either she was entirely confident of her innocence, or she was admitting guilt, and wanted to get it over with.

After an awkward silence, the men took their hats, excused themselves for interrupting the sister's evening, after such an ordeal as the one they had been through that day, and exited the room. Just as the Mayor had reached the entryway, he turned back and said, "If the crowds become too much, please inform the officers. I shall see that you receive all the protection that the police department can afford."

Emma walked them to the door and said, "Of course we want to do everything we can in this matter."

The courteous exchange that had just occurred obscured the real meaning of the warning Mayor Coughlin had just delivered: they were all, essentially, under house arrest.

Calling Dr. Bowen

[The following scenario is one created by the Author, for the purpose of giving a reason for an action Alice Russell took later that night.]

The explosion Emma had expected from her younger sister was not long in coming. Lizzie was leaning against the back of a chair, her hands gripping the carved wood. Her face was effused with color, and her chest was heaving. It was the quiet before the storm. Suddenly straightening, she turned on her sister, eyes blazing. Alice Russell, who had sat silently at the back of the room throughout the Mayor's visit, her hands twisting a handkerchief into a tightly wound cord, looked at Lizzie in shock. This was a Lizzie she had not seen.

"You kept it from me?" Lizzie screamed. "You KEPT it from me? Don't you think I had the right to know? Don't you think I might have conducted myself differently if I had known?"

Emma stood her ground, but her frame seemed smaller. Her face was twisted in pain. "I'm sorry, we thought it was best."

"WE? So, you have all betrayed me!" she screamed. "You have betrayed me, and thrown me to the wolves."

Lizzie ran from the room and up the front stairs, her square heels coming down hard on the carpeted rungs. Alice was standing now, visibly shaking. John's face was one of anger. Female histrionics was the last thing he needed. He walked heatedly into the entryway and grabbed his hat from the hall tree. Emma looked after him in surprise. They had just been told to remain inside the house. The slamming of the back-screen door announced her Uncle had chosen to ignore those orders.

Gripping the railing, Lizzie careened around the curve of the staircase, and ran into her room, slamming the door. She shoved the bolt on the inside of the door into place. Her breath coming in bursts, she ran around her bed and jerked the portiere aside, where she quickly hooked the door separating her room from Alice's. She collapsed on the lounge, taking great gulps of air, her fists clenched in fury.

Emma knocked on Lizzie's door, begging her to talk to her. Alice waited nervously downstairs. Lizzie was hysterical; Emma heard great sobs coming through the door. After several attempts to calm her sister, she came downstairs and asked Alice to go across the street for Dr. Bowen. Alice was not considered one of the family under house arrest. After several moments of indecision, Miss Russell took a shawl and reluctantly opened the front door. [End of scenario.]

Dr. Bowen arrived at the Borden house to find Lizzie in a state he had never seen her in before. It had taken her several minutes to unlock her door and admit him. She was shaking, her nerves completely shattered. She sobbed as she told her dear friend the Mayor had just told her she was suspected of murdering her father and stepmother. As Dr. Bowen had, no doubt, kept up with the papers, and the suspicions levied against Lizzie, it may have come as no surprise. His heart went out to her. He asked Emma to bring him a glass of water. He doubled the dose of morphine he had given Lizzie the day before. Dr. Bowen sat with her a few minutes, holding her hand, and reassuring her that it would be alright. When he walked from the room to return home, he told Emma to call him if she needed him. He was called back to the house later that evening.

1890s bottle of Morphine Sulphate

[Author's scenario continued:]

The doctor had barely left the house when the accusations toward Emma began anew. Lizzie, not yet dulled by the sedative, was railing against her sister, accusing her of betrayal.

"I don't want you near me!" she yelled. "I want you out of my sight!"

Emma stood helplessly in the room. Her own bedroom was just to her left. As she turned to go into it, Lizzie spat, "I don't want you in here!"

Alice finally stepped forward.

"Here, Emma," Alice said, her voice quaking. "I will change rooms with you. You can sleep in your parent's room; I will sleep in yours."

Without a word, Emma gathered her night clothes and toiletries, and exchanged rooms with Alice. Lizzie lay on the lounge, her back turned to the room, and to the sister she had branded a Judas. [End of scenario.]

During the Inquest, Alice Russell was asked why she had exchanged rooms that Saturday night.

Knowlton: "Where did you sleep that night?"

Alice: "The first two nights I slept in what was Mr. and Mrs. Borden's room; the next two nights I slept in what was Emma's room."

Knowlton: "After you found that stick, you changed?"

Alice: "No, that did not make me change."

Knowlton: "You did change after that."

Alice: "Yes. Saturday, I found the stick."

[Alice remains vague as to why she changed rooms that Saturday. There is no report of what occurred to make her do so. The above scenario of Lizzie's accusations toward Emma, although a creation of the Author, when weighed against Lizzie's typical response to betrayal, and her treatment of Emma two weeks later in the matron's room at the Fall River police station, is not an unreasonable deduction. Alice is reluctant to give a reason as to the exchange of rooms, perhaps feeling stories of Lizzie's rage would not be in the girl's best interest. Alice, at this point, has not lost full belief in Lizzie; an attitude that will be tested to its limits the following morning.]

John Morse's Stroll Through Town

Sometime Saturday, two acquaintances of John Morse's from South Dartmouth, came to visit him at the house. South

Dartmouth is home to William A. Davis, the butcher with whom John resides, and with whom a major horse trading and cattle deal was in the works. We do not know what transpired during their conversation.

Postcard of South Main Street showing City Hall (right with clock tower), Fall River, Mass. The buildings on the right are part of the Borden Block. You can see the Academy Building on the right, in front of City Hall.

The New York Herald ran the following snippet Saturday, August 6, 1892: "Late tonight, John V. Morse left the Borden house and walked rapidly down Second Street and toward the business portion of the town. There was an officer at his heels. He wandered around for nearly an hour and then returned to the house, the detective never leaving him for an instant. Whether he wished to get the air or merely to test the closeness of the espionage to which he is subject is not certain."

Sometime that eventful Saturday, Bridget packed the last of her things and left the Borden's attic room for good. A cousin, Patrick Harrington, had offered a room at 95 Division Street in Fall River; walking distance to the police station, although still a fair stretch. She was summoned to the house on Monday, but she would no longer call 92 Second Street, home.

Also, that day, Marshall Hilliard and Dr. Dolan visited the receiving vault at Oak Grove cemetery. Nothing was done at that time, other than to look at the bodies in general. Were they taking another look at the wounds, or was the visit for more nefarious motives? Were the two men interested in seeing if a small gold ring still circled Andrew Borden's little finger? Or, did they check to see if a murder weapon or blood-stained dress had been secreted inside the coffin Saturday morning, as Lizzie wept, and bent over her father's casket to kiss him? What more clever way to dispose of evidence, than to bury it, along with the murder victim, six feet beneath the ground?

The two men walked through the cemetery toward their carriage, and discussed the case. Inside the cool cavern of the vault, Andrew and Abby Borden lay in their caskets, not yet at peace. Their final degradation was yet to come.

Chapter Twenty-Five
Sunday, August 7, 1892

The Fall River Herald, August 7, 1892—Sunday was a quiet day around the house. Emma Borden appeared at the door at 8 o'clock to take in the milk. The servant girl, Bridget Sullivan, could stand the strain no longer and left the house Saturday night to join her friends. None of the family ventured out to church, and there was nobody visible at the windows.

The event of the day was the arrival at the house of Detective Hanscom of the Boston Pinkerton agency, who entered with Lawyer Jennings during the forenoon. He had been hired by the Borden's to look after their interests. He had questioned Lizzie, but found her too exhausted physically for a searching examination.

If the *Fall River Herald* thought the "event of the day" was the arrival of Detective Hanscom at 92 Second Street, they were not privy to Lizzie Borden's movements that Sunday morning. Hanscom's appearance would have paled in comparison to the events about to take place within the Borden's kitchen.

Alice Russell was questioned during the Superior Court trial as to what occurred on Sunday, August 7th:

Mr. Moody (for the Defense): "Who got the breakfast Sunday morning?"

Alice: "I got the breakfast."

Moody: "After the breakfast had been got and the dishes had been cleared away, did you leave the lower part of the house at all?"

Alice: "Yes, sir."

Moody: "Afterward, did you return?"

Alice: "Yes, sir."

Moody: "About what time in the morning was it when you returned, Miss Russell?"

Alice: "I don't know."

Moody: "Was it before noon?"

Alice: "Yes, sir."

Moody: "Will you state what you saw after you returned?"

Alice: "I went into the kitchen, and I saw Miss Lizzie at the other end of the stove; I saw Miss Emma at the sink. Miss Lizzie was at the stove, and she had a skirt in her hand, and her sister turned and said, "What are you going to do?" and Lizzie said, "I am going to burn this old thing up; it is covered with paint.""

Moody: "Covered in paint,"—is that the expression?"

Alice: "I don't know whether she said "covered in paint" or "covered with paint.""

Moody: "Do you recall anything else said then?"

Alice: "No, sir."

Moody: "What did you do then?"

Alice: "I am quite sure I left the room."

Moody: "Did you speak to either of them at the time?"

Alice: "No, sir, I don't remember that I did."

Moody: "Did you come in the room again?"

Alice: "Yes, sir."

Moody: "What did you see then?"

Alice: "Miss Lizzie stood up towards the cupboard door, --the cupboard door was open, and she appeared to be either ripping something down or tearing part of a garment."

Moody: "What part?"

Alice: "I don't know for sure; it was a small part."

Moody: "A smaller part? Go on and state."

Alice: "I said to her, "I wouldn't let anybody see me do that, Lizzie." She didn't make any answer. I left the room."

Moody: "Did she do anything when you said that?"

Alice: "She stepped just one step farther back up towards the cupboard door."

Moody: "Did you notice where the waist of the dress was when she held the skirt in her hands as you first came in?"

Alice: "I didn't know that it was the waist, but I saw a portion of this dress up on the cupboard shelf."

Moody: "Inside the cupboard?"

Alice: "Yes, the door was wide open."

Moody: "When you came back the second time and she was tearing the smaller part, did you see the skirt?"

Alice: "Well, I am not positive; I think I did."

Moody: "Did you have any more talk with her that day, or did she say anything to you about it?"

Alice: "No, sir."

Moody: "At that time were there any police officers in the house?"

Alice: "No, sir."

Moody: "Were there any police officers about the premises?"

Alice: "Yes, sir."

Moody: "Do you know whether there was anyone else in the house except yourself and Miss Emma and Miss Lizzie Borden?"

Alice: "I don't think there was."

Moody: "Miss Russell, will you tell us what kind of a dress— give us a description of the dress that she burned, that you have testified about, on Sunday morning?"

Alice: "It was a cheap cotton Bedford cord."

Moody: "What was its color?"

Alice: "Light blue ground with a dark figure—small figure."

Moody: "Do you know when she got it?"

Alice: "In the early Spring...of that same year."

(**Cross-examination** by Governor Robinson for the Defense):

Robinson: "You called it a Bedford cord, is that right?"

Alice: "Yes, sir."

Robinson: "Is that what we call a calico?"

Alice: "No, sir."

Robinson: "Quite different from a calico?"

Alice: "Yes, sir."

Robinson: "And is it a cambric?"

Alice: "No, sir."

Robinson: "The dress you saw Sunday morning was not a calico, was it?"

Alice: "I judged not. I suppose it was the same dress that I have reference to her having made in the spring. That was the Bedford cord."

Robinson: "Were you three the only persons in there at breakfast?"

Alice: "No, sir."

Robinson: "Was Mr. Morse?"

Alice: "Yes, sir."

Robinson: "And did I understand you to say that you went out; did you go out of the house after breakfast?"

Alice: "I didn't go out of the house. I think I went to my room, or the room I occupied the night before, and put it in order."

Robinson: "Did you help in washing the dishes?"

Alice: "No, sir. Not that morning."

Robinson: "You left that to Miss Lizzie and Miss Emma to do?"

Alice: "Miss Emma. I can't say sure about Lizzie."

Robinson: "When you came back from your chamber you came into the kitchen and saw Miss Lizzie with the Bedford cord dress? And some other part of the dress was over on the mantel or a chair, was it?"

Alice: "It was on the cupboard shelf."

Robinson: "Did you see blood on that dress?"

Alice: "No, sir."

Robinson: "Did you see any blood on the remaining part of it?"

Alice: "No, sir."

Robinson: "Did you see that it was a soiled dress?"

Alice: "The edge of it was soiled as she held it up. The edge she held towards me like this (illustrating), and this edge was soiled."

[Governor Robinson's clever location of the dress did not work. He says "part of the dress was over on the mantel or a chair, was it?" He is trying to get Alice to say the dress was out in the open, not suspiciously hidden away in a closet used for storing cleaning supplies and fuel for the stove. But Alice doesn't take the bait. She restates, "It was on the cupboard shelf."]

 **Lizzie's Burning of the Dress**

Lizzie's burning of the dress took place the morning after the Mayor announced she was suspected as the murderer of Andrew and Abby. They could arrest her at any time. She knows the police are coming back Monday morning for another search in the cellar. She has worn the torn Bedford cord beneath her clothing for three days. Alice is still hovering over her.

The fire in the stove is always hottest during breakfast when it is first built for the day. Alice sees her at the right of the stove, near the dining room door—the location of the firebox, where the fire is. It is interesting that Lizzie holds up the skirt to show Alice "an edge" that was soiled. Lizzie selected the portion of the skirt to show her. Why? Because the hem was missing. It was one of "the pieces" Alice saw on the cupboard shelf. She stated:

Alice: "The cupboard door was open, and she appeared to be either ripping something down or tearing part of a garment...it was a small part."

Could the pieces Alice saw, be the torn sleeves and hem Lizzie removed from the Bedford cord the day of the murders, in order to wear it beneath the blue calico dress?

Lizzie is desperate. She is out of time. There is no more hoping the police are going to go away and look for the real murderer. The Mayor has accused her the night before. They could come for her at any time. Lizzie knows they are coming the next morning to search the cellar chimneys. They could take her then. Also, Alice is now sleeping in Emma's room, next to her. What if she sees something suspicious? She has to get rid of the dress now.

She waits until breakfast is over, and John and Alice have left the dining room and kitchen. She hurries while the fire in the stove is still hot, trusting that Emma will not give her away.

Also, notice Alice sees Emma at the sink in the kitchen, where she "turns" to talk to Lizzie; not down the entry hall in the old sink room.

The kitchen stove at the Lizzie Borden house in Fall River, Ma.
The firebox is found at the right of the stove where the hand irons are. Lizzie
stood here to burn the dress. She moved around to the left end of the stove and
took the dress pieces out of the closet, seen here in the corner. At Alice's
admonition, Lizzie moves closer to the open closet to screen herself from
policemen, who may be outside the window. My thanks to Danielle Cabral for
the reenactment. Photo by the Author.

Emma's question to Lizzie, as she sees her standing at the stove
with the skirt, "What are you going to do?" takes on a different
slant when Emma testifies during the Superior Court trial. Alice
states she heard Emma say nothing after Lizzie tells her sister she
is "going to burn this old thing up." Emma, under oath, testifies a
year later at the trial, that she responded to Lizzie's statement by
saying, "Why don't you?" or, "You better," or "I would if I were
you," or "something like that."

Emma steps way over the ethical, and legal line, during this same testimony to state she saw the stained Bedford cord dress hanging in the clothes press [closet] Saturday night, after the funeral. She states she went into the closet looking for a peg to hang her dress on she had worn that day, and noticed the Bedford cord hanging there. This is after the police did an intensive search of that closet earlier that day, and did not see the dress. She goes on to say it was her idea that Lizzie burns it, as it was not good for anything, as it was so badly faded and soiled. Attorney Knowlton must have felt physically sick at this blatant lie.

The burning of the dress gives us a few interesting insights. Lizzie's faith in her sister's complicity is absolute. She knows Emma will see her burning the dress—she is right there at the sink. Emma is probably still off-balance from Lizzie's outburst the night before—screaming of betrayal. Yet, Lizzie has not one doubt her older sister will stand by her.

Another thing worth noticing, is that the dress was never carried away to be disposed of. Many Lizzie fans have postulated that Bridget, or Mrs. Holmes, or even Alice, covered for Lizzie, and secreted the dress away. It is still here, and she must burn it to destroy the evidence. What we don't know…and may never know…is what became of the calico she wore over the Bedford cord, once she was arrested, and taken away. Did she find a way to remove the blood stains from inside the lining? Did she continue to wear it, or did she find a way to destroy it as well?

Alice Russell has seen much since the time Bridget Sullivan breathlessly knocked on her small cottage door the morning of Thursday, August 4th. Seeing the burning of the dress, after witnessing Lizzie's changing stories to officers and friends, along with the frightening scene the night before—one that required Dr. Bowen to come running twice with a strong sedative—is all running through her mind. She will wrestle with it until the next day.

During the time the Pinkerton Detective was in the sisters' employ, a disconcerting newspaper report came out of Hastings, Iowa—John Morse's home for 25 years before moving back to Massachusetts.

The Hastings Dispatch stated, "Miss Lizzie Borden has sent Detective Hanscom out here to investigate relative to

Morse's past life. The people of Hastings, and particularly John Davidson, Morse's brother-in-law, are awaiting the arrival of the Pinkerton expert with much interest." Lizzie has gone after John!

A Trip to the Receiving Vault

The Fall River Herald, Sunday, August 7, 1892—Assistant Marshall Fleet, Drs. Dolan and Leary, visited the receiving vault Sunday and made a further examination of the bodies, taking measurements of the wounds and notes of other matters which will be of use when testimony is needed in these directions.

The visit to the cemetery was an important one. The axe was taken along with Dr. Dolan and Assistant Marshall Fleet and was fitted into the wounds, with what conclusions cannot be stated at once. The blow which was delivered over the temple of both victims was with a dull edge, and it was impossible to tell whether the axe would fit the wound or not, so shattered was the bone. The cut which extended down the front of Mr. Borden's nose was in a soft part of the face, so that the entire edge of the weapon cut into the flesh. It was an easy matter to measure that, and it was found that while the exact length of the gash did not correspond with the width of the axe blade, yet it could readily have been made by such a weapon. None of the cuts on Mrs. Borden was so clean as that on the face of her husband. In every instance the axe had brought up against the skull; and it was not embedded the entire width.

[The axe taken to compare to the Borden's wounds was likely the long-handled axe that Mayor Coughlin studied under a microscope. He found "three suspicious stains" that "may be blood" upon the handle. It was later ruled out as the murder weapon. If the article is referring to the clawhead hatchet, that did have a long 17" handle, it's blade too was later found to be too wide to fit the incisions.]

Dr. Dolan's Findings on Abby's Death

The Fall River Herald stated that Medical Examiner, Dr. Dolan, "said the only discovery of importance made during the thorough investigation Saturday afternoon was in the spare room, where Mrs. Borden's body was found. Out near the window, drops of blood were found, which indicated that the murdered woman had moved after the first blow was delivered. It is thought that that blow was the glancing one which has been described. The supposition is that the axe fell on the right side of the head, taking off the flesh and hair, and that the woman turned and reeled to the space between the dressing case and bureau where the mortal wound was delivered. After that, the blows fell thick and fast. It is believed that when she was approached, Mrs. Borden stood looking out of the window in this room, and her blood which stained it at this point bears out that view."

Dr. Dolan says that the more he reflects on the small quantity of blood that was spilled, the more at a loss he is to account for it. The same condition prevails in the sitting room below where Mr. Borden was butchered, and there was nothing to raise the suspicion that the murderer had cleaned anything, except the dripping axe.

[Actually, the first blow fell on the left of Abby's face, near her ear, not the right.]

Officer Medley Returns to Westport, Massachusetts

Officer Medley went to Westport on Sunday, August 7th, and spoke to Mrs. Cyrus (Augusta) W. Tripp at her home there. She was the old school friend Lizzie visited with the Poole's during her trip to New Bedford, nine days before the murders. Officer Medley asked Augusta some questions, to which she answered, "Lizzie told me she thought her stepmother was deceitful, being one thing to her face, and another to her back. Lizzie told me her stepmother claimed not to have any influence with her father. "But she must have influence with my father, or he never would have given my stepmother's half-sister such a very large sum of money," she said. She said, "I do not know that my sister and I would get anything in the event of my father's death." This conversation took place at different times, during former visits; nothing being said during her visit July 26th."

While Officer Medley was in Westport, he stopped to talk to the horse traders that were rumored to be in business with John Morse. They denied any knowledge of such a claim. As the horses had been surreptitiously moved to Fairhaven, without the Officer's knowledge, Medley could find nothing suspicious.

Lizzie and Emma received calls from a few friends throughout the day. Meanwhile, the police scurried about town, holding meetings and going over evidence they hoped would convince Judge Blaisdell that there was sufficient cause to arrest Lizzie Borden, and hold her over for a Preliminary Hearing. Marshall Hilliard ordered a man named William Niles to be at the Borden's at 2:30 to dig up the clothes that had been buried behind the barn. What happened to them at that time is unknown; they were buried again several minutes later.

Sunday Admonitions from the Pulpit

Reverend W. Walker Jubb of the Central Congregational Church gave a heartfelt plea to his parishioners that Sunday morning. The First Congregational Church was also in attendance within the stone building on Main Street. Lizzie's pew was obviously vacant, and rumors had been swirling amongst the public, both outside, and inside, the church.

Reverend W. Walker Jubb

The Central Congregational Church, Fall River, Mass.

"Let us ourselves curb our tongues and preserve a blameless life from undeserved suspicions," he intoned. "And while we hope," he continued, "for the triumph of justice, let our acts be tempered with mercy. Help us to refrain from giving voice to those insinuations and innuendoes which we have no right to utter. Keep us from keeping the sweetness of a future by our ill-advised words, and let us be charitable as we remember the poor grief-stricken family and minister unto them."

Reverend Buck stepped to the side of the pulpit and, leaving the Bible behind, addressed the congregation with the words they had been waiting to hear.

"I cannot close my sermon this morning without speaking of this horrible crime that has startled our beloved city this week, ruthlessly taking from our church household two respected and esteemed members. I cannot close without referring to my pain and surprise at the atrocity of the outrage. A more brutal, cunning, daring and fiendish murder I never heard of in all my life. What must have been the person who could have been guilty of such a revolting crime? One to commit such a murder must have been without heart, without soul, a fiend incarnate, the very vilest of degraded and depraved humanity, or he must have been a maniac.

"The circumstances, execution, and all the surroundings cover it with mystery profound. Explanations and evidence as to both perpetrator and motive are shrouded in a mystery that is almost inexplicable. That such a crime could have been committed during the busy hours of the day, right in the heart of a populous city, is passing comprehension. What was the motive? Gain, enmity, sudden anger or revenge? Strangely, nothing of this nature enters into this case. I hope the criminal will be speedily brought to justice. This city cannot afford to have in its midst such an inhuman brute as the murderer of Andrew J. Borden and his wife. Why, a man who could conceive and execute such a murder as that would not hesitate to burn the city."

Did some of the churchgoers that day wonder if, perhaps, the good Reverend might be referencing the same person in both his summations? Could the "blameless life" also be capable of wielding a hatchet, and leaving behind "a mystery that is almost inexplicable?"

Reverend Jubb's final words, that the murderer "would not hesitate to burn the city," was prophetic; its meaning manifesting later, during Lizzie's residence on "the Hill."

Chapter Twenty-Six

Monday, August 8, 1892

Monday found the household at 92 Second Street on edge. Another search was to be done, one that would actually dismantle part of the cellar.

At 10:00 that morning, Officers F.L. Edson, Desmond, Medley, Connors, and Quigley arrived at the Borden house.

With them was Charles H. Bryant, a mason. Their mission in the cellar that day was to look for any weapon, clothing, or anything else that related to the murder, within the chimney cavity. To do that, it was necessary to remove some of the masonry. Upon their arrival, Officer Desmond asked Lizzie for her consent to search the premises. This is Officer Desmond's report:

"I told her [Lizzie] that we had been sent by Marshall Hilliard to make some further search of the premises. Lizzie said "if there is going to be anything done, or anything said, Mr. Jennings must be here." This took place in the sitting room. Hanscom [from the Pinkerton Agency] was sitting in the room at the time. While waiting for Mr. Jennings, Emma came into the sitting room from the front hallway, and said "if you only want to do some searching, you can go right ahead and search any place you wish; but if there is any conversation to be had, Mr. Jennings better be here." I told her we came only to search. About the time we got ready to search, Mr. Jennings came. I told what Lizzie said, also what Emma said.

Mr. Jennings said "that's all right, go right ahead." We went down to the cellar. We had only been there a few minutes, when Mr. Jennings and Hanscom came down. Mr. Jennings spoke about the lumber pile in the yard, and wanted us to be sure and search that before we got done.

"Mr. Bryant [the mason] and myself looked over the chimneys. After finishing the east chimney, which is the one in the kitchen, we went to look at the one in the west of the building. This runs up between the parlor and dining room. The side in the dining room seemed to be bricked up or cemented. While we were looking it over, Emma and Lizzie both said "if this front is in your way, tear it out." Mr. Jennings was there at the time. Emma spoke about a "lumber pile in the yard," and thought it would be a good place to search. Mr. Bryant and myself went into the cellar; and it was thoroughly searched by Edson, Connors, Quigley and Desmond. From there, we went and searched the barn, lumber pile, yard, privy vault, and well, also John Crowe's yard, which is on the side of the Borden house."

According to Officer Edson's police report, "we searched the cellar, chimneys, sounded walls and floor; after which we searched the barn, outhouse, under the outhouse, yard, lumber pile in the yard, and adjoining yards. We found no weapon, or anything suspicious. The search was completed about 1:30 p.m."

[Did Lizzie show any signs of anxiety as the men searched her fireplace? Would they notice the loose brick she removed during the times she eavesdropped on her family? No mention was made of it.]

Marshall Hilliard, Assistant Marshall John Fleet, Mr. Jennings, Dr. Dolan, Detective Seaver and Officer Desmond arrived at the house at 3:00 that afternoon. It was, to say the least, a full house. At that time, they started in the attic, and overhauled everything, piece by piece. From there they went to the second floor, and gave it a thorough search. This was continued until the cellar was reached; the same persons, with the exception of D. Desmond doing the searching there.

Of course, the papers reported the day's events. According to the *Fall River Herald*, Chares H. Bryant, the mason, was called in and every fireplace was opened and examined. Nothing could be found of the axe, and nothing looked as though it had been disturbed. The wood in the cellar was turned over, and every inch of the building was sounded in the endeavor to find some recent hiding place, but once more the police were baffled and the conclusion was arrived at that the weapon had been conveyed from the premises.

The strange request from Emma Borden and Mr. Jennings that Monday morning may relate to the notion "the weapon had been conveyed from the premises." *Both* found it necessary to ask the officers to search the lumber pile out back. Why? It had been gone over several times since the day of the murder. It seems odd Emma and Mr. Jennings would make the request. Could it be that Lizzie told them something in private? Perhaps, that she had heard a "scraping" sound the morning of the murder, as she was out in the barn? A "scraping" noise, that she may have told her sister and attorney, that sounded like it came from the vicinity of the lumber pile.

"Perhaps the murderer was climbing the fence there, and made that noise as he stepped up the lumber pile," she may have told them. Did Lizzie want the policemen to climb up on that stacked pile of boards at the rear of the property (in the southeast corner next to Crowe's barn), and look over? Was she hoping they would find the hatchet she had thrown and finally give up searching the house? Would they think the murderer had escaped that way, tossing the weapon as he went, just as the newspaper predicted? And, a sober thought to ponder, did Emma and Mr. Jennings know she had killed Abby and thrown it there? Were they helping her by asking the police to "search the lumber pile?" It is remarkable that with police and civilians alike climbing over, and along, the back fence, no one saw the hatchet lying on Crowe's barn roof beneath the protective branches of Chagnon's pear trees.

Trial exhibit photo by James Walsh of Borden yard looking southeast. The grape arbor is to the right. The lumber pile is at the rear behind the trees. You can see Crowe's barn (ribbed metal) between the trees behind the barrel. This was taken in 1893 for the trial.

The Handleless Hatchet Comes to Light

During the Monday morning search of the cellar, the most significant find, in the way of evidence, was located inside a dusty box in the middle cellar of the basement. It had lain there since Officer Mullaly and Assistant Marshall Fleet first looked it over the day of the murders. Throughout the following four days, a broken hatchet, covered in white ash, lay in the darkness of the cellar.

Officer Desmond gives this significant discovery a scant three lines in his report of the Monday morning search: "At the outset of the search in the cellar, Officer Medley found a small hatchet. I wrapped it up in a newspaper, and gave it to Medley to put in his pocket. It had no handle to it."

The hatchet head would become the prosecution's star witness during the Superior Court trial. It had received no mention during the Inquest or Preliminary Hearing. At that time, the District Attorney and police were waving the clawhead hatchet before the Judge's eyes as the probable murder weapon. After all, it was sharp, relatively new, appeared to have been recently washed and "swiped," it had to be the instrument of death. There was one problem with it—it didn't fit the wounds—its 5" blade was too wide.

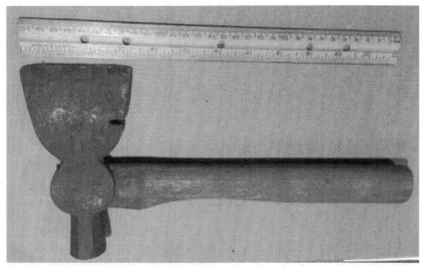

A shingling hatchet, like the handleless hatchet, is shown here. The blade on a shingling was 3 ½"-4" (photo shows 3 ¾"); the clawhead was a 5" blade.

The production of the handleless hatchet at the Superior Court trial in June of 1893, would be one that Edgar Allan Poe would have approved. There was comedy, tragedy, and a mystery befitting the skills of the greatest macabre writer of the 19th century. We will showcase it in the chapter on the great trial.

Alice Struggles with a Lie

During the morning, as the drama unfolded with the hatchet head in the basement, another was transpiring in the parlor of the Borden house. Detective Hanscom called Alice in to talk to her in private, as Lizzie and Emma waited in the dining room. Unless speaking in whispers, it is quite possible the sisters overheard the conversation, as the two rooms were separated only by a wall.

Alice Russell sat nervously pursing and un-pursing her lips, her facial tics betraying her highly nervous state. Ever since she witnessed Lizzie burning the dress the morning before, she had struggled with its implications. The wooden club she found beneath her bed had been bad enough. Lizzie's erratic behavior and volatile nature had unnerved her completely. And now—a detective from the famous Pinkerton Agency had her sequestered in the little-used parlor. She felt the Detective Agency's all-seeing eye, featured in their logo, staring into her soul.

Hanscom asked Alice if all the dresses that were in the house the day of the murders were still here. The poor woman's body must have frozen in terror. After a few moment's hesitation, she replied they were, as far as she knew.

Lizzie and Emma turned to see a frightened Alice Russell walk briskly into the dining room, and close the door. Sitting down dramatically in a spare chair, she hissed, "I have just told Detective Hanscom a falsehood." If the sisters had overheard the conversation in the next room, they kept their poker faces.

Parlor at the Lizzie Borden House and Museum, Fall River, MA.
Photo by Ron Bueker.

"What was there to tell a falsehood about?" Emma asked.

"He asked about the dresses, if all of them were in the house that were here on the day of the murders. I said 'Yes!' Oh, Lizzie," she said, turning her attention to the woman across from her, who was showing signs of anxiety, "I'm afraid the worst thing you could have done was to burn that dress."

Lizzie blinked, color rouging her cheeks. In a loud voice, perhaps for Detective Hanscom's hearing, she yelled, "Oh! What made you let me do it? Why didn't you stop me?"

Alice may have blanched at having the tables of guilt turned on her. Before she could retort, a carriage arrived out front to take her on some errands. She left the house flustered and frightened.

Upon Alice's return, she was asked to sit down and talk with the sisters and have a talk about her conversation with Detective Hanscom. Emma advised her to go into the parlor and tell the Pinkerton man the truth. Further, she told Alice to tell him she and Lizzie had instructed her to do so. Alice disappeared into the parlor and returned in a few moments, terribly flustered. She announced she had told him. What Lizzie must have been going through knowing the Detective now had that piece of damning evidence is not known. Did she hope it would remain a secret, as Hanscom had been hired by the sisters? He would, no doubt, tell Mr. Jennings. Lizzie's panic grew.

Whether Alice had been away from her accounting work for too long, or the past four days had been too much for her, she chose that Monday to pack her small bag and return to her boarding house on Borden Street. Lizzie may have been relieved to see her go.

Meetings and Warrants

The New York Herald, Fall River, Mass., August 8, 1892—For a long time this evening, the Borden horror hung upon a climax as startling as the crime itself. In a private room at police headquarters, District Attorney Knowlton and Chief Hilliard conferred from five o'clock in the afternoon until late at night, and the subject of their conference was whether there is enough evidence to warrant the arrest of three persons well known in Fall River on the charge of murder. They had before them all the facts which the police have been able to collect, along with Detective Seaver and Rhodes, who have done some of the collecting.

Chief Hilliard further exhibited some articles of testimony which throw a new light on the work of the police. The conference had not been going on long when a patrolman came in with one of the registers in which druggists are required to enter all sales of dangerous drugs. He took this book directly into the room where Knowlton and Hilliard were at work. What it shows nobody knows but the police and the District Attorney, but ever since the murder, there has been talk of some such book said to contain a record of the purchase of poison by a member of the Borden household.

Sensations in Plenty

There was rather a sensational beginning in the view of Chief Hilliard's repeated declaration that he was all in the dark for clews [ms] or testimony. In a few minutes, there were more surprising developments. Medical Examiner Dolan came to the back door of the headquarters and carried under his arm a box in which were a hatchet and a dress. It was not intended that anyone should know either of Dolan's coming, or what he brought with him, but two or three reporters happened to be at the rear entrance to headquarters when he drove up, and the lap robe which covered the box fell to the ground as he was lifting the box from the carriage. The dress and the hatchet were plainly seen. There was something else in the box which they could not make out. Dr. Dolan whisked into the conference room as rapidly as possible. It has been strenuously asserted for the last two days that the police have in their possession a dress found in the Borden house on which was a drop of blood. The police have strenuously denied it. It has also been asserted that the stained axe or hatchet found in the Borden house, as described in yesterday's *Herald*, had been discovered to be stained with blood. The police have vigorously denied this also.

Dig 'Em Up!

Before Dr. Dolan delivered his "secret" evidence to Marshall Hilliard Monday afternoon, he had first gone to the Borden house and enlisted a man to dig up the clothes, yet again, that had been recently buried behind the barn. The victim's bloody apparel, and artifacts from the crimes, were spread out on the grass for examination. There were certain parts he wanted for further investigation, and he carried them away with him, and had the remains buried again behind the barn. Hairs found on the victims clothing were carefully picked from fibers and placed in an envelope. Other things were taken away as well.

The Fall River Herald ran the story of the bloody clothes being, once again, buried. *The New York Herald*, sending stories via telegraph to the *Fall River Herald*, stated without hesitation that meetings were being held, evidence gone over, and three arrest warrants were being prepared. What this news must have created in the form of sheer panic in the three accused can only be imagined.

We do know Bridget Sullivan was asked to return to the Borden house and spend the night Monday, so she would be available— under police guard—until she was needed the following morning to appear at the Coroner's Inquest. If Bridget had read the news, and realized she might be one of the three mentioned for an upcoming arrest, it is no wonder that on Tuesday morning, when Officer Doherty came to pick her up for her appearance at the court, she totally broke down. She thought they were about to arrest her.

The newspapers ran a report stating John Morse met some friends and chatted with them downtown for a while Monday night. This may have been the time he later testified to meeting Mr. Charles Holmes and his wife in front of City Hall. Mr. Jennings for the Defense caught John Morse in a lie during his Preliminary Hearing testimony, when Morse claimed he did not talk with Mr. Holmes about seeing the cellar door open the day of the murders, when he first arrived at the house at noon:

> Mr. Jennings: "You were asked the other day when you were on the stand whether you had informed any person about seeing the cellar door open, and you were asked by me whether you had informed Mr. Holmes or not, and you remember of course what reply you made to the questions; I now want to ask you if you have thought the matter over since?"
>
> Morse: "I have."

Jennings: "State what it is."

Morse: "I met Mr. Holmes and his wife down in front— "

Jennings: "What person did you mention it to?"

Morse: "Mr. Holmes."

Jennings: "Where and when did you mention it to him?"

Morse: "I think at the house after we got through."

Jennings: "Did you meet him at the house?"

Morse: "I met him first down in front of city hall."

Jennings: "Did you walk with him to the house?"

Morse: "Yes, sir."

Jennings: "After you got to the house, what did you do?"

Morse: "Went into the house and showed him over it."

Jennings: "Did you go outside afterwards with him?'

Morse: "Yes, sir."

Jennings: "What did you do outside?"

Morse: "Went to the barn."

Jennings: "Did you go into that with him?"

Morse: "Yes, sir."

Jennings: "Now what time was it during those proceedings that you told him about the cellar door being open?"

Morse: "I think it was after we went out of the house, after being in; I think it was."

Jennings: "While you were going out to the barn?"

Morse: "Yes, sir, I think it was."

Jennings: "Was that the day of the murder?"

Morse: "No, sir…it was after the murder; I do not know but several days after."

Jennings: "What did you do, if anything, at the time you told him about this cellar door? I mean as to whether you pointed it out or anything of that kind?"

Morse: "I do not know as I pointed it out, I told him I thought the cellar door was open."

Jennings: "As to whether you pointed the door out to him at the time you told him?"

Morse: "I think I did."

[The fun part of John's testimony, is that Charles Holmes is seated in the audience, within Morse's eye line, watching him on the stand. It makes it hard to lie under the circumstances, but John Vinnicum Morse manages to do it, all the same.]

Charles Jarvis Holmes
Edwin Porter, Fall River Tragedy

John may have talked over another matter with Charles Holmes that night. Mr. Holmes and Dr. Handy were close friends. Handy was telling his wife and others, the night of the murders, of seeing a strange man pacing in front of the Borden house that day. If Dr. Handy has related this story to Mr. Holmes, it is possible that Holmes informs John of it, as a way to offer up a suspect for the murders.

The response he would have gotten from John would be a surprise. Rather than showing appreciation for the news, Morse may have been mortified. The stranger pacing in front of the Borden house Thursday morning was Joseph Chatterton—the man Morse had sent to pick up Abby. The last thing he needed is for the police to find Chatterton and expose the Swansea deal, thus implicating Morse with a possible motive for murder. He may have asked Mr. Holmes to tell Dr. Handy, that the man he saw is innocent of wrong-doing, and to please, in a word, "Shut up!" about him. We do know that when the police approach Dr. Handy on August 10, only four days after Morse's meeting with Mr. Holmes, Handy is suddenly acting strangely, and avoiding identifying anyone.

Chapter Twenty-Seven

The Inquest

Five days after the brutal murders of Abby and Andrew Borden, the people of Fall River realized the wheels of the court system were finally beginning to spin. Rumors of an imminent arrest, or arrests, were everywhere. The streets between the Borden's home and the Police Station, where the courtroom was housed, was packed with people, as though lining a parade route. Once again, horse-and-buggies had to pick their way through the milieu.

The Fall River Police Station and Second District Court.

The Marshal, District Attorney, and Mayor had struggled with what to call the investigation they were about to begin within the courthouse walls. An Inquest, by definition is "a judicial or official inquiry, especially before a jury, to determine the cause of a violent or unexpected death." This is typically called a Coroner's Inquest, and is often held over the dead body. In the Borden's case, the cause of death seemed pretty obvious: blunt force trauma from a heavy, sharp-edged instrument, most likely a hatchet. Calling the witnesses they had on the subpoena list would shed no light on that.

As the reporters circled like buzzards, demanding to know the nature of the sudden announcement of impending events, word went out that the proceedings were merely a judicial inquiry to collect all the evidence through the witness's statements. The public was not fooled, and the authorities finally admitted it was, indeed, an Inquest.

The Fall River Herald was delivering the news, from the beginning day of the Inquest, as fast as anxious readers could devour it.

"District Attorney Knowlton, Medical Examiner Dolan, and Detective Seaver had arrived [at the court house] and were in earnest consultation with the city marshal [Hilliard]. Officers started from the station in all directions, and it was soon apparent that something of importance was about to take place. The members of the party who had been in consultation in the marshal's office proceeded upstairs and the first legal proceedings in the case commenced. Miss White, the stenographer, took notes for Mr. Knowlton. Nobody outside of the officials was allowed in the room and it was impossible to obtain any information as to what took place.

"Bridget Sullivan, the domestic, was the first to arrive at the station. She was escorted from the house by Officer Doherty. Miss Sullivan was dressed in black [green], and her countenance indicated that she thoroughly realizes the position in which she is placed. If an honest appearing face was to acquit a person of a crime, Miss Sullivan has that face.

"From the time Miss Sullivan went upstairs, 9:45 o'clock, until 11:20, nothing indicated that an inquest was being held. At 12:15, a recess was taken until 2 o'clock, the witness being placed in [the] charge of Matron Russell." [It was at this time Bridget told the Matron about the bloody towels in the cellar.]

Officer Doherty, upon arriving at 92 Second Street, found a young woman completely in tears. Bridget Sullivan supposed she was being taken away to be locked in a cell and charged with murder. Her composure crumbled before the police officer, as he repeatedly tried to assure her she was merely coming with him to answer some questions in the Marshal's office. She would not be placed behind bars. Knowing the crowds and reporters outside were salivating for any glimpse of the major players in the Borden murder case, Bridget decided to deny them her tears. She stepped out the door with Officer Doherty, and kept her gaze on the sidewalk, watching her small black shoes as they clicked along.

When they arrived at the station, she was shocked to see the crowd choking off the entrance to the courthouse. They shouted at her, pushed and shoved for a better view, and impeded the progress of anyone going into, or coming out, of the dismal grey building. She was escorted, finally, into Marshal Hillard's office, where Dr. Dolan, Attorney Knowlton, and Detective Seaver awaited her. Once she was asked to take a seat, she broke down again, in near hysterics.

Word had come from Professor Wood that the blood staining the small towels found in a bucket of water in the cellar on the morning of the murders was indeed, human blood. It was this announcement, and others, which the police were anxious to question Bridget.

According to *The Pittsburgh Dispatch*, August 10, 1892— "Bridget Sullivan was summoned immediately to the police headquarters. She went willingly. Speaking of the identity of the murderer, she said she "was too worn and worried to talk of that." Then she exclaimed suddenly, "The murderer should clear me!" After that, she would say nothing, so Bridget was taken before Judge Blaisdell where she told, and retold, her story.

"The girl stood as long as she could. Then she broke down. She told her examiners, it is said, that she did not believe Lizzie Borden left the house at all. She was asked why she thought Miss Borden had not gone out. She answered with sobs. The District Attorney waited in vain for her to regain her composure, and at 12 o'clock, the inquiry was stopped.

Lizzie was called to testify in the afternoon to re-tell her story."

Bridget Sullivan illustration from *The Fall River Herald* front page article, on the first day of the Inquest, August 10, 1892.

In a letter written to Attorney General A. E. Pillsbury on May 5, 1893, shortly before the Superior Court trial was to begin, to determine Lizzie Borden's innocence or guilt in the murder of her parents, Attorney Knowlton gives us some vital information into what was said behind the closed doors of the Inquest:

New Bedford, Mass. May 5, 1893
Hon. A. E. Pillsbury:
Dear Sir:
Jennings wants to have his experts see the skulls, and I told him I supposed there would be no objection, and have so written to Dolan.

They also want Bridget Sullivan's testimony at the inquest. We declined to give it to them before the indictment, but I see no objection to giving it to them now. It is almost identical with her story as told before Judge Blaisdell, and will do us no harm. What do you think?

Yours truly,
H. M. Knowlton

[Saying Bridget's Preliminary Hearing testimony, which would occur two weeks after the Inquest, was almost identical with her statements at the Inquest, does give us a sense of what was said that day, with some very glaring omissions, as we will see.]

On May 17th, co-counsel for the defense, Attorney Adams, writes to Attorney General Pillsbury requesting a copy of Bridget's Inquest testimony, and suddenly, neither Pillsbury or Knowlton know where it is. Pillsbury swears he never had it. And thus, the mystery of Bridget Sullivan's missing Inquest testimony began. At the time of this writing, it has never been published. Many believe these records are still hidden away in the files of Governor George Robinson, at his still-existing law firm, Robinson Donovan P.C., in Springfield, Massachusetts, protected by the client confidentiality pact.

Yet, while they claimed "nobody outside of the officials was allowed in the room, and it was impossible to obtain any information as to what took place," leaks to the press did occur. The men present at the Inquest that day, in addition to the presiding Judge, were Attorney Knowlton, Detective Seaver, Marshal Hilliard, Dr. Dolan and "several of the officers first to arrive on the scene." While even court officer George W. Wyatt was excluded from the secret meeting, others, namely the men with strong suspicions as to Lizzie's guilt, were front row and center. Officer Doherty and Harrington were among the very first to arrive the morning of the murders. It has long been suspected the carefully chosen press leaks came from Officer Phillip Harrington.

The Inquest

The Pittsburgh Dispatch, October 18, 1892— "The leak came through one of the officials who was present at the examination. That official said today to an intimate friend: "It is what Bridget saw, not what she heard or what she guessed, that led to Lizzie Borden's arrest. There were two important points, and they did not occur to her mind, agitated and shocked as she was at the time of the discovery of the crime, until she had a well-defined idea of what the police suspected."

Let's take a look at what was so important in Bridget's secret Inquest testimony that a person inside the courtroom that day found it beneficial to leak:

The Fall River Herald— "The first question [to Bridget Sullivan] was in regard to her whereabouts all through the morning of Thursday up to the time of the murder. She answered that she had been doing her regular work in the kitchen on the first floor. She had washed the breakfast dishes. She saw Miss Lizzie pass through the kitchen after breakfast time, and the young lady might have passed through before."

During Bridget's Preliminary Hearing and Superior Court trial testimony, she sticks to one story that flatly contradicts this Inquest testimony: Her story during these two later appearances says she saw Lizzie as she was washing the breakfast dishes as Lizzie came into the kitchen shortly before 9, directly after John Morse leaves the house. As Lizzie is pouring her coffee, Bridget flees the house to the backyard to vomit. When she returns, Lizzie is gone. She does not see Lizzie again, until she appears at the screen door to ask Bridget if she is going to wash the outside windows. That story never changes after the Preliminary Hearing is held.

Yet, in the story leaked about her answers at the Inquest, she says, "she saw Miss Lizzie pass through the kitchen after breakfast time and the young lady might have passed through before." This clearly states *after* breakfast time...a time that she claims not to have seen Lizzie again until 9:30 that morning, when Bridget is outside the screen door with a pail and a brush. Why has this story changed? It may have something to do with the missing 9 pages of Bridget's testimony during the Preliminary Hearing. We will look deeper into this detail in the Preliminary Hearing chapter.

And what other tidbit was important enough to be leaked to the reporters? Believe it or not...Bridget washing windows in the attic.

> *The Fall River Herald,* Wednesday, August 11, 1892— "Bridget Sullivan has proved herself a most valuable witness, and it is no wonder that she is carefully guarded at the house of her cousin on Division Street. It will be remembered that the story told all along has sent her [Bridget] to the third floor of the house to wash windows and that nobody has been able to ascertain when she ascended the stairs. She told the District Attorney she did not go to the third-floor story to wash windows at all."

Really? While Bridget's window washing was committed on earlier in the book, it is here, in her leaked Inquest testimony, that we find a tremendous cover-up concerning Lizzie's movements on the day of the murders. Let's see how often Bridget told her story of washing windows in the attic, *before* she was one of "the three" hinted at in the papers as having an arrest warrant waiting for her:

> Bridget's first statement to Officer Fleet the day of the murders: Bridget: "Went upstairs at 10:55 to fix my room. After I had been in the room about ten minutes, Lizzie called me downstairs, saying that her father was dead, someone had killed him, and get Dr. Bowen."
>
> Fleet: "Did you see anyone that you think would or could have done the killing?"
>
> Bridget: "No, I did not. I was washing windows outside, and did not see anyone but Mr. Morse that morning; and he went away before nine o'clock. Am very sure I was not upstairs more than ten to fifteen minutes. I did not hear the door opened while I was upstairs, *nor did I see anyone from my window.*" [Italics are the Author's.]

The Fall River Herald, Thursday, August 4, 1892 (the first press report on the day of the murders:) "She [Lizzie] rushed to the staircase and called the servant, who was washing a window in her room on the third floor."

The New York Herald, Thursday, August 4, 1892— "Bridget Sullivan, the servant, was up in the third story, cleaning windows."

The Fall River Herald, Friday, August 5, 1892— "At the time Miss Lizzie came downstairs, I went to one of the upper rooms to finish the window washing. I remained there until Lizzie's cries attracted my attention. I came down and went for Doctor Bowen; I never saw anyone enter or leave the house."

The New York Herald, August 7, 1892— "The servant girl says she was at work cleaning windows in the front room upstairs and she heard nothing until Miss Lizzie called her."

Edwin Porter, a police reporter for *The Fall River Globe*, on Bridget's leaked Inquest testimony— "She finished up her work downstairs and resumed window washing on the third floor, which had been begun the preceding day. The witness went up into the third floor, and while washing windows talked down to the sidewalk with a friend. She went on with the windows and might have made considerable noise as she raised and lowered them. She heard no noise inside the house in the meantime. By-and-by she heard Miss Lizzie call her."

Why so much emphasis on Bridget's activities in the attic that day? And why, during the Preliminary Hearing only two weeks later, did Attorney Knowlton ask the most leading question ever allowed during the proceedings:

Bridget: "When I got through with my work downstairs, if I had not anything else to do, I always went upstairs before I started to get dinner, if I had time."

Knowlton (to Bridget): "Did you look out the window when you were upstairs, you did not, did you?"

Bridget: "No, sir."

Knowlton: "You lay right on the bed."

Of all the mysteries surrounding this case, the handling of Bridget's testimony concerning the simple task of washing windows in the attic, the day of the murders, is one of the strangest. For a prosecuting attorney to lead his own witness is odd in itself. Why was it so important to get Bridget away from that window? A window, that as was pointed out in trial testimony, overlooked the backyard, and barn.

The Author's conclusion, has kept her up more nights than she can count. And one you may, or may not, agree with is:

Bridget finished the last of the windows inside, on the first floor, she was expected to clean that day. She did not clean the kitchen and parlor windows. She testified she had nothing to do with the second-floor cleaning. If you read her testimony in the Preliminary Hearing, you will notice she says "I got water and cloths to get to wash them" [the inside windows on the first floor]. She later says she hung up "her cloth" poured out the water from the hand basin, and then went upstairs. She only mentions one cloth. Did she take the other with her? She has a water tank in her bedroom's closet. It would be easy to dip the cloth in the water tank and give the remaining windows in the attic a quick "spit polish."

Bridget's window is at the top, left. The barn door she, Andrew, and, allegedly, Lizzie used, is at the right, front of the photo. Charles Carrol, trial exhibit, 1893.

Bridget mentions cleaning the front window in the attic. She also mentions cleaning the window in her room. Bridget's room has only one window. It does not face the front; however, it faces the back of the house. It was stated while washing the window at the front, she called down to a friend on the sidewalk. This again indicates the front of the house facing Second Street. There are two attic windows at the front of the house, and two at the back: Bridget's, and the spare room where John Morse often slept.

As questioned earlier in this book, did Bridget, while washing the window in her bedroom, look down and see the barn door open? Fearing Mr. Borden would see it, and be displeased that she had not latched it, did Bridget hurry downstairs and go out and bolt the side door to the barn?

Could that be one of the "two things" the police leak to the press referred to? "It is what Bridget saw, not what she heard or what she guessed, that led to Lizzie Borden's arrest. There were two important points, and they did not occur to her mind, agitated and shocked as she was at the time of the discovery of the crime, until she had a well-defined idea of what the police suspected."

The police suspected Lizzie was never in the barn. Officer Medley's experiment with the barn loft hay dust proved no one had been there. Bridget blurted out the morning of the Inquest, while sequestered in Marshal Hilliard's office that she "didn't believe Lizzie Borden ever left the house at all." When Bridget latches the barn door, Lizzie is nowhere around. If she was in the barn, she would now be locked inside and unable to appear several minutes later at the base of the stairs, screaming her father has been killed.

Only as the day of the murder wears on, does Bridget start hearing Lizzie's statement that she was in the barn's loft. She told Bridget she had just been in the yard when she heard "a groan," and came in to find her father dead. As the officers come and go that day, asking Bridget questions and comparing notes, as she stood in her corner of the kitchen, did it begin to occur to her Lizzie could not have been out back, or in the barn? Is this partly why she left the house the night of the murders and slept across the street at the Miller's?

Now, the important question: If Bridget can swear she did not see Lizzie from her window, wouldn't that be a gold mine for the prosecution? Remember, when Fleet asked her, during the early minutes of the investigation, if she had seen anybody that morning, Bridget answers: "No, I did not. I was washing windows outside, and did not see anyone but Mr. Morse that morning; and he went away before nine o'clock. Am very sure I was not upstairs more than ten to fifteen minutes. I did not hear the door opened while I was upstairs, **nor did I see anyone from my window**." [Bold emphasis by the Author.]

Bridget didn't see Lizzie at the crucial time Andrew was being killed. Lizzie said she went out to the barn, after helping her father get settled, and stayed out in the yard eating pears, or up in the loft of the barn, for 20-30 minutes. Bridget left her at 10:55 to go upstairs, and police have decided Lizzie called Bridget, saying her father is dead, at approximately 11:10. That's only 15 minutes, yet Lizzie claims to have been outside an entire 20-30 minutes.

Then why does Attorney Knowlton, the man hired to put Lizzie behind bars through damning testimony, lead Bridget *away* from the window, and her proof Lizzie was never out of the house?

Bridget testifies she spent part of the time at the "front" of the house, and "may have made considerable noise as she raised and lowered the windows," even calling down to a friend. Does Knowlton believe the Defense will use that time to show Bridget was away from her window at the back of the house—long enough for Lizzie to eat a couple of pears in the backyard, and go into the barn, leaving the door open? Will they grill Bridget asking for the specific time she went down to close the barn door? Does the open door prove Lizzie had indeed been out to the barn? Can Bridget swear she didn't close the door after washing the windows that morning? All it takes are those kinds of questions to raise reasonable doubt in the mind of a Judge or jury. Did Knowlton decide it was not worth it to bring it up, and *open that door*?

Did Bridget, not wanting to admit she had forgotten to lock the door when she had finished the window washing, happily go along with eliminating this detail from her testimony? Worse, would it raise suspicion she was downstairs during Andrew's murder, and outside, possibly to dispose of a murder weapon?

We know, from the time of the Inquest forward, Bridget's story of what she was doing during her 10-15 minutes upstairs that morning, has changed to claiming she was lying on her bed for a short rest. This is probably true in part. Based on how long she took per window downstairs, she could have finished the few windows in the attic in five minutes, especially if she had started them the day before. She probably did lie down after finishing, hoping for a full 20 minutes before she had to go down and start the noon meal.

Attorney Knowlton does the lying for Bridget, so that all she has to do is answer:

Knowlton (to Bridget): "Did you look out the window when you were upstairs, you did not, did you?"

Bridget: "No, sir."

Knowlton: "You lay right on the bed."

Bridget's missing Inquest transcript must have been handed over to Mr. Jennings in the month before the Superior Court trial, as the attorney refers to it several times while questioning Bridget. Oddly, she is not asked about what she saw from her window that morning. Did Pillsbury and Knowlton remove that portion? Mr. Adams, co-counsel for Lizzie, only asks Bridget to point out which window is hers in a photograph presented to her, pointing out it overlooks the backyard. Perhaps both sides agreed the mentioning of the open barn door was a sticky wicket that could go both ways, and they tucked it away.

Bridget's window overlooking backyard at the Lizzie Borden House and Museum.

464

As a final note to this strange segment: Mary Doolan, the Kelly maid, who talked with Bridget over the fence the day of the murders, was subpoenaed to appear before the Superior Court trial in June, 1893. She was never called to the stand. Was she the friend Bridget called down to while washing the attic windows? Was Attorney Knowlton afraid that under cross-examination Mary would be asked about Bridget's movements that morning, and mention she saw, or talked up to her, as she washed the attic window? We may never know.

Another strange report concerning Bridget's testimony was addressed by Edwin Porter, the reporter for the police, and a man who undoubtedly received the lion's share of inside information. One of Bridget's statements leaked from the Inquest states she said, "By-and-by, she heard Miss Lizzie call her. She answered at once, and went downstairs to the first floor, not thinking of looking about on the second floor, where Mrs. Borden was found dead shortly afterward, because there was nothing to make her look around as she obeyed Miss Lizzie's call. **She found Mr. Borden dead and Lizzie at the door of the room.**" [Bold emphasis is that of the Author.

Did Bridget see Andrew Borden's mutilated body? Was Lizzie standing at the sitting room door near the kitchen, instead of leaning against the back door, as Bridget stated multiple times during her three judicial appearances that followed? It is interesting that Bridget is questioned repeatedly during the Superior Court trial by prosecuting attorney Mr. Moody, as to where Lizzie was standing when Bridget came down the stairs. Did they know her original story was quite different?

Lizzie Borden's Inquest Testimony

Marshal Hilliard and Officer Doherty arrived at the Borden home at 1:40 with a subpoena for Lizzie Borden. In an effort to keep the two from comparing testimonies, and to have Bridget nearby if they needed to recall her to the stand that day, Bridget was being held in the matron's rooms at the police department.

As the Marshal's buggy pulled up before number 92, the ubiquitous crowds pushed forward. Something was finally happening. They had seen Bridget led away, now they were here to arrest Miss Lizzie! The men were let into the house. Moments passed, as the breathless crowd waiting in anticipation. When the front door opened, and they caught a glimpse of skirt, the excitement reached a climax. If it had been a generation of cell phones, the cameras would have been flashing.

Instead of Lizzie Borden, the throng of onlookers saw Mary Ella Brigham, Lizzie's friend from childhood, exit the house, and make a mad dash across the street to Dr. Bowen's.

"Did Lizzie faint?" the crowd murmured excitedly.

"Maybe she killed herself before they could arrest her!"

Once again, the morbid gawkers were kept in suspense, as Mrs. Brigham returned to the Borden's without the Doctor, shutting the door behind herself. Agonizing minutes passed. Finally, the door opened, and Marshal Hilliard and Officer Doherty escorted Lizzie from the house. Mrs. Brigham was close behind as they climbed into the waiting carriage.

The Fall River Herald was quick to jump on this historic event. They reported "In the past few days Lizzie has terribly aged. The full round cheeks that friends of her former days remember have entirely disappeared, although the bright eyes and haughty expression are still retained. There was not a falter in the step as she came down the stairs."

Lizzie was attired in black—a departure from her preferred blue color, as she gave a meager nod to the mourning requirements of the day. There was no veil, no crepe, and no tears.

By the time the Marshal's carriage entered Court Square, the crowds were waiting for them. It was tough going down the narrow alley leading to the Police Station's back entrance. As Lizzie finally stepped down from the buggy, reporters noted her pale complexion, and that she was nibbling her bottom lip; a trait she inherited from her father, and seen often throughout the upcoming ordeal.

Lizzie's heart was pounding as she climbed the stairs to the second floor, and walked past the policeman standing guard outside the Second District courtroom. The sedative Mrs. Brigham had just mixed for her, after returning from Doctor Bowen's, was just now sending a chilled feeling through her veins. Her head felt fuzzy, and things around her seemed to be part of a bad dream.

Judge Blaisdell, *Fall River Herald*, August 9, 1892.

Judge Blaisdell was seated at his bench next to the witness chair. Across from this were two tables: one for the Defense lawyers, and one for the Prosecutors. Only the Prosecuting team was present. Attorney Knowlton turned to watch Lizzie Borden as she was asked to take "the stand." In his gut, he knew this would be an uphill climb.

Attorney Andrew Jennings, Lizzie's representative, had battled in vain to be allowed to be present during her Inquest testimony. He knew full well this was not just an "informal examination," as the Marshal and D.A. had tried to frame the meeting. His grounds for representing her that afternoon, he said, was that his client had been accused of murder by the Mayor himself. It would not be the first time the Mayor's ill-timed answer to Lizzie's question, "Is someone here suspected?" would come back to bite him.

At a formal Inquest, Lizzie should have been told her rights, and warned about her answers, as they might be used against her. She was not. Later, Judge Blaisdell said he assumed Mr. Jennings had gone over Lizzie's rights with her. No oath was given, possibly in an attempt to downplay how important the proceedings were. The other men in the courtroom that day could have aptly been called conspirators in creating the noose they hoped to see around her neck. Marshal Hilliard, Detective Seaver, Dr. Dolan, and "several of the officers first on the scene," were still in attendance. It was said, some of the officers came and went during the proceedings.

While it is assumed the Prosecuting Attorney would be happy to have his lead suspect in his crosshairs, Mr. Knowlton was not feeling the thrill of the hunt. He was in an impossible position. This was not only a female—accused of a murder so heinous that most men would flinch—but she was a well-respected member of the community, a Sunday School teacher, and a dedicated volunteer to many causes. Above all, she was a Borden! A name that meant something in her hierarchical town.

The Borden's, along with the Durfee's, the Brayton's, and others, had built Fall River. Their money talked, and their power could bury you. Not only that, Hosea Knowlton knew they had no evidence to put before a jury. Everyone who saw Lizzie only moments after discovering her father's body, stated there was not one drop of blood on her. Attorney General Pillsbury had dumped the case in his lap, and he would have gladly unloaded it.

Lizzie Borden's Inquest Testimony

You can read Lizzie Borden's entire Inquest Testimony by going to this link:

Lizzie Borden's Inquest Testimony.pdf

Or, visit www.lizzieandrewborden.com Lizzie Borden's Inquest testimony was transcribed, and is offered as a PDF document, by Stephanie Koorey and Terence Duniho while writing their article: *"Will the Real Inquest Testimony of Lizzie Borden Please Stand Up?"* (*Lizzie Borden Quarterly*; Oct. 2011.) A hardcopy of Lizzie's Inquest testimony is in the Fall River Historical Society. My sincere thanks to all mentioned for making this available to the public.

Lizzie Borden, circa 1892-1893. Fall River Historical Society.

Where Lizzie Dropped the Ball.

Much of Lizzie's testimony is already included throughout the book as it pertains to that story segment. Besides her rambling account of where she was when Abby was supposedly in the guest room for two hours, and her whereabouts when Andrew came home, there are a few "Oops" moments in her testimony not yet highlighted. The page numbers correspond to Stefani Koorey's pdf of Lizzie's testimony, offered in the link on the previous page. In the interest of space, Lizzie's Inquest is not printed in its entirety here. It is recommended you read it, to obtain a full appreciation for her disjointed statements that day:

1) Pg. 54: Lizzie gives away that she was away from the house Wednesday when John first arrived at 1:30, shortly after the noon meal. She states elsewhere that she never left the house Wednesday, as she was sick, other than to go see Alice Russell later that night. This is significant, because Lizzie was reported being seen trying to buy prussic acid Wednesday. Her defense was that she was home all day, sick, in her room.

Knowlton: "When did he [John Morse] come to the house before your father and mother were killed?"
Lizzie: "He stayed there all night Wednesday night."
Knowlton: "My question is when he came there."
Lizzie: "I don't know; I was not at home when he came; I was out."

2) Pg. 55. Lizzie lies about coming down to supper Wednesday night, something Bridget said she did:

Knowlton: "Did you eat supper at home Wednesday night?"

Lizzie: "I was at home; I did not eat any supper, because I did not feel able to eat supper; I had been sick."

3) Pg. 57. Lizzie states she saw nobody around the house the week of the murders, "except the man who called to see him on this business about the store." Lizzie has told Alice Russell, and Emma (in a letter) that a mysterious man was running around the house Monday night.

4) Pg. 58. Lizzie states she finds her father, on the day of murders, in the sitting room reading the *Providence Journal*, when she first comes down for breakfast. According to Bridget, when Lizzie first appears for breakfast, Mr. Borden is upstairs in his room, with "a big basin of water." Lizzie says she first sees Abby dusting in the dining room; she told police she first saw Abby that morning making the bed in the guest room as she (Lizzie) was going downstairs for breakfast.

5) Pg. 58. Lizzie, when asked where Maggie was when Lizzie saw Abby dusting in the dining room, she says, "Just come in the back door with the long pole, brush, and put the brush on the handle, and getting her pail of water; she was going to wash the windows around the house. She said Mrs. Borden wanted her to." It was pointless to add, "Mrs. Borden wanted her to." Of course, Mrs. Borden wanted her to. She always got her cleaning orders from Abby, plus, she always cleaned the windows on Thursday. This is unnecessary information Lizzie gives to take away any notion that it was Lizzie's idea to send Bridget outside the house to wash windows.

She has also moved the timeline of that morning by thirty minutes, saying she saw Bridget with her brush, pole, and pail at the same time she saw Abby dusting. Bridget left the house with the cleaning items at 9:30; 30 minutes later than Lizzie's claim. It also makes it appear as though Bridget was already about to go out to wash the windows when Lizzie first saw her, thus negating Lizzie needing to tell her to.

6) Pg. 60. Lizzie completely distances herself from Bridget during the time Bridget is washing the inside windows. Why? Because this is the time Lizzie tries twice to get Bridget out of the house, by asking if she's going out, and telling her of a sale at Sargent's. Here, she states she didn't see Bridget cleaning in the sitting room, or dining room.

7) Pg. 61. Lizzie says Andrew spoke to Bridget when the maid let him in the front door the day of his murder. Bridget stated that Mr. Borden "did not say a word," as he came in. Lizzie says she heard him tell Bridget "he had forgotten his key." This is significant as it is meant to show why he couldn't get in. The real reason is that Lizzie had all three bolts working on the front door; something not usually done once the family was up, and began their day. Lizzie was in charge of undoing all but the spring lock each morning, as she came down to breakfast.

8) Pg. 68. Lizzie's need to iron handkerchiefs at the time Andrew comes home works for her two-fold: It's an excuse to beef up the fire ("I put in a stick of wood to try to heat the flat"), in order to burn the Swansea deed, and, it gives Lizzie an excuse to be in the dining room where Bridget is cleaning to tell her about the sick note (the reason for Abby's absence), and to coax Bridget out of the house. It also gives her close access to Andrew, without looking like she is just waiting around.

9) Pg. 69. Lizzie states she saw her father "take off his shoes, and put on his slippers." Crime scene photographs show Andrew is wearing his Gator Congress shoes, not slippers. Putting on his slippers was probably his habit, but not that day. That fateful day, he was waiting for Abby to realize she had missed him at the bank, and return home; they would then go out again. As Lizzie hit him over the head, she would not have been able to see his feet from the head of the sofa, back toward

dining room door, where experts said the killer stood. The Author did an experiment with her hapless husband, using their couch, whose arm is the exact height as the Borden's sofa. She could not see his feet planted on the floor as Andrew's were, from the head of the sofa, and the Author is 6' 2" tall; Lizzie was 5' 4".

10) Pg. 72. Lizzie mentions she was going to go out that day and buy fishing lines to take to Marion on Monday. Was that the errand she was referring to when she told Bridget she might go out? Was the purchase of fishing lines to be her alibi of where she was when Andrew was murdered? Only—Bridget refused to leave, and Lizzie was stuck. It is interesting that Dr. Handy said Lizzie was originally expected at Marion on Thursday, the day of the murders. Was she going to buy lines on her way out of town? Was fishing in Marion to be her alibi?

11) Pg. 73. Lizzie mixes up the two containers in the barn containing lead. She states the box was in the loft, and the basket of tin and lead, was on the main barn floor, next to the door. Police, the day of the murders, find the two containers are in the opposite places. Lizzie describes the box in great detail. Why? She saw it on the barn floor near the door when she tossed in the old lock. (In the box, she saw "Nails, some old locks...") Yet, she says in testimony, the box was up on a bench in the loft, where she spent several minutes looking through it for lead. It was the basket police found in the loft.

12) Pg. 75. Lizzie says "I took some pears up from the ground when I went up [to the barn loft]. How does one hold up one's skirt, hold onto a railing or wall, and climb up steep barn steps holding 3 pears? And, why would you?

13) Pg. 77. Every witness who saw Lizzie the morning of the murders states how clean she was. She has been up in a barn loft thick with hay dust, "pulled over a lot of boards," adjusted a dusty window curtain, eaten three pears with sticky pear juice, dug through a box of old iron and tin, and yet, has nothing on her. Her hands and dress are perfectly clean, and her hair in place.

Day One of the Inquest Ends

At the close of the day on Tuesday, August 9th, District Attorney Knowlton posted the bulletin outside the police station that two witnesses had been examined, and the Inquest would continue the next morning at 10:00. The sentence "Nothing to publish" was added. The scant information did little to mollify the frustrated public. Letters to the police, and to reporters, mirrored Fall River's attitude that the police had done a "shoddy job" from the beginning. Marshal Hilliard could feel the hot breath of discontent and anger upon his neck, as he struggled to find more evidence.

Police were dispatched to Somerset, Massachusetts, at 2:30 that Tuesday afternoon to follow-up on a lead about a farm hand at the Brayton farm burying a bloody hatchet. When the police arrived, they found the man had been killing chickens with a hatchet, and it had never "been buried." This did not keep reporters from scouring the nearby Swansea farms, owned by the late Andrew Borden, as they searched for clues and weapons. Nothing came to light.

Old well at the Borden's Lower Farmhouse. Reporters
searched this for a bloody hatchet, and possibly other evidence.
Photo courtesy of Shelley Dziedzic.

Professor Wood, of Cambridge, arrived the day before, in case he was needed at the Inquest. He had been sent the stomachs and

milk recovered on the day of the murders. He was closeted with
Dr. Dolan for a while on Tuesday. The bits of clothing and other
souvenirs taken from the pile buried behind the Borden barn, were
turned over to him for further examination. He dodged reporters'
questions as to whether he had examined any axes while he was
there that day. He retorted, "I do not expect to. I could not very
well bring down my laboratory."

Attorney General Pillsbury, who came to town at 2:30 that
afternoon, at the request of Attorney Knowlton, was said to be
there to advise the D.A. as to certain aspects of the case. This
caused many to think the prosecution's case was weak, and there
was not enough evidence to proceed with an arrest. The fact the
warrants were made out, and traveling around in Marshal Hilliard's
coat pocket, was not known—not even to Mr. Jennings.

Mr. Knowlton and the Attorney General met at the Mellon
House, during a brief recess. At 3:40, the Inquest was resumed,
and Mr. Pillsbury left the building, where he was met by reporters.
He told the eager journalists that the case was not so mysterious as
had been reported, and bantered with them concerning their clues.
The reporters bantered back that the murder was mysterious
enough to baffle the police, and that five days had elapsed and
there was no arrest. Someone took the pains to further inform the
Attorney General that the evidence was purely circumstantial.

"You newspaper men know, or ought to know," said Pillsbury,
"that you may not be in a position to pronounce on the case. There
may be some things which you have not heard of and which may
have an important bearing." The reply was to the effect that the
head men, working on the case, had conceded at noon that day,
that they had no other evidence, and that they ought to be a pretty
good authority. "Police officers do not always tell what they
know," was the parting shot of the Attorney General as he
withdrew.

Edwin Porter with *The Fall River Globe*, wrote the
following: "At 5 o'clock, Bridget Sullivan left the police
station in company with Officer Doherty, and passed down
Court Square. She was dressed in a green gown with hat to
match, and appeared to be nervous and excited. Nobody knew
her, however, and she attracted no attention. She went into the
Borden house for a bundle and, still accompanied by Officer

Doherty, walked to No. 95 Division Street, where her cousin, Patrick Harrington lives, and where she passed the night. She was allowed to go on her own recognizance and seemed to be much relieved to get away from the Borden house.

"The Government impressed her with the necessity of saying nothing about the proceedings at the Inquest, and she was warned not to talk with anyone regarding her testimony.

"At 6 o'clock, Miss Lizzie Borden, accompanied by her friend, Mrs. George Brigham, and Marshal Hilliard, entered a carriage and drove to Miss Borden's home. The excitement was over for the day, but the District Attorney's bulletin made it plain the authorities would make no further move that night.

"About 7 o'clock that evening, all the prominent officials in the case disappeared to get a little rest. District Attorney Knowlton went to the Mellen House, and Mr. Seaver went down to dine with Marshal Hilliard at his home on Durfee Street. The restless crowds went home to read the reports in the papers. By midnight, the city was quiet."

[The fact that Bridget was allowed to go her cousin's house, and to come and go as she pleased, was a huge sign that the prosecution found her credible and trustworthy. Lizzie and John Morse, however, were still within the walls of the Borden house, with armed policemen rimming the perimeter. Another aside is that Bridget was wearing "a green gown." It was stated by police the servant only had about 3 dresses when they searched her room. If she was in the habit of wearing the green dress when she was outside of work, could the green dye from the dress be the cause of her "frequent headaches?" The dye was made from arsenic, and known to be harmful, if not deadly, during that era.]

The Inquest, Day Two, Wednesday, August 10, 1892

The New York Times, Fall River, Ma., August 10, 1892— "The inquest was continued at 10 o'clock today. The witnesses examined were Lizzie Borden, John V. Morse, Emma L. Borden, Dr. S. W. Bowen, Adelaide B. Churchill, and Hiram C. Harrington. Adjourned until 10 a.m. Thursday; nothing developed for publication.

"This was all that was given out after examinations lasting more than four-and-a-half hours. The principal witness was Lizzie Borden. The change in Miss Borden's appearance after her examination was the chief topic of conversation in the police station tonight. Whatever the police may think of the strength of their clues, it is certain that the opinions of Miss Borden's many friends are entirely in favor of her innocence. This feeling is gaining more adherents every hour. **Dr. Bowen** told a straightforward story, covering the time since he was called to the Borden house a few days before the murder. He incidentally gave some evidence which startled the authorities. The nature of this will not be given for publication, but it was learned that tomorrow an examination of the dead bodies will be made at Oak Grove Cemetery."

Dr. Bowen's Inquest Testimony:

Dr. Seabury Bowen's testimony held few surprises from what has been attributed to him so far. He said only three things that may have "startled the authorities." 1) He said Lizzie told him her father had been "stabbed," when Bowen first arrived that morning. 2) He said he saw Lizzie going "up the street" Wednesday, when she was supposedly buying poison, and 3) he said his first instinct was Abby and Andrew "were killed the same instant." Any of these statements may have sent the Doctors and police to Oak Grove Cemetery Thursday for a full autopsy of the bodies.

John Vinnicum Morse's testimony that day was, to say the least, uncomfortable and confrontational. He answered Attorney Knowlton's questions without wavering, and made a credible witness, albeit losing his temper when he felt a trap closing in. Nothing differed from what he had stated all along as to his alibi that day: "I was at Daniel Emery's at #4 Weybosset Street from

9:30-11:30 a.m." The main portion of his testimony that carried no credibility was his stating he didn't notice any crowds around the house when he arrived shortly before noon.

John is articulate, and appears straightforward. He is not above lying, especially since a Bible was not proffered for an oath to be administered. He avoids, embellishes, and even produces a convenient letter from Andrew to back up his statements.

 ## John Morse's Discrepancies

1) He testifies that he first saw Andrew Borden the morning of the murders, when Mr. Borden came into the sitting room from the kitchen. Bridget said Mrs. Borden was the first down, and went into the sitting room, with Andrew following her "about ten minutes later."

2) John said he walked to the Emery's from the P.O., but his timeline doesn't match up. There is too much extra time left over, and his detailed description of each road he went down, and even stating that he left "the north door of the Post Office" caused suspicion to fall on him early in the case.

3) John lies about picking up his niece at the Warren station and taking her to see the Swansea farm; something that should have been harmless, but he needs to eliminate Swansea, and his dealings with it, altogether.

4) He lies about his intention to come back for the noon meal with Andrew that day. Mrs. Emery said Morse told her he was heading back to New Bedford after leaving her house at 11:30 (it changes to 11:20), but Bowen's message that Andrew is dead, changes his plans, and he heads over to the Borden's to look as if he is accepting Andrew's invitation to dinner, and innocently learns of the murders for the first time.

5) He is evasive about Andrew's will and bequests, and has to be coerced into answering the questions. [Covered earlier]

Emma Borden's testimony elicited much sympathy from the courtroom of men. She looked pale and aged. One newspaper unkindly compared she and Lizzie in appearance: "Lizzie looks a good ten years younger than her age, while her sister Emma looks a full ten years older than her own." Emma's heavy black dress hung on her, threatening to swallow her slender form. She gripped her closed fan and waited for Mr. Knowlton's inquiries.

An inadvertent picture of her sister Lizzie was painted in the minds of the listeners that morning. Without saying it, Emma's remarks showed a younger sister who was lazy, indulged, temperamental, and spoiled. Whenever housework was discussed, Emma tried to disguise that she did it all, when the tasks were supposedly shared by the sisters. She admitted Lizzie spent money freely: "My sister used to order a great many things from John M. Deane's." (Deane's store was in the Borden Block of Fall River, and was considered the best appointed general merchandise store in New England.)

Emma Borden
Courtesy of Stefani Koorey and *The Literary Hatchet*

Emma admitted she was on less cordial terms with Abby than Lizzie. Emma called Mrs. Borden, "Abby," while Lizzie addressed her as "Mrs. Borden," and less frequently, as "Abby."

Attorney Knowlton got her to admit it was the transfer of the Fourth Street house, five years earlier, into Abby's name, that began the major fissure in the household. At that time, Lizzie stopped calling Abby "Mother." Emma also let it slip what the nature of Lizzie and Uncle John Morse's relationship was really like. She said, "He is a very dear Uncle of ours...of mine."

Attorney Knowlton asks Emma if there was any conversation between herself and Bridget upon her arrival from Fairhaven the afternoon of the murders. "I asked her two questions," Emma said, "Would she stay with us, and I asked her if she saw any boy come with a note?" This last question is incredibly telling. Lizzie has told her sister a boy came with a note from a sick friend for Abby. Why is Emma doubting her and asking Bridget for details? Did Bridget wonder about Emma's question, as well?

Attorney Knowlton then asks the question everyone is waiting for:

Knowlton: "Did you see your sister then when you came home?"

Emma: "Yes, sir."

Knowlton: "What did she say about it?"

Emma: "I don't know, there was so much going on."

Knowlton: "I don't think I will trouble you with that question anyhow."

After only a handful of other questions, Mr. Knowlton pauses and looks across at the grieving lady before him. For all that has been said about the attorney in the papers, you cannot say Hosea Knowlton did not have a conscience, and a kind heart.

Knowlton: "I understand you are not feeling well?"

Emma: "No, sir. Not very well."

Knowlton: "So, I have omitted a great many questions I should have asked you on that account."

With that, Emma Borden was excused.

Cutting Away Pieces of the House

During a court recess on Wednesday, August 10th, Maurice Daly, a carpenter, was sent to the Borden house, about 1 o'clock, to remove samples of evidence from the interior. Marshal Hilliard, Detective Seaver, and Officer Harrington pointed out what was needed. Harrington stated "Mr. Daly cut away a marble slat from the west end of the dressing case, a piece of molding that capped the mop-board, and a piece of plaster, to which was adhered the wallpaper. Each of these articles had spots of blood on them." [From the guest room.]

Mrs. Charles Holmes was there, overseeing things while John, Emma, and Lizzie were at the courthouse. She may have been mortified to see the men cutting away pieces of the house. She asked them if they wanted the bedspread and pillow shams? The Marshal replied, "If you please." Harrington stated, "The articles were taken from the northwest room on the second floor, where Mrs. Borden was found. A piece of wood was taken from the west casing of the door which leads from the dining room to the sitting room where Mr. Borden was murdered. The piece of wood had a splatter of blood on it." They also took away a pair of lady's low tie shoes, and one pair of black stockings, which Lizzie wore on the day of the murders. Lizzie handed them to the Marshal upon being escorted home at the end of the Inquest that day. When asked upon the stand, if the stockings she wore the day of the murders had been washed, Lizzie had answered, "I don't know."

Officer Harrington said, "The men continued out to the barn, where they took one willow basket containing two pieces of round lead pipe, and a number of pieces of scrap sheet lead; and one wooden box in which were pieces of round and sheet lead. The basket and contents were found upstairs, and the box and its holdings, downstairs. Everything was brought to the station-house, and locked in the storeroom by Marshal Hilliard."

Officer Harrington then summoned Mrs. Churchill, Hiram C. Harrington, and Allen Eagan to appear in court at 4 p.m.

Mrs. Churchill's Inquest Testimony

Adelaide Churchill's testimony has been given throughout the book. The only statement that raises eyebrows is Mrs. Churchill reporting she arrived before Dr. Bowen, after going over to Hall's Stables to ask Thomas Bowles to find a doctor. Dr. Bowen stated he arrived *before* Mrs. Churchill, on her second visit to the house that morning. The significance of this is it gives Bowen time alone with Lizzie. Bridget and Alice Russell have not yet arrived. Mrs. Churchill's version was corroborated by Bridget's and Alice's testimony.

Mrs. Churchill's description of Lizzie's dress that morning is the most coherent. She described it as "light blue, gingham or calico, with a darker blue diamond figure." Lizzie said her dress was navy blue. The other witnesses describe the dress as light blue, other than the Bowen's. The odd thing is both Alice Russell and Adelaide Churchill say this is the first time they have seen this dress, yet they are frequently at the Borden house visiting the sisters. Did Lizzie have a dress made that would be long enough to conceal another dress beneath it, and loose in front?

Dr. Handy's Discontent

As the Inquest wrapped up for the day, Officers Harrington and Doherty were on the hunt for Dr. Handy. The police were still very much interested in the doctor's description of seeing a strange "exceedingly pale" man hanging out across from the Borden house the morning of the murders.

According to Officer Phillip Harrington's report, Dr. Handy was finally located: "I went in search of Dr. Handy; found him at Charles J. Holmes'. Asked him, would he accompany an officer to Boston to see a party whom the Boston police located, and who they thought resembled the person whom he saw. He said, "Well, I suppose I must go." I said, "No, there is nothing compulsory about the request." He did not seem to like the idea of going, and said, "It is a very warm night, and I have quite a number of cases on hand, from which I expect births, but then (laughing) I suppose they are as apt to come during the day as well as at night. Wait a minute and I'll see."

"He [Dr. Handy] then went to another part of the house, and talked with the Holmes family for a few minutes. He then returned to the parlor and said, "Well, I'll go. Who is going with me, is it you?" I told him I could not say. "Will the officer call my house, will he come in a carriage, or will we go to the depot in the horse car?" I said I did not know, but whichever way, the officer would be there in time.

"After arriving in Boston, we [Doherty and Harrington] called at Station 4, and learned something of, and the residence of, the man we sought. We then went to Police Headquarters [in Fall River], and after transacting my business there, we retired."

Officer Harrington's report on Dr. Handy continues the following morning of Thursday, August 11, 1892. This was the final day of the Inquest, and the tension was mounting to find any and all evidence concerning the case.

Officer Phil Harrington: "In the morning [Thursday] we [along with Dr. Handy] went again to Station 4, from whence a local officer accompanied us to No. 19 Oxford Street, the home of Henrick Wood, the man wanted. Mr. Wood was not at home; he had gone to Lexington in the morning to see a friend who was building a house near a lot owned by him. From the lady who came to the door, we got a description of Mr. Wood. She also showed us a photograph of him. She handed it to me, and I immediately turned it over to the Doctor, who before he had it rightly in his hand, pronounced him not the person. There were three persons on the card, two men and a child. The child was in Mr. Wood's arms. Owing to the position in which he sat, his face was very much shaded, which made it difficult for observation. This, together with fact that Dr. Handy so readily pronounced him not the man, is, to my mind, very significant. His social relations with Miss Lizzie are very close. She was to spend her vacation at Dr. Handy's cottage at Marion, with his daughter. He left Boston for home at 8:30 a.m."

Dr. Handy's Behavior.

Officers Harrington & Doherty find Dr. Handy with the Holmes. Mrs. Holmes has been at the Borden house each day since the murders, and has full access to John Morse. John admits talking to Charles Holmes a few days after the murders, and giving him the Grand Tour of the crime scene. Did John, as posited earlier in the book, hear of Dr. Handy's description of a short, pale man, agitatedly waiting out in front of the Borden home the day of the murders, and panic that his testimony would point to James Chatterton, and Morse's involvement in a clandestine scheme involving the Swansea farms? This would account for Dr. Handy needing to consult with the Holmes before he answered Harrington's request to go to Boston to identify a man. It also addresses why Handy so quickly negated recognizing the man in the photo. He needs to back away from him, as per John Morse's request.

Hiram Harrington was next called to the stand on that Wednesday afternoon. His story varied little from what was reported earlier in the book, concerning Lizzie's temperament, and the family relations within the Borden walls. Although he softened his words slightly for the Inquest, it was clear he was not a fan of Lizzie's. Since he was not involved the day of the murders, he had nothing to offer in way of evidence, other than to slaughter Lizzie's image. Attorney Knowlton did not spend much time with him.

Allen Eagan, who was summoned, does not appear in the Inquest testimony documents. It is probable the name Allen is a misprint. **Ellen Eagan**, was summoned, and she spent a scant three questions on the stand. Her testimony was that she was coming down Second Street on the morning of the murders and became ill. She had been experimenting with some pills to rectify an illness she had, and about the time she reached the Kelly property, the medicine rebelled. She dashed into the Kelly's bushes and vomited. Her appearance in court was in answer to Hyrum Lubinsky's claim that he saw a woman coming from the barn area of the Borden's yard at 10:30 the morning of the murders. It was quickly ascertained Mrs. Eagan was in the Kelly yard, not the Borden's, and was not the woman the ice cream peddler saw. Her testimony did not warrant making it into the court documents that day.

At the end of the day, once again, the crowd went away grumbling that no arrest had been made.

Day Three of the Inquest, Thursday, August 11, 1892

As Lizzie Borden left her house at 92 Second Street that Thursday morning, the last day of the Inquest, did she think she may not be returning home? The newspapers and rumor mills were rife with the notion an arrest was imminent; a sentiment the police may have fostered. As she walked through the sitting room to the front door that morning, in answer to Marshal Hilliard's bell, was the ghost of Andrew Borden's body, lying on a now absent sofa, playing through her mind? Or did she still feel the hangman's noose about her neck?

Edwin Porter with *The Fall River Globe* gave the following report concerning the events of the Inquest's final timeline:

"The same impenetrable secrecy was maintained all day long, and no one knew what progress was being made behind the grim stone walls of the Central Police Station where-in Judge Blaisdell and the chosen few sat in solemn conclave. The scenes of the day before were enacted in the guard room and the streets about the building. Crowds surged about the doors and a double guard of patrolmen were doing duty in the hallways. The forenoon session developed nothing so far, as the public was concerned. Eli Bence, the drug clerk, Fred Hart, another clerk, and Frank Kilroy, who saw Mr. Borden on the morning of the tragedy, strolled into the guard room and were shown upstairs.

"Later, Bridget Sullivan, escorted by two officers, walked up the alley. She attracted no attention, and appeared to be at her ease. The fact Bridget walked from her temporary residence at 95 Division Street to the police station, a distance of more than a mile in the heat of an August day, while other women witnesses rode in a hack from the Borden house, a distance of less than an eighth of a mile, caused some comment.

"At three o'clock in the afternoon, the closed carriage which had become almost as a familiar sight as the police patrol, rattled over the rough pavement. Half a dozen men were in sight, and in a twinkling, two hundred men, women and children, swarmed around the coach. The City Marshal gave an order, Steward Gegan cracked the whip, officers hustled the crowd back, and Mrs. George S. Brigham alighted. She was followed by Miss Emma and Miss Lizzie Borden.

"There was nothing remarkable in the appearance of the party, Miss Emma Borden being evidently the most agitated. The excitement grew as the hour passed, and there was no movement from the courtroom. In the meanwhile, information arrived that an expert safe opener had arrived from Boston, and had driven directly to the Borden house on Second Street. Investigation showed the truth of the story, and the further fact that he had commenced work upon the safe in which Andrew J. Borden kept his books and papers. The safe was found locked at the time of the tragedy, and the secret of the combination died with the murdered man. The expert believed he could easily open the safe, but he found the combination most intricate, and he worked away without apparent success.

"At 5 o'clock Marshal Hilliard and District Attorney Knowlton came from the courtroom and entered a carriage. Soon, the Marshal returned, but the District Attorney was absent for nearly an hour, and it was reported that he had visited the Borden house and had learned that the safe opener had not completed his work. Outside the courtroom, the stalwart officers kept guard, and at the foot of the stairs in the station house the large force of newspaper representatives were on guard. The subordinate officers who had been working upon the case, expressed their convictions that the long-delayed arrest was about to be made, and that Lizzie Borden would not depart from the station with the remaining members of the household.

"Soon, Bridget Sullivan emerged, and escorted by a police officer, walked slowly down the street. Soon, the inquisition was apparently ended, and then Lizzie Borden, her sister, and Mrs. Brigham were escorted across the entry from the courtroom to the matron's room, which is situated upon the same floor. Miss Lizzie Borden threw herself upon the lounge in the room, and the repast was disturbed but little."

Lizzie Borden is Arrested

As Lizzie waited once again, to be escorted back to her home, the wheels of justice were turning just across the hall from where she lay on the matron's lounge. After only ten minutes of consultation, the decision of the authorities was to arrest Lizzie Borden. The court clerk was called, and a warrant quickly was drawn. Reporters, suspicious, but not certain enough to call their papers with the scoop of a lifetime, hung around the hallways, pencils poised. The crowds outside sensed something was in the air, and the tension was palpable.

Marshal Hilliard and Attorney Knowlton soon departed the station. A call had been placed to Attorney Jennings that the two men were on their way to see him. Upon arriving at Lizzie's attorney's home on "the Hill," they informed Jennings a warrant had been made out for Lizzie's arrest. They told him they thought it preferable for him to be there as the warrant was read to her at the police station. The two men returned to the station, and Mr. Jennings arrived a few minutes later. George Brigham also came, perhaps to be there for his wife, who was in the room with Lizzie.

Marshal Hilliard and Detective Seaver entered the matron's room, and informed Lizzie she was to be held by the Government on the charge of murdering Andrew J. Borden. Oddly, the warrant was for Andrew only. They asked Mrs. Brigham to leave the room, and turned to Lizzie. In the gentlest possible manner, the Marshal said, "I have here a warrant for your arrest—issued by the Judge of the District Court. I shall read it to you if you desire, but you have the right to waive the reading of it?" Marshal Hilliard looked at Attorney Jennings, as he completed the latter part of the statement. Mr. Jennings turned to Lizzie and said, "Waive the reading."

Edwin Porter with the *Fall River Globe* gives this fascinating account of what happened next: "The first and only time during the scene the accused woman uttered a word was in response to the direction of her attorney. Turning slightly in her position, she flashed a look at the Marshal, one of those queer glances which nobody has attempted to describe, except by saying that they are a part and parcel of Lizzie Borden, and replied: "You need not read it."

"The information had a most depressing effect upon all the others present, particularly upon Miss Emma Borden, who was greatly affected. Upon the face of the prisoner there was a pallor, and while her eyes were moist with tears, there was little evidence of emotion in the almost stoic countenance. The remaining members of the party prepared to depart, and the effects of the arrest became apparent upon the prisoner. She still displayed all the characteristics of her peculiarly unemotional nature, and though almost prostrated, she did not shed a tear."

The New York Herald ran their version of the arrest, and added the following: "Lizzie did not say anything, and still paid no heed to what was going on about her. Emma Borden looked into her sister's face, and the tears began to roll down her face, but she did not say anything. Mr. Jennings addressed a few words of hope and comfort to his unfortunate client, and bade her goodbye. Emma Borden went with him. She did not kiss her sister or even bid her goodbye, but went crying downstairs and through the police guard room filled with curious people."

[That Emma would not hug, kiss, or tell her sister goodbye, may show that Lizzie had still not forgiven her for withholding the information in the newspapers concerning her guilt. Based on Lizzie's past behavior of not forgiving easily, Emma may still be considered unworthy of her love at this time, even though the break came on Saturday evening, five days prior. It would not be the last time Emma would feel Lizzie's wrath.]

The Fall River Herald reported "A carriage was ordered and Miss Emma Borden, and Mr. and Mrs. George Brigham, prepared to leave. As they emerged from the station into the view of the curious crowds, the women, particularly Miss Emma, looked about with almost a pathetic glance. The people crowded forward, and the police pushed them back. Miss Emma appeared to be suffering intensely. Mrs. Brigham was more composed, but was evidently deeply concerned. The parties entered the carriage and were driven rapidly towards Second Street."

Lizzie was left behind. Her first real indication of the gravity of the moment was when the matron informed her she must now be searched. The formalities of an arrest were administered, but Lizzie was not placed in a jail cell. According to *The New York Herald*, "The Chief stood and looked at her, after the serving of the warrant, he concluded that a cell was no place for a human being so crushed and broken. He gave orders instead that she should occupy the matron's sleeping room, a large, well-furnished apartment on the second floor."

Lizzie Borden's arrest paper contains the following information:

> Born: June 9, 1860 [It should read July 19, 1860] Name: Lizzie A. Borden. Age: 32. Female. Height: 5'4". Parents: daughter of Andrew J. Borden. Complexion: Light. Hair: Light. Eyes: Gray. Born in Fall River. Occupation: at home with parents. Charge: Murder of Father and Stepmother. Officer Making Arrest: R. B. Hilliard. Disposition of the Case: Ordered Committed to await action.

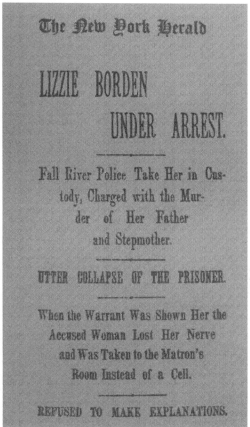

The New York Herald's headline August 11, 1892. The news of
Lizzie Borden's arrest would make headlines around the world.

No sooner had Matron Russell secured her bedding, than Lizzie
fell apart. She broke down and cried as though her heart would
break. The sobbing soon gave way to fits of violent vomiting. The
matron tried, without success to help her, and finally, in
desperation, Dr. Bowen was called. He was, by now, familiar with
Lizzie's emotional lapses, when her steady veneer peeled away to
reveal a woman dominated by her nervous conditions and mood
swings. He gave her a sedative and remained long enough to see
her quiet. Dr. Bowen left behind him an exhausted Lizzie Borden.
The sound of the matron's room door being securely locked was
the last sound Lizzie heard as the warm, fuzzy haze of morphine
overtook her. It was one week to the day that a hatchet had
dispatched Abby and Andrew Borden.

Chapter Twenty-Eight

Behind Bars

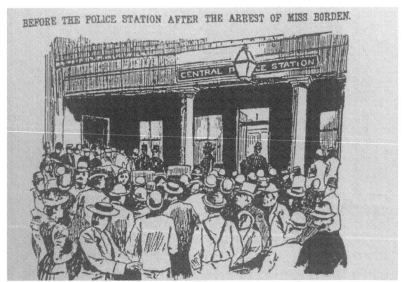

The New York Herald's, August 13, 1892, illustration of the crowds at the police station after the announcement of Lizzie's arrest.

The Final Autopsy

As the town reeled from the news Lizzie Borden was arrested for the murder of Andrew Borden, the dead man's remains were being, once again laid open, in the Lady's Comfort Chamber at the Oak Grove Cemetery. He and Abby were subjected to the ubiquitous "Y" incision, which cut them open from the collar bone down to the "pubis." Doctors Dolan, Cone, Leary, and Medical

Examiner Draper of Boston, worked over the couple in minute detail.

Ladies' Comfort Chamber at Oak Grove Cemetery where the autopsies were performed. Photo courtesy of Shelley Dziedzic & FriendsofOakGroveCemetery.org.

It was a gruesome job. The bodies had not been embalmed, and their decomposition was "much advanced." Abby's head was shaved to get a better look at her wounds. It was shocking to see the number of haphazard cuts that seemed to go in every direction. This was a frenzied attack. To their surprise, a wound appeared on her back, between the shoulder blades. It was an extremely deep cut, showing the hatchet blade would have buried under her skin almost to the helve. It alone would have produced instant death.

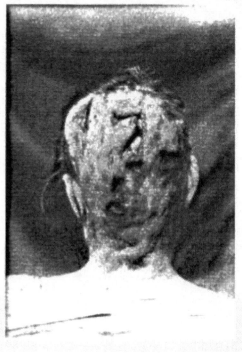

James Walsh's photo of Abby Borden's head during the autopsy
at Oak Grove Cemetery, August 11, 1892.

The doctors conferred over the Borden's bodies, and decided the heads would need to be removed in order to study the skulls, and possibly retained for court evidence. Dr. Dolan took possession of the two heads, taking them home, where their skin and hair was removed, and the skulls boiled. The white skulls were then photographed.

The Arraignment
Friday, August 12, 1892

Lizzie Borden was arraigned in the Second District Court of Fall River, Massachusetts, the morning following her arrest, on Friday, August, 12, 1892. A crowd was already assembled outside the courthouse by 9 o'clock, despite a drenching rain. A few minutes later, a hack arrived carrying Emma Borden and John Morse who alighted and entered the police station. Upon reaching the matron's room at the top of the stairs, they were told they could not enter to see Lizzie. She was in conversation with the Reverend E. A. Buck—a gentleman who would become a fixture on her arm; as ever present as a woman's handbag.

Judge Blaisdell climbed the stairs, and passing Emma, entered the courtroom where Attorney Knowlton was already in attendance. Marshal Hilliard entered next, carrying with him his big book of complaints. In the meantime, the door to Lizzie's room was opened and Emma, John Morse, and Mr. Jennings entered, to spend a few minutes in consultation with "the prisoner." Mr. Jennings left and hurried across the hall to the courtroom, where he asked for a blank sheet of paper. As he quickly wrote across the page, the Marshal approached him and asked if Lizzie was ready. Mr. Jennings nodded, and continued to write.

Edwin Porter with the *Fall River Daily Globe* gave the following account: "Lizzie Borden entered the room on the arm of Rev. Buck. She was dressed in a dark blue suit and her hat was black with red flowers on the front. She was escorted to a chair. The prisoner was not crying, but her features were far from firm. She has a face and chin betokening strength of character, but a rather sensitive mouth, and on this occasion, the sensitiveness of the lips especially betrayed itself. She was constantly moving her lips as she sat in the courtroom in a way to show that she was not altogether unemotional. Clerk Leonard called the case of the Commonwealth of Massachusetts against Lizzie Borden, on the complaint of murder. Mr. Jennings, who was still writing, asked for a little more time. He soon arose and went over to the prisoner. He spoke to her, and then gave her a pen. She signed the paper.

"Mr. Jennings then addressed the court saying: "Your Honor, before the prisoner pleads, she wishes to present the following."

He then read as follows:

"Bristol Second District Court. Commonwealth vs. Lizzie A. Borden. Complaint for homicide. Defendant's plea.

"And now comes the defendant in the above-entitled complaint and before pleading thereto say that the Hon. Josiah C. Blaisdell, the presiding Justice of the Second District Court of Bristol, before which said complaint is returnable, has been and believes is still engaged as the presiding magistrate at an inquest upon the death of said Andrew J. Borden, the person whom it is alleged in said complaint the defendant killed, and has received and heard and is still engaged in receiving and hearing evidence in relation to said killing and to said defendant's connection therewith which is not and has not been allowed to hear or know the report of, whereof she says that said Hon. Josiah C. Blaisdell is disqualified to hear this complaint, and she objects to his so doing, and all of this she is ready to verify.

Lizzie A. Borden, by her attorney, Andrew J. Jennings, (Her signature) Lizzie A. Borden. Sworn to this the 12th day of August, A.D. 1892, before me, Andrew J. Jennings, Justice of the Peace."

When Mr. Jennings concluded, Attorney Knowlton rose and asked the Court if this paper was to delay the prisoner's plea. The Court said it was not to, and ordered the Clerk to read the warrant.

"You needn't read it," said Mr. Jennings, "the prisoner pleads not guilty."

"The prisoner must plead in person," said Judge Blaisdell. At a sign from City Marshal Hilliard, the prisoner arose in her seat.

"What is your plea?" asked the Clerk.

"Not guilty," Lizzie said in a low voice. The Court did not hear her and she was asked the question again. In a loud voice, Lizzie said, "Not guilty," with a clear emphasis on the word "Not."

Mr. Jennings then arose and accosted the Judge with the unfairness to which his client had been treated. She had been denied counsel during the Inquest, even though for all intents and purposes she was under arrest at the time. He went on to say that the Judge should recuse himself from any further participation in an upcoming Preliminary Hearing, as there was no way he would not be prejudiced after hearing all the evidence presented at the Inquest.

"By all the laws of human nature, you cannot help but be prejudiced from the character of the evidence which has been submitted to you. The constitution does not allow a Judge to sit in such a double capacity and it guarantees a defendant from a prejudiced hearing."

After hearing Mr. Knowlton's negation of Mr. Jennings' claims, the Judge agreed with the D.A. and said, "I think Mr. Jennings is mistaken. The statutes make it my imperative duty to hold an inquest and upon the testimony introduced at that hearing, to direct the issuance of warrants. The motion is overruled and the demurrer sustained."

"Then your Honor," Mr. Jennings declared, "we are ready for trial."

Attorney Knowlton blanched. "The evidence in this case could not be completed at once. It could hardly all be gathered by next week," he said. He moved for a continuance until one week from Monday, August 22, at 2 o'clock, when the State hoped to be entirely ready with the case.

"We are very anxious to proceed at once," Mr. Jennings said. "We ask for a trial at the earliest possible moment."

"I didn't know but what you would waive examination here, so I am not ready now," Knowlton said flatly.

It was finally agreed the Preliminary Hearing would take place in the same courtroom, August 22.

Attorney Knowlton immediately moved the prisoner be committed until that date. Judge Blaisdell agreed, as the defense was not a bailable one. But Mr. Knowlton was not finished. He looked at the back of the room where Bridget Sullivan and John Morse were seated. He told the Judge the importance of Mr. Morse and Miss Sullivan to the case of the State was so great that he wished to move that they be placed under bonds to guarantee their presence inside the Court's jurisdiction. Judge Blaisdell said he would grant the request, and asked how much the bonds should be.

"Three hundred dollars is the usual amount," Mr. Knowlton said, "but on account of the gravity of this case, I suggest the amount be $500. Mr. Morse can procure bail, we suppose, but we don't know about Bridget Sullivan."

Bridget had gone pale. It was obvious she did not know what was happening. They were both read the Order of the Court. Mr. Jennings dispatched one of his Notary Publics to go downtown and return with a bondsman. As Bridget and Morse waited, Lizzie was allowed to return to the matron's room, on the arm of Rev. Buck.

John Morse obtained bail from Mr. Almy and Mr. Milne with the *Fall River Daily News*. He soon left the building with Emma, who had spent twenty minutes in the matron's room with her sister, and the Reverend. Morse and Emma threaded their way through the huge crowd, and took a carriage home. Bridget was finally released, and with great relief stepped out of the police station into the rain, to walk to her cousin's home on Division Street.

Over at the Borden house, John A. Maier, a mechanic from the Diebold Safe Company, of No. 72 Sudbury Street, was still struggling with the combination of Andrew Borden's old safe. Officer Harrington watched him anxiously as the day wore on. Finally, the tumblers fell into place and the door was swung open. As Officer Harrington looked on, the contents were pulled out. "Inside was a small amount of cash and some few papers...bundled and tied with strong cord." No will was found. The motive for Lizzie Borden's guilt had just gone up in smoke.

1890s cast iron combination safe.

According to the initial probate, which the sister's filed shortly after Andrew's death, Mr. Borden died intestate. He left real estate valued at $8,190, and a personal estate valued at $13,408.04. Why this record falls far short of listing Andrew's true worth is a mystery. The Fall River accessor's books showed a total valuation of local real estate at $173,650, and a personal estate between $175,000 and $250,000. It was accepted locally that Andrew Borden left an estate valued at near $500,000, a staggering amount in 1892. In 2016, it's the equivalent of nearly $14 million dollars.

Lizzie Borden remained in the matron's room as her family and friends departed. Men's voices were always prevalent outside the door, as she heard the police coming and going about their business. There would be occasional bouts of laughter, which angered her. Her life had just changed forever, and she was going to jail. There should be no laughter. Her lips worked nervously as she tried to picture what lay ahead. *What did a jail cell look like? How long would she be held there? Perhaps they would realize it was a big mistake and let her go home. This wasn't supposed to happen to her. She had always managed to worm her way free of complications.* As the noise of a police station surrounded her, all she could do was to await transportation to the County Jail in Taunton.

Off to Jail

Matron Russell helped Lizzie prepare for her transfer. Lizzie looked at her with those cat-shaped grey eyes, and said, "So, they are going to take me to Taunton, are they?"

"I believe they are," replied Mrs. Russell.

"Well," Lizzie said, a touch of the old haughtiness in her voice, "they seem to do about as they please with me. They were up to my house, and brought me down here—to the inquest, twice, and then they brought me here for a rest, and I did not know what it all meant. Now, they are going to take me to jail. They are having their own way with me now, but I will have mine, by and by."

The strong-willed woman, who could not tolerate a hand in her face, is seen plainly in those words. It is as if it is incomprehensible to her that she be treated this way—murder suspect, or not.

Reverend Buck, once again visited Lizzie, in the matron's room at the Central Police Station, as she waited to be taken to Taunton jail on the 3:40 train. He brought her a bouquet of flowers, which she displayed in her window sill.

As the time arrived for Lizzie's departure from the Police Station, Court Square was once again choked with people. A carriage drew up to the main entrance and Emma Borden, and Andrew Jennings climbed in. Lizzie's carriage was waiting at the side entrance. She stepped inside, quickly flanked by Marshal Hilliard, State Detective Seaver, and Reverend Buck. A small valise of her belongings sat beside her. She appeared calm and resolute.

The Boston Adviser's illustration of Lizzie leaving for jail, escorted by Reverend Buck and Marshal Hilliard.

The route taken to the train station was instigated to outrun the press, and deny the curious a glimpse of the prisoner. Instead of the straight route from the station to the Bowenville depot, the carriage turned up one road, then down another, through side streets and thoroughfares, skirting the river. It was, alas, for naught. As Lizzie's buggy neared the depot, a crush of people could be seen, along with the tenacious press. There was a squad of officers there on duty, and as the crowd surged, the police pushed back.

The Fall River Herald reported "The train for Taunton was a few minutes late, and until its arrival, Lizzie Borden and Mr. Buck remained in the carriage. As the clang of the engine bell was heard, the Marshal pulled up the carriage curtains and assisted Lizzie Borden to alight. She was prettily dressed and appeared quite prepossessing. She wore a blue dress of new design, and a short blue veil. At the realization that the moment for departure had arrived, she was overcome by a momentary weakness, and almost tottered. She was at once supported by the Marshal and Mr. Buck, and leaning upon the arms of the two, she walked through the ladies' waiting room and towards the cars.

"The eager crowd pushed and stared and gossiped as the party entered the rear car of the train. Rev. Buck carried a box containing a number of religious, and other papers, and magazines, and also some books. A telescope bag containing Miss Borden's apparel was placed in the cars. The prisoner sat near the window in a seat with Mr. Buck, and behind them was Mr. Hilliard. The blinds were drawn in order to prevent annoyance to Miss Borden by curious persons. Her glance was vacant and her thoughts were manifestly removed from her present surroundings. Not a word was exchanged between the members of the party, and the prisoner still remained in the same position, staring at nothing. In some manner, the information that Miss Borden was on the train spread, and at a few stations at which it stopped, small knots of inquisitive people were gathered."

At 4:20, the train from Fall River bearing the most famous prisoner in New England history, pulled into the Taunton station. Hundreds of people crowded around each car. Officer Seaver, who was acting as a decoy, hurried to the north end of the station, and the crowd quickly followed. Marshal Hilliard and Rev. Buck assisted Lizzie from the south end of the depot and into a waiting carriage. By the time the disappointed crowd caught on, the buggy was racing toward the Taunton jail, with hacks full of newspaper reporters in hot pursuit.

The sight of her final destination may have somewhat cheered Lizzie. This was not the austere, grey, and foreboding façade of the Central Police Station. Rather, the Taunton Jail was a picturesque stone building, not far removed from the city, with a profusion of ivy growing, and lovely gardens. There were accommodations for sixty-five prisoners, with the women's department housing nine cells; five of which were occupied.

Marshal Hilliard accompanied Lizzie into the corridor and left her for a moment with Rev. Buck, while he turned over the paperwork to Sheriff Wright, the jail keeper. The Reverend offered Lizzie words of cheer, later stating she did not look surprised at the sight of her jail cell, feeling she would be vindicated soon. The Marshal and Rev. Buck departed, leaving Lizzie in the care of the Sheriff's wife. Lizzie looked around her small room which measured nine by seven feet. It contained a bedstead, chair and washbowl. Lizzie requested that none of the daily newspapers be brought in to her.

As Matron Wright helped Lizzie adjust to her new surroundings, she thought she saw something familiar about her eyes and countenance. After several questions, Mrs. Wright asked, "Are you not the Lizzie Borden who used as a child to play with my daughter Isabel?" Lizzie remembered the Wrights as neighbors in Fall River from many years ago, when Mr. Wright held the position of City Marshal. She answered that she was. The matron left the cell with tears in her eyes.

Lizzie Borden in her cell, illustration by
The New York Herald, August, 13, 1892.

The afternoon drew to a close. Lizzie was told she could have visitors, her own bedding from home, and food brought in, or purchased from wherever she wanted. Subsequently, many of her meals were brought in from the City Hotel, a privilege that quickly found its way into the newspaper. An article printed on August 29, 1892, by the *Fall River Daily Globe* was headlined: *"Money Does Wonders/Lizzie Borden Allowed Too Many Privileges by the Police."*

Another article from the *Taunton Daily Gazette,* on August 13, 1892, read "Scores of curious people have walked by the jail today to see where Miss Borden is held. They saw a neat, ivy-clad building, that was all."

The Taunton Jail in Taunton, Massachusetts, 1892.
Photos courtesy of the Fall River Historical Society/*Parallel Lives*.

Taunton Jail with Porte Cochere. Courtesy Fall River Historical Society.

Lizzie Reaches Out Through the Bars

Lizzie's first night within the whitewashed walls of the Taunton Jail may have been bittersweet. The enormity of what she was facing was now a very real thing. All her cunning and planning had not fooled the police. Mr. Jennings assured her repeatedly that the prosecution had no evidence that would convict her—they had simply been unable to run down anyone else to pin it on.

The blessing the confinement brought was a sudden respite from the people who surrounded her life from the morning she called Bridget downstairs and sent her for Dr. Bowen. The crowds had been relentless; peering up at her windows, asking for interviews, shouting at her from the streets. The police had ransacked her room on numerous occasions, and looked through her personal toiletries and undergarments. Her life had been put on display. But, here, with the impenetrable bars and protection of the jail keeper, she was safe. No one could get at her here, without her consent. Oddly, it was a small sense of control in a situation designed to remove it from her.

Lizzie declined all interviews. She did, however, cleverly get her declaration of innocence into the papers, via her friends.

The Fall River Herald printed an interview with Mrs. George Brigham, the friend who had accompanied Lizzie to the Inquest, under the heading "**Miss Borden's Friend**." The timely release of this interview was only a few days before the Preliminary Hearing was to start. You can hear Lizzie's version of events clearly through her friend, Mrs. Brigham's words:

"I wish you would stamp a lie the allegation that Lizzie was not happy with her father and mother—her stepmother I mean," Mrs. Brigham said. "She has told me many times that these latter years have been her happiest. The story that she would not sit at the table with her father is a falsehood of the blackest sort.

"It has been said that Mr. Borden was angry with and did not speak to Lizzie upon her return from Europe. That, too is a falsehood, distorted out of facts that were as contrary to the statement as could be. On the night Lizzie arrived, the family had given her up and Mr. and Mrs. Borden had gone to bed. Lizzie was very tired and only spoke a few words to Emma that night and retired. The next morning Mr. Borden found her steamer chair in the hall and bounded upstairs three at a time to see and greet her, and Lizzie told me her hand ached all day he pressed it so hard. Going downtown, he met a man who said to him, "Well, I would guess that someone had come home judging from your bright face this morning."

"Mr. Borden was, as they say, not a demonstrative man, but he loved his daughters and showed it at such times when they came back after being away. He did not like them being away from home. I could give you very many illustrations of this, showing Lizzie's kind consideration for her father and he for her. For instance, both the girls would have much preferred to live in this part of town to where they did [the "Hill"], and often expressed the wish of course, but said that it was better for their father, more convenient to live where they did, as it was near his business interests, and so they did not urge it. On the other hand, the father knowing the wish, told them only a short time ago to look for a house in this neighborhood.

"Now as to Mrs. Borden. While she was a very good woman, she was not at all affectionate or calculated to draw the children to her. She was simply mild and good, and so long as things went smoothly she would have very little to say about the house. So, that should not be taken as proof of any bitterness of feeling between them, for there was none. Lizzie Borden was a kind and generous girl—very generous—who would do anything in the world for anyone she thought much of. Whenever there were subscriptions to be made up she contributed liberally, and I have seen her assume debts at the church all by herself. These stories of her being skimped for money are equally false with the others. While her income was scarcely in keeping with the wealth of her father, she had more money than she needed. She had the best clothes, her room was fitted luxuriously as a parlor and bedroom, and she bought books by the set rather than the volume.

"Now let me tell you about the arrangement for her outing to Marion just previous to the tragedy. I was invited to be of that party, and like her I could not go with those who went first, although the fact that she couldn't have been spoken of as so singular. She couldn't go because her father and mother were going to Swansey [ms]. Her mother was depending upon a certain companion, as Mr. Borden spent so much time in town that she would not remain over there alone. They found they couldn't get the woman and so gave up the idea, and Mrs. Borden told Lizzie to go on with her plans. Previous to this, Lizzie had promised to act as a substitute for the secretary of the Christian Endeavor Society at its meeting on Sunday—it was an important consecration and business meeting. Had it not been for this she would have gone to Marion on Saturday, but she would not break her word. It was early in the week when her mother told her she might go on with her plans, and she determined to visit her mother's cousin, Mrs. Morse, at Warren, for a couple of days, and wrote to that effect. She was taken violently ill on Tuesday morning, and Wednesday morning, not feeling well enough, she wrote to Mrs. Morse that she could not come.

"And as to insanity? There has never been a trace of it about her. She was a girl of very even temper. She never became excited. She had ideas, spoke them quietly and clearly. She could not be insane for the instant of committing the murder, and then return to her own normal self instantly—and after each of the two murders, for I think Mrs. Borden was murdered first, as do the others.

"Her conduct since the murder has been just what anyone would expect. They speak of her dry eyes. Is it not all too awful to cry about? We might weep, as all of us have, for the death of Mr. and Mrs. Borden, but this, this is too terrible; even I cannot weep in the face of it. Her pride was touched at the first sign of suspicion being directed against her, and the horror of it has kept her as she is."

When Mrs. Brigham was asked during the interview, "Can you tell me how the murders might have been committed?" you get the feeling the reporter had an inkling that Mrs. Brigham's words were actually coming from Lizzie's mouth, and that perhaps he might hit pay dirt with this question.

"I do not wish to add to the many theories which have been discussed," Mrs. Brigham said, but then goes on in what can only be Lizzie's version of an intruder, "but I know that Lizzie herself has often spoken to her mother about the arrangement of the rooms and halls of the house, and how anyone might come in and go all over the house without anyone knowing it. Members of the family have often done so and spoken of it. The house is a very solid old building, and any noise or jar is not easily heard. A man could have entered by the cellar way or the side door, gone upstairs and killed Mrs. Borden, and afterward gone down and hidden in the parlor, which was rarely entered by any of the family. From there he could see anyone in the sitting room and, taking the opportunity, have killed Mr. Borden and passed out either by the cellar way of (which would have been easier) turned the spring latch and walked out of the front door and down the street, as would a caller to the house.

The reporter asks, "Knowing the family and its history as you do, have you no theory as to who committed this murder?" [He has already asked Mrs. Brigham twice if Lizzie suspects anyone. Here, he may be again looking for Lizzie's insights through her friend's words, and he finds them.]

"No, I have not," Mrs. Brigham said. "Mr. Borden was a man who spoke his mind very freely to anyone, and if they attempted to reply, he would shut his teeth and walk away. Of course, he had enemies, but none that I could suspect of such a deed."

Mrs. Brigham Makes Lizzie Case

1) Lizzie's affection for her father, and his for her. That the girls sacrificed their wishes to live in a more desirable neighborhood for his convenience. He told them to start looking for a house on "the Hill," which plays nicely into Lizzie's intent for the near future.

2) Abby was not affectionate to the girls. There was no bitterness, just a quiet co-existence.

3) Lizzie was generous and had her own money, showing she was kind and money was not a motive. The interesting phrase here is: "Lizzie Borden was a kind and generous girl—very generous—who would do anything in the world for anyone she thought much of." Who Lizzie "thought much of" was the elite society she courted, with her money and time.

4) Lizzie's entire alibi for not going to Marion, and being home the day of the murders, is laid out in detail; details Mrs. Brigham could have only gotten from Lizzie.

5) The case for insanity has been brought up. Lizzie slips in an argument for that as well, through her friend.

6) The papers have made much of not seeing Lizzie cry. Her faithful friend covers for her by saying she hasn't cried either, because the deaths "were so horrible."

7) Lizzie puts forth her theory of an intruder hiding in the parlor, the strange layout of the house, even the spring latch (although all 3 locks were found bolted). This is clearly inside information from a woman who lives there.

8) Mr. Borden has an enemy—Lizzie's story all along.

This amazing interview is a window into Lizzie's mind. She continues to manipulate, even when confined to a jail cell. Her dear friend, and constant supporter, Reverend Jubb, also manages to get her words out, as another strike against Lizzie needing to kill her father for money:

The Fall River Herald, a few days before the Preliminary Hearing—Reverend Jubb: "Lizzie was very fond of her father. She asks why don't they go to the bank and find out just how much ready cash she has to her credit? That would dispose of the question of money. They said that her father would not give her what money she wanted to take a vacation. What folly! She wanted to go to Marion for a few days. How much do you suppose she would need for that, and is it reasonable that with the pleasures of the holiday in her thoughts, she would turn to thinking of murder?"

Lizzie's Money & Vacation

This is a brilliant move! Lizzie cashed in bonds, and sold back the Fourth Street house to her father only two weeks before his murder; much of the money in her account was from those transactions. She claimed to have $10,000 in the bank.

The vacation she mentions (through Rev. Jubb) was not the trip to Marion, but her Grand Tour of Europe two years earlier. Rumors had it that Lizzie wired home twice for more money for the trip, as she made her way through the elegant cities. Mrs. Brigham hints at this in her letter in the preceding section, where she negates that Andrew was mad with Lizzie upon her return from Europe. Instead, we see this over-the-top description of his pressing Lizzie's hand so hard "it ached for days," and an unnamed man commenting on how happy Andrew was to have her back.

Emma, ever faithful, puts the final spin on Lizzie's innocence through one or her rare interviews with the press.

New Bedford Daily Mercury, Saturday, August 13, 1892—"Emma Borden made the following statement at the conclusion of the Inquest: "I believe firmly in my sister's innocence. She will have my full support and cooperation, because I am certain she deserves it. The blow has been terrible for me to bear, but I cannot help it. My resources will be at her command."

Emma Borden was put in charge of Andrew's vast wealth, as Lizzie was legally not able to touch it. She paid half of her younger sister's legal expenses, which was formidable. Not only were there the costs of the imprisonment charges, but the fees of the myriad attorneys representing Lizzie were staggering. The former Governor of Massachusetts, George D. Robinson, would take the helm for Lizzie's defense during the Superior Court trial.

Emma Waits

As Lizzie waited out the ten days before the Preliminary Hearing began, sequestered away from the burdens of the press, and the handling of the Borden home, Emma Borden was not so fortunate. Lizzie spent her days reading, or visiting. Mrs. Wright even brought in a rocking chair, stool and feather pillow for Lizzie's comfort. Fresh flowers and a bowl of fruit decorated her room.

Emma's days were quite different. The crowds, although diminished, still milled about the house. The police guard had been removed, once Lizzie was jailed. John Morse was still in residence, unable to leave town due to his bond. The two of them had hired two servants. Emma often cooked for Lizzie and spent long hours with her sister in Taunton.

92 Second Street was an area attraction. Small boys dared each other to touch the siding, or enter the yard. Now that the police guard was gone, the curious came closer, peering into windows and searching for clues in the backyard, usually under the cover of darkness. Emma's nerves were forever on edge, worrying someone would break into the house.

Her fears were confirmed on September 20, 1892, when she was forced to call the police station. Officer Chase filed the following report: "I, this day, visited the Borden house under instructions from the City Marshal. I saw Miss Emma Borden, and she went down cellar with me, and showed me a window in the northeast corner room, nearest to the barn, and next north of the cellar door, which she wanted to have fastened up, and wanted me to note the condition that it was in before anything was done. I found one light of glass broke in the upper sash, the lower sash bad, the appearance of being pushed in, and raised up about five inches."

What comfort John Morse was to Emma, we don't know. A home that once contained a father, stepmother, sister and Bridget, was now down to herself, her Uncle John (a reluctant houseguest), and two strangers she had hired to help with the house. The memories of her former life were in each piece of furniture and small item of décor. One item of furniture refused to relinquish its memory of that tragic day. The calendar dial on the large grandfather clock had mysteriously stopped on the day of the murders, something the omnipresent newspapers reported:

Fall River Evening News, August 9, 1892— "A singular coincidence in the connection with the Borden murders is that the calendar, painted on the old-fashioned clock, at the residence on Second Street, stopped on the fourth, the date of the murders, and still points to that date. The other works of the clock are not impaired, but tick off the minutes and hours with usual regularity."

Chapter Twenty-Nine

The Preliminary Hearing

In the days leading up to the Preliminary Hearing, the newspapers filled their pages with whatever fodder they could find. Fall River was forced to content itself with a recapping of the Borden murders, theories, police running down leads, and a few scant offerings of Lizzie's days in the Taunton Jail. The public, both on, and below, "the Hill," were running out of breakfast conversation. Anticipation was building as each day brought them closer to the sensationalism that would, temporarily, lift them from their boring routines.

Interestingly, the psychics and clairvoyants took advantage of the lull to spring forth in full force. Attorney Knowlton, the Marshal, and Attorney Jennings, were besieged with letters from those "gifted with special powers." These purveyors of the ether world, using Ouija boards, cards, and telepathy, claimed they had received messages from the departed Borden's, particularly, Andrew. Clues as to where the bloody hatchet could be found and who the murderer was, were sent in; many requesting a monetary reward should their revelations bear fruit.

Meanwhile, in the real world, an important hearing in the Borden case was about to take place. In Massachusetts, a preliminary trial, or hearing, was held in a District, or lower, court of the state. Its purpose was to determine if there was probable cause for charging a defendant with a crime which is beyond the jurisdiction of the District Court. Today, it is called "a probable cause" hearing. Serious crimes had to be heard by the Superior Court, and murder was a serious crime. Therefore, Judge Blaisdell, through a Preliminary Hearing, had to determine whether there was sufficient evidence to judge Lizzie Borden "probably guilty" of the murder of her father, Andrew J. Borden.

A Preliminary Hearing also allows a defendant the opportunity to hear the evidence against them. This is called "discovery." Unlike a Grand Jury examination, the defendant has the right to be present at a Preliminary Hearing, and her counsel is allowed to cross-examine the prosecution's witnesses.

The New York Times, on August 15, 1892, gave the public a taste of what was to come. "City Marshal Hilliard said today "This case will depend on circumstantial evidence wholly, and the people's interest cannot be served by throwing the evidence into the hands of the defense until a hearing of the trial takes place. The District Attorney and myself are satisfied that the public authorities have ample cause for the holding of Miss Borden, and she has not been imprisoned in haste nor without a full understanding of what her arrest meant."

"The Marshal's statement has given rise to much speculation as to the character of the evidence that the prosecution submits at the trial. The preliminary trial is not now regarded as of special importance in fixing the responsibility for the crime, except that it gives the defense an opportunity to measure the strength of the Government's case. It is an even chance that the verdict will be "probably guilty." If the verdict should be "probably not guilty," the Government could still insist on placing the case before the Grand Jury, and demand an indictment over a discharge ordered by the lower court.

"A great deal is being published in connection with the case about the Borden family honor. On this point the most important member of the Borden family said for publication this morning: "The honor of the Borden's, whose names are so closely allied with the prosperity of the town, is not to be affected by a police suspicion perhaps resting justly on Miss Lizzie Borden. No true Borden has ever placed a stumbling block in the way of the law and no member of my family will in any way hamper the police in their investigation."

And with that, the prestigious Borden clan shut their door firmly in Lizzie's face. The sentiment portrayed by the words "suspicion perhaps resting justly on Miss Lizzie Borden" and "no true Borden has ever placed a stumbling block in the way of the law," was patently designed to put distance between the "true Borden's" and the woman who had tarnished the Fall River founding fathers' name.

Andrew Jennings felt the weight of the burden placed upon his shoulders by Andrew J. Borden's youngest daughter. It was a strange position in which to be. Mr. Borden had been Jennings' client for a good many years. He was privy to Andrew Borden's personal, as well as commercial concerns, whenever legalities were involved. That he would be defending his friend's daughter from the charge that she had brutally murdered him with a hatchet, was a very surreal event. His heart went out to Emma Borden, particularly. She suffered greatly beneath the strain.

Mr. Jennings, feeling perhaps his legal expertise was not quite up to a murder trial, called in Melvin O. Adams as co-counsel. Colonel Adams was from Boston, and a former District Attorney of Suffolk County, Massachusetts. Adams was a no-nonsense attorney who was not inclined to suffer fools gladly. He instigated more than one sparring contest as the hearing progressed.

Lizzie's Back in Town!

As if Ringling Brothers had rung the bell, the crowds headed for Court Square on August 22. Lizzie arrived from Taunton, on the 11 o'clock train to her hometown amid the same fanfare as when she left. She was dressed in the same blue dress she wore ten days earlier when she was transferred north. The papers were uncharacteristically quiet regarding her refusal to be seen in the traditional black mourning; typically worn for a year after a loved one died. With her usual iron-clad will to do as she pleased, she flaunted her independence, even when a show of sensitivity toward her father's death would have served her better in the public's opinion, and perhaps, the judge's.

Once again, Lizzie was taken to the matron's room at the Central Police Station. She was put in the charge of Matron Reagan. The jail lacked suitable amenities for Lizzie, so she claimed her place on the lounge within the locked room, and waited.

The continual hum of voices floated to Lizzie, as three hundred people made their way into the courtroom. Unlike the Inquest, the hearing was open to the public, and the crush of people trying to obtain a seat that day was akin to a riot. Many were well-dressed women carrying picnic baskets and knitting bags. That a woman was on trial for a heinous murder did not dim the carnival atmosphere filling the room, along with a flurry of skirts. Makeshift tables had been brought in for the nearly 50 reporters who were forced to share chairs in the small room. Gloved hands fluttered fans continually as the 80-degree heat, aided by a healthy dose of humidity, caused the courtroom to feel like a day on the African veldt.

At 2 o'clock, Judge Blaisdell arrived and took his seat. He did not look pleased to see the picnic baskets, and general air of frivolity. Twenty minutes went by. The heated crowd squirmed in their seats. The door opened and three hundred faces turned to see Lizzie Borden enter the room. But, it was not Lizzie. Attorney Jennings walked in, looking none too happy. Colonel Melvin Adams was right behind him. They entered the Judge's chambers where Attorney Knowlton was waiting. Finally, thirty minutes later, the three attorneys returned to the courtroom, and Mr. Knowlton addressed Judge Blaisdell.

"If it pleases Your Honor," Mr. Knowlton said, feeling the 300 sets of eyes staring into his back, "there are some things used as evidence in this case which are wanting at the present time. Consequently, we have agreed with the defendant's counsel to adjourn this hearing until Thursday, if it meets Your Honor's approval."

The crowded courtroom let out a collective groan. They had been here since 12 o'clock, and it was now 3. They would have to do it all over again in three days, and hope to get a seat.

Judge Blaisdell agreed to Mr. Knowlton's request, and the room emptied.

Lizzie asked if she could remain at the Central Police Station, in the Matron's room, rather than return to Taunton. The Marshal, tired of ducking crowds, agreed. Emma brought her sister some bedding, and a home-cooked meal. Lizzie spent the next two days reclining on the lounge, writing letters, and reading. Reverend Jubb was a daily visitor, along with her older sister and a few loyal friends.

"Emma, You Have Given Me Away!"

On August 24th, the day before the hearing began, a dramatic scene unfurled in the Matron's room between Lizzie and her sister Emma. Matron Reagan, accustomed to seeing the two sisters interact in a calm and supportive attitude, was shocked at the exchange that occurred shortly after Emma entered the small room.

"You've given me away, Emma!" Lizzie exploded, either unaware or unconcerned that Matron Reagan was only four feet away cleaning the small toilet area.

"No, Lizzie, I haven't," Emma said, worriedly. She had feared this exact reaction from her sister. Trying to mollify Lizzie, she said, "I only told Mr. Jennings what he needed to know for your defense."

"That is false and I know it," Lizzie shouted. "But remember, I won't give in one inch! Never!"

Lizzie, reportedly, held up her small finger, indicating an "inch" mark on it, as the emphasis of her final words. With that, she lay on the lounge and turned her back to the room, facing the wall. Emma slumped into a chair, and sat, head bowed. Matron Reagan stated that the silence lasted an hour and a half, until Mr. Jennings arrived to confer with Lizzie. According to the *Fall River Herald*, "Mr. Jennings talked with Emma, and later he called on Lizzie in order to clear up certain matters on which he has not been able to secure satisfactory information."

What could Emma have told Mr. Jennings that would incite Lizzie's outburst? Emma had been away during the murders, and had little evidentiary information to offer. In the Author's opinion, there are two things Emma might know about: the location of the Bedford cord dress, and, the information about the "dress pattern" Mr. Knowlton asked about during the Inquest.

"Emma, You've Given Me Away!"

There are two things, and probably more, that Emma may have been privy to, that Mr. Jennings may have asked her about in order to prepare Lizzie's defense, so as to be prepared for anything the prosecution might throw at them:

1) The Bedford Cord dress. Alice told Detective Hanscom on Monday, August 8, that she witnessed Lizzie burning a dress in the stove. Hanscom undoubtedly reported this to Mr. Jennings, as Jennings and the sisters hired the detective. Mr. Jennings would have asked Lizzie and Emma about the dress, and while the explanation of burning "an old paint-stained dress that was good for nothing," may have seemed innocent enough, there was a glaring problem. The police found no such dress during 4 intense searches of the house and dress closet, prior to the dress being destroyed on Sunday, August 7. Where had it been? If Emma told Jennings she had not seen it in the clothes closet, or anywhere else, before she saw it in Lizzie's hands in front of the stove Sunday morning, that's an issue that must be addressed. The salient point here, however, is that the prosecution is unaware of the dress burning incident at this time. Alice has only informed Detective Hanscom, and he is Jennings' man. Jennings may be fearful Alice will buckle under examination and "tell all," and he needs to have a good rebuttal in place.

2) The dress pattern: Lizzie buys some cheap dress material while on her New Bedford visit 9 nine days before the murders, on the only day she is out of view of her hostess. This fabric was her alibi for being gone an hour and a half: she was shopping. When Knowlton questions Lizzie on the stand during the Inquest, he mistakenly asks her if she bought a dress pattern, not material. She takes advantage of his mistake and agrees she did buy a dress pattern, and it is in a trunk in the attic of the house, "unmade." When asked to describe it, her frantic mind goes to the last dress pattern she used, the

one for the Bedford Cord and the Pink Wrapper that was made during May—3 months before the Inquest. The only reason Lizzie would lie and admit to buying a dress pattern, that if found will surely show it has already been cut up and used, is the dress fabric she bought has been made into a dress—one designed to cover another dress, and has blood spots on the lining, or has already been destroyed. It would have been much simpler to correct Knowlton and tell him the truth: she bought fabric not a pattern, and tell him where his men can find it, than put herself in a pickle with admitting to a dress pattern that would unmask her as soon as they saw it. Officer Fleet has been to the house to talk to Emma and ask for the dress pattern while Lizzie sat in the Taunton Jail. He first shows up on August 20th. Emma must have told him she would look for it. His last visit to the house, requesting the dress pattern, was on August 22nd, the day the Preliminary Hearing was to begin, but was postponed for 3 days. Emma, now in a panic, would have told Mr. Jennings that the dress pattern Lizzie described is not new, and she did not buy one in New Bedford. She was sure to have asked Lizzie about it, and if Lizzie told her she bought fabric instead, then the question is, "Where is it?" There is no innocent reason to its being gone. Emma needs Mr. Jennings advice, as it is obvious the police will keep returning, asking for a pattern that will catch Lizzie up in a lie. As Mr. Knowlton is later handed an intact dress pattern, it may be Mr. Jennings did his job in protecting Lizzie.

The Show Down Begins

On August 25, 1892, the hearing finally began. Twenty-three witnesses were called to testify over a 6-day period, in what was to be a dress rehearsal for the Superior Court trial that would follow—if Lizzie was found "probably guilty."

Edwin Porter, our ever-vigilant reporter for the *Fall River Globe*, got the story from Matron Russell concerning the argument between Lizzie and Emma, and ran with it. It made headlines the next day, exactly when the Preliminary Hearing was to kick off.

Mr. Jennings and the sisters were mortified. The remarks of "giving me away," and "I won't give in," sounded like the words of a guilty person. Mrs. Brigham, Reverend Judd, Mrs. Holmes, and others came after Matron Reagan. She had unwittingly released a maelstrom of controversy. Her only recourse, under the onslaught, was to deny she reported any such conversation between the sisters. The papers circled their wagons with taunts of "of course she is going to deny it," and other slaps against the retraction.

Mr. Jennings was frantic. He had a paper drawn up for her to sign, stating the whole thing was a lie, and she never witnessed any such exchange between the sisters. He asked the good Reverend to hand it to her. When she looked it over, she panicked. She had not lied about what she saw, but she had never imagined it would be in the papers. Porter was always hanging around—he was the police reporter. She may have forgotten for an instance, that what went in his ear, came out of his pen, and onto the world forum that was a newspaper.

Mrs. Reagan, looked at the official-looking form Jennings had drawn up and balked. She took it downstairs to the Marshal, and asked him what to do. Should she sign it? Marshal Hilliard read it over and blew up. Upset at the mess she had gotten herself into, he ordered Matron Reagan not to sign it, and to only testify about her story on the stand. He also told her to mind her business and sent her back upstairs to handle her famous ward.

Mr. Jennings, incensed that Hilliard had blocked his efforts to do damage control, snatched up the paper from the Marshal's desk and waving it dramatically in the air, declared before a dozen reporters—and a crush of spectators—that he and his defendant were being unfairly treated. Mrs. Raegan did tell her story, under oath, during the Superior Court trial ten months later. She testified she told the truth…the conversation between Lizzie and Emma had occurred. And thus, the lead-up to the much-anticipated hearing took center court; the drama the crowds had hoped for already in full sway.

In an effort to break the tension inside the walls of the small matron's quarters at the Fall River Police Department, Matron Reagan playfully asked the small group of friends in Lizzie's waiting area if they could meet her challenge that they could not break an egg with their hands. It was the last afternoon before the hearing and nerves were taught.

Mrs. Holmes, Mrs. Brigham, Lizzie and Emma were present. Lizzie, after hearing Mrs. Reagan's challenge, spoke up, "Well, I can break an egg," she said confidently.

"Not the way I would tell you to break it," Mrs. Reagan said, smiling, and bet her a dollar. Lizzie, in a manner of which her father would have approved, bartered her down to a quarter.

Mrs. Brigham went for the egg. Upon her return, she placed it into Lizzie's eagerly outstretched hands. Mrs. Reagan told Lizzie how to hold it. "Put it between your two clasped hands and crush it," the Matron teased.

Lizzie, in true Borden stubbornness, pressed at the egg over and over. Mrs. Raegan warned Emma, who was seated closest to her sister, to move aside, in case the egg broke and ruined her dress. She needn't have worried. The egg would not break.

Lizzie reluctantly handed the egg back to the beaming Matron. With words ripe with meaning, she said, "There, that is the first thing that I undertook to do and never could."

Edwin Porter interrupted them, asking Mrs. Reagan to step out into the corridor. Upon returning to the room, Mrs. Brigham testified Matron Reagan said, "That reporter has come after me again, and I told him that I had nothing to tell him." The following morning, as the Preliminary Hearing began, the *Boston Globe* trumpeted the story of the sister's quarrel, citing Edwin Porter as its source, and Porter citing Matron Reagan, as his.

Please Take the Stand

Beginning August 25, 1892, witnesses were called to bear their testimony concerning the murder of Andrew J. Borden. While evidence concerning Abby's murder was also introduced, and in particular, the amount of time that had transpired between her death and her husband's, her name did not appear on the Arrest for Murder, should Lizzie be found "probably guilty." Lizzie, at this time, was only being held for the possible murder of Andrew Jackson Borden, her father. It was one of many oddities concerning the early days of the case.

Much of the pertinent testimony of the witnesses has already been presented throughout this book as it applied to the various chapters. There were, however, some truly poignant moments in the Preliminary Hearing that bear noting.

Dr. Dolan: The Medical Examiner was second to take the stand that Thursday morning. He followed Civil Engineer **Thomas Kieran.** The engineer merely testified to the drawings and measurements he made of the house and property for the benefit of the trial.

Dr. William A. Dolan answered Attorney Knowlton's questions with succinct information concerning what he saw on the day of the murders. The audience was spared nothing when it came to the details of the blood and gore. From blood splatter to brain-rending slashes, measurements of wounds to stained furniture and wallpaper, it was all laid out in minute detail. The papers reported that the sisters held up remarkably well, considering the brutal details of their parents' death were on display for all to see.

Then came the most-traumatic moment of the hearing, during the cross-examination by Attorney Adams, Lizzie's co-counsel:

Mr. Adams: "Have those bodies been interred?" [Referring to Abby and Andrew Borden's bodies after the full autopsy was performed a week after the murders.]

Dolan: "Yes, Sir."

Adams: "When?"

Dolan: "I do not know just what date it was; I think it was a week last Tuesday."

Adams: "Did you remove anything from those bodies, or either of them?"

Adams: "Yes, sir. I removed the skulls, the heads."

A gasp from the shocked spectators erupted. All heads turned toward Lizzie and Emma who were seated next to each other. Emma immediately placed a gloved hand over her face as her head dropped to her chest. Lizzie turned a startled face to her sister before hiding her own behind her black fan. Reverend Buck, notably hard of hearing, did not miss the doctor's statement. He, the Holmes, and the Brigham's turned incredulous faces toward the two sisters who sat in stunned silence. Tears flowed behind Emma's gloved hands. Lizzie finally looked up, trying valiantly to regain her composure. Attorney Adams tried to regain the court's attention.

Adams: "When?" [As to the removal of the heads]

Dolan: "The day of the autopsy."

Adams: "For what purpose?

Dolan: "Because I was instructed to do so, by the Attorney General."

Adams: "What did you do with them?"

Dolan: "I cleaned them."

Adams: "Do you mean to say these bodies are buried without their heads?"

Dolan: "Yes, sir." His voice dropped; the courtroom spectators gasped again.

Adams: "Has it been said to any member of this family, or any friend, that these people were buried without their heads?"

Dolan: "I do not know."

Adams: "Have you said it, or cause it to be said?"

Dolan: "No, sir."

Adams: "Did you photograph them, or cause them to be photographed?"

Dolan: "Yes, sir...by James A. Walsh...a photographer from this city."

Doctor Dolan was then asked if he was present when the safe was opened. He replied that he was. Mr. Adams made a point of stating no will was found; a point that weighed in Lizzie's favor. If Andrew had not gotten around to making a will, there was no fear of him disinheriting his daughters in favor of Abby.

Mr. Adams addressed the taboo subject of the bloody towels found in the pail in the cellar. Dr. Dolan said he saw them, looked "at them casually," and asked Officer Mullaly to take them. He said they were left downstairs in the Marshall's office, and "nothing further done with them." He said he did examine them there, and was satisfied they had no connection with the case.

Dr. Dolan did "fudge" about the use of the hatchet during the autopsy at Oak Grove Cemetery. Mr. Adams asked him if "they [axes and hatchets] at any time were used by you or any person in your presence, with reference to the wound?" Dr. Dolan answered, "No, sir." Mr. Adams tried again, "They never have been tried, or attempted to be fitted to those wounds?" "No, sir," Dolan answered.

It was reported that he and Assistant Marshal Fleet took the clawhead hatchet to the cemetery receiving vault and laid it up against the wounds to see if it would fit the incisions. Where Dr. Dolan dodged the question, is when Adams asked if he had attempted to fit the hatchet to the wounds *during* the autopsy. In truth, Dr. Dolan did not try the hatchet during the autopsy. He and Officer Fleet, along with Dr. Leary, tried the hatchet against the wounds Sunday, August 7th, four days *before* the autopsy. Mr. Adams may have read about it in the *Fall River Herald*, which ran the story, but gotten the day wrong as to when the "hatchet fitting" took place. Dr. Dolan did lie when he answered, "No, Sir," to the question if the hatchet had *never* been tried or "attempted to fit those wounds."

His one-two punch came when he declared the murderer of Andrew might not be splattered with blood, as it shot toward his feet and the end of the couch. Dr. Dolan stated the murderer stood between the open dining room doorway and the sitting room, at the head of the couch. He said that due to the leverage action of a long-handled instrument, it would not take extraordinary strength to crush in a skull with a hatchet. He also said the murderer's hands would not necessarily be covered in blood. A point was made that the only blood on the clothes Lizzie wore that day, and handed over to the police, showed only a pinhead-sized drop on the petticoat on the "outside" of the underskirt, not the inside where you would expect to find a menstrual spot.

The autopsy reports of both Andrew and Abby were read in mind-numbing brutality as to each wound, its measurements, and the probability of causing death on its own.

The newspapers following Dr. Dolan's time on the stand reflected the barometer of the public's feelings. They were outraged that the sisters had not been asked or told that their parents' bodies were beheaded and buried in that manner. It was called "barbarous." At that moment, the tide turned in favor of Lizzie Borden, more than it had at any other time. The only damning evidence against her was the timeline of the murders; that Abby died so much earlier than Andrew. Most people could not wrap their minds around an intruder hanging around for an hour and a half to take a shot at a man, who wasn't expected home until 11 o'clock.

Dr. Dolan was asked to identify the ring of keys, and the two spare keys, found in Andrew's pocket. He was then asked to leave them with the court for future use. An inconsequential question as to Andrew's partially used package of "fine cut chewing tobacco," found in the dead man's pocket, was asked: merely if Dr. Dolan knew Mr. Borden chewed tobacco; he answered he did not know. Was it to hint that perhaps it belonged to another male...possibly the real killer? With that, Dolan stepped down.

The Star Cast of Witnesses

There were the auxiliary witnesses that caused little stir in the minds of the sensation-seeking crowds that filled the courtroom each day. The bank clerks who saw Andrew Borden the day of the murders; Joseph Shortsleeves and James Mather, the two carpenters working on Mr. Borden's store where he picked up a lock that day; Charles C. Cook, his property manager; neighbors flanking the Borden property; a few doctors; and an endless parade of police officers. The spectators fanned themselves, stole a nibble from their picnic baskets, yawned, laughed and watched Lizzie Borden's profile, or the back of her head, depending upon where they were seated. The women, who made up 80% of the gallery, shifted beneath the confinement of their corsets in the wilting heat.

Bridget Sullivan: Those who watched Bridget Sullivan on the witness stand were favorably impressed with the Irish domestic's unfaltering cadence. She answered each question given to her with as much detail as was asked of her; never contradicting any information she had given over and over again to the police, newspaper interviews, or during her Inquest testimony. She went over the days leading to the day of the murder, remembering meals she prepared, who arrived, who departed, what was worn, and what time they ate. The courtroom learned all the intimate details of the Borden family's daily routine—including slop pails, menstrual cycles, and 101 ways with mutton. As Bridget recited the numerous times mutton appeared on the Borden table, she and Lizzie exchanged looks and a small smile.

Attorney Adams for the Defense did his best to shake Bridget's memory of the murder day. Her recollection of what happened that morning differed widely from Lizzie's in several ways:

1) Did Bridget have male callers who may have sat with her on the side steps or in the backyard? [The purpose was to show it may have been one of Bridget's beaus that Lizzie saw when she said she saw a man running around the house. It was damage control for the now awkward "stranger in the night" scenario she had been trying to sell.]

2) When Lizzie ate with her parents at the table and when she didn't. Bridget and Lizzie's stories of when Lizzie was at the table were different, especially Wednesday lunch when Lizzie said she was too sick to be at the table, but Bridget said she not only ate with the family, she was there early. [In order to show Lizzie was not up and around, let alone may have just come in from a visit to a drug store for poison.]

3) Mr. Adams tried to push the poisoned pear theory. He asked Bridget if she was sure pears weren't eaten during the time leading to the murders. She shut him down repeatedly.

4) Bridget's most formidable volley with the acerbic attorney came when he tried tenaciously to get her to say she had seen Lizzie in the kitchen the morning of the murders reading, just as Lizzie claimed she was while "waiting for my irons to get hot."

Adams: "Did you see her reading there any time that forenoon?" [In the kitchen.]

Bridget: "No, sir."

Adams: "Was not there some old Harper's magazines with pictures in it?"

Bridget: "Yes, sir."

Adams: "You had seen her there looking at them, or reading them?"

Bridget: "Sometimes I would."

Adams: "You have seen her sitting down in the kitchen doing that?"

Bridget: "Not very often."

Adams: "She came into the kitchen and sat down there?"

Bridget: "Not very often."

Adams: "She had done that before, and you have seen her sit down and read there, and look at these magazines?"

Bridget: "Once in a while."

Adams: "Do you remember whether that morning she sat down in the chair there and read?"

Bridget: "I did not see her."

Mr. Adams had met his match with Bridget. The fiery Irish temper, while in control, flashed often as he tried to throw her in his efforts to support Lizzie's timeline of that morning.

Adams: "Do you not think you went to the barn and got a pail, then came back into the house, and met Miss Lizzie at the screen door?" [This is Lizzie's version]

Bridget: "No, sir."

Adams: "You do not think you said so yesterday?"

Bridget: "No, sir."

Adams: "If you did say so yesterday, you were mistaken?"

Bridget: "I did not say so."

When that tactic didn't work, Mr. Adams tried another. This is called, "rotate the questions out of sequence to trip her up" …it didn't work either.

Adams: "Who tended the bell?"

Bridget: "I tended it when nobody was in the house. When Mrs. Borden was in, she went. Mr. Borden went always when he was in the house."

Adams [shifting gears]: "You made a coal fire that morning?"

Bridget: "Yes, sir."

Adams: "Those stairs are carpeted, and have been for years?" [The stairs leading from the kitchen to Abby's room.]

Bridget: "Yes, sir."

Adams: "Do you know what dress Mrs. Borden had on that morning?"

And on, and on, he tried. Only once did Mr. Adams score a major point. He asked Bridget if anyone had approached her yesterday, after her testifying on the stand, to talk to her about her testimony. She said she had been down in the Marshal's office area waiting for the carriage that would take her home. Mr. Adams went on the attack, his voice raised and confrontational:

Adams: "Did anybody have any talk with you; did he, the District Attorney talk to you last night?"

Bridget: "Yes, sir, he said a few words to me down in the Marshal's office."

Adams: "Was the Marshal there?"

Bridget: "He was around there; I do not know whether he was listening to me."

Adams: "Did they have any testimony, or anything, written out, or on any paper which they showed you last night?"

Bridget: "Mr. Knowlton showed me a little paper."

Adams: "What kind of little paper?"

Bridget [squirming now]: "I do not know what is was."

Adams: "Did you look at it?"

Bridget: "Yes, sir."

Adams: "Was it in writing?"

Bridget: "In printing, I think." [Probably stenographer's transcript.]

Adams: "Was it something that you had said somewhere?"

Bridget: "Yes, sir."

Adams: "It was. And had you made some mistake?"

Bridget: "No, sir."

Adams: "You read it, did you not?"

Bridget: "No, sir."

Adams: "You said he showed it to you?"

Bridget: "I said I saw it. He read a little of it."

Adams: "Was that something that you had said?"

Bridget: "Yes, sir."

Adams: "When did you say it? Did you say it yesterday, or at that other time when you were in this room?" [The

Inquest was held in the same room as the Preliminary Hearing.]

Bridget: "I do not know."

Adams: "Had you said it at all at any time?"

Bridget: "Yes, sir."

Adams: "How much do you think he read to you, quite a little?"

Bridget: "About half a dozen words."

Adams: "What were those half a dozen words?"

Bridget: "I don't know."

Adams: "Was it about the note? The laugh upstairs? The groan? Her saying words slowly?" To each of those questions, Bridget answered, "No, sir." He could not get her to budge.

During Bridget's missing Inquest testimony, and the 9 missing pages of her Preliminary Hearing, we know, through leaks, that she said Lizzie came down the back stairs just after Andrew came home that morning at 10:40-10:45. The door between the Borden's bedroom and Lizzie's was always locked, on both sides. Bridget was surprised to see Lizzie coming down that way, as the girls were forced to use the front stairs, due to the locked bedroom door.

Bridget testified she heard Lizzie laughing at the top of the front stairs when Andrew came home that day. Mr. Knowlton asks her (during the Preliminary Hearing), "How soon did you see her?" [After hearing Lizzie laugh.]

Bridget: "It might be five or ten minutes after, she came down stairs; she came through the front hall. I don't know whether she came from upstairs. She came through the sitting room. I was in the sitting room."

Knowlton: "Where was Mr. Borden?"

Bridget: "In the dining room. He sat at the head of the lounge in a chair when I saw him."

Bridget made a slip in the previous testimony. Attorney Knowlton is trying to prove Bridget saw Lizzie come from the front stairs, where Bridget heard her laugh. This puts her near Abby's body. But, Bridget, knowing she saw Lizzie come down the *back* stairs, as she went into the kitchen to get more cleaning water, has a hard time telling a straight out lie; especially one that could get "the girl" hanged.

So, Bridget throws in, "I don't know whether she came from upstairs." "She came through the sitting room," works for either staircase. If Lizzie came down the back way, she entered the sitting room from the kitchen, and probably placed the key to Andrew's bedroom door back on the fireplace mantel so he wouldn't find it missing. He has come home unexpectedly early. She does not want him to know she has unhooked the doors upstairs as she went about killing Abby.

If Lizzie came down the front stairs, she would enter the sitting room from the front entry. It is there Bridget hedges. And it may be those *half a dozen words*, "I don't know whether she came from upstairs," that Knowlton showed to her on a piece of paper in the Marshal's office. He was not happy with the disclaimer she threw in.

To underscore that Lizzie came down the front stairs, Knowlton hits it again a few statements later in the hearing:

Knowlton: "Did you see her when you let Mr. Borden in, or only hear her?"

Bridget: "No, sir; heard her."

Knowlton: "When she came down, what room did she come into from the front hall?"

Bridget: "In the sitting room where I was; then she went into the dining room."

She had just answered which room Lizzie came into a few statements earlier, but Knowlton is intent on getting his "front hall" theory in.

When Bridget is asked about the paper Knowlton showed to her, she says, "I said I saw it." She also says, "He read a little of it to me." Perhaps, Bridget cannot read. It would not be unusual for a poor immigrant who may not have had much schooling. Many foreigners who came to America went into domestic service, which did not require the ability to read and write, or take on clerical positions.

As stated earlier, Mr. Knowlton was careful to keep Bridget away from her bedroom window in her testimony.

His leading question, "Did you look out the window when you were upstairs, you did not, did you?" may have caused a few people to wonder. Mr. Adams merely asks Bridget if her room overlooks the backyard.

Bridget's testimony did not help Lizzie, nor did it harm her, except to confirm her version of the morning's happenings. Remember, Bridget testified first at the Inquest, and it was supposed to be a secret session. She was not in the room when Lizzie testified, and vice versa. The only knowledge she would receive on Lizzie's story would come from Mr. Knowlton. Lizzie never took the stand again.

Illustrated American Drawing of Lizzie (l), Emma (center), and Reverend Buck, during the Preliminary Hearing. Courtesy of the *New York Times*.

John V. Morse: John's testimony may have aptly been labeled "The Artful Dodger." He is adept at couching his answers in a way that just manages to slide under the radar; while others are outright lies. We do get a better sense of him in the Preliminary Hearing as to his attachments to Fall River. It is easy to forget, due to his 20 years away in Iowa, that he is a native of Fall River and Swansea, and he has many, many relatives in the area.

John states he moved back to Fall River, from Hastings, Iowa, in 1890. This may be a significant date. It was in 1890 that Lizzie was away on the Grand Tour for almost 5 months; plenty of time for Andrew and John to begin piecing together their farm enterprise. He lived in Warren, Rhode Island, for one year, when he first moved back, and was living in South Dartmouth, Massachusetts, for the year leading up to the murders. At the time of the hearing, he is still living under house arrest at the Borden's.

As Knowlton hammers away at John's whereabouts the Wednesday he arrived from South Dartmouth, one day before the murders, it is interesting to note John's ubiquitous answer:

Knowlton: "On the occasion of this tragedy, when did you come to the house; I am assuming that you did come."

Morse: "Before this? On the third."

Knowlton: "What time on the third?"

Morse: "I left New Bedford on the 12:35 train."

John Morse used the same statement over and over in his other testimonies. "I left New Bedford on the 12:35 train." One sentence; no embellishment. What that does is leave it open. Even though Knowlton is asking about Wednesday, the 3rd, John's answer is vague. At other times, Wednesday is not specifically mentioned, just "what time did you arrive in Fall River?" Leaving "New Bedford on the 12:35 train" is probably a true statement, the question is, which day did he leave? He may have been in the area longer than he wanted to admit.

The rest of John's testimony pertaining to him, has been provided in earlier sections of the book. He is articulate, quick on his feet, and, at times, confrontational. The only time in his Preliminary Hearing that he loses control is when he is closely questioned about his knowledge pertaining to Andrew's intentions for a will, or bequests. Suddenly, he is all over the place, and obviously avoiding the question. The other land mine placed before him was by Mr. Jennings, when he tried to pin him down as to what time he actually arrived back at the Borden's for the noon meal on the day of the murders. When John stated he saw no crowds, "nothing that drew my attention," it was obviously a lie.

His relationship with Lizzie was finally brought out. While he and Emma had close ties, he finally admitted, "I do not think I ever had a letter from Lizzie in my life!" This is odd, as John is Lizzie's Uncle on her mother's side. A mother she lost early in life. Yet, it is also obvious, that John has been involved in every major real estate dealing in which Andrew has undertaken—including the purchase of the house on Fourth Street for Abby's half-sister. It seems when John comes to town, things get very heated at the Borden homestead.

Alice Russell: Attorney Knowlton had a rough time as he trudged his way through Alice Russell's Preliminary Hearing testimony. The witnesses had changed since their Inquest testimonies. They were lead to believe the Inquest was just a casual gathering of information to aid the police in their search for the murderer. By the time the Preliminary Hearing rolled around, two weeks later, they realized their 15 minutes of fame has just been extended, and thrown into the national limelight. This is serious now. None showed their unhappiness in being in that spotlight more than Alice Russell—Emma and Lizzie's close friend for over eleven years.

Perhaps it was Alice's witnessing of the burning of the dress, her later knowledge of Lizzie's nocturnal trip to the cellar without her, her private insight into Lizzie's tantrums and lies that followed the murders (as Alice camped out at the house for four days), it was evident, Alice Russell did not want to impart any more information than was absolutely necessary during her testimony.

Attorney Knowlton: "Was Mrs. Churchill there when you got there?" [The day of the murders.]
Alice: "I cannot remember whether she was or not."
Knowlton: "Did you say anything to Lizzie, or she to you?"
Alice: "I do not remember."
Knowlton: "Do you remember anything you did? Did you go in and see either of the bodies?"
Alice: "No, sir."

Knowlton: "Do you remember how Lizzie was dressed?"
Alice: "No, sir."
Knowlton: "Do you remember anything that took place at all?"
Alice: "I remember nothing very connectedly."

During Mr. Jennings cross-examination, Alice's answers had a little more meat to them, but they were still mostly broth. Each question was met with meager detail. Most astonishing, is she remembers nothing of the dress Lizzie wore, even though she spent 45 minutes with her, fanning her, rubbing her hands, and even trying to loosen her blouse, before she changed into the pink wrapper. For Mr. Knowlton, Alice was as hard to crack as Andrew Borden's safe.

Adelaide Churchill: Where Alice Russell's testimony had been vague, and at times, non-existent, Adelaide Churchill was articulate, and filled with detail. Her relevant information has been offered elsewhere in the book. Two of the more damaging aspects she proffered, as to Lizzie's guilt, was her testimony concerning Lizzie asking people twice to go upstairs and look for Mrs. Borden, and, that Bridget called her into the kitchen to tell her about Abby's "sick friend" note:

Knowlton:" Do you remember anything more being said about that note, than what you have testified to?"
Churchill: "Yes, sir. Bridget told me that Mrs. Borden had a note to go to see someone that was sick, and that she was dusting the sitting room and hurried off. She said, "she did not tell me where she was going; she usually does."

Mr. Jennings, during his cross-examination of Mrs. Churchill, tried to hone in on the note:

Jennings: "Now you say Bridget told you something about this note, when was that?"
Churchill: "We were in the kitchen, she called me into the kitchen."
Jennings: "Called you in the kitchen?"
Churchill: "Yes, sir."
Jennings: "Who was there at that time?"
Churchill: "Lizzie."
Jennings: "Anybody else?"

Churchill: "I don't think so."

Jennings: "Won't you tell us again just what Bridget said to you. Do you recollect how it happened that you said anything to her; state that."

Churchill: "I did not."

Jennings: "She told you voluntarily, without anything being said to her?"

Churchill: "Yes, sir."

Jennings: "Now tell us again, as near as you can recollect, just what Bridget said?"

Churchill: "She said Mrs. Borden had a note to go and see someone that was sick. She was dusting the sitting room, and she hurried off. She said she did not tell me where she was going; she usually does."

Jennings: "Now as to the statement which you say Bridget made to you with regard to the note, whether she did or did not state whether Miss Lizzie, or Mrs. Borden told her that?"

Churchill: "She did not say who told her. She said to me, "Mrs. Borden had a note to go see someone that was sick. She was dusting the sitting room, and she hurried off. She did not tell me where she was going; she usually does."

During Bridget's Preliminary Hearing testimony, she was asked about the note:

Adams: Mrs. Borden had told you she had a note from somebody, and was going on a sick call, and went away without telling you where she went?"

Bridget: "No, sir. Mrs. Borden did not say anything to me about a note."

Adams: "Whether you said to Mrs. Churchill that? Do you remember of talking with her about it?"

Bridget: "I might tell her what Miss Lizzie told me."

Adams (Angry): "Never mind about the might. I want to call to your mind, if I can, whether in the talk you had with Mrs. Churchill, you said to her that Mrs. Borden was away; that she told you that she had got a note, and had gone off on a sick call; and she went away without telling you anything about it?"

Bridget: "I do not know if I told her that."

Adams: "You do not remember saying anything of the sort?"

Bridget: "No, sir."

Adelaide Churchill had lived next to the Borden home all her life. Yet, after the day of the murders, she returned only for the funeral service. She admitted to not returning to the house after she left to fix the noon meal for her family that fateful Thursday. She did not come over the next day to offer assistance. Did Mrs. Churchill already feel Lizzie was more involved that she led those around her to believe? Or, did she really see something that day, as was rumored, something that she would never tell, "even if they tear my tongue out."

Eli Bence: The young drug clerk's testimony that Lizzie Borden came into D.R. Smith's Drug Store on Wednesday, August 3, one day before the murders, asking for prussic acid, was allowed during the Preliminary Hearing. His testimony, and his other two clerks who were there that day, have been reported earlier in the book. They were not allowed to speak during the Superior Court hearing before a jury of 12 men. The reason given was two-fold: it was too far removed from the day of the murder (it was only the day before), and, the murders were committed with a hatchet, not poison, so it was not relevant. If the three men had been allowed to testify, it may have made the difference in Lizzie's verdict.

Dr. Seabury Bowen: Dr. Bowen's testimony was rather dull and uneventful. At times, he was vague, and on a few occasions, got the arrival time of certain people wrong. He was clearly biased as to Lizzie's innocence. It was also evident he took some of his "memory of events and fashions" from his wife, while articulating the information as if it were his own. He deftly sidestepped his embarrassment concerning the finding of Mrs. Borden's body, and telling the first policemen on the scene that he thought she had "fainted," or "died from the shock" of finding Mr. Borden murdered. It was only after Officer Doherty informed the doctor, that "her head has been caved in," that Bowen realized she had been attacked as well.

Professor Edward S. Wood: There was palpable anticipation as Professor Wood, of Boston, took the stand. This was the man who had studied all the hard evidence and would now state his findings. If ever Lizzie Borden's heart raced, it was now, as she waited to hear the results of her parent's possible poisoning and any evidence found on the hatchets and axes.

Mr. Knowlton for the Prosecution: "Did you receive a package containing two stomachs at any time?"

Wood: "On the fifth of August I received a box by express, and opened it, and found that it contained four jars. One jar was labeled "milk of August 3rd," and another jar labeled "milk of August 4th." The third jar was labeled "stomach of Andrew J. Borden," and the fourth jar labeled "stomach of Mrs. Andrew J. Borden." All of these jars were properly tied and sealed, with seals unbroken."

Knowlton: "Have you preserved the seals?"

Wood: "I have." [These seals are now on display at the Fall River Historical Society, in Fall River, Massachusetts.]

Knowlton: "What did you do with those stomachs, Professor?"

Wood: "The stomachs were both unopened. I opened them; carefully examined the stomachs, and carefully examined the contents which they contained. I found that both stomachs were perfectly normal in appearance. They were in the condition of perfect health. There was no evidence of the action of any irritant, or anything of that kind...I tested Mr. Borden's stomach also for prussic acid, with a negative result. There was no evidence of any irritant poison having been in the stomachs at all, no irritation. There is no other ordinary poison which would prove fatal immediately; that was the only one I considered it necessary to test for, under the circumstances."

Knowlton: "Have you analyzed the milk?"

Wood: "I have not...I have not opened the jars; I have not had time to."

[This was a major victory for Lizzie. No prussic acid found in the stomachs. There are two salient points here, however. Wood did not test for arsenic. Lizzie was unable to purchase prussic acid, but Andrew and Abby's sudden vomiting, and other symptoms, pointed to a possible poisoning by arsenic. If no irritation was found in the stomachs, this is not unusual. The stomachs were removed a full two days after the sickness began. They had thrown up most of the contaminated food and liquid. Experts state that the signs of arsenic may begin to diminish as quickly as four hours after consumption, especially if it has been expectorated.]

Lizzie must have felt a rush of relief at Professor Wood's testimony. The poison theory was the only one that might have sunk her case, as the police had no other evidence against her at this point; only a druggist's story. The hatchets and axes were next, but one has to wonder if she was concerned about them at all. The hatchet used to kill Abby was still lying on the roof of Crowe's barn, and the police had skipped over the hatchet she broke in the cellar; it was not among the four presented at the hearing.

Wood: "On the 10th of August, I received a trunk from Dr. Dolan. It contained a hatchet, two axes, a blue dress skirt, a blue dress waist, a white skirt, a starched skirt, a lounge cover, and a large envelope which contained three small envelopes, these envelopes being marked, one of them "hair taken from A.J. Borden," the second one, "hair taken from Mrs. A.J. Borden," and the third one "hair taken from the hatchet." On the 16th of August, I received from Marshal Hilliard personally in Boston, a paper box containing a pair of shoes or ties, and a pair of black stockings."

In order, Professor Wood rattled off the words that the court had been waiting to hear. Lizzie listened tensely:

Hatchet: "No blood, no trace of blood."

Both Axes: "No blood."

Blue Dress Skirt and Blouse: "No blood."

White Skirt (petticoat): "One very small spot, which looked like blood, on the outside of the skirt, in the front, six inches from the bottom, 1/16th of an inch in diameter. That was blood."

Hairs from Andrew and Abby compared to hair found on the hatchet: "It was not a match to either person. It was, in fact, not a human air, but bovine; belonging to an animal, probably a cow."

Lizzie sat back in her seat. Her mask was in place, but the news had to have made her heart leap. That was it. Nothing! Not one damning piece of evidence—with one exception: Professor Wood gave Abby's time of death, based on her stomach contents, and the rate of digestion, as 1 ½ to 2 hours, before her husband's demise.

Professor Wood's theory as to where the assailant stood when the first blow was given, was "somewhere in the dining room, they stood in the dining room doorway."

The reaction to Professor Wood's testimony, concerning the blood evidence and stomach findings, was far-reaching:

The Fall River Herald, August 30, 1892— "The announcement [of Professor Wood] sent a tremor throughout the courtroom. The dignified precincts of the court would permit no outbreak of emotion, such as characterized this same announcement, as it appeared a few moments later on the bulletin boards of the newspapers in Boston, where the crowd paused to read and cheered the words, which they firmly believed established beyond a doubt that an innocent woman had been unjustly accused. Newspapermen, within hearing of the Professor's words, dropped their pencils for an instant and lost unimportant words. They did not, however, lose two very significant sentences which followed: "There are no bloodstains on the dress or shoes. The hair is not a human hair."

The rain had dampened most of the early days of the Preliminary Hearing. It did nothing to squelch the enthusiasm of the crowds who fought daily for entrance into the courtroom. Most of these spectators were the ever-present women of Fall River, showing up in their best hats and dresses, as if attending a lawn party. *The Fall River Herald* quipped:

"Is it curiosity or sympathy that attracts so many women to the district courtroom? Some women are blessed in not having any household cares to bother them."

Assistant Marshal Fleet: On day four of the Preliminary Hearing, Officer Fleet took the stand and went over the events of the day of the murders, and after. As he was testifying, something happened inside the courtroom to bring the wheels of justice to a temporary halt:

The Fall River Herald— "At this point some confusion was created by the fainting of Mrs. Bowen, wife of the physician. Mrs.

Bowen has been a regular visitor to the courtroom during the hearing, and is credited with being a firm believer in the innocence of Lizzie Borden. The heat in the room, combined with the nervous strain of the affair, caused her momentary weakness Monday afternoon. She was carried into an adjoining room and the hearing proceeded.

"The scene at this time was very dramatic. Every eye was directed toward the Assistant Marshal [Fleet], and each person was bending eagerly forward to catch every word of the slowly uttered sentences. Lizzie herself bit her lips constantly, and her sister's hands were nervously moving up and down a fan which lay in her lap. At this time, the gas was lighted, and this brightened the effect of the situation."

Officer Fleet at that time, was describing the finding of the hatchets and axes in the cellar. That Lizzie was showing her nervousness at this time, by biting her lip, is not surprising. When the handleless hatchet is not introduced, she may have felt, once again, that Providence had smiled upon her.

Lizzie wasn't the only one celebrating, although she was noticeably happier as the Defense's turn at the witnesses took center stage. *The Fall River Herald* announced "The close of the fifth day of the trial of Lizzie Andrew Borden found the prisoner's friends triumphant. All morning they sat in the courtroom and heard blow after blow delivered to the government's theory, shattering it piece for piece, until only a ragged framework remained."

The testimony for the Defense has been given where applicable throughout the book. There were no big headline-grabbing revelations. Mr. Jennings believed the prosecution had not proved its case, and his time spent wrapping up a few loose ends, was brief.

The New York Times, Fall River, Ma., August 31, 1892—
"The preliminary trial of the great Borden case is practically at an end. There yet remains the arguments of the attorneys, and tomorrow morning District Attorney Knowlton will sum up

the evidence advanced by the prosecution and will endeavor to show that the evidence is of a nature that will warrant the return of Lizzie Borden to the Bristol County Jail, there to remain at least until November, when the Grand Jury will be opened. The argument for the defense will be advanced by Col. Melvin O. Adams of Boston.

"It took just four hours for the defense to put in their case today. Nobody pretended that the testimony presented was of such a nature that the attorneys for the prisoner would care to go before a jury upon it as their complete answer to all the allegations of the defense. What they did endeavor to show was that it was possible for some unknown man to have committed this murder; that the actions of Lizzie Borden after her discovery of the body of her father was natural, and that there were no blood stains visible upon her garments. They endeavored to make clear the fact that the failure of the Government to find the weapon was virtually ample proof that she did not leave her yard upon the morning of the murder, and that search after search of the premises failed to reveal any weapon of a suspicious nature, with the exception of the hatchets and axes.

"What has become of that weapon if Lizzie Borden is guilty?" said Mr. Adams in a private conversation. "Did it vanish into mid-air? No. The natural presumption must be that the murderer carried the instrument away with him."

The Closing Arguments

The Herald was incorrect in reporting Mr. Adams would offer the closing summation for Lizzie's defense. Her family's longtime attorney, Andrew Jennings, felt he could add the passion needed during this final attempt at her freedom.

"I must say I close this case with feelings entirely different from those I have ever experienced at the conclusion of any case," Mr. Jennings said. "This man was not merely my client, he was my friend. I had known him from boyhood days, and if three short weeks ago, one had told me that I should stand here defending his youngest daughter from the charge of murdering him, I should have pronounced it beyond the realm of human credibility...

"I suggest that even the learned district attorney himself cannot imagine that any person could have committed that crime unless his heart was as black with hatred as hell itself."

Lizzie flinched. Her face convulsed, and she burst into tears. The woman who had shown no emotion after the discovery of her father's mutilated body, nor during the trial—even when told that her father's body had been buried without its head, or when his stomach contents were so graphically recalled—now, before the entire courtroom of startled onlookers, cries. It is interesting that her tears are for the description her attorney has just delivered of the murderer of her father—someone with a "heart as black with hatred as hell itself." Her tears are for herself, at hearing herself described in such a way. A sociopath only feels his own pain, and it was never more evident than here, when Lizzie's façade slips away.

Mr. Jennings went on to attack the prosecution's failure to show motive or means in their presentation. He stated that "it was almost impossible for a person to commit these crimes without being almost covered with blood, from the waist upward in the case of Mr. Borden, and from the feet upward in the case of Mrs. Borden…. Here was a girl they had been suspecting for days. She was virtually under arrest and so, for the purpose of extracting a confession from her to support their theory, they brought her here and put her on the rack, a thing they knew they would have no right to do if they placed her under arrest.

"Day after day the same questions were repeated to her in the hope to elicit some information that would incriminate her. Is it a wonder," Jennings asked, "there are conflicting statements?"

"They haven't proved this girl had anything to do with the murder. They can't find any blood on her dress, on her hair, on her shoes. They can't find any motive. They can't find the axes and so I say, I demand the woman's release."

"Don't," he begged, "put the stigma of guilt upon this woman, reared as she has been and with a past character beyond reproach. Don't let it go out in the world as the decision of a just judge that she is probably guilty."

There was a pause as Mr. Jennings took his seat. Suddenly a ripple of applause started at the rear of the room, and by the time it made its way forward, had swelled to a crescendo. Lizzie wept openly, and many in the courtroom joined her. Judge Blaisdell waited, his gavel poised, allowing Attorney Jennings this moment. Then he rapped upon his bench, and the court was adjourned for a two-hour recess.

Outside the rain continued, but the crowds would not be denied. On this day, the fate of Lizzie Borden would be announced. She would either exit the door with her sister, and return to her home, or, if found "probably guilty," she would exit on the arm of Marshal Hilliard and be returned to her cell in the Taunton Jail.

Andrew J. Jennings, Lizzie's Attorney. Photo courtesy of
The Fall River Historical Society.

Hosea P. Knowlton, Attorney for the Prosection.
Private collection.

When the court resumed, Attorney Knowlton took a deep breath, and addressed Judge Blaisdell. He hoped the recess had allowed Mr. Jenning's emotional impact to dim somewhat.

"The crime of murder touches the deepest sensibilities of feeling," he began. "There is the deepest feeling of horror about it, and above all, in the unnaturalness that brings the thrill of horror to every mind. There was not a man, woman, or child in the world of whom we could not have said, they would have done it. But it was done. There is no motive for murder," he admitted. "There is reason for it, but no motive."

Mr. Knowlton went on to address Mr. Jennings accusation of unfair bias toward Lizzie as the murderer. He stated she benefited from the deaths, she was on the scene when both deaths occurred, and she was the only person with whom Abby was not in accord. He went on to point out that the police had followed every clue and rumor, expending copious hours of manpower and resources to track down the murderer. And then, he pointed an accusatory finger at Lizzie's demeanor:

"While everybody is dazed, there is but one person who, throughout the whole business, has not been seen to express emotion. These facts do not point to a woman who expressed any feminine feeling.

"We are constrained to find that she has been dealing in poisonous things," he concluded, "that her story is absurd and that hers and hers alone has been the opportunity for the commission of the crime. Yielding to clamor," he said, in reference to the applause afforded Mr. Jennings' summation, "is not to be compared to the greatest satisfaction, that of a duty well done."

The gallery was silent as Attorney Knowlton sat down. He felt the weight of the situation and the expectations that hovered over the room like a dark cloud. Judge Blaisdell furrowed his forehead, and took a moment before delivering his verdict.

"The long examination is concluded and there remains but for the magistrate to perform what he believes to be his duty," he said. "It would be a pleasure for him, and he would doubtless receive much sympathy, if he could say, 'Lizzie, I judge you probably not guilty. You may go home.' But upon the character of the evidence..." (Emma's head went down, as Lizzie steeled herself) "...presented through the witnesses who have been so closely and thoroughly examined, there is but one thing to be done—painful as it may be. The judgment of the court is that you are probably guilty and you are ordered committed to await the action of the Superior Court."

The courtroom sat in shock. Emma's tears could not be held back. Lizzie was ordered to stand as the clerk read the decision of the court ordering her back to Tanton Jail to await the Grand Jury scheduled to meet on November 7. She would sit in a jail cell for a little over two months.

A Matter of Timing

There was yet another underlying factor to the case; it was the matter of who died first—not just as evidence as to the murderer's access to the victims, but as a monetary milestone.

The Fall River Herald, September 1, 1892—"The examination before Judge Blaisdell has furnished evidence on one important point, and upon this all the experts agree. It relates to the question of priority of death and was a matter of the greatest importance to the relatives of Mrs. Andrew J. Borden. If she was left a widow, for only a moment, she would be entitled to a widow's interest in a large property. It is called a Widow's Dower. If she was killed before her husband died, it has been pointed out that her heirs would receive nothing. These heirs are Mrs. George Whitehead, and Mrs. George Fish of Hartford. Their counsel, James F. Jackson, Esq., was in consultation with Mr. Jennings this morning. The latter maintains that unless the woman died first, the entire theory of the government, upon which was based, Lizzie's Borden's arrest would fall through. Mr. Jackson did not state whether or not he would contest the question in the courts. There are about $5000 to go to Mrs. Borden's heirs of property in her name at the time of her death."

Is it at all possible Lizzie planned Abby's murder first, knowing it would leave Andrew Borden's estate fully to her and her sister? It has always been assumed Abby died first due to opportunity. She was always at home in the mornings, and Andrew was always away conducting business. On this particular morning, it was necessary to kill Abby before she was driven to the meeting at the bank. But, did it occur to Lizzie that their order of death would matter in terms of inheritance? Would disallowing Abby's relatives a share in the estate be just another feather in Lizzie's blue bonnet? It's a chilling thought.

The Fall River Herald, September 1, 1892—"Lizzie Borden passed a night similar to those she has passed during the trial. Not being able to sleep, she has been taking opiates, and in this way has been able to maintain her strength. When she returned to the matron's room after the pronouncement of the judgment she gave way to a single outbreak of grief at the prospect of continued imprisonment, but her friends assured her that she would be free at the end of that time, and this cheered her.

"At 12:45 o'clock a carriage was driven around to the north entrance of the station-house, and the crowd that was on the watch rushed to see what was going on. In a few minutes the prisoner appeared, escorted by Mr. Buck. She wore the blue flannel gown she has worn during the trial. She was handed into the carriage, and Marshal Hilliard and Detective Seaver followed closely after her, the former bearing the necessary papers issued by the court to warrant her committal. The crowd made way, and the carriage was driven rapidly to the station. The party boarded the 1:29 train for Taunton. Lizzie's appearance had not changed materially, except perhaps that care had deepened the facial lines a little."

Lizzie's Shiny New Hatchet

On September 8, 1892, Officer Phil Harrington sent a letter to Attorney Knowlton with one of the stranger revelations in the case:

Fall River
Sept. 8, 1892

H. M. Knowlton, Esq.

Dear Sir,

Not knowing Marshal Hilliard's whereabouts, I forward this to you.

The F.R. Daily Globe has another story of a letter sent by Lizzie Borden to her friends at Marion. They claim, that without any introduction to or comment upon, the following sentence appears: "When I come I will chop all the wood, for I have a new sharper ax."

To this I would not pay much attention, but my informant told me he thought the Globe could and would produce the letter.

Tomorrow, or in a few days a representative of the F.R. Globe is to call on you and state the facts of the above. Possibly Mr. Thurston or Mr. Porter.

Yours etc.

Officer Phil Harrington

Four days later, on September 12th, Knowlton sent the following letter to Attorney General Pillsbury:

Sept. 12, 1892

My Dear Pillsbury,

…It is doubtless true that Lizzie Borden wrote to her Marion friends the day before the murder that she should be over Monday; and would chop all their wood for them for she had been looking at the axes in the cellar and she had found one as sharp as a razor.

If this is so, it means insanity.

Yours,

H.M. Knowlton

Lizzie's love of chopping things appeared again in a letter to Mr. Knowlton from a Mrs. George O. Walker, who wrote that her friend had told her of Lizzie's time in Swansea:

"She told me of a family in Swansea, whom Lizzie visited in younger days, and who tell, with bated breath, of her one day taking a nest of robins, and "chopped off their heads," because she "wanted to have a funeral." From an entirely remote, but equally authentic source, I am told of a lady, who called at the Borden house one day, and was much annoyed by a kitten, who kept jumping into her lap. It became so troublesome that Lizzie finally took it from the room, and on her return, said, "That kitten won't trouble you any more. I've chopped off her head."

There were several rumors of Lizzie killing a kitten belonging to Abby that kept coming into the sisters' sitting room in the guest chamber, and bothering their guests. It was reported even Alfred Johnson, the Swedish farmhand from Swansea, who brought their milk and chopped wood for them, stated it was true—Lizzie had beheaded a cat.

As to the letter that Lizzie purportedly sent to her friends at Marion, on September 12, 1892, Officer Medley wrote the following report:

"I visited Miss Lizzie [Elizabeth] Johnston at Myricks on Saturday. She refused to make known to me the contents of the letter she received from Lizzie Borden on the day of the Borden murder, until she had consulted with Mr. Jennings. I talked with her for two hours, but was unable to make her change her mind. She met Mr. Jennings Saturday night. I saw her again today, when she informed me that Mr. Jennings told her she need not tell me the contents of the letter if she did not want to; and she did not want to. I have seen the other girls who were at Marion at the time. None of them will talk. I have made all this known to Mr. Knowlton, and that gentleman instructed me to procure all their names, and give them to you, in order, that they may be summoned to appear before the Grand Jury. The names are as follows: Mary L. Holmes, Isabel J. Fraser, Lizzie Johnston, Louise Remington, and Mabel H. Remington."

On September 25, 1892, Officer Harrington visited Elizabeth Johnston to ask her about the letter Lizzie sent to her the day before the murders, regarding an "axe as sharp as a razor." Ms. Johnston, of 24 Ridge Street, said, "I have said all I think I should about the letter."

Whether or not the girls were called at the Grand Jury, we don't know. It was a highly secretive meeting, and other than one person's testimony, presented to Attorney Knowlton before it began, this time, there were no leaks.

The Grand Jury

On November 15, 1892, the Grand Jury took up the charges against Lizzie Borden. Attorney Knowlton, hoping beyond hope that he could rid himself of the case, had been in constant contact with Attorney General Pillsbury in the two months between the Preliminary Hearing and the Grand Jury session. Letters, phone calls, and meetings filled up their calendars. Knowlton was desperate to find a way to avoid the Grand Jury trial. The question of Lizzie's sanity was even considered.

Mr. Pillsbury, in what some saw as a heartless disregard for Knowlton's feelings, told him they were going on with the plans. The finding of Judge Blaisdell made the Grand Jury a "done deal." Attorney Knowlton's faith in the Government's case was not as firm as that of his higher up. The fact that Pillsbury had backed away from the prosecuting table, claiming health issues, was just added weight on Knowlton's shoulders.

The Grand Jury listened to Hosea Knowlton's unenthusiastic case. Pillsbury had written to him:

"I still favor holding back all that can be prudently held back, especially as I now think that what you have absolutely determined to put in will make the case as strong to the public as if everything went in."

As the biggest testament to Knowlton's fervent wish to unburden himself of this albatross, he did something unheard of. Knowlton invited Attorney Jennings to present his defense case as well to the Grand Jury. This was basically unheard of. A Grand Jury's purpose is to hear all the evidence *against* the prisoner, in order to determine if there is enough to warrant a Superior Court trial. Yet, Attorney Knowlton was standing aside for Attorney Jennings to give it his best shot. And, Jennings took it. Granted, it was also a way for the Prosecution to determine what the Defense had in the way of evidence, but it had all been brought out previously in the Preliminary Hearing. It was all for naught.

The Grand Jury, after hearing both sides, adjourned six days later, without reaching a decision. As it was November 21st, it may have been a Thanksgiving break for the judicial system. It was enough time for a former friend of the Borden sisters to come forward with a story she had long held to herself.

Alice Russell asked Attorney Knowlton for a meeting. He listened in astonishment, and perhaps with a sinking heart, as she told him of witnessing Lizzie burning a "paint-stained Bedford cord dress" the Sunday after the murders. She told him she had told Detective Hansom about it, but nothing was done. Her conscience would not allow her to go on, as she now feared Lizzie was indeed, guilty of murdering her parents. Knowlton had no choice; he asked for the Grand Jury to reconvene.

How Lizzie must have viewed her friend's betrayal is not known. That the Grand Jury had dismantled without a decision had, no doubt, given her great hope, as she "celebrated" Thanksgiving in her jail cell. On December 1st, 1892, the powerful body handed down three indictments for murder: one for the murder of Andrew J. Borden, one for the murder of Abby Borden, and one charging Lizzie with the murder of both of them, just for good measure. The vote was 20 to 1, and had taken only ten minutes of deliberation. Alice Russell's damage was done.

Attorney General Pillsbury sent Knowlton a letter of congratulations for his work on "this accursed case." It is doubtful Knowlton was celebrating. He was now looking at taking on a monster of a trial, with the same mixture of confusing and conflicting evidence. Lizzie's circle of friends, in religious and feminist groups, had grown, and the papers were serving Knowlton up ala mode to the delight of the public.

Attorney Jennings quickly pleaded with Pillsbury that Lizzie is allowed to furnish bail, as she was no threat to flee the country. Pillsbury, in his typical fashion, dismissed Jennings request, writing to Knowlton, "Jennings spent the afternoon with me Friday on the question of bail, but I think I have quieted him."

Attorney Jennings then begged the Attorney General for the trial to begin as soon as humanly possible. Despite repeated appeals to both Knowlton and Pillsbury, the Government took no steps to schedule the Superior Court trial. It would later be claimed that both men held the hope that extended imprisonment of the accused might bring about a physical or mental breakdown, and make a trial unnecessary. If the public ever found out, decapitating the Borden's heads would be but one outcry of "Barbaric!"

Chapter Thirty
The Superior Court Trial

The fallout from the findings of the Grand Jury went beyond Lizzie's incarceration. As always, her life had a trickle-down effect on those within her reach; none more so than her sister Emma.

On December 3, 1892, two days after the Grand Jury indicted Lizzie, Attorney Jennings wrote the following letter:

> My Dear Pillsbury,
>   Mr. Morse wishes to go out West and wants to know if any chance of his being needed this month. As he wishes to go Tuesday, wire or write me so I can get it Monday. I spoke to Knowlton about it and he said he had no objection if he would come back.
>
> A.J. Jennings

And with that, Emma was left alone in an empty house. New carpet had been put down in two rooms where her parents' bodies had lain. The sitting room had been repapered. She was to spend Christmas with her two servants, unless they had family plans elsewhere.

92 Second Street was still a major curiosity in Fall River. While the crowds outside its walls did not number in the hundreds and thousands any longer, the traffic finding its way past the front door was unrelenting. The Borden house was the haunted house every small town claimed, and for Emma, it was a nightmare. The evenings were the hardest. With John's departure to Iowa, she faced the hecklers and Peeping Toms on her own. She feared someone would throw a rock through the window, or befoul the

side of the house with some type of graffiti. She kept Lizzie's room waiting for her, just as she left it; it was the only reminder there had been a family here once.

Lizzie, meanwhile, spent her days writing letters, and ordering food from the City Hotel. With the indictment handed down by the Grand Jury, had come the removal of two constants in her life: Alice Russell and Elizabeth Johnston. Elizabeth, her friend that was to vacation with her in Marion that fateful August, had stood steadfastly by Lizzie's side. She refused to show the letter she received from Lizzie on the day of the murders, and spent long hours with her friend at Taunton Jail. Elizabeth brought treats, magazines, and books, and would talk with Lizzie as long as Matron Wright would allow. She proclaimed Lizzie's innocence to all who would listen.

But this was all to change after Alice Russell's damning evidence of the dress burning hit the papers. Elizabeth suddenly distanced herself from Lizzie. While not speaking out against her one-time friend publicly, she ceased all communication with her, as did Alice Russell. Emma and Lizzie never heard from them again. When Lizzie was later interviewed by Mrs. Mary A. Livermore at the jail, she said sadly, "What hurts me most is the malignant feeling that has been shown...Is my character of 30 years to count for nothing?"

The months wore on. Lizzie's few remaining supporters sent candy and other items to keep her cheered as she waited inside the white-washed walls, facing an uncertain future. There was no date set for trial. If she felt at one time, as she told Matron Reagan in Fall River, that "they do what they want with me," this blatant disregard for her peace of mind would have been torture. She relied on the kindness of her jailkeepers, the Wrights, who tried to make her Christmas as pleasant as possible. And, as always, Emma was by her side.

A letter from Lizzie to her dear friend, Annie Lindsey (Mary Ella Brigham's sister), written while incarcerated in the Taunton jail, shortly after Christmas, shows Lizzie's depression over her circumstances:

Wednesday, January 18, 1893—2:00 p.m.

My Dear Annie,

I meant to have written long ago, but my head troubles me so much I write very little.

I think soon they will take me up the road, to the insane asylum [Taunton Lunatic Hospital].

A box of nice candy came to me Tuesday, and no one but my friend Annie sent it. Thank you dear very much.

Do you know I cannot for the life of me see how you and the rest of my friends can be so full of hope over the case.

To me, I see nothing but the densest shadows.

It is fine sleighing here, the bells jingle all night long.

I must say good-bye for this time.

With much love for my loyal friend.

L.A.B

[Letter courtesy of the Fall River Historical Society/*Parallel Lives*]

The Great Trial Begins

Attorney Andrew Jennings' pleadings for a trial were finally answered, and the date for the Superior Court to hear the case was set for June 6, 1893. Lizzie had now been in jail since the end of the Inquest, on August 11, 1892.

In 1891, legislation was passed, mandating a panel of three judges were required to sit the bench in the event of a capital case. Lizzie Borden's murder trial may have been one of the first cases, if not the first (in Massachusetts), to have three judges in residence. The three men selected were Chief Justice Mason, Associate Justice Celeb Blodgett, and Associate Justice Justin Dewey. Attorney Jennings and his famous client were doubtless happy to see fresh faces sitting the bench. Gone was the judge who had overseen Lizzie's Inquest and Preliminary Hearing: Judge Blaisdell. If her Inquest testimony was kept out, the three new judges might look at her with unbiased eyes.

The Three Superior Court Judges: Blodgett, Mason, and Dewey.
Fall River Herald, June 5, 1893.

The three men sitting at the bar were fatherly-looking in appearance. Judge Mason sported a flowing white beard, and sad eyes. He was married and the father of three daughters who were close in age to Lizzie Borden. Judge Blodgett was described as "genial and unaffected in manner." He was a graduate of Dartmouth College and practiced law in Boston. Justice Dewey of Springfield, Massachusetts, was the father of three daughters, all in their twenties. Judge Dewey had been appointed to the Superior Court in 1886, by then-Governor George D. Robinson, the man who was to represent Lizzie Borden in the Superior Court trial the three learned judges were about to hear.

And thus, the stage was set. Lizzie's fate would be determined by a 12-man jury, but the presiding magistrate—two with grown daughters mirroring Lizzie's age and sensibilities—and one put there by Miss Borden's attorney, would play a part in her outcome.

The counsels were chosen. Lizzie would be represented by her loyal friend, Attorney Andrew Jennings; Melvin O. Adams, who had represented her ably in the Preliminary Hearing; and Ex-Governor George D. Robinson. The Prosecution team included Attorney Hosea Knowlton, and William H. Moody. Mr. Moody came to the case with an impressive resume: he was District Attorney of Essex County, and a graduate of Harvard, where he had known Theodore Roosevelt. Many felt he was the ablest attorney to sit on either side of the courtroom.

For the Prosecution

William H. Moody   Hosea Knowlton

For the Defense

Andrew Jennings   Gov. George D. Robinson

Melvin O. Adams

The location for the trial, despite Attorney Jennings' pleadings that it be held in Taunton, was set in New Bedford, Massachusetts, at the Bristol County Superior Court House. The courtroom was on the second floor, and accessed by a staircase that opened directly into the room; leaving a large cavity in the courtroom floor. The spectators' seats were wooden benches in the rear which rose in tiers. The witness box and the jury box were to the left of the judge's position. To accommodate the wealth of journalists that had descended on New Bedford for the trial, a series of long tables with four-legged stools have been placed along the courtroom wall, separated from the jury area by only the court crier's box. Four large, brass, gas-burning chandeliers hung from the courtroom ceiling.

New Bedford courtroom where Lizzie was tried. Photo by the Author.

Outside the building, the town of New Bedford had taken on a carnival-like atmosphere. Businesses practically ground to a halt. People congregated on sidewalks and in restaurants, and everywhere the sole topic of conversation was the murder case. Thirty extra temporary lines, serving New Bedford for the use of the newspaper men, were installed at the Western Union and Postal Telegraph offices. It was obvious this was to be no normal trial. This was a murder trial involving a socially prominent woman accused of double parricide, in which the victims were dispatched in a most brutal manner. Even the World's Columbian Exhibition (the World's Fair), which had opened in Chicago, was taking a back seat in the headlines of the summer of 1893.

Hear Ye, Hear Ye!

Robert Sullivan, in his book *Goodbye Lizzie Borden,* published by Penguin Books in 1974, described the opening day:

"Picture this singular scene on the first Monday in June 1893, the clerk and the bailiffs standing so stiffly that they seemed part of the court fittings, the spectators' seats crowded to full capacity, the press tables so swarmed that some of the correspondents shared the tiny stools or stood. The unseasonably torrid weather was amplified by the body heat generated by the pressing crowd, which fluttered palm-leaf and folding fans to provide a semblance of coolness. At 11:25 A.M. the detention room door opened and Lizzie Borden was led to, and placed at, the bar for trial. At 11:28, with a resounding crash of the bailiff's staff, the Court entered and took its place upon the bench, Chief Justice Mason in the center, flanked by Justice Blodgett to his right, and Justice Dewey to the left. The court crier, from his box at the side of the courtroom, gave the cry:

"Hear ye, hear ye, hear ye! All those having anything to do before the Honorable, the Justices of the Superior Court gather round, give your attention, and you shall be heard. God save the Commonwealth of Massachusetts! Be seated!"

The trial was favored by one particular journalist with star power. Joseph Howard was probably the first syndicated news columnist of the nation. Known for his flamboyant style, and over usage of adjectives dripping with detail, he was a favorite of the reading public in 1893. He represented the *Boston Globe, The New York Recorder*, and Pulitzer's *New York World*. His columns stood out in each paper by his bold black signature:

One hundred and forty-five prospective jurors crammed the courtroom on the first day of the trial. The gawkers were left outside as the serious business of selecting 12 men to sit the panel was chosen. After four hours of mind-numbing examination, in the end, they were, George Potter, Willaim F. Dean, John Wilbur, Fredric C. Wilbar, Lemuel K. Wilber, William Westcott, Louis B. Hodges, Augustus Swift, Frank. Cole, John C. Finn, Charles I. Richards, and Allen H. Wordell.

The 12-Man Jury for the Lizzie Borden Case. Courtesy of Dialtant.media.com

Joseph Howard kicked off the sensationalism of "the trial of the century" in grand style. Writing from the courtroom on June 5, the opening day of the trial, he wrote:

"After Sheriff Wright had drawn up in real New Bedford state with the judges, a modest little carryall stopped at the door, from which alighted the heroine of the day. Heretofore, from the morning of the murder until her last appearance, Miss Borden has worn a blue serge dress. Her costume today was becoming and of fashionable cut. Her hat was a model for theatergoers, flat built, of lace, ornamented with blue rosettes, a tiny blue feather. Her frock was of black merino, fastened at the neck with a modest brooch. She wore dark undressed kid gloves and very neatly-fitting shoes. Her self-possession was remarkable, and she ascended the long flight of stairs leading to the courtroom quickly, briskly in fact, and took her place in what is called the "dock," which in reality is nothing but a space between two rails, where two chairs are placed, one of which is occupied by the deputy sheriff, the other by herself.

Lizzie Borden on trial, drawn from life by Louis F. Grant.
(Wide World Photos)

Lizzie illustration, *Wide World Press.*

"Life here has a face. Her dark brown hair was modestly coiled behind. Her full forehead was very pale, her wide-apart eyes had an unpleasant stare. Her cheeks, which are overfull, hang down below the line of the chin, making a pronounced mark on either side of the face, carrying the line from the lower part of the ear a long distance down to the point of an obstinate and stubborn chin."

Lizzie Borden, wearing the modest brooch described by Joseph Howard, the opening day of the trial. Photo courtesy of the Fall River Historical Society.

Lizzie and Emma Borden wearing matching pansy pins. Emma's photo courtesy of lizzieandrewborden.com, and the *Literary Hatchet*.

[As an interesting aside, photos of the sisters, taken at different times, show identical pansy pins. Did Emma loan the pin to Lizzie to wear (perhaps for luck during the trial), or vice versa? Was it a gift to the sisters—matching pins, perhaps from Andrew? Or, was it merely a popular accessory in 1893? The photo of Emma was found by Stefani Koorey with lizzieandrewborden.com in the Swansea Museum, amid Borden family photos. Emma and Lizzie have the same catlike eyes.]

Joseph Howard went on to describe the scene that day in the courtroom in prosaic fashion: "Outside in a neighboring field was a most demonstrative cow, who's mooing is almost continuous, frequently interrupting the learned judge, often drowning the responses of mild-mannered witnesses, and causing as far as eye could see the one and only smile that changed the impassiveness of the Borden countenance from morning until night."

Lizzie was alone that day. Emma and her friends were not allowed inside the courtroom during the jury selection, nor any other time, if they were to be called as a witness. The face of her dear friend Sheriff Wright, who had been so kind to her at the Taunton Jail, must have cheered her, while others found his manner in riding roughshod over the gallery a bit pompous and overbearing.

The day ended at 6 o'clock. Attorney Knowlton would begin the trial in earnest the following morning at 9 o'clock, when he would present his opening arguments.

The Prosecution Opens

Attorney Hosea Knowlton could have aptly been labeled "The Reluctant Counsel." His attitude toward his role was summed up in a letter to Attorney General Pillsbury shortly before the trial, upon hearing Pillsbury would not be joining the fray due to health concerns:

Hon. A. E. Pillsbury, Attorney General

My Dear Sir:

I have thought more about the Lizzie Borden case since I talked with you, and think perhaps that it may be well to write you, as I shall not be able to meet you probably until Thursday, possibly, Wednesday, afternoon.

Personally, I would like very much to get rid of the trial of the case, and feel that my feelings in that direction may have influenced my better judgment; I feel this all the more upon your, not unexpected, announcement that the burden of the trial would come upon me...

Yours truly,
Hosea Knowlton

And so, District Attorney Moody took the helm for the prosecution, and opened the case, much to the surprise of some. At 39-years-of-age, he was the youngest of the professional participants at the trial, and he was about to try his first murder case. That being said, many called his opening remarks "a masterpiece."

The prosecution's approach to proof of guilt was three-fold:

1) Lizzie Borden was pre-disposed to, and had pre-determined to murder, Andrew J. Borden and Abby Durfee Borden.

2) Lizzie Borden did in fact murder Abby Durfee Borden and Andrew J. Borden, in that order, and with a substantial interval of time between the two killings.

3) That by her statements and by her actions after the murders, and each of them, Lizzie Borden by word and act placed herself in a position which was entirely inconsistent with innocence. In fact, by her words and by her deeds after the murders, and each of them, Lizzie Borden had displayed a consciousness of guilt of the murders to the point that she revealed herself to be guilty beyond reasonable doubt.

Moody told the jury that the witnesses would support one or more of the three basic premises of guilt. He stated Lizzie's motive was her hatred of Abby, and her general fear of loss of inheritance. Her state of mind at the time of the murders would be proven by her actions and words prior to the tragedy. Moody declared the prosecutions' witnesses would show Lizzie Borden had the strength and the means available to commit the crimes, and more importantly, she had the exclusive opportunity to carry out the murders.

Finally, Mr. Moody told the jury that the witnesses would testify as to Lizzie Borden's lies to prevent the detection of the first murder; her lies and inconsistent statements as to her own whereabouts; her lies and inconsistent statements as to her discovery of her father's corpse, and as to the inevitability of her knowledge of the first murder; and very significantly, witnesses would testify as to unusual acts and statements in the several days following the murders and before her arrest.

Although the temperature outside the courtroom on that June 6th morning was 93 degrees by noon, and even hotter inside the small room, the court sat spellbound by Moody's declaration of proof against the woman who sat, almost disinterested, in a seat only a few feet from him.

Lizzie's detachment soon dissolved as Mr. Moody inadvertently caused a major sensation during his opening. At one point, the attorney was holding up Lizzie's blue dress that was to be offered into evidence. It was the dark blue Bengaline she handed over to Marshal Hilliard. He tossed it carelessly aside as he moved on in his speech; however, as he did so, the dress hit a tissue-covered handbag that rested on the prosecution table. The tissue fell away, exposing to plain view the hideous, sightless eyes of the fleshless skulls of the two victims. Lizzie at first covered her eyes with her fan, then her head fell against the police matron seated next to her, in a dead faint. Reverend Jubb, who was seated before her, separated only by the railing, turned around to assist her. Attorney Jennings ran for water and smelling salts, while Deputy Sheriff Kirby, who sat beside her, fanned her. After several minutes, Lizzie sat up, "her face as pale as marble."

Mr. Moody showing the jury the dress, with the two skulls in the handbag, drawn at his right. *Fall River Herald*, June 6, 1893.

A fanciful illustration titled, *"Lizzie Faints Away,"* used in a story appearing in the *"Police Gazette,"* the man's magazine of the 1890s.

Attorney Moody ended his opening with these words: "We shall ask you to say, if say you can, whether any other reasonable hypothesis except that of guilt of this prisoner can account for the sad occurrences which happened upon the morning of August 4th."

The first witness called was **Thomas Kieran**, the Fall River engineer who did the drawings of the house and grounds to facilitate trial testimony. His words were ones of measurements—not only of the Borden residence, but of the closest neighbors to them.

VIEW OF THE VICINITY OF THE MURDERS.

I. Borden house.
II. Borden barn.
III. The well.
IV. Fence with barbed wire on top.
V. Side entrance.
VI. Churchill residence.

VII. Dr. Bowen's house.
VIII. Dr. Chagnon's house.
IX. Kelley house.
X. Yard from which officers watched the Borden house.
XI. Kelley's barn.
XII. Pear orchard.

Thomas Kieran's drawing of the Borden neighborhood.
The Borden house is marked I.

After Mr. Kieran's testimony, Mr. Knowlton stood and asked that the jury now be taken to Fall River to view the house and grounds. Lizzie declined the offer to attend the viewing of her home. Mr. Jennings and Mr. Moody accompanied the panel of 12 men to 92 Second Street. As usual, the crowds followed.

THE JURY GOES TO FALL RIVER TO VIEW THE BORDEN PREMISES

Drawing of the jurors viewing the Borden house.
Boston Daily Globe, June 6, 1893.

Day Three of the Trial, June 7th

As the third day of trial began, it was evident the spectators within, and without the courtroom were ready for the real drama to begin. They had listened to measurements and the boring preliminaries, now they wanted to hear from the principle people involved in the murders of Abby and Andrew Borden. They were surprised when, instead, Mr. Knowlton recalled the engineer, Thomas Kieran to the stand. Many became restless.

In a curious move, Attorney Knowlton asked the engineer if he had conducted an experiment with the hall closet next to the front door of the Borden home interior. He said he had. He was asked to state what he had done. Mr. Kieran said he had placed a man inside the closet, and with the door ajar the witness, Kieran, had failed to see the man inside while standing eight or ten feet away from the closet and looking directly into it. If Mr. Jennings and Governor Robinson exchanged looks of surprise at the testimony, it was no wonder. This was the prosecution's witness, yet here he was, providing proof for the defense that an intruder could have hidden in the house the day of the murders. Further, no evidence had been given yet in the trial, other than some floor plans and measurements—nothing that would warrant this type of testimony. If Knowlton was tipping his hand that his heart was not in this trial, he was off to a great start!

James Walsh: The photographer James Walsh was next. He testified to being called to take photos of both Borden's, including those of their partial autopsies. He arrived around 3:00 the afternoon of the murders, and left close to 5:30. Charles Carrol took the interior and exterior photos of the house and grounds just prior to the start of the trial, and they were presented to the jury.

Finally, one of the star witnesses took the stand. There was a shift in the gallery, as they perched on the edge of their seats. John Vinnicum Morse, the evasive, mysterious Uncle from the West, walked in in his rumpled suit to take the stand.

John Morse during the trial. *Fall River Herald.*

John V. Morse: The formalities were gone into. Mr. Morse stated he was now sixty-nine-years-old, a brother to the late Sarah Morse, Lizzie's biological mother. He recited the same details he had in the Preliminary Hearing, as to arriving at the Borden's the day before the murders "on the 12:35 from New Bedford." He spoke of the breakfast Thursday morning, including that there were bananas on the table. He said he left by the side door around 8:45, saw Bridget cleaning in the kitchen as he went, and was asked by Andrew to come back for dinner. His trip to the Post Office, detailed walk to Weybosset Street, and return to Andrew's were laid out. He stuck to his story that he did not notice any crowds around the Borden house when he got there close to noon. He went into the yard, ate a pear, and saw a man at the side door who told him, for the first time, Andrew was dead. He went in immediately where he viewed both bodies.

"I first saw Lizzie and then I passed into the sitting room and saw Mr. Borden's body," Morse testified. "Then I went part-way up the stairs, far enough to see Mrs. Borden's body lying on the floor with blood on her face. Lizzie was sitting in the dining room on the lounge. Mrs. Churchill and Miss Russell were with her, but then they went into the sitting room where Mr. Borden's body was lying on the sofa. There were two or three police officers in the house and I saw blood spots leading from the sitting room into the dining room and above Mr. Borden's head. I think Emma washed those off Sunday."

John Morse's testimony was oddly without drama, compared to the confrontational atmosphere that prevailed during the Preliminary Hearing. His answers were taciturn and by rote. The only curious thing during his time on the stand was that neither Robinson, nor Knowlton asked him a single question as to whether he had any conversation with Lizzie that day, after discovering the murders. It is also the first time we hear Mrs. Churchill and Alice Russell went into the sitting room where Andrew lay. Perhaps the sheet covering him gave them some comfort.

The next five witnesses were called to testify to Andrew's whereabouts the morning of his murder, between 9:30 and 10:30 a.m. Their testimony has been presented in the book under Andrew's timeline that morning. The witnesses were (in order): **Abraham C. Hart, John T. Burrill, Everett M. Cook, Jonathan Clegg, Joseph Shortsleeves, and James Mather.** While their collective testimony did little to shed light on the murders, it did showcase one important point: the three banking institutions, and the two stores owned by Mr. Borden, that he visited that morning, were all located close together in the business district near City Hall, which was only 900 feet from Number 92 Second Street; an easy five-minute walk home.

Bridget Sullivan: No other witness held as much interest to the court as the young Irish domestic who had witnessed so much the day of the murders.

According to *The New York Times*— "A buzz of excitement went around the room at 12:30, when Mr. Moody called "Bridget Sullivan." She was dressed in a maroon colored, fashionably-made dress, and wore a large hat, with a large feather, and black kid gloves. She leaned on the left side against the rail, looked straight ahead, and spoke so low that he had to tell her to speak louder. The prisoner changed posture so as to see the witness plainly, and watched her steadily with large eyes wide open."

Bridget only spoke for thirty minutes before a recess was called at one o'clock. She was back on the stand at 2:15 and testified until 4:55 that day, until court was adjourned until the following morning.

Drawing of Bridget on the stand. *Fall River Herald.*

Bridget's testimony was, once again, clear, forthright, and unchanged. There was no mention of washing windows in the attic, looking out her bedroom window, or seeing Lizzie come down the back stairs into the kitchen.

> *The New York Times*— "Then I went up to my room and lay down. The first notice I took of any time was when I heard the City Hall clock strike eleven. I think I had been there three or four minutes. I don't think I went to sleep. Heard no noise. Am able to hear the screen door if it is closed by a careless person. The next thing I heard was when Lizzie called me to come down, as her father was dead, that was at least fifteen minutes after."

Bridget's testimony recapped her testimonies from before. She was clearly polished by now, knew what to say—and what not to say. She rattled off the details most people could recite by heart: She was called "Maggie" by the girls; had been with the Borden's two years and seven months at the time of the murders; had no chores on the second floor of the house; Lizzie was in charge of sweeping and dusting the parlor in the summer months; Bridget's chores were washing, ironing, cooking, and a little scrubbing.

She was reciting the events of the morning of the murders, and had gotten to Mr. Borden throwing his slops on the grass, when she was interrupted. Mrs. Caroline Kelly needed to be called at that time, as she had a pressing engagement. Bridget stepped down.

Mrs. Caroline Kelly: Mrs. Kelly's testimony was brief. She lived next door to the Borden's and had a dentist's appointment the morning of the murder. As she hurried down Second Street to her appointment, she saw Andrew Borden coming around the side of his house to the front door. He was carrying a small white parcel, which she described in detail as to its measurements.

"When I saw him at the front door," she said, "I was opposite his front gate, near enough to touch him, but his back was turned toward me; he was stooping down. This was exactly twenty-eight minutes to eleven."

Bridget Sullivan (re-called): Bridget continues to go over the events of Thursday, August 4th. There is no change in her testimony since the Preliminary Hearing. She is now careful to say she saw Lizzie come into the sitting room from the *front* entry, five minutes after hearing her laugh at the top of the stairs. There are no surprises in her testimony.

It was not until Mr. Moody asked her what dress Lizzie was wearing that day that the fireworks begin:

> Mr. Moody: "What was the usual dress that Miss Lizzie Borden wore mornings? Will you describe it?"
>
> Mr. Robinson: "Wait a minute; we object to that."
>
> Moody: "Not as having any tendency to show what she had on that morning."
>
> Robinson: "I object."
>
> Moody: "I don't care to press it against objection."
>
> Bridget: "Well, she wore a – "
>
> Robinson and Mr. Moody: "Wait a moment."
>
> Moody: "I will call your attention, not asking you when it was worn or what part of the time it was worn, to a cotton or calico dress with light blue groundwork and a little figure. Does that bring to your mind the dress I am referring to?"
>
> Bridget: "No, sir; it was not a calico dress she was in the habit of wearing."
>
> Moody: "I did not ask about the habit, but— "
>
> Robinson: "That should be stricken out."
>
> Moody: "Certainly."
>
> Judge Mason: "Let it be stricken out."
>
> Moody: "Do you remember a dress of such a color?"
>
> Bridget: "Yes, sir."
>
> Moody: "Will you describe that dress that I have referred to as well as you can?"
>
> Bridget: "It was a blue dress with a sprig on it."
>
> Moody: "What was the color of the blue; what was the shade of blue?"
>
> Bridget: "Light blue."
>
> Moody: "And what was the color of what you called the sprig on it?"

Bridget: "It was darker blue, I think, than what the under part was."

Moody: "Did it have any light spots or light figures in it?"

Robinson: "This is very leading now— "

Bridget: "I don't remember."

Moody: "When did she procure that dress?"

Bridget: "Last Spring, I guess."

Moody: "Was it made at the house or made somewhere else?"

Bridget: "I think it was made at the house...Generally the same dressmaker has been there since I have been in the house."

Moody: "Let me ask you in this connection, if you are able to tell us what dress she had on that morning?"

Bridget: "No, sir, I couldn't tell what dress the girl had on."

[Bridget may, or may not have noticed Lizzie's dress on the morning of the murders. She was not feeling well, and barely turned toward Lizzie to ask her what he wanted for breakfast, before bolting out the screen door to throw up. When Bridget returned to the kitchen, Lizzie was gone. The next time she saw Lizzie, Bridget was on the outside of the screen door and heading for the barn. Finally, she saw Lizzie as she raced down the stairs when Lizzie called her, saying Mr. Borden had been killed. She was told to hurry away for Dr. Bowen. The only time Bridget really had a chance to notice Lizzie's dress was during the 45 minutes between being sent for Bowen and Miss Russell, and Lizzie going up to her room to change into the pink wrapper. With all that was going on with people and police coming, she may not have noticed.

Or, if she did, she kept quiet, rather than see Lizzie hang. One word from her saying Lizzie had changed from the Bedford cord that morning, into something else, would be all it would take for a noose to be fashioned. It is evident in the previous testimony, when Bridget says, "it was not a calico dress she was in the habit of wearing," that she was referring to the ribbed cord dress, one that was "light blue" with a "darker sprig," exactly like the one Alice Russell described as the Bedford cord Lizzie burned that Sunday.]

Bridget gave the following damaging evidence, based on what she saw and heard that day: the bell had not rung when Mr. Borden came home that morning at 10:40; he said nothing as he came in about forgetting his key; the front door was triple locked; she heard Lizzie laugh at the top of the stairs, in the vicinity of where Mrs. Borden lay dead; she did not see Lizzie in the kitchen reading a magazine as Lizzie testified she was; Lizzie tried to entice her out of the house twice that morning, including telling her of a sale at Sargent's—something Lizzie had never done before; she had not seen Lizzie cry, and most damaging of all, Bridget claimed the only person she heard from about the note, was Lizzie, not Abby. She also said she had seen no one come to the door to deliver a note. (Bridget was out back throwing up when the messenger came, so she would not have known someone came to the door.)

Mr. Robinson, on cross-examination did his best to get Bridget to say the Borden family was a pleasant place to be, where everyone was civil to each other, ate meals together, and even planned Christmas together. Bridget admitted to not hearing quarrels, but would not budge that the girls often ate their meals alone. She also denied ever saying they planned Christmas together.

He pushed to say Lizzie was sick on Wednesday as well; Bridget would only admit that Lizzie complained about being sick. She did say Lizzie was at all the meals Wednesday, including being there for dinner [lunch], which was unusual.

Robinson next pressed Bridget on the layout of the house, trying to make it look as if she was in the back part of the kitchen doing dishes in the sink room, instead of in the kitchen proper, intimating she may not have seen Lizzie reading at the kitchen table. Bridget didn't bite. Next, he walked through the washing of the outside windows, and her talking with the Kelly girl. His point was that someone could have come into the side door on the north, while Bridget was gabbing and washing windows on the south side of the house. Bridget admitted someone could have. He also established that Bridget had made at least six or seven trips to the barn for water, and that the windows on the north side of the house were too high up to see inside the house. She agreed.

His final victory in the intruder theory was to elicit from her that the door to the parlor had been closed all morning, and that she had no business in the front entry, until she let Mr. Borden in. His point: someone could have been hiding inside the parlor the entire morning, between the time Abby was killed and Andrew was murdered. Bridget did not mention she had testified at the Inquest that she went through the parlor before opening the front door, presumably to peek out the window to see who was fumbling with the lock.

Bridget admitted to seeing no blood anywhere on Lizzie that morning, or that her hair was disarrayed in any way. Robinson did score a major point when he got Bridget to admit that on Wednesday, she saw Lizzie in the Bedford cord when she came down to breakfast and when she was there for the noon meal. His point was, Eli Bence and his clerks described Lizzie as coming into the drug store between 10:00 and 11:30 that morning, wearing a dark dress, not a light blue wrapper. Unless Lizzie changed her dress, twice, that morning, it made it look as though Lizzie never left the house.

Robinson asked where Bridget had lived since leaving Fall River after the Inquest. She said she had been living in New Bedford, employed at the jail keeper's house as a cook. Marshal Hilliard and Detective Seaver had put up her security.

Moody asked Bridget if Mrs. Borden was in the habit of telling the servant when she was going to leave the house. Robinson objected to it, and Bridget's ordeal was over. She gratefully stepped down, and the court adjourned for the day.

Bridget's employment at the New Bedford jail keeper's home was a source of contention for the lady. She told Officer Harrington on October 1, 1892: "Yes, I left New Bedford for good. I did not like the way the papers spoke of me, said I was in the New Bedford jail. And I got a postal card from the Court, requesting me to call for my witness fees, and that was addressed to the New Bedford jail. I did not like this, so I thought I would show them I would not stay any longer. I think I will try to get a place here [Fall River], through Mrs. McKenney's Agency; if not, I may go to Newport, R.I. and work in the hotel where I was employed before. I have relatives in South Bethlehem, and as I worked there before, I may go again." In a joking manner she said she "may go back to Ireland." She promised wherever she would go, she would let me know through Mrs. Harrington of Division Street.

"She saw nobody about the case since the trial, but several called at New Bedford, and she would not see them; neither would she in the future, for she was tired of the whole thing.

"I think," she said, "it will be hard for me to get a place, for no one wants to hire a person for one month. I think the District Attorney should give me something for my time. The papers and the postal card made me feel badly; but aside from them, I got tired over there. I had nothing to do but look at the walls of the prison, and I found seven grey hairs in my head. I would rather have a place where I would have something to do."

[Bridget was not imprisoned at the jail, she was a cook in the jail keeper's house, but mail was sent to the jail's address. Her reference to not finding work for one month, is that she was to stay in the area until the Grand Jury in November opened. Bridget stated that she had not seen Miss Lizzie or Miss Emma since leaving the Borden house on Monday, August 8, 1892. As she was the Government's witness, it may have been due to a restriction on her visiting the sisters. Or, she may have cut them off. We do see a stronger Bridget through her words to Officer Harrington. She, more than any witness, evolved throughout the months following the crime.]

Lizzie at the trial. Frank Leslie's *Illustrated Weekly*.

Chapter Thirty-One

Superior Court Trial
Day Four, June 8, 1893

Hosea Knowlton plowed on through the ensuing days of the trial. The weight of it pressed upon him; he was no less troubled on the home front. He had written to Attorney General Pillsbury three weeks before the trial began concerning his young daughter's health:

My Dear Atty. General—
...I find myself seriously and unexpectedly handicapped. Our little 3-year-old came down with scarlet fever last Monday. She is doing well: but she is at the age when I would not trust her with hired nurses, for all the world has in the way of reward or glory. That means the home is broken up, children out, Mrs. K. quarantined, & I under the highest obligation to be at home nights, for six weeks—so the Doctor fixes the time. Isn't it wicked, just at this crisis. That was why I had to have Moody come to New Bedford, instead of meeting him, as I originally intended and appointed, in Boston...

Yours very truly,
Hosea M. Knowlton

Sunday P.M.
May 14, 1893

If Hosea Knowlton hoped his piteous words would fall on sympathetic ears, he was mistaken. No reprieve from his duties as head counsel in "the accursed case" was offered. Mr. Pillsbury merely wished him well at home, and it was back to business as usual.

On May 17th, shortly before the Superior Court trial began, there were also letters flying back and forth between the D.A. and Pillsbury concerning Bridget's missing Inquest testimony. Mr. Jennings and Mr. Adams asked for it, but were told neither Knowlton nor Pillsbury had it. As Lizzie's attorneys quoted from it during the trial, it was evidently found. Why they waited until only three weeks before the trial to ask for it, is strange.

Joseph Howard, that bombastic journalist with a flair for words, turned his pen to Lizzie's health as the trial continued on:

"Lizzie alone maintained an unflagging interest, her hacking cough serving to stimulate curiosity as to her condition. It seemed odd enough to see this little woman unattended by one of her sex to support her while she endured the merciless scrutiny of the old women and maidens who stared and stared as though she was a petrification or a mummy from the pyramids of Egypt."

Howard

[Emma was not at Lizzie's side, as all witnesses that were to be called were sequestered outside the courtroom, to eliminate their hearing other's recitals of the events.]

The Cast of Witnesses First on the Scene

Day four of the trial began with a different manner of people attending. Mr. Howard commented that "the country roads were alive with farmer's teams, from early dawn, hurrying toward the courthouse. There were two or three very pretty women, and an especially attractive bride from Boston, but a large majority were vinegar-faced, sharp-nosed, lean-visaged and extremely spare. It was a totally different audience from any that has gathered before."

Lizzie's cough was once again remarked upon. She had been suffering from a bout with bronchitis, and after her fainting spell on Tuesday, kept a small vial of smelling salts in her lap.

Dr. Seabury Bowen: The first witness called that day was Dr. Seabury Bowen. Mr. Howard wrote that "when he took the stand he smiled upon Lizzie, who, wrapped in an outer jacket, seemed tired and presently hid her face behind the fan as her quick eye detected Mr. Moody's reaching for the faded dress concerning which so much has been said."

Dr. Bowen looked uncomfortable as he began his testimony. He had barely begun going over a few minor details about his relationship with the Borden's, when Mr. Moody pounced.

Moody: "On the day preceding August 4, did you see Miss Lizzie Borden at any time on the street?"

Bowen: "I saw her after six o'clock—between six and seven o'clock."

Moody: "Going in which direction?"

Bowen: "Going north, going down the street."

Moody: "Going down?"

Bowen: "Yes, sir."

Moody: "Did you at any time see her coming up the street?"

Bowen: "No, sir."

Moody: "By the street you mean Second Street, I presume?"

Bowen: "Yes, sir."

Moody: "Doctor, you testified at the Inquest, did you not, the private hearing?"

Bowen [squirming now]: "Yes, sir."

Moody: "That time was very soon after these occurrences that are under inquiry?"

Bowen: "Yes, sir."

Moody: "Do you recall whether you said anything at that inquest as to seeing Miss Lizzie Borden coming up the street on Wednesday?"

Bowen: "No, sir; I did not."

Moody: "Perhaps I may aid you: Do you remember being asked the question and replying in the manner that I state, "Where did you afterward see Mr. Borden? Did you see him Thursday?" Answer: "I don't remember seeing him Thursday; I might possibly. I saw him Wednesday walking along between the side street and gate. Lizzie I saw walking up the street and I concluded they were all right, all of them."

Bowen: "Down the street it should have been. I made a mistake."

Moody: "It was a mistake then?"

Bowen: "Yes, sir."

[Bowen not only lies about his statement regarding seeing Lizzie walking "up the street," but as to the time he saw her. The emphasis on Lizzie's direction that day, is that the drug store where she tried to buy prussic acid Wednesday is "up the street," not downstreet where Miss Russell lives, and where Lizzie was headed Wednesday evening. Mr. Moody realizes the significance of the direction she walked that day. Secondly, it was Dr. Bowen's wife, Phoebe, who saw Lizzie walking downstreet at 6 o'clock. She remembered the time because they had just finished dinner. Dr. Bowen now changes the time from 6 o'clock, to between 6 and 7 o'clock. Why? Because it is now known that Lizzie did not arrive at Miss Russell's until 7 o'clock. Where did she go between 6 and 7 that evening? Dr. Bowen has altered the time for her.]

Dr. Bowen states in his testimony that the sofa upon which Andrew Borden's body lay was "even with the door frame." Many have speculated that the location of the sofa in the room looks off-kilter. It is not centered beneath the wall picture, and the head is actually several inches into the dining room door frame. This is how Dr. Bowen found it that morning. If it was moved, it was done so before he arrived, and the only ones there upon his arrival were Lizzie and Mrs. Churchill. Ample room is given between the end of the sofa and the door leading to the kitchen. Perhaps Abby's girth played into its placement.

Mr. Moody gets the doctor to admit that Lizzie blurted out "that father has had trouble with his tenants," and that "Abby had a note and went out," within minutes of his arrival that morning.

Dr. Bowen is then asked if he had any conversation with Lizzie while Bridget and Mrs. Churchill were upstairs on their errand to procure a sheet to cover Mr. Borden. He replied, "No, sir." The doctor then states he left to go and telegraph Emma. When asked how long he had been at the Borden house before he left to do that, he said he didn't know. In earlier testimony, Dr. Bowen first said he arrived at the house that morning close to 11:25. As he ascertained the timeline he needed to cover his tracks in later testimony, he changes his arrival to a good ten minutes earlier. Why? To facilitate how long he was at the house before sending a telegram with an 11:32-time stamp. He was actually gone from the home during that errand longer than he wanted to allow, as it included a quick trip to the Emery's and to talk to John Morse, who was visiting there.

Mr. Moody asks Dr. Bowen about his first view of Abby after Mrs. Churchill tells him they have found her up in the guest room. The doctor testifies he placed his hand on her head and felt the wounds, and then took her pulse, finding her dead. This is a huge departure from his original testimony in the Inquest, and his statements to the police that day. When Moody asked him if he had originally stated that he thought Mrs. Borden had fainted from shock, he emphatically denied saying so. Bowen also changes his original Inquest statement from, "I told them I thought they were both killed at the same instant," to, "I told them I thought they were both killed by the same instrument." This is to save face now that it is common knowledge they died almost two hours apart.

The biggest showdown in Dr. Bowen's testimony came when Mr. Moody pressed him to describe the dress Lizzie had on that morning. He reminded the doctor he had described it as "sort of drab, not much color to it to attract my attention; a sort of morning or calico dress." Moody hounds him to state what he meant by "drab, or not much color," and Bowen dodges him. Finally, Mr. Moody shows Bowen the dress that Lizzie turned over to the police, as the one she wore the morning of the murders before changing into a pink wrapper. After many objections as to his questioning, and that he was, in fact, badgering his own witness, he pinned Bowen down:

Moody[exhibiting dress]: "Does that appear to you, doctor, to be a sort of drab, or not much color to is, sort of morning calico dress? Is that the dress she had on that morning?"

Bowen: "I don't know."

After several more objections, and Dr. Bowen's refusal to say anything but "I don't know," Moody finally got his point across:
Moody: "What color do you call that dress?" [In his hands.]
Bowen: "I should call it dark blue."

[The dress Lizzie wore that morning over the sleeveless Bedford cord, was described by everyone else as light blue, with the exception of Lyman Lubinsky, the ice cream peddler, who remembered it as dark blue, and the Bowen's. Bridget was wearing dark blue, and Lubinsky claimed to see both women at the same time. Was it Bridget's dress he was describing?]

Dr. Bowen was asked by Mr. Adams the state of the shutters in the guest room where Abby's body was found. He said, "they were both thrown together loosely; shutters that fold, the same as these do, but were made of wood. It was only the shutters on the north window, facing Mrs. Churchill's that were partly closed."

[This is significant because Mrs. Churchill testified she was actually in the upper bedroom of her house that morning at the time Abby was being killed. The bedroom where she stood, making the bed, faced the Borden's guest room. Had Lizzie seen her, and quickly thrown the upper and lower shutters to?]

Dr. Bowen testifies as to the position of Abby's body, and that he and Dr. Dolan lifted it to check the wounds, and the photograph was taken later that day may have shown her in a slightly different position, especially her arms. He was also asked about Andrew's body in the photograph, and he said Mr. Borden's head was lower in the picture; that the body had slipped down somewhat from when he first saw him.

He testified to giving Lizzie bromo caffeine on Thursday to quiet her nerves, but increased it Friday to morphine sulfate, a dose that was doubled on Saturday. Mr. Adams (Lizzie's attorney) then got the doctor to testify to Lizzie taking morphine from that Saturday, all throughout the Inquest, and her arrest. He elicited the information that morphine "given in double doses can affect the memory and change and alter the view of things and give people hallucinations." Mr. Moody, for the prosecution, was able to get Bowen to admit he only saw Lizzie actually take the dose twice.

Bridget Sullivan (recalled): Bridget is recalled to clear up a few things. Mr. Robinson for the defense begins by asking her about going down to the cellar with the officers the morning of the murders. She is asked who those officers were.

Bridget: "Mr. Doherty, Mr. Fleet, and Mr. Medley."

Robinson: "Those three men? Mr. Doherty, Mr. Fleet and Mr. Medley?"

Bridget: "I think they was. I didn't know them: I learned since that they were."

Robinson: "You know now?"

Bridget: "Yes, sir; I heard they were the officers."

Robinson: "Well, you have seen the same men again several times?"

Bridget: "Yes, sir, but I wouldn't know them again, until I was told they were the men."

Mr. Knowlton: "What did you say?"

Bridget: "I wouldn't know the men again, but I heard they were the officers that went down with me."

[If you look at Bridget's wording, you get the sense she knows she has been told a lie as to who accompanied her to the cellar that morning. It was not Officer Medley, it was Officer Mullaly. They chose another name beginning with 'M' to confuse her. Mullaly is an officer who will play a major role in the upcoming testimony, and he was the one who originally found the handleless hatchet the morning of the murders. They need Bridget to get him away from the cellar, and the hatchet, with her testimony. Officer Medley did come across the broken hatchet, but not until three days later, on Monday.]

Bridget sticks with her story that she only showed the men where the hatchets were, but did not touch them. Officer Mullaly stated she handed them down to him. Robinson shows Bridget the cellar floor plan and asks her if it helps locate where the hatchets were; she claims "it doesn't help me at all." She says she doesn't know what was done with the hatchets after they were found, never saw them lying on the cellar floor, and pretty much distances herself from any knowledge concerning them.

She is asked about the dress she wore that morning (dark indigo blue calico with a white clover leaf figure). She later changed that afternoon to a blue gingham with a double border of white at the bottom. She couldn't remember what time in the afternoon she changed. She ended her testimony by claiming she did not see Lizzie cry that day, despite Mr. Robinson reminding her she said during her Inquest that Lizzie was crying when Bridget saw her standing at the bottom of the stairs.

Mrs. Churchill: Mr. Howard gave a concise description of Mrs. Adelaide Churchill as she stood to testify before the jury.

"The next witness was Mrs. Churchill, who testified that she was a widow who rented rooms and did her own work, enjoying life as she passed through it, and she looked it.

"When Governor Robinson questioned her as to the dress worn by Lizzie, she was inclined to be very positive as to Lizzie's dress, which she described as a light blue and white mixed groundwork woven together as it were, with a dark navy blue diamond figure on which there was no spot of blood or anything else."

MRS. CHURCHILL

Fall River Herald's illustration of Mrs. Churchill on the stand.

And then, Mrs. Churchill dropped the bombshell.

Mr. Moody (Showing the dark blue dress Lizzie turned over to the police as the one she wore that morning): "Was that the dress she had on this morning?" [Morning of the murders.]

Mrs. Churchill: "It does not look like it."

Lizzie's composure, after hearing her longtime friend betray her in such a way, is not reported upon. Mrs. Churchill also testified the dress Lizzie wore that day was "not snug." It "had a box pleat or something down the front..it was loose." Mrs. Churchill further stated she never saw Lizzie cry that day.

Mr. Robinson took over and asked Mrs. Churchill if the street outside the Borden's, and her own home, was a noisy street. She replied it was. He asked her "if the windows to her house were open to that noise, you might not be able to hear noises in the house?" She said that was true. Interestingly, Mrs. Churchill testified only minutes before that Lizzie told her she heard "a distressing sound" that morning coming from the house, while she was out back, and that noise caused her to come in to find her father murdered. Robinson opened the door for the prosecution to point out a noisy street works both ways; no one walked through it.

Mrs. Churchill recounted the events of the morning, all of which have been provided earlier in the book. She offered nothing new, other than to describe Mrs. Borden as "a very fleshy woman, not much taller than I am." She said Lizzie told her twice she wished someone would go and look for Mrs. Borden that morning—the second time after Miss Russell came. She saw no blood on Lizzie nor did she see another dress beneath the one she wore.

Mr. Robinson asked Mrs. Churchill whether it was Lizzie or Bridget that spoke to her in the kitchen about the note Abby received from "a sick friend." Robinson hammers home that it was Bridget, not Lizzie, who said Mrs. Borden had a note and hurried off. Mrs. Churchill repeated Bridget's words, "She was dusting in the sitting room, and hurried off. She didn't tell me where she was going, she generally does." She stayed with Lizzie until 12 o'clock that day, until she finally went home. She said Lizzie was sitting in the dining room, and had not gone upstairs, when she left.

A final follow-up question was asked Mrs. Churchill by Mr. Moody, which shed some light on Mr. Jennings efforts early on to get some of the witnesses to testify the dress Lizzie turned into the police was the one she wore that morning:

Moody: "Mrs. Churchill, was your attention called very soon after this to the question of what dress Miss Lizzie Borden had on the morning of this homicide?"

Churchill: "I was asked at the Inquest what dress, and I described it."

Moody [exhibiting dress]: "Was this dress called to your attention soon after that, this particular dress?"

Mr. Robinson: "Wait a moment."

Moody: "When did you first see this dress?"

Churchill: "Mr. Jennings showed it to me the first time that I saw it."

Moody: "How soon was that after the homicide?"

Churchill: "I don't know how soon, before the public hearing, I think...after the Inquest."

Moody: "And did you have some talk with Mr. Jennings about the dress (I don't ask you what was said)? Did some talk pass between him and you with reference to the dress?"

Churchill: "Yes, sir."

Mr. Robinson (for the defense): "Did you happen to know that all the dresses, this one included, were taken by the officers on Saturday, the day of the funeral?"

Churchill: "No, sir, I didn't know anything about it."

Robinson: "And had been kept in the possession of the government ever since; did you know that?"

Churchill: "No, sir."

Robinson: "Did you know it was produced by the officers at the Inquest?"

Churchill: "No, sir. I didn't see any dress at the Inquest."

Robinson: "Well, you don't know about that?"

Churchill: "No, sir, I don't know."

Mr. Knowlton: "Do you mean to imply that was so?"

Robinson: "I do not mean to imply anything. I ask the witness what she knows about it, and I am not testifying."

[This is the first we hear that they kept all of the dresses from the closet the day of the second search, after the sisters are back from the funeral. It was reported there were close to eighteen dresses in the "clothes press." If the dresses are gone, then Emma Borden's testimony (yet to come) about what occurred that Saturday night in the dress closet is highly suspicious.

It is clear Mr. Jennings had tried to encourage Mrs. Churchill to "recognize" the blue dress Lizzie handed in as the one she saw her wearing that morning. Mrs. Churchill stuck to her guns, and described the dress she saw. Of all the witnesses, hers is the most detailed description of Lizzie's dress that morning.]

While the tension mounted inside the courtroom, outside it was another hot day in New Bedford. Joseph Howard, with typical aplomb, described the "temperature" of the ongoings:

> "By the side of the courthouse runs one of the busiest thoroughfares of the city, along which ramshackle mill teams and rattlebang wagons incessantly do roll. Crowds stand there all day long, birds sing, the cow moos, and a regular monkey-and-parrot time is perpetually on the go. No wonder the court declined to sit all day. No wonder that at this point a recess was taken and all hands rushed pell-mell for the dining rooms, where, in spite of the crowds, an appetizing and satisfying lunch was neatly and correctly served."

Alice Russell: Word was out Miss Alice Russell would next be called to the stand. Mr. Howard wrote, "The interest all along has been intense, but the intensity was made vivid by the report that Miss Alice Russell, for many years, so to speak, bosom friend of Lizzie Borden, who had testified and sworn to tell the truth, the whole truth and nothing else at the Inquest, had had her conscience gnawed some months ago, and had made up her mind to moult the wing of friendship and literally obey the mandate implied by the phraseology of her oath.

"To men and women ordinarily constituted such an experience as Miss Russell had today would be tolerably tough, but with unmartingaled manner she threw up her head with lofty disdain and told her story again and again.

"Miss Russell, who is very tall, angular and thin, with a lofty forehead and pale blue eyes, is extremely trim in her manner and holds her mouth as though prisms and prunes were its most frequent utterances. As she took the oath, Lizzie hitched her chair up closer to brother Adams, removed her coat, and gave her a look."

The New York Herald's drawing of Alice Russell.

Miss Russell retold her story from the Preliminary Hearing, tapping her black fan against the railing for emphasis. She gave a detailed account of Lizzie's visit the Wednesday night before the murders—where Lizzie told of poison and enemies, and her postponed trip to Marion. The courtroom heard how the young woman felt "as though something is hanging over me that I can't throw off." She repeated Lizzie's story of the Marion girls asking her why she didn't join in with the conversation, and how her father had mistreated Dr. Bowen when he called to check on the family that morning.

Thursday's events were told as reported earlier in this book: Miss Russell saw the policemen force the hook from Lizzie's bedroom door; she tried to loosen Lizzie's dress blouse in the dining room when she thought Lizzie was heated, but Lizzie said, "I am not faint," and stayed her hand; she went with Lizzie to her room and was immediately sent to tell Bowen to ask for Winward for the funeral services; she saw Lizzie come out of Emma's room tieing a pink wrapper; she and Lizzie took the slop pail to the cellar that night, and she was unaware that Lizzie returned a few minutes later alone.

It is here that Alice falters as Mr. Moody asks if they went straight upstairs after their return from the cellar. Alice keeps saying, "I don't know...still I don't know..." that they went straight upstairs, after arriving on the first floor from the cellar. The Author's thoughts on this were offered earlier. It was a strange confession to make on Miss Russell's part.

Alice tells of the dress burning, and confessing to Detective Hanscom about it. When Mr. Moody asks her if she mentioned the dress burning at the Inquest, or Preliminary Hearing, she admits she did not.

Miss Russell is asked if she heard about the note Abby was to have received that day, as to the search made for it. She answered that Dr. Bowen had come into the dining room and asked Lizzie if she knew where it could be. He had looked all over and in the wastebaskets. Alice said she volunteered that Abby "probably burned it," and Lizzie readily agreed that must be what happened to it. She went on to say that she did not see Lizzie cry, or faint. She saw no blood on her clothing, hair or hands. The searches were gone over, and how Miss Russell saw a "small bundle" on the floor of Emma's closet, as the police pushed against it with the door.

Alice's last moments on the stand were taken up with the detailed information of where Lizzie stood in the kitchen as she burned the dress the Sunday morning after the murders. Alice was asked to mark on a diagram where Lizzie stood at the stove, and where the cupboard was that held the torn pieces of dress. She did so, and it was shown to the jury.

Mr. Moody: "What was that cupboard used for? What was its use?"

Alice: "As near as I remember, there was coal and wood kept in the closet, and on the other shelves I remember seeing flat irons; that is all I remember, there were kitchen utensils."

With that, Alice was released. She avoided looking at the Defense table, and walking ram-rod straight, exited the courtroom, and Lizzie's life.

John Cunningham: Mr. Cunningham, the newsdealer who found himself thrown into the center of the murder case of a lifetime, testified next.   His story was the same as he reported in the Preliminary Hearing.   Only when he spoke of looking through the grass on the south side of the house for clues, and finding no one had walked there, did a ripple go through the courtroom.   As Joseph Howard aptly put it, "A new dealer testified that he carefully examined the grass about the Borden house immediately after the tragedy, but could not discover any footprints, which is unfortunate for the reputation of his eyesight, as both Bridget and Mr. Morse had been out there in the morning."

Officer George W. Allen: Mr. Allen was the first policeman to show up that fateful Thursday morning. He testified as he had earlier. He saw Mr. Borden before the sheet had been called for to cover him; he checked the first floor closets for a murderer; saw Lizzie and said she was not crying; deputitzed Charles Sawyer to stand guard at the door; went to the station to inform the Marshal of what he found; returned with Officer Mulally and saw Mrs. Borden dead upstairs; saw a bloody handkerchief between her feet and the window (it was probably moved when the doctors straightened her); he saw no blood on the furnishings of the sitting room, other than the sofa. He went away shortly before noon, after his second visit to the house.

Officer Francis H. Wixon: Joseph Howard described Officer Wixon as "a cheeky deputy sheriff who told of frightful wounds on the bodies and contrasted the thinness of the blood on Mr. Borden with that of Mrs. Borden. His idea was to prove that the woman was killed long before the man. This inference he was asked to give as an opinion, and after a long argument between the learned brothers, having come to a conclusion that they would hear it, directed the witness to give it, whereupon, he promptly replied, "I have none." The courtroom laughed…and the cow mooed.

Assistant Marshal John Fleet: Mr. Fleet's testimony has been entered before. He kept to the story of his arrival that day, his two conversations with Lizzie in her room—underscoring her acerbic statement, "She is not my mother! She is my stepmother!" He spoke of seeing Officer Medley in the side yard as he arrived that day, and of going to the cellar twice. On his first visit he found Officers Devine and Mullaly. There were two hatchets and two axes laying on the washroom floor. He picked up the clawhead hatchet and studied it. It stood out to him due to its sharpness, a few stains that could be blood, and that it looked as if it had been freshly washed and "wiped down." He hid it in the keeping cellar next to the wash room behind some barrels, to make sure nothing happened to it.

During his second trip to the cellar, he found the same policemen there, along with Dr. Dolan. He asked Officer Mulally to show him where the hatchets and axes had been found. Mullaly took him to the middle cellar where the wood was stored, and pointed out the box the hatchets had been in.

ASST MARSHAL FLEET EXAMINES AN AXE

Fall River Herald's drawing of Assitant Marshal Fleet with one of the axes.

Mr. Fleet was shown the two axes and hatchets and asked if they looked like the ones he saw that day. He said they did. He was asked if the spot of blood he thought he saw on the clawhead hatchet was still there. He said he did not see it now.

Mr. Fleet was then asked to describe in detail what happened after Officer Mulally showed him the box where the two hatchets had been found.

Fleet: "In the middle cellar, on a shelf, or a jog of the chimney—an old-fashioned chimney—I found the head of a hatchet. It was in a box, I should say, about a foot or fourteen inches long, perhaps eight or ten inches wide. It might be a little larger, and I should say about four inches deep. There were some other tools, and pieces of iron."

He is shown the hatchet head and asked if that is the one he saw.

Fleet: "This looks like the hatchet I found there; pretty sure that that is the one. This piece of wood was in the head of the hatchet, broken off close. It was covered with white ashes, I should say, upon the blade of the hatchet--not upon one side, but upon both. The other tools in the box had dust upon them. It was a light dust. That is, the dust on the other tools was lighter and finer than the dust upon that hatchet. The piece of the handle had a new break. There seemed to be ashes on the break as well. I put it back in the box, looked around the cellar, and went outside.

Mr. Fleet testified to his searching Lizzie's room on the day of the murders with Officer Minnehan (who was at the time of the Superior Court, deceased) and Officer Wixon. He stated Lizzie's unhappiness to see them there, and about her telling them it was a waste of time to look in her room as she always kept the door locked and no one could get in, or throw anything in. He then described the searches of Saturday, and in particular, the search of the dress closet at the end of the second-floor hallway. Mr. Fleet had a hard time remembering if there had been a white cloth hanging over the dresses (as he testified at the Preliminary Hearing). He now said "he thought not" about them being covered.

Mr. Robinson asks Mr. Fleet if he saw any paint on any of the dresses. When Mr. Fleet says he did not, Robinson said, "Would you have seen any blood the way you looked?" referring to Fleet saying they did not do a careful search of the dresses on Thursday, the day of the murders. Mr. Fleet answered, "Not without it was on the outside, right before my eyes. I didn't look at them closely."

Governor Robinson had made his point: Lizzie's paint-stained dress could have been hanging there, and the men missed it. The double-edged sword here, is it also meant they could have missed one with blood stains. Governor Robinson closed for the day with the facetious question "Were you looking for a man in that clothing?" Fleet answered, "If he was there, yes we were." Robinson shot back that the door to the closet was locked and required a key to get into it.

At 5:00 P.M. the court was adjourned to Friday, June 9th, at 9:00 a.m.

Chapter Thirty-Two

The Superior Court Trial
Day Five

The saga of the hatchet head is a compelling one. It became the ugly step-child as the trial progressed. Bridget distanced herself from the hatchets completely, still cognizant that, should Lizzie be found "not guilty," the fickle wheels of suspicion could roll her way. There were only two people home that day who could have committed the murders, and she was one of them.

Assistant Marshal Fleet, with his self-important attitude, had taken the credit for finding the handleless hatchet on the day of the murder, eager to claim the spotlight for the weapon now being branded the likely candidate for the murders. The clawhead hatchet—the favored star of the Preliminary Hearings—had been thrown out, due to the fact its 5"-wide blade was too broad to have done the deed. Fleet leaped completely over Officer Mullaly's part in showing him the box where the hatchets had been found, and that both men discovered the hatchet head at the same time. Mr. Fleet came to rue the fact he had taken full credit for its discovery that grizzly morning.

Day Five of the Superior Court trial began with the recalling of Fleet to the stand to continue his testimony. Obviously, during the night, he had realized an error he made in the previous day's testimony—or a member of the prosecution firmly pointed it out. It was time to do damage control. Governor Robinson had other plans.

Robinson: "Were there any ashes there?" [In the middle room of the cellar where the hatchet head was found.]

Fleet: "There was. In the middle cellar."

Robinson: "Where you found the box?"

Fleet: "Yes. The box with the hatchets in it. There might be six bushels [of ashes], within a few feet of the chimney."

Robinson: "So that the pile of ashes was right near—within a few feet of that chimney where the box was in which these hatchets were found, and in which you found that one without a handle—is that right?"

Fleet: "Yes, they were coal ashes."

Robinson [Showing hatchet without a head]: "When did you find that?"

Fleet: "The afternoon of the 4th of August, the second visit [to the cellar]."

Robinson: "Why didn't you tell me before when you went on to tell about the second visit, why didn't you tell me that you found this?"

Fleet: "You didn't ask me."

Robinson: "I didn't ask you! You didn't know that I was trying to find out all you did in the cellar at each of these times down there? You didn't understand that, did you?"

Fleet: "I have already stated when and where I found that."

Robinson: "Who were there when you found this?"

Fleet: "Officer Mullaly,"

Robinson: "Mr. Mullaly you said stood right by?" [When Fleet found the hatchet head in the box].

Fleet: "He was there and showed me the box where the hatchets was taken from."

Robinson: "Did you take it out in his presence?"

Fleet: "I don't recollect whether he saw me take it out or not. He may have done so."

Robinson: "Had you noticed whether either of the other two hatchets were covered with ashes?"

Fleet: "The smaller one was somewhat dusty."

Robinson: "Now about this one, the clawhead."

Fleet: "That one had apparently been cleansed. It looked damp. The hatchet looked to me bluer than it does now, and there was one red spot upon the blade [the clawhead]. I think it was rust."

Robinson: "Did you take out the other tools that were in the box?"

Fleet: "I did not."

Robinson: "Did you see whether they were dusty or not?"

Fleet: "They were dusty...some dust on them."

Robinson: "Was there any dust on this one, the one without a handle?"

Fleet: "There was. All over it. It looked as if it might have fell into that ash barrel."

Robinson: "And that little piece of the handle was on there at that time, wasn't it?" [The small piece that fit into the eye of the hatchet had been taken out by Professor Wood to look for blood.]

Fleet: "Yes."

Robinson [About to spring the trap]: "And that end there had ashes on it just the same way as it indicates now?"

Fleet: "Not so much as it had on the other end here."

Robinson: "Which end do you mean?"

Fleet: "This piece here was new, apparently a new break." [Indicating the end of the broken hatchet head handle where the break was.]

Robinson: "Had ashes on it, hadn't it?"

Fleet: "I didn't notice any ashes, on the new break."

Robinson: "Now, what did you do with that after bringing it out of the box?"

Fleet: "I didn't bring it out."

Robinson: "What did you do with it?"

Fleet: "I let it remain in the box after looking at it."

Robinson: "You didn't take it along with you?"

Fleet: "I did not."

Robinson: "Did you show it to Mr. Mullaly? Was Mr. Mullaly there?"

Fleet: "He was there."

Robinson: "Did you show it to Mr. Mullaly?"

Fleet: "I can't say that I did. I think I did. I think he saw it."

Robinson: "Did he see you put it back in the box?"

Fleet: "I presume that he did, sir."

Robinson: "And you didn't take it out and lay it down with these others?"

Fleet: "No, sir."

Robinson: "You went off, and left this in the old ashy box just as you found it, did you?"

Fleet: "Yes."

[Mr. Fleet is against the ropes. He has just contradicted his testimony from the day before that he saw ashes on the end of the handle where the new break was seen. If ashes were found on the part of the handle piece, it would show that Lizzie did not just break it the morning of the murders, to make it look as if it could not have been used as a murder weapon; ashes on the break would make it appear dusty and used like the other tools in the box. Fleet realizes that now, and changes his testimony to say he saw no dust on the broken edge.

Robinson catches him out in another lie. He asks Fleet what he did with the hatchet head after bringing it out of the box. Fleet replies, "I didn't bring it out." How could Fleet have known the hatchet head was coated with ashes on both sides without removing it to look at it? Robinson catches him up again by asking if Mullaly saw him put it back in the box. Fleet says, "I presume he did." Fleet's testimony was a mess, and it was about to explode in his face when Officer Mullaly takes the stand later that day—the officer he just tried to show did, or did not, witness his actions with the hatchet head.]

Robinson then goes in for the kill:
Robinson: "Well, do you say this morning, having it called to your attention, that were no ashes on that broken end at that time?"
Fleet: "Not that I discovered."
Robinson: "Will you swear they were not there?"
Fleet: "No, I couldn't really do that."
Robinson: "You don't really do that?"
Fleet: "No, sir."
Robinson: "What did you say yesterday about ashes on the end?"
Fleet: "I don't know that I said anything yesterday about ashes on that end. I said that the hatchet was all covered with dust."
Robinson: "Do you remember being asked by Mr. Moody yesterday: "At that time did you observe anything with reference to ashes upon the point of the break of the handle,

upon the wood where it was broken?" And you answered, "There seemed to be ashes there like the other."

Fleet: "I might have said that, yes, sir."

Robinson: "Were you telling it as it was yesterday or as you tell it now this morning?"

Fleet: "I tell it this morning just as I saw it."

Robinson: "Then you didn't tell it yesterday as you saw it?"

Fleet: "Well, I suppose I did yesterday as I thought. I may have misunderstood about the break. I understand this was a new break."

After much badgering from Robinson, and many disclaimers from Mr. Fleet, the final answer was arrived upon:

Robinson: "I know you keep saying that [that it was a new break], but I am after the ashes on the break. Now, which one of those answers will you take, or do you want to make another one?"

Fleet: "No, sir; I will take the answer—this answer: that I didn't discover or didn't notice any ashes upon the break."

Robinson: "That is this morning's statement?"

Fleet: "Yes; while there *might* have been ashes on there."

Robinson [Yelling]: "Oh, are you going to put that in?"

[The clunk sound in the room may have been Attorney Knowlton's forehead hitting the prosecution table. Fleet's testimony was a disaster.]

Robinson [Giving up, having made his point]: "Do you know who took it away from the place where you put it?"

Fleet: "Only as I have heard...Officer Medley. It was in possession of the Marshal."

Governor Robinson goes on to trap Fleet again by reminding him that in his Preliminary Hearing testimony, Fleet said he found no other weapon in the cellar other than the four laying on the cellar floor. He did not mention finding the handleless hatchet at all. Fleet dances around it saying he "didn't think it came into play."

With that, a humiliated Assistant Marshal stepped down from the stand. His feelings of embarrassment and anger would pale compared to what was coming later.

Officer Phil Harrington: Officer Harrington retold his story from the Preliminary Hearing offered earlier in the book. He had questioned Lizzie, and found her answers so unusual that he had cautioned her to wait until the next day to submit to any more inquiries. She had courtsied, and said she could answer them just as well at that time. He said she was never in tears, and described her attitude as "cool."

Harrington recites his amazingly-detailed description of Lizzie's pink wrapper. The smiles went through the gallery, and Mr. Moody couldn't resist asking at the end of it, "That finishes it, does it?" Even Lizzie smiled and laughed softly. Harrington then told of seeing Dr. Bowen reading a torn note with the word "Emma" written in the top left corner, stating it was only something "about my daughter going through somewhere," and then watching as the doctor tossed the scraps of paper into the stove fire. At that time, Harrington said he noticed a roll of burned paper inside the stove. At that point, Dr. Dolan entered the kitchen with "two or three cans in his hands, and three hatchets." He called Harrington over to stand guard over the cans. Fleet then sent him off on an errand.

After returning, he joined the others in searching the barn. He testified the barn was "very hot, suffocating, with considerable dust." Harrington then searched the yards flanking the Borden's property and spoke with the people there. He found no weapon, and no marks of blood "of any kind."

Mr. Robinson, during his cross-examination of Officer Harrington, elicits the information that Lizzie said her father had returned from the Post Office that morning, and she asked him, "Any mail for me?" and she said he replied, "No." [Bridget said she did not hear Andrew answer Lizzie about the mail.] Robinson then asks Officer Harrington if he noticed what shoes Andrew had on that morning:

Harrington: "He had a laced shoe."

Robinson: "Do you mean a low shoe?" [Hoping to show Andrew had changed into slippers, with Lizzie's help, just as Lizzie said.]

Harrington: "No, sir."

Robinson: "A laced high shoe? It was not a congress boot?"

Harrington: "No, sir."

Robinson then shows him the photograph of Andrew laying dead on the sofa, wearing congress boots.

Robinson: "Seeing this [photo], having this to refresh your recollection, do you change your statement?"

Harrington: "No, sir."

Robinson: "You leave it that he had on laced boots?

Harrington: "My impression was laced boots."

After a few more questions as to the cellar and barn, Officer Harrington stood down. The man who could describe a woman's pink wrapper in such detail that it rivaled that of any fashion diva, could not recall the shoes a *man* had on. So far, it had not been a banner day for the police.

CAPTAIN HARRINGTON UNDER CROSS EXAMINATION.

Officer Phil Harrington being cross-examined by Governor Robinson.

Officer Patrick H. Doherty: Next up was Officer Doherty, the gentleman who became closest to Bridget Sullivan as he escorted her to and from the Inquest, and made sure she was guarded at her relative's residence on Division Street during the Preliminary Hearing. Perhaps their Irish heritage made them kindred spirits.

Doherty went over the day's events, from his arrival until his departure. He testified Lizzie told him she had been in the barn and heard "a scraping noise." She told the officer Mr. Eddy and Mr. Johnson from the Swansea farms would never hurt her father, and that Mr. Eddy "is sick."

Officer Patrick Doherty

Officer Doherty said he later went up to her room and opened the door a few inches to enter. She stopped him, and said, "One minute,' and shut the door in his face. A full minute or two later, she opened it, and he went in and looked around. Miss Russell was there.

Doherty was asked by Mr. Moody to describe the dress Lizzie was wearing downstairs when he first interviewed her in the kitchen:

Doherty: "When I saw her downstairs, I thought she had a light blue dress with bosom in the waist, or something like a bosom. I have a faint recollection; that is all I can say about it. I thought she had a light blue dress. I thought there was a small figure on the dress; a little spot, like."

Moody [showing Doherty the dress Lizzie turned in]: "Was it this dress?"

Doherty: "No, I don't think so."

The dress with "a bosom in the waist" was called a Pigeon dress in 1892 (l). Compare it to the tight fit of the 1892 dress in the photo on the right. Mrs. Churchill said the dress Lizzie wore the day of the murders was not tight, it was a "box pleat, loose." Photo courtesy of The Dresstress.com.

Officer Doherty states that he did not get to look in Emma's room during the time he went into Lizzie's room, after she closed the door on him. The door to Emma's room was locked. Had Lizzie hurried and locked it before letting him in? Perhaps telling a confused Alice Russell who was sitting there, something like "Emma would not want strange men in her room." We do know that the first team to search the room found Emma's door open, but only "peeked in."

Was it because of the bundle on Emma's shelf, that may have contained the torn sleeves and hem from Lizzie's Bedford cord? Was it that she had temporarily hung the blue dress she had been wearing all day there, as she slipped into the pink wrapper? It is strange that the door was unlocked one minute, and locked later.

Officer Doherty stated he saw Lizzie the next day, on Friday, and she was wearing the same light blue dress as the day before. He had been on guard duty at the house all night, beginning at one a.m. At six the next morning, Friday morning, he watched Officer Edson take away the four hatchets and axes. He was also in the kitchen when Lizzie entered and asked Bridget if she was sure the cellar door had been locked the morning before. Bridget answered,

"Yes, marm." Doherty said Bridget was wearing a dark calico, possibly brown.

Doherty told the court the only search he joined in was the day of the murder, including the barn, which he called "stifling hot." He did not search on Friday, Saturday, or Monday.

Officer Michael Mullaly: The twentieth witness to take the stand was Officer Michael Mullaly. Mr. Mullaly would turn out to be the case's most sensational witness, next to Alice Russell and Professor Wood. Yet, of all the police officials that worked on the Borden case, he was the only one not to be advanced in rank. Some of the men were promoted the very day after the murders. Officer Mullaly's police report, called "The Witness Statements," is also curiously missing. Could this all be due to what was about to happen in that stuffy courtroom, on Friday, June 9th, 1893?

Mr. Moody opened the questioning of Officer Mullaly by asking him how long he had been a policeman with the Fall River Police. He answered "fifteen years."

Moody: "And your position in the force is what?"

Mullaly: "Patrolman."

Moody: "It was last August, was it?"

Mullaly: "Yes, sir."

Was Mr. Moody underlining that Officer Mullaly had not been promoted as the other officers?

The day of the murders Officer Mullaly had arrived at the Borden's at "23 minutes to twelve." He first spoke to Lizzie when he stuck his head into the dining room and asked her if she knew what personal effects her father might have on him. She answered him "a silver watch and chain, a pocketbook with money in, and a gold ring on his little finger." He then asked her if she knew if there was a hatchet or ax on the premises; she said there was, and Bridget would show him where they were. Before they went to the cellar where the hatchets were, he, Doherty and Bridget searched the attic area, finding nothing of interest.

Officer Mullaly, along with Bridget and Officer Doherty, went to the cellar. He stated the following:

Mullaly: "Bridget led the way. She went into the cellar there, and she took from a box two hatchets."

A ripple went through the room. Bridget had claimed emphatically during her time on the stand, she did not touch the hatchets.

> Mullaly: "She reached up and took them out and gave them to me. She had to reach up, and didn't have to stand on anything to get it. I took them out into what I call the wash room and laid them on the floor, and I stayed there with them until Mr. Fleet came. The ax handles were covered with ashes at the time. I called Mr. Fleet's attention to them when he came. He looked at them. [Laying on the wash cellar floor.]"

Officer Mullaly said he then went upstairs and out into the yard, and searched the yard, the wood pile, the barn and fences, "all around and back into the house again." He went into the guest room with Officer Hyde and searched around in there where Abby lay dead. He then went back down to the cellar; Officer Hyde went with him. He searched around the cellar again, and did not find anything. Officer Fleet then came down again.

Mr. Moody then leads Mullaly carefully into what happened after Fleet spoke to him:

> Moody: "What did you do after Mr. Fleet spoke to you?"
> Mullaly: "I showed him where them hatchets were taken from."
> Moody: "What did you show?"
> Mullaly: "I showed him a box where Bridget had taken them from."
> Moody: "What did you do after you showed him the box?"
> Mullaly: "He took a hatchet out of there. It looked to me as if it was smaller than one of them [indicating the four on display]. The handle was broken and he put it back, and it was covered with dust or ashes, or something like that. It had a clean break, it looked fresh, as if just broken."
> Moody: "How did that [the break], in respect to the dust and ashes, compare with the sides of the hatchet? How did the freshly broken wood in respect of dust and ashes, compare with the sides of the hatchet?"
> Mullaly: "It was cleaner, the hatchet."

The noon recess was called, bringing a welcome, yet an anti-climatic end to the morning's testimonies of hatchets and ashes.

The newspapers reported that Lizzie "looked wilted" and "pale." The noise outside the open windows of the courtroom was reported as unrelenting: stonemasons chipping away, horse and buggy traffic, birds singing, and the unhappy Bessie mooing in the background.

When court reconvened at 2:15, the judges and gallery looked refreshed. Lunch had been served, and the weekend lay only a few hours ahead. For Lizzie, the thought of a bed, even one shadowed with bars, must have seemed like a welcome reprieve to the grueling week.

Officer Mullaly stepped back onto the stand and waited for Mr. Moody to begin.

Moody: "Mr. Mullaly, you had been describing the appearance of the hatchet without a handle. Was there anything you noticed with reference with it?"

Mullaly: "The handle was broken fresh. Both sides of the blade was covered with what I call ashes. It looked so as though it was rubbed on there, wiped on, would be my way of expressing it."

Moody: "What did Mr. Fleet do with it after each of you had observed it?"

Mullaly: "I believe he put it back."

Moody: "Did you see the hatchet again afterward?"

Mullaly: "Not in the house."

Moody: "Wherever you saw it, if you saw it at all, you saw it after it was taken away from the house?"

Mullaly: "Yes, sir."

Moody: "Then where did you go?"

Mullaly: "Then went upstairs to this room where Mrs. Borden lay; Officer Hyde and myself searched it, and there I saw Miss Borden, and I had some conversation with her there. I inquired of her whether she saw somebody around the premises, and she told me she did. She said she saw a man around there with dark clothes on. She said he was a man about the size of the Officer Hyde, or about as large as Officer Hyde. I then went to the attic with Mr. Fleet and searched. Then I went into the yard, over the fence into the Kelly's yard. I didn't find any weapon or appearance of blood."

Mullaly's final statements concerning the hatchets, was that the box, from which Bridget retrieved them, was up high, and without a lid. He had not looked in it, merely accepted the two hatchets from her.

Governor Robinson hefted himself from his chair, and adjusted his glasses importantly. Fans fluttered throughout the courtroom, an occasional cough broke the momentary silence, and Lizzie waited. If Alfred Hitchcock had scripted the suspense surrounding the following testimony, he would not have improved upon it.

Robinson: "Were you looking yourself, helping him [Mr. Fleet] to find anything [in the cellar]?"

Mullaly: "He came down in the cellar and asked me where Miss Sullivan got those hatchets from, and I showed him."

Robinson: "In that same box?"

Mullaly: "In that same box."

Robinson: "And then he looked in the box?"

Mullaly: "He went there and he took it out."

Robinson: "And you had not been there to look before?"

Mullaly: "No; I had been there to look in the box."

Robinson: "Nothing else was taken out of it while you were there?"

Mullaly: "Nothing but the hatchet and parts of the handle."

Robinson [dismissively]: "Well, parts. That piece?' [Indicating the little piece that was in the eye with the fresh break on one end.]

Mullaly: "That piece, yes."

Robinson: "Well, that was in the eye, wasn't it?"

Mullaly: "Yes; then there was another piece."

Robinson: "Another piece of what?"

Mullaly: "Handle."

A collective gasp filled the room. The Governor stared at the Officer on the stand as if he had just sprouted tentacles. Even the Judges' heads swiveled in the witness' direction— three incredulous faces turning in unison. The cow mooed for emphasis, but this time, no one laughed.

Mr. Robinson composed himself and thundered, "Where is it?"

Mullaly: "I don't know."

Robinson: "Don't you know where it is?"

Mullaly: "No, sir."

Robinson: "Was it a piece of that same handle?"

Mullaly: "It was a piece that corresponded with that."

Robinson: "The rest of the handle?"

Mullaly: "It was a piece with a fresh break in it."

Robinson: "The other piece?"

Mullaly: "Yes, sir."

Robinson: "Well where is it? Did you see it after that?"

Mullaly: "I did not."

Robinson: "Well, did you take it out of the box?"

Mullaly: "I did not."

Robinson: "Did you see it taken out?"

Mullaly: "I did."

Robinson: "Who took it out?"

Mullaly: "Mr. Fleet took it out."

The courtroom was electric. The buzz of whispers filled the air, as once again, Governor Robinson struggled to rebound from the shock.

Robinson: "Mr. Fleet took it out?" he finally managed.

Mullaly: "Yes, sir."

Robinson: "You were there?"

Mullaly: "I was there."

Robinson: "Anybody else?"

Mullaly: "Not as I know of."

Robinson: "Did Mr. Fleet put that back too?"

Mullaly: "He did."

With an expansive breath that threatened to pop the shirt buttons straining against the Governor's barrel chest, he turned his reddened face to the prosecution table.

Robinson: "Have you that handle here, gentlemen?"

Knowlton: "No," was all the attorney could muster.

Robinson: "You haven't it in your possession, may I ask?"

Knowlton: "Never had it."

Robinson: "The government does not know where it is?" obviously convinced a cover-up is going on.

Knowlton (with obvious humiliation): "I don't know where it is. This is the first I ever heard of it."

The courtroom erupted in excited whispers. The tension between the opposing attorneys was palpable. Robinson whirled on his heel, and faced a nervous Michael Mullaly.

Robinson: "Did you ever tell anybody about this before?" he barked.

Mullaly: "No, sir, never did."

Robinson: "Do you know where Mr. Fleet is now, this minute?"

Mullaly: "I do not. I saw him downstairs...before the adjournment."

Robinson: "That is all. I would like to have Mr. Fleet come in. I would like to have him sent for."

Knowlton: "We were proposing to do it."

Mr. Moody: "Mr. Officer, call Mr. Fleet."

Robinson: "I would like to have this witness [Mullaly] in the room until Mr. Fleet comes. He need not stay on the stand."

Moody: "You may take a seat in that room. (Pointing to the rear.) Do not leave that room or that seat."

Michael Mullaly stepped down. It was impossible to ignore the sensation his testimony had brought to the courtroom. What was he feeling? Had he been told to lie about the hatchet handle? Fleet was the Assistant Marshal—his superior. Had Officer Mullaly refused to lie under oath, and for that noble decision, had he been passed over for a promotion, and his police report of his actions that day, destroyed? Perhaps, there was a small sense of vindication, and not a little fear, as to what would happen to him back in Fall River.

Assistant Marshal John Fleet entered the room. The looks on the faces of the spectators and the prosecution may have been a tip-off that something had gone wrong.

Robinson wasted no time, once the cocky officer was seated on the stand.

Robinson: "Mr. Fleet, returning to the subject we had under discussion this morning, about what you found in that box downstairs: You know the box by the chimney?"

Fleet: "Yes, sir."

Robinson: "Will you state again what you found there at the time you looked in?"

Everyone was perched on the edge of their seats. The incessant fluttering of fans was stilled as the people crammed into that small room waited for his reply.

Fleet (looking none-too-happy, but keeping the haughty expression firmly in place): "I found a hatchet head, the handle broken off, together with some other tools in the there and the iron that was inside there. I don't know just what it was."

Robinson (showing hatchet): "Was this what you found?"

Fleet: "Yes, sir."

Robinson: "Did you find anything else, except old tools?"

Fleet: "No, sir."

Robinson: "Sure about that?"

Fleet: "Yes, sir."

Robinson: "You did not find the handle, the broken piece, not at all?"

Fleet: "No, sir."

Robinson: "You did not see it, did you?"

Fleet: "No, sir."

Robinson: "Did Mullaly take it out of the box?"

Fleet: "Not that I know of."

Robinson: "You looked in so that you could have seen it if it was there?"

Fleet: "Yes, sir."

Robinson: "There was no hatchet handle belonging to that picked up right there? Or any piece of wood beside that that had any fresh break in it?"

Fleet: "Not that came from the hatchet."

Robinson: "Or in that box anyway? Or round there anywhere?"

Fleet: "No, sir, not that I am aware of; I did not see any of it."

Assistant Marshal Fleet was excused, amid the whispered excitement of the crowd. Attorney's heads from both tables bowed together and conversed in urgent undertones. After several minutes, **Officer Charles Wilson** was called to the stand. His testimony was mundane and anti-climatic. It was clear both sides of the case only wanted his information on the record, as their heads were still whirling from the previous testimony given by Fleet and Mullaly. After some cursory questions about Mr. Wilson helping Mr. Fleet search the dress closet, and his look around Lizzie's room, shortly after Lizzie admitted he and Fleet inside, he was dismissed.

Before Mr. Wilson's back had barely exited the courtroom door, Mr. Knowlton was on his feet.

> Knowlton: "If your Honors please, I think that it is important that an investigation should be had to see whether the piece of wood that had been described by Mr. Mullaly is still in that box. In order that it be done with entire fairness, I ask that somebody be designated to go over with an officer to do it. I make this motion with no other interest than that of justice."
>
> Robinson: "Justice is what we want," he said acerbically.
>
> Knowlton: "Do you object to the appointment of an officer for that purpose?"
>
> Judge Mason: "The court cannot interfere with the preparation of the case."
>
> Mr. Moody: "Miss Annie M. White will take the stand."
>
> Basically, Judge Mason had told Mr. Knowlton, "You made your ash pile, you lay in it."

The newspapers lapped up the day's events like a starving cat. Their headlines screamed about what had been nicknamed "the hoodoo hatchet." The unfolding case was the stuff from which journalistic dreams are made.

Newspaper typeset letters. Each letter was placed by hand.

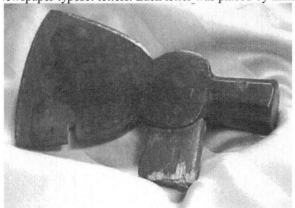

The handleless hatchet now on display at the Fall River Historical Society.

Miss Annie White entered the room. She was described as stout, pleasant-looking, and mild. She carried with her a folder of papers. Her time on the stand was short-lived.

Moody: "Were you present at a proceeding at Fall River sometime in August of last year?"

White: "Yes."

Moody: "I am referring now to August 9th. Did you see Miss Lizzie Borden?"

White: "I did."

Moody: "And Mr. Knowlton?"

White: "Yes."

Moody: "In what room were you in?"

White: "In the district courtroom in Fall River."

Moody: "Who was there besides those whom you have named?"

White: "Judge Blaisdell, Mr. Leonard, the clerk of the court, and Dr. Dolan, and Mr. Seaver was there part of the time, and Marshal Hilliard was there all of the time, and there was one or two persons came in there I didn't know—strangers."

Moody: "Now was there some conversation between Mr. Knowlton and Miss Borden at this time?"

Mr. Robinson: "Wait right there!"

And with that, Miss White's testimony ended. Governor Robinson said the point he needed to make should be outside the jury's hearing, and deferred until the next morning.

Robinson: "Now the court, I have no doubt, have anticipated this question, which was likely to arise."

The Judges conferred in whispers, and agreed to have the matter heard without the jury present. Miss White was excused.

The issue in question was the eligibility of the introduction of Lizzie Borden's Inquest testimony. Her defense attorneys were emphatic that it was inadmissible due to the violation of her rights at the time she was subpoenaed to appear in court. Miss White had with her a copy of the stenographic record she took the day of Lizzie's testimony, and was prepared to read it in court, in front of the jury. It would be a hotly debated item that would take up a good portion of the following Monday, June 12th.

**JUDGES MASON AND
BLODGETT CONFER**

Newspaper rendering of the two judges discussing the
admissibility of Lizzie Borden's Inquest testimony.

George A. Pettee was called after Miss White exited the room. The afternoon was waning, and the gallery stirred restlessly in their seats, sensing the fireworks of the day were over, and down to a few snap, crackle, and pops.

Mr. Pettee stated that he was in a unique position as he had once owned 92 Second Street, the scene of the brutal murders. He had known Andrew Borden for many years. He had passed the house at 10:00 that morning and saw Bridget washing windows. It was shortly after 11:00 when he heard about the murders at Wade's store, only two buildings away. He had gone to the house, and Dr. Bowen, at times performing as Ring Master, pulled back the sheet and showed Mr. Pettee Andrew's gruesome wounds. He testified that he saw movement in Mr. Borden's blood; that is was still fresh and flowing. When Dr. Bowen showed him Abby's body upstairs, he placed his hand on her head and stated the hair was dry with matted blood. He told the doctor, "This is where it started," meaning Abby had been dead longer. There was a "skin" that had formed on the pool of blood around her head.

Mr. Pettee was excused after only a handful of questions, without cross-examination.

Mr. Augustus P. Gorman was called. He owned the paint shop on the corner of Borden and Second Street. His only purpose was to say the clock in his store, the one John Cunningham had looked at as he called the Marshal that morning to report Andrew's death, was not a good clock, and did not keep very good time at all. He was excused, without cross-examination.

Adelaide Churchill was recalled. Mr. Moody asked her if she knew what a Bedford cord dress was. She replied, "No, Sir." When pressed to describe Lizzie's dress that morning, she said, "I thought it was a cotton dress of some kind."

Mr. Robinson asked what kind of dress Bridget had on, and Mrs. Churchill replied, "I think a light calico or gingham. It looked as if it might have faded some. I would not call it an indigo blue, very much lighter, a light summer dress."

Mrs. Churchill was excused. Mr. Knowlton stood and addressed the Judges. "We expected to fill the afternoon with the testimony of Miss White, which I understand my friend wants to have a conference about, as we have no other witnesses to call at this time. Miss White's testimony would occupy more than two hours if she was called.

Judge Mason then admonished the jury before dismissing them, not to discuss the case, or form any opinions yet, based on the evidence they had heard, as they had only heard a part of the case thus far.

At 3:40 p.m., the court was adjourned to Saturday morning, June 10th, at 9:00 a.m. A battle-weary courtroom exited.

Chapter Thirty-Two

The Superior Court Trial, Day Six
Saturday, June 10th, 1893

A special dispatch to the *Boston Herald*, June 10, 1893—
There was another exciting contest outside the courtroom
between the two sets of lawyers. The district attorney, Mr.
Knowlton, sent two officers to the Borden home to get the box
in which the blade was found, and the handle, if it was in it.
Miss Borden's sister, Emma, still lives in that house, and her
lawyer saw to it that their antagonists were kept out. That was
what happened. Miss Lizzie's chief counselor, A.J. Jennings
had better luck, he got the box, but lo! The highly important
handle was missing. Who took it can only be guessed at. Had
it been found, it would have played hob with the theory that
Miss Borden burned it. However, the policeman who saw it
proves a good witness for Miss Borden as the handle itself.

If the handle had been found in the box, along with the broken
head, it would have faired well for Lizzie. The handle, if found
without blood stains, would make the broken tool look just as
innocent as was planned. If the handle was missing it would look
suspicious. The new break in the hatchet head's small handle
section, pointed to recent activity. If the matching handle is not
with it, then it was taken away for mysterious reasons—the most
popular theory being that it had blood on it that could not be
washed off.

Then why leave it there at all for the officers to find Thursday?
Had Lizzie been in a hurry, and felt that in its broken state no one
would consider it? Had the repeated trips to the cellar by the
police concerned her? Perhaps word got to her through Bridget that
Officer Mulally and Fleet had seen it on Thursday. At any rate,

between the murder day, and Monday morning when Officer Medley found the hatchet and was told to take it to Marshall Hilliard, the handle had disappeared.

The Boston Herald, June 10, 1892, New Bedford, Ma.— The famous box, marked "Muscatel Grapes" in blue—the dominant color in this case—was on the table before the jury this morning. A new glass of flowers was before the judges—a bunch of heliotropes, along with the glasses of carnations that have lasted all the week. It stood between the deep red carnations that typify bloody guilt and the gentle pink ones that stand for maidenly sufferings. A change in the carnations was noticed. The guilty ones were dropping, and their heads hung down around their vase. The others, emblematic of distressed maidenhood, were rigid and erect. Miss Lizzie Borden had been likened to a barometer, because heretofore her spirits at early morning have corresponded with what the day was to bring forth for or against her. It was not so today. She was limp and inert this morning. She seemed depressed. The dress which she wears in court every day is black crepe.

It will interest both sexes to hear that Bridget Sullivan, as she visits her friends in the kitchens on the Hill, is fond of saying that she scarcely knew Lizzie Borden when she saw her in court the first day, she has grown so fat. Evidently, as the district attorney would say, prison fare is better than the routine of mutton, cold soup, cookies and green peas she used to get in her cheerless hole in Fall River.

The saga of the hatchets and handles continued with the testimony of Officer Edson on Saturday morning.

Officer Francis L. Edson: Mr. Moody guided Officer Edson through his movements of Friday morning when he arrived early at the Borden home to collect the two hatchets and two axes from the cellar wash room. Bridget, who had been summoned by John Morse to return to the house, after she had slept the evening of the murders across the street with the Miller's, allowed Officer Edson into the back screen door.

Moody: "That was Friday morning?"

Edson: "Yes, sir."

Moody: "What did you take?"

Edson: "Two wood axes, a hand axe, and a small shingle hatchet."

Moody: "Where did you take them from?"

Edson: "From the cellar. Three of them were in the wash room on the floor. The other one, the hand hatchet [clawhead] was in the vegetable cellar on a scaffold or shelf. I carried them to the police station and put them into Marshal Hilliard's custody."

Moody: "Have you had anything to do with the handleless hatchet, any possession of that at any time?"

Edson: "I have not."

Mr. Moody asked Officer Edson if he was present during the search of the cellar on Monday, August 8th. He said he was, along with Captain Desmond, Connors, Inspector Medley, Officer Quigley, and the mason Charles H. Bryant. He also said Mr. Jennings and Detective Hanscom were present.

Mr. Robinson cross-examined Officer Edson as to the thoroughness of the cellar search.

Edson: "Well, that part that I took part in, I searched in the vegetable cellar, removed all the barrels, boxes and shingles underneath the stairs. I also searched the coal pile, and in the wood cellar: around the furnace. The back of the chimney is in the middle cellar—the wood cellar. Looked in boxes at the base of that chimney that contained ashes and cinders, sifted coals. There was a niche in the chimney and some ashes in there."

Robinson: "Did you or any other of the party to your knowledge on that Monday take away anything from the house?"

Edson: "Yes sir. Officer Medley had a hatchet head in his pocket."

Robinson: "Did you see it?"

Edson: "He showed it to me partly."

Robinson: "Do you know where he got it?"

Edson: "I do not."

Robinson: "When did he show it to you?"

Edson: "Just as he was about to leave he came to me and pulled it out of his pocket, and it was in a paper, and says, "I am going down street—"

Robinson: "He took it out of his pocket?"

Edson: "Yes, sir. It was wrapped in paper. Glanced at it, that is all. It was only the small hatchet—no handle. He didn't have any handle in his possession. I didn't see a loose handle around there, and I didn't find one."

Robinson: "Did you find anything in that cellar in any way that will help us at all in this case?"

Edson: "Outside those hatchets and axes, no sir."

Robinson: "You carried the two axes and two hatchets in a bag down to the police station on the morning of the 5th?"

Edson: "No, sir."

Robinson: "I beg pardon, I thought you said so?"

Edson: "No, sir. I carried them to the station."

Robinson: "What did I say?"

Edson: "In a bag."

Robinson: "Did you see anybody carry them in a bag?"

Edson: "No, sir."

Robinson: "How were they carried?"

Edson: "In my hands, openly."

Robinson: "You didn't see anybody around there with a bag putting anything in?"

Edson: "No, sir. Captain Harrington, and Doherty, Officer McCarty, Reagan J. Linneham, and J. Minnehan saw me."

Officer Edson stated he also searched the barn, the privy vault and the woodpile that Monday, while the dismantling of the chimney in the cellar was taking place.

Edson: "We opened the top of the [wood] pile and opened down a foot or more into the center of it, and we saw through the boards where space had been made and strips laid to allow the air to circulate, and we could see through the pile, if anything should be seen there. We were satisfied there was nothing there."

This may have been in response to Mr. Jennings and Emma asking the officers to take a closer look at the woodpile. Their interest in it, even after it had been searched three times, seems odd.

They checked the well and found only dirt and debris. They looked for freshly-turned sod in the yard, and found only the section where the bloody clothes had been buried. Officer Edson also scaled the fence into Crowe's yard, being careful not to tear his clothes on the barbed wire. If Lizzie was watching as he did this that Monday, four days after the murders, she may have held her breath—the hatchet lay on the barn roof only a few feet away. Once again, her actions remained clothed in secrecy. He did not see it.

Next up was **Officer Benjamin F. Mahoney**. He testified that it was he and Mr. Edson that were sent to the Borden house at quarter of four Friday afternoon to try and retrieve the box where the hatchet head was found. A servant girl answered the door and they were denied admittance. His only other testimony referred to his taking custody of the blue dress Lizzie handed the police on Saturday, August 6th, when Marshal Hilliard requested it during their second search of the day. Officer Mahoney had taken the dress from the custody of Professor Wood on May 30, 1893, under the instructions of the D.A. and the Marshal. He returned it to Professor Wood on June 2nd, 1893. He kept it in his possession during that time.

Officer William H. Medley took the stand, with Lizzie Borden's "peculiar and singular" gaze upon him. This was the officer who had interviewed her the morning of the murders, and then runs to the barn loft to test her story of being up there for 20-30 minutes on that stifling hot day. There he found no prints in the thick layer of hay dust. After placing his hand in the dust, and walking about in it, he could clearly see his own prints. Lizzie's defense had done its best to eradicate his testimony by bringing in several "witnesses" to claim they had been up in the loft before Medley, obviously leaving copious tracks in the dust. One by one, their testimony was demolished by Attorney Knowlton, who, with renewed vigor, took the reins from his co-counsel, Mr. Moody. Officer Medley stated "it was a very hot day," and went on to say the two windows and the hay door in the loft were both closed when he went up.

Officer Medley testified that he participated in the search of the cellar on Monday, August 8th, while the mason was at work on the chimney. He answered Mr. Moody as to his actions at that time:

Medley: "I examined all I could in the wash cellar, then I helped to put out some barrels and things that were in a corner of the wash cellar in another little cellar, and after putting part of those back in place, I think there was a large pile of wood in that particular corner of the cellar, and in there while searching I found a small hatchet head. It was in a box, perhaps fifteen or sixteen inches long and four or five inches deep. It was on a block—I am not sure whether it was a chopping block or a block made from a box, but it was some piece that rested above the level of the cellar floor, perhaps about a foot and a half high, and this box was on top of that. It was filled with old rubbish—irons of different kinds, and one or two tools, I have forgotten just what they were; and some nails, I think."

Moody: "Was there any other officer in the same cellar when you found the head of the hatchet?"

Medley: "No, sir."

Moody: "Where was Captain Desmond?"

Medley: "In the passage way in the cellar...two or three feet from me."

Moody: "Did you take it from the box?"

Medley: "I did. I showed it to Captain Desmond right away. After some instructions from Captain Desmond, I put it in a paper and wrapped it up, and showed it, I think to some other officer [Edson], and carried it immediately to the City Marshal's office."

Moody: "Did you find any handle or anything having the appearance of a handle to this hatchet, except the piece that was in the eye of the hatchet?"

Medley: "No, sir."

Moody: "Now, sir, I wish you would describe without any further question, the appearance of that hatchet as you found it?"

Medley: "It was all covered with dust, as I took it from the box—a coarse dust. It was a coarse dust, and seemed to me like the dust of ashes...it was on the whole of it, both sides. I noticed there was a new break. I did not notice if there were ashes or dust on the new break."

[The box, when Officer Medley saw it Monday morning, was now sitting down lower on a ledge. It may be where Fleet and Mulally left it after looking it over the Thursday before—or– perhaps someone else took it down to remove the handle and take it away.]

Governor Robinson cross-examined Officer Medley and walked him through his actions upon finding the hatchet head. The officer stated that he had shown it to Captain Desmond, and they both walked with it to the water closet where some papers were kept for sanitary reasons. He claimed he wrapped it in a piece of brown paper, and placed it in the side pocket of his sack coat jacket and carried it away to the police station.

Governor Robinson then had Officer Medley take the actual head and wrap it in a piece of newspaper to demonstrate how he wrapped it that day. Medley did so, handing it back to the counsel, saying "I am not very tidy at such things. That is, as near as I can think, is about how I did it."

[Medley hands Robinson a neatly wrapped package.]

Officer Medley stated he was a patrolman at the time of the murder, and was promoted to Inspector in December. He was asked how he left the barn door after going up to look at the hay dust, and he stated he closed it, and left it as he had found it, with the hasp on, and a piece of iron through it, "It hung from a chain or rope or something, just to keep the hasp on the staple."

[The other people who claimed to have gone into the barn before Medley, said the barn door was open. He was the only one to find it locked with a hasp and staple, just as it was always kept when none of the Borden's were inside.]

Officer Medley of the Fall River Police Department. A patrolman at the time of the murders (l), and as an Inspector after his promotion in December, 1892 (r). Courtesy of Edwin Porter, the *Fall River Daily Globe*.

Captain Dennis Desmond, Jr. was up next. Sporting a full mustache, the custom of the day, he took the stand, and stated, upon questioning that he too had been promoted since August 4th, from Acting Captain, to Captain.

Mr. Moody, after establishing that Captain Desmond had been part of the searches of the Borden home, in particular the dress closet, asked:

Moody: "Did you see any dress that was soiled with paint or with spots of any kind?"

Desmond: "No, sir."

Moody: "Upon the Monday following did you take part in any search?"

Desmond: "I did, yes, sir. I was in command of the squad that went there to search."

Moody: "Among others was Officer Medley there?"

Desmond: "He was."

Moody: "I will call your attention to anything that Mr. Medley showed you during the progress of the search in the cellar?"

Desmond: "A small hatchet. He called me from what I was doing to a room in the cellar...just west of the kitchen cellar. It had been broken and the wooden part had been left...the piece of iron and wood in the head. I looked it over, examined it quite closely. We took it to the north side of the building, directly opposite to where he said he found it. [Water closet] It was all dirty: that is, it was covered with a dust which was not of a fine nature, that is, it was too coarse to be called a fine— what I mean is, it wasn't any sediment that might have collected on it from standing there any length of time. The dust that we found in general throughout the cellar was nothing at all such as was on this hatchet. This was a much coarser nature."

He then testified that Officer Medley carried the hatchet head away, wrapped in a newspaper.

Mr. Robinson, on cross-examination, asked Desmond if he was sure there was no hatchet handle in the box when Officer Medley showed him where it was found. "There was nothing but iron in the box; an old bolt, some nails, a chisel. No handle."

[As a side note, it would seem the things Lizzie claimed she needed from the barn—nails and iron—are right there in a box in the cellar.]

The next section of testimony brought some much-needed comic relief to the proceedings. Captain Desmond, while describing the coarseness of the ashes on the hatchet blade, let it slip that he wrapped the head up in the newspaper and handed it to Medley. Officer Medley testified only minutes before that he had wrapped the blade in brown paper and took it away.

Robinson: "Are you certain about taking it up?" [Picking it up]"

Desmond: "Yes, sir. I got the paper from the water closet there to do it up with."

Robinson: (Handing witness the handleless hatchet.) "Well, won't you wrap it up in about as large a piece of paper?"

Desmond: "I shall have to get a full-sized newspaper to do it, much larger than that, sir. (Referring to a piece of paper handed witness by counsel.)

Robinson: "You got a piece out of the water closet?"

Desmond: "Yes, sir."

Robinson: "Brown paper?"

Desmond: "No, sir, regular newspaper, but a larger paper than that."

Robinson: "You wrapped it in newspaper?" the Governor said, prolonging the comedy, to the gallery's amusement.
Desmond: "Yes, sir. A very large newspaper."
Robinson: "Larger than that? (Exhibiting a *Boston Globe*.)
Desmond: "Yes."
Robinson: "Well, take that and give us the way you wrapped it up."
Desmond: (Witness does so.) "I wrapped it up in such form as that, and passed it to him." [The head is wrapped up into a huge mass.]
Robinson: "Made as big a bundle as that, did it?"
Desmond: (Sensing the sarcasm and smiles in the courtroom) "No, sir, not as large as that."

The Boston Globe reported on the incident—Today the hatchet laid out more policemen. Mr. Robinson actually made the two policemen show the jury how each one wrapped it up. The two officers went through the performance, each one swearing positively to his details. One made a brown bundle the size of a five-cent cut of pie, and other made a great newspaper bundle, big enough to conceal a pair of longshoreman's shoes.

Why do two officers both claim they wrapped the hatchet? Had it been wrapped twice, with perhaps one of them unwrapping it to show it some other officer before Medley left to take it to Hilliard?

Officer Medley (l) and Captain Desmond (r) folding the hatchet into the paper. Illustration by *The Boston Globe*, June 10, 1893.

Detective George F. Seaver was the last witness to go before the court that Saturday. He was a member of the State District Police force, living in Taunton, Massachusetts. He testified that Assistant Marshal Fleet showed him the handleless hatchet on Saturday, during the second search done after the funeral. He said he took it out of the box, looked it over, and put it back. He described the dust on the hatchet head as coarse, unlike the other dust around it. He said the break on the handle portion looked "fresh, a bright break, as though it had not been done very long."

Mr. Moody then led him to the testimony about the dresses in the clothes press on the second floor.

Seaver: "I first went into the closet and the closet blinds were shut, that is, the outside blinds. I opened the blinds—there were cloths around the window—hoisted the window and took the cloth down and opened the blinds, and then I went to the hooks. Captain Fleet was there with me. He had gone in two or three minutes before me.

"I commenced on the hooks and took each dress, with the exception of two or three in the corner, and passed them to Captain Fleet, he being nearer the window, and he examined them as well as myself, he more thoroughly than myself, and I took each garment then and hung it back as I found them; all with the exception of two or three which were heavy or silk dresses in the corner. I didn't pass those down. I just looked at them and let them remain as they were."

Moody: "Those were silk dresses?"

Seaver: "Those were silk dresses, I am very sure, heavy dresses, and they hung there, and I didn't disturb them."

Moody: "Did you discover anything upon any of those dresses?"

Seaver: "I did not."

Moody: "Did you see a light blue dress, diamond spots upon it, and paint around the bottom of the dress and on its front?"

Seaver: "I did not."

Detective Seaver is then asked to go into great detail about the myriad blood spots found in the two locations where the bodies lay that day. While 86 spots of blood sprayed across the wallpaper above Andrew's head was mentioned, the account of Abby's room was more graphic:

Seaver: "On the face board of the bed, it was besmeared with blood, the space—so many spots were found I did not attempt to count them—very many of them. We found the lower board of the dressing case besmeared with blood spots, very thick, and also some matted hair, stuck on the blood. That was very near the floor. On the glass of the dressing case there was fifteen blood spots. The heavier parts of each spot were at the bottom. Nine inches from the window casing and two and one-half feet from the floor was a spot of blood. There were two spots upon the dressing case and the window."

Mr. Robinson stood up for the cross-examination:

Robinson: "When you looked down in the box that day down cellar, you found this, or saw this hatchet head, did you?"

Seaver: "Yes, sir."

Robinson: "Saw it in the box?"

Seaver: "In the box. No, sir. At the time I first saw it, Mr. Fleet took it out of the box. I saw him take it out of the box, and I looked at it."

Robinson: "What day was this, Mr. Seaver?"

Seaver: "This was Saturday afternoon right after we got through with the search upstairs. After we left the closet, we went directly downstairs, or very soon after...me and Mr. Fleet."

[This is the first we hear that Mr. Fleet looks at the handleless hatchet again, other than on the day of the murders. He does not testify to looking at it on Saturday, let alone showing it to Detective Seaver. Yet, both men still leave it behind, even though both find the coarse ashes coating it suspicious, and that it appears to have been freshly broken.]

Governor Robinson now goes for the jugular. With rapid-fire questioning, he asks about Mr. Fleet and Detective Seaver's search of the dress closet. He hammers the Detective as to the colors of the dresses, how many, if there were boxes and trunks, and on and on. Over and over, the Detective admits he doesn't know what color the dresses were, what material, how many. "Was there a pink one? Was there a blue one? Any black ones? How about the green one here? Silk, alpaca, wool?" Seaver answers each with an "I don't know." He *is* certain none of them had paint stains or blood.

Robinson: "Were you there at the clothes room when the city marshal made a request for the production of the dress Miss Lizzie had on Thursday morning?"

Seaver: "I was downstairs at the time, not at the clothes room. It was brought to Mr. Hilliard by some person, I think."

Robinson: "Right in your presence?"

Seaver: "Yes, sir."

Robinson: "You heard the request made, and it was brought immediately, wasn't it?"

Seaver: "I think it was, yes."

Robinson: "Don't you know it was brought right out of that clothes room? Wasn't it right after the search? Didn't that blue dress hang right up on the second hook from the window?"

Seaver: "I wouldn't swear; I don't remember it."

Robinson: "Well, were you present when Dr. Dolan examined it?"

Seaver: "No, sir. I don't know about his examining it. I don't recollect it excepting at the station."

Chapter Thirty-Four

Superior Court Trial, Days 7 - 15
Doctors and Blood Spatter

The Superior Court trial rumbled on; a trainload of evidence with one final destination—the conviction, or acquittal of Lizzie Andrew Borden. During the time of the trial, a serial killer was hacking up tourists, who were staying at his torture chamber in a hotel in Chicago, while they visited the World's Fair. H. H. Holmes confessed to 27 murders at his World's Fair Hotel, only 3 miles from Jackson Park where millions were attending the 1893 World's Columbian Exposition. It was estimated that the actual body count was closer to 200. He was captured in November of 1894, and found guilty of four counts of murder in the first degree, and six counts of attempted murder; a mild conviction based on his actual deeds. Yet it was Lizzie Borden, a Sunday School teacher from Fall River, who was capturing the lion's share of headlines in 1893.

Will Lizzie Be Heard?

Monday, June 12th, at 9 A.M., the court opened its doors to a select few. The jury was not in attendance, nor was the gallery. The attorneys for both sides argued the admissibility of Lizzie Borden's Inquest testimony be read before the jury. The arguments consumed the morning, but in the end, the Judges ruled it inadmissible due to the nature in which Lizzie was treated, and most importantly, she was denied legal counsel or advised of her rights, after being told she was a suspect in a murder investigation. That Miss White, the stenographer from the Inquest, would not be reading Lizzie's confusing and contradictory testimony was a God-send to the defense. Lizzie put her head down on the railing of the dock, and wept with relief.

The Doctor's Weigh In

The courtroom was about to be thrown into a Jekyll and Hyde laboratory when the humid days of June 12th and 13th arrived on the calendar. With the exception of Officer Joseph Hyde, the policeman who watched Lizzie's nocturnal movements in the cellar the night of the murders, the rest of the docket was made of up of Professors and doctors.

As the jury, gallery and newspapermen arrived inside the small courtroom, shortly after lunch on Monday, June 12th, they were surprised to see the transformation of the stuffy surroundings. The blood speckled bedspread from the guest room was hung over the juror's railing, the bloody pillow sham was on display, and other articles that were smeared with blood. It was obvious, the gloves were off and the meat of the case was about to hit the sensation-seeking public full-blast.

Much of these learned men's testimonies have been provided earlier in the book. For the sake of brevity, their latest findings are offered in the order of their appearance:

Dr. Albert C. Dedrick: Dr. Dedrick's time on the stand was brief. He testified to arriving at the Borden home sometime after 2 in the afternoon. He found Mrs. Borden's blood "ropy" and "coagulated," while Mr. Borden's blood was "more cozy." He estimated the time between the two deaths was "several hours."

Dr. William A. Dolan:
1) Lizzie told him the "sick note" Abby received that morning was probably burned in the stove.
2) The sofa where Andrew lay was up against the jam of the dining room door, not centered on the wall.
3) The sofa is now at the courthouse.
4) Andrew's hand was still warm, and his blood was bright red and still oozing at noon, when Dr. Dolan arrived.

5) Dr. Dolan pulled the Prince Albert coat up a little to get in the inside pocket.

6) Under Andrew's head, in order, was a doubled-up afghan, the Prince Albert coat, and then a sofa cushion with a little white tidy on it.

7) He had Mr. Kieran, the civil engineer, take measurements of the area where Abby Borden lay between the bed and dressing case.

8) He stated Abby's hands were around her head; her head was not resting on them; nearer the wall than her head. They were an inch or two apart. Dr. Bowen stated her arms were beneath her bosom.

9) Dr. Dolan took away the bloody handkerchief after he had it, and other things, dug up, after they had been buried behind the Borden's barn, and had it with him at the courthouse in a satchel, in Mr. Moody's office. He stated the handkerchief was found near Abby's head.

10) Dr. Dolan participated in the autopsies at the house at 3:00 the afternoon of the murders. He removed their stomachs, tied them off at both ends and put them into separate, clean jars, which he sealed.

11) On August 11th, a more thorough autopsy was performed at Oak Grove Cemetery. Joining him was Dr. Francis Draper of Boston. Dr. Draper made casts of both skulls at that time. They examined the intestines of both bodies, measured and inspected each wound on the skulls. The wounds varied from one to five inches in length.

12) Dr. Draper decapitated both bodies and prepared the skulls by removing flesh and cartilage without interfering with the integrity of the bone.

13) He testified he believed Mrs. Borden died "from one and a half to two hours, or from one hour to one and a half hours before Mr. Borden."

14) He told Mr. Adams that the bodies were interred on August 11th, after the heads had been removed. The family, the daughters Emma and Lizzie, were not notified that the internment had been performed with headless bodies.

The court adjourned at 5 o'clock until Tuesday, June 13, at 9:00 A.M.

Tuesday, June 13, 1893

Dr. Dolan was recalled and interrogated for the Defense by Mr. Adams, during which a lengthy discourse took place in which each wound was reviewed, including whether it had penetrated the brain cavity. Many women in the courtroom were feeling the heat of the day and nausea associated with the graphic descriptions that seemed to go on and on. The room was overbearingly hot and fans fluttered faster with each gory detail.

Finally, the testimony turned to the hatchet without a handle, and everyone breathed a little easier, but not for long.

Adams: "Have you examined the hatchet?"

Dolan: "I have."

Adams: "Do you consider it a good edge, a sharp cutting edge?"

Dolan: "I do. It is sharp. As to the position of the murderer, from the appearance of things, I would place the assailant of Mr. Borden at the head of the lounge, between the parlor door and the head of the lounge, and the blows were swung from left to right."

Adams: "If the assailant, using the instrument you have described, or a similar one, had cut the artery which you have described, would it not have been natural that the assailant would have been covered in blood? Or would have been splattered or sprinkled with blood?"

Dolan: "Not necessarily."

Adams: "How do you explain that they would not have been?"

Dolan: "Because the blood would not spurt in that direction. It would not necessarily spurt in the direction of the assailant."

Mr. Adams now brings out the cast made of Andrew's skull and a nervous twitter goes through the gallery.

Adams: "No more than the ordinary strength of a person was required to administer these blows?" he asked incredulously.

Dolan: "Moderate force was used; no more than moderate force to give those blows was used."

So far, Mr. Adams questions were doing more for the prosecution than for Lizzie's cause. The jury had heard the assailant would not necessarily be splattered with blood, and only moderate strength was necessary to inflict the myriad wounds.

Adams: "Now, taking the position of Mrs. Borden, the pillow shams, the bedspread, the spots on the pillow shams, mirror and baseboard, where in your opinion did the assailant stand when inflicting these injuries?"
Dolan: "Astride the body."
Adams: "And over it?"
Dolan: "Yes, sir."
Adams: "How did the assailant face?"
Dolan: "The east wall."

At this moment, there was a stir in the jury box. All eyes turned to see Juror Hodges in a near faint. The grizzly testimony, white skull cast, and the heat, had overwhelmed him. The jury was dismissed for a short recess and he was taken out to their small room. The rest of the courtroom may have appreciated the reprieve from the morbid testimony. Many stared at Lizzie's profile to gauge her reaction to the accounts of the murders in such graphic detail.

After five minutes, the jurors were seated once again, Juror Hodges returned holding a small cup of water. Dr. Dolan was asked about blood spots pertaining to the garments and shoes Lizzie had handed over as being worn the morning of the murders. He said there was a "smooch" near the skirt pocket, that was not blood. Blood found on the soles of the shoes was found to have been put there during the tanning process of the leather, and the white petticoat had just the one pinhead-sized spot, on the outside of the skirt near the bottom. Other than the statements regarding the timing of the two deaths, Dr. Dolan had done nothing to damage Lizzie's case.

The Experts Arrive

The prosecution's sole purpose for introducing the next three experts was to elicit testimony that would underscore their "proof of guilt" trifecta: 1) Lizzie was physically capable of inflicting the wounds, 2) the murders of the victims were committed while she was at home, and in Abby's case, alone in the house with her stepmother, and 3) there was an appropriate weapon available to her in the house to commit the crimes. First up, was Professor Wood.

Professor Edward S. Wood:

1) Professor Wood was a chemist and physician, who for twenty-two years had been the Professor of Chemistry at Harvard Medical School, and had testified in a large number of capital cases.

2) He received a box containing four jars on August 5, 1892, from the Railroad Express: one jar labeled milk of August 3, 1892, one labeled milk of August 4, 1892, one labeled stomach of Andrew J. Borden, and one labeled stomach of Mrs. Andrew J. Borden. They were examined.

3) After testimony concerning the rate of digestion, the two stomach's contents, and other descriptive internal details, the Professor said he estimated Abby died one and one-half hours before her husband.

4) He stated he received on August 10th, two axes and two hatchets, a blue dress, skirt and waist, a white skirt, a piece of the sitting room carpet, a piece of the bedroom carpet, a piece of false hair, a braid or switch, a hair from Mrs. Borden's head, a hair from Mr. Borden's head, and a hair taken from the head of a hatchet. He found no blood on the weapons, the hair was from an animal, probably a cow.

5) The spot of blood on the white underskirt was human blood, on the outside of the skirt, not the inside. This was significant as Mr. Robinson's defense explanation for the blood was that it was menstrual blood, which would more likely be found on the inside of the skirt, not the outside. The prosecution did not press the matter, mostly because the subject was too indelicate in that era.

6) Professor Wood stated, "On August 30th, I received the hatchet head or handleless hatchet, and it has been in my possession ever since. My examination revealed that both sides of the hatchet head were uniformly rusted, that there were several reddish spots upon the head, although I could not determine that these were blood stains. I soaked the hatchet for several days in a solution which accounts for the darkening of the fractured part of the wood handle. When I received it, there was white dirt, like ashes, clearly visible with a substance resembling ashes, and was, and continues to be at this time, strongly adherent to both sides of the blade. It resisted rubbing. The hatchet, in my opinion, had been wet when placed in, or in contact, with the white material, and this white material had permeated the many crevices of the blade's surface and had stuck very tightly."

7) Professor Wood said if the hatchet had been used as the murder weapon, rubbed with ashes and *then* broken, it would account for no blood or ash being found on the "fresh break." When asked if the head could have merely fallen into the ashes and looked as it did, he said, "No." The ashes had been forcibly rubbed onto it, which accounted for them being still lodged in the blade's crevices.

8) He described prussic acid as "one of the most-deadly poisons we know; any solution which contains one grain of prussic acid is a fatal dose."

9) Mr. Adams got the Professor to admit he could not tell how recently the hatchet had been broken.

10) Mr. Adams asked about the blood spatter the assailant might have received. "The assailant standing behind Andrew Borden would almost certainly receive spatters of blood on the upper part of his body; if the assailant stood astride Mrs. Borden, he would receive spatters on the lower part of his body." The Doctor, however, could not form an opinion as to the number of spatters of blood, *if any*, which the assailant would receive.

Dr. Frank W. Draper, M.D. was next. We preface his testimony with a letter he wrote to Attorney Hosea Knowlton a few days before the trial began.

F.W. Draper, M.D.   May 31, 1893
104 Marlborough Street
Boston

My Dear Sir:

Dr. Cheever and I have had a conference today with the Borden photographs and skulls before us. We are in entire accord and he will testify:

1) That the cause and manner of the deaths were the same in both cases, namely, fracture of the skull and injury to the brain by blows to the head.

2) That the weapon was an edged tool of some weight, like a hatchet.

3) That the length of the edge of the weapon was about 3 ½ inches.

4) That Mrs. Borden was killed by blows inflicted from behind, the assailant standing astride the body.

5) That Mr. Borden was killed by blows given by the assailant standing at the head of the sofa just within the door.

6) That the assailant was right handed and used his right hand, or, if using both hands, that the left hand was foremost, or in front of the right hand, on the handle.

7) That Mrs. Borden died first, and the supposition of an hour's interval is not inconsistent with the facts relating to the stage of digestion, the body temperature and the condition of the blood in the two cases.

8) That the deaths were instantaneous.

9) That a woman would have sufficient physical strength to inflict the blows, assuming that she was of normal adult vigor.

I write especially to inform you of two important discoveries which I made upon a careful examination of the two skulls. On Mr. Borden's skull, I found that the blow just in front of the ear left its mark on the base of the skull within the cavity, that its depth was 1 7/16 inches and that it cut directly through the internal carotid artery; this wound was necessarily and immediately fatal from hemorrhage. The other discovery is still more important; on one of the cuts in Mrs. Borden's skull, near the right ear, there is a very small deposit of gilt metal with which hatchets are ornamented when they leave the factory; this deposit (Dr. Cheever confirmed the observation fully) means that the hatchet used in killing Mrs. Borden was a new hatchet, not long out of the store. Perhaps this is not new information, either to you or Dr. Dolan; it was new to me and seemed important enough to justify immediate conveyance to you. The shining deposit can be seen with the naked eye; it is plainly visible with the use of a lens, when once its situation is indicated.

I see by the morning papers that killing people with hatchets is a Bristol County habit. I am sorry that this latest homicide comes just now when you and Dr. Dolan are so much occupied with other matters.

Very truly yours,
F.W. Draper

[The underlining of the word "new" is Dr. Draper's.]

Attorney Knowlton received this letter on May 31st, 1893. Dr. Draper testified in the Superior Court trial only 13 days later. Yet he is never asked, nor does he testify to finding the gold gilt material in Abby's skull. Why? Because the handleless hatchet, although sharp, was not new. There was no gold embossed emblem upon it, no gilt along its edge. It had been chiseled down often over the years. At this late stage, Knowlton could not switch gears again, when they had already eaten crow by announcing during the Preliminary Hearing that the clawhead hatchet was the murder weapon, only to have it proven its blade was an inch and a half too wide for Andrew's cuts.

They switched gears for the Superior Court trial, and had been waving the broken hatchet as their new star. If they switched again, to a new, fresh-out-of-the-store hatchet, *that they didn't even have*, they would have been a laughing stock and the jury would have had a more than reasonable doubt about the prosecution even having a case. Therefore, Dr. Draper's finding of gold residue in Abby's cut was not mentioned.

Two days after Dr. Draper testified on the stand, a newspaper article shook Fall River, and rattled both Mr. Jennings and Mr. Knowlton:

Another Hatchet Found

Fall River, June 15, —Last night a boy named Potter, son of C.C. Potter, clerk in the Fall River Water Works office, while looking for a ball, found a hatchet on the top of John Crowe's barn, which is located just in the rear of the Borden property.

Mr. Potter this morning reported his find to the police and also sought an interview with the counsel for the defense, but was unable to find Mr. Jennings. He still has the hatchet in his possession and describes it as an ordinary implement, with a hammer head. The hatchet was weather-beaten and the blade covered with rust.

Some of the particles of rust being removed, a slight coloring of gilt was disclosed which would either indicate that the hatchet was at one time used as an ornament or was quite new when lost or discarded.

Another article by *The Daily News Bulletin* stated "The hatchet is an ordinary shingle hatchet with a blade 3 3/8 inches in length. It has the appearance of having been comparatively new or little used. The handle, which is 13 ½ inches long, looked weather-worn as if it had been long exposed to air, sun and storm.

"If the murderer of Andrew J. Borden and his wife escaped from the Borden premises by the rear, and it was a very easy way for him to escape, he could easily have thrown the hatchet to the place where it was found.

"So far as is known, no man has been on the roof within two years. Mr. Crowe knows of none; all telegraph, telephone, electric light wiremen, roofers, and several photographers agree on this. The police did not visit it in their thorough search.

"The police are examining it this morning. They thought they could tell whether there had been blood on it or not. They confirm that they are baffled.

"But one of them, who has been an important witness in the Borden case, admits that with the new find and the exclusion of the Bence story [Lizzie buying poison], everything has gone up for the government so far as a possible conviction of Lizzie Borden is concerned.

"The defense has opened its case. Now look for important and vital contradictions of government testimony.

The story of the hatchet being found, and the evidence of finding gold gilt in Abby's skull, were never heard within the courtroom. Shortly after, the Crowe's barn hatchet disappeared from the police station, never to surface again.

Why wouldn't Mr. Jennings want to bring in this valuable last inning reprieve? Because it was a double-edged sword. Yes, as the papers hinted, it could have been tossed there by an escaping murderer, but, as the prosecution could point out, it could just as easily have been thrown there by Lizzie Borden, a woman seen coming from the backyard that morning by a Russian ice cream peddler.

And Mr. Knowlton? As already stated, it would have sunk his credibility and the case he had built. The hoodoo hatchet had a brother. It is interesting that both murder weapons, the Crowe's barn hatchet and the handleless hatchet, are both shingling hatchets with a 3 ½ - 3 3/8-inch blade. This is a smaller, lighter hatchet—one a woman would gravitate toward. It is very possible Mr. Jennings and his co-counsels never heard about Dr. Draper's finding of the gilt material...he was the prosecution's man, and discovery had already been submitted.

Dr. Frank W. Draper, M.D. had practiced medicine in Boston for twenty-four years. He was a graduate of Harvard Medical School, and had been the Medical Examiner for Suffolk County, Massachusetts.

1) He received a plaster cast of the skulls of the Borden's and while at the cemetery, had drawn pencil marks upon the skulls, indicating the exact location and length of each of the many wounds. He had found the bodies, at that time, very much decomposed. He could not testify as to the sequence of the blows, and stated the numbers they were given were not indicative of the order in which they were received. There had been 11 blows to Mr. Borden's head.

2) He testified the length of the blade that killed Andrew Borden was 3 ½ inches.

3) Using the plaster cast of Abby's skull, he went over her various wounds, 18 in all. The first wound, which was a flap over the left ear, had been delivered from the front to the back and was a long cut. There were two wounds on the top of the head in the back of the crown; both of them had penetrated the skull and entered the brain. The next wound had entered the ear and was deep enough to penetrate the skull. There had been a group of twelve wounds above the right ear "distributed in a fan shape;" varying in depth, these wounds altogether resulted in a complete smashing of the skull. The final wound was the on the body, near the neck, where the neck meets the shoulders. It had been delivered right to left as the assailant stood over the body.

At this time, there was a pause in the testimony. Lizzie Borden was, mercifully, allowed to leave for the next portion of Dr. Draper's testimony. She was seated in a small room next to the courtroom.

Mr. Moody picked up a large package from the floor near the prosecution table and placed it on his table. He looked over some papers, then without preamble, took from the package the fleshless skull of Andrew Borden. The room gasped. It was one thing to see a plaster cast; to see the discolored head of the victim was another. The gruesome relic shocked spectators, jurors and the Court alike.

Dr. Draper accepted the skull with the detachment of a seasoned Medical Examiner. He produced from his pocket a piece of tin plate which he said measured exactly 3 ½ inches in length. Using the piece of tin plate, he then inserted it into each of the many wounds on the crushed skull, showing how each blow had been administered. The 3 ½" tin plate fit each wound perfectly. Not only did it fit the cuts exactly, Dr. Draper said, no other blade width would facilitate those same cuts. To test the theory, Mr. Adams handed him a new hatchet, unrelated to the case, with a similar blade width. It was not ground the same way the handleless hatchet had been, and it did not fit the cuts in the skull. In other words, only that broken hatchet head could have made those wounds. It was like comparing a bite mark where the molar had a worn edge. It was an imprint born of its singular usage. Without the grinding the hatchet head had had, it was too thick. It was an extraordinary moment.

Mr. Adams for the defense, took one more shot at the Doctor. He went into gruesome detail about the beheading and boiling of the heads, hoping to gain the sympathy and repulsion of the jury. He then asked Dr. Draper to take a piece of chalk and mark on Mr. Adams' jacket back, exactly where the blow to Abby's neck area had been. Dr. Draper stepped up behind the attorney, and taking a piece of chalk, drew a line onto his suit jacket, indicating the location of the horizontal blow to Abby's back, between her shoulder blades. As he was drawing the line, Mr. Adams in his usual caustic manner quipped, "I trust that I shall not be numbered and marked as an exhibit."

The courtroom gallery erupted in laughter, including the jury. After a long day of graphic and gory detail, it was some much-needed comic relief.

Mr. Adams wrapped up his questioning of the doctor by asking if the fake hair braid and Abby's thick hair, would alter the strength needed in cutting through it with the blows. Dr. Draper said it would not, and the blows were within the physical capability of a woman.

Many of the females seated about the courtroom that day may have marveled at the information they were capable of inflicting such damage, and no doubt, more than one glanced at Lizzie's arms.

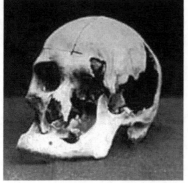 

Andrew Borden's skull (left), Abby's (right).
Courtesy of the Fall River Historial Society.

Dr. David W. Cheever: Dr. Cheever was a Boston physician, and the Professor of Surgery and Anatomy at the Harvard Medical School.

1) On May 31st, 1893, for the first time, he viewed the skulls of Andrew and Abby Borden. He concluded that the weapon used had a blade of 3 ½ inches, and no longer. He stated the handleless hatchet fit it perfectly.
2) He testified the scalp wound inflicted on Abby occurred when she was face-to-face with her assailant.
3) All the wounds he saw, he testified, could have been inflicted by a woman.
4) With regard to the spattering of blood, "I can say with certainty that no one can tell the direction of blood spattering or its radius."
5) Dr. Cheever conceded the assailant would in all likelihood have blood on his shoes, in the matter of Abby's murder.

The medical evidence was now all in. The prosecution's three-legged stool of probable guilt had withstood the grueling testimony: Lizzie had the strength to carry out the murders, she may not have been spattered in blood, and the murder weapon—the handleless hatchet—came from her own cellar.

The court adjourned at 5:00 p.m., until the next morning, June 14, 1893, at 9 a.m. It would be the ninth day of the trial.

Wednesday, June 14, 1893

The ninth day of the trial opened with the usual heat and humidity of New Bedford in the summer months. Ladies fluttered their fans, men flapped their lapels in hopes of a breeze. The cow's unhappiness was clearly heard through the open windows. The climate in the courtroom mirrored the oppressive heat outside. The case was looking bleak for the defendant; in particular, the testimony from three of the east coast's most-prominent medical men, concluding Abby had been dead an hour and a half before Andrew. It put her death at the time Lizzie was alone in the house, with a servant outside washing windows, with plenty of hatchets and axes in the cellar. She also had ample time to clean up—an entire hour, before Bridget came inside to clean.

Marshal Rufus B. Hilliard was called by the prosecution. He had been the City Marshal of Fall River for 14 years. A walrus of a man, he was weary of the case, and ready to move on to other matters. Hilliard testified to being at the Borden house to supervise and help in the various searches; including the barn and grounds. He stated he had asked Mr. Jennings on the day of the funeral for the dress Lizzie had worn the day of the murders. Mr. Jennings had gone out of his sight for a few minutes, and returned with a blue dress waist, skirt and white underskirt, and handed them to the Marshal. Hilliard turned them over to Dr. Dolan.

On the evening of the funeral, August 6th, Hilliard and Mayor Coughlin had gone to the Borden house to speak with the residents there. "I sent for officers to clear the street, and then the Mayor and I saw Lizzie and Emma and Mr. Morse in the parlor. Mayor Coughlin asked that the members of the family remain in the house for a few days, and he offered them police protection and suggested that they send persons for the mail rather than go to the post office for it."

"Lizzie then said, 'What! Is there anybody suspected in this house?' The Mayor said, "Well, perhaps Mr. Morse can answer that question as the mob had accosted him the night before.""

"Then Lizzie said, 'I want to know the truth!' and she repeated that twice. With that Miss Emma spoke up and said, 'We have tried to keep it from her as long as we could.' Then Lizzie said, 'I am ready to go at any time."

The cross-examination of Marshal Hilliard was lengthy, with Mr. Adams trying to ascertain if the Marshal told Miss Emma at the end of the search Saturday evening, that they had done a complete and thorough search, and with the exception of the mason looking at the chimneys Monday morning, they were through. Hilliard danced around it for a while and admitted that was essentially what was communicated. He also said a warrant for Lizzie's arrest was not offered Saturday night—it had been drawn up Monday, August 8th. This played into Mr. Jennings' point that at the time of Lizzie's Inquest testimony there was a warrant ready for her, yet she was denied counsel, or a warning of her rights.

Mayor John W. Coughlin was next. He stated he was a physician, surgeon, and Mayor of Fall River. He basically backed up Marshal Hilliard's telling of the conversation in the Borden's parlor on Saturday evening, August 6th.

Mrs. Hannah H. Gifford took the stand and testified to being Lizzie's dressmaker for seven or eight years. She retold Lizzie telling her that Mrs. Borden "was a mean, good-for-nothing."

Miss Anna H. Borden, Lizzie's traveling companion for the Grand Tour of Europe stood at the railing, looking uncomfortable. She once again distanced herself from being a close relative of Lizzie's. While the witness was there to testify to Lizzie's tales of an unhappy home, and her dread of returning there after the European trip in 1890, the Judge ruled it inadmissible, due to the grounds "the statements were too ambiguous in character and too remote in point of view of time." The not-so-close relative stood down.

The next four witnesses: **Lucy Collet, Thomas Bowles, Patrick McGowan,** and **Aruba Kirby** were all brought on as witnesses to anyone being seen in the Borden yard that Thursday morning. Patrick was the pear thief, Lucy sat on Dr. Chagnon's patio during the murder timeline, Thomas Bowles was washing Mrs. Churchill's carriage next door, and Aruba Kirby was in her sink room next door to Dr. Chagnon, looking out on his driveway, just northeast of the Borden's home. None of them saw anyone suspicious.

Mrs. Hannah Reagan, Matron of the Fall River jail.
Photo courtesy of Edwin Porter, *The Fall River Daily Globe.*

Mrs. Hannah Reagan was one of two jail matrons at the Fall River Police Station. Lizzie had been put in her care, and had been given the use of Matron Regan's sitting room during the Inquest and Preliminary Hearing. She was questioned about the alleged quarrel she heard between Emma and Lizzie on the morning of August 24th, the day the Preliminary Hearing was to start.

Mrs. Reagan testified to the following conversation:

"Miss Emma Borden came to my room about twenty minutes to nine o'clock on the twenty-fourth of August, and I let her in, and she spoke to her sister Lizzie. I left the two women talking together, and I went into a toilet room about four feet from where Lizzie Borden was lying on a couch, and I heard very loud talk, and I came to my door, and it was Miss Lizzie Borden; she was lying on her left side, and her sister Emma was talking to her, and Lizzie says, "Emma, you have given me away, haven't you?

"She says, "No, Lizzie, I have not."

"You have, "Lizzie says, "and I will let you see. I won't give in one inch." And Lizzie sat right up and put up her finger, and I stood in the doorway, looking at both of them. Lizzie spoke in a loud voice. She laid down on the couch and faced out the window and closed her eyes. Emma got a chair and sat down beside her sister and stayed until sometime after eleven o'clock in the morning. Miss Lizzie did not speak to her again, or tell her goodbye when she left. They both saw me.

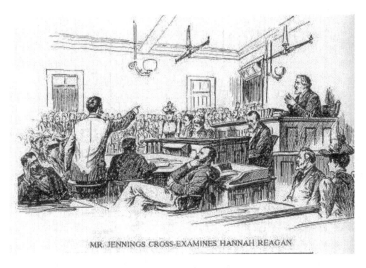

MR. JENNINGS CROSS-EXAMINES HANNAH REAGAN

Mr. Jennings, who came to where Lizzie was, shortly after Emma left that morning, tried to get Matron Reagan to play down the hurt feelings between the two sisters to which she had testified, by getting her to admit they had all played a crushing an egg trick in the same afternoon, and everyone laughed, and was having a good time. Mrs. Reagan admitted that the mood was better, but that Emma had not joined in. She repeated Lizzie's statement, upon not being able to break the egg, that "it was the only thing I've ever attempted to do that I could not."

Mr. Jennings tried again. He reminded Mrs. Reagan that he, himself, had offered her a paper to sign regarding the retraction of her story about the quarrel, that she had recklessly told to reporter Edwin Porter. While admitting Mr. Jennings drew up a paper, she denied signing it, or agreeing with it. He pushed her to admit the only reason she did not sign the document was that Marshal Hilliard had forbidden her to do so. She denied that was the reason. She stuck by her story of the quarrel, under oath.

The final witnesses of the day were called upon to speak of poison, and Lizzie's interest in it. First up was **Eli Bence,** the young clerk from D. R. Smith's drug store in Fall River. The prosecution was ready to show that Lizzie Borden, on Wednesday, August 3rd, one day before the murders, tried not once, but twice, to buy prussic acid, the deadliest poison of all, from two drug stores within an easy walking distance of her home.

Mr. Bence only managed to get his name and occupation out, before Mr. Robinson was on his feet, asking the Judge to have the jury excluded for *voir dire. Voir dire* is a legal term meaning "to see what is to be said." The jury left the room, and the prosecution went over its poison case, asking Mr. Bence to retell his story of Lizzie's trip to his drug store on August 3rd. He did so. Robinson argued its admissibility as the Borden's were not killed by poison. Moody claimed it went to show premeditation and a determination to kill. Robinson said it was too remote in time, (even though it was only a day before).

Charles H. Lawton, Nathaniel Hathaway, and **Henry H. Tillson** were called on June 15th for day ten of the trial. Lawton was a pharmacist, Hathaway an analytic chemist, and Tillson, a furrier, dealing in women's furs. They offered details concerning prussic acid, and that it had never been used to clean fur capes.

In the end, Judge Mason threw it out. The jury would not hear the story of Lizzie's attempt to buy poison. Once again, Lizzie wept with joy.

> *The Boston Globe*—June 15, 1893, New Bedford—At the conclusion, she burst into tears—into a convulsion of pleasure, gratitude, and sudden relief that wracked her body. She had learned to brace herself against adversity and unkindness, but mercy and active friendliness were so new to her that she broke down then.

At this time, District Attorney Knowlton rose and said, "The Commonwealth rests its case, in chief."

The Prosecution had done all it could to prove its case against Lizzie Andrew Borden. While they could ask questions of the Defense's witnesses in cross-examination, and hope to score some points, or raise some doubts, their cannon shots had been fired. The closing summation would carry home their points. They only hoped it would be enough.

A rumor was going around that the Defense might not even present a case, saying the Prosecution had failed to prove theirs. The jurors waited hopefully; dreams of resuming a normal life in their minds. They had seen things of which nightmares are made. With temperatures in the 90's, the courtroom was anxious to be unpacked from its sardine-like state, and go home.

They were to be disappointed. While only two days in duration, Lizzie's lawyers did, indeed, present their string of witnesses. In what can only be called a lame attempt at some redemption against the points made against her, Mr. Jennings rallied his co-counsel, and began.

Chapter Thirty-Five

Superior Court Trial
The Defense

On day 15 of the trial, while the temperature outside sizzled, the barometer inside the courtroom had changed. With the Defense about to take its turn, there was a noticeable difference in Lizzie Borden's behavior. She giggled behind her handkerchief, spoke with her attorneys and sat upright, no longer wilting, or keeping her eyes downward. The rest of the room sensed the change, and there was a general feeling of lightness, despite the perspiration-stained clothing and restrictive corsets.

The description of the attendees during the final days of the trial had also swung in a different direction. The country bumpkin crowd had given way to the upper crust of New England. Ladies in chiffon and silk, their hats looking like the latest in millinery fashion, filled the seats. Instead of cheap paper fans, as the ones that had crackled during most of the trial, theirs were of ivory and bamboo, some edged in lace and decorated with exotic scenes. Perhaps Lizzie looked around and felt a rush of joy—was this indicative of the elite finally accepting her? Were they here to champion her?

The stenographic system of the courtroom ran like a well-oiled machine. The on-duty stenographer, one of several men, sat at a desk in front of the witness, and worked a five-minute shift. As soon as his time limit approached, another typist would nudge him out of his chair, and take his place, never missing a word of testimony. The replaced stenographer then sped from the room, down the stairs and into a room where a bevy of secretaries took his pad of notes and typed them into a polished document. A third man was already running back up the stairs with the previous set, all bound and stitched, to hand over to both attorneys, and the three

Judges. The system was so efficient, the legal teams had the previous witness's statements in their hands within an hour of their appearance on the stand. Today, some of these documents are on display, and copies may be purchased, at the Fall River Historical Society. You can see the attorney's hand-scribbled notes in the margins, as they went over prior testimony for their rebuttals.

A typical day in the Superior Courtroom. Lizzie is in the foreground.
The Boston Globe.

Andrew Jennings opened for the defense. A small, slender man, Jennings gave off a nervous energy. He was described as "resolute with a face full of anxiety." He had let Mr. Adams hammer home most of the cross-examination during the prosecution's case, but he was now on his feet and ready to dismantle Knowlton's case against his client. Sadly, it was not much of a case, and it had all been heard before, with the exception of Emma Borden's testimony, which would come last.

Mr. Jennings' Opening Argument

Mr. Andrew Jennings opened his argument for the defendant by giving his personal relationship to Andrew Borden as his client and friend. He stated the brutality of the crime, "the audacity by the time and place," and played upon the jurors' conscience that the daughter of a man could not possibly do this heinous crime—it had to be the work of "an insane person or fiend."

His points that would be presented to the jury as proof of her innocence were:

1) Lizzie's spotless reputation in the community, a member of the church; she was interested in church matters and was connected with various organizations for charitable works.

2) "There is not one particle of direct evidence in the case from beginning to end against Lizzie Borden. There is not a spot of blood, there is not a weapon that they have connected with her in any way, shape or fashion. Their case is wholly circumstantial."

3) "There is no motive for the commission of this crime. Even if the prosecution furnishes you with a motive on her part to kill the step-mother, they have shown you absolutely none to kill the father."

4) The clawhead hatchet, which the prosecution first put forth as the murder weapon, was eliminated after Professor Wood proved there was no blood upon it, nor could it have been washed in such a way as to remove all traces. "They have got to produce the weapon, and having produced it, connect it in some way directly with the prisoner, or else they have got to account in some reasonable way for its disappearance."

5) As to exclusive opportunity, the prosecution has provided witnesses from all around the house testifying they did not see anyone at the time of the murder. Mr. Jennings points out that none of them, saw Mr. Borden walking up Second Street that day. [In point of fact, several *did* see him coming along Spring Street, and Mrs. Kelly saw him as he came around the house.]

6) Lizzie burned the dress due to its being badly stained with paint. In fact, Mr. Jennings points out, it doesn't matter, because the Bedford cord is not the dress she had on that morning—it is the blue dress she handed over to the police when they asked for it.

Thus, was the case Mr. Jennings put forth, stating he would back it up with his witnesses. He jumped in with the intruder theory.

The Witnesses for the Defense

Martha and Marianne Chagnon, mother and step-daughter, who were neighbors to the Borden's to the northeast, testified to hearing a loud banging noise against the fence separating their property from the Borden's at 11 o'clock the night before the murders. It was pointed out, although they claimed the noise lasted five minutes, their large dog parked outside near the fence, never barked. It was also pointed out that the Fall River Ice Company, only one lot over from them, made the same type of noise as the ice was loaded down their chutes.

Next came the **Kirby's**, neighbors to the north of the Chagnon's, who found a stranger, senseless and unresponsive, laid out on their steps leading to the Third Street sidewalk. Mr. Kirby yelled at him and shook him, with no success. This testimony was quickly dispatched.

Delia Manley and **Sarah Hart** were called to testify to seeing the strange, pale young man loitering inside the Borden's gate post at 9:45-9:50 a.m. the morning of the murders, as they looked at pond lilies in the back of a peddler's cart parked in front of the Borden's home. The description of their testimony has been presented earlier in the book.

Dr. Handy came on-board to report his sightings of a similar extremely pale, young man walking sporadically across from the Borden house, around 10:20 that morning. While earlier reports said the man was thought to be Mike the Soldier, the town drunk, they were later disproven, and the mysterious man Mrs. Manley, Hart, and Dr. Handy reported was never found.

[It is the Author's belief that man was Joseph Chatterton, nephew to John Morse, who was there to pick up Abby Borden for her meeting at the bank, transferring a Swansea farm deed into her name.]

Attorney Knowlton, giving Mr. Moody a well-deserved reprieve, showed a new spirit as he went after the Defense's witnesses. Perhaps Pillsbury had been writing to him, from his lounge chair on a beach in Florida, where the Attorney General was convalescing, lighting a fire beneath the reluctant D.A. Or, maybe Knowlton, seeing light at the end of the tunnel, and knowing his re-election was nigh, decided to put on a memorable grand finale.

He reiterated that the Chagnon women's window was closed the night they heard banging on the fence, their Newfoundland dog, resting on the patio, never barked, and the noise from the ice house was formidable.

As for the three witnesses who saw the man loitering outside the Borden's on the morning of the murders, he pointed out that Mrs. Manley barely noticed him, not even enough to describe his face, whether he had a mustache, or how old he was. She finally managed to say he was probably 30. That he was pale and wearing light clothing were her most salient points.

Poor Dr. Handy was hammered, and ridiculed, as he tried, without success to describe how the man he saw, was oscillating back and forth, as he walked. Knowlton ran him through the ringer.

Finally, Handy said, "He was moving very slowly, and I imagined that he was..."

Knowlton cut him off: "I beg your pardon. I didn't ask you what you imagined." Knowlton was on a roll.

Mark Chace was another witness to testify to a mysterious stranger hanging about at the time of the murder. He said he saw a strange buggy parked in front of the Borden's house that morning. Knowlton took him apart, by finally eliciting the buggy Chase saw was farther up the road, and not, in fact, in front of the Borden property. On a street comprised more of businesses than homes, a strange buggy was not a smoking gun.

Finally, **Charles N. Gifford** said he saw a man, with a straw hat pulled down over his eyes, weighing 180 – 190 pounds, sitting on the side steps of the Borden's the night before the murders.

Charles Sawyer took the stand and told of his lengthy stay, holding the fort at the rear screen door the morning of the murders. He spoke of seeing Lizzie in the rocking chair, with Mrs. Churchill and Miss Russell, "administering" to her. He saw no bloodstains on her dress. This was a man who had been in a unique position that morning, to see and hear more than most. Yet, his testimony is common, and unembellished. One gets the impression he became increasingly nervous as the day wore on, as reports came to him that two people had been brutally murdered and were within steps of him. His bolting of the kitchen cellar door, and stepping outside the house to stand on the back-porch steps, were clues to his state of mind. He stated he had handled the clawhead hatchet, and even rubbed off a tiny swatch of rust, when he found himself alone in the kitchen, as the partial autopsies went on in the nearby sitting room and dining room.

Jerome Borden was called. He was a relative of the Borden's and had arrived at the house the day after the murders, "about 2 o'clock." Mr. Borden's testimony was to show the front door of the Borden house could be opened without a key, due to a faulty spring lock. If the door wasn't slammed hard, one could simply push it open if the lock hadn't caught. John Morse and Mrs. Brigham also testified that the lock had issues.

The next string of witnesses was brought in to discredit one of the more damaging aspects of Lizzie's guilt: Medley's finding no footprints in the barn loft dust that morning. They were as follows: **Walter P. Stevens**—a reporter for the *Fall River Daily News,* claimed he had heard three people up in the loft, while he was looking around the barn's first floor, *before* Officer Medley came into the barn. Mr. Knowlton dove in by asking what time Stevens arrived on the scene. "I don't know." What time did you see Mr. Medley? "I don't know." Did you see him enter the premises? "No." Knowlton: "So that all of Mr. Medley's movements you know is that at one time while you were there you saw him going into the kitchen?" "Yes." Knowlton: "Where he had been before that, you don't know?"

Stevens: "No." Stevens admitted the barn door was wide open when he went in. Officer Medley had found it locked. And then Knowlton offered his knock-out punch: "Do you certainly recall any of your movements or the order of them?"

Stevens: "Yes, sir. I remember the first part. I don't remember just when I tried the door, whether it was before or after I entered the house." Next...

Alfred Clarkson—is a steam engineer who claimed he was one of the three men up in the loft that morning before Officer Medley arrived on the scene. Mr. Knowlton discredited the witness by showing a discrepancy in the time he said he arrived at the Borden house. He has just announced he arrived there at 11:30 the morning of the murders, and spoke with Charles Sawyer at the back door for about 5-8 minutes before going into the barn. Knowlton reads back Clarkson's testimony from the Preliminary Hearing where he said he arrived that morning at 11:40. The witness says he wouldn't swear he had not said that, only two weeks after the murders at the Preliminary Hearing. That would mean he went into the barn a good five minutes or more *after* Officer Medley stated he was there, when you add in the time Clarkson spoke to Sawyer. Moving right along...

Everett Brown and Thomas E. Barlow—tagged "Brownie and Me" by the local papers, were the two boys mentioned earlier during the Preliminary Hearing. They testified they were messing around that day, "pushing down" along the Second Street sidewalk, bumping each other off into the gutter. They saw Officer Doherty race across the street to make his call at the undertakers to Marshal Hilliard, and made their way to the Borden yard. They looked around for clues, after being told a murder had taken place, eventually finding their way into the barn. By the time Knowlton finished with them, it was obvious they had been coached as to their testimony. Thomas Barlow's was especially telling: "Went in the barn and went right up to the hayloft. I went over to the front window on the west side and looked out the window. Then we went and looked in under the hay, and after that we came downstairs and went out."

Knowlton: "How was the heat up there up in the barn compared with it out in the sun?" Barlow: "It was cooler up in the barn than outdoors." Smiles went around the courtroom. Every single witness had said the temperature and environment in the loft that day was "stifling, oppressive, extremely hot, and close." Mr. Knowlton's work was done. The case against Officer Medley's claim to being the first in the barn had just melted beneath the August sun.

Hymon Lubinsky, Charles E. Gardner, and **Charles V. Newhall** were next called by the Defense to show evidence that Hymon Lubinsky saw Lizzie coming from the barn area at 11:05-11:10 the morning of the murders, just as she had claimed. First up, the Russian ice cream peddler.

Hymon Lubinsky—He claimed he picked up his team from Charles Gardner's stable at the corner of Second Street and Rodman, only a few blocks from the Borden house, on the morning of August 4th, "a few minutes after 11:00 o'clock." He stated, that as he drove past the Borden house, he "saw a lady come out the way from the barn right to the stairs back of the house—the north side stairs, from the back of the house. She had on a dark colored dress. She had nothing on her head. She was walking very slow." He stated he knew who the servant was, as he had delivered ice cream to her two or three weeks before the murders.

Lubinsky then dropped the statement that should have been pounced on, but wasn't: "I saw the servant and the woman too," as he drove by that morning. Mr. Jennings asked, "Was the woman you saw the day of the murder the same woman as the servant?" "No, sir."

Mr. Knowlton, after a lengthy question-and-answer about where Lubinsky had gone after he saw "the woman" and when he broke for dinner, etc., finally asked, "Who did you tell about that?" "I told Mr. Wilkinson. And then I told Mr. Mullaly, the policeman…two days after the murder, in Mr. Wilkinson's boot store. Mr. Wilkinson is my boss. I also told a reporter."

Mr. Knowlton gets the foreigner to admit that he spoke with Mr. Phillips on the Defense team just before the trial, in Mr. Jennings office. He also had Mr. Lubinsky state that the time he usually picked up his team from Gardener's was at 10:30, not 11:00. Lubinsky said he was running late that day, as the horses had not finished eating when he got there. It was all for naught. Officer Mullaly was later recalled to show in his police report, Hymon Lubinsky had told him two days after the murders, that he had passed the Borden's at 10:30 that morning, not 11:00, and saw a woman fitting Lizzie's description coming from the barn area. Lubinsky also told a reporter, who ran the story, stating the time was 10:30 a.m. Once again, the witness had been coached, and asked to move his timeline up a half an hour to foster Lizzie's alibi for her father's murder.

Charles Gardner—owned the stables Lubinsky went to that morning to pick up his team. He backed the Russian's story 100%. Knowlton was unable to shake him. By then, the obvious lie told by Lubinsky as to what time he was actually passing the Borden's house was still ringing in the juror's ears. It is hard to say how much credence they gave this witness, or **Charles V. Newhall**, a saddlery hardware maker, whose short testimony only served to say he was in Mr. Gardner's company from around 11:00 until 11:50, and saw "a reporter" heading up Second Street" shortly after he heard Mr. Borden had been stabbed. His testimony did little to add or detract from the case.

Joseph Lemay was called next. After stating his name, and that he lived on a farm of 56 acres at Stony Brook, Fall River, his testimony was interrupted by Mr. Knowlton, claiming the witness was about to introduce new evidence, something the Court had to rule on. The counselors approached the bench and conferred with the judges in private, with Mr. Jennings offering the following order of proof:

"This witness will testify that on the 16th day of August, at his farm, about four miles north of City Hall, while travelling into the woods for the purpose of cutting poles, just before he reached a turn in the road, he heard the words "poor Mrs. Borden" repeated three times, and immediately saw sitting upon a rock behind a wall and some brushwood, a man." Mr. Jennings continued by saying the man picked up a shingling hatchet and shook it at Mr. Lemay. He had spots of blood upon his shirt. He turned away, as Mr. Lemay brandished his own axe, and leaped over a wall, and disappeared into the woods.

By direction of the court, the witness left the stand, and the jury was excused until the next day, at nine o'clock. Knowlton and Jennings then argued their reasons for allowing the witness to go on with his testimony. Knowlton claimed it was hearsay evidence, without validation. Jennings argued that a man found with a hatchet, blood on his clothing, and mentioning Mrs. Borden was fair game. The judges said they would take it into consideration, and adjourned the court until the following morning, Friday, June 16.

Mr. Joseph Lemay does not make a repeat appearance, so it is assumed the testimony was ruled inadmissible.

Friday, June 16th

Friday morning brought with it a welcome respite from the heat. Overnight, the temperature had dropped 37 degrees; from 92 on Thursday evening, to 55 on Friday morning. The end of the trial was in sight, and that, along with the cool weather, brought an air of impending release from the long, graphic trial. Newspapers weighed in with their opinions, psychics and headline wannabes wrote copious letters to the prosecution, police and reporters; all stating they knew the answer to the murder mystery. Women's suffrage movements, and Christian organizations denounced Knowlton for the "witch hunt;" not the first to give a nod to neighboring Salem. The amount of ink dedicated to this world-famous trial, would rival that of Jack the Ripper's notoriety.

Everyone took their places and the day's events began, with most of the day's testimony spent on debunking Matron Reagan's story of Lizzie and Emma's argument August 24th, 1892, within her private rooms at the Fall River Police station.

Thomas F. Hickey, a reporter for the *Fall River Globe* was called and asked about his conversation with Matron Reagan regarding the truth of her story in the *Boston Globe* concerning a quarrel she overheard between the sisters when Lizzie allegedly said, "Emma, you have given me away." He stated when he spoke to Mrs. Reagan, a woman he knew, the morning following the publishing of the story, he said "I see you are getting yourself into the paper," and that she laughed, and said, "Yes, but they have got to take it all back." He went on to say Mrs. Reagan told him there was no truth at all to the story printed about the alleged quarrel.

Mr. Knowlton, on cross, took the tactic that the newspapers of the day were highly competitive—each trying to get "the scoop." Hickey agreed that was so. Knowlton tried to get him to admit that he was out to discredit the *Boston Globe's* "scoop" on a highly explosive story. Mr. Hickey finally admitted "I was sent to get Mrs. Reagan's story." Knowlton: "That was what you were after, to have something to offset the *Globe* scoop, wasn't it?" "Yes, sir." Knowlton: "If you could get it?" "Yes, sir." Knowlton (triumphantly) "Exactly."

James E. Winwood was then called. He was the undertaker who had charge of the Borden's funeral. Mr. Jennings asked him, if while he was preparing the bodies for burial, whether or not he had seen any ring on Mr. Borden's finger? Mr. Winwood said, "I cannot remember so long ago." He was excused.

Mrs. Marianna Holmes was sworn. After giving the oath, Mr. Jennings dove into her relationship with Lizzie, having her state that Lizzie had been friends with Mrs. Holmes' daughter since childhood. Jennings then had her state all the charity work Lizzie was involved with, including teaching Chinese children in Sunday School, and helping at the hospital. She stated she had seen Lizzie and Abby sit together at church within a year prior to the murders.

Mrs. Holmes said she arrived at the Borden's around 1 o'clock in the afternoon, the day of the murders. She went over the day's events without offering any new information. She left the house at half-past eight that evening. She testified that she was at the house part of the time, every day until Lizzie's arrest.

Lizzie's blue dress that she had turned over to Marshal Hilliard was brought in and shown to Mrs. Holmes. Mr. Jennings asked, "Did you at any time see this dress there?" Mrs. Holmes stated, "Miss Lizzie had that dress on Friday morning, and I think also on Saturday morning for a short time. She wore a black net over silk dress to the funeral Saturday morning."

[Note here that Mrs. Holmes says the dress turned in is the dress Lizzie wore for three days. She also says Lizzie had it on "for a short time Saturday morning" before changing into the black dress. Oddly, Mr. Knowlton did not challenge her on her testimony concerning the dress Lizzie wore, and the one she turned in. Others described it as light blue. The dress on display is a navy blue, a darker blue dress. Hymon Lubinsky testified the woman he saw coming around the house that morning was wearing a dark dress. Had Lubinsky and Mrs. Holmes been "nudged" as to their memory of the dress the defendant wore?]

Mrs. Holmes was then questioned exhaustively as to her presence during the time Mrs. Reagan had been given a paper by Reverend Buck, and asked to sign it, stating she had never told a reporter about a quarrel between Lizzie and Emma Borden. Mrs. Holmes stated she was in the room when it happened, and also saw Mrs. Reagan go out into the hallway to talk to reporters. She said Mrs. Reagan talked more to Mrs. Brigham after the incident than to herself.

Mr. Jennings ended his examination of Mrs. Holmes by making sure he got on the record that Lizzie had come down to the sitting room the morning of the funeral, and kissed her father as he lay in his casket.

Mr. Charles Holmes (Marianna's husband) was called. His entire testimony was his recollection of the events following Mrs. Reagan's refusal to sign the paper written up for her by Mr. Jennings, denouncing her story to the paper about an argument between Lizzie and Emma, where Lizzie declared, "You have given me away, Emma." He stated Mrs. Reagan said she would sign it if Marshal Hilliard said it was alright. Marshal Hilliard had yelled at her and Mr. Jennings, and told her to go back to her room, and for she and Reverend Buck to mind their own business. Hilliard also told her to state what she knew on the stand, under oath, which she did. Mr. Holmes said she did not sign the paper proffered to her by Mr. Jennings.

John Caldwell, a reporter who was there that day, and witnessed the hoopla in the Marshal's office, testified he heard Hilliard tell Mrs. Reagan, "If you sign that paper it will be against my express orders. Then he turned and saw me and ordered me out of the office. I went, after explaining I did not know it was a private office."

Mary Brigham, Lizzie's close friend, testified that Mrs. Reagan came into the Matron's room after returning from Marshal Hilliard's tirade. Mary said, "She acted mad. She sat down in a rocking chair as near me as she could sit. She said to me, "It is all a lie from beginning to end. I was willing to sign that paper but the Marshal wouldn't let me do it. He told me to go to my room and obey orders. I would rather leave a place than stay here where I have been so lied about." That was all Mrs. Brigham had to offer.

Miss Emma Speaks

Joseph Howard, our favorite journalist, weighed in on the sensation Emma Borden's upcoming testimony caused about New Bedford:

"It being noised about the town that Emma Borden was on the stand, everybody made a rush for the courthouse, but they might as well have rushed to the spire of the nearest church, for the good people already favored with seats knew a good thing when they had it, and not a soul stirred during the entire recess save such as knew they would have no difficulty in getting back.

"Next to the interest felt in Lizzie Borden, with a possible exception in favor of well-meaning Bridget Sullivan, the popular desire has been greatest to see Miss Emma Borden, daughter of the murdered man and sister of the accused.

"She is over 40 years of age, and looks it; a prim, little, old-fashioned New England maiden, dressed with an exceeding neatness in plain black with the impress of a Borden in every feature. Self-reliance and personal dignity, I should say, are conspicuous factors in her composition. There was no swaying of her slender form, no drooping of her straight eye, no quivering of her tight-shut mouth. Everybody looked at her, but she looked at the counsel only."

The Emma Borden who entered the New Bedford courtroom on that Friday afternoon was not the woman the public had grown accustomed to seeing. This was a stronger woman, with the Borden traits of iron will showing in the firm set of her mouth, and the direct eye contact with which she met each inquisitor. She stood straight, confident and self-possessed, for two hours. Only during a recess did she accept a chair for a moment. It was clear— Emma Borden was here to be heard, and to make it known that she would not be intimidated.

While the newspapers were unrelentingly cruel in their description of her, Emma Borden could not be faulted for her quiet demeanor, and strength. This was a woman who had walked into a home splattered with the blood of her father and stepmother, asked to take over the funeral arrangements, to take care of her younger sister—who by then had hidden away in her bedroom—while a physician from across the street had feed her a daily supply of sedatives. She had wiped up the blood, dealt with the police, and spent every spare moment at his sister's side: in jails, and in courtrooms. Yet, the papers could only point out that she had a large forehead, weak chin, and looked much older than her 42 years.

EMMA BORDEN ON THE STAND

Newspaper depiction of Emma Borden on the stand,
during the Superior Court trial, June 16, 1893.

Mr. Jennings started the questioning of Lizzie's older sister by asking Emma Borden the state of Lizzie's assets. He wanted the motive for murder out of the way—Lizzie had plenty of her own money. She had no need to kill for it.

Emma produced records showing Lizzie had $170 on deposit at the B.M.C. Durfee Bank, $2,000 in the Massasoit Bank, $500 in the Union Savings, and $141 in the Fall River Five Cents Savings.

This, in addition to various shares of stock. In 1892, this was a substantial amount.

Mr. Jennings went for the sentimental side of the testimony. He led Emma through a short discourse underscoring Andrew's wearing of the little gold ring Lizzie had given him "10-to-15 years" before the murder. Emma testified it was the "only article" of jewelry he ever wore, and that he had been buried with it upon his little finger.

Emma stated the sisters owned between 18 or 19 dresses, in various closets. All of those within the clothes press closet, with the exception of one of Abby's dresses hanging there, belonged to Lizzie and Emma. When asked how many of the dresses were blue, Emma answered, "Ten. Two of them to me, and eight to my sister." [This may have had a more sinister meaning than Emma realized. Eight blue dresses gave Lizzie a selection that could mirror the dress she claimed she wore that day. Would people notice the difference between one blue dress with a darker figure, or another?]

Mr. Jennings asked her about the search done Saturday afternoon after the funeral. Emma stated that Dr. Dolan told her, "The search had been as thorough as the search could be unless the paper was torn from the wall and the carpets taken from the floor." She went on to say that she and Lizzie gave the officers full permission to search everywhere, and even assisted when a trunk with a tricky lock wouldn't open.

Emma was asked about the blue Bedford cord dress Lizzie was in the habit of wearing around the house in the mornings. She described it as a blue cotton Bedford cord dress, very light blue ground with a dark figure measuring about an inch by three-quarters of an inch. It was made of cheap material costing only 12 ½ cents a yard. She stated the dress had gotten paint on it shortly after its creation by the dressmaker, who had worked on it at the Borden house, sewing in the guest room, as was the custom.

Mr. Jennings next question, while appearing innocuous, was about to detonate a bomb as loud as the one dropped when Officer Mullaly said he saw the handle to the hatchet head on the day of the murders.

Jennings: "Now, where was that dress, if you know, on Saturday, the day of the search?"

Emma: "I saw it hanging in the clothes press over the front entry."

If one could see the look on Knowlton's face, when Emma Borden stated she saw the stained Bedford cord hanging in a closet the officers had just turned inside out, it would be worth its weight in gold. The courtroom sat in stunned silence, as Mr. Jennings hurried on.

Jennings: "How come you to see it at that time?"

Emma: "I went in to hang up the dress that I had been wearing during the day, and there was no vacant nail, and I searched around to find a nail, and I noticed this dress."

As the prosecution table reeled, the best was yet to come.

Jennings: "Did you say anything to your sister about that dress in consequence of your not finding a nail to hang your dress on?"

Emma: "I did, I said, "You have not destroyed that old dress yet? Why don't you?"

Jennings: "What was the condition of that dress at that time?"

Emma: "It was very dirty, very much soiled, and badly faded."

Jennings: "When did you next see that Bedford cord dress?"

Emma: "Sunday morning, I think, about nine o'clock. I was washing dishes and I heard my sister's voice and I turned around and saw she was standing at the foot of the stove, between the foot of the stove and the dining room door. This dress was hanging on her arm, and she says, "I think I shall burn this old dress up." I said, "Why don't you?" or "You had better," or "I would if I were you," or something like that. I can't tell the exact words, but I meant, do it. And I turned back and continued washing dishes and did not see her burn it and did not pay any more attention to her at the time. The kitchen door and windows were all wide open, screens in, and blinds open. Officers were all about the yard."

Mr. Jennings tried to establish that it was a custom in the Borden house to burn old dresses, rather than keep them as rags, as most houses did, but Mr. Knowlton objected, and the question was ruled out.

Emma then testified about Alice Russell coming to her and Lizzie as they sat in the dining room on Monday morning, the day after the dress burning, to tell the sisters Detective Hanscom had just asked her about Lizzie's dresses. Alice was in a state, saying she had just lied to the Detective, telling him all the dresses were still in the house that were there the day of the murders. "The worst thing you could have done was burn that dress, Alice had told Lizzie. "Oh, why did you let me do it?" Emma said was her sister's reply. She claimed she and Lizzie sent Miss Russell back into the parlor where Mr. Hanscom was seated, to tell him the truth, that the dress had been burned due to old paint stains.

Emma took it one step further. She stated she had not seen Lizzie wear the Bedford cord "for several weeks before I went away." Bridget had testified that Lizzie wore it Wednesday, the day before the murders, and was in the habit of wearing it almost every morning.

[Food for thought: Emma said she noticed the stained Bedford cord as she looked for an empty nail to hang her dress. Why were all the nails taken? Had Lizzie purchased a new dress while Emma was gone, or had one made? One that looked almost identical to another one, perhaps longer than her others, so she could hand the police a similar dress? Mrs. Churchill and Miss Russell stated they had never seen the dress Lizzie was wearing the day of the murders. Another obstacle to Emma's testimony is the earlier testimony by the police that all the dresses were taken away Saturday afternoon. Had they been returned by Saturday night?]

Two dangerous bombs had been defused, as far as Jennings was concerned: Lizzie had no financial motive to kill her parents, and, the burning of the dress was not a suspicious thing to do in the Borden household, and had, in fact, been instigated by Emma, not Lizzie. The sisters had even insisted Alice admit to her lie concerning it.

Bomb three was still smoking when Jennings went for his final series of questions.

Jennings: "Now, Miss Emma, do you recall a story that was told by Mrs. Reagan about a quarrel between yourself and your sister?"

Emma: "Yes, sir."

Jennings: "On that morning, did you have any conversation with Miss Lizzie, in which she said, "Emma, you have given me away, haven't you?"

Emma: "I did not."

Jennings: "And did you say, "No, Lizzie, I haven't." "You have," she says, "and I will let you see I won't give in one inch." Was there any such talk as that?"
Emma: "There was not.
Jennings: "Anything like that? That morning or any morning?"
Emma: No time. Not any time."
Jennings: "Was there ever any trouble in the matron's room between you and your sister while she was there?"
Emma: "There was not."

An uncomfortable tension swept the room as Attorney Knowlton stood for the cross-examination. He looked across at this little woman with the receding chin and large brown eyes. He had underestimated her. She returned his gaze with the steely intensity for which the Borden's were known. The game was on…and the gloves were off.

Mr. Knowlton began by asking Emma how long she had been in Fairhaven, and when she had returned to the Borden house. She stated she had been away two weeks, and returned the afternoon of the murders at 5:00 o'clock. She admitted Lizzie had come to see her in Fairhaven on Saturday while Lizzie was staying a few days in New Bedford. She stated she now lived alone in the Borden house, with the exception of two servants. She was asked to list the Morse relatives living nearby, which she did.

Mr. Knowlton now waded into murky water. He asked Emma about the transfer of the Fourth Street house into Abby's name, and the friction it had caused between the sisters and their parents. Emma admitted to some bad feelings, but turned the tables by saying it was she who had the strongest feelings against Abby— Lizzie's were actually more cordial toward their stepmother than her own. Knowlton flipped them right back around by having Emma's earlier testimony read to her from Miss White's stenographic documents, where she said the relationship between Lizzie and Abby was not cordial. They volleyed back and forth on the issue until Emma weaseled out by saying she didn't remember saying that, and she felt the relationship between the two had been cordial for the past three years.

Tension hung tight in the air. The two opponents squared off, as if waiting for the next round bell to ring.

Mr. Knowlton then tried to insert an ominous motive to explain Emma and Lizzie exchanging rooms after Lizzie's return from Europe. He asked Emma if Lizzie had asked to take over the larger room, hinting at Lizzie's demands. Emma stated flatly it was her idea. End of story.

The District Attorney asked Emma about the guest room where Abby's body was found, and to its purpose as a sitting room for the sisters.

Knowlton: "And didn't you usually receive Miss Russell there?"

Emma: "Very often." [There may have been pain in that statement.]

Knowlton: "Didn't you usually receive Miss Anna Borden there?"

Emma: "No, sir; she was never in that room in her life."

There was a 1 o'clock recess taken until 2:15 p.m. The feeling in the room as the break was announced was akin to the release of air from an overblown balloon.

When the afternoon session began, Mr. Knowlton ran Emma through the house chores, while Bridget was still there. It was determined the servant had no duties on the second floor. The girls took care of their own rooms, as did Abby of hers. The guest room was cleaned depending on who used it. Lizzie was in charge of unlocking the three front door locks each morning.

Mr. Knowlton asked Emma if she had caused any search to be made for the note Abby supposedly received that morning. Emma answered, "I think I only looked in a little bag that she [Abby] carried down street with her sometimes, and in her work-basket." She said she instigated the advertisement offering a reward for the writer, or messenger, of the note. None appeared. It ran for several days.

Emma answered Mr. Knowlton's question about whether she knew there was a broken hatchet in the cellar, by saying, "Not until you told me about it...at the Grand Jury." She testified that she, Lizzie, and Abby had "waterproofs" (raincoats), and that she had taken hers with her to Fairhaven. Abby's usually hung in the clothes press near the front door at the base of the stairs, and Lizzie's blue and brown plaid, hung in the clothes press upstairs.

Mr. Knowlton's next attempt was more forceful. He was after the truth concerning the quarrel between Emma and Lizzie reported by Matron Reagan. Emma's answers are not as forceful as those she gave Mr. Jennings, and they are evasive:

Knowlton: "Do you remember any talk that passed between you and Lizzie?" [On that morning of August 24th, 1892, in the Matron's room.]

Emma: "No, sir."

Knowlton: "Nothing, whatever?"

Emma: "No, sir."

Knowlton: "How long did you remain there?"

Emma: "I think an hour and a half or two hours."

Knowlton: "And your attention was called very promptly to the circumstances of that morning's interview, was it not?"

Emma: "It was called to me the next morning."

Knowlton: "And even then, could you recall anything that was said at all?"

Emma: "I don't remember now whether I did or not. It was nothing but ordinary conversation, and I didn't remember it as I didn't tax my mind with it."

Knowlton: "And there was no sitting silent for any length of time that morning?"

Emma: "I don't remember. I don't know."

Knowlton: "Do you remember whether it did or not?"

Emma: "I think not."

Attorney Knowlton now pours salt on the wound when he goes over how close Alice Russell had been to the sisters. After several questions in that area, he turns to the night of the murder, and receives some interesting answers from Emma:

Knowlton: "Miss Russell stayed with you three days after the Thursday?"

Emma: "Yes, sir."

Knowlton: "Night and day mostly?"

Emma: "I think so."

Knowlton: "Slept in the house Thursday night?"

Emma: "Yes, sir."

Knowlton: "Was that at anybody's request?"

Emma: "I don't remember."

Knowlton: "Did she sleep in the house Friday night?"
Emma: "Yes, sir."
Knowlton: "Did she stay there Saturday night?"
Emma: "I don't know. I think she did, but I am not sure."

["I am not sure?" Saturday night is the night Alice switched rooms with Emma. How does she not remember that? Was she distancing herself from it, as it was due to an explosion by Lizzie after the Mayor accused Lizzie of the murders? Or, for some other reason? It's certainly a very strange answer.]

Hosea Knowlton is now entering hostile territory. He knows Emma has lied about seeing the Bedford cord in the clothes closet Saturday evening after the search is over. If she is not lying, then it means Lizzie has successfully hidden it for three days, despite myriad searches of the house. There is no witness to Emma's finding the dress in the closet Saturday night, so no one to verify Emma's statement. If he brings it up, he risks the jury wondering why the police didn't see it. Was it due to an incompetent search? What else did they miss? He is already dealing with the mess Mr. Fleet put them in with the hatchet head and missing handle. Emma will only lie to him. He decides to go for the testimony that did have a witness—one willing to stand up before the Grand Jury, and a private investigator, to tell the truth.

Knowlton: "Do you recall what the first thing you said was when Miss Lizzie was standing by the stove with the dress?"
Emma: "I said, "You might as well," or, "Why don't you?" something like that. That is what I meant. I can't tell the exact words."
Knowlton: "Wasn't the first thing said by anybody was, "Lizzie, what are you going to do with that dress?"
Emma: "No, sir. I don't remember so."
Knowlton: "Do you understand Miss Russell so to testify?"

[His careful groundwork of showing Miss Russell to be a longstanding friend of the sisters will now pay off. This is a woman who would do nothing to hurt them, except to lie on the stand.]
Emma: "I think she did."
Knowlton: "Do you remember whether that was so or not?"

Emma: "It doesn't seem to me. I don't remember it so."

Knowlton: "Why doesn't it seem so to you, if I may ask you?"

Emma: "Why, because, the first I knew of it, my sister spoke to me."

Knowlton (sarcastically): "That is what I thought you would say. Now, you don't recall that the first thing that you said to her, the first thing that was said by anybody was, "What are you going to do with that dress, Lizzie?""

Emma: "No, sir. I don't remember saying that."

Knowlton: "Miss Russell was in the room, was she not?"

Emma: "I don't know. When I turned to hear what my sister had to say, I saw Miss Russell, but she wasn't in the room with her then. She was in the dining room with the door open."

Knowlton: "The reason you think you didn't say so was because you had previously spoken to her about destroying the dress?"

Emma: "Yes, sir. I had previously spoken about it. I don't think I had thought of the dress at the time. I had spoken to her about it."

Knowlton: "Now, isn't that the reason that you say you didn't say that, that argument?"

Emma: "The reason that I say I didn't say so is because I didn't say so," Emma shot back.

Knowlton: "You swear you didn't say so?"

Emma: "I swear I didn't say it."

Knowlton: "Didn't you just tell me that you didn't remember of saying it?"

Emma: "I did."

Knowlton: "Do you mean to put it any stronger than that?"

Emma: "I think I may truthfully."

Knowlton: "What has refreshed your recollection since?"

Emma: "Nothing; only thinking, I am sure I didn't."

Knowlton: "Did you see your sister burn the dress?"

Emma: "I did not."

Knowlton: "Did you see Miss Russell come back again the second time?"

Emma: "I don't remember; I think she was wiping the dishes and came back and forth and I didn't pay attention."

Knowlton: "Did you hear Miss Russell say to her, "I wouldn't let anybody see me do that, Lizzie?"
Emma: "I did not."
Knowlton: "Do you mean that you don't remember it or that it was not said?"
Emma: "I don't say it was not said. I say that I didn't hear it."
Knowlton: "And did you notice that for any reason your sister Lizzie took and stepped away after something was said by Miss Russell?"
Emma: "I didn't see my sister at all after she left the stove."

[This was Mr. Knowlton's, or anyone's first chance to ask about the dress burning incident, as it had been first heard of at the Grand Jury five months earlier. We do not know if anyone questioned Emma after Alice came in at the final hour to make her announcement after the Grand Jury recessed for Thanksgiving. Mr. Knowlton may have felt he came away with an empty sack. Or, perhaps the jury would recognize a sister desperately trying to save her younger sibling's life.]

Mr. Jennings had two follow-up questions for Emma. The first was very odd, and left hanging:
Jennings: "You remained in the kitchen yourself all the time washing dishes?"
Emma: "I was."
Jennings: "Then did you go to the stove?"
Emma: "Yes, sir."
Jennings: "Do you know where the waterproof of Miss Lizzie's was on the day of the search?"
Emma: "Hanging in the clothes press that has been spoken of so often."
Jennings: "Do you know where it is now?"
Emma: "It is there now."
Jennings: "Been there ever since?"
Emma: "Every day since."

[The first question set is very strange. Why did Jennings ask Emma if she went to the stove? Why are there no follow-up questions pertaining to it? Was Jennings worried someone had seen Emma go to the stove? An officer, Alice? Did Alice testify at the Grand Jury that she saw Emma go over to the stove, perhaps to see if the dress had burned? Was he worried Knowlton might bring it up on re-cross? It would look less suspicious if Jennings put it out there first. Knowlton threw in the towel on this one, and let it go. It is never heard of again.]

As the diminutive spinster made her way down from the stand that day, did Attorney Knowlton look at her with grudging respect? She had taken all this "bear of a man" had leveled at her, and not flinched. *What was it with these Borden women,* he may have thought, *that they can bear up so well in the face of adversity?* Emma smiled at her sister, and exited the courtroom.

Mrs. Mary Raymond was sworn in to testify. Her story concerning the making of the Bedford cord dress in May, 1892, has been included earlier in the book. She stated that she made two dresses for Lizzie during that sewing session: a blue Bedford cord dress with full sleeves and a narrow ruffle, and a pink and white striped wrapper. The Bedford cord had gotten paint on it shortly after she made it. When Jennings tried to find out what the Borden's usually did with their old dresses, he was met with objections from Mr. Knowlton. He finally managed to get his question in by asking what Lizzie did with the old dress the Bedford cord replaced. Mrs. Raymond replied, "She cut some pieces out of it, and said she would burn the rest."

Jennings: "Could she get that dress on under any of her other dresses?"

Raymond: "No, sir. Her dresses were always made too snug for that, the waist and the sleeves both."

Phoebe Bowen was next called. The wife of Dr. Seabury Bowen, had only played a small part in the tragic aftermath that day, as her husband sent her home not long after she arrived. Her time on the stand, however, was long enough to do some damage:

Knowlton: "You noticed her [Lizzie's] hands, you say?"
Phoebe: "Yes, sir."
Knowlton: "They looked white?"

Phoebe: "They did."

Knowlton: "Did you notice they were clean?"

Phoebe: "Yes."

Knowlton: "Clean and white?"

Phoebe: "Clean and white."

Knowlton: "The whole of the hands?"

Phoebe: "Yes, sir."

Knowlton: "Nothing on them at all?"

Phoebe: "No, sir."

Knowlton: "Did they present to you the appearance of having been out in a dusty barn?"

Phoebe (realizing the trap too late): "I did not notice anything upon them."

Knowlton: "Noticed nothing of that kind whatever?"

Phoebe: "No, sir, I was not thinking of it."

Knowlton: "Clean and white, were they?"

Phoebe: "I think they were."

[While Jennings may have cringed, it would probably pale to how her husband would respond when he found out, as Dr. Bowen was one of the few people still trying to save Lizzie's life.]

Mr. Knowlton managed to rattle Mrs. Bowen further when he reminded her of her Preliminary Hearing testimony, where she described the dress Lizzie wore that morning as "a blouse waist of blue material with a white spray running right through it." Phoebe Bowen then changed by testifying to the white spray as "Oh, it was blue, a dark blue." When Knowlton shows her the dress Lizzie turned in, and he asks, "That would not be described by you in any way as a blouse waist of blue material with a white spray running through it?"

Phoebe (helplessly): "That would not."

Knowlton: "Were you an intimate friend of the family, Mrs. Bowen?"

Phoebe: "Yes, sir."

Knowlton: "And at that time when you gave that testimony, you did not know that any question was made as to whether the right dress had been produced to the officers, or not?"

Phoebe: "I did not know anything about the dress."

Mrs. Mary Brigham is recalled and asked a few more questions about the incident in the Matron's room in respect to the quarrel. She testifies she went for the egg that afternoon for the trick, and that afterward, Edwin Porter came back into the corridor outside the room, and beaconed to Mrs. Reagan. The Matron went out into the hallway, and upon returning said, "that reporter has come after me again, and I told him that I had nothing to tell him." She stated this was the afternoon before the Preliminary Hearing began, and the story of the sister's quarrel ran in the paper.

Mrs. Brigham then said she and John Morse had done an experiment where Morse lay on the floor between the bed and the dressing bureau in the position where Abby's body's lay. Mary stood on the stairs at the position Bridget and Mrs. Churchill stood, and claimed to see Abby's body under the bed. She said someone of her height could not see him from the hallway, over the top of the bed, but you could once you walked into the room a little way. She also said they ran some experiments with the spring locks on the front door, and found it didn't close properly and could be popped open if it hadn't been shut hard enough for the lock to catch.

Miss Annie White, the stenographer was recalled and asked to read back Bridget's Inquest testimony answer when she was asked if Lizzie was crying that morning when Bridget hurried down the stairs after Lizzie yelled for her that "Father has been killed." Miss White read it back, and Bridget did say, "Yes, sir, she was crying." Bridget denied saying that in all other testimonies.

With that, the Defense rested. Articles of evidence offered in the case were requested, for the Government's short rebuttal. A fifteen-minute recess was called.

The Government's Rebuttal

Mr. Moody recalled **Rufus Hilliard**, the Fall River Marshal. It was a very short testimony going over Marshal

Hilliard's orders to Matron Reagan to not sign the paper drawn up by Mr. Jennings to refute her story running in the papers concerning the quarrel between the sisters. He testified there were many witnesses who overheard him.

Next was **Officer Michael Mullaly**, who was questioned by Mr. Moody about obtaining some information from Hymon Lubinsky, the ice cream peddler, on the 8th of August. Mullaly said Mr. Lubinsky told him he passed the Borden's at 10:30 that morning, and saw a lady coming from the area of the barn toward the side steps. Mr. Mullaly produced his book of reports where he wrote down the information at the time of the interview. He said he also reported those details to Mr. Fleet the same day.

Miss Annie White is called to the stand again, and asked a few follow-up questions, that have been stated before.

Mr. Robinson, after a consultation with Attorney Knowlton stood and said, "The evidence is closed on both sides." With that, the trial of the century was over. All that remained were the closing arguments, and the charge to the jury. The battle-weary attorneys picked up their satchels of papers, and left the building.

Closing Argument for the Defendant
June 19, 1893

Governor George Robinson stood and addressed the jury. He wasted no time in imprinting upon them (unnecessarily after the myriad crime photos and bloody detail of the trial) that this was a gory murder. He went over the number of blows to each head, the crushing of the skulls and the penetration of the brains.

"The terrors of those scenes no language can portray," he said, with great feeling. "And so, we are challenged at once, at the outset, to find somebody that is equal to that enormity, whose heart is blackened with depravity, whose whole life is a tissue of crime, whose past is a prophecy of that present. A maniac or fiend, we say. Not a man in his senses and with his heart right, but one whose abnormal productions Deity creates or suffers, a lunatic or a devil. So, do we measure up the degree of character, or want of it, that could possibly prompt a human being to such acts."

Lizzie shuddered, and wept. The description would have touched all but the blackest of hearts. This was her attorney, describing a monster that God Himself would abhor. It was a reality too close to home.

Mr. Robinson then fired a volley at the police department of Fall River for their ineptness. "Policemen are human, made out of men, and nothing else; and the blue coat and the brass buttons only cover the kind of man that is inside. And you do not get the greatest ability in the world inside a policeman's coat. You may perhaps get what you want, and what is sufficient, but you must only call upon him for such service as he can render."

Robinson went on the popular "rush to justice" mantra, stating the public was hounding the police for a murderer: "Look here, Mr. City Marshal, these murders were committed yesterday. Haven't you the murderer in the lock-up? Get somebody in!" Robinson intoned. And so, they choose the youngest daughter, who was home at the time."

The jury was given charge of Lizzie's fate, Mr. Robinson told the twelve men. "There she stands, protected, watched over, kept in charge by the judges of this court and by the jury who have her in charge."

Mr. Robinson spotlighted again a case built on circumstantial evidence, not direct evidence. There were no eyewitnesses to these murders, no dripping, bloody hatchet, no blood upon the suspect. He then hit his strongest point, in the mind of the Defense: "And I shall expect the learned District Attorney to withdraw the things that Brother Moody said he was going to prove, because he has not proved them. Mr. Moody said the Government was going to claim and prove that this defendant was preparing a dangerous weapon on August the 3rd, the day before the murders. You heard him say that. I did. He said it. They have not proved it, have they? Was there a thing about it in evidence?"

[This was a low blow. The evidence to be proven through the testimony of two druggists, who stated Lizzie Borden came into their stores "the day before the murders" to buy prussic acid, never made it to the stand. The reason the jury never heard it, was because it was excluded while they were out of the courtroom.]

Governor Robinson then goes after the murder weapon—the handleless hatchet. "For the handle is in it [the box] and it is out of it. Fleet didn't see and Mullaly did see it. Fleet didn't take it out of the box and Mullaly saw him do it. And it is in the box now, and they run over to Fall River to get it; or they wanted to, and can't get into the house, and explain about it. So, we rather think that that handle is still flying in the air, a poor orphan handle without a hatchet, flying around somewhere. For heaven's sake, get the 125 policemen of Fall River, and chase it, till they drive it in somewhere and hitch it up to its family belongings."

The courtroom grinned, as did Lizzie, behind her fan.

The location of Lizzie and Abby's body that morning was gone into. Robinson pointed out that someone standing on that landing would not be able to see over the bed of the guest room and view Abby's prone body. He reminded the jury that they had all gone to the house and stood in the same place, and that a person could leave Miss Lizzie's room, and pass down the stairs, and not have seen Abby lying there, unless she turned her head at the turn of the stairs to deliberately look beneath the bed.

He even had a reason for the "tight board shutters" in the guest room being partially closed that morning. "The New England housewife does not like her carpet to fade. They don't let the light in."

Mr. Robinson tries to sell the story to the jury that both Bridget and Lizzie were told by Abby that she received a note from a sick friend, and went out, even though Bridget stated flatly she did not receive the information from Mrs. Borden, but rather from Lizzie. He re-reads Mrs. Churchill's testimony to the jury, omitting the fact that Bridget told her about the note voluntarily, after calling her inexplicably into the kitchen, where Lizzie sat. He also stated that it was Miss Russell, not Lizzie who suggested Abby must have dropped the note in the fire after reading it.

Lizzie's story of being in the barn is gone over, and said to be a perfectly natural thing for her do while she waited for her irons to heat. She ate some pears beneath the shade of a tree for ten minutes, and then went into the barn. She happily has a witness this time. An ice cream peddler sees her. Robinson then attacks Officer Mullaly's timeline of the peddler, discrediting him as "the Knight of the handle."

Lizzie's testimony of hearing a scraping noise, and a groan, are tossed away as the excitement of the moment: "such noises are a common occurrence—it is not a serious matter." Lizzie hearing Abby come back "before her father came back," and sending people to go upstairs in the front room to look for her, is "natural."

[He forgets that when Andrew comes in, Lizzie tells him Abby had a note from a sick friend and went out; not that she may have come back, because "I think I heard her come in."]

Mr. Robinson then attacks the theory that just because Lizzie stopped calling Abby "Mother" some five years ago, is nothing. Lizzie is now a 32-year-old woman. Mrs. Borden was her step-mother. "She is not my mother, she is my stepmother," is a natural thing to say. "I suspect that never a man lets into the inner chamber of his heart the feeling that anybody else in the world can stand where his own mother did." He then reminds the jury that Bridget said she never heard a word of complaint between the two women. He tells of the dressmaking parties the two sisters had with their stepmother in the guest room. He takes a shot at Officer Harrington, which causes the courtroom to erupt in laughter: "Phillip Harrington ought to have been there and had the whole style developed to him, to learn more than he knows, if it is possible to put anything in his head on the subject."

The jurors' heartstrings were once again plucked, as Mr. Robinson said that Andrew Borden "was an old-fashioned man, lived in a simple way, did not care anything about the frivolities of life, had worked himself up to what would be called a fortune, had taken care of it, was then superintending its use and income, and for all that on his little finger was that ring which belonged to his little girl."

The indelicate position the pail of bloody cloths played in Lizzie's suspicion was gone into briefly, in an attempt to play down her second visit to the cellar that night without Alice Russell. "Taking again her own sickness at that time, the fact that that pail was standing right by the sink—I am not going to make any suggestions, but I am quite certain that you will guess what she was there for. I will leave it there."

[He has omitted that his co-counsel said Lizzie's "sickness' [menstrual cycle] ended Wednesday night, and her trip to the cellar was Thursday night, the evening of the murders.]

Mr. Robinson then tried to defuse the number of witnesses who said Lizzie was wearing a light blue dress that morning, not the dark colored dress that has been turned over to the police. "Now there is a difference of recollection, just as good people on one side saying it was a dark blue as those on the other who say it was a light blue. But you will remember that at that time there were several ladies in there and Bridget was there with a lighter colored dress, so that those who speak of a lighter colored dress may have had in mind what Bridget had on." [Bridget had on a dark blue dress.]

The next shot taken at the Government's case was their assertion that Lizzie was alone in the house with Abby, and alone with Andrew, once Bridget went upstairs. Robinson points out the screen door was unlatched while Bridget was out washing windows. He points out how Bridget was talking with the Kelly girl for a while, out of view of the side door. Lizzie was inside "doing ordinary work, going up and down stairs, going to the water closet in the cellar." He then goes into an elaborate hypothetical of how an assailant came in and where he could have hidden.

Officer Medley's finding that no one had walked on the barn loft floor that morning had to be taken apart. Robinson mentioned the half-dozen witnesses who had testified to being up in the loft before Medley arrived, perhaps hoping the jurors would forget that all of their statements had been discredited.

Governor Robinson wrapped up with "It is enough, as I have said, if the Government fails to prove the charge. Then your duty is to find her not guilty. There is reasonable doubt, and you must think 'I cannot go to the length of a verdict of guilty on this evidence.'" As to Lizzie's lack of tears he quoted from a song:

> "The eyes that cannot weep
> Are the saddest eyes of all."

"Take care of her as you have and give us promptly your verdict of "not guilty" that she may go home and be Lizzie Andrew Borden of Fall River in that bloodstained and wrecked home where she passed her life so many years."

Judge Mason allowed the jury to retire for a brief recess before Mr. Knowlton's arguments began.

The Argument for the Prosecution

Hosea Knowlton, the reluctant District Attorney, stood before the jury with mixed feelings in his heart. His calling by the Government to present a case guaranteed to procure a verdict of guilty was his mantle. Yet, the outcry of the public against him, that he would endeavor to put an innocent, well-bred, Christian woman behind bars, and then tie the noose that would hang her, rang in his ears from morning until night. Her blood would forever be on his hands, just as it had been on the murderer, of Andrew and Abby Borden.

He also opened by speaking of the atrocity of the crime, and this heartrending case, "which lacerates the heartstrings of humanity." Mr. Knowlton went on to say: "My distinguished friend says, "Who could have done it?" The answer would have been, "Nobody could have done it." If you have read the account of these cold and heartless facts in any tale of fiction, before this thing had happened, would you not have said, "Mr. Foreman, that will do for a story, but such things never happen." It was in impossible crime. But it was committed."

"The prisoner at the bar is a woman, and a Christian woman, as the expression is used. It is no ordinary criminal that we are trying today. It is one of the ranks of a lady, the equal of your wife and mine, of your friends and mine, of whom such things had never been suspected or dreamed before. I hope I may never forget, nor in anything that I say here today lose sight of the terrible significance of that fact. We are trying a crime that would have been deemed impossible but for the fact that it was, and are charging with the commission of it a woman, whom we would have believed incapable of doing it but for the evidence that is my duty, my painful duty, to call to your attention.

"But I beg you to observe, Mr. Foreman and gentlemen, that you cannot dispose of the case upon that consideration. Alas, that is so! But no station in life is a pledge or a security against the commission of a crime, and we all know it. Those who are entrusted with the most precious savings of the widow and orphan, who stand in the community as towers of strength and fidelity, suddenly fall, and their wreck involves the ruin of many happy homes."

[Mr. Knowlton hit the very nerve of this case. He knew instinctively that these 12 men hearing the case were all husbands and fathers. They had seen evidence of gore and brutality beyond measure, and at each photograph, or bloody piece of carpeting and clothing, Knowlton knew they were measuring it against the women in their own lives. *Could my wife or daughter be capable of this?* He addressed it masterfully.]

Attorney Knowlton attacked the punch Mr. Robinson had leveled at the Fall River Police Department. "A blue coat does not make a man any better; it ought not to make him any worse. They are men; Mr. Fleet is a man, Mr. Mullaly is a man, Mr. Medley is a man; and they are not to be stood up in a row and characterized as good or bad because they are officers, but upon what you think of them as men. There is no presumption that any class of people do not tell the truth."

As to the Government's case being built upon circumstantial evidence, Mr. Knowlton said, "I have heard many an honest man say that he could not believe circumstantial evidence. But, gentlemen, the crime we are trying is a crime of an assassin. It is the work of one who does his foul deeds beyond the sight and hearing of man. Direct evidence is the evidence of a man who sees and hears: circumstantial evidence is all other kinds. Murder is the work of stealth and craft, in which there are not only no witnesses, but the traces are attempted to be obliterated. And yet murder must be punished."

Attorney Knowlton then laid out the proof he believed his case had provided as to Lizzie's guilt:

1) Abby came to her death by a period of an hour and a half before her husband. "Andrew Jackson Borden probably

never heard the clock strike eleven as it pealed forth from the tower of City Hall."

2) The obstacles an intruder would have to surpass to commit the two murders, while hiding for an hour and a half in that "house of locks," and go undetected by Lizzie, Bridget, and the busy street of people outside.

3) Abby Borden had not an enemy in the world.

4) "There was a skeleton in the closet, with grinning eye balls and the dangling limbs. It is useless to tell you there was peace and harmony in that family." Others had spoken of Lizzie's hatred toward her stepmother.

5) "No thief did this thing, there was no object of plunder. There was nothing in those blows but hatred. A great strong man would have taken a blow of that hatchet and made an end of it. Yet here, we see some struck at an angle, badly aimed; some struck here in the neck, badly directed; some pattered on the top of the head and didn't go through..."

6) Abby was struck from the front and fell onto the floor. The sound of her body hitting the floor would have been heard throughout the house, yet Lizzie heard nothing.

7) Bridget was obviously telling the story of the note as Lizzie told her to tell it to Mrs. Churchill.

8) Mr. Knowlton takes an unusual stand: "There may be that in this case which saves us from the idea that Lizzie Andrew Borden planned to kill her father. I hope she did not. I should be slow to believe she did. But Lizzie Andrew Borden, the daughter of Andrew Jackson Borden, never came down those stairs. It was not Lizzie Andrew Borden, the daughter of Andrew. She came down those stairs, but a murderess, transformed from all the thirty-two years of an honest life, transformed from the daughter, transformed from the ties of affection, to the most consummate criminal we have read of in all our history or works of fiction." [He practically offers up an insanity defense for Lizzie, but he has hit the heart of it...this woman who murdered her father, has changed. The killing of another human being only an hour and a half earlier, has changed her.]

9) Lizzie had no duties around the house, "so Emma tells us. There was nothing for her to do."

10) Officer Harrington reported seeing a small fire in the stove at noon. There was heat enough to warm a small hand iron to iron 9 or 10 handkerchiefs. There was no need to leave the house to wait for them to heat. When Bridget went upstairs she had already ironed most of them. Miss Russell said about three of them were still sprinkled, and had not been done. So why stop ironing the minute Bridget went upstairs? "What for, gentlemen?"

11) Lizzie's heated remark to Mr. Fleet that "she is not my mother, she is my stepmother," even though the woman, who had raised her from the age of two, lay only a few feet away, dead, in the next room.

12) Lizzie said she assisted her father to lay down, and helped him remove his shoes and put on his slippers, when he was found with his street shoes on.

13) That Lizzie Borden went up into that stifling hot barn for twenty to thirty minutes is "simply absurd, I assert that story is not within the bounds of reasonable possibilities. She went out of the house and up in that barn, to the hottest place in Fall River, and there remained during the entire time that was covered by the absence of Bridget upstairs. It was necessary that she should be in the loft...it was the only place where she could put herself and not have known what took place."

14) Show us the screen that needed fixing, as she told Miss Russell for her visit to the barn for iron; Show us the fish lines that those sinkers went on. It was easy to do if they were in existence; if there was any truth to the story.

15) Hymon Lubinsky saw Lizzie coming from the backyard at 10:30. It was entered into a report the minute he stated it. He told a reporter, I presume it was published. Later, he tells his story to Mr. Phillips in Mr. Jennings' office, and the time of his passing of the Borden house, is now changed to "a little after 11 o'clock."

16) Charles Sawyer, a big, burly man, was so nervous about the butchery of these people, that he locked the cellar door inside the kitchen entry and waited outside the door. Yet, Lizzie, after just discovering her father hacked to death, blood pouring, and having just seen him less than 30

minutes earlier, remained in the house, and sent away the two women who were there to help her. There was no fear of a murderer remaining in the house. She knew who the murderer was, and she was in no danger.

17) Lizzie had ample time to clean up after Abby's murder. While Knowlton cannot account for how she managed to have no blood on her after Andrew's death, he does make the ominous statement: "Perhaps one of the pregnant facts in this case is that when the officers had completed their search and in good faith had asked her to produce the dress she was wearing that morning, they were fooled with that garment which lies on that trunk, which was not upon her when any human saw her. Knowlton then reads Mrs. Churchill's statement of the dress she saw Lizzie wearing that morning, when they were alone, and Mrs. Churchill was the first to arrive: "It looked like a light blue and white ground work; it seemed like calico or cambric, and it had a light blue and white ground work with a dark navy blue diamond printed on it." Showing Mrs. Churchill the dress Lizzie turned in, "Was that the dress she had on this morning?" "It does not look like it," Mrs. Churchill said.

18) The paint-stained Bedford cord is not anywhere in the house Saturday when the police undertake two searches. It was definitely not in the clothes press with the other dresses. Where was it? The fact that Emma says she saw it there, and suggested Lizzie burn it, falls within the perimeters of a sister's love, and trying to save her life. And, she burns the dress the morning after the Mayor tells her she is suspected of murder.

19) The handleless hatchet shows signs that someone adhered white ashes to it on both sides to make it appear dusty and ill-used. The ashes, according to Professor Wood, look as though they were wiped onto a wet blade, and forced into the crevices. The hatchet head is found in the Borden cellar. It fits the wounds perfectly; in fact, it would be doubtful any other blade could have fit the wounds, due to its singular grinding. An intruder would have carried the weapon away, not spent all that time on disguising an instrument of murder

20) Mrs. Reagan's story of the sister's quarrel was told under oath. She was seen speaking to the reporter shortly before the story ran in the newspapers, and she was reluctant to sign the paper Mr. Jennings drew up, asking her to perjure herself. It was waved away as self-evident. She did overhear the argument of Lizzie accusing her sister of giving her away.

Attorney Knowlton, with a great inner sigh of relief, rested his case, and lifted the albatross from his neck. It was in the hands of the jury. He had done all he could.

The Charge to the Jury

Judge Dewey, the man Governor Robinson had put on the bench, gave one of the most unique, and biased, charges ever given to a jury. Many stated his charge was better than the Defense's entire case in the realm of freeing Lizzie Borden from the hangman's noose. Instead of merely admonishing the jurors to look over all the evidence, and come to a fair finding, the lengthy charge held some of the following statement:

1) Judge Dewey gives an overview of Lizzie's past character, and habits. He then says, "In other cases it may raise a reasonable doubt of a defendant's guilt even in the face of strongly incriminating circumstances."

2) As for Lizzie's hatred of Abby, and the things she had spoken of her to others, he said, "Imputing a motive to the defendant does not prove that she had it. What according to common observation is the habit of young women in their use of language? Is it not rather the use of intense expression? Whether or not they do not use words which, strictly taken, go far beyond their real meaning?"

3) As for the note from the sick friend, Judge Dewey practically handed the juror's proof of the intruder theory on a platter: "Contemplate the possibility of there being another assassin than herself; might it not be part of the plan or scheme of such a person by such a document or paper to withdraw Mrs. Borden from the house?" After killing her, "might he not have a reasonable and natural

wish to remove that note as one possible link in tracing himself?"

4) He dismissed Lizzie's contradictory statements alluded to her from her Inquest testimony "as to be received with great caution. Repetition of oral statements, is subject to much imperfection and mistake..."

5) The most astonishing blow was dealt to the learned men of Harvard who had testified as witnesses. Judge Dewey said, "Now the Government has called as witnesses some gentlemen of scientific and medical knowledge and experience, who are termed experts. They sometimes manifest a strong bias or partisan spirit in favor of the party employing them."

6) As to Lizzie not taking the stand on her own behalf, he defended her decision by saying, "She is exposed to the peculiar danger of having her conduct on the stand and her testimony severely scrutinized and perhaps misjudged..."

7) Judge Dewey's final salute to Lizzie was asking the gentlemen of the jury if they "can extract from the testimony such a description of a dress as would enable you from the testimony to identify the dress?"

Judge Dewey then excused the jury to go and deliberate their findings, and render a verdict.

The charge was so incredible, that Joseph Howard took his pen to it on Wednesday morning, June 21, 1893:

Judge's Plea for the Innocent

"The judge's charge was remarkable. It was a plea for the innocent. Had he been the senior counsel for the defense making the closing plea on behalf of the defendant, he could not have more absolutely pointed out the folly of depending upon the circumstantial evidence alone. With matchless clearness, he set up the case of the prosecution point by point and, in the most ingenious manner possible, knocked it down...and like the saints he continued to the end throwing bombs of disheartenment into the range of the prosecution and causing smiles of great joy on the lips of Lizzie's friends. I doubt there was such a charge before. There never was a prosecution so handicapped before."

The jury made their decision on the first ballot. Out of respect for the prosecution, they delayed ringing the bell that would signal they were ready to publish their verdict. For an hour and a half, they talked. The exhibits had not been touched. The two fleshless faces of Andrew and Abby Borden sat among the pieces of bloody carpet, axes and hatchets, silent in their waiting for the announcement concerning their daughter. Would the jury believe Lizzie Borden capable of murder?

At 4:30 in the afternoon of June 21, 1893, the bell rang, and the twelve men were led into the jury box. Thousands crowded the sidewalks outside. The tension inside the small courtroom was reaching the boiling point, and for once, it had nothing to do with the June heat. The three judges took their seats, while all eyes scanned the faces of the twelve bewhiskered jurors in hopes of a sign of their findings.

Chief Justice Mason blurted, "Have the jurors rise as their names are called, Mr. Clerk." The court crier called each juror by name from his high perch.

Simeon Borden, a cousin of Lizzie's, stated officially, "Lizzie Borden stand up." Lizzie rose, the nibbling of her lips giving away her anxiety. She was adorned with a large, wide-brimmed hat, pushed toward the front of her forehead, and festooned with a large feather.

"Gentlemen of the jury," Clerk Borden said, "have you agreed upon a verdict?"

"We have," Foreman Richards intoned.

"What say you, Mr. Foreman---"

Foreman Richard cut him off, no longer able to hold it in, "Not guilty!" he shouted.

The courtroom erupted in thunderous applause and great shouts of joy. It passed through the open windows and out to the street where New Bedford took up the cry. There was a scene of exultation such as the city had never seen. Sheriff Wright gave up maintaining order in the courtroom, and sat back in his chair, resigned to the chaos. His eyes rimmed with tears, happy to see the young woman who had played with his daughter as a child, and who had been his ward at the Taunton jail for ten months, set free.

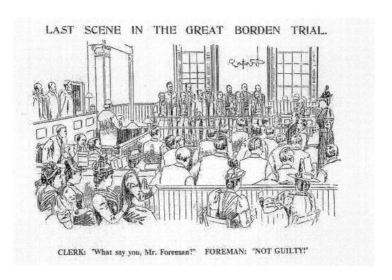

LAST SCENE IN THE GREAT BORDEN TRIAL.

CLERK: "What say you, Mr. Foreman?" FOREMAN: "NOT GUILTY!"

Lizzie collapsed against the railing flanking her chair. She leaned upon it and hid her face in her arms as she sobbed. Emma reached for her. "Take me home," Lizzie sobbed, "take me home. I want to go to the old place tonight."

"Not Guilty!" - THE PRISONER CRIES WITH JOY

New Bedford Standard-Times illustration.

Actual view of the railing where Lizzie placed her head (right front). Her Defense table is in front of her, the prosecution's table is to the left. The jury was to her right (not shown). Photo by the Author, courtesy of the Bristol County Superior Courthouse, and Richard George.

Mr. Jennings, overcome with emotion, turned to Mr. Melvin O. Adams, his co-counsel, took his hand and said, "Thank God!"

Lizzie was lead out of the room, where men and women alike were waving handkerchiefs and cheering. She was taken to the judge's chamber where she took some time to regain her composure. After an hour, a carriage arrived to take her and her sister to the New Bedford station. As usual, a crowd surrounded her, while Emma tried valiantly to push through the people pressing against her sister. They managed finally to board the train that would carry them back to Fall River, a place Lizzie was sure would embrace her now. Mrs. Susan S. Fessenden, whose voice had been heard from so often during the trial, captured Lizzie's future in one succinct sentence: "Some people will hold aloof from her as tainted; some will lionize her as though it were some triumph to have suffered long and bitterly at the hands of the state." Lizzie herself, in a letter to a friend, said prophetically: "Of course, my life will never be the same."

The jurors from the trial had been through much, and during that time they had formed a bond, and decided to have a yearly party to keep in touch with one another. In July, 1893, Juror Augustus Swift, took a 30-by-20-inch photograph of the 12 jurors who had decided Lizzie's fate, to her home in Fall River, and presented it to her. Captain William Lewis was with him. Lizzie was touched, and it was said she and Emma placed the portrait in their parlor. Lizzie wrote to one of the jurors, Frederick C. Wilbur, and thanked him, and the others, for the portrait, calling them her "faithful friends and deliver's."

Portrait of the jury presented to Lizzie Borden upon her acquittal. Photo courtesy unknown,

The Taunton Courthouse today, in Taunton, Massachusetts.
Photo by the Author.

Home Sweet Home

"Now take me home. I want to go to the old place and go at once tonight."
Lizzie Borden leaving the courthouse to go home to Fall River.
The Boston Advertiser

While Lizzie had told Emma to take her straight home, the sisters were taken instead to the residence of Charles J. Holmes. He and his daughter, Annie, accompanied Lizzie and Emma, and helped them navigate the knots of people who were everywhere. At the Holmes house on Pine Street, Lizzie's friends gathered to congratulate her (including the women from the Marion group), and welcome her back to Fall River. The loneliness she had experienced for 10 long months, melted away, and she saw the faintest glimmer of a happy future: a future without Abby, without fear of financial uncertainty, and one where she would be welcomed into the society she craved. Hadn't they all cheered for her in New Bedford when she was found innocent? The fine ladies with their expensive gowns and richly adorned hats had taken her hand in their gloved grasps and joined in her happiness. It had all been worth it.

Lizzie and Emma spent the night at the Holmes, sequestered from the media and crowds, sure to be holding vigil outside the walls of 92 Second Street. Lizzie placed her head upon the feathered pillow, and for the first time in over a year, she slept with no fear of the dawn. As the sunlight streamed in through the lace curtains of the Holmes guest room, she rose, to finally return home. The papers stated she did just that, "at 9:49 a.m."

The Holmes residence today in Fall River, Massachusetts.
Photo by the Author.

According to the *Fall River Daily Evening News,* Lizzie had "returned to her household duties in her Fall River home," and hopes for "nothing so strongly than that she may be forgotten by the newspapers and left in peace by the curious." Mrs. Mary A. Livermore said of her friend that "the poor girl feels herself under surveillance even now" in spite of the fact she had been liberated by the courts. All about the Borden property, individuals peered over the fence and from every vantage ground to catch a glimpse of her" until the outlandish behavior became "maddening."

There was still some unfinished business concerning the bodies of Andrew and Abby Borden. They were buried, yes, but without their heads. In accordance with Lizzie and Emma's wishes, Mr. Andrew Jennings, who was still their legal representative, addressed Mr. Hosea Knowlton, and made a request. Based on that, Mr. Knowlton wrote to Dr. Dolan:

Dear Sir—
Mr. Jennings insists that the skulls of Andrew and Abbie [ms] Borden be returned to his clients. As there is no pending case and they were held for evidence only, I see no reason why they should not be returned.

Hosea Knowlton
July 14, 1893

The sisters may have contacted undertaker James Winward to carry out the proper burial of the skulls. It was handled in the most secret of undertakings, as for once, the newspapers did not emblazon the event across their pages. While no evidence of the burial was documented at the time, some recent events may prove the victim's heads were rejoined with their caskets.

Modern Skullduggery

The Sun-Journal, from Lewiston, Maine, wrote on Wednesday, August 5, 1992, that James Starrs, a professor at George Washington University, made a surprising statement during the 100-year anniversary of the butchery of Andrew and Abby Borden. He stated that six months prior, he had scanned the two graves of the murdered couple, with a radar probe, in search of the skulls. His findings? "I am as sure as science will allow that the skulls are buried at Oak Grove Cemetery in Fall River, about three feet above the rest of the remains of the Borden's," Starrs claimed. He used charts to show some "anomalies" in the soil. Once word got out about his skullduggery, relatives of the Borden family let it be known that his actions would not be tolerated, and any further investigation on his behalf, be halted.

A Short Trip to Newport

Lizzie and Emma, finding the crowds and notoriety hard to handle after such a grueling ordeal, accepted the invitation of some dear friends to come to Newport and recuperate. William K. Covell and family welcomed the sisters, and encouraged them to relax, away from the curious gaze of the sensation-seekers. As always, the reporters were there to document Lizzie's every move:

The New Bedford Evening Journal, July 5, 1893—Lizzie "with the daughter of Mr. Holmes...went for a week's outing to Newport a fortnight ago, very quietly" so that the fact of her going "was scarcely known. The two young people spent the days in resting and riding, and the change of scenery and relief from persistent surveillance was greatly appreciated." *The Newport Mercury* reported on July 8, "Misses Lizzie A. and Emma L. Borden have returned from a week's visit to Newport." [Articles courtesy of *Parallel Lives*/Fall River Historical Society.]

Lizzie and Emma may have been invited to the Covell's to celebrate the 4th of July. The first fireworks in America were in 1777 on July 4th, just one year after the signing of the Declaration of Independence, and were instigated every year since. As the "bombs bursting in air" rattled the seaside town of Newport, did Lizzie celebrate her own recently-found independence with family and friends? A two-week vacation from cares was just what she and Emma needed. Yet, in the end, the house on Second Street, with its memories, missing sofa, newly carpeted guest chamber and sitting room, were waiting for her.

The sisters secretly hoped the crowds were tired of watching their windows and doors in hopes of seeing a member of the family. John Morse had gone home to Iowa, and Bridget was beginning a new life, away from the Borden tension and limelight, the blood-splattered walls, and the police scrutiny.

Lizzie Borden on the piazza at the Covell's, July, 1893.
Photo courtesy of the Fall River Historical Society.

The Covell house in Newport, R.I., where Lizzie and Emma spent a week after the trial. The photo of her above may have been taken on this porch.
Photo courtesy of Shelley Dziedzic.

The All-Seeing Eye

Wherever Lizzie went, her actions were commented upon. Her dear friend Charles J. Holmes tried to run interference for her. He told the multitudes that were on the lookout for her that he did not expect she would be seen "at church, a concert, or at a public gathering for many weeks to come. She does not wish to intrude in public under the present circumstances." In the weeks following Lizzie's acquittal, the crowds staked out the Central Congregational Church on Rock Street, in hopes of seeing her. Many may not have known she was away at Newport. It did not stop the vicious gossip:

"Not at Church," the headlines read. "Did not see her," and on it went. Yet, when she finally did appear within the church doorway, on July 23rd, escorted by Dr. Seabury Bowen and Charles J. Holmes, the pendulum of scandal swung the other way:

Fall River Daily Herald, Monday, July 24, 1893— "Miss Lizzie Borden attended morning and evening services at the Central Congregational Church yesterday." Another paper was quoted as saying "her appearance was a surprise to most of the congregation." One sharp tongue was quoted as saying, "The town was all astir Sunday because Lizzie Borden went to church. I don't see why it should bother people so, for if she is guilty is not church the best place for her?"

The surprise that first day back at church was probably Lizzie's. After the accolades and well-wishes of the public at the "not guilty" announcement, she may have expected a warm greeting from her fellow parishioners. What she found was a section of empty seats surrounding her family's pew, number 22. Although their pews were paid for, their family's names engraved upon small gold plaques, the religious and pious congregation distanced themselves from her. The message it sent was more indelible than any newspaper headline.

Like dominoes falling one right after the other, Lizzie's friends fell away. Women who had worked with her in her many charitable endeavors, silently removed themselves from her realm. Some who had written to her in jail, now ignored her attempts to reach out to them in social settings. The loss of Alice Russell had been great, although Lizzie's anger felt over her betrayal burned hotter. With her had gone Elizabeth Johnston, one of her dear friends from the Marion circle. She stopped her attendance at the Christian Endeavor Society, as the members there cut her. Problems with the Young Women's Temperance Union caused their final removal from the upper floor of the Andrew J. Borden building, where they had been paying $120 in rent. Lizzie, once acting as Secretary of that organization, and once the recipient of their support during her trials, was suddenly cut by them. Whether it was their idea or hers, they removed to another location.

One of the reasons for the committee's decision to move was that Charles C. Cook, Mr. Borden's (and now the sisters') property manager, had refused to make some repairs the Union asked for, as the property had not yet been put into the sisters' name, and he did not want to bother Emma at this time (during the trials). For whatever reason, the YWTU moved away, as did their friendship to Lizzie.

For Fall River, the verdict of "not guilty" may have been published, but there had been no murderer arrested to take her place in the crimes. The papers had railed against Judge Dewey's biased charge to the jury, causing many to believe Lizzie skated by on the squeaky wheels of an unjust judicial mandate. She was, literally, in a "No Man's Land"—acquitted, but still very much under the umbrella of suspicion in the public's mind. The Borden's of the "Spindle City" were ashamed and angered that their birthright had been tainted by this woman, who had been an outsider, living in the wrong part of town. Emma merely picked up the pieces, as she always did.

Putting It in Print

Barely two months after the Superior Court trial ended, a book hit "the stands" that would cause a sensation throughout the small town. Edwin Porter, that tenacious reporter for the Fall River Police Department, put his copious notes and newspaper reporting into one damning book called, *The Fall River Tragedy*. Here it was, in permanent black and white, the telling of the Borden murders, complete with leaked testimony from the Inquest—many believing Officer Phillip Harrington as the mouthpiece. The book left no doubt as to Porter's belief that Lizzie had wielded the hatchet.

Attorney Jennings flew into action to put a stop to the book before its release; sending notices to both Porter and the publishing house of John D. Monroe. He threatened that "any false statement or colorable description" would be prosecuted. No photos of Andrew J. Borden, his daughters, John V. Morse, or any of the defense attorneys would be allowed. Porter and Monroe lawyered up. They went ahead with crime scene photos, and other black and whites, the first of their kind to be seen in print, as opposed to hand-drawn illustrations. They did steer clear of printing Lizzie, Emma or John's likeness. Abby Borden and Bridget's photographs were not mentioned in Jennings' warning, and were fair game.

The book was published, and ready for sale on August 10, 1893. Sadly, it found its way into the libraries of the elite on "the Hill," and into the hands of Andrew Jennings, Mrs. George S. Brigham, Anna and Carrie Borden, and others who were anxious to see what damage had been done. For the asking price of $1.50, Lizzie's "untold story" was laid out for the world to see.

An Olive Branch

The legal question of who died first, Andrew or Abby, had come home to roost, as the Borden sisters went about handling the paperwork of their inheritance. Abby had died intestate, leaving no will, as had her husband. Therefore, when Abby died first, anything in her name was automatically transferred to her husband's estate. When Andrew died, his heirs became sole owners of all of it. So, Abby's real estate holding of "one undivided half of a house and land at Number 45 Fourth Street, valued at $2,000, and her personal assets valued at $1,716.05, went to Lizzie and Emma, and Abby's family received nothing.

The sisters decided to transfer Abby's estate to her heirs, perhaps partly to head off any more salacious publicity, and to move on with their lives. *The New York Times*, under their column called "Personal Gossip," wrote: "Miss Lizzie and Emma Borden have voluntarily transferred, it is said, about $4,000 worth of property, which belonged to their murdered stepmother, to Mrs. [George W.] Whitehead of Fall River, and Mrs. [George B.] Fish of Hartford, Connecticut, who were sisters of Mrs. Borden." Abby's relatives were satisfied with the settlement, and Emma and Lizzie closed the door on that chapter of their lives.

On January 22, 1894, Lizzie and Emma submitted "the first and final account" of Andrew J. Borden's estate, valued at between $300,00 and $500,00. In today's dollars, it amounted to close to $14 million. The Borden ladies were wealthy, and able to do as they pleased. And what they wanted most, especially Lizzie, was to move away from the tainted house on Second Street, and up to Fall River's echelon of wealth and power: "the Hill."

Maplecroft

Chapter Thirty-Six

A New Address

Emma and Lizzie Borden had lived under the same roof all their lives. Emma's attendance at school, Lizzie's Grand Tour of Europe—and her incarceration—were the only times the sisters were separated, barring a few short vacations. In Victorian New England, spinsters, and unmarried sisters living together, was practically the norm. Spinster schoolteachers were ubiquitous, and several of Lizzie's friends filled those positions.

Every family had maiden aunts, and many women preferred a life without the domineering hand of "the head of the house." Subservience, within the pristine walls of well-ordered households, was alive and well in the 1890s. But Suffragettes were moving ever closer through the brush, as they gained momentum for women's rights. In the television movie, *The Legend of Lizzie Borden* (1975), the actress playing Hosea Knowlton's wife says to him, "You have no idea how unbearably heavy these skirts can be at times." Her reference was to the subservient role women played in the Gilded Age—not to the weight of the fabric.

Shopping for a Home

Without hesitation, the Borden sisters took Charles Cook in hand and pointed him to Fall River's Hill area. Rock Street, once the epicenter of the lush mansion enclave, had been usurped by Highland Avenue as "the place" to own a home. While Lizzie and Emma did view a home on Rock Street, the houses they migrated toward were not on a grand scale, compared to many jaw-dropping edifices sprawling across manicured lawns.

One of the first homes the sisters visited was 99 Rock Street. It belonged to William H. Chace, a successful dealer in leather goods for the Union Belt Company. The Borden's made him an offer of $15,000 for the house, but he turned them down, stating he had another offer made to him prior to their arrival. It was basically "under contract." Whether that was true, or not, the sisters moved on.

Next on the list was the home of a locally-famous man by the name of Henry W. Peabody. Mr. Peabody was a member of the Salem, Massachusetts, Peabody's who were known far and wide for their wealth and position. *"You're a Peabody or you're nobody,"* was a well-known mantra. The Peabody Essex Museum in Salem is named for them, as is a mansion in that city. Peabody, Massachusetts, a nearby town to Salem, stands as testament to the family renown.

To the door of 12 Underwood Street on July 5th, 1893, Lizzie and Emma knocked and were afforded a tour of the house. Mrs. Peabody, nee Nannie J. Brayton, was sister to Elizabeth H. Brayton, one of Lizzie's fellow passengers on the *RMS Scythia* on her return trip from Europe in 1890. Lizzie must have looked at the rich furnishings and small accouterments with a voyeuristic eye. She was finally within the walls of a Brayton; perhaps a home that had, at one time, hosted a party to which she was not invited. Nannie was a member of the Troy Book Club, and probably knew Emma from that association. For whatever reason, the sisters kept looking.

The largest home Lizzie and Emma considered was a breathtaking Italianate marvel at 85 High Street, owned by Junius P. Prentiss, treasurer for the Fall River Board and Trade. The home was originally built for Charles O. Shove, whose daughter Ellen had also traveled with Lizzie to Europe. Once again, Lizzie ran her gloved hand over the marble and glass of homes to which she had never gained access.

The sisters later viewed a home for sale just a few doors down from the Prentiss house, at 62 High Street. The large two-and-one-half story Queen Anne was the dwelling place of another Fall River tragedy. The home's owner, fifty-six-year-old Alfred D. Butterworth, a traveling agent for the Hargraves Soap Company in Fall River, hanged himself on April 14, 1892. His body, hanging from a tree limb in a wooded area of northeast Fall River, was seen by a Mr. Joseph B. Peacock, who was out strolling. He ran to the police station to report his sighting. In an ironic twist, it was Officer Mullaly, the same policeman who found the handleless hatchet, who was called to look into it.

Mr. Butterworth's death was a mystery, as he was known to be a happy man, with a loving family, and beautiful home. No one knew why he suddenly chose to climb a tree in his grey suit and light overcoat, and release his hold, allowing the noose to take his life. The home's tragic past made it an odd choice for the Borden sister's consideration.

Meanwhile, back on Second Street, the interest in the "murder house" was just as prevalent as ever. People climbed the fences, tried to get into the barn, and did their own "recon" throughout the property. Charles C. Cook was finally told by the sisters to put up a sign out in front of the house that read: "Trespassing on these premises is strictly forbidden by the owners." Alas, it was akin to putting up an "X marks the spot;" number 92 was now as conspicuously stamped as "You are Here."

7 French Street

It was not lost on Lizzie and Emma Borden that gossip and headlines followed their every move. Emma hoped the sensationalism would die down as time passed and other tantalizing bits of news found their way into ink. But, the trial had only ended a few weeks earlier. The obvious dislike of the Borden women, shown by of some of the people they were hoping to call neighbors, was harder to ignore. Many on High Street were not pleased when the sisters made an offer on the infamous Butterworth house. After much haggling over the price, Lizzie and Emma moved on, and the monied denizens of that street breathed a sigh of relief.

The home of Charles Marion Allen at 7 French Street, next caught their eye. It was only a few yards from Highland Avenue, that desirable mansion-lined street where the Who's Who sipped tea and passed judgment on those outside their social realm. Ironically, Charles Allen and Andrew J. Borden shared the same great-great-grandfather, John Borden, making the two men distant cousins. This may have appealed to the sisters, and they made an offer.

In July of 1893, the sale was procured through G. M. Haffards & Company, with the price set at $13,000. The transaction was finalized on August 10, 1893. Lizzie had finally gotten what she always wanted: a house on "the Hill." Surely now she would be accepted and afforded all the prestige and clout the Borden name afforded her through her lineage.

Charles Allen, ironically became the owner of the Chace home—the one on Rock Street the sisters had bid on and been denied—after he bought it from William W. Stewart, who had purchased, and owned, the house for only two months. Had it been a clandestine way to block the Borden ladies from ownership, or had Stewart merely had other circumstances arise to warrant his quick sale?

The Allen's needed three weeks to move out. Lizzie and Emma busied themselves with packing and buying new furniture to supplement the few pieces they would retain from the old place. The newspapers happily reported the sale of the French Street house, and "the Hill" got its first taste of life living near the infamous Lizzie Borden. People began showing up, strolling by the house, and finding myriad excuses as to how "they just happened to be in the area."

7 French Street (Maplecroft).
The Swift house is to the left. Photo courtesy unknown.

The area newspapers, nipping at Lizzie's heels like a tenacious bulldog, followed her everywhere. News feeds went out far and wide, including one posted in the *New York Post* regarding the sister's movements, which read, "both are seen on the streets almost daily." It was noted the sisters were actively visiting various homes on "the Hill," in the hopes of living there. As always, Lizzie's attire was mentioned. Many commented on the fact that she still refused to be seen in mourning black. Emma, it was mentioned, was always wearing black, as a nod to her departed father. It would appear Lizzie's thumbing of her nose at other's expectations of her behavior had not changed.

Moving Day

September came to Fall River. A smattering of the autumn colors for which New England is famous, began making their debut. Winds from the ocean swept across the face of Massachusetts, spiraling dead leaves to the ground. Lizzie Borden watched the dance of nature from her second-floor bedroom window at 92 Second Street, as a half-moon shone down on the changing landscape. The pear trees were shedding their leaves, exposing the secrets they had hidden for over a year. Lizzie pushed the lace curtain aside a little farther and pressed her face to the window. A shard of moonlight shot off a metal ridge pole as it ran the length of the roof of Crowe's barn. Her heart skipped a beat. And then she remembered. The hatchet had been found a few months ago. It was gone. The wind moved through the bare pear tree limbs, that pointed with skeletal fingers toward the place where the abandoned murder weapon had lain.

Taking a deep breath, Lizzie turned to face the stacks of books, packed trunks, and stuffed satchels littering her room. Emma kept coming in to ask "Do you think we should keep this?" or "What should we do with the old cookware?" kind of questions. The sisters were busy packing, eager to begin a new life on French Street. At every turn of the corner at their old home, ghosts rose up to block their way. The memories were thick: some wonderful, most stained by tension. Abby's relatives had come and taken away her things; the sisters had to deal with their father's, and it had not been easy.

Finally, moving day came. A crowd assembled outside the house on Second Street to watch with maudlin curiosity as the movers brought out each piece of furniture and carefully packed trunk. The spectators may have been disappointed to find sheets and blankets covering most things. Lizzie, especially, refused them the right to peer at their personal belongings.

On September 6, 1893, the wagonloads of Lizzie and Emma's belongings pulled up in front of 7 French Street. The window curtains of neighboring houses were cautiously pulled aside as the Swifts and Davenports peered out at the "new kids on the block." The movers carried the covered furnishings and packed bundles into the house, with both Lizzie and Emma rapidly pointing out the location for each large piece. Constantly reminding the men to "mind the polished wood floors," the house began to fill with items brought from the Borden home. Next were shopping trips to buy new pieces, art for the walls, linens, monogrammed silverware, and towels for the ball and clawfoot bathtub.

Lizzie & Emma's bathroom at *Maplecroft* with original fixtures.
Photos by the Author.

A bathtub! Perhaps of all the modern amenities the Borden's found awaiting them in a home scarcely four years old, was a modern bathroom. There would be no more hip baths in front of the stove on Sunday morning; pouring hot water from a tea kettle into a metal tub. They ran their fingers over the porcelain surface of the sides, turned the faucets on and off, luxuriating in the feeling of hot running water.

The kitchen was fitted with all the newest equipment. While home use refrigerators would not hit the market until 1913, the house on French Street had a modern ice box with large compartments and a stylish front. There was even a small door behind it where the iceman could deliver the ice from outside, without bothering the resident.

The ice box delivery door at *Maplecroft.*
Photo by the Author.

As the movers placed the last trunk inside the front hall and received their pay and departed, there came that strange feeling one always has when the rush and stress of packing and moving is over, and you stand inside the strange walls of someone else's home. Lizzie and Emma paused in their scurrying and stood inside the main hall, light playing through the stained-glass window above the stair landing, and looked at each other—a mixture of emotions playing across their faces. The look said, "This is ours?

We live here now? This is who we are?" And with that, they turned to look at their shiny new home, and began to unpack.

Back on Second Street, the shadows played across the austere boards of the Drab green siding and even darker Drab green trim. The shutters to the windows had all been closed; the house looking as if it was now in eternal slumber. When the pears dropped next summer, who would harvest them? Would the worn cellar steps echo another "Maggie's" footsteps, as she labored beneath a hod of coal and a bundle of wood for the stove? And all those locks. Would the keys be needed now as they had been before?

The house remained closed up. As soon as the sisters caught their breath, they ordered it remodeled—spinning back the hands of time and returning it to a two-family dwelling. By October, 1893, it was ready, and the two new renters, Louis L. Hall and Willard B. Peckham, and their families, moved in. A newspaper remarked upon it, saying, "heads of the two families do business within two blocks of the gloomy house and they smile derisively when their customers question them about ghosts."

Inside 7 French Street

The original home Emma and Lizzie purchased on French Street had an open front porch, or "piazza," as it was called in that era. The steps from the sidewalk leading up to two simple doors of oak. Lizzie has the initial "B" engraved over the keyhole of the front door lock. The entry into the home was spacious, with a set of stairs to the west, lit by stained-glass windows. A built-in hallway bench nestled against the steps and hosted a horse-hair cushion, that is now found in the north room of the second floor, above the back porch. If one sat on the bench and looked up, you could see through to the third-floor stairwell. The entry floor was parquet in beautiful golden hues. An ornate fireplace sat across from the stairs, giving the area a formal and yet welcoming feeling.

> Full-color photos of *Maplecroft* and the Lizzie Borden B&B can be seen at www.rebeccafpittmanbooks.com. Click the Color Photos tab next to the book's bio. Photos courtesy of the owners.

The view of *Maplecroft's* entry, looking down from the staircase.
Photos © by the Author, courtesy of Twilight Enterprises, LLC.

Front entry stairs & bench seat *at Maplecroft*. Photo by the Author.©

Front entry hall tree and chairs (top), and entry hall fireplace (bottom). Radiators
were in place in 1893 when the Borden sisters moved in.
Photos © by the Author, and courtesy of Twilight Enterprises, LLC.

The Parlor at Maplecroft

The parlor at 7 French Street is twice the size as the one in the
Second Street home. Filled with light from windows on two sides
of the room, its rich William Morris wallpaper (in hunter green

with pastel blue and rose flowers), and lush area rugs set off the natural wood floors to perfection. A double inlay of darker wood rims the floors, making the room an enclave of its own. Balloon-backed chairs, sofas, tables and display cabinets sat in inviting vignettes about the parlor, while red velvet curtains puddled on the floor. A baby grand piano holds court in one corner of the room, while a detailed mantled fireplace rests along the wall flanking the entry. Here the sisters entertained, and here, in one brief golden moment, the famous actress Nance O'Neil, and her troupe, laughed and drank into the wee morning hours, with Lizzie playing the delighted hostess.

The south side of the parlor has windows facing the street and through the lacy sheers one can see the traffic as it slows to peer in wonder at the infamous home of Lizzie Borden. The author was fortunate enough to spend two nights at *Maplecroft* during the writing of this book, and witnessed the curious who still travel past, and stop and stare, even today. It was a room filled with beauty and art, but it may have left the owners feeling somewhat vulnerable to the invasiveness of French Street and its voyeurs.

The Parlor looking in from the west entryway. The piano is to the left. ©

Parlor archway looking west to the front entry.
Photos © by Author, courtesy of Twilight Enterprises, LLC.

Original stain-glass window at top of entry stairs.
Photo © by Ron Bueker, courtesy Twilight Enterprises, LLC.

Parlor fireplace with its blue tile and columned wood. A torchiere lamp is to the right. Photos © by the Author, and courtesy of Twilight Enterprises, LLC.

Parlor window facing French Street (r), and one facing the Kenney house (l) where it sat in 1893. A photo of Nance O'Neil rests on the table. ©

The Dining Room at *Maplecroft*

The dining room at *Maplecroft*, nestled in a bay window setting, is lovely. The arched entry into the room can be seen upon entering the front door.

The entry hallway looking north into the dining room.
Photo © by the Author, courtesy of Twilight Enterprises, LLC.

The wallpaper in the room is original to the house, and may have been selected by Emma and Lizzie themselves. They were only the second owners of the home and it had been built only four years before they took ownership. The paper is in a lattice-work motif with cornflower blue background and pastel fruit and floral clusters. It adds a softness to the dark molding and ceiling beams that encase a soft-brushed linen lining. It was popular in the 1800s to place linen over ceiling plaster, that was known to crack. It was a cost-effective way to maintain an elegant look without constant plaster refurbishment.

The dining room at Maplecroft. Note the quartered oak wainscoting. The fireplace sported green tile and a metal sliding firebox door.
Photos © by Kristee Bates, courtesy of Twilight Enterprises, LLC.

Just some of the attention to detail at Maplecroft (l), and a nod to Lizzie's affinity for collecting and giving Sun Bonnet Babies dishware (r). The child's chair is reminiscent of the children who loved to visit & host small tea parties.©

The Kitchen and Pantry

To the left of the dining room fireplace is a door leading into a large pantry where the ice box delivery door was found. It also houses a radiator, which would be a strange thing to have next to an icebox, hinting that the room may have become something else (perhaps a dinette) when a modern refrigerator replaced the icebox and was located in the kitchen proper. The windows of the pantry overlook the side yard and the Swift house to the west.

A cupboard in the Pantry at *Maplecroft*. The old ice box and tongs can be seen at the left. Photo © by the Author, courtesy Twilight Enterprises, LLC.

The kitchen at *Maplecroft* is airy and filled with sunlight. The high white tin ceiling reflects the light and gives the room a spacious feeling. The current owner, Kristee Bates, has chosen to refinish it in the period Lizzie enjoyed in her later years: the 1920s. Here, we get a wonderful glimpse of life in the roaring 20s, when new modes of modernized kitchen equipment were in vogue. From a refrigerator, to the one-piece sink and modern stove, the room was full-functioning. A large table sat in its center, perfect for food preparation, or morning coffee. The walls are painted in a soft buttermilk gold color. Two doors lead to the cellar, and out to the back porch, with steps going down to the porch and garage, respectively.

Two views of the kitchen: (l) looking past the stove into the pantry; (r) the refrigerator, with the cellar entry to the left, and closet door to the right. Photos © by the Author, courtesy of Twilight Enterprises, LLC.

One-piece white enamel sink with pantry to the right. ©

The embossed white tin ceiling in the kitchen. ©

The Second Floor Bedrooms

Lizzie and Emma Borden had something in their new home they must have reveled in...hallways! No more interconnecting rooms and lack of privacy. Here, they found wide hallways with walls covered in soft, ecru wallpaper, with polished wood floors, hallway runners, and a radiator that covered one entire wall. There were doors separating the sleeping quarters from the rest of the second floor and the back stairway, complete with...locks.

Two views of the 2nd-floor hallway: (l) looking north to the bathroom. Emma's bedroom is on the left; (r) looking south toward the library/sitting room double doors. Lizzie's bedroom door is on the left. The stairs to the 3rd floor are at right. Photos © by the Author, courtesy of Twilight Enterprises, LLC.

Close-up of the frosted glass door with keyhole lock leading
from the back stairs to the 2nd-floor bedroom area.
Photo © by the Author, courtesy Twilight Enterprises, LLC.

At the top of the front entry stairs, to the right, is a large room that extends the entire length of the front of the house. It is thought to have been the library and sitting room for the Borden sisters. The myriad windows in the room, looking east, north and west, made a perfect setting for relaxing and if one were so inclined, to spy on your neighbors from three advantage points: the south-facing window overlooked the Lake house across the street, the east window overlooked the Kenney house, and from the window seat area one could see both the Brayton's on the corner and the Swift house next door.

The room also boasted a fake fireplace. It is interesting that it is not a functional piece, and may have been installed to give the room a feeling of gentility and "warmth." It has a lovely faux carved verse upon the front piece, that has given Lizzie scholars something to interpret for years:

And Old-Time Friends, And Twilight Plays
And Starry Nights, And Sunny Days
Come Trooping Up the Misty Ways
When My Fire Burns Low.

Mantelpiece in the *Maplecroft* library with the poem mentioned above.
Photo by the © Author, courtesy of Twilight Enterprises, LLC.

While the poem may have come from one of Lizzie's favorite books of poetry, if she had it custom made, perhaps there is a hidden meaning to the words. "Old-Time Friends, and Twilight Plays." This may have referred to her time with Nance O'Neil, the actress, whose many "plays" Lizzie attended. "Starry Nights" might refer to Vincent van Gogh's famous painting that was created in 1889, shortly before the Borden girls bought the home, and only one year before Lizzie's tour of Europe. The oil painting may have been a favorite of Lizzie's, who adored art and may have seen the masterpiece hanging in a European museum. The rest of the verse shows her loneliness, and a yearning for the past when memories smolder like a fire burning low.

Library fireplace with poem. Photo by Ron Bueker.

The *Maplecroft* library and sitting room looking west. The room today is furnished as a bedroom. The fireplace with poem is at the left. Photo © by Kristee Bates, Twilight Enterprises, LLC.

Maplecroft library and sitting room looking east. The windows on the right face French Street, the window on the left faced the Kenney house. Photo © by Kristee Bates, Twilight Enterprises, LLC.

To the left of the library on the second-floor landing, is a double room suite "divided by a set of mullioned glass doors." The southern-most room boasts a bay window, with views of the east, which would have been facing the Kenny house. During Lizzie's residency, the middle window housed a jewel-toned stain-glass pane. A closet with dress hooks is housed in this room, with a door leading out to the stairway landing.

The front part of the bedroom suite, showing the bay window. The stain-glass that filled the middle pane is no longer there. These windows overlooked the Kenny yard, where Lizzie complained of their barking dog bothering her. Photo © by the Author, courtesy of Twilight Enterprises, LLC.

Through the double doors to the north of this room was the second half of the suite. This portion housed an ornate fireplace with "glazed tile in mottled shades of blue, green and gold, and a decorative brass and iron grate." [Quotes are from *Parallel Lives*/The Fall River Historical Society.] A sentimental verse graced the fireplace mantle, and may have hearkened to Lizzie's visit to Scotland during the Grand Tour, or to her Old English lineage:

"AT-HAME, IN-MY-AIN COUNTRIE."

The fireplace in what is believed to be Lizzie's bedroom at Maplecroft.
The verse "At-Hame, In-My-Ain Countrie" can be seen on the mantelpiece.
Note the "Boston Terrier" on the chair.
Photo © by the Author, courtesy Twilight Enterprises, LLC.

"My Ain Countrie" referred to one's homeland; a place of comfort, and, if you will, ownership. This may have been Lizzie's bedroom, and the verse was a personal one for her. At last, she had her own home—her own domain. She was "at hame (home)" in her "own countrie." This room also emulates her bedroom on Second Street. It too housed a fireplace, and an alcove, which she turned into a private toiletry area. The *Maplecroft* alcove is home to built-in drawers, which would have held gloves, handkerchiefs, undergarments, and hosiery, along with other personal items. The wallpaper is a deep blue with sprays of red, blue, gold, and green foliage.

The connecting room with a closet and bay windows could have held her lounge, writing desk and a bookcase. She may have basically copied her set-up from the old place, albeit on a grander scale.

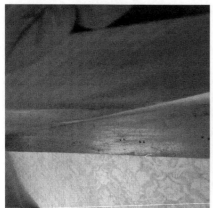 

Inside the bay window room's closet. You can still see the holes made by the dress hooks (l). One of Lizzie's dress hooks, presented to the Author by *Maplecroft's* owner, Kristee Bates (r). Photos © by the Author.

Original *Maplecroft* doorknob presented to the Author by Kristee Bates. Photo © by the Author.

Lizzie's bedroom. A cozy corner by the fireplace (l), and her dresser alcove (r).
Photos © by the Author, courtesy Twilight Enterprises, LLC.

Looking from the bay window room into Lizzie's sleeping area. You can see the
dresser alcove in the back. The wallpaper on this side is a deep cobalt blue with
multi-colored nose gays. Photo © by the Author, Twilight Enterprises, LLC.

Across the hall from Lizzie's suite was Emma's bedroom. It is a large and airy room, its window facing west. As the sisters grew older, they spent more and more time apart, traveling on their own with friends or, in Lizzie's case, a paid companion. The room is decorated to reflect Emma's new-found love of travel.

Emma's room, with its large west-facing window.
Photo © by the Author, courtesy of Twilight Enterprises, LLC.

The wallpaper in Emma's room is of a much lighter feeling than the dark blues of Lizzie's. The area has a fresh appeal, with a sense of lightness: something the older Borden sister was possibly desperately trying to find in her life. The bed is in the raised colonial style, with a footstool to assist her as she climbed into bed. Area rugs of collaborating motif are placed about the room.

Two views of Emma's room: (l) a nod to her wardrobe style of that era, and her packed travel trunk; and (r) an ornate mirror and sitting area. The trim and area rugs in the room sport a cooling deep blue. Photos © by the Author, courtesy of Twilight Enterprises, LLC.

Coming from Emma's room and traveling to the north along the second-floor hallway, one passes through a doorway that could have locked off the bathroom area from the bedrooms. The bathroom was shown earlier, with its small hexagon-shaped tile floor and art nouveau blue tile trim. The sink sits upon legs, as was the fashion in the Gilded Age. The mirror and fixtures are original.

Lizzie added a back porch in 1909, four years after Emma departed. Above it, she created a long room, emulating the front library and sitting area, but vastly different in décor. This room was almost void of decoration or enhancement. There is no wood molding, only a wallpaper border in its place. The exposed brick fireplace, so simple and stark, seems jarring compared to the rest of the house. Perhaps at one time it sported an ornate front piece, that was carried away sometime over the years. Today, a closet has been turned into a private bath area.

It may be this new addition was designed to move her farther and farther away from the front of the house where strangers constantly stopped and ogled her home; hoping for a glimpse of her. The room overlooks the back of the property, and would have been much quieter: safe from backfiring cars, horns, and pedestrians.

The brick fireplace in the back bedroom/ sitting area at *Maplecroft*.
Photo © by Ron Bueker, courtesy of Twilight Enterprises, LLC.

Back bedroom in new addition overlooking the backyard.
Photo © by Ron Bueker, courtesy of Twilight Enterprises, LLC.

This room may have doubled as a sitting room and library, just as it did in the front of the house. It is also rumored Lizzie used it as a bedroom in summer months, and may have passed away here. Just outside the door to the room is the back staircase to the kitchen, making it easier for a maid to bring food to the room in Lizzie's later years, or for her to reach the back-porch area without going through the front of the house. She was using a cane later in life, and getting around was becoming more cumbersome.

Original horsehair cushion in the new addition bedroom that was first located on the front entry hall bench. Photo © by the Author, courtesy of Twilight Enterprises, LLC.

The Rear Porch

Lizzie's need to sit quietly among the birds and squirrels, far from the prying eyes of French Street may have prompted the addition of a large verandah, with a wide river rock wall on one end. It commanded the full length of the back side of the house. Its rounded curve on one end gave it an elegant, softer feeling, with its turned spindles and low railing. Here, near the stone wall, Lizzie could sit in her rocker, secreted away from the voyeuristic gaze of neighbors and traffic. With her Boston Terrier in her lap, and book in her hand, she spent many tranquil moments here.

Rear view of new porch addition with stone wall and chimney.

The back porch at *Maplecroft*, installed in 1909.
Photos © by Ron Bueker.

The outside ice delivery door on the back porch.
Photo © by Ron Bueker, courtesy of Twilight Enterprises, LLC.

Outside the second-floor addition is a funny little step that was put in when the room was created. It sits off by itself, away from the back stairway, instead of meshing with the landing. It is almost as if Lizzie was cutting costs with this new wing, including the stairs. Perhaps the abhorrence of spending unnecessary money on a house's amenities, was a trait she inherited from her father. This is the only part of the house Lizzie had a hand in building.

Odd little step into the back addition over the porch.
Photo by Kristee Bates, Twilight Enterprises, LLC.

The Third Floor

Another set of steps leads from the second-floor back staircase to the third floor where the servants slept. Here the maids and coachman each had their own room, with a small toilet room for their use. A bathtub, toilet and water tank were in the cellar, a far more luxurious setting than Bridget was afforded.

The first room to the left of the third-floor back stairs is a large room facing east. It may have housed two beds. It has two dormer windows, a closet and a door leading to the third-floor landing and the front stairs. This was probably the maid and cook's room.

The large third-floor room facing east. The door to the left is a closet with dress hooks, the door to the right leads out to the landing and front stairs.
Photo by Ron Bueker©, courtesy Twilight Enterprises, LLC.

Alcove in third story maid's room. Photo © by the Author.

To the north of this room is what may have been the coachman's room. It has two doors which open to the front landing and rear landing, respectively. A shared toilet area sits next to it.

Coachman's room on the third floor. Photo © by the Author.

The other sleeping area is a room in the southwest corner of the third floor. It was reserved for Lizzie's traveling companions. It is designed today to reflect the era between 1911 and 1913 when Trudy Russell, Lizzie's companion, lived at *Maplecroft*, and read with Lizzie in the library, which was directly beneath this room. There is a private sink room with running water in a small alcove, with shelves for toiletries. A stain-glass window overlooks the lot where the Kenney house stood. Another window faces French Street. Just outside the door is the landing, with stairs leading directly down to the library and sitting room where Trudy and Lizzie spent their most wonderful moments sharing stories and poetry.

Traveling companion's room with private sink room. Photos © by Ron Bueker, courtesy of Twilight Enterprises, LLC.

Portrait of Trudy Russell in the Companion's room. ©

The last room on the third floor was used as the clothes press. This room, as did the one on Second Street, has a solitary window, and dress hooks around the room. You can still see the hook holes around the entire perimeter. Room for trunks, hat boxes and satchels was available.

Today, the room reflects a time when mysticism was at its peak during the Gilded Age of America. The wealthy hired mediums and psychics to hold séances in their parlors, and conjure dead loved ones. Table tilting, rattling tambourines, and disembodied voices were sought after entertainment for week-long parties. It was during this time that Edgar Cayce and the likes of Houdini made names for themselves.

Houdini speaking from the grave. Photo courtesy unknown.

Séance during the Gilded Age. Photo courtesy unknown.

The Séance Room at *Maplecroft*, once the close press for Lizzie and Emma's dresses, capes and furs. Photo © Ron Bueker, courtesy of Twilight Enterprises, LLC.

View looking down from the third-floor landing. Photo © by the Author.

The cellar at Maplecroft is eerily reminiscent of Second Street. Here we find the barred windows, so prevalent during that era. The brick is whitewashed, and there are separate rooms. A large zinc-lined double sink rests against the wall where the laundry was done—a larger set-up than Bridget probably had. There is a bath area with a clawfoot tub, toilet and water tank. A door leads to the outside backyard, reflecting the Borden house's layout.

A coal shoot was used, so the delivery man could shovel coal into it from the outside. The maid could then lift its hatch and take what she needed from inside. A story exists that Lizzie would leave a piece of chocolate cake and a glass of milk for the delivery man, who would enter the cellar through the back door, eat his cake and take his payment from a shadowy figure on the back stairs. Lizzie was known for her kindness to the "lower class."

The basement currently sports original windows, spindles and other wonderful items waiting to be restored.

The *Maplecroft* cellar with its whitewashed brick and old windows. Photos © by the Author, courtesy of Twilight Enterprises, LLC.

The outside front piazza was originally open, and wrapped the south and west side of the house. The current owner has lovingly left a segment of the siding here to show the original color of the home when Lizzie owned it and its transformation through the ages.

A New Address

The section below the window shows the original paint color. ©

The front porch facing French Street and the west.
Photo © by Ron Bueker, courtesy of Twilight Enterprises, LLC.

The Garage

In 1911, Lizzie contracted for a garage to be built at the back of the lot where the Kenney house once stood. It has double doors and white columns, looking more like a summer cottage than a garage for her two cars. The floor has a trap door that may have been used to facilitate oil changes. An antique gas pump stands in one corner of the large, open area. Her original plan was to build it in the lot to the back and west of her home that she shared with the Swifts next door. The contract made with her, however, was that the shared property was to remain "park-like" with no structures built upon it. To retaliate, Lizzie built a 10'-high lattice work fence that blocked the light into the Swift's front room and entry. It was one of several "spite fences" she would erect. The original smaller wrought iron fences outlining her property boundaries are still there today.

Maplecroft's garage, built in 1911. Photo © courtesy of Kristee Bates.

Spite fence (l) separating Lizzie's lawn and the Davenport's house. (r) is the original Gilbert Barker Visible Gas Pump, circa 1910. Photos by Ron Bueker. ©

A framed photo of *Maplecroft* with a Ford Model T out front, possibly from the early 1900s. Photo courtesy of Twilight Enterprises, LLC ©.

Maplecroft in 2016. Photo © by Ron Bueker.

Replacing "Maggie"

If Lizzie and Emma needed one more stamp of authority to underscore they were their own women—with their own rules, and household—it came with the interviewing of acceptable servants to run their French Street home. A maid-of-all-work, a cook, and a handyman (who also doubled as a groomsman) were typically required. Other homes on "the Hill" might also have a governess, butler, and nurse on staff, but for the two sisters, their needs were few. There were Employment Offices in Fall River to whom one could turn for employees. Bridget Sullivan mentioned she had gone through Mrs. Mary McKenney to find work, and it may be to her the sisters turned.

The servants of the mid-1890s, were typically paid two-to-five dollars a week. They were given an evening off each week, and every other Sunday. They rose before their employers and were often still doing some mending or ironing, after the rest of the house was in bed. A popular pastime for these hard-working individuals, was to gather around the kitchen table at each other's places of employment, sip a cup of tea, and exchange gossip;

usually concerning their employer's habits and pastimes. This was a tradition to which Lizzie would soon use to her advantage

We do not know if Emma brought with them the two domestics she hired at Second Street, while Lizzie was in jail for almost a year. By 1900, the census showed 29-year-old Annie E. Smith, from Massachusetts, living in the house as a maid. Interestingly, Alfred C. Johnson, the hapless farmhand from Swansea (that may have indirectly been poisoned by Lizzie in her 1892 attempt to kill her parents), became the Borden sisters' first groomsman, when they moved onto French Street. Alfred later married and left their employ. During the time he worked for Lizzie and Emma, he lived on the third floor of their new home. Had Lizzie hired him out of a sense of guilt, or did it go further? Perhaps the farmhand had approached her with a secret knowledge of seeing her about the Lower Farmhouse that Sunday morning. And, of course, it could be Lizzie was just trying to help someone who had worked for her father.

Replacing Alfred in 1900, was a young man by the name of Joseph H. Tetrault, a recognized lady's man. At 37-years-of-age, he was only four years Lizzie's senior, and came from nearby Rhode Island. The sisters had broken from the norm of hiring Irish immigrants, or other foreign domestics—at least for now. In 1903, they hired Hannah Bostron Nelson, a thirty-two-year-old immigrant from Sweden. It may be that Alfred Johnson, being Swedish himself, recommended her. She was newly single, after her short marriage to Samuel Pearson ended. Hannah took back her maiden name of Nelson and sought employment in Fall River, where she found herself knocking on the door of 7 French Street. She would become one of Lizzie's strongest attachments.

Freedom!

As Lizzie Borden went about her days, decorating her home, and ordering books and knick-knacks by the dozens, the sense of freedom she felt was intoxicating. There would be no more jail matrons to watch her every move, no police officers going through her private things, and no limited space. She was free! The only cage that still surrounded her was the ever-present media. *The Fall River Globe*, Lizzie's nemesis, insisted on rehashing the murders in morbid headlines on the anniversary of the Borden's death each year. Her presence, once recognized, was reported in each city she visited.

"The White City" at the Chicago World's Fair
Photo courtesy of www.nikolatesla-inventor.com.

In October of 1893, Lizzie, joined by her good friend Reverend Buck's daughter, Alice, and Caroline Borden, Lizzie's cousin, headed off to Chicago to see The Columbian Exposition, or more commonly known as, the World's Fair. Why Emma did not go along is unknown. The fair boasted a central court of white stucco buildings, called "The White City." It was historically lit with a new invention called electricity—courtesy of Nikola Tesla and George Westinghouse, Jr. The crowds gasped as the night sky was filled with thousands of lights, reflecting in the canals and lagoons of the courtyard. It was a momentous occasion for the country. The Louisiana Purchase Exposition, informally known as the St.

Louis World's Fair, would not happen until 1904, where it too showcased an electric backdrop.

With 27,300,000 visitors, spread across 690 acres of attractions, Lizzie could finally lose herself and find some glimpse of anonymity. The buildings may have reminded her of her Grand Tour of Europe and happier days. Although Lizzie traveled under an assumed name, the Fall River papers were never far behind her. *The Fall River Daily Globe*, on October 3, 1893, reported Lizzie as having "been doing the World's Fair." Lizzie, no doubt, had a small debt of gratitude to the artists who peppered her image across the daily rags, as her trials dragged on. With newspaper photography in its infancy, the tabloids relied on illustrations—none of which were flattering, or resembled her all that much.

Two of the many sketches of Lizzie Borden during her trials.

Another trip was taken the following summer; this time with Emma in tow. Phoebe Bowen, wife of Dr. Seabury Bowen—the flustered neighbor of the Borden's who testified at Lizzie's legal proceedings—also joined Lizzie on a trip to Niagara Falls. It was dutifully reported in *The Fall River Evening News* column "Our Folks and Other Folks": "Mrs. Dr. S. W. Bowen and Misses Lizzie A. and Emma L. Borden have gone to Niagara Falls for a brief outing."

As Lizzie and Emma tried to reorder their lives into something that resembled normalcy, the stain of a double murder case was never really cleansed. The curious continued to make their way along the sidewalk outside the steps of 7 French Street, some boldly ringing at the front door.

Annie Lindsey, nee Brigham, and her sister Mary Ella, had been friends with Lizzie since her childhood. They had been her neighbors long ago on Ferry Street, both growing up to become strong, independent women, who married well. Annie would come to own several mansions, and one day, be presented to the Queen of England. It is to her Lizzie often wrote, and we get a glimpse of the ongoing circus that surrounded the acquitted murder suspect:

> My Dear Annie,
> A gentleman called Friday and left his card saying he was a friend of yours. If Emma had been home I would have sent her down first to see if it was all right. But as she was out of town I declined to go down for fear it was a made-up story, as he had no line from you. Gov. Robinson insists on my doing this for fear of reporters. Three times the past month, people have come saying Mrs. Mary Livermore sent them. I did not see them and have found out later she had sent no one. I am very, very sorry if he is your friend, and hope you will tell him <u>why</u> I could not come down. Your friends are welcome when I am sure, and I dislike to be discourteous to anyone. If he ever cares to come again, I shall receive him with pleasure. So please let me know if he <u>is</u> your friend, and I will remember.
> Ella [Mary Ella, Annie's sister and Lizzie's good friend who stood by her throughout the trials] was in this morning looking bright and rosy. Now I wish you lived here. I have so few friends in Fall River.
>
> Yours with love,
L.A. Borden
Saturday, Feb. 24, 94

[Letter courtesy of the Fall River Historical Society/*Parallel Lives*.]

Mrs. William Lindsey, Jr., aka Annie, had moved to Boston, into an elaborate mansion, where she was renowned for hosting parties attended by the socialites of that city. Lizzie is never mentioned among the guest lists: for the galas, or the simple dinner gatherings. She may have gone, and wished not to be mentioned, for fear the papers would report on it and cause her dear friend unwelcome celebrity. Or, Annie and Lizzie may have quietly admitted her attendance, at any social function, would bring unwanted attention, and thus, she stayed home. It was clear from her letters; she was a very lonely woman.

Property and Problems

Charles C. Cook had been Andrew Borden's right-hand man when it came to managing Mr. Borden's growing portfolio of properties. Upon Andrew's death, Mr. Cook was retained by Lizzie and Emma Borden to continue in that capacity. For the two women who found the ownership of one house on Ferry Street daunting, the burden of maintaining and overseeing city blocks of buildings, farm acreage, and sundry homes would have caused more than one sleepless night.

Arson

While Fall River was no stranger to fires—indeed the "Spindle City" had more than its fair share of flames—the plethora of fires that scorched the Borden sisters' properties would fall close to being unbelievable.

Two weeks after Lizzie's acquittal on June 23, 1893, a fire of "undetermined origin" broke out in Andrew Borden's newly acquired "Birch Land" properties. The buildings at 94 through 98 South Main, suffered structural damage in the sum of $434 dollars; the tenants lost $645 in inventory and furnishings.

On November 28, 1893, shortly after Lizzie's return from the Chicago World's Fair, the A.J. Borden Building came close to going up in flames when a row of wooden buildings to its north burned. The firefighters determined the blaze was of an "incendiary nature," meaning it had probably been the work of an arsonist. Among the fallen properties were an apothecary (Charles A. Baker), an undertaking firm (Luke and James Watson), a bookseller and stationary shop (Robert Adams), and a boots and shoes store (Humphrey and William Henry Preble). The row of buildings had been nicknamed "asbestos row," due to the many fires set there by arsonists.

That two of Andrew's dearest holdings were in an arsonist's crosshairs is unique. It was just the beginning.

The Andrew J. Borden Building, at the corner of Anawan and South Main Streets, in Fall River, Ma. Photo courtesy of the Fall River Historical Society.

Over the next eight years, six more fires would break out in the Andrew J. Borden Building and other properties the sisters inherited. Their respective dates are interesting, as they tend to coincide with traumatic events in Lizzie's life.

1) The Birch Land fire in early July, 1893, may have coincided with a possible exclusion from the wedding list of Lizzie's cousin, Mary Emma Borden. Her father Jerome Borden and Andrew J. Borden, both sat on the board of directors at the Union Savings Bank. Whether Emma and Lizzie were invited to the December wedding is not sure, as it was reported the nuptials were only attended "by the immediate family," but we do know Lizzie's wedding gift of $100 went unrecognized. There was no Thank You card, or visits from the newly married Mrs. Charles D. Peirce. [Information courtesy of the Fall River Historical Society.]

2) On October 12, 1903, a fire broke out at the A.J. Borden Building, at the E.P. Charlton & Company offices there. It was logged in at the fire station under "Explosion of Boiler." 1903 was the year Lizzie was forced to remove Joseph H. Tetrault from her home. Tetrault had been a hairdresser in Fall River, and many women about Fall River fell to his charms. He was living at the time in one of Lizzie and Emma's buildings at 394 Spring Street, that was operating as a boarding house. In 1899, he was offered the job as coachman at the Borden's new house on French Street, where he unpacked his things in their attic room. Gossip began circulating soon after, some hinting that Emma was none-too-pleased with the handsome Tetrault's "position." The insinuations finally caused Lizzie to let him go in 1903, and replace him with Frederick W. Coggeshall. Mr. Coggeshall did not last long. Joseph Tetrault was reinstated the same year.

3) A more serious fire blasted out the windows of Anawan Street, as the A.J. Borden Building once again ignited on January 28, 1905. Once again, E.P. Chapman & Company were the recipients of the epicenter of the fire. A rag, or something flammable, resting close to the steam pipes below the Chapman & Company offices, was said to be the cause. The destruction of the Borden building was vast, with many businesses housed there, ruined. Oddly, the office of Charles C. Cook, the Borden's sisters' agent, was spared. The damages resulted in $12,655.64 paid out in insurance to Lizzie and Emma, with an additional $24,167.93 paid by the tenant's insurance for destroyed contents. 1905 was the year Emma left Lizzie and French Street behind, a split that had been building for at least two years. The fire was reported early in the morning at 8:10. The following morning at 7:48, the firemen were called back when it "rekindled." A fire would not be the only thing marking 1905 as "coincidental" in Lizzie's orbit of strange happenings.

4) On May 3, 1905, another fire at one of the Borden's sisters' properties, made of brick, was reported. The strange entry of "Unnecessary" was listed as the cause.

5) August 24, 1906, another fire on Borden property, this time a wooden structure, and again the culprit was listed as "Unnecessary."

6) 1907 was rife with smoke and flames. Interestingly, it is the year Lizzie's favorite chauffeur, Joseph Tetrault, departs her employ for good. August 3rd of that year, the A.J. Borden building was once again the destination of the Fall River fire department. The Rogers & Allen's School of Business sustained minor loss compared to the Charlton fire: $143 in damages. The Borden property at 394 Spring Street (the residence of Lizzie's chauffeur in 1899), was called in, with "soot in the chimney" listed as the cause.

7) In 1908 and 1909, two more fires hit properties owned by Lizzie and Emma: Samuel Jones' Jewelry Store at 234 South Main Street, and Leopold Tillis' tailor shop and home at 228 South Main Street, respectively. Both resulted in minor damage.

8) Earlier, in December and January of 1901, two fires threatened the late Andrew J. Borden's properties: 184 South Main Street exploded after a workman set a match to a new gas meter beneath the store of McManus & Company, "Clothing and Men's Furnishing Goods." The gas had been leaking for some time before the meter man struck the match that December morning. Two months later, in February, a fire threatened to destroy several buildings as a strong wind fanned the flames of 238 South Main Street, at the corner of Spring. This corner, Andrew Borden's "Birch land," was hit again, fifteen years later.

That Fall River had its share of fires is an understatement, but that so many befell Andrew Borden's properties (16 fires in all) may have caused more than one person to raise an eyebrow. Perhaps, just like the Ferry house, money was preferable to property ownership, or was the arsonist acting out for emotional reasons only? We have no proof, only surmises, that once again shroud the saga of Lizzie Borden in mystery.

A Monument for the Borden's

With money in hand, Lizzie and Emma Borden commissioned the Smith Granite Company of Westerly, Rhode Island, to create a monument solidifying the Borden's position in Fall River. Oak Grove Cemetery, where Abby and Andrew Borden were buried, along with Sarah Morse Borden, their mother; and little Alice Ester Borden, their sister who had died so young, was the resting place of Fall River's elite. The Borden monument must be in good taste, utilizing the best in materials.

Lizzie and Emma settled on a tall structure with a concave base and four grave markers set at an odd angle to the monument. The finest New England blue marble was used, with a total cost of $2,124. On January 4, 1895, the final resting place of the two murder victims was anchored by the stately monument, bearing the name BORDEN in chiseled letters. It was not the most ornate in the cemetery: it was simple and of classic design.

As would always be the case, a small crowd gathered to watch the workmen erect the statue. They were rewarded by a brief glimpse of Lizzie and Emma Borden, as the sisters stepped quickly from a carriage to critique the placement of markers and the overall presentation. They hurriedly returned to the carriage, and exited the grounds. The onlookers, however, did not. It was reported that no less than 50 people swarmed the newly marked graves, leaving it a muddy mess. A constant stream of visitors filed past the monument throughout the day.

The Borden gravesite. At the right are (from l to r) Alice, Sarah, Andrew & Abby. Lizzie (Lizbeth) and Emma are above at the left. Photo by Ron Bueker.

The Borden Monument at Oak Grove Cemetery, in Fall River, MA.
Photo © by the Author.

Wedding Bells for Lizzie

For Lizzie Borden, the local press would forever use their black ink to stain her reputation and inflict pain. Among the cruel jokes laid down at her expense, were two reports of her wedding nuptials. *The Fall River Daily Globe*, once again, in order to create a sensation, ran the following:

"WEDDING BELLS"

The Fall River Daily Globe, Fall River, Ma.; December 10, 1896—A rumor to the effect that Miss Lizzie A. Borden of French Street is soon to marry a Mr. Gardner, of Swansea, has gained wide circulation about the city and Swansea, where it is pretty generally credited. A local modiste is now engaged in making an elaborate trousseau for Miss Borden. It has been given out that the garments are for a European trip, but as one of the dresses is known to be a beautiful white satin creation the knowing ones simply smile when asked about the matter. It is said the affair will take place about Christmas or New Year's.

Another wedding announcement made the papers on Feb. 21st (no year was given), stating she was engaged to one of the jurymen who acquitted her. It is probable the piece from December 10, 1896, caused her the most embarrassment, as the Mr. Gardner they mention, was no doubt her cousin, Orrin A. Gardner, the elusive bachelor of Swansea. Orrin would later become a dear friend and confidante to Emma Borden. He was years younger than both sisters and was undoubtedly humiliated by the wedding announcement linking him with one of Fall River's most infamous ladies.

Lizzie wrote to the "modiste" hinted at in the *Globe's* ugly rumor, a Mrs. William Cummings (Emma L. Holmes) to apologize: "I am more sorry than I can tell you that you have had any trouble over the false and silly story that has been about the last week or so. How or where it started, I have not the least idea." It was signed, "Sincerely, L.A. Borden."

There Goes the Neighborhood

By January of 1896, Lizzie and Emma could already gauge the temperature of their Hill residents. Although only residing on French Street for less than three years, they were acutely aware that the society divas, who wrote out party and wedding invitations on gilded stationary, did not include the Borden sisters on their guest lists. Only a few old friends called to see their beautiful parlor and dining room, or to exclaim with delight and awe at the lovely stained glass windows and Tiffany sconces. It was perhaps this periphery shut-out that caused Lizzie to go on the warpath. If Emma had hoped for a quiet, invisible existence, after all the exposure and pain she had gone through on her younger sister's behalf, it was not to be. In fact, it was just heating up.

Lizzie's first target was her neighbor, Mr. James Kenney. She wrote to him complaining of his chickens in her yard, and his small dog barking throughout the summer. She had the audacity to ask the man to get rid of the dog, or keep him full-time within the house.

Maplecroft (center), the Swift home (l) and a glimpse of the Kenney home (r). This shows how closely packed the homes are to each other. A barking dog would certainly annoy after a time. Photo courtesy of lizzieandrewborden.com.

Mr. John H. Brayton was the recipient of another of Lizzie's poison pen letters on May 31, 1900, when she wrote him to complain of his bird keeping her awake and making her nervous. The Brayton's lived across the street and to the west of Lizzie, a distance that would impede most bird's songs, especially "a little bird," but, with her library windows open wide, the shrill tweeting could have carried across the street.

Lizzie's love of animals has been a long-standing assumption, evidenced by her involvement in the Animal Rescue League of Fall River; an organization to which she left over $30,000 when she died. It is possible it was not the animals that bothered her so much, as it was their owners. If her neighbors would not include her in their social gatherings, then she would retaliate by making their lives miserable—if it was through their pets, so be it.

The furry and feathered friends of "the Hill's" populace were not Lizzie's only target. Her neighbors' children were up for grabs, as well.

A New Address

In the Spring of 1902, Lizzie called the Fall River police to put an end to the taunting and vandalism she had been subjected to for years. Her complaints were against the neighborhood children who played "despicable tricks, such as trampling over her lawn, lambasting the side of the house with decayed eggs, ringing the doorbell at late hours, tieing [ms] the doors, and calling Miss Borden vile names when she came to the door." As the report appeared in the *Fall River Daily Globe*, it appears Edwin Porter was still getting "the scoop" from the local police department. Nothing came of the reports, although the police did stake out Miss Borden's home (dressed in plain clothes, which fooled no one). As the children were the offspring of "the Hill's'" elite, no arrests or warnings were forthcoming.

Chapter Thirty-Seven

Spinning Out of Control

The allegations of Lizzie's affinity for theft are legion. Some were proven, others attached to her by opportunity, means, and intent. Officer Harrington approached Andrew Borden in 1891, informing him that the burglary of Abby's things on Second Street was committed by none other than Andrew's own daughter: Lizzie. Another theft, six years later, when Lizzie's father was no longer around to hush it up, made headlines:

"Charged with Stealing--
Warrant Issued for the Arrest of Lizzie Borden"

The newspaper banners were everywhere, none happier to announce the scandal than the *Fall River Daily Globe*. The story centered around a prominent jewelry store in Providence, Rhode Island, the Tilden-Thurber Company. In February of 1897, the newspapers reported that Lizzie "a frequent visitor to that city and customer" of that jeweler, had allegedly shopped there, and after leaving, it was noted two small painted porcelains were missing. Mr. Henry Tilden was informed about the missing items.

Sometime afterward, a woman, believed to be Mrs. Preston Hicks Gardener, a friend of Emma and Lizzie's, brought one of the porcelain pieces in to be cleaned. It was recognized as one of the art pieces missing. Upon questioning, Mrs. Gardener told the establishment the porcelain was a gift from Lizzie Borden. The police were notified and Detective Frank H. Parker was called in. Upon arriving at Lizzie's residence on French Street, he soon discovered the second painted porcelain. When asked about the piece, and the one brought in by Mrs. Gardener, Lizzie said "she had bought them both at the store of the Tilden & Thurber Co, paying $16 a piece for them." The jeweler claimed the price tag for the porcelains was $100 for the pair. The disparity in price tags gives one to doubt Lizzie's estimate. Was it possible she never looked at the price, but merely saw something she liked, and took it?

The Fall River Globe ran the story, adding "the most strenuous effort" was made to squelch the story; even the Boston papers were silenced. The Providence Chief of Police confirmed the arrest for Lizzie was legitimate, and had been issued, but never served. Andrew Jennings, still on retainer, refused to speak to reporters, other than to say he did not believe the story. The matter was handled in a discreet manner and the headlines went away. It was believed Lizzie settled with the prestigious jewelry store, and full restitution was made.

Stories of Lizzie's sticky fingers abounded. Area papers reported she was "being shadowed by Pinkerton detectives on suspicion that she has been seen shoplifting in Boston." Fall River gossip mongers declared the stores there kept a watchful eye on Lizzie as she perused their aisles. Kinder tongues called it "a compulsion," while harsher minds labeled her "insane."

The papers hounded Lizzie Borden in the years following her acquittal. In the various gossip columns, any reporting of "the Hill's" inhabitants (even if it was a simple excursion about town) would somehow mention they were "neighbors of Lizzie Borden." Her name appeared like a watermark: faint, but always obvious beneath the print.

The rumor, that no doubt, caused Lizzie the highest anxiety was one run by the *New Bedford Mercury*:

—Although Miss Borden was arraigned and tried, she was not tried on the charge of having murdered her mother, this charge having been dropped when the jury returned a verdict of not guilty in the Andrew J. Borden case. The only way in which the matter could possibly be reopened was a mistrial on the charge of murder of Mrs. Borden."

When Attorney Knowlton was interviewed, concerning the story, he stated the case could not be reopened, under any circumstances, even if new evidence was found. A sigh from 7 French Street (which was renumbered 306 when the addresses changed in 1898) was probably heard all the way to Swansea.

All Hallow's Eve, 1902

"Come away from the window, Lizzie," Emma said, a scene reminiscent of the first year they had lived in the house. She pulled the lace curtain from her sister's hand, where she had been holding it aside, as she watched the French Street parties. Windows were aglow with gas lights, and pumpkins lined the carved stone steps outside the festooned mansions. Children, adorned with straw masks and oversized costumes, darted about the streets, their elongated shadows following closely behind them. Laughter and music wafted into the Borden sisters' second-floor library through the open window. Emma shivered in the autumn chill and quickly closed it, as a swirl of orange and red leaves rose on a soft breeze and kissed the window pane.

The two women sat in the soft glow of the sitting room that ran the length of the front of the house. Bookcases, laden with classics and poetry, adorned the walls, giving a dual purpose to the room. It was here Emma and Lizzie spent their evening hours, when they were both in residence, which had become less frequent. A strain as insidious as poison ran through their relationship. The unbreakable bond, that had never faltered during the long ordeal of Lizzie's arrest, imprisonment and trials, now began to fracture. Emma longed for calm, and to fade quietly from public judgment and voyeurism. Lizzie, in typical fashion, turned her back on her detractors, and did as she pleased, usually to the detriment of those in her orbit.

As the two sisters sat in their Victorian elegance, perhaps wishing the fireplace that anchored the room was functional, the sound of singing came from the front of the house, just beneath the sitting room windows:

"Lizzie Borden took an axe,
Gave her father forty whacks,
When she saw what she had done,
She gave her father forty-one."

As the sisters pushed themselves from their chairs to a standing position, the front doorbell shrilled. The high-pitched noise went on without reprieve, until Lizzie crammed her palms against her ears, her face red with anger. Emma hurried out through the double doors and down the front stairs. Moments later, the sound of the front door opening preceded the sudden cessation of the bell. Lizzie slowly lowered her hands, her heart pounding. She pushed the pin curls from her broad forehead and tugged on her blouse waist. Her ears were still ringing, but not enough to miss what came next:

> "Andrew Borden now is dead,
> Lizzie hit him on the head,
> Up in heaven he will sing,
> On the gallows she will swing."

Hilda Gifford and Florence Brayton, circa 1903.
Photo courtesy of The Fall River Historical Society.

Emma ran up the stairs to find her sister doubled over, clutching the back of a sofa. An odd restraint came over her. Where once she would have reached for Lizzie to comfort her, her hands remained at her side, limp with resignation.

"They can't hurt you, Lizzie," she said, her voice thick with exhaustion. "They're only children acting out what their parents have told them. Stay away from the window."

With that, Emma left the room and walked the few steps to her bedroom. As she turned to shut the door, she caught sight of Lizzie's back, once again straightened in determination. Just as she eased the large wooden door to, the sound of splatting eggs hitting the side of the house could be heard.

The Borden sister's house at 306 French Street had become Fall River's haunted house. Hilda Gifford, whose home was only a few streets over on Lincoln Avenue, was one of the children who delighted in playing pranks on Lizzie. The daughter of a Fall River jeweler, she, along with her sisters Dorothy and Helen, would draw straws with other "Hill" children in a dare to see who would have to dash up to Lizzie's door and put a pin in the doorbell, causing it to ring incessantly. They would then back away, hiding behind trees and bushes, to see if "the murderer" would answer the door. According to the wonderful book *Parallel Lives*, Hilda recalled decades later that she "envisioned an axe coming out of every window."

View of French Street looking west from Highland Avenue, 1891. Beginning from the home on the right and going down, are the homes of William Hooper; Honorable James Davenport, James Kenney; George Allen (Lizzie's new home); and Attorney Marcus G.B. Swift. Photo: Fall River Historical Society.

The early 1900s

As Fall River rang in the New Year, celebrating the turn of the century in 1900, there were rapid changes on the horizon. The city was the largest cotton cloth manufacturing center in America, with eighty-seven mills. Women's fashions were becoming more daring, the corset less restrictive, and bloomers were being worn for the new-found thrill of "biking." Inside the home, modern conveniences and mass-manufactured furniture, were giving the happy homemaker more free time, and an inexpensive way to decorate. For someone with money, travel was an ever-present luxury to be plumbed to the dregs. Ford Model T's, and Stanley Steamers rumbled and belched their way along macadamized roadways, while electric trolley cars were taking over the horse-drawn variety. The shrill twill of phones, and the bright light of electricity now filled most homes and businesses.

Mail was still delivered twice a day, but now one could have it delivered to their door, instead of making a dual trip to the Post Office each morning and afternoon. The world was getting smaller, perhaps no more obvious than within the walls of 306 French Street. Lizzie's bizarre behavior, rather than being quelled after her acquittal, intensified. It may have been a frightening time for Emma, who, aware of her sister's mood swings and blind rage, was seeing the behavior acted out in ways she could not have expected. Lizzie was making enemies throughout "the Hill," with her poison pen letters, and overt actions. The first head to roll was Mr. James Kenney, who lived in the home to the east of her.

Lizzie's letters to the gentleman, asking him to sell or "shut up" his dog, as well as wrangle his stray hens, culminated in her asking the man to move his entire house! She bought his home, through her agent Charles Cook, rented it back to Kenney, and then asked him to move it away so she could own the lot next to her and have "the space." In 1898, after many heated exchanges, the Kenney's had their home relocated to Madison Street, with one caveat on Lizzie's end: she wanted to retain the stone that had been their home's foundation, or wall. She got her way. Elizabeth Kenney, James. F. Kenney's granddaughter, recalled years later that "if things did not go the way Lizzie wanted them, she would complain." It may be these are the same stones that now line the back property of *Maplecroft*.

Maplecroft in the early 1900s. You can see the empty Kenney lot
next to it, and a "spite fence" bordering the property between the lot
and the Davenport house, home to former Mayor, James F. Davenport.

Lizzie now had more acreage, separating her home from the Davenport house, that sat just east of the now-vacated Kenney lot. She joined with the Swifts to the west of her in purchasing the small lot abutting her home on the west, giving her even more space. In a gesture of friendship, Emma Lake, wife of Edward B. Lake, who lived across French Street from Lizzie, offered to buy the lot west of the Lake's home that separated their house from the Brayton's and half it with Lizzie. The desire was to give the area around the Lake's and Lizzie's homes a spacious park-like atmosphere. And, so, in 1898, Lizzie joined Emma Lake and bought up even more of her French Street neighborhood.

Edward. B. Lake's Queen Ann home at 2 French Street, in 1892.
Courtesy of the Fall River Historical Society.

In Emma Lake, Lizzie found a friend. The two women ran back and forth to each other's homes, shopped together, and became close companions. In 1895, at the age of forty-one, Emma Lake gave birth to a son, Russell, and he became a fixture at the Borden's house. Russell recalled that Lizzie came over to their house frequently, and he and his mother visited hers just as often. He remembered her as kind and "a good woman." Lizzie was his best customer at his lemonade stands. Emma Borden, he remembered as a "quiet, unassuming lady."

Russell remembered sitting on his veranda at the Lake house on French Street, seeing the hacks pulling up in front of Lizzie's house, pointing to it with their whip and telling their paying customers that the notorious Lizzie Borden lived there. He said people would gather outside stores to watch for her, when they saw her coach parked in front. She began to avoid the public, retiring farther into the shadows of her home and moving into the rooms farthest removed from the street.

The newly acquired part-ownership in the lot west of the Lake's house was confirmed in writing, with both Emma Lake and Lizzie Borden affixing their signatures to it in 1898. In 1911, they had a more formal agreement drawn up, utilizing Lizzie's neighbor, John Tuttle Swift (an attorney), stating that neither party will sell off their half without the consent of the other. So far, so good. But as it always was with Lizzie, things never remained calm for long. A fall-out occurred between the friends. In 1913, Lizzie erected one of her famous "spite fences" along the property division line of her half of the lot, effectively ruining the park-like setting. The tension between the two women, which was reported in the *Boston Sunday Herald* "had been strained for some time," may have been the result of some strange occurrences happening on French Street in 1905.

Strain Between Emma and Lizzie

Emma began spending more time away from Lizzie. One of her favorite destinations was *Holmlands*, the summer home of her dear friends, the family of Charles Holmes. The Holmes were there for the Borden sisters all throughout the trials and it was to their home in Fall River Lizzie and Emma first came after the acquittal. Emma stayed in close contact with the family visiting their spacious farm setting in Rochester, Massachusetts, as often as possible. The Holmes were famous for their parties, and their invitations were much sought after. Oddly, by 1898, Lizzie's name no longer appears on their guest list, but Emma "was always welcome." It was rumored, that for whatever reason, the Holmes had "cut Lizzie." In 1902 and 1904, Emma had overnight visits at *Holmlands*, both occurring near the anniversary date of the murders of her father and stepmother; leaving Lizzie to deal with the tragic shadows of the past on her own.

For Emma Borden, the ties she had forged with friends grew stronger, while Lizzie's frayed and became "cut" altogether. Emma had always been the family liaison, writing to Borden and Morse relatives, and keeping in touch. John Morse deferred to her for family information; referring the police to her when they asked about nearby relatives. John also admitted he "had never had a letter from Lizzie in his life." It was clear that people were more to Emma than stepping stones to success; they offered unconditional love and a safe harbor—two things missing from her life with Lizzie. Whether it was due to their disparate personalities, Lizzie's on-going feuds with their neighbors, the ubiquitous spotlight that played upon their lives, or other, more upsetting reasons, the strain between the two sisters was growing.

Rumors of Lizzie's closeness with her coachman and chauffeur, Joseph Tetrault, who was in residence at the Borden home on French Street in the early 1900s, was still causing Fall River tongues to wag. With Emma's more frequent departures from home, had Lizzie found companionship in another denizen of her Victorian home? It would not be the last relationship that provided the gossip for many a breakfast table on "the Hill."

Beyond the Gaslights

In a world filled with voyeurs, literally peering through the windows of Lizzie's life, is it any wonder she found solace and escape within the darkness of theaters? She attended plays at the Academy from her home on Second Street, often securing tickets the moment they went on sale from her friend Alice Russell, who worked for the owner. With Fall River now reporting her every move, she chose theaters in nearby Boston, and New York City. As the gaslights dimmed, and the curtain rose, Lizzie lost herself amidst the fake sets and dramatic orations. The tragedies, played out before the audience in grand gestures and climatic effects, titillated her psyche so prone to drama. Here, in the darkness, she was invisible, with a world of fantasy providing an escape from a life all too-fraught with reality.

It was here amidst the accolades and adulation of the theater-going audience, that Lizzie first saw and became obsessed with, the famous actress, Nance O'Neil.

Nance O'Neil was born Gertrude Lamson in Oakland, California, on October 8, 1874. Her sister Lilian, had garnered success as a stage actress, and Nance soon followed in her footsteps, making her debut in 1893. She was introduced to noted director-actor, Arthur Rankin, who took her under his wing. Their relationship was a roller-coaster ride of triumph and financial strain. The world of the actor in the Gilded Age came without a safety net. If the ticket sales were good and the reviews even better, you were rolling in cash. Just as quickly, if the seats were vacant and the critics vicious, you found yourself living in abandoned rooms, or at the generosity of friends. It was the latter role that Lizzie Borden was to play a part in a tragedy of her own creation.

Nance's fame grew as an enigmatic actress whose face could portray any emotion. She was soon playing to audiences in Australia, New Zealand, Egypt, South Africa, and England. 1900 saw her rise to glory…1902 saw her fall. The company's fortunes were in trouble. Reviews of her performances were mixed, and in 1902, the actress and her troupe returned to America. But, in 1904, as the fickle hand of fate turned once again, Nance's star glittered; this time in Boston. *The Boston Globe* enthused:

Her hair is of a beautiful light and natural golden hue, her eyes of deep blue, and wonderfully attractive, and her face, strongly marked in feature…has a mobility such as scarcely more than one actress in a generation is privileged to possess.

Nance O'Neil. Photo of unknown origin.

In Boston, Nance played the Columbia, Colonial, Hollis Street, and Tremont theaters. Her Lady Macbeth was hailed as "a superb performance," while her Magda was touted as "realistic and thrilling." Her sold-out performances were met with up to a dozen curtain calls. And among the fans rising to their feet and cheering with unabashed enthusiasm, was Lizzie Andrew Borden.

After one such performance, Lizzie returned to her Boston hotel and wrote to the actress, telling her of her admiration, and asking permission to meet her. A floral bouquet accompanied the note. Lizzie was granted permission, and met the actress backstage at the Tremont Theater. We do not know if Nance knew who her new admirer was, but a friendship was formed. Fourteen years Lizzie's junior, Nance (at 30) and Lizzie (at 44) began a friendship that may have had an additional advantage for the actress, and one which a woman such as Lizzie, unaccustomed to letting people gain access to her, may have misunderstood.

Lizzie Borden in her 40s. Photo courtesy of the Fall River Historical Society.

Nance continued to play New England, with stops in Fall River. On February 3, 1905, she played at the Academy, amid tepid reviews. She was said to be suffering from a cold and her performance of Elizabeth, the Queen of England, suffered for it.

It was this performance in Fall River that started the rumor mills churning faster than the spindles in the city's cotton factories. Newspapers reported "Miss Borden's carriage awaited after the play, and together they went to Miss Borden's home." The "entertainment afforded Miss O'Neil is said, however, to have been of the quietest character," owing to the actress being "ill from overwork," and was conducted "such as one friend might give another." This paled in comparison to another visit from the actress to Lizzie's home where she and her company were entertained in high style. An orchestra, caterer, hired palm trees, and amenities—the best money could buy—were all lavished on the theater troupe. For once, it was Lizzie's house whose windows blazed with lights, and music could be heard along French Street wafting through her lace curtains. It must have been a moment she cherished. Had she finally arrived?

Lizzie once again opened her pocketbook to fund a week-long house party in Tyngsboro, Massachusetts. Miss O'Neil had a country place there, where Lizzie had been an invited guest on occasion. She named it "O'Neil Manor" and filled it with dogs, parrots and monkeys. Its 200 acres accommodated horses, which the actress loved to ride. Lizzie invited the entire troupe to her rented house in Tyngsboro, and for a week, wined and dined her new "friends."

The relationship between Lizzie and Nance has been one of speculation. In later years, when asked about Miss Borden, Nance said of Lizzie, she had "gray eyes and graying hair," with "an unmistakable air of refinement and intellect." She spoke of Lizzie's fondness for travel and her kindness to animals. Nance went on to mention her insight into Lizzie's life: she "seemed utterly lonely...she was always so alone." Nance stated that they "became friends and remained friends, though only in memory," and they "never met again after she finished her season in the East." She admitted to being "rather a poor correspondent," and never exchanged letters with Lizzie, saying "we were like ships that pass in the night and speak to each other only in passing."

While the ships "passed," Nance gave Lizzie hope that the friendship was one of lasting fondness. In 1904, Nance presented Lizzie with an expensive book of poetry, edged in gold gilt and festooned with laurel wreaths. The Poems of Thomas Bailey Aldrich, bore a dedication to Lizzie, in Nance's own hand:

> For my dear Lizbeth with love from
> Daphne
> O'Neil Manor. Tyngsboro, Mass.
> June 13, 1904

Here, we see the first glimpse of the name Lizzie would come to call herself only one year later: Lizbeth. It may have been a reflection of Old English homage, or simply an affectionate nickname, but Lizzie loved it, and adopted it to alter the image she now sought to present. Daphne may have been a nod to the Greek nymph, daughter of the river god, Peneius, pursued by Apollo. Nance may have portrayed her once in a play. The inscription is one of affection, and doubtless, filled Lizzie's lonely heart with happiness. Thenceforth, she became Lizbeth Andrews Borden. [The addition of the 's' to Andrew is correct.]

Sadly, the façade of friendship began to melt, like snow beneath the early sunlight of Spring. Two of Nance's troupe asked Lizzie for loans, of which were never repaid. By 1906, the actress and her friends disappeared from Lizzie's life. It is analogous to the story of *The Great Gatsby*, by F. Scott Fitzgerald, and the friends who came for his parties, but were gone with the rising sun.

Left behind was the scent of scandal. Many Puritans in Fall River hinted of a homosexual affair between Lizzie and the actress. Nance at one time had referred to Lizzie as "a quiet, reserved, frail little old-fashioned gentlewoman," which does not smack of sensuality.

Whatever the relationship, it appears Emma made herself scarce whenever Nance was to visit their French Street home. The actress claimed she never met Lizzie's sister. Emma's disapproval of the friendship may have been the final straw that drove her from the house. It was thought "the trouble originated from a disagreement in winter after Lizzie…had given a dinner and entertainment to Nance O'Neil and her company." [Quote from *Parallel Lives*/The Fall River Historical Society.]

Thespians, known for their love of parody, may have begun teasing Lizzie during a winter dinner party about her notoriety. Fueled with drink, perhaps a few of the actors took it too far by reenacting the murders through a humorous sketch. If Emma overheard it from the sanctity of her room, it would have been too much. She was already dealing with Lizzie's unconventional friendship with Joseph Tetrault, their coachman, and now this. As mentioned, Lizzie had sent Tetrault away, only to rehire him, setting tongues wagging all over Fall River.

Emma Leaves

Emma's decision to finally leave her forty-four-year-old sister is one that must have come after agonizing soul-searching. She had been with Lizzie through the toughest times imaginable. Finally, she turned to her dear friend Reverend Buck for counsel. Emma admitted "matters reached such a pass that I could not stay longer in the same house as Lizzie." Reverend Buck listened carefully to Emma's concerns, and said finally, "it was imperative that I should make my home elsewhere."

It is interesting, that even though Reverend Buck passed away in 1903, Emma stayed in the house until 1905. Nance O'Neil was not on the scene in 1903. Perhaps Lizzie's friendship with Mr. Tetrault was what caused Emma to confide to the Reverend. As a man of the Church, he would not likely advise her to leave Lizzie, unless the transgression she shared with him was one likely to hurt her soul. Although Lizzie had troubles with stealing, a sin the Church would frown upon, unmarried fornication would be far more serious. The split was so grievous, that Emma later stated, "I do not expect to set foot on the place while [Lizzie] lives."

Emma's words were from a rare interview she granted to the *Boston Sunday Herald* in 1913. She was living with the late Reverend Buck's five unmarried daughters, "the Misses Buck." She told the reporter she would do her "duty in answering the cruel slanders that have been made against her [Lizzie] both in public print and by gossiping persons who seem to delight in saying cruel things about her...I am still going to do it in defending my sister even though circumstances have separated us."

Thus, according to newspaper reports, in May, 1905, "Miss Emma packed up her belongings, called a moving wagon and shook the dust of the French Street home...from her feet. Ever since her departure, the tongues of gossip have been wagging tremendously, even for Fall River, which is saying a great deal." By 1906, Emma is listed as living in Providence, Rhode Island, spending time with the Gardener's at their Touisset home, *Riverby*, only minutes from Andrew Borden's Upper Farm. During this time, the Gardener's, relatives and friends of the Borden sisters, estranged themselves from Lizzie, as did the Buck sisters. Lizzie's friends were all but gone.

The Gardner's *Riverby* home in Touisset, Massachusetts.
Photo courtesy of Shelley Dziedzic.

A Thief in the Night

As the New England snow was settling onto the manicured lawns of Fall River's elite in December of 1905, everywhere were the signs of Christmas. Store windows laid out sumptuous displays of toys, food and clothing. The latest in modern conveniences were highlighted and stores were festooned with garlands and lights. Elaborate animated scenes filled department store windows, turning the season into a fairyland. For those who were happy, it was a magical time of year; for those who were lonely, it was torture.

Lizzie decorated her home, trying to put from her mind that this Christmas would be her first without Emma in her life. Forty-four years with her sister, shopping together, opening presents and talking over plans, had ended. Neighbors' windows were ablaze with warm lights and candles. The sound of horses adorned with bells filled the air as sleighs laden with laughing families traveled throughout "the Hill." A growing panic must have filled Lizzie's head. Changing her name to Lizbeth had done nothing to alter a personality that would snap when faced with abandonment. And Emma, her one constant, had abandoned her.

Maids who serviced the large homes surrounding 306 French Street, often congregated in the kitchens of their various employers, during their time off. Lizzie welcomed them into her home, often laying out tea and pastries for them. They filled the house with much-needed laughter. They also provided her with gossip about their employers. Offered up in a mood of joviality, the domestics were unaware they were furnishing information as to the comings and goings of the people who hired them. Lizzie, whether in the kitchen where the women were gathered, or close-by in the dining room or pantry, may have listened, to ascertain when her neighbors would be away from home.

On December 18, 1905, *The Fall River Herald* reported "Mr. and Mrs. Charles T. Kirby, of number 39 Belmont Street, and their family, had been away for the day. They returned in the evening around 10:30 o'clock." Upon arriving home, they were "somewhat surprised on noticing...that several of the rooms on the second floor were aglow with light, and it only took a few minutes to ascertain that they had had unwelcome visitors in their absence." They found that "every room showed traces of visits from the intruders, the contents of closets and drawers...strewed about the rooms, in an evident search for money and jewelry. The police and inspectors" believed the thieves "were people well acquainted with the Kirby house and the fact that the family was away. They were not professionals as they did not molest any of the silverware." They "left several gas jets burning," and had "left no clues." A dining room window was found open, "forced by use of a jimmy," allowing access to the house.

The objects taken are suggestive: A gold ring, a lady's gold watch, a string of gold beads, a silver bracelet watch, two gold studs, three gold stick pins, two silver stick pins, an amethyst ring, a gold bracelet, two belt buckles of gold and silver, and a Smith and Wesson revolver. The police believed the burglar was probably female. The items stolen spoke to a woman's interest in jewelry. A rumor that a female had been canvassing houses lately had been reported, but by whom?

Lizzie's view of the Brayton house today, across the street, from her 2nd-floor sitting room. The Kirby house was two houses to the left of it.
Photo by the Author.

The Kirby house was only two houses south of the Brayton's, the home across from Lizzie on the corner of French and Belmont. The lot she owned with Mrs. Lake abutted the lawns of the Brayton's and their neighbor, with towering pines and multiple bushes. A perfect place to walk one's Boston Terrier in the evening hours.

On December 19, the following night, Lizzie's neighbors across the street from her, the Lake's, with whom she co-owned the lot to the west, were also robbed. Newspaper reports stated Edward and Emma Lake, with their family, and two visiting houseguests,

Abbie B. Marrin, and Mrs. F. A. Jenkins, were having dinner in their home. Mrs. Jenkins "returning to the second floor...discovered an open window, which no one recalled having opened." A quick inventory showed over $400 in valuables missing. The open window was next to a veranda post, suggesting the intruder had entered that way.

Again, the items stolen were strangely familiar to a burglary at the Andrew J. Borden home in 1891:

"A gold watch, valued at $300, a stick pin worth $17, $12 in money, and a gold chain," had been taken from Mrs. Marrin. Mrs. Lake's purse on the hall table was missing $35, and "her desk had been forced open and rummaged through." Interestingly, the thief had piled together some silver souvenir spoons, but had forgotten them in "their haste to escape."

A gold lady's watch, money was taken from a purse, a desk broken into... Lizzie collected souvenir spoons, as did many people in that era. The craze began with the World's Fair, and the spoons were highly sought after.

Had the burglar seen a returning maid from the window of the upstairs room? Was the open window near a veranda post just a ruse, when the culprit had actually walked right in the side kitchen door on the east side of the house by the driveway, and crept up the back stairs while the family and their guests were dining? Perhaps the perpetrator knew the maid was allowed some time off that evening after dinner was served, or that she had run an errand.

This was a house Lizzie knew well. She and Emma Lake spent many hours together, shopping and roaming each other's houses. Perhaps Lizzie had watched Mrs. Lake purchase some of the items and had coveted them. She certainly would have known exactly where they were kept. Did Lizzie's opera glasses lay ready on the window seat of her second story library?

Both burglaries happened roughly a week before Christmas; a Christmas without Emma; a Christmas filled with angst.

There is no proof Lizzie was involved in these burglaries, and the Author has taken some liberties in describing scenarios she believes are plausible, especially when compared to a chain of events that followed in later years. Did Emma Lake suspect Lizzie of being the burglar? Did it prompt their falling-out resulting in Lizzie building a spite fence down the middle of their shared lot?

Emma Travels

In 1906, Emma Lenora Borden found her wings. After dedicating her life to her younger sister, the spinster, at age 55, set out to see the world. Purchasing a first-class ticket aboard the White Star Liner *SS Cymric*, she departed Boston and arrived in Liverpool, England on June 2, 1906. Letters to her friends, the Brigham's, show her touring Europe, until her return to Fall River, in October of that same year. Mary Ella Brigham hosted a party in her honor upon her return. That the Brigham home was so close to *Maplecroft*, only a few houses over on Belmont Street, may have caused Emma some pain. She once again visited Mary Ella on the morning of December 29, along with the Buck sisters. While Lizzie "celebrated" another Christmas season alone, Emma was surrounded by friends, only a few houses over.

With the local papers continually reporting the excursions of the "Spindle City's" citizens, it is possible Lizzie kept track of her older sister's new-found freedom. What effect it may have had on her "nerves," is a question to ponder.

Tetrault Departs

For reasons unknown, Joseph Tetrault, the infamous coachman who may have played a part in Emma's removal from French Street, left Lizzie's employ in 1907. Coincidentally, two fires broke out that year inside the Borden sister's properties.

Mr. Tetrault was replaced by Walter Clayton Fogg. He would act as coachman until 1909, when he was "let go," due to a complication brought about by his wife, Honora. It seems Mrs. Fogg purchased some new furnishings for their home on Barnaby Street, using credit she procured by using Lizzie Borden as a reference, as her husband Walter, was employed by her. When Mrs. Fogg fell behind on her payments, the store went to Lizzie, who paid off the bill, but subsequently told Walter he needed to find employment elsewhere. She may have provided him with a letter of recommendation, and remained cordial with him, knowing the situation had been outside his control.

Walter Fogg died in 1921, leaving Honora a widow with four children. Eventually, she ran out of money and reached out to relatives who turned her away. Finally, in desperation, two of her daughters appealed to Lizzie Borden for help. They were denied. With Lizzie, "once burned" is more than "twice shy"—it is an unforgivable offense.

Maplecroft is Born

The tradition of naming one's grand manors, or sprawling farmlands, was not new to Fall River. Indeed, two of Emma's favorite retreats, owned by her friends, were *Holmland*s and *Riverby*. *Interlachen*, the Spencer Borden mansion, was a well-known estate in the area. Stationary sometimes bore the name of these fanciful addresses, and perhaps a discreet sign hung near a gate, but no one on "the Hill" had ever emblazoned a home's name across the front of the property.

Enter Lizzie Borden. Perhaps with fond memories of Nance O'Neil's *"O'Neil Manor,"* Lizbeth set out to create a new image for herself. In the tradition of Jane Austen settings and romantic novels such as *Wuthering Heights*, Miss Borden christened her French Street home *Maplecroft*. The word *croft* is of Old English origin, a lineage of which Lizzie appeared to be fond. The word means a small, enclosed field, usually adjoining a house. She had certainly procured additional lands around her home and it was the stately maples there that had probably leant their name to the house. Maples are native to New England and they added to her feeling of "roots" there.

By 1908, the calling cards and stationary emanating from 306 French Street were embossed: Lizbeth of *Maplecroft*. Lizzie had formed an identity to her liking; one that reflected stature and importance. On September 18, 1909, she made it official by having the name *Maplecroft* carved into the newly-created granite steps leading up to the front door. According to William Henry Savoie, the mason, Lizzie's instructions were very clear, including into which step she wanted the name carved.

Lizzie's *Maplecroft,* carved in granite, at her home at 306 French Street.
Photo by Ron Bueker.

It was also in 1909, Lizzie added the large back piazza, with an overhead room, to the house. In order to make changes to the house, Lizzie was required to contact Emma for permission, as the sisters still jointly owned the home. Permission was granted, and on September 15, construction began on an addition measuring "fourteen feet wide by fifteen feet in length, set on a stone foundation." The Lake's had recently added on to their home across from her, perhaps prompting the decision in a Victorian "keeping up with the Jones'" move.

Lizzie now had her new piazza, complete with stone corner piece; a place to hide from prying eyes. Her new home had a new name—one set in stone for all the world to see. Unfortunately, Fall River, and especially her neighbors on "the Hill," found the chiseled name not only ostentatious, but a grievous mistake. Now every curiosity seeker traveling up the toney streets in search of the famous Lizzie Borden's home would know exactly where to find her. Once again, the wealthy circled their wagons, and Lizzie was shut out.

New Servants & Companionship

Lizzie's world was shrinking. More and more, she found companionship within the walls of *Maplecroft,* turning to her staff and occasional travel companions for solace and friendship. Her

Boston Terriers were constantly at her side, and she filled her days with quiet moments on her back piazza, or reading within the security of the large room overhead. She erected birdhouses and fed the squirrels that ran rampant on the tree-lined streets. Perhaps, for Lizzie, her domestic help and the animals around her, had something in common; something in which she found comfort and peace. They all relied on her for their well-being. In essence, Lizzie held all the cards. She was in control. While it may not have been unconditional love, it was close enough.

Perhaps the person within Lizzie's employ who had the strongest impact upon her, was a domestic named Hannah Bostron Nelson. This dark-haired Swedish immigrant came to work at *Maplecroft* during the turbulent years when Emma was still in residence. Hannah witnessed much sorrow, and doubtless, many outbursts and theatrics. With her soft, sing-song cadence, she spoke to Lizzie in ways that must have touched the deeply lonely woman. Letters from Lizzie in 1908, to others speak of her fondness for Hannah.

Hannah Bostron Nelson.
Photo courtesy of the The Fall River Historical Society.

We can begin to feel some empathy for this lonely lady of *Maplecroft*, when tragedy once-again stains her happiness.

Hannah passed away of dysentery on June 3, 1908, in a Rhode Island Hospital, where she had languished for some time. She was only thirty-seven years of age. Lizzie was inconsolable, and as before, left alone to roam her opulent rooms on "the Hill."

The two Mary's: Mary S. Boucher, and Mary A. S. Reynolds, came to *Maplecroft* to fill Hannah's missing shoes. They may have occupied the large, spacious room on the third floor that would easily house two beds. Lizzie wrote they "are doing very well but no one knows how I miss my Hannah." Mary Boucher remained with Lizzie for eight years, Miss Reynolds for two, when she departed to marry James E. Dynes. Servants typically came and went through a revolving door as their lifestyles, and needs, changed. For any employer, who formed attachments, these sorts of transitions could be difficult at times.

Lizzie lost herself inside the pages of her beloved books. Her initials, L.A.B. appear on the flyleaf of many of her favorite tomes. She stated once, "I spend much time reading and building castles in the air." Sadly, the castle she built with the inheritance left her by her father's death, had become a prison. There would be no reprieve from public condemnation. The verdict they handed down was possibly crueler than the one the jury of 1893, could have voiced.

Emma's Journeys of Happiness

While Lizzie found solace in her books, pets and domestic servants, Emma, with an unlimited pocketbook, indulged her love of travel. There was a bright, shiny world out there that she had previously only glimpsed in postcards sent her from well-meaning friends.

In early 1908, she found herself on the Golden Coast of California, a place she had dreamed of visiting ever since her friend Mary Ella Brigham sang its praises through her vacation postcards. For several months, Emma visited the beaches and cliff sides of the state, and hopped over to Catalina Island. Did she have any regrets about leaving Lizzie and the drama behind? If she did, she managed to bury them beneath the glistening sands of the coastline, at least for a time.

Orrin Gardener, the hapless fellow who found himself "engaged" to Lizzie in the Fall River headlines, was extremely close to Emma. They often visited friends together, as they did on the evening of September 15, when they called on Mary Ella Brigham. Once again, Emma was within walking distance of *Maplecroft*, yet there is no record she stopped there.

On February 2, 1910, the *Fall River Daily Evening News* ran the following blurb under its "Our Folks and Other Folks" gossip column:

> Miss Emma Borden of Providence, formerly of this city, and Mrs. Preston H. Gardner, left Wednesday for New Orleans. They will be attending Mardi Gras festivities, and will later spend time in Florida at the winter resorts, returning in about a month.

It is highly probable that Lizzie read the article. While strange fires had licked the bricks and wooden structures of Andrew J. Borden's properties in 1908 and 1909, 1910 shows no destruction. If Lizzie had been behind the myriad fires, there is no record she acted out in retaliation for Emma's travel and friendships.

Another Addition to *Maplecroft*

On February 18, 1911, Permit number 33 was assigned to Lizzie in response to her request to build a garage at the back of her property. Having once been turned down by the Swifts next door to erect a building on the lot she shared with them, she instead set about having one constructed at the rear of the lot that once housed the Kenney home.

Inside Lizzie's Maplecroft garage on French Street.
Note the radiator system along the back wall.
Photo by the Author.

The edifice was not an ordinary box-like garage. With white columns and double doors, it reflected taste and a desire to impress. It still stands today. Its dimensions' measure twenty-eight- feet wide and thirty-seven-feet long. Complete with running water and a steam radiator that ran the length of the back wall, it was a modern wonder for that era. A trap door in the room may have been to enable the chauffeur to maintain the undercarriage of a car, or it may have been the home of the machinations that ran a turntable that enabled the car to be rotated, instead of backed out of the structure. F.O. Stanley, the famous inventor of the Stanley Steamer Motor Car had just such a device in his garage at his home in Estes Park, Colorado, in 1908. Perhaps, Lizzie had read about it.

Chapter Thirty-Six

Reaping the Rewards

As the second decade of the 1900s began, Lizzie may have watched the rapid changes around her with increasing tension. The world she knew was gone. Automobiles were replacing the horse and carriage in increasing numbers, women were in the workplace, the corset had been flung to the winds and modern appliances were finding their way into the home; including dishwashers, gas ranges, and vacuum cleaners.

President William F. Taft visited Fall River to commemorate its Cotton Centennial, as the city was enjoying the fruits of its cotton-manufacturing labors. 10,000 mill stockholders, including Emma and Lizzie Borden, watched the money pour in. Andrew, who had owned stock in Troy Mills and others, would have appreciated seeing his fortunes grow. It was rumored that President Taft asked to be driven past the home of the city's living legend. If the story is true, did Lizzie see the nation's president peering up at her curtained windows.

For Lizzie, the "rewards" she reaped, in the realm of material goods and luxuries were great. When measured against the yardstick of friendships, family, and happiness, she fell tragically short.

On the twentieth anniversary of the murders, the *Boston Sunday Herald* ran a feature article entitled: "Lizzie Borden Twenty Years After the Tragedy." It labeled her "a recluse, as damned by public opinion and as ostracized by former friends and enemies alike." It went on in the harshest of words, calling her "an outcast, an Ismael, a social pariah…shut off from the world as if she were behind prison bars…the silent, inexorable censure of her fellow men and women." Even Emma, in a rare interview in 1913, admitted, "Queer? Yes, Lizzie is queer."

Articles rehashing the Borden murders had run every year on the anniversary since 1892. Finally, in 1914, they stopped, with the *Fall River Globe*, Lizzie's constant nemesis, giving the story its last "hurrah."

Friendships

By 1916, Lizzie's closest ties were to the employees who worked for her and their families. To these companions, she became "Auntie Lizzie," or "Auntie Borden," creating a family of her own invention. She opened her heart and her purse strings, especially to the children, bestowing gifts of Sunbonnet Babies dishware to the girls and gold rings to the boys. If there was some hidden symbolism dating back to the murders in the selection of gifts, it may have been subliminal. The Sun Bonnet Babies depicted a tranquil world of tidy housekeeping, each day relegated to a certain chore, with Sunday as a day of fun and fishing. Thursday, showed the washing of windows, an ironic twist. The gold rings were quite possibly the means of giving love over and over, as she had given one as a token of such to her father, long ago. Her little Boston Terrier Laddie Miller Borden was her constant companion.

Mrs. Dr. James Wardle Hartley and her daughter, Grace, became close friends with Lizzie. Little Grace frequented *Maplecroft,* attending small tea parties in the dining room and parlor and bringing much-needed joy into Lizzie's lonely life. It was a friendship that endured for the last ten years of Lizzie's life; a life increasingly fraught with nervous spells and depression. Grace married Louis McHenry Howe and remained Lizzie's friend until she was buried in the Borden plot.

In 1919, Lizzie hired Ernest Alden Terry to serve as her chauffeur. His, and his family's, friendship would be one of lasting happiness for her. She became "Auntie Borden" to his children, Grace Lorraine and Alden, presenting them with her favorite gifts of Sunbonnet Babies dishes, and other trinkets. Alden remembered being invited to "Auntie Borden's" for little tea parties.

In 1922, Lizzie picnicked with the Terry's and Alden, along with her two domestic servants, Nellie and Florence, and an unidentified woman. Lizzie's Boston Terrier was in tow. Lizzie had her family: one consisting of employees, their offspring and her beloved pets.

Headstone of Lizzie's Boston Terriers: Donald Stuart, Royal Nelson, and Laddie Miller. They are buried at Pine Ridge in Dedham, Ma. The name "Nelson" was in homage to Hannah and "Miller" was a nod to another maid, Ellen B. Miller. Photo courtesy of Shelly Dziedzic.

Someone is in the House

On April 8, 1920, two homes within walking distance of *Maplecroft* were burglarized. The first home was that of Andrew H. Gardner on Rock Street, two blocks from Lizzie's door. Between 4 o'clock and 11 p.m., an intruder entered the Gardner home and took their time going through each room. The maid had the day off and Mr. Gardener was absent, showing inside knowledge of the family's movements that day.

"Three costly watches, valuable silver plate, jewelry, and jewelry boxes," were stolen. Oddly, "they departed with most of the cigars in the house, leaving three cigars in each of two boxes, and a single cigarette of a nearly full good sized box." Again, the items taken were largely feminine in nature. The theft of tobacco may have been reminiscent of a pouch of fine cut chewing tobacco found in the pocket of Andrew Borden as he lay murdered upon his sofa. Had the thief left behind a few cigars, unable to deprive the head of the house of all his tobacco?

Just one block from Lizzie's house, at 222 Belmont Avenue, was the home of James Fitzgerald, a treasurer and father to three small children, and his wife, Mabel. His home was also broken into during the evening, but from appearances, the thief had been frightened away "by the approach of someone in the house."

The homes were close in proximity, both had windows jimmied and raised to show entrance. A wooden chisel, little used, was found in a vacant lot that would be purchased by Lizzie in July of that same year, through her agent, Charles Cook. Known as the Baker lot, it was found to hold the stolen pink leather jewel case, tossed aside after its jewels had been removed, and a chisel. The lot sat near Lizzie's home. The break-ins were never solved.

After each series of break-ins, Lizzie hurriedly departed for Washington, D.C. A letter sent April 19, only a week after the burglaries, to her friend Amada P. Thelen was very telling.

> My dear Manda, you may be surprised I'm here. I was tired and nervous so ran away for a while. Nellie [Lizzie's maid, Ellen B. Miller] wrote me you called...Am not sure but may stay here a month [D.C.]. My love to you dear, L.A.B.

Over the years, following fire break-outs in Lizzie's business properties, she once-again ran to D.C., always staying at the Cochran (which later became the Franklin Square Hotel), and writing Manda that her "nerves" were to blame for her escape.

The Cochran Hotel, later renamed the Franklin Square Hotel, in Washington, D.C. to where Lizzie escaped. Photos of unknown origin.

1923 Goes Up in Smoke

On Sunday, March 5, 1923, fire once-again broke out in the Andrew J. Borden Building. It became apparent the blaze began in the cellar beneath the Modern Shoe Store, a business leasing the site from Emma Borden. At 7 o'clock that evening, flames and smoke billowed from the first floor, the second and third floors sustaining smoke and water damage. While not as extensive as the great fire of 1916, it burned down a large portion of the businesses framed by South Main, Spring, Pearl, and Columbia Streets. Among the lost buildings several belonged to Emma and Lizzie Borden. The 1916 fire was called the worst inferno in the city's history. Reports of damages were close to a million and a half dollars. Once again, the Birch land buildings were hit, with no explanation for the devastating fire.

The fire of 1923, which started in the basement of the Modern Shoe Store coincided with a lawsuit between the two sisters. Emma, "with Lizzie's full knowledge," filed a petition on April 14, 1923, to hire her own agent, Jacob Donis, in effect separating herself from Charles Cook, her long-standing agent. Mr. Cook would remain in charge of Lizzie's properties. It is interesting Lizzie was made aware earlier that year that Emma had issued leases to the Modern Shoe Store, Inc, and others. Lizzie in turn had asked for "an equal distribution of the property known as the A.J. Borden block, wishing to hold the property in severalty, retaining it without a joint interest with any other person."

The suit went back and forth, resulting in Emma selling her share of the building to her new agent, Jacob Dondis, and Lizzie retaining her interest until she died. Was it a coincidence that the fire started beneath the shoe store to which Emma had just provided a lease, thus showing her independence in her dealings, without her sister's involvement. Lizzie fled to D.C., citing "nerves."

The End of the Borden Saga

Emma Borden, sometime in the 1920s, moved to Newmarket, New Hampshire, to live out her remaining days in peace, residing on Main Street at the boarding house of Miss C. Connor. In her early 70's, Emma was described as "about five foot four, and weighing about 130 to 138 pounds, usually attired in loose shifts of light colors." Her hair was quite gray, and styled in such a way that it was up on the head, held with hairpins above her oval face. While cordial and refined, she was said to possess a surprisingly "harsh voice." Emma stayed true to her father's memory: "Every Memorial Day I carry flowers to father's grave," she said. "And Lizzie does not forget him. But she generally sends her tribute by a florist." No mention is made of flowers for Abby.

Andrew Jennings, Lizzie's attorney and knight, died on October 19, 1923. The *Fall River Daily News* ran his obituary, and if Lizzie saw it, it may have caused her a moment of pain. Jennings was 74 and died at his summer home at Westport Harbor.

On June 1, 1927, Lizzie Borden died at *Maplecroft*. Her heart had given out, and at 8:30 in the evening, she was gone. She was sixty-six years old. Did the residents on "the Hill" breathe a sigh of relief? Did many have a hard time accepting their town's legend was actually gone? The funeral was a strictly private affair. Mrs. Vida Turner was asked to sing the single hymn Lizzie had requested. It was *"My Ain Countrie,"* a song whose title was still carved on the mantelpiece in the upstairs bedroom. The singer was hastily called to *Maplecroft* on Saturday, June 4. The Undertaker let her in, ushered her into the dining room, although Lizzie's remains were in the parlor. She was told to sing, then ushered back out the door, with orders not to tell anyone she had been there.

Lizzie had friends. They were there in the spacious floral-scented parlor of *Maplecroft*. Some were servants and their families, some, a loyal few, had stayed close to her through the end. She had asked to be buried at her father's feet, and that request was carried out. Lizzie's casket was carried from *Maplecroft* and conducted to Oak Grove Cemetery beneath the watchful eye of James Winward & Company; the same establishment she had requested to handle her father's funeral. Only after her death, did the people of Fall River hear of a different side to the woman they denigrated. Laughlin McFarland, the owner of a Fall River bookstore, let it be known that Lizzie had purchased hundreds of books over the years for the city's poor children. In her will, she left $30,000 to the Fall River Animal Rescue League. It is reminiscent of the verse from the song *"Bless the Beasts and the Children"*: Bless the beasts and the children, for in this world they have no choice; they have no voice." It was to the helpless Lizzie reached out, and to the ones who could not hurt her, or pass judgment—animals and children.

Lizzie died without the one thing her money could not buy:

"I would give every cent I have in the world and beg in the streets, if it could only be proved while I live that I did not kill my father and stepmother."

Sadly, it was rumored upon notice of her death, many asked, "Did she confess?"

On the morning of June 10, 1927, Emma L. Borden died in her bed in Newmarket, New Hampshire, at the age of 76. The coroner's report stated Chronic Nephritis, with which she had been suffering for two years. Senility was listed as a contributing factor. Annie C. Connor, the woman with whom Emma had resided since her move to New Hampshire, was at her side, as was Orrin Gardener, Emma's cousin and constant friend. Her body was taken for her wake to the Gardner home, *Riverby*, in Touisset, only a half a mile from Andrew Borden's Upper Farm. She had passed away only ten days after her sister. And thus, Andrew J. Borden's posterity was gone.

Emma's funeral was attended by friends who had remained steadfastly by her side. Mary Ella Brigham and her husband George, Florence Bowen (daughter of Dr. Seabury Bowen), Alice Buck, and many others were there. Emma's body was buried, at her request, at the feet of her mother Sarah, only a few feet from Lizzie.

Lizzie left behind a sizeable fortune: $310,513. Emma's totaled $447,099. Neither sister left the other any bequests. Lizzie's 1924 Buick sedan was left to her chauffeur, Mr. Terry, and her 1923 Lincoln, to her agent Charles C. Cook. Other bequests were left to her friends, in both property, personal possessions, and cash.

Workers at Oak Grove Cemetery following the burial of Lizzie (Lizbeth) Borden, June 4, 1927. Photo courtesy of the Fall River Historical Society.

Epilogue:

No concrete evidence has ever surfaced pertaining to Lizzie's guilt in the double murders of August 4, 1892. It is a mystery many love to contemplate. The question remains, what drove her to the actions for which she is held responsible in the court of public opinion? Was she a victim of an unstable mind? One subject to the whims of emotions and outbursts of rage? Certainly, her family and friends report a woman who was "queer," "peculiar" and "sullen." Others label her with the stronger emotions of anger, a temper when crossed, and a propensity to do anything to get what she wanted.

Was Lizzie a sociopath? A look at the traits pertaining to that title may be enlightening:

1) Manipulative and Cunning: They never recognize the rights of others and see their self-serving behaviors as permissible.
2) Grandiose Sense of Self: Feels entitled to certain things as "their right.
3) Pathological Lying: Has no problem lying coolly and easily and it is almost impossible for them to be truthful on a consistent basis.
4) Lack of Remorse, Shame or Guilt: A deep seated rage, which is split off and repressed, is at their core. The end always justifies the means and they let nothing stand in their way.
5) Shallow Emotions: When they show, what seems to be warmth, joy, love and compassion, it is more feigned than experienced and serves an ulterior motive. Outraged by insignificant matters, yet remaining unmoved and cold by what would upset a normal person.
6) Need for Stimulation: Living on the edge. Promiscuity, stealing, early signs of delinquency. Verbal and physical outbursts are normal.
7) Callousness/Lack of Empathy: Unable to empathize with the pain of their victims, having only contempt for others' feelings of distress, and readily taking advantage of them.

8) Poor Behavioral Controls/Impulsive Nature: Rage, no concern for their impact on others. Impulsive behavior (stealing, acting out, no filter or braking system).
9) The problem in Making and Keeping Friends.
10) Irresponsibility/Unreliability: Not concerned about wrecking others' lives and dreams. Oblivious or indifferent to the devastation they cause.
11) Criminal Versatility: Changes their image as needed to avoid persecution. Changes life story readily.

In the 1830s, this disorder was called "moral insanity." By 1900 it was changed to "psychopathic personality." More recently it has been termed "antisocial personality disorder" in the DSM-III and DSM-IV. Psychopaths fall under this definition when meeting certain criteria. "They don't discriminate who it is they lie to or cheat. There is no distinction between friend, family and sucker," according to Michael Seto, a psychologist at the Centre for Addiction and Mental Health in Toronto, Canada.

That Lizzie Borden exhibited these personality traits seems obvious when looking at her life. Setting fires, stealing, outbursts, pathological lying, and even murder for gain, all fall within the realm of possibility. Her desire for acceptance into "the Hill's" bosom found her doing charity work and offering her services in what was deemed unselfish and generous. Yet, when those avenues bore no fruit, she quit, rescinded her largesse and retaliated. The need for drama and stimulation can be seen in her actions. Setting fires, animal cruelty, and lying are traits many juveniles exhibit who fall inside the criteria for a disturbed mind. Was the fire in the barn of Mrs. Churchill, and others near Lizzie's home on Second Street (shortly before the murders), the beginning of her need to quench the desire for elevated stimulation? Certainly, her disregard for her sister's pain never entered her mind. Repeatedly she lashes out at Emma when things don't go her way, never once feeling empathy for the trials her sister is also going through.

Lizzie Borden will continue to fascinate us. To peek behind the curtain at minds who dare to do the unthinkable is a voyeuristic thrill for the rest of us who remain safely cosseted within the walls of normalcy. That they "get away with it" may cause us periodic nightmares, and a need to take a second look at the people next door.

The fallout of the murders of Andrew and Abby Borden went far beyond the walls of 92 Second Street. The Swansea deal, put together by John Morse and Andrew Borden, was to have favorably impacted the lives of dozens of their relatives. Gone now was the dream of a major horse and cattle enterprise, years in the making. Abby's relatives mourned her loss, while Andrew's business endeavors teetered for a time. The police and attorneys sucked into her vortex sacrificed their professional and family time on her behalf. The reach of her actions may never be totally contemplated.

Bridget Sullivan moved to Anaconda, Montana, and married John Sullivan (no relation) in 1905. She died there on March 25, 1948. She bore no children, and left this world without revealing her secrets about what she saw that day, August 4, 1892. Where she was between that year and her marriage in 1905 is a mystery. Rumors say she returned to Ireland, and helped her family pay for a farm. The source of the money to do so, has been theorized, to no avail. Many in 1892, close to her, were in a position to help financially, including Lizzie, Emma and John Morse.

Bridget Sullivan, in her 70s, in Montana. *Fall River Herald.*

John Vinnicum Morse died in 1912, in Hastings, Iowa. He returned there after the trial, and picked up where he left off—his dreams of a large cattle business in Fall River, dashed to pieces.

Hosea Knowlton, Lizzie's trial prosecutor, who suffered greatly throughout her many legal dealings, died at his summer home on December 19, 1902, in Marion, Massachusetts. He had enjoyed the new estate for only two summers before his death. It is reported his ashes were scattered in the waters behind his home.

Hosea Knowlton's home in Marion, Ma. Photos by Ron Bueker.

A sobering thought: Did the plot to kill Abby and Andrew Borden begin in April, when Lizzie first learned of the deed transfer? The poison was stolen from the barn in May, after Lizzie insisted on a green paint color. She may have pushed to have the house painted. Did she deliberately brush up against the wet paint to ruin the dress, giving her an excuse to later burn it?

With rumors of movies and other books coming out shortly, based "loosely" on her life, it is evident the fascination with Lizzie Borden will likely never die. At the writing of this book, Fall River is gearing up for the 125th anniversary of the murders in 2017. Salem has its witches and Fall River has Lizzie:

"A woman with her face pressed up against the window of a world she could not enter."

Rebecca F. Pittman

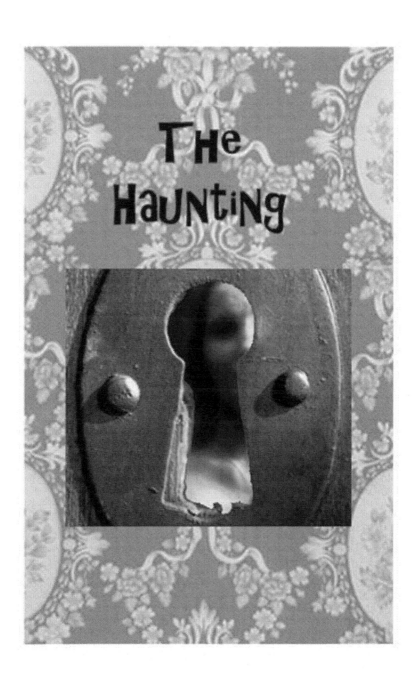

The Haunting

The Lizzie Borden B&B Museum Hauntings

After spending the night in some of the most haunted venues in America, I have noticed one thing: each house or hotel, has its own atmosphere. You can feel it the minute you walk in the door. It isn't something that can be captured with a tape recorder or EMF reader; not even something that moves a planchette across an ancient board. It's a presence. Without fail, each venue owner I've interviewed has mentioned this "presence;" the feeling of someone always watching. You will feel it, turn quickly, only to find you are alone in that darkened hallway.

Other hauntings are more overt. While researching the Myrtles Plantation in St. Francisville, Louisiana, I watched my earrings move the length of a mantle and saw my blanket jerked from the bed by an unseen hand. At the Stanley Hotel in Estes Park, Colorado, I've had pipe tobacco smoke blown into my face, a 4" square burned into my bare shoulder (which disappeared four hours later), and my watch halted at 1:30 each morning. By far, the happenings at Lemp Mansion in St. Louis, Missouri, rattled me the most. My bed in the third-floor attic was kicked, and something sat on my feet; a chandelier played light games with me; and I heard the sound of gunshots and a large dog barking outside my room on the second floor. Unnerving, as this home is renowned for three suicides by gunshot—and one bullet taking the life of a dog.

When entering the Lizzie Borden B&B Museum, you are first struck with awe. The house, remarkably frozen in time, is real. You can see the sitting room and black sofa—in the location where Andrew Borden was murdered—the minute you cross the front door threshold. The owner has stayed true to the room's layouts and furnishings, going largely off crime scene photos and the secrets houses give up; in the way of hidden wallcoverings, boards, and bricks. 92 Second Street is filled with memorabilia from the era and the murders, and it requires a couple of trips to take it all in. Lee-Ann Wilber, the manager, has done a fantastic job of finding authentic antiques and décor, allowing you to step back into the Fall River of 1892.

But, is the house haunted? Let's hear what people are saying:

Danielle Cabral, has been a tour guide at the Lizzie Borden House for five years. She is a history major in college and wants to teach. Danielle feels she and the others working there are part of the house now. Their pride in the home is obvious, and well deserved. I asked her about the paranormal activity in a house that witnessed two such brutal murders.

"I have experienced things," Danielle said. You hear footsteps quite often. It sounds like a man's boots. My tours have heard the footsteps coming down the back stairs behind them, that run next to Andrew Borden's bedroom. They will stop, look behind them, see no one, and ask me "Did you hear that?" I smile and say, "The footsteps? Oh, yeah." I think the best things happen in the daytime. When the house is locked, and only the staff is downstairs, you can hear a door on the second floor go "Wham!" When I just started working here, I was cooking, and I was asked to go upstairs and change the bedding. As I was going up the front stairs, I heard a female voice behind me go "Ahem," with a small cough. I thought it was my boss. There was no one there. I later wondered if it was Abby, showing displeasure at my housekeeping ability.

"I always hear two people talking at the top of the front stairs; sometimes two females, and sometimes a male and a female. We hear children in the attic room, known as the Knowlton room. It may be the children who were drowned in the cellar next door in the Kelly house, which was once owned by Eliza Borden. Eliza (named after her mother) and Holder may be the two kids whose voices and laughter we capture on EVP's. People staying in the room where Abby died report a strong male presence, and sometimes a strong female presence. The female gives off a caring, nurturing vibe. One man, who was sick and lying on the bed, felt a female hand on his forehead, as if caring for him. The male presence seems upset. I don't know if it's John Morse, who slept in that room, or if it's Andrew.

"In the Andrew Jennings' room on the third floor, the staff have seen large handprints on the bedspread, spread apart like a man is leaning on the spread, with his hands planted there. The activity in the house is interesting; it tends to be more active two weeks before the murder anniversary, or Halloween. We get people all over the world that just come to America to see this house. It's very humbling to know I get to work here every day," Danielle said.

"Why do you think Lizzie is still such a hot topic all these years later?" I asked her. "It's still America's biggest unsolved murder," Danielle stated. "If a man had done it, it may not still be so sensational."

Danielle told of an occurrence when Lee-Ann Wilber, the manager, was watching TV in the parlor, and at 3:30 in the morning, she sees a shadow moving up the front stairs, just outside the parlor door. At the same time, the entry chandelier blew out all the bulbs.

"People see a shadow man walking through the house all the time, like Mr. Borden is doing his final walk," Danielle reported. "I saw a man at the top of the back stairs, and I thought it was Tim, our Assistant Manager. But, then I realize it was a shadow form and I jumped back. I hear his voice over the voice boxes, and on my cell phone that I used to record my tours to go over them. I had just mentioned Mr. Borden being a good businessman, and we heard a deep throaty growl. The recorder on my phone picked it up. Tim heard a giggle from the back stairs, and no one was there. These are things that happen all the time. The daytime tours get just as much stuff happening as the nighttime tours."

Sue Vickery is another tour guide at the Lizzie Borden B&B and Museum. "I have had voices speak in my ear, I feel Mr. Borden hit me in the back when I'm talking about him. During an overnight stay, I did in the attic, the lights suddenly went off on that floor. It spooked me, so we came down to the second floor. Just as we did, the lights in the attic came back on, the second-floor lights went out. We go down to the first floor, and the second-floor lights come back on. It was as if someone is shooing you down the stairs by shutting the lights off. I have picked up Abby's "voice" and she tells me Lizzie did it, and that John was not part of it, and that Bridget knew about it after the fact. She gets these statements by using dowsing rods and asking questions. I feel my grandmother is here watching out for me," Sue says. "She protects me."

"An older couple were sleeping in the Borden's bedroom" she continued, "and the man had a sleep apnea apparatus on his face. He woke up to someone tapping him on the forehead and whispering in his ear "Oh, you poor dear." His wife was turned on her side away from him, asleep.

"Mr. Borden will mess with the security cameras, and once we tell him that they are there to take care of his house, he stops. We have mediums tell us that Abby is surprised so many people are still interested in her home. She told us she wants us to do a good job cleaning.

"When I finished a tour in Bridget's room in the attic, I had just said that Bridget had liked working here, when a medium in the group piped up, and said, "Oh no, she didn't! She was afraid of Lizzie!" I wasn't sure about her, until she interrupted me during my tour in the kitchen, and told me my grandmother was there, and described how she died and who was with her. It made me take her seriously.

"I was in the attic putting out the towels in Bridget's room, and there was a big swirling black mist in front of the Hosea Knowlton room. It lasted a few minutes, and then faded away. Tim was in the cellar, and I was alone up there." Sue is at peace working in the house. She feels her grandmother's presence with her every day.

People write to me, the Author, through Facebook, and my *Ghost Writings* newsletter, at my rebeccafpittmanbooks.com site. Some send photos, such as two shot back-to-back, by Lynn Chumack, in the sitting room. In the second, even though it was taken a second after the first one, there is a white mist in front of the fireplace.

Many of the stories I receive concerning paranormal activity at the Borden house revolve around black shadow people seen on the stairways, and especially, in the hallway outside the Borden's second-floor bedroom.

Andi Hovermeyer, Dayton, Ohio: "My friend and I were spending the night in the Andrew and Abby Borden bedroom. You get to use two bedrooms there, which is nice. My friend got the room that was once Abby's dressing room. The suite has its own bathroom. I got up to use the bathroom around 1:25 in the morning. Just as I passed the door that leads to the second-floor landing, I hear this scratching noise on the door. I opened it, and standing at the end of the hall, where a window is, is this tall thin form of a man. It's funny that you can sense that a black shadow is turned toward you, but I could. I could see it was wearing a long coat that came to his knees, and that the cuffs of the sleeves were a little flared. It turned, and walked up the stairs to the attic. I slammed the door, locked it, and bolted to my friend's room, where I spent the remainder of the night holding onto her arm."

Jeff Daniels, Lynn, Massachusetts: "I was on one of their tours at the Lizzie house. We were standing in the room where Abby died. I'm watching the guy talking, who is standing in the spot where the body was found, and something kept flashing across the mirror behind him. I turned to see if anyone was taking pictures. No one was. It happened again, only this time the flash in the reflection broke into a dozen little green lights that flew across the glass. The lady next to me saw them, too. There wasn't anything going on to cause it. Everyone was standing still. It was night, so it wasn't sunlight coming in. The shutters were closed anyway. Freaky."

Debbie Layton, San Diego, California: "Did a tour. Standing at the top of the stairs outside Lizzie's room, hearing about people being able to see under the bed in the murder room. I'm last in line, still standing on the second step to the top. I hear this sigh in my ear. I mean, a deep, sad sigh that felt like it moved my hair. Dumb, I know, but I swatted at it, and freaked out. I jumped up the stairs and stood at the head of the group. One lady looked at me like I was rude and butting ahead. I'll never forget what that felt like."

Mercedes Ramirez, Phoenix, Arizona: "My boyfriend and I stayed the night at the Lizzie Borden house. It was fall and we were also going to Salem for the madness there. He wanted the room where Abby Borden died. I wasn't real crazy about that.

When we went into the room, I got nervous and asked him to ask if we could have a different room. They were booked solid. He teased me, said he was there if I needed him (big thrill!) and I was forced to stay there. We were getting ready for bed. I think it was 10:30 or so. I'm propped up in bed looking over brochures for Salem, when he says he has to go to the bathroom. It's out in the hallway. I told him "No way I'm stayin' in here alone!" He sighed and left me there. He left the door to the room open and walked a few steps to the bathroom that used to be the old dress closet for Lizzie.

"I'm watching every corner. I kept looking out at the staircase, sure something was going to come up. Like, two minutes later, my boyfriend comes bolting into the room, slams the door, and jumps into the bed. He looks scared to death. For a few minutes, he wouldn't talk to me. When I finally got mad, he said he was sitting in the bathroom, and this shadow comes out of the shower, and stands in front of the mirror over the sink. He said he could make out a big wide skirt that went to the floor, and puffy sleeves and her hair was piled up. There was the smell too that appeared when "she" did...something he said smelled unpleasant, kinda musky-like. I've never seen him like that. He didn't sleep all night. He usually goes to the bathroom first thing in the morning, but this time he said he would stop at a gas station on the way to Salem."

Marshall Clayton, Williamsburg, Virginia: "I am writing you because I think it would be fair to offer something from a skeptic. I think many of these "haunted" hospitality venues play off the paranormal and people's love of being scared. That being said, there is something about being in a home where two people were brutally murdered, and having the rooms just as they were that day. The owners did an incredible job of reproducing the layouts seen in the crime photos. The rooms are really nice, and in broad daylight, you sometimes forget you are looking at a sofa in a location where a man was hacked to death. I do confess to feeling a different energy in that room, and in the guest room upstairs, where Mrs. Borden died. Not some rattling chains type of experience, but one, I feel, is more impactful—a sense of sadness, of fear, of loss. There is a strong atmosphere in the house. But ghosts? I'll get back to you if I ever see one...anywhere."

John Alden Taylor, Peabody, Massachusetts: "I come from an area synonymous with the Witch Trials. I have been subjected to folklore and spooky stuff since I was small. Some of the accused witches were from here. So, I went to the Borden house not expecting much. It was just to see where the murders happened and to say I had been there.

"My girlfriend and I took the tour, which I will say, you get your money's worth. No skimping on time. You get to see the whole house and ask lots of questions. I'm sure the guides have heard it all. One lady asked if Lizzie's presence was ever felt on the potty. (Eyeroll) We did have one thing happen in the attic that I can't explain. The guide had finished up there, and we were all trooping back down the stairs (there were about 10 of us). Carrie and I were last. We went down about three steps when she grabs me. I turn to look at her, and she is pointing at a pillow that has magically ended up on the stair right behind her! We just walked down that step. There is no one else up there. She ran past me, nearly falling down the stairs. I wanted to tell the guide, but Carrie just wanted to leave. I heard there were cookies in the kitchen at the end of the tour. Thanks to her, I didn't get one."

Mike Randal, Salt Lake City, Utah: "I was in Boston on business, and I decided to drive the hour to Fall River to see the famous Lizzie Borden house. After seeing so many pictures of it, it's surreal to actually pull into the driveway. I've read a lot of the books on the case, and I found myself wishing Dr. Bowen's house and Mrs. Churchill's were still there. It's cool that the Kelly house is still there.

"The tour was really informative and the lady that gave it was really good. She said she was going to college and was a history major. You could tell she loved her job there as a tour guide. I finished the tour, and was walking back to my car. On a whim, I stepped to the window where I think Officer Hyde watched Lizzie the night of the murders, come down in the dark for the second time. You can't see in very good. I was straightening back up, when this...I don't know how to put it...a face, I guess, sort of fluttered across the window, from the inside. It wasn't a woman. It looked like a young man, with a big mustache. I got a glimpse of a thin white collar, and then dark shoulders. It was really fast. There are bars on the window there, but I could see it distinctly behind them. It wasn't a real person walking around in the cellar. It was gray, and only his shoulders and head were floating up higher than the sill. I wondered if it could have been the ghost of one of the policemen there that day in the cellar."

Shelley Dziedzic, Mystic, Connecticut: is a seasoned Lizzie Borden historian, with her own website, LizzieBordenwarpsandwefts.com. In 1998, she began working as a tour guide at the house under the former owner, Martha McGinn. Many have seen Ms. McGinn's video concerning the paranormal activity she had seen at the house, including the window on the second-floor landing opening and shutting in rapid succession, and a gray lady floating across the cellar floor. "I have been working the night shift and had to check people out of the house for seeing things in the mirror, and hearing noises," Shelley said. "I have even had to escort guests to and from the bathroom." Then you have the pranksters. "People on the street think it is fun to call out things and groan through the letterbox in the front door. And of course, a guest may play a prank on someone. Employees never do, however—it would be an insurance risk."

"While I believe people come into haunted houses predisposed to being terrorized, I still have to admit, there is a creepiness to being in the Borden house alone, which I have been for many hours. Sometimes I think I hear footsteps overhead, when no one is there. Sometimes I think I hear voices at the top of the stairs, which cease when I go to the bottom of the stairs. Once or twice, I have felt a chill, or smelled the scent of perfume which hangs briefly in the air—all when the house is empty. One evening, while alone, I felt something cold behind my chair in the dining room—then a sigh. My mind rationalized most of this, but there is always a tiny margin of wondering, is there something there?"

Shelley went on to mention the many séances held in the house. While many are dubious, brought in by many professed psychics, a few stand out as authentic. One such occasion involved a woman who had traveled from England to see the house.

"She gave her impression of a presence, an old man standing in the driveway who had a message. She described the man and his age. While most mediums channel Lizzie, this lady was describing Southard Miller, an old friend and neighbor of Andrew Borden. I was somewhat impressed by this. She gave us a message from the old man. He told her to tell me that the repair job on the street out front of the house was not done properly. Miller was a carpenter and house builder; he actually built the Borden house. She could not have known about the repair work 2 weeks prior! The same evening, two motion detectors went off."

"I am a historian," Shelly stated. "But, I guess to steal from the great Edith Wharton, "I do not believe in ghosts, but I am afraid of them."

Colleen Johnson, a tour guide at the Lizzie Borden B&B and Museum: "On the first day I worked at the house in 2006, I was giving a practice tour to the guide who was training me, and I used the word "cheap" to describe Andrew, several times. Later while following a tour she was giving, the tour guide used the word "frugal" in the same room. Each time she did, I began to cough and felt as if I couldn't breathe. The final time, I literally felt a hand on my throat.

"On occasion, when sleeping in Bridget's room, I will hear footsteps coming up the stairs, when I'm alone in the house. Those stairs are carpeted now, but they weren't in the Borden's time, and the steps I hear are of boots on wooden stairs. I have stood looking down the stairs, as I've heard these sounds, and no one is there!"

Angel Brigham, Dallas, Texas: "My Mom and I did the tour in 2015. I wanted to spend the night, but they were booked. The tour was really good...longer than I expected. I was enjoying it, and really looking over all the furniture and stuff...there's a lot to see there...when I hear a sobbing sound next to the room they said was the dress closet. It's a bathroom now for some of the bedrooms on the second floor. I mentioned it to the tour guide and he said he didn't hear anything. There were five people on the tour, and they looked at me like I was nuts. I stood there a minute, not wanting to go into the room where everybody went, cuz it's where Mrs. Borden's body was. I hear the sobbing again! It's really sad, like, heart-wrenching stuff. It was right next to me, not on the other side of the bathroom door. I moved away from it, and it got louder. My Mom was in the room with the others and I motioned for her to come out on the landing. She did, looking miffed I was making her miss the tour. I asked if she heard the sobbing, which was still going on. She said she didn't hear anything. Now I'm freaking out. When the tour came out and went into the Lizzie bedroom, I went downstairs and waited in the parlor. It really got to me. I felt sad the rest of the day."

Darrin Hutchinson: In October 2011, my wife and I spent the night there and had a few things happen to us. My wife felt nauseous from the moment we stepped into the house and the unexplained feeling did not go away until we left the following day. On the evening of our stay they gave us a tour of the house explaining what happened in each room. A couple of things occurred overnight. While starting to fall asleep in the Andrew Borden room, where my wife and I stayed, I had the feeling of a hand pressing against the middle of my back, which was turned toward the bedroom door. It kept me awake for a little while and I was somewhat afraid to turn over in case I might see something. Eventually, I did fall asleep because I was so tired from our drive there that day, but was awoken during the night by a commotion in the adjoining room followed by the sound of someone running down the stairs. We didn't get up to see what was going on at that time but found out the following morning from one of the other guests in the room next to ours, a paranormal investigator had freaked out during the night because he said the covers had lifted off of him and he then bolted out of the John V. Morse room (where Abby died) and down the stairs. He later made his way back upstairs but would not go back into his room. Instead, he asked the guest in Lizzie's room if he could sleep on the couch, which he did.

There is a strong atmosphere in the Borden house. Our knowledge of what occurred there certainly plays a part, and yet there is feeling as you walk the floors Lizzie, Emma, Bridget, Andrew and Abby walked, that you are not alone. For those of you who have not visited this amazing venue, may I highly recommend it? The owners have done an incredible job of recreating the actual environment of August 4, 1892. The doors, woodwork, and some of the hardware are original to the home. Every detail is fastidiously gone over. The rooms are beautiful, and the breakfast, first-class (shout-out to Tim Reyes). Perhaps you'll come away with a ghost story of your own. The Author.

Some of the amazing staff at the Lizzie Borden B&B Museum.
Top left: Danielle Cabral; Top Right: Nikki & Sue Vickery
Middle left: Tim Reyes; Middle right: Colleen Johnson
Bottom center: Rick Bertoldo

𝒯𝒽𝑒 𝒮𝓃𝓉𝑒𝓇𝓋𝒾𝑒𝓌𝓈:

There are amazing people who have spent copious hours involved in one aspect or another concerning the Lizzie Borden murder mystery. Whether penning a book, running a venue, offering a website and blog, performing on stage, or proffering a museum, the wealth of information they offer is a true gift to all of us who can't get enough of this case. Several of these people took time to share their knowledge with me, along with photos pertaining to the crime, and the people involved with it. Everyone I spoke with in Massachusetts opened their doors to me, and went out of their way to help me gather the information I needed. While I have listed them in the Acknowledgments, I wanted to offer you a closer look at the major players in this saga that is Lizzie Borden.

The Fall River Historical Society

The Fall River Historical Society is located at 451 Rock Street, in Fall River, Massachusetts, only minutes from the Lizzie Borden House, and *Maplecroft*. Michael Martins and Dennis Binette are the curators there, and along with an amazing staff (shout-out to the two Kathy's) they lovingly care for the history that made Fall River great, and infamous. The museum houses the largest collection of Lizzie Borden memorabilia, both from her personal life, and from the murder trials. The famous handleless hatchet is on display there, along with other artifacts from the murders. It is only a small part of a mansion crammed full of beautiful furnishings, art and historic artifacts. It is a must-see!

I asked Dennis Binette, co-author of *Parallel Lives: A Social History of Lizzie A. Borden and Her Fall River*, and curator at the museum, some questions:

1) **What is your favorite piece in the Rock Street mansion that houses the Fall River Historical Society, and why? (This does not have to be Lizzie related):**

"There are so many wonderful things in the collection that it's tough to pick one. One of my favorites, though, is a sampler in silk thread done by Delana Borden while a student at Mary Balch's Female Academy. If Michael could own one piece in this house, it would be the John Cotton portrait by Sanford Mason, a Rhode Island painter who painted in the 1820s and 1830s.

2) **What item in the Lizzie collection captures your interest the most, and why?**

"In the Lizzie collection, we think the prison letters, no doubt. They present a totally different side to her character than has ever been supposed and are the first examples of personal primary source material dealing with her imprisonment."

3) **If you could ask Lizzie one question, what would it be?**

"I would hope that it would be a civil conversation and not an inquisition. Michael would like to ask her about her dogs, seeing as how he also has Boston Terriers."

4) **What annual event put on at the FRHS is your favorite, and what new event would you like to offer?**

"There are so many annual events that are each appealing for different reasons. Not much of an answer, huh?"

5) **How long did *Parallel Lives* take to research and write? Besides the prestigious Kirkus review, what are you most proud of, regarding the book?**

"*Parallel Lives* took ten years to research and write. A look at the acknowledgments shows how many great people were forthcoming with their assistance and information. And this book had to be completed along with all the other tasks at hand: running a museum, curating a collection, decorating for a phenomenal Holiday Open House, running a seasonal tea room, buying for and running a museum shop, maintaining a library and research center, planning events, etc. There are a lot of hats here. In retrospect, we wonder how we ever had a chance to write the book.

"The Kirkus Starred Review was a total surprise, but we would never have ever anticipated being named to Kirkus's

"Best of 2012" list. The thing that I am personally proud of is that, finally Lizzie's life as a woman is told, placing her against the backdrop of her times, and finally putting her story in perspective.

6) **Are there any new books coming out?**

"There are a few books on the horizon, but nothing in the immediate future. But, keep in touch, you never know what will come along."

My sincere thanks to Dennis Binette for taking the time to answer my questions. After looking at his list of duties, I felt a little guilty. He and Michael Martins offer their collective 60 years of experience to every author who comes tapping on their door. They are amazingly generous.

If you haven't read *Parallel Lives*, I highly recommend you do. You can find information for it at www.lizziebordenparallellives.com. For information on the Fall River Historical Society, including upcoming events, go to www.fallriverhistorical.org, or www.lizzieborden.org.

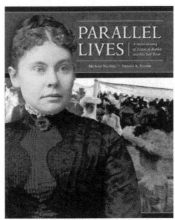

Michael Martins (l) and Dennis Binette, curators at the Fall River Historical Society, with their book *Parallel Lives*.

The Websites and Blogs:

Shelley Dziedzic at the Lizzie Borden house,
with Max, the house mascot.

Lizzie Borden: Warps and Wefts

1) What is your name, and what occasioned your interest in the Lizzie Borden saga?

Shelley Dziedzic. I am from Maryland originally, and lived there until I was 21. I had heard of Lizzie Borden only in the context of the little 40 whacks ditty. We used to jump rope to it. I moved to New England in 1972 and lived on Aquidneck Island during my husband's Navy years. We would shop at Fall River Knitting Mills and visit the city often but I still was not particularly interested in Lizzie. It was not until 1991 when I saw Legend of Lizzie Borden on TV, while ironing one Sunday afternoon, that I became obsessed with the case. I raced up to Fall River the next day to visit the historical society only to find they are closed on Mondays. On Tuesday, then curator Florence Brigham, opened the door to the historical society and filled me in on the Borden case. The timing was great because the next year was the Borden centennial and I attended the week-long seminar every day in costume and was the first to walk through *Maplecroft* when it opened to the public on August 4th. I formed a group called the

Second Street Irregulars in 1993, mostly composed of people I had met at the 1992 conference, and the group is still going strong. We usually meet at the Second Street house in the Spring as we did this year, to discuss and investigate the case. I also began a theatrical group called The Pear Essential Players which, up until this year, performed at the murder house on August 4th and in area Borden-related venues.

In 1998 I went to work for the McGinn family who owned Second Street and wrote and directed the annual August 4th production and worked as a night tour guide and innkeeper from 1998- 2016. In 2007 I created a blog site called **Lizzie Borden: Warps and Wefts** to honor the textile heritage of the city and to put out truthful research on the case after finding so many errors in published work and television documentaries.

In 2014, I published the History of Oak Grove, which focuses on the cemetery history and all the Borden-related people buried there. There are more Lizzie projects in the works.

2) **When did you first create your forum and what did you envision for it? Do you posit whether you see Lizzie as guilty or not?**

Lizzie Borden: Warps and Wefts was launched in 2007 as a place for people to read, free of charge, my research, see photos of Fall River, the murder house, and Lizzie-related material. It was created to counteract so much total falsehood, exaggeration and misinformation on the internet. It also provided readers an avenue to comment or contribute information. Warps and Wefts is still going strong. Both guilty and innocent platforms are explored-mostly the site deals in facts.

3) **If you could ask Lizzie one question, what would it be?**

My inclination over years of study of this case is to lean on the side of a guilty verdict. I also maintain there is some missing information we are not privy to surrounding the motive, and that we may never find out those missing bits which lit the fuse on that Thursday morning, so my question to Lizzie would be **"WHY?"**

4) **How do you account for the ongoing fascination with the Borden murder case? What keeps people interested after 124 years?**
After lecturing to probably several thousand people on the topic, both as a house guide and area lecturer, I have made note of the reaction to the Borden case by the general public. In order of continuing interest, I would say that Lizzie keeps 'em coming back for more because:
a. It's a woman accused.
b. It is unsolved.
c. It is a hatchet, used by a woman in a brutal, bloody and unusual crime
d. The woman was acquitted despite damning evidence
e. The murder house is still intact and one might stay overnight since 1996
f. There has been a huge paranormal interest in the murder house since 2005
g. Both parents were murdered with the child accused of the murder (not unusual)
h. Nobody else was ever brought to justice for the murders
i. Lizzie never confessed and stayed in the city, shunned by old friends.

5) Do you feel there will be new information forthcoming in the future that could impact the impression of the public concerning this case?
Having been present during a few discoveries, I cannot help but hope there is more out there about the Borden case, yet to be made public. It would be great to see the Robinson papers. I believe there may well be letters which are kept private, in the hands of people in the city which might shed light on Lizzie. The release of the **Knowlton Papers** and **Parallel Lives** gave valuable insight. No individual is one-dimensional. I think Lizzie was a very complex person: both capable of murder, and also a loyal and sweet old lady who could be kind to animals. I believe that there is something *yet unseen* which would support a guilty Lizzie rather than an innocent one. I hope I live long enough to see it.
Check out Shelley's various sites:

www.pearessentialproductions.org

www.lizziebordenwarpsandwefts.com
www.secondstreetirregulars.com
www.friendsofoakgrovecemetery.org

Faye Musselman

www.phayemuss@wordpress.com
website
Tattered Fabric: Fall River's Lizzie Borden: blog

1) **What is your name, and what occasioned your interest in the Lizzie Borden saga?**

My name is Faye Musselman.

"In 1969, when I was pregnant with my son, I used to take long walks to the Library and one day cited Victoria Lincoln's book; "A Private Disgrace: Lizzie Borden by Daylight". The book jacket had a lace fan with a hatchet superimposed. I checked it out and read it cover to cover that day. I went back the next day and asked "What else ya got?" I was hooked. Within 7 years I was making twice-annual trips to Fall River and meeting some people who actually knew Lizzie through the graces of the Historical Society Curator Emeritus, Florence Brigham.

2) **When did you first create your forum and what did you envision for it? Do you posit whether you see Lizzie as guilty, or not?**

"July of 2007. Serious research, humorous musings, theoretical postulating; interesting images; and a splash of Fall River history. It's no mystery. Oscam's razor stuff.

She wanted money, daddy had it, she got it.   Short
answer: Yes, I posited that she was guilty.

4) **If you could ask Lizzie one question, what would it be?**
"How did you like the Roman Coliseum? No, seriously
I would ask her what she did with the hatchet because I
don't believe it was ever found.

5) **How do you account for the ongoing fascination with
the Borden murder case? What keeps people
interested after 124 years?**
"This case is not so much a "Whodunnit" as it is a
masterly, real-life "How dunnit." Classic solved and
unsolved crimes always have had a mass appeal. This one,
framed in the Victorian era, is born in an era when so
many "classics" were born. But this one is a pip. It has it
all; the virginal spinster, the somewhat miserly father, the
dreaded stepmother, the yearning for independence but
stuck without the financial means or skillsets to achieve it,
the mysterious uncle, the name Borden and its' social
cache, the dichotomy of the have and have-nots, i.e. the
mill workers versus the upper class who owned or
otherwise controlled most everything.   Now add to it the
missing murder weapon, a 10-15-minute window between
the second murder and the shout-out, disbelief that a
Borden female could do such a thing, the hushed and
huddled society playing out against the newspapers'
coming of age with cross-country tentacles able to publish
in 24-hour news cycles, and, mostly, the oddity of Lizzie
herself.   This case has legs.   It has transcended the
generations and now her persona has emerged into a pop
culture icon as a one-dimensional psychopath wielding a
bloody axe.   She's our Jack the Ripper, but 15, and in a
dress with a comely grin on her face.

6) **Do you feel there will be new information forthcoming
in the future that could impact the impression of the
public concerning this case?**
"There already has been. It's a massive book "Parallel
Lives – A Social History of Lizzie A. Borden and Her
Fall River" published by the Fall River Historical Society.
Previously, we only knew about her first 33 years.   For

the first time, we learn details of not only the first but the entire **second-half** of her life. It reveals a woman of depth and feelings and kindness and years of sadness and depression. But as much as that content thrills case purists, it doesn't sell in today's TV's true case drama presentations. It's not sexy enough. So, we are fed misinformed pabulum or outrageous exploding rock candy inside the mouth and mind of a Christina Ricci portrayal. I think Lizzie acted alone and took it to her grave. More letters and photographs will come out which might alter that savage and raging persona into a more formidable matron of the Jazz Age holding on to the social deportment of an Edwardian society.

"Viewing my blog is without registration or cost. But, I also post Lizzie Borden collectibles there for sale, and soon will be listing more. www.phayemuss@wordpress.com.

Stefani Koorey

Lizzie Andrew Borden Society Forum
www.lizzieandrewborden.com

1. Stefani Koorey. I was born and raised in Florida, although both my parents are Yankees, from north of the Mason/Dixon line. My parents were voracious readers and all of the kids in my family inherited their love of books. We especially enjoyed reading true crime non-fiction. When I was about fifteen years old, my father read Robert Sullivan's *Goodbye, Lizzie Borden* and asked us one night at dinner what we thought of her guilt or innocence. None of us had ever heard of her. So, we were instructed to read the book and then we would be able to have a more informed discussion on the case. We passed the book around, one to the other, until we were all hooked on the story. Those dinner hour discussions on the Lizzie Borden case are fond memories to me.

2. The Lizzie Borden Society Forum started sometime in 2001, through a free online forum system named Arborwood. After a time, this company started to charge for its services and it was then that I decided to have my own set-up where I could have much more control over design and formatting. The first post on the new site was December 1, 2003. We had a small group of dedicated armchair detectives sharing their theories and research with one another. I envisioned the forum as a safe place to discuss all things Lizzie Borden, Fall River, and Victorian America. With almost 100,000 posts, 6,000 topics, and nearly 500 registered users, The Lizzie Borden Society Forum is rare in that it has lasted so long! I think it is one of only two true-crime oriented forums in the world (the other being Casebook Jack the Ripper) that is still in operation after 13 years. Most discussion forums crumble with infighting, trolls, bad behavior, and perceived insults in the way people speak to one another. This forum is about respecting each other even as we disagree. Every once in a while, someone has to be scolded or banned, but that is a rare occurrence.

I do not have an opinion about Lizzie's guilt or innocence. I push no theory or idea one way or the other. I don't feel that the answer to this mystery will ever be determined and at best it is an intellectual pursuit that fascinates and engrosses those who care to pursue it. And like Jack the Ripper, I don't think anyone will ever solve it.

3. If I could ask Lizzie Borden one question it would be, of course, did you or didn't you kill one or both of your parents. Not that she would give me a straight answer! My curiosity about her is currently focused on what she sounded like (did she have an accent, was her voice high-pitched, etc.) and moved like. I would love to discover film footage of her or a recording of her speaking. I need to hear her. I just need to.

4. The ongoing fascination of the case stems from it being unsolved and unsolvable. Without our modern forensic investigative techniques, the police of that era were stymied in their ability to ever truly get close to the truth. In addition, the Fall River police force of 1892 was more of a constabulary——they spent most of their time keeping the peace. They had very little experience in murder investigations and the only real "detectives" at the time were the Pinkertons—a paid detective agency. The police in Fall River never secured the crime scene, jumped to conclusions about Lizzie's guilt based on their misogynistic feelings of her and her reaction to the murders, and created more chaos than clarity. The newspapers of the day were steeped in yellow journalism and most stories were riddled with factual errors. They sensationalized this event from the first moment and the story has continued to sensationalize ever since. It was the first trial to be covered by the AP wire services, so newspapers nationwide were carrying day by day coverage of Lizzie's trial in 1893. Everyone knew who she was in this country. She became a part of the water supply.

There are always those who feel they have solved the case, and I find all of them interesting but deeply flawed. Authors tend to decide her guilt or innocence and then use the sources at hand to prove their theory instead of the other way around. Even well-respected internet sites and magazines continue to proffer factual inaccuracies as they spin the tale. The mythology that surrounds this case is enormous!

5. I don't expect there will be anything "new" to add to the story except perhaps discovery of new photographs of the cast of characters or family stories revealed by those who knew her best during her lifetime. The only thing we know is that on Thursday, August 4, 1892, in Fall River, MA, two people, Andrew Jackson Borden and his wife Abby Durfee Gray Borden, were brutally killed in their home at 92 Second Street. That's it.

I have personally found previously undiscovered photographs of the Borden's, including Lizzie, Emma, Andrew, and Sarah. In addition, I found a cache of books that once belonged to Emma Borden and personal family photograph albums of the Borden and Morse families. These folks are in the process of being identified, so stay tuned for info on those!

I am currently working on a biography of Bridget Sullivan, the Borden maid. She died in 1947 and there are still those alive who personally knew her, unlike those who have since passed away in

Lizzie Borden's circle. Bridget Sullivan's story is a fascinating one and what we think we know about her is far from the reality of her life.

Anyone can join the forum at:
http://lizzieandrewborden.com/LBForum/index.php.

We welcome all polite conversations on the case and are eager to share our ideas and theories with anyone who wishes to join in the fun.

We want everyone to have a level playing field when discussing the case and that is the reason why the primary source documents are given away. The late Harry Widdows, myself, and my sister, Kat Koorey, were the first to transcribe these documents into a searchable format in Word and as a PDF so that scholars and interested parties could use the information in new ways to help them in their research.

Lizzie Borden B&B Museum
Owner: Donald Woods   Manager: Lee-Ann Wilber

I spoke with Lizzie Borden B&B Museum owner, Donald Woods. He was kind enough to give me some of his time, and tell me about his involvement with the historic house. My first question to him was what drew him to purchase the home at 92 Second Street:

"I'd always had a dream of owning a home where I could dig up the yard and look for artifacts. I was watching ABC News, and they announced the Lizzie Borden house was up for sale. The Leery Press and Martha McGinn owned it at the time. The Press business was literally attached to the south side of the house.

Once word got out I had bought it, every newspaper was chasing me, all shouting the same question, "What are you going to do with it?" You can only answer that question so many times before your caustic side kicks in. So, when the Boston Globe asked me, I retorted, "Probably a B&B, with a Starbucks on the side." Not one of my better moves. It was suddenly popping up on TV. I get a call from Starbucks basically saying "Say WHAT?" I learned a lesson.

"We get over 10,000 people here year around, from all over the world. Our tours are $18 an hour at this time. We typically have

10-15 people per tour. The paranormal reality shows are always calling and wanting to do investigations. We've allowed a few. It's an interesting process. Basically, the house is the star.

"Lee-Ann Wilber manages the house and does a fantastic job. She was in sales for GNC and knows how to handle things. She's also decorated it with a keen eye for historical detail.

"As for future plans, I would say more online presence, utilizing the Web. Also, primarily is to care for the house. It's a responsibility we don't take lightly. Huffington Post named the house one of the most-haunted places in the WORLD! That brings a lot of people to your door...and you want them to be glad they came."

You can make reservations to stay at the B&B, or book a tour by going to www.lizzie-borden.com. They also have gifts and memorabilia for sale.

Kristee Bates. Photo courtesy of the
Fall River Herald.

Maplecroft Owner: Kristee Bates

Kristee Bates bought Lizzie's *Maplecroft* in 2012. She has restored it to its Gilded Age image, a time when Fall River's elite called "the Hill" home. You literally step back in time, and feel as if Emma and Lizzie will walk into the various rooms at any moment. She was gracious enough to let my husband Ron, and myself spend two nights there in October, 2016. It is a treat I will never forget. Here are her answers to a few of my questions:

1) What prompted you to purchase *Maplecroft*?

"My girlfriend and I visited Fall River in June of 2014. We stayed at the B&B... we always wanted to see that huge house on the hill that she moved to. My friend looked it up online and it was for sale. The rest is history. Everything came into place to buy it... it was a once in a lifetime opportunity and as mentioned earlier, everything from the inspection to renovation of the home fell into place.

2) Did you know a lot about the Lizzie Borden story when you bought her home?

"I was familiar with the case. I had read quite a bit and felt like visiting the B&B would help me "solve the murder" in my own mind.

It did and while renovating *Maplecroft* I learned even more. The majority of information I learned from renovation has focused more on Lizzie's later years at *Maplecroft*. It's amazing how much the house reveals about Lizzie and Emma.

3) Where do you feel the most comfortable in the house? Do you feel welcome there?

"I feel very welcome in the house....at different times during the renovation I felt more comfortable in specific rooms. Oddly, I've always felt most comfortable and welcome in the basement and parlor.

4) When restoring certain features of the house, such as wallpaper, etc., what guided you as to your purchases? Were there tell-tale signs in the house that showed what the previous colors or patterns had been?

"Miraculously, I found her original wallpaper behind her corner radiators in the foyer. That helped with the foyer selection. When I purchased the home, there were remnants of her second and third floor main walls. I chose a similar pattern, however I selected more of a gold cast in the paper than the grayish white of the original paper."

5) What is your vision for the home? Do you plan to open it to the public?

"I plan to open it to the public and offer lodging, tours, events and so much more.

6) You did an interesting thing with your renovation of the kitchen. What made you decide to furnish it in the 1920s motif?

"Maplecroft's former curator Bill Pavao, suggested we add a 1920's refrigerator and stove to show the changes that occurred in the many years she lived at Maplecroft. We wanted to show how much appliances changed during her lifetime.

7) Do you have any plans of offering Maplecroft to the public in the near future?

"That is a dream of mine. So many people drive by, or stop, and want to peek inside. We are in the process of looking into permits and legalities of opening it as a B&B, and offering tours. If permits allow, I would love to have special events here, in a tasteful setting, and high tea on the back porch and lawn would be lovely. Stay tuned.

Thank you, Kristee for your amazing hospitality and generosity.

You can find out more about the upcoming plans at *Maplecroft* by writing to lbmaplecroft@gmail.com, or go to their FB page. We are so privileged to have two such amazing venues, lovingly restored to look as they did in 1892-1893. Both homes are beautifully furnished, and you have to look closely so as not to miss all the wonderful artifacts and décor. It's like a glorious treasure hunt that continually unfolds Lizzie's life before your eyes.

Yet, the homes are very different, which is as it should be. 92 Second Street is exactly as it was the day of the murders. *Maplecroft* reflects Lizzie's rise to riches, and her desire to be counted among the wealthy and socially prominent residents on French Street. By visiting both homes, you get the fullest sense of her journey...one that ended within the walls of *Maplecroft* in 1927.

Appendix I:

𝓗𝓲𝓰𝓱𝓵𝔂 𝓡𝓮𝓬𝓸𝓶𝓶𝓮𝓷𝓭𝓮𝓭:

Recommended Reading:

Parallel Lives. Michael Martins and Dennis A. Binette; Fall River Historical Society Publication
The Commonwealth of Massachusetts vs. Lizzie A. Borden: The Knowlton Papers 1892-1893. Michael Martins and Dennis A. Binette. Fall River Historical Society.
Lizzie Borden Past and Present. Leonard Rebello. Al-Zach Press, Fall River, Massachusetts.
The Lizzie Borden Sourcebook: David Kent, in collaboration with Robert A. Flynn. Branden Publishing Company, Boston.
Lizzie Borden and the Mysterious Ax. Robert A. Flynn. King Philip Publishing Company.
Forty Whacks. David Kent. Yankee Books, Pennsylvania.
The Fall River Tragedy: *A History of the Borden Murders*. Edwin Porter. 1893.
Lizzie Borden: Resurrections. Sherry Chapman. Pear Tree Press. Fall River, Massachusetts.
Goodbye Lizzie Borden. Robert Sullivan. Penguin Books.
Yesterday in Old Fall River: A Lizzie Borden Companion. Paul Dennis Hoffman.CarolinaAcademicPress.
Lizzie. Frank Spiering. Random House.

Research Publications:

Witness Statements: For the Lizzie Borden Murder Case
    ©Stefani Koorey
Lizzie's Inquest Testimony. ©Stefani Koorey
Inquest Testimony of Other Witnesses. ©Stefani Koorey
The Preliminary Hearing. The Fall River Historical Society.
The Superior Court Trial: Volumes I, II and III. The Fall River Historical Society.

Recommended Lizzie Borden websites and blogs:

Lizzie-Borden.com: The Lizzie Borden House and Museum. Reservations for tours, overnight accommodations, merchandise, and events.

LizzieBorden.org: The Fall River Historical Society's websites. Information on hours, tours, special events and merchandise.

LizzieAndrewBorden.com: Website and blog. Information, documents, blogs, The Literary Hatchet, photos and more.

LizzieBordenWarpsandWefts.com: Website and blog. Information, blogs, photos, and documents.

TatteredFabric.com: Website and blog. Blogs, memorabilia for sale, documents, photos, and information. phayemuss@wordpress.com.

Recommended Places to Visit to Learn More:

Carl Becker
The Swansea Museum
Victoria Road
Swansea, Massachusetts

The Swansea Library
69 Main Street
Swansea, Massachusetts

The Fall River Historical Society
451 Rock Street
Fall River, Massachusetts

A big "Thank You" to these people for their time and efforts on my behalf.

Recommended Places:

The Fall River Grill is just one block up from the Lizzie Borden B&B at 363 2nd St. **"Killer Service. Killer Food."**

Lizzie Borden's Maplecroft, her mansion "on the Hill" will be opening as a B&B in 2019. 306 French St. Fall River, MA. 02720. Call 774-357-5160 for information.

Appendix II:

Important Locations:

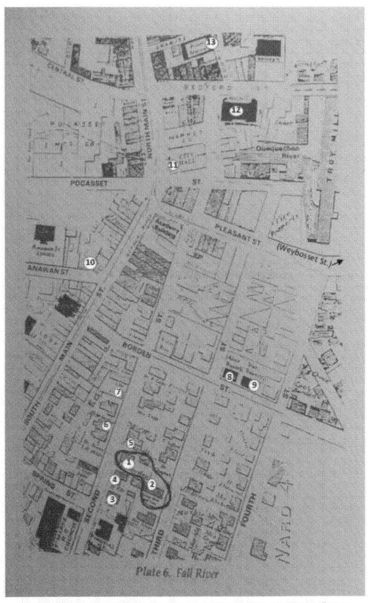

Lizzie's Neighborhood: 1) Borden House; 2) Crowe's Barn; 3) Wade's Store;
4) Kelly House; 5) Churchill House; 6) Dr. Bowen; 7) Hall's Stables; 8) Alice
Russel's House; 9) Starr Bakery; 10) A. J. Borden Building; 11) City Hall Clock;
12) Post Office; 13) Police Station & Court Room

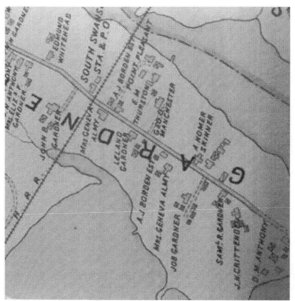

The Lower Farm area in Swansea. Andrew's summer home is at the center of the map. The South Swansea train depot can be seen at the top of Gardner's Neck Road.

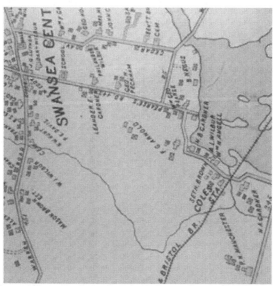

The Upper Farm, where Andrew Borden's large farm was located. Mr. Eddy's house is at the left, the corner of Old Warren and Pearse Roads. Today, the area houses the Touisett Golf Course. Coles Station is at right. Maps courtesy of Leonard Rebello.

Appendix III:

The Breaking of the Hatchet

Lying a shingle hatchet on the chopping block (l). Hitting hatchet w/ back of 17"-long handle (r). Hatchet wood is hickory, and harder to break. Hickory required a long-handled hatchet to break it. It took one try.

 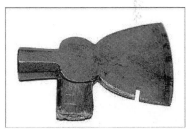

The result of hitting hickory wood hatchet with the back of long-handled hatchet (l). Handleless hatchet from 1892, considered Andrew's murder weapon (r).

Hitting an ash wood hammer with back of short-handled hatchet (l). 1890s short-handle clawhead hatchet (center). Result of break (r). Hammer wood is ash & softer than hickory. Police testimony said handleless hatchet was "hardwood," probably ash or hickory. The clawhead hatcet handle was 17" long, according to testimony. Both breaks resemble murder weapon.

Lizzie said she "picked up a chip" off the floor. She may have placed it beneath the hatchet to elevate it before striking (l); snapping its neck (r).

The break in the handleless hatchet has mystified Borden aficionados for years. Typically, when a hatchet or axe breaks, it splinters along the grain, like a broken baseball bat, as can be seen in the above photographs. Andrew Borden's murder weapon is a horizontal break that we could only replicate by placing a small chip or wedge beneath the head and striking it at its narrowest point—the neck. The murder weapon presented during the Superior Court trial, and now on display at the Fall River Historical Society, is broken exactly like the experiments on the previous page prove.

Each shown on the preceding page took only one strike. It would have taken Lizzie seconds to accomplish. Other tests without the wedge resulted in the splintering shown above.

THE HISTORY & HAUNTING SERIES

The Stanley Hotel

The Myrtles Plantation

Lemp Mansion

Lizzie Borden

COMING IN 2017

The Crescent Hotel

Salem

www.rebeccafpittmanbooks.com

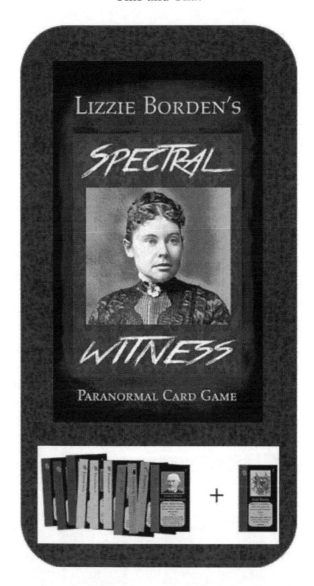

**The Lizzie Borden Spectral Witness Paranormal
Card Game. Now on sale!**

Can you solve the Borden murder mystery
using actual crime scene photos and evidence?
This Rummy-style card game is never the same twice!
Available at www.rebeccafpittmanbooks.com.

ABOUT THE AUTHOR

Rebecca F. Pittman's interest in historical places has been with her since she discovered the Winchester Mystery House in San Jose, California, at the age of 10. Her father took her to see the mysterious home, and the love affair with mysteries, history, and the paranormal was born.

This is her 12th book; 4th in the History and Haunting Series. *The History and Haunting of the Stanley Hotel, The History and Haunting of the Myrtles Plantation,* and *The History and Haunting of Lemp Mansion,* are popular books about some of the top-10 most-haunted venues in America. *The History and Haunting of the Crescent Hotel,* and *The History and Haunting of Salem,* are slated for a 2019 release. Rebecca is also working in the fiction arena with her release of *T.J. Finnel and the Well of Ghosts*: a book geared to audiences 10 and up, which has been compared to *Fablehaven* and *Harry Potter.* Coming soon are several mystery novels with a supernatural bent for adults: *Don't Look Now! The Diamond Peacock Club,* and *Hourglass.*

Rebecca has been featured on *Coast to Coast AM* with George Noory, *Fox News, Jim Harold's Campfire,* Travel Channel's *Legend Hunter,* and other TV, radio, and print media. She was a TV talk show host on a show for women, called *Troubleshooting Men: What in the World Do They Want?* A book of the same name teaches single and married women how to have a life of abundance, and the relationship they've longed for.

You can visit Ms. Pittman's website at rebeccafpittmanbooks.com, and sign up for her free monthly newsletter, *Ghost Writings,* where she reports on paranormal events and venues, often sharing her reader's stories. She lives in the Colorado Rocky Mountain's foothills.

The Ancient Arms of

Borden

The last piece of irony, in a case fraught with it: The Borden Coat of arms bears two hatchets, along with a hatchet-wielding lion.